# North American Linkages:
## Opportunities and
## Challenges for Canada

GENERAL EDITOR:
RICHARD G. HARRIS

# North American Linkages:
# Opportunities and Challenges for Canada

The Industry Canada Research Series

University of Calgary Press

ISBN 1-55238-106-4
ISSN 1700-2001


University of Calgary Press
2500 University Dr. N.W.
Calgary, Alberta, Canada T2N 1N4

**National Library of Canada cataloguing in publication data**

Main entry under title :
North American linkages : opportunities and challenges for Canada

(Industry Canada Research Series ; v. XI)
Issued also in French under title : Les liens en Amérique du Nord.
Includes bibliographical references.
Co-published by Industry Canada.
ISBN 1-55238-106-4

1. North America – Economic integration.
2. Free trade – North America.
3. Investments – Canada.
4. Canada – Economic conditions – 1991-    .
I. Harris, Richard G.
II. University of Calgary.
III. Canada. Industry Canada.
IV. Series.

HF1766.N67 2003          382.917          C2003-980091-1

---

**Canada**   We acknowledge the financial support of the Government of Canada through the Book Publishing Industry Development Program (BPIDP) for our publishing activities.

---

Published by the University of Calgary Press in cooperation with Industry Canada and Public Works and Government Services Canada – Canadian Government Publishing.

---

EDITORIAL AND TYPESETTING SERVICES: VSES Communications.
COVER DESIGN: Paul Payer/ArtPlus Limited

Printed and bound in Canada
∞ This book is printed on acid-free paper.

# Table of Contents

# PART II: THE NAFTA COUNTRIES AS A COMMON MARKET

COMMENT ON:

CAN THE NAFTA PARTNERS FORGE A GLOBAL APPROACH TO INTERNET GOVERNANCE? 681

STEVEN GLOBERMAN

# Acknowledgments

A S GENERAL EDITOR, I WOULD LIKE TO ACKNOWLEDGE the assistance and support of a number of people who were instrumental in the North American Linkages project and this research volume. Senior Assistant Deputy Minister Andrei Sulzenko and Deputy Minister V. Peter Harder supported the North American linkages initiative within Industry Canada as a research priority and translated the need for policy analysis into action. Renée St-Jacques, Someshwar Rao and Prakash Sharma from the Micro-Economic Policy Analysis Branch of Industry Canada were instrumental in the initiation of the research projects, and in the planning and organization of the conference in Calgary at which the papers were first presented. They also provided useful advice on various aspects of the direction of the project and with the organization of the conference. I would also like to thank Andrew Sharpe of the Centre for the Study of Living Standards, who was responsible for the logistics of the Calgary conference, Victor Spassov and his team at VSES Communications, who did the copy editing, page setting and translation of the volume, and Joanne Fleming and Varsa Kuniyal, who assisted me and the authors with the overall preparation of papers and editing process. I also extend my thanks to John King, of the University of Calgary Press, for his support in the publication of this volume. Finally, I wish to thank the authors for participating in the project and the conference, as well as for their own excellent contributions to the volume.


Richard G. Harris
Simon Fraser University

*Richard G. Harris\**
*Simon Fraser University*

# Introduction

THE SUBJECT OF NORTH AMERICAN INTEGRATION is one of the most durable themes of Canadian economic, social and political debate. This volume reports on the current state of research with respect to the economic linkages between Canada, Mexico and the United States, and presents a number of analyses of how changes in these linkages might affect the Canadian economy. The perspective is primarily on Canada and the implications of the change in the linkages for Canadian policy. The extent to which trade volumes between Canada and the United States accelerated after the Free Trade Agreement (FTA) and the North American Free Trade Agreement (NAFTA) surprised almost all analysts. It seemed timely to review the extent of these developments, given that almost a decade has passed since the NAFTA came into effect. This was the intent of the research program organized by Industry Canada, whose results comprise the studies in this volume. We note, too, that the research reported here was carried out before the tragic events of September 11, 2001, which have raised awareness of the deep interdependence between Canada, Mexico and the United States in the economic sphere as well as others. Security issues, border controls and immigration have dominated the media since the attacks and have served only to heighten public awareness of this interdependence.

The studies in this volume are largely positive in focus. Most do not take a position on whether or not deeper economic integration of the North American economies is desirable. For our purposes, it is convenient to group them into three categories. A first group is primarily empirical and attempts to assess the current state of economic integration. This is not as easy as might be imagined. New data sources, statistical methods and theories are brought to bear on the question of how to measure and interpret the observed changes in the flows of trade, investment and people, and their impact on the Canadian economy. A second group of studies deals with the policy dimensions of the integration process. There is a wide range of approaches taken here. One is to ask how deeper economic integration has affected existing national policies. Taxation, for example, is an important example of the three countries' ever-growing interdependence. In areas like social

\* *During the period in which the research program of this volume was carried out, the author was a fellow of the Canadian Institute for Advanced Research. Their generous support is gratefully acknowledged.*

policy and the environment, some argue that deeper linkages are constraining national sovereignty, while others maintain that such constraints already exist as a matter of fact, and optimal policy design requires more formal policy coordination or harmonization between countries. On balance, the authors do not resolve the case decisively for either harmonization or national independence. A third group of studies deals with what might be called the deepening of NAFTA institutions. What would be the impact of pushing the NAFTA countries toward a customs union or common market, for example? This could include the establishment of an integrated labour market through formal labour mobility links between Canada and the United States, a common currency or a common external trade policy.

We warn the reader that some of the more difficult issues in North American integration are not discussed in the studies that follow. First, they are concerned primarily with economic as opposed to political issues. The complex interdependencies running between the politics and economics of integration would be another volume. Second, some of the economic issues are not covered: these include border arrangements, transportation, communications and service market integration. Some of these are dealt with tangentially, but in general, another research program dealing with specific sectoral questions would be useful. Last, there is no attempt here, either by the authors or the editor, to arrive at some concluding welfare-benefit analysis of deeper Canada-U.S. or North American integration. Canadians may someday need to undertake exactly such a calculation and the research in this volume could help show them how.

The volume comprises 17 studies organized into three parts: I. *Measuring Integration: Trade and Investment*, with seven studies; II. *The NAFTA Countries as a Common Market*, with four; and III. *Policy Convergence or Divergence?*, with six. We begin with a look at Part I.

## MEASURING INTEGRATION: TRADE AND INVESTMENT

THE INCREASED TRADE INTEGRATION between Canada and the United States after the FTA is well-known and draws the specific attention of several studies. For example, the first one, by Acharya, Sharma and Rao, provides a useful summary of several important trends during the 1990s, while debunking a number of myths. First, much of the increase in trade is intra-industry, more or less as predicted by the trade theories used by this editor and others during the 1980s. Somewhat surprisingly, however, there is no significant increase in intrafirm trade, although it remains very important in the Canada-U.S. trade flows. In general, the authors also find that the structure of comparative advantage for Canada remains in commodity-intensive sectors, although some non-resource manufacturing sectors like machinery and autos have seen significant gains. They attempt to identify the source of the increased trade volume — the million-dollar question in this area.

Their answer is that the FTA and the NAFTA do not appear to have as much to do with this increase as other factors. In their statistical analysis, the depreciation of the Canadian dollar appears to explain a lot, but as noted, trade theory does not provide any good reason why trade volumes (as opposed to the trade balance) should be related to the exchange rate. The authors also look at the tough question of the relationship of productivity to trade and find some evidence that trade growth has promoted productivity growth in Canada. We are nevertheless left with a difficult question: why did the productivity gap between Canada and the United States grow during the 1990s? This problem is addressed by Industry Canada research in other volumes the reader would find useful as companions to this one.

Mexico's role in the evolution of NAFTA trade patterns is discussed in the second study, by Schembri and Vesselovsky, and the third, by Sawchuk and Sydor. Standard Hecksher-Ohlin theory predicts that trade between the NAFTA partners should see Mexico, with its abundant pool of unskilled labour, export goods intensive in unskilled labour to Canada and the United States, whose strengths are in capital and skilled labour. This is certainly evident. But Schembri and Vesselovsky also find that productivity effects are important. As in the Ricardian model, they treat productivity as exogenous. One strongly suspects, however, that Mexico's trade expansion is due to a strong two-way interaction between its trade liberalization process and upgrade in productivity. In either case, Mexico has been gaining market share significantly in both Canada and the United States. Sawchuk and Sydor use shift-share analysis to find out whether Canada is losing out to Mexico in the U.S. market. Their answer is yes. While one may therefore view Mexico as a competitive threat to Canada, it would not be wise to draw this conclusion. Generally, one would expect labour-intensive manufacturing activities to relocate to Mexican locations when possible. Given that pre-NAFTA trade barriers were much higher in Mexico than in Canada or the United States, much of the trade adjustment process has occurred in Mexico. The increase in Mexican exports (and imports) is to be expected, given the origins of the process, and benefits not only Mexico but also Canada and the United States.

In the fourth study, Head and Ries look at whether the post-FTA data support particular theories of international trade. Their analysis suggests that, contrary to Acharya, Sharma and Rao, the FTA was a major factor in explaining the increase in trade volumes. Many of the "new trade" theories predict a potential "home market effect" — that is, trade liberalization between a large and small country is biased against small-country exports of differentiated goods produced under conditions of increasing returns to scale. In the Canada-U.S. case, these theories suggest Canada would have been forced out of non-resource intensive manufacturing. In some cases, they even suggest this effect can be welfare-reducing for the small country. The "reverse home market effect" is when the market access enjoyed by the small country actually increases output and exports of the differentiated goods it produces. Head and Ries find evidence that the Canada-U.S. case in fact demonstrates the reverse home market effect. In general, they conclude that the welfare effects of the FTA were positive for Canada.

More generally, the potential impact of agglomeration on the location of economic activity has been one of the most difficult research questions to answer. Similar to the home market effect, strong agglomeration effects could work against firms choosing to locate in Canada. In the fifth study, one of the first to look at detailed regional and city linkages between Canada and the United States, Proulx documents the emergence of regional networks involving linkages between Canadian city regions and their proximate neighbours to the south on the basis of a Porter-type cluster analysis. In Proulx's view, the benefits of agglomeration are at the cluster network level. Canadian locations, therefore, do not suffer from any particular disadvantage and, as in Head and Ries, integration into the corresponding U.S. clusters confers a major benefit on Canadian locations. Both papers strongly suggest that trade integration has not been detrimental to Canadian-based producers.

A major debate in the United States during the 1990s was whether increased trade has contributed to the growing inequality between the incomes of high- and low-skill workers. While the income inequality trend has not been as strong in Canada, the same basic question could well be asked here. In the sixth study, Beaudry and Green have taken a novel tack on this issue: they focus not on the direct trade impact on wages, but on the potential indirect effect through capital formation. Using a new theory in which capital is allocated between a modern and traditional sector, they show that countries with higher levels of investment per worker will have more modest wage inequality. They use this theory to explain the differences between wage inequality trends in Canada, the United States, the United Kingdom and Germany. The intriguing implication of their analysis is that flows of physical capital across borders may have had, and may have in the future, stronger effects on income inequality than trade flows. In particular, they argue that deeper economic integration with the United States, which is generally a net importer of capital, given its low savings rate, may reduce investment in Canada and lead to greater wage inequality. In general, more research on the linkages between income distribution and economic integration is required.

Global foreign direct investment (FDI) flows have grown at a pace that exceeds even the growth in trade. The North American data show a similar trend, although its causes remain unclear. In the seventh and last study of this section, Globerman and Shapiro discuss the troubling fact that Canada's share of inward FDI to North America has fallen, with the United States being the destination of choice for most firms. The worry for Canada is that this development may reflect a large-market bias on the part of global firms, which would place Canada at a disadvantage in the competition for North American investment. In their discussion of the data, they point out that this "fact" is due to a sudden jump in U.K. and West European acquisitions of U.S. firms during the late 1990s boom in the United States. Whether this will turn out to be a longer-term trend remains uncertain at this point.

## THE NAFTA COUNTRIES AS A COMMON MARKET

THE FOUR STUDIES OF PART II OF THIS VOLUME deal with what are often referred to as common market issues. These are a set of formal government-to-government arrangements which would move the NAFTA countries from the status of a free trade area to some deeper form of integration. A number of commentators and politicians have raised the possibility of moving the NAFTA countries toward a common market, including President Fox of Mexico. The three important characteristics of a common market like the European Union that go beyond free trade are 1) labour mobility, 2) a common external trade policy, and 3) monetary integration or a common currency. A common market falls short of political union but has many of the institutions one typically associates with a federal state.

Labour mobility within North America is minimal. Governments continue to use migration controls as an instrument of national policy. As Harris and Schmitt note in the first study of Part II, the current levels of migration between Canada and the United States are quite low in relation to other periods in history. There are some limited forms of labour mobility within the NAFTA countries covering certain types of professionals under the TN visa program. The apparent one-way flow of high tech professionals from Canada to the United States raised considerable alarm as to the possibility of a serious "brain drain." The obvious question is: what would happen if labour mobility were extended to cover most professions — would Canada become a backwater, with most of its talent moving to large U.S. centres? Harris and Schmitt conclude that the historical evidence is not decisive. The welfare benefits of additional labour mobility could well be captured primarily in the form of higher wages to skilled labour in the smaller country — Canada — without a mass exodus from Canada. On the other hand, if Mexico were to be included, it is almost certain that the northward migration of unskilled labour from Mexico to the United States and Canada would lower the wages of unskilled labour here. On theoretical grounds, one can argue that most welfare gains from integration can be captured through trade liberalization rather than liberalizing factor flows. The evidence on this issue, however, is quite weak and more research is required.

Brown, Deardorff and Stern use the Michigan World Trade Model to assess a variety of trade policy initiatives within the NAFTA, as well as a range of bilateral and multilateral initiatives. The trade diverting effect of virtually all regional deals is one of the central themes of their results. The movement toward world free trade is generally the best trade policy because it leads to an absence of trade diverting effects. Regionalism in trade policy, however, is probably here to stay. One of these authors' most interesting results is that a common external tariff for the NAFTA countries appears to have very limited impact, although the details are sensitive to the methods by which a common external tariff is determined. As is common in this class of models, efficiency gains are offset by the terms of trade effects. If Canada and Mexico experience, on average, tariff cuts against third countries under a common external NAFTA tariff, the Michigan model predicts that welfare in both countries would decline — despite some efficiency gains from a common external tariff.

Within Canada, and to some extent Mexico, the possibility of a common currency or some form of North American monetary integration has been discussed extensively. In the next study, Arndt looks at the pros and cons of this complex set of issues and the available evidence. The cost-benefit analysis of Mundell's optimal currency area theory sets the benefits of an independent monetary policy against the costs of exchange rate instability and multiple currencies. Arndt notes that several studies point to the commodity-intensive nature of the Canadian economy to suggest (at least qualitatively) that there are still substantial benefits in a floating Canadian dollar. However, the extensive trade integration of the two countries is inevitably tipping the scales in favour of a common currency. In the case of Mexico, a common North American currency would have the added benefit of substantial financial stability, including a reduced risk of events like the peso crisis of the early 1990s. He concludes by noting that at this point, the major stumbling block to any move toward monetary union is a reluctance on the part of the United States to consider such an arrangement.

Most Canadians tend to be wary of any further formal moves toward deeper economic integration arrangements, like a common market. In the fourth and last study of Part II, Hart argues vigorously that it is in Canada's best interest to push further on integration rather than maintain the status quo. While falling short of recommending a push toward a common market, he argues that a major bilateral (Canada-U.S.) initiative is needed to address a number of remaining unresolved issues, including countervail and subsidy, border restrictions and security issues. The softwood lumber dispute certainly is vivid evidence of the validity of this position. Whether such an initiative would be feasible, given the current mood in Washington, is unclear. Hart argues, however, that Canada has no serious alternative other than to engage the Americans in these discussions. It is clear that without some response by the United States to these types of initiatives, both Canada and Mexico are left in the position of unilateral adjustment of their own domestic policies to the de facto integration that is occurring.

We now turn to the last six studies, which comprise Part III of this volume. They deal with Canada's policy options.

## POLICY CONVERGENCE OR DIVERGENCE?

ONCE ONE MOVES BEYOND TRADE, currency and factor mobility, the literature on economic integration moves outside the common market framework to policy areas that, historically, have been driven by domestic considerations. In today's world, however, such policy areas are increasingly affected by integration — driven either by formal intergovernmental arrangements like the NAFTA, or simply by the de facto integration that accompanies large increases in international trade and investments with lower transport and communication costs.

This literature takes two major approaches. The first, which we might call the policy convergence approach, holds that greater integration creates incentives for policy convergence between countries. This convergence is accomplished by a variety of mechanisms, from specific treaties to informal collaboration. The second is associated with what is called competitive federalism. In this literature, governments are assumed to compete with each other for mobile factors of production by choosing the policies most likely to attract incremental investment and jobs in light of the policies chosen by other governments. The typical prediction of this type of theory is either a "race to the bottom" result, with policies which impose the smallest burden on mobile factors (for example, the country with the lowest tax rate and least restrictive regulations benefits the most), or the opposite, a policy divergence. The latter, often referred to as the Tiebout hypothesis, occurs when governments differentiate themselves optimally in policy space. It is a model widely used to support decentralized government in federations. For regionally integrating national governments, this model supports the argument that policy divergence among states works and improves their welfare without formal policy coordination. The popular language commonly used to discuss these issues is the much-abused term "national sovereignty." Room to manoeuvre on domestic policy is equated to preserving national sovereignty. A lack of sovereignty is equated to policy convergence brought about either by formal treaties or by competition.

The six studies in Part III cover a number of domestic policy issues. They all illustrate the considerable tension in Canada between the pressures toward policy convergence with the United States versus the benefits of policy independence and hence divergence. The first two (Collins and Davies, and Dahlby) deal with taxation. While some areas of taxation are covered by international treaty, tax policy is largely determined by the national government, which sets tax rates independently — that is, without consulting the other governments, subject to the pressures to remain competitive.

Collins and Davies provide some important new estimates of the marginal effective tax rate on human capital in Canada and the United States. They find that, accounting for the costs of education, marginal effective tax rates are higher on human capital in Canada than in the United States at most income levels. They find that the marginal effective tax rates on human capital income in Canada and the United States are 15.9 and 8.5 percent, respectively. Given that higher education is more heavily subsidized in Canada, they note that this creates a powerful incentive for individuals who are educated in Canada to move early to the United States — a potentially important driver of the "brain drain" noted above. To date, however, these differences have not caused the convergence of the personal income tax systems of the two countries.

Dahlby specifically addresses the question: Is international competition for mobile capital creating a race to the bottom for business taxation? He argues that in the late 1980s and early 1990s there was evidence that tax rates were being lowered as a response to U.S. and U.K. tax cuts. He notes that there are still substantial divergences between countries on effective tax rates on inbound and outbound FDI. In the case of North America, he argues that integration will ultimately bring greater pressure on Canada to harmonize its rule for the allocation of corporate income with those of the other NAFTA countries.

In the third study, Boychuk and Banting ask similar questions with respect to income maintenance programs in Canada and the United States. They make the important argument that a proper analysis must account for both national and subnational variations to reach valid conclusions. Looking at a range of programs, they detect some convergence in the area of unemployment insurance and family benefits, but generally find little evidence of convergence in social policies. To the extent convergence is important, it seems to be occurring in areas controlled by the federal government rather than provincial governments: this contradicts the popular notion that the smaller the government the stronger the incentive to harmonize.

Environmental policy exhibits a similar lack of convergence, as Olewiler notes in her study. She finds no evidence of a race to the bottom for environmental standards, and to the extent that there is convergence, it is at the level of the most stringent environmental standards under the NAFTA. Interestingly, she argues that Canada, which has seen a substantial decentralization of environmental policy to the provincial level, has in fact created a status quo bias, so that Canadian standard-setting policies are lagging behind those of the United States.

Competition policy is one area in which the history of economic integration is quite varied. European integration began with a move toward a common competition policy, ahead of movement in other areas like trade and currency, but the NAFTA has virtually no mechanisms for a common competition policy. One unfortunate consequence of this is that dumping and subsidy issues remain largely unresolved and the source of considerable friction between the NAFTA countries. Replacement with a common predatory pricing rule within a common competition policy would be more desirable on economic grounds. Nevertheless, the United States continues to view competition or antitrust policy as a domestic instrument and in the case of cross-border mergers this is creating a new set of intergovernmental conflicts. In fact, both the United States and the European Union have been involved in a number of disputes involving the extraterritorial application of their own antitrust rules.

The fifth study, by Ware and Musgrave, reviews the theory and evidence on these issues and notes that some particularly thorny problems emerge for small open economies like Canada's. The very costly nature of merger reviews and the potential for costly delays as a result of intergovernmental competition through extra-territorial application of domestic competition law has created demands for global competition agencies. Both the Organisation for Economic Co-operation and Development and the World Trade Organization are pursuing global competition agency initiatives. At the North American level, however, there are no such initiatives; in practice, Canada is faced with a U.S. government which has been more vigorous in pursuit of its own interest through extra-territorial application of its laws. How should Canada respond? Ware and Musgrave argue that there is still a considerable amount of room for manoeuvre on the part of the Canadian competition authorities. They also posit that preservation of domestic competition should continue to be an important policy objective despite the increased levels of integration.

No discussion of integration would be complete without at least one paper on the Internet, which is viewed by many as one of the principal technological drivers of globalization. In the last study, Mann takes us through the difficult issues that multinational regulation of cyberspace potentially would create. For this new and incredibly important communications medium — the backbone of the "knowledge economy" — she poses the important questions: Should the Internet be regulated? If so, where and by whom? Does a global technology require a global regulator? She restricts herself to two issues — taxation and informational privacy. E-commerce over the Internet creates potential tax problems for both direct and indirect taxes. Since physical location does not necessarily coincide with value creation, the natural definition of residency for the purposes of income taxation becomes problematic. The Internet poses an even more direct challenge to existing systems of indirect taxation which are highly differentiated across regions and commodities. She argues that there is a natural case here for a trilateral NAFTA tax agreement covering Internet taxation, with rules of apportionment built on existing rules of origin procedure.

There has been substantial pressure to regulate the collection and dissemination of personal information on the Internet. Mann points out that in this rapidly evolving technology there are incentives to protect privacy — but it

9

is important to preserve the incentives for innovation. Canada has tended to focus on a legislative approach which gives privacy rights more weight than in the United States, which thus far has relied more on Internet self-regulation, hoping to preserve market incentives for innovation. Mann argues that these different approaches can be preserved within an overall, NAFTA-defined approach to data protection. She concludes that a NAFTA-based approach to Internet governance within the NAFTA region is the only practical alternative, which moreover is supported by both the existing levels of integration and policy coordination in other areas. By contrast, she argues that a global governance regime for the Internet is neither desirable nor realistic.

## CONCLUSION

THERE IS NO SINGLE CONCLUSION that emerges from the rich set of data and hypotheses in these studies. The state of North American linkages is complex and it is evolving in a number of ways. While economic integration has proceeded at a rapid pace over the last two decades, the NAFTA partners still maintain distinctive national policies in a wide range of areas. There are clear pressures emerging to forge some uniquely North American approaches toward the formation of a common North American market, but these are still in the early stages. The events of September 11 have had an enduring impact on the debate about North American linkages in a number of ways. The concept of a North American perimeter has been proposed and is still under consideration. Within this perimeter, Canada, the United States and Mexico would share a common external border with respect to security, immigration and the checking of goods being shipped into the North American zone. Some steps in that direction have been made already. If the three NAFTA countries move significantly in the direction of a North American perimeter, it will be an important step in the direction of a common market. Preserving Canada's distinctiveness while leveraging the economic benefits that economic integration brings will continue to be the single most important item on the national policy agenda for the foreseeable future.

# Part I
## Measuring Integration: Trade and Investment

*Ram C. Acharya, Prakash Sharma & Someshwar Rao*
*Industry Canada*

*1*

# Canada-U.S. Trade and
# Foreign Direct Investment Patterns

## INTRODUCTION

R APID ADVANCES IN INFORMATION AND COMMUNICATION TECHNOLOGIES, the sharp drop in transportation and communication costs, and fierce international competition for markets, capital and skilled professionals have accelerated the pace of globalization of business in Canada and all other countries. Canada has participated actively in this process. International trade (goods and services) as a share of Gross Domestic Product (GDP) increased dramatically in the 1990s. It now represents nearly 90 percent of Canada's GDP. Similarly, Canadian firms are investing heavily abroad: in fact, since 1996, Canadian direct investment abroad (CDIA) has exceeded foreign direct investment (FDI) in Canada.

However, much of the increased trade and investment orientation came in the form of increased commercial linkages with the United States and Mexico, perhaps as a result of the Free Trade Agreement (FTA), the North American Free Trade Agreement (NAFTA), the strong U.S. economy and the depreciation of the Canadian dollar. Despite the growing economic linkages, Canada's productivity and real income performance lagged far behind the United States in the 1990s, and the Canada-U.S. productivity and real income level gaps widened significantly — the exact opposite of expectations.

The objective of this study is an in-depth analysis of Canada's trade and investment patterns with the United States, our dominant and most important trading partner. Our analysis hopes to shed some new light on the puzzling trend of the widening economic performance gap between Canada and the United States despite the growing commercial linkages. This study addresses the following key research and policy questions:

- What are the patterns of merchandise trade between Canada and the United States, by industry and by region?

- Is the recent large increase in trade between the two countries a structural or cyclical phenomenon?

- What role does intrafirm trade play in the Canada-U.S. trade relationship?

- What are the patterns of trade in services and foreign investment between Canada and the United States?

- What has happened to the factor content of Canada's exports over the years?

- How has the comparative advantage position of Canadian manufacturing industries changed over time?

- How has intraindustry trade between Canada and the United States changed over time?

- Has the expansion of trade with the United States led to increased product specialization and higher productivity growth?

- Who are Canada's main competitors in the U.S. goods market and how well is Canada doing?

Our findings indicate that Canada-U.S. trade and investment links deepened in the 1990s across all provinces and industries. The buoyant U.S. economy and the depreciation of the Canadian dollar were mainly responsible for the dramatic increase in Canadian exports to the United States. Nevertheless, the FTA and the NAFTA increased Canadian exports to the United States by about 9 percent. Contrary to expectations, however, the share of intrafirm trade in total trade of U.S. affiliates in Canada and Canadian affiliates in the United States has declined significantly. This decline suggests that the reduction of tariff and non-tariff barriers might have increased outsourcing by Canadian and U.S. multinationals in search of cost reductions. Our results also show that the skill content of Canadian exports of goods and services has risen steadily over the past 20 years. The two free trade agreements have led to a slight expansion in intraindustry trade (an indicator of increased specialization) and improved Canada's productivity. Canada has gained market share in the United States, primarily in resource-based and labour-intensive products. However, Canada has lost market share in the paper and allied products, non-electrical machinery, and non-metallic mineral industries. Over the same period, China expanded its market share in all of these industries significantly, as did Mexico, with the exception of the paper and allied products industry, which saw an expansion of the market shares of the European Union (EU), Japan and East Asia.

The study is divided into seven sections. After the introduction, the second section analyses the patterns of the Canada-U.S. goods trade, disaggregated by province or state and industry, and looks at the role of intrafirm trade in the growing trade linkages between the two countries. The third section discusses Canada's service trade and FDI linkages with the United States, disaggregated by industry. The fourth section considers the factor content of Canada's exports and the country's revealed comparative advantage (RCA) positions. The fifth section sets out trends in intra- and interindustry trade between Canada and the United States, as well as the contribution of the FTA and the NAFTA to Canada's product specialization and productivity improvements. The sixth section analyses the trends in Canada's market shares of U.S. imports, disaggregated by industry and competitor. The concluding section summarizes the key findings of the study and discusses their implications.

## MERCHANDISE TRADE PATTERNS

CANADA'S TRADE FLOWS HAVE RISEN DRAMATICALLY since 1980. In 2000, Canada's exports of goods and services reached $473.9 billion, up from just $87.7 billion in 1980, a 5.4-fold increase. Similarly, imports of goods and services reached $425.9 billion in 2000, a 5.2-fold increase over the same period (Figure 1). As a result of this phenomenal growth, Canada's merchandise trade rose from 25 percent of GDP in 1980 to 42 percent in 2000. Merchandise imports also rose to 35 percent of GDP in 2000, from 22 percent in 1980 (Figure 2). In the service trade, exports rose to 5.4 percent of GDP in 2000, up from 2.8 percent in 1980, and imports reached 6 percent of GDP in 2000, up from 4 percent in 1980 (Figure 3).

Few bilateral economic relationships in the world today approach the Canada-U.S. commercial linkages. In 2000, the two-way trade of goods and services between Canada and the United States amounted to $700 billion: $627.2 billion in goods, $72.8 billion in services. Canada sent 86 percent of its merchandise exports to the United States, which was the source of 73.7 percent of its imports (Figure 4). Two decades earlier, less than 70 percent of Canadian merchandise exports were destined for the American market. The United States accounts for a much smaller share of Canada's service trade: 59 percent of exports and 63 percent of imports in 2000, not significantly different from 1980 levels.

# FIGURE 1

## TOTAL VALUE OF EXPORTS AND IMPORTS OF GOODS AND SERVICES, 1980-2000

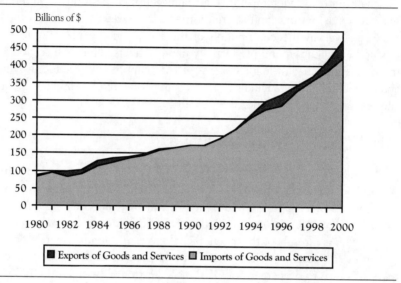

Source: Statistics Canada.

# FIGURE 2

## RATIO OF GOODS TRADE TO GDP, 1980-2000

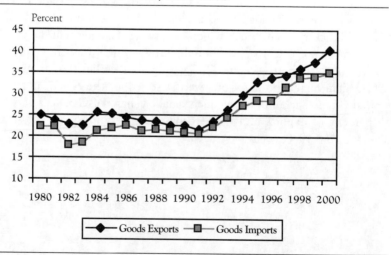

Source: Statistics Canada.

FIGURE 3

## RATIO OF SERVICE TRADE TO GDP, 1980-2000

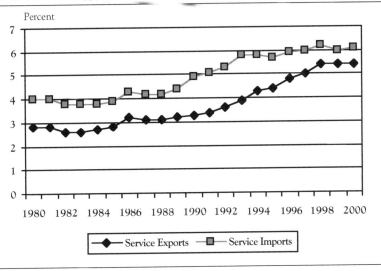

Source: Statistics Canada.

FIGURE 4

## THE U.S. SHARE OF CANADIAN TRADE IN GOODS, 1980-2000

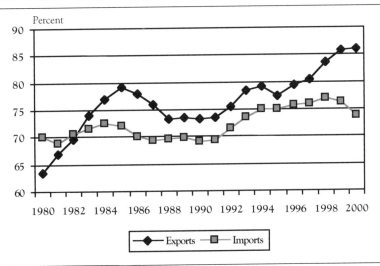

Source: Statistics Canada.

## MERCHANDISE TRADE LINKS BETWEEN CANADIAN REGIONS AND THE UNITED STATES

CANADA'S STRONG ECONOMIC PERFORMANCE over the 1980-2000 period was powered by an annual growth of 9.5 percent in merchandise exports to the United States. Of the five Canadian regional markets,[1] Ontario is the main supplier to the U.S. market, currently shipping over 56 percent of Canada's total goods exports to the United States. The province's share has remained relatively flat over the last 20 years. Quebec has the second-largest share of Canada's goods exports to the United States, followed by the Prairies (Table 1).

### TABLE 1

### THE CANADIAN REGIONAL SHARE OF THE GOODS TRADE WITH THE UNITED STATES, 1980-2000 (PERCENT)

| | Exports to the United States | | | Imports from the United States | | |
|---|---|---|---|---|---|---|
| | 1980–1989 | 1990–1994 | 1995–2000 | 1980–1989 | 1990–1994 | 1995–2000 |
| Atlantic | 4.1 | 3.9 | 3.8 | 1.4 | 1.7 | 1.3 |
| Quebec | 16.8 | 17.6 | 17.8 | 11.5 | 11.6 | 9.8 |
| Ontario | 56.1 | 56.7 | 56.5 | 72.4 | 70.9 | 73.3 |
| Prairies | 15.5 | 15.0 | 15.5 | 9.0 | 8.7 | 9.4 |
| British Columbia and the Territories | 7.5 | 6.8 | 6.4 | 5.7 | 7.1 | 6.2 |
| Total | 100 | 100 | 100 | 100 | 100 | 100 |

Source: Statistics Canada.

### TABLE 2

### THE U.S. SHARE OF THE CANADIAN REGIONAL GOODS TRADE, 1980-2000 (PERCENT)

| | Exports to the United States | | | Imports from the United States | | |
|---|---|---|---|---|---|---|
| | 1980–1989 | 1990–1994 | 1995–2000 | 1980–1989 | 1990–1994 | 1995–2000 |
| Atlantic | 60.1 | 66.5 | 71.9 | 20.3 | 26.9 | 23.8 |
| Quebec | 65.8 | 76.8 | 82.8 | 43.0 | 44.0 | 43.0 |
| Ontario | 86.5 | 88.1 | 91.4 | 79.9 | 76.1 | 75.7 |
| Prairies | 73.4 | 69.4 | 76.4 | 86.1 | 83.1 | 82.1 |
| British Columbia and the Territories | 40.0 | 48.3 | 58.6 | 40.4 | 45.9 | 48.4 |
| Total | 73.0 | 77.5 | 82.9 | 67.1 | 65.8 | 66.9 |

Source: Statistics Canada.

On the import side, Ontario absorbs almost three-quarters of Canadian merchandise imports from the United States, while Quebec and the Prairies each accounts for about 10 percent. The U.S share of all Canadian regional exports rose during the 1995-2000 period, as compared to 1980-89 and 1990-94. On the other hand, imports from the United States fell in all Canadian regions between 1990-94 and 1995-2000, except in British Columbia and the Territories (Table 2).

In Table 3, we evaluate the performance of Canadian merchandise exports to the United States, disaggregated by region. For analytical purposes, we group the American states into four regions: Northeast, Midwest, South and Northwest.[2] Canadian exports to the South increased 12.3 percent per year during the 1980-2000 period. With overall export growth to the United States at 9.5 percent, both Ontario and Quebec registered higher-than-average growth, powered by a strong expansion of trade with the South and Northwest. Atlantic Canada also increased its trade linkages with the South, Midwest and Northwest significantly, and Prairie exports to the South and Northeast rose at an annual rate of 15 percent. However, exports from British Columbia and the Territories rose at a significantly slower rate than those from other Canadian regions. To sum up, the export growth of the Atlantic region was fastest in the South, that of Quebec, Ontario and British Columbia in the Northwest, and that of the Prairies in the Northeast. The U.S. South was the second-fastest growing export market for Quebec, Ontario and the Prairies.

## TABLE 3

## AVERAGE ANNUAL GROWTH OF GOODS EXPORTS FROM CANADIAN TO U.S. REGIONS, 1980-2000 (PERCENT)

| From/To | Northeast | Midwest | South | Northwest | United States | World |
|---|---|---|---|---|---|---|
| Canada | 8.3 | 9.3 | 12.3 | 9.7 | 9.5 | 9.3 |
| Atlantic | 7.2 | 13.1 | 14.0 | 11.9 | 9.2 | 7.9 |
| Quebec | 8.8 | 8.5 | 13.1 | 13.8 | 9.9 | 7.4 |
| Ontario | 7.6 | 9.9 | 11.8 | 15.3 | 10.0 | 9.4 |
| Prairies | 15.1 | 7.6 | 15.0 | 5.9 | 8.6 | 9.1 |
| British Columbia and the Territories | 6.2 | 9.2 | 7.9 | 8.3 | 8.2 | 4.9 |

Note:   The compound growth rate was obtained by 1) fitting the trend by means of the equation $\ln x_t = \ln x_0 + \ln(1+g)t + u_t$ ,where $x_t$ denotes exports of goods from Canada and $g$ represents the instantaneous (at a point in time) growth rate, and then 2) computing the compound growth rate = (Antilog of $g - 1$) * 100. The trend factor is highly significant for all trend equations estimated for exports of merchandise from all Canadian markets to all U.S. markets for a period of 21 years.

Source: Statistics Canada.

Canada's exports to the Northwest and South grew faster that those to the Northeast and Midwest: as a result, the shares of total Canadian exports declined for the latter, while rising for the former (Table 4). The Northwest and the South regions accounted for 30 percent of Canada's total merchandise exports during the 1995-2000 period, up from about 23 percent during the 1980-89 period. However, almost half of Canada's exports are still destined for the Midwest. The Northeast and Midwest regions account for more than two-thirds of exports from all Canadian regions except the Prairies and British Columbia and the Territories: they receive 60 percent of total U.S. exports from the Prairies and less than 30 percent from British Columbia and the Territories. The Northwest is the latter's most important export market; it takes 52 percent of this Canadian region's exports to the United States. Similar shifts, albeit small ones, are observed for Canadian import shares from the U.S. regions; the South and Northwest shares have increased, while the importance of the Northeast has declined (Table 4).

## TABLE 4

## REGIONAL DISTRIBUTION OF CANADIAN TRADE WITH U.S. REGIONS, 1980-2000 (PERCENT)

| | | Exports | | | | | Imports | | | |
|---|---|---|---|---|---|---|---|---|---|---|
| | | NE | MW | South | NW | | NE | MW | South | NW |
| Canada | | | | | | | | | | |
| | 1980-1989 | 30.2 | 46.0 | 11.7 | 11.8 | | 22.0 | 43.4 | 15.1 | 10.3 |
| | 1990-1994 | 26.0 | 47.4 | 12.6 | 12.5 | | 20.9 | 44.6 | 19.7 | 11.4 |
| | 1995-2000 | 24.9 | 44.0 | 16.4 | 13.6 | | 19.5 | 44.5 | 23.7 | 11.4 |
| Atlantic | | | | | | | | | | |
| | 1980-1989 | 76.4 | 5.7 | 15.6 | 1.8 | | 35.3 | 20.6 | 32.9 | 10.4 |
| | 1990-1994 | 66.4 | 8.6 | 18.5 | 3.1 | | 30.1 | 23.6 | 32.0 | 10.2 |
| | 1995-2000 | 59.5 | 10.2 | 25.3 | 3.0 | | 36.8 | 18.3 | 36.9 | 7.6 |
| Quebec | | | | | | | | | | |
| | 1980-1989 | 51.3 | 27.9 | 16.4 | 3.8 | | 43.9 | 21.9 | 20.5 | 10.8 |
| | 1990-1994 | 47.5 | 25.3 | 17.2 | 8.1 | | 47.9 | 15.7 | 22.3 | 9.0 |
| | 1995-2000 | 45.4 | 23.6 | 23.8 | 5.9 | | 47.7 | 14.5 | 24.8 | 10.6 |
| Ontario | | | | | | | | | | |
| | 1980-1989 | 28.7 | 56.2 | 10.3 | 4.6 | | 21.0 | 48.6 | 13.5 | 6.1 |
| | 1990-1994 | 21.9 | 59.3 | 9.9 | 7.4 | | 18.7 | 51.9 | 18.7 | 7.4 |
| | 1995-2000 | 21.0 | 54.8 | 13.4 | 9.7 | | 17.5 | 51.2 | 23.2 | 7.4 |
| Prairies | | | | | | | | | | |
| | 1980-1989 | 8.3 | 53.7 | 7.8 | 30.0 | | 8.9 | 48.1 | 20.4 | 15.5 |
| | 1990-1994 | 13.2 | 50.4 | 13.9 | 21.2 | | 10.2 | 46.6 | 26.2 | 13.8 |
| | 1995-2000 | 13.1 | 46.5 | 16.1 | 23.3 | | 10.9 | 43.9 | 30.2 | 14.4 |
| British Columbia and the Territories | | | | | | | | | | |
| | 1980-1989 | 14.0 | 16.7 | 17.7 | 51.0 | | 8.4 | 19.3 | 11.7 | 54.8 |
| | 1990-1994 | 10.5 | 20.5 | 15.7 | 51.7 | | 8.8 | 21.1 | 14.2 | 53.0 |
| | 1995-2000 | 10.3 | 19.1 | 16.8 | 52.2 | | 8.5 | 18.7 | 16.0 | 56.2 |

Note:  NE is Northeast, MW is Midwest and NW is Northwest.
Source: Statistics Canada.

## MERCHANDISE TRADE LINKS WITH THE UNITED STATES: INDUSTRY DIMENSIONS

IN THIS SUBSECTION, we present Canada's goods trade in the U.S. market for the 21 industries at the Standard Industrial Classification (SIC) 2-digit level.[3] The U.S. share of Canadian exports for these industries is found in Appendix A, Table A1. It is interesting to note that the U.S. share either rose (in 18 industries) or remained constant (in rubber and plastics, and transportation equipment) during the second half of the 1990s — except for tobacco products. Between 1995 and 2000, the U.S. share of Canadian exports was more than 90 percent in seven industries: furniture, refined petroleum, transportation equipment, rubber and plastics, clothing, non-metallic minerals and printing. On the import side, the U.S. share rose in some industries and fell in others. There is not a single industry in which the United States supplies 90 percent of Canada's imports.

To demonstrate the regional dimension, we compute the U.S. share of each of 21 industries' exports for each Canadian region by using average annual data for the 1995-2000 period. We then divide this share by the U.S. share of the corresponding region's goods exports (in the last row of Table 5). An industry with a value greater than one would tell us that this Canadian industry, for that region, has a greater-than-average orientation in the United States — a rough indicator of comparative advantage. The results are presented in Table 5, where industries with a value greater than one are denoted by a check mark.

Even though a clear-cut picture does not emerge, it could be interpreted that Atlantic Canada specializes in industries other than machinery, mining and food products. Quebec has a revealed comparative advantage in labour-intensive industries such as textile products, clothing and primary metals. Ontario, on the other hand, concentrates on transportation equipment (autos), furniture, paper and allied products, and refined petroleum. Prairie exports are dominated by mining, refined petroleum and clothing. Agriculture, fishing and forestry, transportation equipment, non-electrical machinery and non-metallic minerals dominate the exports of British Columbia and the Territories.

## MERCHANDISE TRADE: INDUSTRIAL AND REGIONAL DIMENSIONS

This subsection presents some facts on the merchandise exports of Canada and its five regions to the four U.S. regions, by industry. The details for Canada and each Canadian region are set out in Appendix A, Tables A2 through A7. On the basis of Table A2, Table 6 compares Canada's change in export share for 1990-2000 to its export share for 1980-89. An upward arrow means that the export share of the corresponding industry rose, while a downward arrow means that it fell during the 1990s. A similar table can be constructed for each Canadian region.

**TABLE 5**

**REGIONAL DISTRIBUTION OF INDUSTRIES WITH HIGHER-THAN-AVERAGE MARKET SHARE IN THE UNITED STATES, 1995-2000**

| Industry | Canadian Region | | | | |
|---|---|---|---|---|---|
| | Atlantic | Quebec | Ontario | Prairies | British Columbia and the Territories |
| 1. Agriculture, Fishing and Forestry | √ | | | | √ |
| 2. Mining | | | | √ | |
| 3. Food and Beverages | | | | | |
| 4. Tobacco Products | √ | | | | |
| 5. Rubber and Plastics | √ | √ | | | √ |
| 6. Leather and Allied Products | √ | √ | | √ | √ |
| 7. Textile Products | √ | √ | | | √ |
| 8. Clothing | √ | √ | | √ | √ |
| 9. Wood | √ | √ | | √ | √ |
| 10. Furniture and Fixtures | √ | √ | √ | √ | √ |
| 11. Paper and Allied Products | | | √ | | |
| 12. Printing, Publishing and Allied Products | √ | √ | | √ | √ |
| 13. Primary Metals | | √ | | | |
| 14. Fabricated Metal Products | √ | √ | | √ | √ |
| 15. Machinery (except Electrical) | | | | | √ |
| 16. Transportation Equipment | √ | | √ | √ | √ |
| 17. Electrical and Electronic Products | | | | √ | √ |
| 18. Non-metallic Minerals | √ | √ | | √ | √ |
| 19. Refined Petroleum and Coal | √ | √ | √ | √ | √ |
| 20. Chemical Products | √ | | | | √ |
| 21. Other Manufacturing | √ | | | | √ |
| Average Export Share to the United States | 71.9 | 82.8 | 91.4 | 76.4 | 58.6 |

Note:  The data in the last row are taken from Table 2.
Source: Statistics Canada.

It is clear from Table 6 that overall, the shares of Canada's goods exports during the 1990s fell for the Northeast and the Midwest regions, while those for the South and Northwest rose. The export shares of agriculture, fishing and forestry, food and beverages, furniture and fixtures, printing, publishing and allied products, and transportation equipment rose for all markets except the Northeast. None of the six industries whose market share rose in the Northeast during the 1990s were able to raise their share in more than one regional market. Even though the overall share in the Midwest fell, the shares of many industries rose in this region. In the South, the export shares of rubber and plastics, leather and allied products, wood, electrical and electronic products, and chemical products fell during the 1990s despite the region's rise in overall export share. Similarly, in the Northwest, the shares of food and beverages, fabricated metal products, machinery (except electrical), transportation equipment, and refined petroleum and coal shrank.

---

**TABLE 6**

**CHANGE IN CANADA'S INDUSTRIAL EXPORT SHARE TO U.S. REGIONAL MARKETS: 1990-2000 COMPARED TO 1980-89**

| Industry | Northeast | Midwest | South | Northwest |
|---|---|---|---|---|
| 1. Agriculture, Fishing and Forestry | ↓ | ↑ | ↑ | ↑ |
| 2. Mining | ↑ | ↓ | ↑ | ↓ |
| 3. Food and Beverages | ↓ | ↑ | ↑ | ↑ |
| 4. Tobacco Products | ↑ | ↓ | ↓ | ↑ |
| 5. Rubber and Plastics | ↓ | ↑ | ↓ | – |
| 6. Leather and Allied Products | ↑ | ↓ | – | ↑ |
| 7. Textile Products | ↓ | ↓ | ↑ | ↑ |
| 8. Clothing | ↓ | ↓ | ↑ | ↑ |
| 9. Wood | ↓ | ↑ | ↓ | ↑ |
| 10. Furniture and Fixtures | ↓ | ↑ | ↑ | ↑ |
| 11. Paper and Allied Products | ↓ | – | ↑ | – |
| 12. Printing, Publishing and Allied Products | ↓ | ↑ | ↑ | ↑ |
| 13. Primary Metals | ↓ | ↑ | ↑ | ↓ |
| 14. Fabricated Metal Products | ↓ | ↑ | ↑ | ↑ |
| 15. Machinery (except Electrical) | ↓ | ↑ | – | ↓ |
| 16. Transportation Equipment | ↓ | ↑ | ↑ | ↑ |
| 17. Electrical and Electronic Products | ↑ | ↓ | ↓ | ↑ |
| 18. Non-metallic Minerals | ↓ | ↑ | ↑ | – |
| 19. Refined Petroleum and Coal | ↑ | ↓ | ↑ | ↓ |
| 20. Chemical Products | ↑ | ↓ | ↓ | ↑ |
| **Overall Change** | ↓ | ↓ | ↑ | ↑ |

Note: "Other Manufacturing" is not reported; (–) = no change.
Source: Statistics Canada.

---

## THE ROLE OF INTRAFIRM TRADE IN CANADA-U.S. MERCHANDISE TRADE

IS THE DRAMATIC INCREASE IN TRADE FLOWS between Canada and the United States due to the expansion of intrafirm (cross-border trade between parents and affiliates) or intercorporate trade? As there are no good Canadian time-series data on intrafirm trade of goods, we have used data from the U.S. Bureau of Economic

Analysis to examine the trends in intrafirm trade between Canada and the United States.[4] These data show that the share of U.S. intrafirm trade in total U.S. goods trade (exports and imports) to the world changed little between 1983 and 1997: it fluctuated with no sustained trend. The share of intrafirm trade as a proportion of total Canada-U.S. goods trade, however, has declined substantially.[5] The U.S. intrafirm export share of total U.S. exports to Canada declined from 51 to 36 percent between 1983 and 1997 (Figure 5). Similarly, the intrafirm import share of total U.S. imports from Canada decreased from 47 to 40 percent over the same period (Figure 6).

Much of the intrafirm trade between the two countries is carried on by U.S. multinational companies (MNCs), and there was little change during the 1990s. Table 7 shows that U.S. MNCs ship about 95 percent of U.S. intrafirm exports to Canada and receive more than 80 percent of U.S. intrafirm imports from Canada. Canadian MNCs contribute the rest of the intrafirm trade. As expected, U.S. MNCs dominate in all industries, especially in transportation equipment and chemical products.

## TABLE 7

## SHARE OF U.S. MNCS AND AFFILIATES IN U.S. INTRAFIRM TRADE WITH CANADA (PERCENT)

| Industry | Exports Shipped by U.S. Parent Companies to Affiliates in Canada | | Imports Shipped to U.S. Affiliates in Canada by U.S. Parent Companies | |
|---|---|---|---|---|
| | 1992–95 | 1995–98 | 1992–95 | 1995–98 |
| All Industries | 95.7 | 94.7 | 84.1 | 81.6 |
| Petroleum | 95.3 | N/A | 79.1 | N/A |
| Total Manufacturing | 96.3 | 95.4 | 90.0 | 89.3 |
| Food and Kindred Products | N/A | 92.5 | N/A | N/A |
| Chemical and Allied Products | N/A | 98.5 | N/A | 88.8 |
| Primary and Fabricated Metals | 53.1 | N/A | N/A | 40.7 |
| Machinery (except Electrical) | 99.4 | N/A | N/A | 97.8 |
| Electrical and Electronic Equipment | 75.2 | 55.4 | N/A | N/A |
| Transportation Equipment | 99.7 | N/A | N/A | 98.7 |
| Wholesale Trade | 94.2 | 92.7 | 34.7 | 29.2 |
| Services | N/A | 78.9 | 86.6 | 50.5 |
| Other Industries | N/A | 91.4 | 66.0 | 27.8 |

Note:   In this table, some service industries have been included. This is because some service industries carry on some trade in goods, even though their share might be very small. In addition, some data were kept confidential and are therefore reported as not available (N/A).

Source:   U.S. Bureau of Economic Analysis.

FIGURE 5

U.S. INTRAFIRM EXPORTS OF GOODS AS A PERCENTAGE OF TOTAL U.S.
GOODS EXPORTS, 1983-97

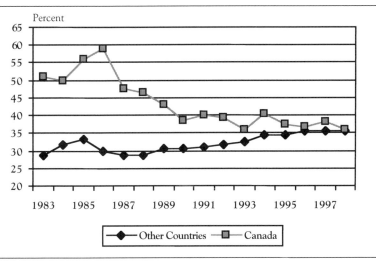

Source: Statistics Canada.

FIGURE 6

U.S. INTRAFIRM IMPORTS OF GOODS AS A PERCENTAGE OF TOTAL
U.S. GOODS IMPORTS, 1983-97

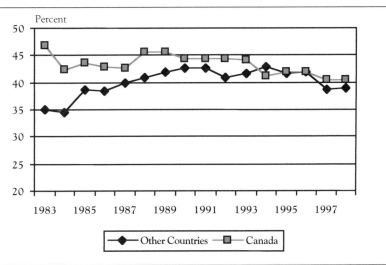

Source: Statistics Canada.

Hence, contrary to expectations, the dramatic increase in Canada-U.S. two-way trade during the 1990s was not due to a rise in intrafirm trade. These results suggest instead that the fall in tariff and non-tariff barriers might have increased outsourcing by U.S. MNCs seeking cost reductions.

## THE IMPACT OF THE FTA ON CANADA-U.S. MANUFACTURING TRADE FLOWS

IN THIS SUBSECTION, we analyse the role of economic growth in Canada and the United States, the depreciation of the Canadian dollar, and the role of the FTA and the NAFTA in the expansion of manufacturing trade flows between Canada and the United States during the 1980s and 1990s by estimating equations for Canadian exports and imports, disaggregated by industry. To quantify the contribution of various factors to the growth of exports for each industry $i$, we estimate the following growth equations for Canadian exports to the United States:

$$\frac{dx_i}{x_i} = \beta_1 \frac{dy^*}{y^*} + \beta_2 \ln r_i + \beta_3 c_i + \beta_4 FTA + u_i, \quad i = 1,\ldots,20,$$

where $x_i$ is the Canadian export of industry $i$, $y^*$ is the U.S. real GDP, $r_i$ is the industry-specific real exchange rate, $c_i$ is capacity utilization in Canada of industry $i$, and FTA is a dummy assigned a value of zero from 1980 to 1988 and a value of one from 1989 to 1999. The real exchange rate is defined as $p_i/ep_i^*$, where $p_i$ denotes the output price index in Canada of industry $i$, $p_i^*$ is the U.S. output price index, and $e$ refers to the nominal exchange rate, defined as the number of Canadian dollars per U.S. dollar. Therefore, $r_i$ = U.S. *goods/Canadian goods*. In general, we expect a negative relationship between the growth of real exports and real exchange rates.[6] For the estimation, the growth of real exports and U.S. real GDP are expressed as percentages. The equation is estimated with data from 1980 to 1999. For details on the estimation of export and import functions, see Goldstein and Khan (1985) and Magee (1975).

We estimate two regressions for the overall manufacturing sector — one with the transportation sector and the other without it. We exclude the transportation sector because as a result of the auto pact, the U.S. tariff rates for the automotive sector were almost zero (even at the SIC 2-digit level of aggregation) at the time of the FTA. It is thus desirable to exclude the transportation sector to demonstrate the impact of the FTA, which did not affect this sector at all. The results are presented in the following panels. Both empirical models do a good job (and produce similar results). All four explanatory variables are statistically significant in the regression equation for total manufacturing exports. These results suggest that it was strong U.S. economic expansion that was mainly responsible

## EXPORT EQUATIONS

| DEPENDENT VARIABLE | INDEPENDENT VARIABLES | | | | | |
|---|---|---|---|---|---|---|
| Canada's Real Export Growth to the U.S. Market | U.S. Real GDP Growth | Log of Real Exchange Rate | Capacity Utilization in Canada | FTA Dummy | $R^2$ | D–W |
| Total Manufacturing | 2.451 (4.07)[a] | −0.517 (−3.56)[a] | −0.002 (−3.44)[a] | 0.078 (3.23)[a] | 0.68 | 1.60 |
| Total Manufacturing (without Transportation Sector) | 2.710 (4.53)[a] | −0.319 (−2.21)[b] | −0.002 (−3.06)[a] | 0.090 (3.76)[a] | 0.69 | 1.79 |

| Canada's Real Export Growth to the U.S. Market | U.S. Real GDP Growth | Log of Real Exchange Rate | Capacity Utilization in Canada | U.S. Tariffs to Canada (percent) | $R^2$ | D–W |
|---|---|---|---|---|---|---|
| Total Manufacturing | 2.208 (3.34)[a] | −0.481 (−2.99)[a] | −0.001 (−1.58) | −0.015 (−2.42)[b] | 0.60 | 1.27 |
| Total Manufacturing (without Transportation Sector) | 2.380 (3.81)[a] | −0.290 (−1.93)[c] | 0.000 (−0.55) | −0.018 (−3.36)[a] | 0.66 | 1.51 |

Notes: The number in parentheses below each coefficient is a t-ratio.
[a]Significantly different from zero at the 1 percent level, on the basis of a two-tailed test.
[b]Significantly different from zero at the 5 percent level, on the basis of a two-tailed test.
Source: Authors' estimations.

for the large rise in Canadian exports to the United States during the 1990s. The regression results imply that an increase of 1 percent in U.S. real GDP growth leads to a rise of 2.5 percent in Canadian manufacturing exports to the United States (2.7 percent without the transportation sector).

The depreciation of the Canadian dollar stimulates exports. The capacity utilization variable coefficient is negative, implying that Canadian business relies more on exports to the United States during periods of weak domestic demand and vice versa. The FTA dummy coefficient is positive and statistically significant. However, the impact of the FTA on Canadian exports to the United States, after controlling for other variables, was modest — exports rose by about 9 percent. The FTA dummy coefficient seems rather low, but this is not the only study to find that trade liberalization between Canada and the United States has had a low impact. On the basis of Canada's exports to the United States between 1971 and 1986, Rao and Lemprière (1992) found that 75 percent of Canada's export growth to the United States was accounted for by the increase in U.S. consumption. In addition to 15 percent of trend growth, the rest of the increase was due to other factors, like changes in unit labour costs and U.S. capacity utilization rates. The 1992 study found that the role of tariff reduction was negligible. Our result may not be surprising, given that the average U.S. world manufacturing tariff rate was already at a low 3.88 percent in 1988, and we would expect the rate to be slightly lower for Canada.

In another exercise, we estimated the above equation using U.S. tariff rates for Canada instead of the FTA dummy, both with and without the transportation sector.[7] The results are presented in the panels below under the same headings as in the panels above. As expected, the U.S. tariff rates have a negative value, implying that it was the fall in U.S. tariff rates that led to the rise in Canada's real exports to the United States. The results, whether we use the FTA dummy or U.S. tariff rates for Canada, are basically the same, with the following two differences:

1. The capacity utilization variable, although it has the same negative sign, turns out to be statistically insignificant once we use U.S. tariff rates.

2. U.S. real GDP and log of real exchange rate coefficient values fall slightly if we use U.S. tariff rates instead of the FTA dummy.

Note that the coefficient on U.S. tariffs is -0.018 when the transportation sector is excluded. This means that a fall of 1 percent in U.S. tariff rates raises real Canadian exports by 0.018 percent. With U.S. tariff rates at 4.54 percent in 1988 and 0.07 in 1999, there was a fall of 4.47 percent in U.S. tariff rates during the 1988-99 period. The resulting change in real Canadian exports would be equal to 8 percent. Note that when we use the FTA dummy, its coefficient is 9 percent. The effect of the FTA on Canada's real exports is thus almost the same, whether we measure it on the basis of U.S. tariff rates or the FTA dummy.

The details for equations estimated with the FTA dummy for all 19 industries are presented in Appendix A, Table A8. At the industry level, the export growth of different industries responded to a variety of combinations of the four explanatory variables. Only for fabricated metal products were all four determinants of export growth statistically significant.[8] U.S. real GDP growth was significant for wood, furniture and fixtures, fabricated metal products, machinery (except electrical), non-metallic minerals and refined petroleum. The real exchange rate was significant for rubber and plastics, clothing, paper, printing, fabricated metal products, transportation equipment and refined petroleum. The capacity utilization variable was positively significant for the real export growth of food and beverages, rubber and plastics, printing, fabricated metal products and non-metallic minerals. The dummy variable FTA was positively significant for food and beverages, rubber and plastics, fabricated metal products, non-metallic minerals, chemical products and other manufacturing.

We now turn to the estimation of Canada's imports from the United States, disaggregated by industry. The real growth of Canadian imports from the United States is regressed in terms of the growth of Canadian real GDP, the log of the real exchange rate, capacity utilization in the United States and the FTA dummy. Complete estimation results are presented in Appendix A, Table A9. Different combinations of the three explanatory variables have propelled the import growth throughout Canada's industries.

For total manufacturing imports, the estimated regression equation is as follows:

## IMPORT EQUATIONS

| DEPENDENT VARIABLE | INDEPENDENT VARIABLES | | | | | |
|---|---|---|---|---|---|---|
| Canada's Real Import Growth from the U.S. Market | Canadian Real GDP Growth | Log of Real Exchange Rate | Capacity Utilization in the United States | FTA Dummy | $R^2$ | D–W |
| Total Manufacturing | 3.626 (5.90)[a] | –0.166 (–0.96) | –0.001 (–1.96)[c] | 0.058 (1.93)[c] | 0.72 | 1.51 |
| Total Manufacturing (without Transportation Sector) | 3.504 (6.18)[a] | 0.138 (0.87) | 0.000 (–0.71) | 0.055 (1.96)[c] | 0.74 | 1.81 |

| Canada's Real Import Growth from the U.S. Market | Canadian Real GDP Growth | Log of Real Exchange Rate | Capacity Utilization in the United States | Canadian Tariffs to the United States (percent) | $R^2$ | D–W |
|---|---|---|---|---|---|---|
| Total Manufacturing | 3.210 (4.90)[a] | –0.085 (–0.49) | 0.000 (–0.11) | –0.014 (–1.32) | 0.68 | 1.31 |
| Total Manufacturing (without Transportation Sector) | 3.136 (5.49)[a] | 0.189 (1.23) | 0.001 (1.61) | –0.011 (–1.83)[c] | 0.73 | 1.64 |

Note: The number in parentheses below each coefficient is a t-ratio.
[a]Significantly different from zero at the 1 percent level, on the basis of a two-tailed test.
[b]Significantly different from zero at the 5 percent level, on the basis of a two-tailed test.
[c]Significantly different from zero at the 10 percent level, on the basis of a two-tailed test.
Source: Authors' estimations.

As expected, the coefficient for real GDP is positive and highly statistically significant. An increase of 1 percent in Canadian real GDP growth raises real manufacturing import growth from the United States by more than 3 percent (whichever specification we use). The real exchange rate coefficient has an unexpected negative value for all manufacturing and an expected positive value if we consider manufacturing without the transportation sector: however, these coefficients are all statistically insignificant. The capacity utilization coefficient is significant only if we consider all manufacturing and use the FTA dummy instead of U.S. tariff rates. The FTA dummy is significant for both specifications, with or without the transportation sector. The coefficient for Canada's tariff rates to the United States, however, is significant only if we consider manufacturing without the transportation sector. It has the expected negative value, as one would expect Canada's imports from the United States to rise with the fall in Canada's tariff rates on exports from the United States. On the whole, we could conclude that the FTA has had a significant impact on real Canadian imports of U.S.-manufactured goods.

The industry-wise regressions are presented in Appendix A, Table A9. We do not use U.S. capacity utilization here, as this variable is not significant in three out of four cases in the above regression. In 17 out of 19 industries, the real GDP coefficient is statistically significant, with the exception of tobacco products and printing, publishing and allied products. The real exchange rate variable is significant for food and beverages, textile products, clothing, and electrical and electronic products, while the FTA dummy is positive and significant for food and beverages, textile products, clothing, electrical and electronic products, and other manufacturing.

## Are These Estimates Reasonable?

We are of the view that our estimates of the impact of the FTA and the NAFTA on Canada-U.S. trade flows are fairly reasonable. Much of the trade between the two countries was already free of trade barriers before the two agreements. For instance, according to Magun, Rao and Lodh (1987), the average Canadian tariff rate on U.S. imports was only 3.8 percent in 1987, as compared to an average U.S. rate of 2.3 percent on Canadian exports. Similarly, non-tariff barriers were not large — under 2 percent. Furthermore, not all the tariff and non-tariff barriers were eliminated under the FTA and the NAFTA. Nor do all the reductions in trade barriers translate into reductions in export and import prices, because many prices are set globally and are affected by the fear of fierce competition. Producers are expected to absorb some of the tariff reductions into profit margins. Therefore, even with a full pass-through in trade prices, Canada's exports and imports to the United States can be expected to rise by a maximum of less than 10 percent in real terms, given reasonable assumptions about trade elasticities. The ex ante general equilibrium impact of the FTA on Canada's real exports and imports was 2.7 and 4.9 percent, respectively, in a hypothetical case involving the complete removal of tariff and non-tariff barriers under the FTA, in an optimistic scenario of an Economic Council of Canada (ECC) study (Magun et al. 1987). Even so, our estimated impacts on real exports are more than three times larger than the ECC estimates. Our estimates for imports, however, are significantly smaller than the ECC ones, which were based mainly on the large income effect on imports. In the ECC simulations, Canada's real GDP increased by 2.5 percent. In short, our estimated impacts are in line with previous estimates and are reasonable. More importantly, Canada's share of U.S. total imports remained more or less constant during the 1990s, despite a dramatic increase in Canadian exports to the United States. This suggests that the two trade agreements have had only a modest impact on Canada's exports to the United States.

It is possible, however, that the FTA and the NAFTA have done more than remove many of the trade barriers. They may have created a major change in the mood and psychology of Canadian and U.S. business, which has contributed to the expansion of trade between the two countries. One could argue that our estimates will not pick up these important changes. However, our dummy variable technique is meant to capture not only the impact of the removal of trade barriers, but also the underlying motivating forces of trade flows. Nevertheless, it is difficult to disentangle precisely the contribution of changes in real income, real exchange rate and trade barriers to changes in trade flows between Canada and the United States.

## THE SERVICE TRADE AND FOREIGN DIRECT INVESTMENT PATTERNS

THE STUDY SO FAR HAS BEEN BASED on the evolution of merchandise trade links between Canada and the United States over the last 20 years. However, the deep economic integration between Canada and the United States is also reflected in the service trade and FDI linkages between the two countries.

### CANADA-U.S. SERVICE TRADE PATTERNS

ON THE GLOBAL SCALE, it is expected (and to some extent already reflected in the data) that services will play an increasingly larger role in international trade, especially the new knowledge and skill-intensive commercial services. To understand the dynamics of the service trade, we have analysed Canada-U.S. service trade patterns with a focus on commercial services.[9] It should be noted that even before the current initiatives by the World Trade Organization, both the Canada-U.S. FTA and the NAFTA had included a number of provisions to facilitate the growth of the North American service trade.

Table 8 shows that over the last 20 years, the percentage of Canadian services exported to the United States has held steady at about 58 percent, while the percentage of U.S. services in Canada's total service imports has increased marginally, from 61 to 63 percent. It also shows that the 1990s saw a decline in both exports and imports of commercial services. Nevertheless, the decade has seen commercial services keep their place as the single largest Canadian service trade, with 52 and 54 percent of total service exports to and imports from the United States, respectively (Table 9).

## TABLE 8

## THE U.S. SHARE OF CANADA'S SERVICE TRADE, 1980-2000 (PERCENT)

| Type of Service | Exports to the United States | | | Imports from the United States | | |
|---|---|---|---|---|---|---|
| | 1980–1989 | 1990–1994 | 1995–2000 | 1980–1989 | 1990–1994 | 1995–2000 |
| Travel | 68.0 | 56.9 | 58.9 | 66.3 | 70.6 | 63.8 |
| Transport | 40.1 | 47.3 | 54.4 | 36.6 | 41.1 | 43.8 |
| Commercial | 63.0 | 63.9 | 60.6 | 74.8 | 71.0 | 71.9 |
| Government | 29.9 | 21.0 | 23.1 | 34.4 | 25.7 | 24.5 |
| Total | 57.3 | 56.7 | 58.1 | 60.9 | 63.3 | 62.8 |

Source: *Canada's International Transactions in Services,* Catalogue 67-203-XPB, Statistics Canada, 2000.

## TABLE 9

## BREAKDOWN OF THE TRADE IN SERVICES WITH THE UNITED STATES, 1980-2000 (PERCENT)

| Type of Service | Exports to the United States | | | Imports from the United States | | |
|---|---|---|---|---|---|---|
| | 1980–1989 | 1990–1994 | 1995–2000 | 1980–1989 | 1990–1994 | 1995–2000 |
| Travel | 40.3 | 31.2 | 29.2 | 34.5 | 40.1 | 30.1 |
| Transport | 17.8 | 17.4 | 17.8 | 14.8 | 14.2 | 15.2 |
| Commercial | 39.5 | 50.1 | 52.2 | 48.3 | 44.7 | 54.2 |
| Government | 2.5 | 1.3 | 0.8 | 2.5 | 0.9 | 0.5 |

Source: *Canada's International Transactions in Services,* Catalogue 67-203-XPB, Statistics Canada, 2000.

As Table 10 shows, Canada's major commercial service export categories include insurance, architectural and engineering, management, communications, research and development (R&D), and computers and information. Together, they accounted for nearly 67 percent of commercial service exports in 1990-94, which fell to 63 percent in 1995-99. However, they were still the most important Canadian service exports to the world. On the import side, the same categories predominated (except for R&D), although royalties and licence fees also figured prominently.

The breakdown of Canada's commercial service trade with the United States was more or less similar to that with the rest of the world, except for a few categories. Overall, commercial service exports to the United States fell from 64 to 61 percent between 1990-94 and 1995-99, while imports from the United States held steady at 71 percent throughout these two periods. If we compare the U.S. share for each category to the total U.S. share in commercial services given in Table 11, we find both exports and imports concentrated in the computer, R&D and audio-visual categories, with significant imports in royalties and licence fees.

TABLE 10

BREAKDOWN OF THE TRADE IN COMMERCIAL SERVICES TO THE
WORLD, 1990-99 (PERCENT)

| Service Category | Exports | | Imports | |
|---|---|---|---|---|
| | 1990–94 | 1995-99 | 1990–94 | 1995-99 |
| Communications | 11.6 | 8.9 | 8.5 | 8.1 |
| Insurance | 21.8 | 16.0 | 18.9 | 18.0 |
| Other Financial | 5.9 | 5.2 | 6.9 | 7.2 |
| Computers and Information | 7.1 | 6.3 | 3.4 | 3.7 |
| Royalties and Licence Fees | 2.4 | 6.1 | 14.0 | 12.8 |
| Management | 9.0 | 9.2 | 11.2 | 13.6 |
| R&D | 7.8 | 9.5 | 3.8 | 3.7 |
| Architectural, Engineering and Other | 9.4 | 13.4 | 4.4 | 4.9 |
| Miscellaneous | 13.1 | 13.2 | 15.6 | 14.4 |
| Audio-visual | 4.1 | 5.5 | 5.1 | 6.1 |
| Total | 92.1 | 93.3 | 91.7 | 92.5 |

Note: To focus on large export items, we have excluded five categories from the study, as their share in total trade was very small: construction, non-financial commissions, equipment rental, advertising, and personal, cultural and recreational. Together, these five categories contributed about 7 percent of Canada's total exports to the world and 6 percent of Canada's exports to the United States.

Source: *Canada's International Transactions in Services*, Catalogue 67-203-XPB, Statistics Canada, 2000.

Trade in services can take place among related parties as well as with foreign third parties (arm's-length client trade).[10] Table 12 shows the share of Canada's total service trade with the United States that is carried on by related parties. About 43 percent of Canada's total service exports to the United States was carried on by related parties. In other words, 43 percent of shipments making up Canada's total commercial service exports to the United States went either from U.S. subsidiaries in Canada to their parent companies in the United States or from Canadian parent companies to their subsidiaries in the United States. The remaining 57 percent was accounted for by either Canadian companies or foreign country MNCs (other than the United States). On the import side, 58 percent of shipments from the United States was carried out by related parties. These proportions were almost stable during the 1990-99 period. Hence the percentage of Canada's related-party commercial service exports to the United States is lower than its share of related-party imports from the United States.

Canada's related-party exports to the United States were very high in R&D, management, and royalties and licence fees, as was the related-party import share. Over time, the percentage of related-party exports in computer and information, management, royalties and licence fees, and R&D fell. On the import side, however, only the R&D percentage decreased between 1990-94 and 1995-99.

## TABLE 11

### THE U.S. SHARE OF CANADA'S EXPORTS OF COMMERCIAL SERVICES, BY CATEGORY, 1990-99 (PERCENT)

| Service Category | Exports to the United States | | Imports from the United States | |
|---|---|---|---|---|
| | 1990–94 | 1995–99 | 1990–94 | 1995–99 |
| Communications | 67.4 | 54.0 | 51.3 | 51.9 |
| Insurance | 57.0 | 56.1 | 50.8 | 49.1 |
| Other Financial | 47.5 | 48.1 | 48.3 | 52.3 |
| Computers and Information | 74.3 | 75.0 | 94.3 | 85.4 |
| Royalties and Licence Fees | 51.0 | 61.5 | 83.4 | 76.9 |
| Management | 64.4 | 64.5 | 84.9 | 86.7 |
| R&D | 76.2 | 73.7 | 73.5 | 81.5 |
| Architectural, Engineering and Other | 34.8 | 28.3 | 51.3 | 62.4 |
| Miscellaneous | 79.1 | 71.1 | 88.1 | 90.5 |
| Audio-visual | 86.2 | 87.5 | 83.6 | 86.7 |
| Total | 63.9 | 60.6 | 71.0 | 71.7 |

Source: *Canada's International Transactions in Services*, Catalogue 67-203-XPB, Statistics Canada, 2000.

## TABLE 12

### SHARE OF TRADE TO THE UNITED STATES CARRIED ON BY RELATED PARTIES, BY AFFILIATION, 1990-99 (PERCENT)

| Affiliation | Exports | | Imports | |
|---|---|---|---|---|
| | 1990–94 | 1995–99 | 1990–94 | 1995–99 |
| Computers and Information | 49.0 | 47.7 | 39.0 | 40.3 |
| Royalties and Licence Fees | 72.0 | 56.0 | 86.5 | 86.7 |
| Management | 79.8 | 74.8 | 88.8 | 86.9 |
| R&D | 93.6 | 90.0 | 94.1 | 87.6 |
| Miscellaneous | 68.9 | 68.3 | 87.5 | 89.0 |
| Total | 42.1 | 43.0 | 58.0 | 57.5 |

Note: In this table, we have included only categories of commercial services whose shares of related-party trade were higher than the related-party share of total commercial services for at least one time period.

Source: *Canada's International Transactions in Services*, Catalogue 67-203-XPB, Statistics Canada, 2000.

The largest volume of commercial service trade in Canada is carried on by Canadian-controlled resident companies, with the next-largest held by U.S.-controlled firms. Together, they account for about 90 percent of Canada's exports and imports of commercial services (Table 13).[11] This table also shows clearly that the share of Canada's commercial service exports held by Canadian-controlled firms was much higher than their share of Canada's commercial service imports. The situation for U.S.-controlled firms was the reverse: their share of Canada's commercial service exports was lower than their share of Canada's commercial service imports.

On average, the export share of Canadian-controlled companies rose from 67.6 percent in 1990-94 to 69 percent in 1995-99, while the share of exports by U.S.-controlled firms fell from 22.3 percent to 21 percent over the same period. On the import side, the share of Canadian-controlled firms rose from 46 to 47.4 percent, while the share of U.S.-controlled firms fell from 43 to 41 percent over the same period. The remaining trade share was accounted for by foreign (non-U.S.) companies.

On the export side, the Canadian-controlled company share of computers and information, royalties and licence fees, architectural and engineering, and management rose during the second time period (compare the percentage in column 1 with that in column 3 in Table 13). The share of Canadian-controlled firms fell in communications, insurance, R&D and audio-visual. In most cases, but not always, the Canadian company share losses were made up by U.S. firm share increases (and vice versa).

## TABLE 13

## SHARE OF COMMERCIAL SERVICES, BY CATEGORY AND COUNTRY OF CONTROL, 1990-99 (PERCENT)

| | Exports | | | | Imports | | | |
| | 1990–94 | | 1995–99 | | 1990–94 | | 1995–99 | |
| Service Category | Canada | United States | Canada | United States | Canada | United States | Canada | United States |
|---|---|---|---|---|---|---|---|---|
| Communications | 97.5 | 1.7 | 93.8 | 2.1 | 97.4 | 0.7 | 93.5 | 1.0 |
| Insurance | 57.9 | 24.0 | 56.3 | 22.6 | 50.1 | 31.6 | 47.9 | 32.1 |
| Other Financial | 98.1 | 1.9 | 94.9 | 4.4 | 97.7 | 2.1 | 93.8 | 3.6 |
| Computers and Information | 56.3 | 38.6 | 62.8 | 27.7 | 59.3 | 33.0 | 59.2 | 30.4 |
| Royalties and Licence Fees | 57.5 | 31.6 | 70.8 | 19.3 | 5.8 | 75.9 | 10.5 | 66.3 |
| Management | 75.8 | 14.5 | 78.9 | 12.6 | 22.1 | 63.0 | 31.0 | 56.3 |
| R&D | 69.4 | 16.4 | 68.0 | 17.5 | 30.3 | 48.8 | 28.0 | 56.1 |
| Architectural, Engineering and Other | 75.2 | 11.7 | 79.1 | 12.1 | 62.9 | 18.4 | 68.0 | 17.5 |
| Miscellaneous | 35.6 | 57.4 | 41.2 | 52.5 | 17.5 | 81.4 | 14.9 | 83.5 |
| Audio-visual | 85.2 | 14.8 | 82.7 | 17.3 | 80.6 | 17.9 | 78.1 | 19.5 |
| Total | 67.6 | 22.3 | 69.1 | 21.0 | 46.1 | 43.3 | 47.4 | 41.1 |

Source: *Canada's International Transactions in Services*, Catalogue 67-203-XPB, Statistics Canada, 2000.

**TABLE 14**

**CANADA'S SERVICE TRADE, BY COUNTRY OF CONTROL AND AFFILIATION, 1990-99 (PERCENT)**

| | Exports | | | | Imports | | | |
| --- | --- | --- | --- | --- | --- | --- | --- | --- |
| | 1990–94 | | 1995–99 | | 1990–94 | | 1995–99 | |
| Controlling Country | Affiliated | Un-affiliated | Affiliated | Un-affiliated | Affiliated | Un-affiliated | Affiliated | Un-affiliated |
| Canada | 23.3 | 76.7 | 25.2 | 74.8 | 14.7 | 85.3 | 17.6 | 82.4 |
| United States | 67.6 | 32.4 | 62.5 | 37.5 | 84.2 | 15.8 | 84.2 | 15.8 |
| Other | 65.1 | 35.0 | 58.6 | 41.4 | 73.7 | 26.3 | 74.7 | 25.3 |
| Total | 37.4 | 62.6 | 36.3 | 63.7 | 51.0 | 49.0 | 51.5 | 48.5 |

Source: *Canada's International Transactions in Services*, Catalogue 67-203-XPB, Statistics Canada, 2000.

Canadian-controlled companies dealt with clients unaffiliated with their exports, for the most part: 76.7 percent in 1990-94 and 74.8 percent in 1995-99 (Table 14). However, most export transactions by U.S.-controlled companies were between parents and subsidiaries (67.6 percent during the first period and 62.5 percent during the second). On the import side, the share of intrafirm trade between Canadian parents and Canadian subsidiaries was even smaller: 14.7 percent in 1990-94 and 17.6 percent in 1995-99. The share of imports by U.S.-controlled firms in Canada was mostly (about 84 percent) from their U.S. parents. Overall, the intrafirm trade share of Canada's service exports dropped from 37.4 percent in 1990-94 to 36.3 percent in 1995-99. On the import side, the share of intrafirm trade was steady at about 51 percent during both periods.

## CANADA-U.S. FDI PATTERNS

IN 2000, FDI STOCK REACHED $291.5 BILLION, a 4.5-fold increase from $64.7 billion in 1980. Similarly, CDIA rose from $28.4 billion in 1980 to $301.4 billion in 2000, a 10.6-fold increase. Both FDI and CDIA as a percentage of GDP have shown a growth trend between 1980 and 2000 (Figure 7). FDI exceeded CDIA from 1980 to 1996. Since 1997, however, CDIA has outpaced FDI in Canada. These investment linkages with the United States highlight three interesting and contrasting patterns (Figure 8). They show that

1. the U.S. share of CDIA has been declining after reaching its highest level of 69.4 percent in 1985;
2. the U.S. share of the total stock of FDI in Canada began to decline in 1985, remained stagnant between 1990 and 1994, and began a partial recovery but ended on a negative path in 2000; and
3. neither CDIA nor FDI appear to have responded to real GDP growth in Canada and the United States during the 1990s.

## FIGURE 7

## FDI AND CDIA AS A PERCENTAGE OF GDP, 1980-2000

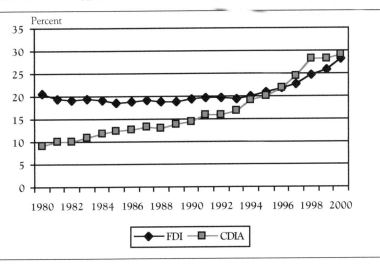

Source: Statistics Canada.

## FIGURE 8

## U.S. SHARES OF CANADIAN FDI AND CDIA, 1980-2000

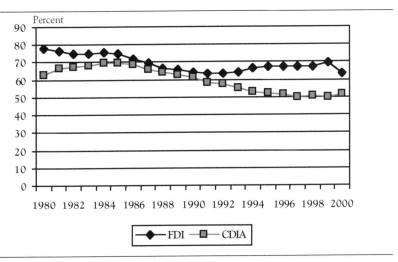

Source: Statistics Canada.

## TABLE 15

### BREAKDOWN OF U.S. FDI IN CANADA, 10 LARGEST INDUSTRIES, 1988-99 (PERCENT)

| Industry | Industry Share of U.S.FDI | | Annual Growth of U.S.FDI | U.S. Share of Total FDI |
|---|---|---|---|---|
| | 1988 | 1999 | 1988-99 | 1999 |
| Petroleum and Natural Gas | 22.6 | 11.1 | 0.4 | 95 |
| Electronic Equipment and Computer Services | 5.4 | 9.1 | 12.3 | 99 |
| Consumer and Business Financing Intermediaries | 3.0 | 8.5 | 17.9 | 98 |
| Insurers | 7.8 | 8.2 | 7.5 | 65 |
| Chemicals and Other Chemical Products | 8.2 | 7.8 | 6.7 | 63 |
| Motor Vehicles, and Parts and Accessories | 11.3 | 7.1 | 2.7 | 79 |
| Wood, Wood Products and Paper, Integrated Operations | 0.9 | 4.3 | 23.4 | – |
| Investment Intermediaries | 1.7 | 3.7 | 15.3 | 50 |
| Wood and Paper Products | 2.0 | 3.7 | 13.1 | 100 |
| Food (except Retailing) | 3.6 | 3.7 | 7.3 | 100 |

Note:   The percentages were calculated by adding up U.S. industry-level data. As the data for some industries were suppressed for reasons of confidentiality, the industry sum amounted to 82.4 percent of the total FDI from the United States.

Source: Statistics Canada.

To get some industry perspective on U.S. direct investment (USDI) in Canada, we selected the 10 industries with the largest USDI in Canada on the basis of 1999 figures (Table 15). Nine of them also held the largest total FDI portfolios in Canada (the exception is wood, wood products and paper, integrated operations). In other words, the largest FDI recipient industries also received the largest amount of USDI. Columns 1 and 2 list the industry share of USDI in Canada for 1988 and 1999. About 67 percent of USDI is allocated to these 10 industries. The breakdown of industry share between 1988 and 1999 has changed, but the total market share of these 10 industries has not changed, which indicates a stable flow of USDI in these industries. The third column shows the compound annual growth of USDI in Canada in 1999, based on 1988 figures. USDI in all industries (except petroleum and natural gas, and motor vehicles) increased by an impressive amount. The last column shows the U.S. share of total FDI in Canada. Five industries received at least 95 percent of their FDI from the United States, while the other five received at least half of theirs from the United States. From the above analysis, three conclusions follow:

1. the largest recipient industries of FDI in Canada are also the largest recipients of USDI;

2. in Canada's 10 largest FDI recipient industries, the U.S. share of FDI is very high; and

3. the growth rate of USDI in most of these 10 industries is impressive.

**TABLE 16**

**BREAKDOWN OF CDIA IN THE UNITED STATES, 10 LARGEST**

**INDUSTRIES, 1988-99 (PERCENT)**

| | Industry Share of CDI in the United States | | Annual Growth of CDI in the United States | Share of CDI in the United States in CDIA |
|---|---|---|---|---|
| | 1988 | 1999 | 1989–99 | 1999 |
| Deposit-accepting Intermediaries | 7.3 | 17.7 | 18.0 | 37 |
| Printing and Publishing | 10.8 | 16.3 | 13.0 | 86 |
| Non-ferrous Metals and Primary Metal Products | 12.8 | 12.3 | 8.4 | 47 |
| Insurers | 12.1 | 11.2 | 8.1 | 73 |
| Petroleum and Natural Gas | 10.7 | 8.5 | 6.6 | 47 |
| Railway Transport | 4.1 | 6.6 | 13.8 | – |
| Investment Intermediaries | 5.9 | 4.5 | 6.2 | 26 |
| Chemicals and Other Chemical Products | 2.7 | 3.7 | 12.2 | 58 |
| Iron, Steel and Related Products | 3.4 | 3.6 | 9.3 | – |
| Wood, Wood Products and Paper, Integrated Operations | 4.3 | 3.5 | 7.0 | 100 |

Note: The percentages were calculated by adding up available industrial CDI data for the United States. In 1999, this amounted to 60.4 percent of the total CDI in the United States.
Source: Statistics Canada.

In Table 16, we repeat the same process with the 1999 Canadian direct investment (CDI) figures for the United States. The 10 largest industries are listed as before. Of these, eight (all except railway transport, and iron and steel) also held the largest overall 1999 CDIA portfolios. The CDI share of these 10 industries in the United States rose from 74.1 percent in 1988 (sum of column 1) to 87.9 percent in 1999 (sum of column 2). The increase in their share could also be understood in terms of the very high annual CDI growth rate in the United States in column 3. The last column shows that unlike the FDI from the United States into Canada, the United States is not necessarily the predominant destination for the 10 largest industries with respect to CDIA.

In the 1990s, Canada's exports and imports of goods and services have expanded rapidly, thereby deepening the linkages between Canada and the United States. This conclusion, however, does not necessarily extend to Canada's international direct investment performance. Overall, Canada's linkages with the United States have remained unchanged or have declined, both in terms of the U.S. share of total FDI in Canada and in terms of the U.S. share of total CDIA.

# FACTOR CONTENT AND RCA

## FACTOR CONTENT OF CANADIAN EXPORTS

THE PATTERN OF CANADA'S EXPORTS is largely a result of specialization changes in the productive activities of firms. Businesses and entrepreneurs respond to the availability of inputs and access to markets. Export flows embody inputs that reflect the total input availability in an economy. In practical terms, a country exports the services of its abundant inputs and imports the services of its scarce inputs when input abundance is measured in terms of a world input-endowment standard. Empirically, changes in the input abundance in Canada would be reflected in its export flows.

We use Statistics Canada's input-output table of the Canadian economy to calculate the factor content of Canada's exports for the years 1985, 1990 and 1997. Since the input-output tables are for the whole Canadian economy, the factor content we arrive at is for Canada's total exports to the world, not to the United States. However, as we saw in Appendix A, Table A1, the U.S. share of Canada's exports is very high and almost symmetric across industries, so we can generalize the results for the United States. For this analysis, we use more disaggregated industry-level data than in previous sections. Our sample consists of 119 industries in the business sector (93 goods-producing industries and 26 service-producing industries).[12] Of the 93 in the goods-producing sector, nine are in agriculture, fishing, forestry and mining, with the other 84 in manufacturing. Note that as there are only 110 industries at the SIC 3-digit level in manufacturing, the 84 manufacturing industries in our study nearly approximate the SIC 3-digit level of industry analysis for the manufacturing sector. However, the 26 service industries in our study are a highly aggregated number, as there are 12 industries at the SIC 1-digit level and 41 industries at the SIC 2-digit level in business sector services.

To calculate total (direct and indirect) factor content in Canada's exports, we proceed as follows (for methodology, see Appendix B): The accounting balance between total supply and total demand is given by Equation (B1) in Appendix B to solve for the equilibrium level of gross output (given by the notation $g$ in the appendix) for each sector. This solution can be used to measure the change in gross output required for each industry (both as intermediate input and final consumption) with a given change in final demand. Note that the changes in final demand will not be met by domestic industry alone. To the extent that the change in final demand is supplied by imports, the impact of change in final demand on domestic industries will be reduced. To measure the impact of a change in final demand for domestic output, therefore, we net out the import leakage for each industry, as measured by the ratio of net imports — net of re-exports — to use for that industry, use defined by the sum of intermediate input use, consumption, investment and inventory additions for the whole domestic economy. This yields Equation (B5), which can be used to compute the level of output change required for an exogenous change in final demand (exports, investment and consumption) net of import leakage. Next, in Equation (B6), we find the level of gross output required to produce the given level of exports by plugging the value of actual Canadian exports for a year into each industry. Once we have determined the level of gross output, we multiply it by the ratio of direct input (capital and labour) to gross output for each industry, as in Equation (B7) for capital and Equation (B8) for labour. This calculation yields the capital and labour embodied in Canada's exports. Its results on factor content are presented in Table 17.[13] Not surprisingly, as exports rise, the amount of capital embodied in them also rises. However, by 1997, the physical capital content in one million dollars of Canadian exports had fallen by some 42 percent from its input content level in 1985. Given that the labour content in one million dollars of exports over the same period had also fallen by 40 percent, the capital-to-labour ratio had decreased only marginally, from $83,582 to $80,705 per employee (the sixth row in Table 17).

The magnitude of the capital-labour ratio decline differs between the goods and service sectors. By 1997, in the goods sector, the physical capital content of goods exports worth one million dollars had fallen by some 44 percent from its input content level in 1985. Given that the labour content of one million dollar's worth of exports over the same period also fell by 42.3 percent, the capital-to-labour ratio decreased only marginally.

By 1997, the physical capital content in one million dollars' worth of Canadian exports had fallen some 43.5 percent from its input content level in 1985 for all Canadian service industries. As the labour content in one million dollars' worth of exports over the same period had fallen by a smaller proportion of 39.7 percent, the service capital-to-labour ratio had decreased much more markedly than the goods-industries ratio. Overall, service-exporting industries use at least twice as much physical capital and labour in absolute terms as goods-exporting industries.

This calculation demonstrates that service-producing industries have a higher level of value-added than goods-producing industries. The input content analysis suggests that both the physical capital and labour content in a one-million-dollar export bundle of both goods and services exhibit a declining pattern. However, the goods-exporting industries have adopted productivity-enhancing technologies that have reduced the use of physical capital and labour services far more than the service-exporting industries have.

The total quantity of labour embodied in exports reveals the structure of an aggregate labour force; but it cannot shed light on the relative composition of the different types of labour in the production process. The labour force can be distinguished by the size of the investment workers have made in their education, training and the acquisition of various other skills. In the early 1970s, Canadian exports were most concentrated in natural resources, physical capital and labour with at most an elementary school education (Postner 1975).

## TABLE 17

### FACTOR CONTENT OF CANADIAN EXPORTS

| | 1985 | 1990 | 1997 |
|---|---|---|---|
| **Total Business Sector** | | | |
| Exports (millions of $) | 125,086 | 159,554 | 312,747 |
| Capital Embodied in Exports (millions of $) | 125,229 | 139,595 | 181,645 |
| Labour Embodied in Exports (thousands of employees) | 1,498 | 1,693 | 2,251 |
| Capital Embodied in $1 Million of Exports ($) | 1,001,141 | 874,906 | 580,804 |
| Labour Embodied in $1 Million of Exports (number of employees) | 12.0 | 10.6 | 7.2 |
| Total Capital-labour Ratio Embodied in Exports | 83,582 | 82,468 | 80,705 |
| **Goods-producing Industries** | | | |
| Exports (millions of $) | 107,974 | 134,171 | 261,037 |
| Capital Embodied in Exports (millions of $) | 95,053 | 104,478 | 130,090 |
| Labour Embodied in Exports (thousands of employees) | 1,123 | 1,233 | 1,568 |
| Capital Embodied in $1 Million of Exports ($) | 880,336 | 778,690 | 498,359 |
| Labour Embodied in $1 Million of Exports (number of employees) | 10.4 | 9.2 | 6.0 |
| Total Capital-labour Ratio Embodied in Exports of Goods | 84,651 | 84,760 | 82,954 |
| **Service-producing Industries** | | | |
| Exports (millions of $) | 17,112 | 25,383 | 51,709 |
| Capital Embodied in Exports (millions of $) | 30,176 | 35,117 | 51,554 |
| Labour Embodied in Exports (thousands of employees) | 375 | 460 | 682 |
| Capital Embodied in $1 Million of Exports ($) | 1,763,391 | 1,383,493 | 996,998 |
| Labour Embodied in $1 Million of Exports (number of employees) | 21.9 | 18.1 | 13.2 |
| Total Capital-labour Ratio Embodied in Exports of Services | 80,385 | 76,327 | 75,537 |

Source: Authors' calculations.

Whether or not there has been any change in the skill content of labour in Canada is an important policy issue. We address it by using the data on labour quality from a Statistics Canada labour force survey. We grouped the labour skill data into four categories for each industry:

1. up to eight years of schooling;

2. high school graduation;

3. post-secondary certificate or diploma training; and

4. university graduation.[14]

## TABLE 18

## PERCENTAGE OF LABOUR SKILL EMBODIED IN CANADIAN EXPORTS

| | Year | Up to Eight Years of Schooling | High School | Post-secondary | University |
|---|---|---|---|---|---|
| Total Business Sector | 1985 | 12.0 | 52.0 | 21.7 | 10.1 |
| | 1990 | 7.6 | 44.3 | 33.8 | 10.0 |
| | 1997 | 4.6 | 36.6 | 40.5 | 13.2 |
| Goods Industries | 1985 | 13.4 | 52.5 | 22.6 | 8.4 |
| | 1990 | 8.5 | 44.8 | 33.5 | 7.6 |
| | 1997 | 5.3 | 37.3 | 40.9 | 10.6 |
| Service Industries | 1985 | 7.8 | 50.6 | 25.1 | 15.2 |
| | 1990 | 5.1 | 42.8 | 34.5 | 16.3 |
| | 1997 | 2.8 | 35.2 | 41.9 | 19.1 |

Note: Percentages do not add up to 100, as some data were suppressed for reasons of confidentiality.
Source: Authors' calculations.

Our results in Table 18 show that the labour skill content of Canada's exports has changed, as measured by the level of education. In the overall business sector (119 industries), by 1997, the percentage of workers with high school education or less had dropped and that of workers with post-secondary and university education had increased significantly.

Canada's goods-exporting industries have reduced their input content of workers with less than a high school education and increased the use of high school, post-secondary and university graduates by a wider margin than service-exporting industries. The incidence of post-secondary graduates rose much more rapidly in the service-exporting industries, however.

To sum up, Canada's exports of goods and services in 1997 were much more high-skill labour-intensive than during the 1970s and 1980s.

### IMPORTED INPUT CONTENT IN CANADIAN EXPORTS

THE PRODUCTION AND EXPORT OF GOODS REQUIRE not only physical capital and skilled workers, but also other goods and intermediate inputs produced elsewhere in the world. One aspect of globalization based on innovation and trade liberalization is the deepening of specialization and niche production of final goods, as well as intermediate inputs and processes across countries. Again, the methodology in Appendix B and the Statistics Canada input-output table for the Canadian economy allow us to compute the imported input content of Canada's exports, which is presented in Table 19. First, we use Equation (B6) to calculate the output required for each of the 119 industries (for both final consumption and intermediate input) at the actual export level for each year, as in the previous subsection. Then we use the input-output table to compute the intermediate input required for each industry to produce that level of output, as given by Equation (B9). The total intermediate input use is then multiplied by the fraction of net domestic imports for that industry to obtain imported intermediate input, as given by Equation (B10). Here we assume that the demand for imported intermediate input in an industry is proportional to the net import use for that industry, where use is defined as the sum of the amount used for intermediate input, final consumption, capital formation and inventory additions.[15]

Although the 26 service industries in our sample did not increase the use of imported inputs in their exports until the 1990s, Canada's goods-exporting industries had expanded the share of imported inputs from less than 24 percent in 1980 to more than 37 percent in 1997. The overall trend appears to be that Canadian exporters of goods and services are making a strong move toward greater use of imported inputs to achieve export sales abroad. The increased use of intermediate inputs might be due to outsourcing — the process of channelling more intermediate inputs produced in foreign countries into domestic production. This is happening in many developed countries, as they are increasingly importing inputs from countries where labour is cheap. We do not expect outsourcing to have much influence on Canada's imports from the United States, as U.S. wages are higher than ours, but it could be an influential factor for imports from developing countries. However, we have no data to check whether Canadian imports of intermediate inputs from the rest of the world are rising proportionately more than those from the United States.

When this trend toward increased use of imported input in Canada's exports is taken into account, the increase in net exports — net of imported input — to GDP ratio is substantially lower than the gross exports to GDP ratio we reported in the introduction. Using data from the input-output table for exports, imports, GDP and imported input, we present the ratio of exports to GDP in both gross and net terms in the panel below (expressed as a percentage).

| Year | Ratio of Exports to GDP | Ratio of Net Exports to GDP | Ratio of Trade to GDP | Ratio of Net Trade to GDP |
|------|-------------------------|-----------------------------|-----------------------|---------------------------|
| 1980 | 29.0 | 23.2 | 56.7 | 50.9 |
| 1985 | 29.3 | 22.3 | 56.9 | 49.9 |
| 1990 | 26.5 | 20.1 | 54.0 | 47.6 |
| 1997 | 40.2 | 27.7 | 80.7 | 68.3 |

Note:   Trade is defined as the sum of exports plus imports. Net trade is defined as the sum of net exports plus imports. The input content is calculated by means of the methodology explained above.
Source: Authors' calculations.

**TABLE 19**

**PERCENTAGE OF IMPORTED INPUT CONTENT IN TOTAL EXPORTS**

|                       | 1980 | 1985 | 1990 | 1997 |
|-----------------------|------|------|------|------|
| Total Business Sector | 22.2 | 25.8 | 26.5 | 32.5 |
| Goods Industries      | 23.7 | 28.9 | 29.1 | 37.2 |
| Service Industries    | 7.0  | 6.4  | 6.8  | 8.4  |

Source: Authors' calculations.

The first column of data shows that the ratio of exports to GDP rose from 29 percent in 1980 to 40.2 percent in 1997. Note that the denominator (GDP) is the value-added, whereas the numerator (exports) is not, as it will count both value-added and intermediate input, including imported intermediate input. For example, when Canada exports a car, its export value will also include the value of parts imported from the United States and anywhere else in the world, as well as the value-added created in Canada. To exclude the imported part, we subtract the amount of imported input from total exports, defined as net exports, and re-port its percentage in column 3. Note the substantial difference: the ratio of net exports to GDP has increased to only 27.7 percent (contrast this to the 40.2 per-cent in column 1). Similarly, the ratio of trade to GDP is only 68.3 percent when we net out the imported input, as opposed to 80.7 percent.

Table 19 provides the summary for the sectors; however, one important as-pect will be to look at how the fraction of industries and their export share have changed for different percentage ranges of imported input content in exports. To decipher this pattern across industries, we compute the percentage of imported input content in the exports of each $i$th industry ($\mu_{xi}$). Then we group the in-dustries in the total business, goods-producing and service-producing sectors into five categories: percentage of imported input content in exports of less than 10; 10-20; 20-30; 30-40; and more than 40 percent for the years 1980, 1990 and 1997.[16] Then, for each of these five categories, we report the number of industries and their percentage of Canada's total exports for each year in Table 20.

Table 20 should be read as follows: Let us look at the first row. In 1980, there were 26 industries in the business sector whose share of imported input content in their exports was less than 10 percent, and they were supplying 28.7 percent of Canada's total exports. Those numbers dropped to 17 and 20.6 in 1997. The table shows that the overall pattern of the imported input content in Canada's export industries was an upward trend. For the overall business sector, the number of in-dustries and the export percentage are falling for the 10, 10-20 and 20-30 percent ranges and rising for the 30 percent and up range. However, the increased im-ported input use is unevenly distributed between the goods- and service-producing industries. The pattern in the business sector is more or less determined by the pattern in the goods sector. In 1980, there were only 18 industries in the goods-producing sector whose exports contained more than 30 percent of imported input. That number had gone up to 41 by 1997. Similarly, the export percentage of these industry categories had risen from 22 in 1980 to 59 by 1997.

This tells us that by 1997, most goods industries had expanded their use of imported inputs to 30 percent or higher. Given that more than 75 percent of Canada's goods are imported from the United States, this is a clear indication that over the course of the 1990s, Canada's exporters have become more linked to U.S. suppliers for intermediate inputs to achieve export sales abroad.

As for the service industries, their use of imported inputs in 1997 has moved up from less than 10 percent to 10-20 percent. Interestingly, industries using more than 20 percent of imported inputs have also moved down to 10-20 percent.

Increased trade in intermediate inputs constitutes an empirical observation of deeper economic links between trading economies. Now the obvious question is: In what types of industries did import content rise? Is the growth in import content strongest where export growth is also strongest? To answer these questions, we compute the growth rate of imported intermediate input and the export growth for each industry in both sectors over three periods: 1980-85, 1985-90 and 1990-97. In the panel below, we list the correlation coefficients of imported intermediate input growth and export growth for each period.

For Canadian goods industries, there was strong evidence of almost perfect correlation between the growth in the use of imported inputs and the export growth in all three periods. For the service industries, this linear association between the growths of imported inputs and exports, despite remaining strong, had eased from a high of 95 percent during the early 1980s to 83 percent in the 1990s. Overall, our analysis of Canada's economy during the 1980s and 1990s shows a sustained pattern of strong growth of imported input use supporting a strong export performance.

| CORRELATION OF EXPORT GROWTH TO IMPORTED INTERMEDIATE INPUT GROWTH | | |
|---|---|---|
| Time Period | Goods Industries | Service Industries |
| 1980–85 | 0.99 | 0.95 |
| 1985–90 | 0.93 | 0.89 |
| 1990–97 | 0.99 | 0.83 |

Note: This is a cross-industry correlation of 93 industries in the goods sector and 26 industries in the service sector. All coefficients are statistically significant.
Source: Authors' calculations.

## TABLE 20

## BREAKDOWN OF INDUSTRIES BY PERCENTAGE OF IMPORTED INPUT CONTENT, 1980-97

| | 1980 | | 1990 | | 1997 | |
|---|---|---|---|---|---|---|
| | Number of Industries | Percentage of Total Exports | Number of Industries | Percentage of Total Exports | Number of Industries | Percentage of Total Exports |
| Total Business Sector | | | | | | |
| $\mu_{xi} \leq 10\%$ | 26 | 28.7 | 26 | 27.4 | 17 | 20.6 |
| $10 < \mu_{xi} \leq 20\%$ | 41 | 24.0 | 41 | 21.0 | 29 | 15.0 |
| $20 < \mu_{xi} \leq 30\%$ | 34 | 26.7 | 33 | 18.9 | 32 | 15.4 |
| $30 < \mu_{xi} \leq 40\%$ | 11 | 6.2 | 13 | 12.5 | 26 | 16.4 |
| $\mu_{xi} > 40\%$ | 7 | 14.4 | 6 | 20.2 | 15 | 32.6 |
| Goods Industries | | | | | | |
| $\mu_{xi} \leq 10\%$ | 8 | 23.2 | 8 | 16.5 | 3 | 11.5 |
| $10 < \mu_{xi} \leq 20\%$ | 38 | 25.6 | 36 | 23.1 | 21 | 12.3 |
| $20 < \mu_{xi} \leq 30\%$ | 29 | 28.5 | 30 | 21.5 | 28 | 17.5 |
| $30 < \mu_{xi} \leq 40\%$ | 11 | 6.9 | 13 | 14.8 | 26 | 19.6 |
| $\mu_{xi} > 40\%$ | 7 | 15.8 | 6 | 24.1 | 15 | 39.1 |
| Service Industries | | | | | | |
| $\mu_{xi} \leq 10\%$ | 18 | 83.5 | 18 | 84.9 | 14 | 66.1 |
| $10 < \mu_{xi} \leq 20\%$ | 3 | 8.4 | 5 | 9.8 | 8 | 29.0 |
| $20 < \mu_{xi} \leq 30\%$ | 5 | 8.1 | 3 | 5.3 | 4 | 4.9 |

Source: Authors' calculations.

## TRADE INTENSITIES OF CANADIAN MANUFACTURING INDUSTRIES

ANOTHER RELATED QUESTION: How did export intensity and import penetration change over time? Here, we will concentrate on only 84 Canadian manufacturing industries, which contribute about 80 percent of Canada's exports. Let $\xi$ denote gross export intensity, or the export percentage of an industry's total shipments, and let $\rho$ denote the import penetration, defined as the percentage of imports in total domestic consumption. Export intensity thus shows the share of gross output used in the foreign market (either for consumption or intermediate input), while the import penetration represents the percentage of Canadian consumption supplied by foreign goods. We list these percentages in Table 21. It is evident from the table that the percentage of industries with larger export intensity and import penetration is rising over time. For example, between 1985 and 1997, the percentage of industry with export penetration of 10 percent or less had fallen from 39 to just 10 percent. Similarly, the percentage of industry with import penetration of less than 10 percent fell from 29 percent in 1985 to 11 percent in 1997. However, the percentage of industries with more than 30 percent of export penetration rose from 36 to 60 percent. A nearly identical change took place on the import penetration side. As the last row in Table 21 shows, on average, export penetration reached 53.2 percent in 1997, an increase of 52 percent from just under 35 percent in 1985. Similarly, import penetration increased from just below 37 percent in 1985 to nearly 55 percent in 1997, a 49-percent increase. We may conclude, therefore, that Canadian production is increasingly shipped to foreign markets, with demand at home increasingly met by imported goods. This trend is probably an indication of intraindustry trade, which we will analyse in detail below.

Because import content of intermediate input is rising, as is gross export intensity, it is worthwhile to evaluate net export intensity, defined as the difference between gross export intensity and percentage of imported intermediate input content. Let $\mu_{si}$ denote the percentage of imported input content in *shipments*. Hence, for industry $i$, the net export intensity is given by $\xi_i - \mu_{si}$. The results are presented in Table 22.

The number of industries as well as the export percentage rise between 1985 and 1997 as we move down to the higher ranges of net export intensity in the first column. For example, there were only 18 industries in 1985 with a net export intensity of more than 30 percent, and these industries supplied 37 percent of Canada's manufacturing exports. By 1997, this number had risen to 36 industries and their export percentage to 42 percent. This suggests that not only were imported inputs in the manufacturing sector rising over time, but that gross export intensity was rising even faster. As a result, Canadian manufacturing industries have become more export-oriented, even if we net out their increasing use of imported input content. In a study using a more aggregated level of data for 1974 and 1993, Campa and Goldberg (1997) show that the tendency of Canadian industry has been to greater net external orientation.

---

**TABLE 21**

**INDUSTRY BREAKDOWN BY GROSS EXPORT INTENSITY AND IMPORT PENETRATION (PERCENT)**

| $\xi$ and $\rho$ | Gross Export Intensity | | | Import Penetration | | |
|---|---|---|---|---|---|---|
| | 1985 | 1990 | 1997 | 1985 | 1990 | 1997 |
| ≤10% | 39 | 35 | 10 | 29 | 25 | 11 |
| 10-20% | 24 | 19 | 11 | 20 | 13 | 19 |
| 20-30% | 11 | 15 | 19 | 15 | 17 | 6 |
| 30-40% | 7 | 5 | 10 | 10 | 6 | 8 |
| 40-50% | 7 | 11 | 7 | 6 | 15 | 11 |
| > 50% | 12 | 15 | 43 | 20 | 24 | 45 |
| Total | 100 | 100 | 100 | 100 | 100 | 100 |
| Average | 34.9 | 39.0 | 53.2 | 36.7 | 40.4 | 54.8 |

Note: The interval is defined by the upper limit of its range. For example, if the export intensity of an industry in 1985 was 20 percent, it is counted in the 10-20, not the 20-30 percent range.
Source: Authors' calculations.

## TABLE 22

## BREAKDOWN OF NET EXPORT INTENSITY FOR
## 84 MANUFACTURING INDUSTRIES (PERCENT)

| Net Export Intensity $\xi_i - \mu_{si}$ | 1985 | | 1990 | | 1997 | |
|---|---|---|---|---|---|---|
| | Number of Industries | Percentage of Total Shipments | Number of Industries | Percentage of Total Shipments | Number of Industries | Percentage of Total Shipments |
| $\xi_i - \mu_{si} \leq 10\%$ | 42 | 39.6 | 38 | 32.7 | 15 | 12.0 |
| $10 < \xi_i - \mu_{si} \leq 20\%$ | 14 | 18.7 | 11 | 17.1 | 22 | 17.0 |
| $20 < \xi_i - \mu_{si} \leq 30\%$ | 10 | 4.3 | 11 | 7.5 | 11 | 29.5 |
| $30 < \xi_i - \mu_{si} \leq 40\%$ | 7 | 17.0 | 10 | 20.1 | 12 | 14.2 |
| $\xi_i - \mu_{si} > 40\%$ | 11 | 20.4 | 14 | 22.6 | 24 | 27.3 |
| Total | 84 | 100 | 84 | 100 | 84 | 100 |

Source: Authors' calculations.

## SPEARMAN RANK CORRELATION OF 84 MANUFACTURING INDUSTRIES

| Rank of | 1985 and 1990 | 1990 and 1997 | 1985 and 1997 |
|---|---|---|---|
| Gross Export Intensity | 0.88 | 0.85 | 0.73 |
| Import Penetration | 0.95 | 0.93 | 0.87 |
| Import-content Intensity | 0.98 | 0.81 | 0.82 |
| Net Export Intensity | 0.83 | 0.78 | 0.70 |

Note: Rank correlation is made between two years across 84 industries (observations).
Source: Authors' Calculations.

By using Spearman rank correlation coefficients for the four trade orientation indicators, we find that the industries with relatively higher percentages in 1985 and 1990 hold their rankings in 1997.[17] The high rank correlation coefficients for all four indicators show that industry rankings did not change significantly over the sample period. Hence, despite the phenomenal increase in all intensities, the relative pattern of gross intensity, import penetration, imported input content and net intensity remained stable over time.

## REVEALED COMPARATIVE ADVANTAGE

IN THIS SECTION, we calculate Canada's RCA vis-à-vis the United States for 84 manufacturing industries. To quantify RCA is not usually a trivial task and there is no clear-cut methodology on how to do so for a multi-country, multi-commodity case. One problem is that the theoretical concept of comparative advantage is usually defined in terms of pre-trade relative prices, whereas real-world data express post-trade equilibria. Even though the Balassa (1977) RCA export share index is not flawless, we use it in our methodology as a first approximation. The use of this index implies that the level of trade barriers between the two countries in the study is equivalent and that each country carries on trade in each industry (Bowen 1983). It could be argued that the first assumption is not far off target for Canada-U.S. trade. The second assumption is satisfied, as only three of 84 industries had no trade data for either country. The export-share measure of RCA is expressed by the equation

$$RCA_{ij} = \frac{x_{ij}}{X_j} / \frac{w_i}{W}, \quad i = 1, 2,...,84 \text{ and } j = \text{Canada and the United States,}$$

where the subscript $i$ denotes an industry and $j$ a country, $x_{ij}$ is the export of commodity $i$ by country $j$, $X_j$ is the total exports of country $j$ to the world, $w_i$ is the export of good $i$ from the world and $W$ is the total export from the world. By using the ratio of the above index for Canada and the United States, we obtain the following index for each of 84 industries:

$$(1) \quad R_i = \frac{x_{i, Canada}}{X_{Canada}} / \frac{x_{i, United States}}{X_{United States}}.$$

Now the next question is: Can the index calculated by means of Equation (1) — i.e., higher (or lower) than one — be interpreted as showing RCA (or relative disadvantage) for Canada over the United States for the given industry? If there are only two goods, there is an exact correlation between comparative advantage (as indicated by pre-trade relative prices) and the observed trade pattern, and it is given by direction of trade. However, with multiple goods and countries, the methodology is again not clear-cut. Hillman (1980) has developed an index which requires correspondence between RCA and pre-trade relative prices in a country comparison for a specific commodity: the transformation performed to the index or RCA has to be monotonic. In another study, Marchese and de Simone (1989) show that this condition is met for the great majority of commodities traded in 1985 by 118 developing countries. We do not test this condition in this study, but make a first guess that the data for Canada and the United States will satisfy the Hillman criteria so that $R_i > 1$ ($< 1$) could be considered to be an industry with an RCA (or disadvantage) for Canada over the United States.

We use Equation (1) to calculate RCA. The industries with a value greater than one (that is, the industries with RCA for Canada vis-à-vis the United States) are given in Appendix C, Table C1. In 1985, Canada had RCA in 31 (out of 84) industries; by 1997, Canada had lost RCA in seven and gained RCA in 13 new ones, for a total of 37 industries, which are listed in Table C1.[18]

Since comparative advantage might be due either to factor endowment or technological differences, we relate industry rank based on $R_i$ to industry rank based on total (direct and indirect) capital labour ratio, which we calculated above in the subsection on the factor content of Canadian exports.

On the basis of the total capital labour ratio embodied in exports, we decompose 84 manufacturing industries into two categories: those with a capital labour ratio higher than the national average for the manufacturing sector (capital-intensive industries), and those with a lower-than-average capital labour ratio (labour-intensive industries). In notational form, an industry $i$ is considered capital-intensive if $k_i/l_i > \bar{k}/\bar{l}$, where $k_i$ and $l_i$ are the total capital and labour embodied in industry $i$ respectively; and $\bar{k}$ and $\bar{l}$ are the average of total capital and labour embodied in the whole manufacturing sector. If this relationship is reversed, the industry is considered labour-intensive.

Note that for industry $i$ the comparative advantage position might well change from year to year: the value of $R_i$ can thus move from greater than one to less than one and back again. Similarly, an industry can be capital-intensive one year and labour-intensive the next, depending on its ratio of capital and labour to the national average manufacturing capital labour ratio.

The results are presented in Table 23. Let us take the case of RCA > 1. In 1985, 31 Canadian industries had RCA over U.S. industries. These 31 industries were producing 70 percent of Canada's total exports, two-thirds of which was produced by labour-intensive industries and one-third by capital-intensive ones. The percentage of exports produced by industries where Canada had RCA fell slightly to 66.6 percent in 1990 and 65.1 percent in 1997, even though the number of industries with RCA rose from 31 in 1985 to 37 in 1997. There was also an interesting change in 1997 as compared to the earlier benchmark years: while the percentage of exports by industries with RCA did not change much, a substantial share of these exports shifted from labour-intensive to capital-intensive industries. Note that the proportion of capital-intensive industries with RCA increased from 24.4 to 41.9 percent between 1990 and 1997, while the share of labour-intensive industries with RCA fell from 42 to 23.2 percent over the same period. There is no similar drastic shift in the industries where the United States had comparative advantage.

## TABLE 23

### TRENDS IN CANADA'S RCA VIS-À-VIS THE UNITED STATES

| | | RCA > 1 | | | RCA < 1 | | |
|---|---|---|---|---|---|---|---|
| | | $\dfrac{k_i}{l_i} > \dfrac{\bar{k}}{\bar{l}}$ | $\dfrac{k_i}{l_i} < \dfrac{\bar{k}}{\bar{l}}$ | Total | $\dfrac{k_i}{l_i} > \dfrac{\bar{k}}{\bar{l}}$ | $\dfrac{k_i}{l_i} < \dfrac{\bar{k}}{\bar{l}}$ | Total |
| 1985 | Number of Industries | 11 | 19 | 31 | 13 | 37 | 50 |
| | Percentage of Total Exports | 22.9 | 46.8 | 69.7 | 10.1 | 19.9 | 30.0 |
| 1990 | Number of Industries | 10 | 21 | 31 | 8 | 42 | 50 |
| | Percentage of Total Exports | 24.4 | 42.2 | 66.6 | 4.7 | 27.9 | 32.6 |
| 1997 | Number of Industries | 14 | 23 | 37 | 9 | 35 | 44 |
| | Percentage of Total Exports | 41.9 | 23.2 | 65.1 | 6.2 | 27.8 | 34.0 |

Note: There are only 81 instead of 84 manufacturing industries in the table because RCA for three of them could not be calculated.

Source: Authors' calculations.

# INTRAINDUSTRY TRADE AND PRODUCTIVITY

INCREASING TRADE ALLOWS COUNTRIES to specialize production. Specialization may occur among industries, among firms within industries and also within firms. In this section, we examine the types of specialization that have taken place as a result of our expanding trade linkages with the United States. We adopt the definitions of Fuentes-Godoy, Hanson and Lundberg (1996) to calculate different specialization indices on the basis of Canada-U.S. trade flows for 84 manufacturing industries between 1983 and 1997. We use Canada's exports to and imports from the United States to compute intraindustry trade.

Let $x_{it}$, $m_{it}$ and $q_{it}$ be Canadian exports to the United States, Canadian imports from the United States and total shipments of production for industry $i$ in year $t$, respectively. Let $g_{it}$, $n_{it}$ and $z_{it}$ be gross international trade specialization, interindustry specialization and intraindustry specialization, respectively. Hence, we have

$$g_{it} = \frac{x_{it} + m_{it}}{c_{it}}, \; n_{it} = \frac{|x_{it} - m_{it}|}{c_{it}} \text{ and } z_{it} = g_{it} - n_{it} \equiv \frac{2 \min(x_{it}, m_{it})}{c_{it}},$$

where $c_{it} = q_{it} + m_{it} - x_{it}$ is consumption.[19] Thus the formula provides an estimate on the extent to which the gross trade, net trade and intraindustry trade are related to (or deviate from) consumption. It is clear from the above definition that if an industry only exports or imports, all gross specialization reflects interindustry specialization, and if an industry's exports are equal to its imports, all specialization will be intraindustry specialization. We can aggregate these definitions across industries and arrive at aggregate concepts of gross, interindustry and intraindustry specialization. Note that the level of specialization indices depends on the level of aggregation: a higher level of aggregation causes the interindustry value to fall and the intraindustry value to rise, and vice versa. What level of aggregation should we adopt to calculate these concepts of specialization? The rationale is that the level of aggregation should be compatible with the production technology. An industry should be defined at a level of factor intensity which is similar throughout its establishments. Thus, the higher the disaggregation level, the more precise the definitions for intraindustry trade can be.

It is clear from Figure 9 that both inter- and intraindustry specialization has expanded significantly between 1983 and 1997. However, the growth in intraindustry trade is much greater, indicating that the main trade focus was between similar industries rather than among different industries defined in terms of comparative advantage. In recent years, that trend is strengthening as the gap between the percentage of intra- and interindustry specialization is widening. The fitted time-trend equations for gross inter- and intratrade specialization are given in the panel below. It shows that on an annual basis, intraindustry trade rose almost twice as fast as interindustry trade. The average percentage of intraindustry trade for 84 industries during the 1980s (1983-89) and 1990s (1990-97), as well as the growth exhibited during the second period, is set out in Appendix D.

## FIGURE 9

### TRENDS IN TOTAL INTER- AND INTRAINDUSTRY TRADE, 1983-1997

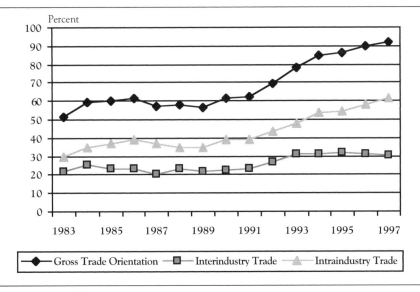

Source: Authors' calculations.

| TIME TREND OF INTER- AND INTRAINDUSTRY TRADE | | | |
|---|---|---|---|
| Time Period: 1983 97 | me-trend Coefficient | | Growth |
| Gross Orientation | 0.039 | (7.99) | 4.02 |
| Interindustry Trade | 0.029 | (5.04) | 2.94 |
| Intraindustry Trade | 0.046 | (8.95) | 4.69 |
| Ratio of Intra- to Interindustry Trade | 0.017 | (3.73) | 1.70 |

Note:   The t-values are significant at 1 percent.
Source: Authors' calculations.

We wanted to examine the causes of intraindustry trade specialization. Intraindustry trade can take place in industries differentiated on the demand side, the supply side or both. Intraindustry trade determinants in the literature include economies of scale, demand for variety, product differentiation and difference in technology. Economies of scale are an important factor for intra-industry trade; however, there are no data available to measure it. As a proxy, we use number of employees per establishment. Similarly, there are no data to capture product differentiation from the demand side. Therefore, we use a variable that could capture the notion of differentiated product from the supply side — the proportion of high school graduates in the total labour force of an industry. Technology difference is captured by means of the capital-labour ratio. We use the FTA as a dummy. We have allowed for industry fixed effects and the time variant effect to be taken by time-trend. We estimated a pooled least square regression (pooling 84 industries for the 15-year period). The results are presented below.

All explanatory variables are significant (with the exception of the FTA), indicating that a labour force with a greater proportion of skilled workers and an increase in the capital-labour ratio lead to a higher level of intraindustry specialization. As the size of the firm (in terms of number of employees) rises, intraindustry trade falls. This may be due to the fact that intraindustry trade is carried on primarily by relatively smaller firms that supply the U.S. niche product market. Note that the FTA dummy is not significant. Using data at the SIC 4-digit level, Trefler (1999) finds a small increase in intraindustry trade during the post-FTA period but, more interestingly, that the FTA did not contribute to this increase in a statistically significant way.

| INTRAINDUSTRY TRADE AND ITS DETERMINANTS | | | | | |
|---|---|---|---|---|---|
| Dependent Variable | Independent Variables | | | | |
| | Proportion of High School Graduates | Capital-labour Ratio | Employment per Establishment | FTA | Time |
| Intraindustry Trade | 108.78 $(2.01)^b$ | 3.75 $(8.91)^a$ | −0.37 $(−2.12)^b$ | 34.04 (1.23) | −7.16 $(−1.76)^b$ |
| | $R^2 = 0.21$ | | | | |
| | n = 1,134 | | | | |

Notes: The dependent variable is in percentage form, defined as $z_{it} *100$. The proportion of high school graduates is the percentage of high school graduates in the total labour force. Capital-labour ratio is the net capital stock (in dollars) per employee. Employment per establishment is the total number of employees divided by the number of establishments in an industry.
[a]Significantly different from zero at the 1 percent level, on the basis of a two-tailed test.
[b]Significantly different from zero at the 5 percent level, on the basis of a two-tailed test.
Source: Authors' estimations.

From the above analysis, it is evident that increased trade has led to intraindustry specialization. However, has trade increased productivity? The interaction of trade and productivity in the economic relationship of two countries is not well understood. However, there is evidence suggesting that an increase in international trade has led to increased productivity for many countries. Edwards (1998) provides a good overview of the existing literature. Some studies on Canada have shown a relationship between the FTA and productivity. Trefler finds that the FTA increased labour productivity in Canada's manufacturing sector, with the greatest increase in industries where tariff cuts were highest. Harris and Kherfi (2000) find that since the FTA, increases in intraindustry specialization appear to have contributed significantly to productivity growth in Canadian manufacturing. We estimated the impact of intra- and interindustry trade, size (as defined above), capital-labour ratio and the FTA on labour productivity for 84 manufacturing industries with 15 years of data (from 1983 to 1997). The results are set out in the panel below.

Our results suggest that the increase in intraindustry trade has raised labour productivity. Employment per establishment is positively significant, meaning that labour productivity rises with the size of the firm. Here, the FTA figure is significant, suggesting that the FTA has had a positive impact on labour productivity in Canada. The dependent variable, labour productivity level, is measured in millions of dollars of real output (in 1992 prices) per employee. The average annual labour productivity level from 1989 to 1997 (the post-FTA period) was $0.0624 million per worker. About 18 percent of this productivity ([0.0112/0.0624] * 100) is accounted for by the FTA.

## LABOUR PRODUCTIVITY AND ITS DETERMINANTS

| Dependent Variable | Independent Variables | | | | | |
|---|---|---|---|---|---|---|
| | Intraindustry Specialization | Interindustry Specialization | Capital-labour Ratio | Employment per Establishment | FTA | Time |
| Labour Productivity | 0.00002 (8.02)[a] | –0.00005 (–3.76)[a] | 0.001 (31.69)[a] | 0.00003 (2.25)[b] | 0.0112 (5.68)[a] | –0.0002 (–0.73) |
| $R^2 = 0.86$ | | | | | | |
| n = 1,134 | | | | | | |

Note: Capital-labour ratio is defined as net capital stock (in dollars) per employee. Employment per establishment is the total number of employees divided by the number of establishments in an industry.
[a]Significantly different from zero at the 1 percent level, on the basis of a two-tailed test.
[b]Significantly different from zero at the 5 percent level, on the basis of a two-tailed test.
Source: Authors' estimations.

# CANADA'S COMPETITIVE POSITION IN THE U.S. MARKET

THROUGHOUT THIS STUDY, we have tried to assess and analyse the importance of the U.S. market for Canada's trade and investment without taking account of other countries. However, Canada's relative competitive position depends on how other market competitors are performing in the United States. For this purpose, we disaggregate the suppliers of U.S. imports into seven countries or regions. They are: Canada, the EU, Japan, Mexico, China, other East Asia and the rest of the world (ROW).[20] To identify the performance of each of these seven competitors, we estimate a time trend using a system of seven equations (one for each country or region) for each of 19 SIC 2-digit U.S. manufacturing industries and one overall manufacturing sector. The estimated system of equations with across-equation restrictions for each industry $i$, $i = 1, \dots ,20$ is

$$x_{ijt}/m_{it}^* = c_{ijt} + \beta_{ijt}t + u_{it}, \quad s.t. \quad \sum_j c_{ijt} = 100 \quad and \quad \sum_j \beta_{ijt} = 0,$$

where the subscript $j$ represents Canada, the EU, Japan, Mexico, China, other East Asia and the ROW. The variable $x_{ij}$ denotes country $j$'s exports of $i^{th}$ industry to the United States, $m_{it}^*$ stands for total U.S. imports from the world in industry $i$ at time period $t$, $c$ represents the constant term, and $t$ denotes the time period from 1980 to 2000. The dependent variable is thus the U.S. import market share for each country or region in industry $i$ for time period $t$, expressed as a percentage. Since the constant term in the equation measures the first-year percentage, the sum of the shares for all U.S. trading partners should add up to 100 (first constraint). In this construct, the coefficient measures the annual percentage change in a country's share of U.S. imports. As the loss of one country's share is another country's gain, the sum of coefficients across countries or regions should add up to zero (second constraint). The constraints are implemented by imposing restrictions on the seventh equation (the equation for the ROW), which is not estimated, but its constant term is given by $100 - \sum_{j'} c_{ij't}$ and its coefficient is given by $0 - \sum_{j'} \beta_{ij't}$, where $j'$ represents all $j$ except the ROW.

The estimated system of equation results for 19 industries is presented in Appendix E, except for the ROW (which is not reported, as our objective is to analyse the six markets, not the ROW). The fitted trend equation for the overall manufacturing sector indicates that Canada, the EU, Japan and other East Asia lost market share, whereas Mexico and China gained. Japan had the largest loss, China the greatest gain. Canada lost U.S. market share at the rate of 0.12 percent per year, whereas China and Mexico gained at a rate of 0.49 and 0.42 percent per year respectively. The fitted time trend for total merchandise is given in the following panel.

| SHARE OF TOTAL U.S. MANUFACTURING IMPORTS FOR DIFFERENT COMPETITORS | | | | | | |
|---|---|---|---|---|---|---|
| | Canada | EU | Japan | Mexico | China | Other East Asia |
| Constant | 20.36 | 23.83 | 24.73 | 1.20 | −1.23 | 16.09 |
| Time | −0.12 | −0.23 | −0.43 | 0.42 | 0.49 | 0.08 |
| | $(-2.61)^a$ | $(-4.93)^a$ | $(-9.31)^a$ | $(9.10)^a$ | $(10.66)^a$ | $(1.78)^b$ |

Note: The dependent variable is measured as a percentage. The constant term for each country could be read as that country's share of U.S. imports in 1980. The second row of numbers is the time coefficient for each country, which measures the country's annual percentage change in U.S. import market share. The number in parentheses is t-ratio for the time-trend coefficient.
[a]Significantly different from zero at the 1-percent level, on the basis of a two-tailed test.
[b]Significantly different from zero at the 10-percent level, on the basis of a two-tailed test.
Source: Authors' calculations.

Canada has gained market share in nine industries (Table 24).[21] The first column in Table 24 shows the industry share of total U.S. manufacturing imports, and the second shows the average annual growth of U.S. industry imports. The third lists the coefficient of time variable, which shows the percentage rise of Canada's U.S. market share. The remaining columns show the market share position of other competitors. A country that gained market share in a given industry is assigned a plus sign, one that lost market share is assigned a minus sign and one that neither lost nor gained is left blank. The industries in which Canada scored gains over the year constituted about 43 percent of U.S. manufacturing imports. Canada gained market share in industries where the EU and Japan lost ground. Other East Asian countries lost market share in seven of these nine industries. Mexico and China lost no market share in any of these industries, and indeed raised their market shares in most of them.

Canada lost its U.S. market share in the three industries shown in Table 25. These industries accounted for 20 percent of total U.S. merchandise imports. The market gainers were China (in all three industries), Mexico and other East Asia (in two), and the EU and Japan (in one).

## TABLE 24

### INDUSTRIES IN WHICH CANADA GAINED U.S. MARKET SHARE

| Industry | Share | Growth | Canada | EU | Japan | Mexico | China | Other East Asia |
|----------|-------|--------|--------|----|----|--------|-------|-----------------|
| Food and Beverages | 3.0 | 8.0 | 0.75 | | | + | | |
| Tobacco Products | 0.6 | 9.5 | 1.09 | − | | | | + |
| Rubber and Plastics | 2.5 | 8.4 | 0.16 | − | − | + | + | − |
| Textile Products | 1.1 | 7.4 | 0.75 | | − | + | | − |
| Clothing | 6.7 | 7.4 | 0.10 | − | − | + | + | − |
| Wood | 1.8 | 9.9 | 0.39 | − | − | | + | − |
| Primary Metals | 5.0 | 8.4 | 0.32 | − | − | + | + | − |
| Fabricated Metal Products | 2.6 | 10.7 | 0.11 | − | − | + | + | |
| Transportation Equipment | 19.9 | 9.8 | 0.10 | − | − | + | | + |

Note:   This table is taken from Appendix E, Table E1. The industries listed here are ones with a positively significant estimated time trend for Canada over the last 20 years. The share is based on the annual average from 1995 to 2000. Similarly, the growth is annual average growth during 1995-2000.
Source: Authors' calculations.

## TABLE 25

### INDUSTRIES IN WHICH CANADA LOST U.S. MARKET SHARE

| Industry | Share | Growth | Canada | EU | Japan | Mexico | China | Other East Asia |
|----------|-------|--------|--------|----|----|--------|-------|-----------------|
| Paper and Allied Products | 2.1 | 9.9 | −0.97 | + | + | | + | + |
| Machinery (except Electrical) | 16.6 | 10.0 | −0.37 | − | − | + | + | + |
| Non-metallic Minerals | 1.4 | 10.4 | −0.15 | − | − | + | + | − |

Note:   The industries listed here are the ones with a negatively significant estimated time trend for Canada over the last 20 years, given in Appendix E, Table E1.
Source: Authors' calculations.

Canada has maintained its market share in a number of industries that account for about 37 percent of total U.S. manufacturing imports, including major import industries like furniture and fixtures and electronic and electrical products. Among this group, U.S. imports of furniture and fixtures, chemicals and chemical products, and petroleum and other coal products increased faster than total U.S. manufacturing import growth, while imports in other industries grew at a rate slower than average U.S. growth. In most of the industries, where Canada was able only to maintain its market share, Mexico and China expanded theirs.

We summarize the above discussion in the following panel. We split U.S. import market share data into two categories based on whether the U.S. total imports for a particular industry grew faster or slower than average U.S. manufacturing import growth. We also break the import market share data down in terms of market loss, market gain and no trend for Canada.

The overall story of the market share changes for major suppliers to the U.S. market is fascinating. As the U.S. economy kept piling up riches during the 1990s, the market share of Japan and the EU kept declining. Japan lost market share in 12, while gaining in only one (paper and allied products) of the 19 U.S. manufacturing import industries. The EU economies also lost market share in 12 industries, while gaining in three (refined petroleum, paper products and chemicals). Other East Asian economies lost market share in eight, while scoring gains in six of the U.S. import industries. Mexico and China made the biggest inroads into the U.S. import market by gaining market share in 13 industries, while losing in none.

At the aggregate level, the above conclusions suggest that the U.S. marketplace is highly dynamic and competitive. Market share champions of the past cannot take the U.S. market for granted. It appears that the large and prosperous U.S. economy is creating deeper links in a large number of Mexican and Chinese industries. By contrast, Canada's exporters were unable to increase market share in a number of large U.S. industries like machinery, electrical and electronic products, and chemicals and chemical products. This may also indicate that Canada's exports scored a below-average performance in increasing market share in the industries often included in the "new economy," characterized by a high degree of product innovation, a high level of new technology and skill intensity, and above-average growth prospects. New players like Mexico, China and East Asia have been successful in challenging Canada's special economic relationship with the United States. They have increased their U.S. economic links in a number of important industries, including parts of the new economy.

| SUMMARY: CANADA'S POSITION IN U.S. IMPORTS | | | | |
|---|---|---|---|---|
| | U.S. MERCHANDISE IMPORT SHARE FOR INDUSTRIES IN WHICH CANADA HAD: | | | |
| Growth of U.S. Industry Imports | Market Gain | Market Loss | No Trend | Total |
| Faster-than-average U.S. Import Growth | 2.6 | 1.4 | 11.1 | 15.1 |
| Slower-than-average U.S. Import Growth | 40.6 | 18.7 | 25.6 | 84.9 |
| Total | 43.2 | 20.1 | 36.7 | 100 |

Note: The average U.S. import growth from 1995 to 2000 was 10.4 percent.
Source: Authors' calculations.

Change in market share, however, should not be understood as necessarily a change in competitiveness. Standard trade theories tell us that the trade volume between two countries rises with an increase in their market sizes (as measured by their GDPs), an increase in similarity between them (smaller difference in their GDPs), a fall in tariff and non-tariff barriers, a fall in transportation costs or an increase in outsourcing. If a competitor country has larger proportionate change with respect to the United States in one of the above factors when compared to Canada, all other factors being equal, that country's export share may rise faster than Canada's, even if there is no change in the competitive position between Canada and that competitor. For example, after the NAFTA, trade barriers between Mexico and the United States fell proportionally more than those between Canada and the United States (which were already close to zero because of the 1989 implementation of the FTA). With the NAFTA, therefore, one would expect Canada's share of U.S. imports to fall and Mexico's to rise. Similarly, given that the Chinese economy has grown faster than Canada's for the last few years, one would expect China's share of U.S. imports to rise faster than Canada's. The hypothesis that when two countries become more similar in size, trade between them increases has found considerable empirical support in both OECD and non-OECD countries (Hummels and Levinsohn 1995). Moreover, a growing body of literature has shown that U.S. outsourcing is increasing. The rapidly rising integration of world markets has brought with it a disintegration of the production process, in which manufacturing or services activities done abroad are combined with those performed at home. Measured as the share of imported input to total purchase of non-energy materials, outsourcing in the United States has risen from 5 percent in 1972 to 12 percent in 1990 (Feenstra and Hanson 1996). As outsourcing is generally to a country with cheap labour, we could see more U.S. imports from countries like Mexico and China, which would reduce Canada's relative share of U.S. imports.

| CORRELATION BETWEEN CHANGE IN MARKET SHARE AND CHANGE IN RCA | | |
|---|---|---|
| | CHANGE IN RCA | |
| CHANGE IN MARKET SHARE | 1990–85 | 1997–90 |
| 1990–85 | 0.310 | |
| 1997–90 | | 0.479 |

Note:   We calculate the change in Canada's 1990 U.S. import market share from its 1985 market share and calculate the change in Canada's 1990 RCA index from its 1985 level. Then we run a cross-industry correlation, using 19 industries (observations). Similarly, we calculate the 1997 change in market share and RCA index from their 1990 levels and obtain the second correlation.

Source: Authors' calculations.

One way to evaluate whether Canada is losing or gaining market share against what the standard trade theories would predict is to run a gravity model that encompasses the trade flows of all foreign competitors in the United States as dependent variables, and their GDPs, distances and changes in trade barriers as independent variables. However, that is not the objective of this study. Accordingly, it does not deal with the whys of Canada's U.S. market share, but rather provides facts on what is happening to Canada's merchandise export position in the U.S. market. Moreover, since we have only seven U.S. trade flows (seven suppliers to the United States) for each year, the number of observations for regression analysis is too small.

Previously, we calculated Canada's revealed comparative advantage vis-à-vis the United States, with an index greater than one showing RCA for Canada. In what follows, we estimate the correlation between change in Canada's U.S. market share and change in Canada's RCA vis-à-vis the United States. The results are presented in the panel below. The results show that the change in RCA position for Canada (increase in RCA index) vis-à-vis the United States and Canada's increase in market share *vis-à-vis* other competitors in the U.S. markets are positively correlated.

## CONCLUSIONS

THE MAIN OBJECTIVE OF THIS STUDY has been to provide an in-depth analysis of Canada's trade and FDI patterns with the United States, Canada's largest and most important trading partner. Our findings highlight several interesting trends. The following are some of the important conclusions:

- Canada's trade and investment links with the United States deepened considerably in the 1990s. This trend is pervasive across all Canadian industries and provinces.

- The importance of the South and Northwest U.S. regions increased steadily for all Canadian provinces and regions, except for British Columbia and the Territories. However, more than two-thirds of all Canadian exports are still destined to the Northeast and Midwest regions.

- Not surprisingly, Atlantic Canada exports mainly resource-based and labour-intensive products; Quebec concentrates primarily on resource-based and labour-intensive manufacturing products and electrical machinery; Ontario's exports are dominated by transportation equipment and non-electrical machinery; agriculture, mining, refined petroleum and chemical products account for much of the Prairies' exports; while British Columbia and the Territories export largely wood products, paper and allied products, non-electrical machinery and non-metallic mineral products.

- Contrary to expectations, the share of intrafirm trade in Canada-U.S. trade flows declined significantly in the post-FTA period, suggesting that the reduction of tariff and non-tariff barriers might have increased outsourcing by U.S. and Canadian multinationals in search of cost reductions.

- The buoyant U.S. economy and the depreciation of the Canadian dollar were mainly responsible for the dramatic increase in Canadian exports to the United States during the 1990s. As expected, the FTA contributed positively to Canada's exports — on average, they increased by about 9 percent. Similarly, the growth in Canadian real GDP was the main driver of the rapid growth of imports from the United States during the post-FTA period. On average, real exchange rate depreciation and the FTA were not significant factors in the import expansion.

- Unlike the situation in goods, the U.S. share of total Canadian exports of services has remained more or less constant at about 58 percent for the past 20 years, suggesting that service exports do not respond much to business cycles and real exchange rate movements. Americans account for slightly less than two-thirds of our total service imports.

- The U.S. share of Canadian commercial service exports declined during the 1990s. However, the importance of commercial services in the overall trade in services with the United States has increased steadily over the past 20 years. They currently represent slightly over 50 percent of Canadian service exports and imports. Canadian and U.S. multinationals account for more than 90 percent of Canada's trade in commercial services.

- Canadian exports of commercial services are carried on mainly by Canadian-controlled firms, while imports are split equally between Canadian-controlled and U.S.-controlled firms. Canadian-controlled multinationals do more arm's-length trade, whereas U.S.-controlled firms engage in intra-corporate trade. Canadian-controlled companies have a higher percentage of intrafirm exports than imports; the opposite is true for U.S.-controlled firms.

- Unlike the situation in merchandise trade, the U.S. share of Canada's FDI has declined steadily during the past 20 years to just over 50 percent of the total Canadian outward direct investment stock. Similarly, the U.S. share of total Canadian inward FDI stock fell until 1990, then remained more or less steady until 1994, but has increased slightly since then.

- Since much of the service trade, especially in commercial services, is carried out by multinationals, it is not surprising that the importance of the U.S. market for service exports has either remained stagnant or declined. The FDI trends do not bode well for future growth of Canadian service exports to the United States.

- The labour and capital requirements to produce $1 million worth of Canadian exports declined steadily both in the goods- and service-producing industries. Service exports use much more labour and capital than goods exports.

- More importantly, the skill content of goods and service exports increased steadily during the past 15 years. For instance, the percentage of employees with post-secondary and university education in total goods exports rose from 31 to nearly 51 percent between 1985 and 1997. For service exports, the percentage of skilled workers more than doubled during the same period, reaching about 36 percent.

- The share of imported inputs in goods exports increased steadily from about 24 percent in 1980 to over 37 percent in 1997. The import content of service exports is considerably smaller than that in goods exports — in 1997 imported inputs represented only 8 percent of service exports, up from 6.8 percent in 1990.

- The industrial structure of import content, export intensity, import penetration and net-export intensity remained fairly stable during the 1985-97 period, suggesting a deepening of the comparative advantage position for Canadian industries.

- Between 1985 and 1997, the number of industries with a revealed comparative advantage increased by six. At the same time, the export share of industries with a revealed comparative advantage declined from about 70 percent in 1985 to around 65 percent in 1997. In addition, the capital intensity of 23 of 37 industries with a revealed comparative advantage in 1997 was below the average capital intensity.

- Both intra- and interindustry trade increased significantly during the 1990s. Intraindustry trade increased faster than interindustry trade, however, suggesting an increase in product specialization faster than warranted by specialization based on the advantage in factors of production. Our pooled industry and time-series regression results suggest that a greater proportion of skilled employees and a positive capital labour ratio contribute positively to intraindustry trade. The coefficient on the FTA dummy is positive but not statistically significant, implying that the FTA at best had only a small positive impact on intraindustry trade.

- Our analysis of interindustry variation in labour productivity over time suggests that the FTA has contributed to Canada's labour productivity significantly, both directly and indirectly, perhaps by stimulating competition and innovation, rationalizing production processes, increasing capital intensity and intraindustry specialization, and raising the average size of business establishments.

- Despite fierce competition, Canada has maintained its market share in a majority of industries, which account for over 55 percent of U.S. imports. Surprisingly, Canada has gained market share in a number of resource-based and labour-intensive industries, perhaps because of the FTA and dollar depreciation. In these industries, the EU, Japan and the East Asian countries have lost a lot of ground. On the other hand, Mexico and China have made huge gains. Canada lost ground in paper and allied products, non-metallic minerals and non-electrical machinery. Here too, Mexico and China have made huge inroads at the expense of Canada, the EU and Japan.

Our findings suggest that the dramatic increase in trade and investment linkages between Canada and the United States during the 1990s was mainly the result of strong U.S. economic expansion and the real exchange rate depreciation. These results imply that future Canadian export growth to the United States will depend critically on the health of the U.S. economy and the competitive position of Canadian industries.

We cannot continue to rely on a weak Canadian dollar to maintain our cost-competitiveness in the U.S. market. Instead, we should deepen and broaden our comparative advantage position in technology and skill-intensive products, while improving our relative productivity performance across all industries. This is the only successful way to face the growing competitive challenge from Mexico and China in the U.S. market and win, while closing the large Canada-U.S. real income gap.

# ENDNOTES

1    The Atlantic region includes Newfoundland and Labrador, Prince Edward Island, Nova Scotia and New Brunswick; the Prairies consist of Manitoba, Saskatchewan and Alberta; British Columbia and the Territories include British Columbia, Yukon, Nunavut and the Northwest Territories.

2    The Northeast region includes Connecticut, Maine, Massachusetts, New Hampshire, Rhode Island, Vermont, Delaware, District of Columbia, Maryland, New Jersey, New York and Pennsylvania; the Midwest region consists of Illinois, Indiana, Michigan, Ohio, Wisconsin, Iowa, Kansas, Minnesota, Missouri, Nebraska, North Dakota and South Dakota; the South region includes Alabama, Arkansas, Florida, Georgia, Kentucky, Louisiana, Mississippi, North Carolina, South Carolina, Tennessee, West Virginia, Arizona, New Mexico, Oklahoma and Texas; and the Northwest region includes Colorado, Idaho, Montana, Utah, Wyoming, Alaska, California, Hawaii, Nevada, Oregon and Washington.

3    There are 31 industries altogether at the SIC 2-digit level of the goods-producing sector (agriculture, fishing, forestry, mining and manufacturing). However, in order to make the industry classification comparable with other sections of the study, particularly with the U.S. classification, we have included all five industries under the agriculture, fishing and logging divisions under one heading: "Agriculture, Fishing and Forestry." Furthermore, we have placed all four 2-digit industries in the mining division under one industry called "Mining." We have combined the food and beverage industries into one. We have also placed rubber products and plastic products under the single heading of "Rubber and Plastics." Finally, the primary textile and textile product industries are grouped under the rubric "Textile Products." As a result, we end up with just 21 industries and one overall merchandise sector.

4    In 1998, intrafirm trade accounted for 35 percent of U.S. exports and 39 percent of U.S. imports. Intrafirm exports consisted largely of transactions by U.S. MNCs with their affiliates, whereas intrafirm imports consisted of transactions by foreign MNCs with their affiliates in the United States. In 1998, of the 35 percent of exports accounted for by intrafirm trade, 27 percent was shipped by U.S. parent companies to their affiliates and 8 percent was shipped by foreign affiliates to their foreign parent groups. On the import side, of the 40 percent share of U.S. intrafirm imports (out of total U.S. imports), 17 percent was imports by U.S. parents from their affiliates and 22 percent was imports by foreign affiliates from their parent groups. However, the intrafirm trade share of U.S. parent companies has increased, indicating a decrease in their transactions with non-affiliated companies over the years. Between 1983 and 1998, the export share has increased from 35 to 46 percent, with the import share rising from 39 to 49 percent over the same period.

5    As there are no data on all affiliates, the following analysis on intrafirm trade of U.S. MNCs is restricted to intrafirm trade between U.S. parent companies and their majority-owned foreign affiliates (MOFAs). In the aggregate, intrafirm exports with MOFAs accounted for about 97 percent of the total for the last 16 years, approaching about 100 percent in recent years. Similarly, intrafirm imports accounted for 95 percent of the total for the last 16 years, and some 98 percent recently.

6    An increase in $r_i = p_i/ep_i^*$, means that a basket of Canadian goods could purchase more U.S. goods and would amount to an appreciation of the Canadian dollar. Similarly, a decrease in $r_i$ would mean a depreciation in the purchasing power of Canadian goods abroad.

7    The U.S. tariff rates for Canada are compiled from two sources. The rates from 1980 to 1988 are computed from the National Bureau of Economic Research (NBER) database. However, these are U.S. tariff rates for the world, and cannot be disaggregated by country. In absence of a better measure, we have taken these rates as a proxy for Canada. The United States had lower tariff rates for Canada than for other countries, at least in the auto sector, so the U.S. world rates (which we have taken as the rates for Canada) will overstate the rate for Canada. For the 1989-1999 period, we were able to obtain U.S. tariff rates for Canada from the United States International Trade Commission Web site. In both cases, the tariff rates are calculated as the ratio of duty collected to customs value.

8    The criterion for statistical significance is set at 10 percent or less.

9    In the absence of detailed regional and industrial data, our discussion here is based on national data.

10    Transactions that take place between Canadian parents and Canadian subsidiaries, and between foreign subsidiaries and foreign parents are said to be "related." However, transactions between Canadian companies and third parties are said to be "other" or "not related."

11    The sum of the entries under Canada and the United States for a given category of commercial services and time period may be less than 100. If so, the remaining share of trade is carried out by companies which are neither Canadian- nor U.S.-controlled.

12    In the input-output table, at the link level of aggregation, there are 167 industries altogether: 154 in the business sector and 13 in the government sector. As the objective of this chapter is to measure the capital, labour and imported input contents of Canadian exports associated with the business sector, we will concentrate on industries in the business sector only. Seven business-sector industries are excluded from the study. These industries do not have capital stock and labour requirement data and do not export or import (except the transportation margin industry which has a very small amount of exports). As a result, this chapter is based on just 147 industries in the business sector. Since the data on capital stock is available for only 119 industries, we have converted these 147 industries into 119 industries for the calculation of factor and imported input contents. The conversion was carried out primarily by rolling up the SIC 4-digit industries in the input-output table into the SIC 3-digit manufacturing industries and rolling up the SIC 2-digit and SIC 1-digit categories into services.

13    In this section, the results presented refer to Canada's exports to the world, as the input-output table does not allow us to calculate patterns for the United States alone.

14    The data set is available at the SIC 3-digit level from 1983 to 1998 for the whole economy. We use only business sector data. The data from 1985 to 1989 and from 1990 to 1998 are based on two different surveys which are not fully compatible. There are six types of labour skills in the first period and seven in the second. We

have aggregated these skills into four categories for each period to make the skill content more comparable over time.

15    This assumption means that the intermediate input fraction for each industry depends only on the fraction of net imports to use, not on the quantity of imports used for final consumption plus the quantity used for intermediate input. In reality, even if the two industries have the same fractions of net imported input, they are likely to have different fractions of imported intermediate inputs simply because they have a different proportion of imports in their intermediate inputs and their finished goods. There is no way to avoid this problem, as the input-output table does not decompose each industry's total imports by intermediate input and finished good. Given the data constraint, this is the best approximation we could use.

16    In the service-producing sector there are only three categories, as there were no industries whose percentage of imported inputs in exports was higher than 30.

17    To calculate Spearman's rank correlation ($r$) coefficient for export intensity for 84 industries between 1985 and 1990, we first ranked the industries in 1985 and 1990 by export intensity (from low to high or high to low). After that we found the sum of the squares of the differences, $d$, between 1985 and 1990 export intensity rankings and substituted in the formula $r = 1 - \left( 6 (\sum d)^2 / (n^3 - n) \right)$, where n is a number of industries (84 in our case) for the two time periods. We repeated the same process for other export intensity year pairs and for other intensities as well.

18    To determine the RCA, we had to get Canada's total exports and U.S. total exports into the same industry categories. As industry classification of the two countries differs, we had to run a concordance. To do this, we first compiled U.S. trade data at the U.S. SIC 4-digit level for 1980 to 1988 from the National Bureau of Economic Research (NBER) database; and for 1989 to 2000 from the United States International Trade Commission database. Then we converted them into Canadian SIC 3-digit data. Many U.S. industries, even at the 4-digit level, do not fall uniquely into a single Canadian 3-digit industry level. As a result, Statistics Canada's "Concordance Between the Standard Industrial Classification of Canada and the United States: 1980 Canadian SIC-1987 U.S. SIC, Catalogue 12-574, was not sufficient. We thus used the augmented concordance table kindly provided for us by Daniel Trefler (Trefler, 1999).

19    When $x_{it} > m_{it}$, intraindustry trade is represented by $x_{it} - m_{it}$ and it will be twice the minority flow $2m_{it}$. Similarly, if $x_{it} < m_{it}$, intraindustry trade will be represented by twice the minority flow, $2x_{it}$. Note that in the first case, if $2x_{it} > c_{it}$ and in the second case $2m_{it} > c_{it}$, intraindustry trade will be greater than 100 percent. Note also that the concept of intraindustry trade defined here is similar to the Grubel-Lloyd index (except the denominator) given by $\left( x_{it} + m_{it} - |x_{it} - m_{it}| \right) / \left( x_{it} + m_{it} \right)$. Actually, the denominator in the above definition could be the output of industry $i$ as well. In the denominator, we have used total shipments instead of shipments related to the U.S. market, as shipment data are not available for the United States separately. Since the shipment data are available only for the years 1983 through 1997, we have analysed the intraindustry trade for these 16 years only. Similarly, since shipment data are available only for the

manufacturing sector, we have had to exclude the agriculture, fishing, forestry and mining industries from the study.

20  We include Hong Kong, Indonesia, Malaysia, the Philippines, Singapore, South Korea, Thailand and Taiwan in "other East Asia." Countries which are not included in the other six categories and have trade with the United States are aggregated into the ROW category.

21  The change in market share position is defined in terms of t-value of the time coefficient. A negatively significant t-value indicates a decline in market share, a positively significant one, an increase. Market share is considered stable if the t-value is not significant, whatever its sign.

## BIBLIOGRAPHY

Balassa, Bela A. "The Changing Pattern of Comparative Advantage in Manufactured Goods." *The Review of Economics and Statistics* 61 (1979): 259-66.

Bowen, Harry P. "On the Theoretical Interpretation of Indices of Trade Intensity and Revealed Comparative Advantage." *Weltwirtschaftliches Archiv* 119 (1983): 464-72.

Campa, Jose, and Linda S. Goldberg. *The Evolving External Orientation of Manufacturing Industries: Evidence from Four Countries.* NBER Working Paper No. 5919. Cambridge: National Bureau of Economic Research, February 1997.

Edwards, S. "Openness, Productivity and Growth: What Do We Really Know?" *Economic Journal* 108, 447 (1998): 383-98.

Feenstra, Robert C., and Gordon H. Hanson. "Globalization, Outsourcing and Wage Inequality." *American Economic Review* 86, 2 (1996): 240-45.

Fuentes-Godoy, Cesar, Paul Hanson and Lars Lundberg. "International Specialization and Structural Change in the Swedish Manufacturing Industry, 1969-1992." *Weltwirtschaftliches Archiv* 132, 3 (1996): 522-43.

Goldstein, Morris, and Mohsin Khan. "Income and Price Effects in Foreign Trade." In *Handbook of International Economics, Vol 2.* Edited by Ronald W. Jones and Peter B. Kenen. North Holland: Elsevir, 1985, pp. 1041-105.

Harris, Richard G., and Samer Kherfi. "Productivity Growth, Convergence, and Trade Specialization in Canadian Manufacturing." Paper presented at the Canada-U.S. Manufacturing Productivity Gap Conference, Ottawa, January 2000.

Hillman, Arye L. "Observations on the Relation between 'Revealed Comparative Advantage' and the Comparative Advantage as Indicated by Pre-trade Relative Prices." *Weltwirtschaftliches Archiv* 116 (1980): 315-21.

Hummels, David, and James A. Levinsohn. "Monopolistic Competition and International Trade: Reconsidering the Evidence." *Quarterly Journal of Economics* 110, 3 (1995): 799-836.

Magee, S. P. "Prices, Income and Foreign Trade." In *International Trade and Finance: Frontier for Research*. Edited by P. B. Kenen. Cambridge: Cambridge University Press, 1975, pp. 115-252.

Magun, Sunder, Someshwar Rao and Bimal Lodh. *Impact of the Canada-U.S. Free Trade on the Canadian Economy*. Working Paper No. 331. Ottawa: Economic Council of Canada, 1987.

Marchese, Serafino, and Franciso Nadal de Simone. "Monotinicity of Indices of 'Revealed' Comparative Advantage: Empirical Evidence on Hillman's Condition." *Weltwirtschaftliches Archiv* 125, 1 (1989): 158-67.

Postner, Harry H. *Factor Content of Canadian International Trade*. Ottawa: Economic Council of Canada, 1975.

Rao, Someshwar, and Tony Lemprière. *An Analysis of the Linkages between Canadian Trade Flows, Productivity, and Costs*. Working Paper No. 46. Ottawa: Economic Council of Canada, 1992.

Trefler, Daniel. *The Long and Short of the Canada-U.S. Free Trade Agreement*. Industry Canada Research Series on Perspective on North American Free Trade, Paper No. 6. Ottawa: Industry Canada, 1999.

# APPENDIX A

# MERCHANDISE TRADE

## TABLE A1

## THE U.S. SHARE OF CANADA'S GOODS TRADE, 1980-2000 (PERCENT)

| Industry | Exports | | | Imports | | |
|---|---|---|---|---|---|---|
| | 1980–1989 | 1990–1994 | 1995–2000 | 1980–1989 | 1990–1994 | 1995–2000 |
| 1. Agriculture, Fishing and Forestry | 17 | 34 | 41 | 66 | 67 | 66 |
| 2. Mining | 64 | 71 | 74 | 31 | 23 | 23 |
| 3. Food and Beverages | 56 | 65 | 72 | 44 | 55 | 58 |
| 4. Tobacco Products | 36 | 74 | 38 | 69 | 40 | 35 |
| 5. Rubber and Plastics | 90 | 94 | 94 | 73 | 77 | 79 |
| 6. Leather and Allied Products | 82 | 85 | 89 | 11 | 13 | 11 |
| 7. Textile Products | 49 | 71 | 84 | 46 | 56 | 64 |
| 8. Clothing | 74 | 88 | 94 | 6 | 13 | 18 |
| 9. Wood | 72 | 69 | 80 | 82 | 85 | 82 |
| 10. Furniture and Fixtures | 94 | 96 | 97 | 53 | 71 | 67 |
| 11. Paper and Allied Products | 68 | 69 | 70 | 78 | 85 | 87 |
| 12. Printing, Publishing and Allied Products | 91 | 84 | 91 | 85 | 86 | 86 |
| 13. Primary Metals | 70 | 65 | 77 | 63 | 65 | 59 |
| 14. Fabricated Metal Products | 77 | 80 | 87 | 68 | 71 | 74 |
| 15. Machinery (except Electrical) | 75 | 75 | 82 | 72 | 71 | 70 |
| 16. Transportation Equipment | 94 | 94 | 94 | 84 | 78 | 80 |
| 17. Electrical and Electronic Products | 73 | 80 | 84 | 67 | 58 | 56 |
| 18. Non-metallic Minerals | 90 | 88 | 92 | 62 | 66 | 68 |
| 19. Refined Petroleum and Coal | 91 | 92 | 97 | 55 | 55 | 66 |
| 20. Chemical Products | 64 | 74 | 82 | 73 | 76 | 76 |
| 21. Other Manufacturing | 71 | 75 | 80 | 59 | 61 | 63 |
| Total Share | 73 | 78 | 83 | 67 | 66 | 67 |

TABLE A2

CANADA'S EXPORT SHARE TO THE U.S. REGIONAL MARKETS, BY INDUSTRY, 1980-2000 (PERCENT)

| Industry | 1980–1989 | | | | 1990–2000 | | | |
|---|---|---|---|---|---|---|---|---|
| | NE | MW | South | NW | NE | MW | South | NW |
| 1. Agriculture, Fishing and Forestry | 41 | 31 | 5 | 24 | 26 | 36 | 6 | 31 |
| 2. Mining | 12 | 51 | 5 | 32 | 18 | 46 | 14 | 21 |
| 3. Food and Beverages | 58 | 22 | 7 | 12 | 44 | 24 | 14 | 17 |
| 4. Tobacco Products | 17 | 6 | 74 | 4 | 63 | 5 | 26 | 5 |
| 5. Rubber and Plastics | 29 | 32 | 31 | 9 | 23 | 39 | 29 | 9 |
| 6. Leather and Allied Products | 59 | 22 | 10 | 9 | 60 | 20 | 10 | 10 |
| 7. Textile Products | 35 | 18 | 41 | 5 | 33 | 16 | 43 | 8 |
| 8. Clothing | 60 | 20 | 9 | 12 | 56 | 17 | 12 | 15 |
| 9. Wood | 32 | 24 | 25 | 18 | 24 | 30 | 23 | 22 |
| 10. Furniture and Fixtures | 38 | 33 | 19 | 9 | 27 | 39 | 21 | 12 |
| 11. Paper and Allied Products | 39 | 36 | 14 | 12 | 36 | 36 | 16 | 12 |
| 12. Printing, Publishing and Allied Products | 76 | 12 | 6 | 6 | 49 | 21 | 14 | 16 |
| 13. Primary Metals | 56 | 28 | 11 | 5 | 47 | 32 | 17 | 4 |
| 14. Fabricated Metal Products | 34 | 39 | 16 | 11 | 26 | 40 | 21 | 12 |
| 15. Machinery (except Electrical) | 23 | 37 | 26 | 14 | 20 | 41 | 26 | 13 |
| 16. Transportation Equipment | 20 | 69 | 6 | 5 | 11 | 73 | 7 | 9 |
| 17. Electrical and Electronic Products | 40 | 19 | 28 | 12 | 46 | 14 | 22 | 18 |
| 18. Non-metallic Minerals | 50 | 30 | 9 | 11 | 31 | 44 | 14 | 11 |
| 19. Refined Petroleum and Coal | 37 | 44 | 4 | 16 | 38 | 32 | 18 | 10 |
| 20. Chemical Products | 22 | 40 | 28 | 10 | 25 | 38 | 25 | 12 |
| Total | 30 | 46 | 12 | 12 | 25 | 45 | 15 | 13 |

Note: Each row shows Canada's export share to the four U.S. regions, out of Canada's total exports to the United States, for each industry during the 1980s and 1990s. The sum of data columns one to four should add up to 100, as should the sum of data columns five to eight, for each industry. However, because of rounding, the sum might be slightly above or below 100. In the case of the last row (Total) the sum does not add up to 100 because "Other Manufacturing" is not included.

## TABLE A3

## THE ATLANTIC REGION'S EXPORT SHARE TO THE U.S. REGIONAL MARKETS, BY INDUSTRY, 1980-2000 (PERCENT)

| Industry | 1980–1989 | | | | 1990–2000 | | | |
|---|---|---|---|---|---|---|---|---|
| | NE | MW | South | NW | NE | MW | South | NW |
| 1. Agriculture, Fishing and Forestry | 94 | 1 | 3 | 1 | 89 | 2 | 4 | 3 |
| 2. Mining | 57 | 10 | 33 | 0 | 66 | 16 | 18 | 1 |
| 3. Food and Beverages | 89 | 4 | 4 | 3 | 83 | 5 | 7 | 4 |
| 4. Tobacco Products | 96 | 1 | 1 | 2 | 71 | 1 | 1 | 26 |
| 5. Rubber and Plastics | 28 | 6 | 62 | 4 | 14 | 21 | 57 | 9 |
| 6. Leather and Allied Products | 76 | 15 | 7 | 3 | 56 | 22 | 11 | 11 |
| 7. Textile Products | 34 | 16 | 44 | 6 | 35 | 11 | 46 | 7 |
| 8. Clothing | 52 | 11 | 13 | 25 | 33 | 30 | 10 | 27 |
| 9. Wood | 94 | 2 | 4 | 0 | 63 | 14 | 20 | 2 |
| 10. Furniture and Fixtures | 86 | 3 | 8 | 3 | 70 | 11 | 8 | 10 |
| 11. Paper and Allied Products | 70 | 10 | 20 | 0 | 57 | 16 | 21 | 2 |
| 12. Printing, Publishing and Allied Products | 64 | 17 | 10 | 8 | 75 | 9 | 10 | 7 |
| 13. Primary Metals | 77 | 6 | 14 | 2 | 63 | 16 | 19 | 1 |
| 14. Fabricated Metal Products | 59 | 9 | 26 | 6 | 59 | 8 | 30 | 3 |
| 15. Machinery (except Electrical) | 40 | 17 | 35 | 7 | 40 | 18 | 32 | 9 |
| 16. Transportation Equipment | 63 | 11 | 20 | 6 | 53 | 13 | 24 | 10 |
| 17. Electrical and Electronic Products | 29 | 22 | 29 | 20 | 28 | 26 | 33 | 13 |
| 18. Non-metallic Minerals | 56 | 2 | 42 | 0 | 69 | 13 | 13 | 4 |
| 19. Refined Petroleum and Coal | 94 | 0 | 5 | 0 | 65 | 1 | 34 | 1 |
| 20. Chemical Products | 53 | 12 | 32 | 3 | 69 | 10 | 16 | 4 |
| Total | 76 | 6 | 16 | 2 | 62 | 10 | 23 | 3 |

Note: Each row shows Canada's export share to the four U.S. regions, out of Canada's total exports to the United States, for each industry during the 1980s and 1990s. The sum of data columns one to four should add up to 100, as should the sum of data columns five to eight, for each industry. However, because of rounding, the sum might be slightly above or below 100. In the case of the last row (Total) the sum does not add up to 100 because "Other Manufacturing" is not included.

## TABLE A4

## QUEBEC'S EXPORT SHARE TO THE U.S. REGIONAL MARKETS, BY INDUSTRY, 1980-2000 (PERCENT)

| Industry | 1980–1989 | | | | 1990–2000 | | | |
|---|---|---|---|---|---|---|---|---|
| | NE | MW | South | NW | NE | MW | South | NE |
| 1. Agriculture, Fishing and Forestry | 85 | 7 | 4 | 3 | 81 | 6 | 5 | 6 |
| 2. Mining | 41 | 37 | 20 | 1 | 41 | 21 | 32 | 3 |
| 3. Food and Beverages | 78 | 12 | 7 | 3 | 66 | 13 | 13 | 6 |
| 4. Tobacco Products | 50 | 8 | 36 | 6 | 79 | 3 | 13 | 5 |
| 5. Rubber and Plastics | 40 | 32 | 22 | 6 | 34 | 32 | 28 | 6 |
| 6. Leather and Allied Products | 67 | 23 | 5 | 6 | 71 | 15 | 7 | 6 |
| 7. Textile Products | 52 | 11 | 33 | 4 | 50 | 11 | 29 | 10 |
| 8. Clothing | 76 | 13 | 7 | 4 | 75 | 9 | 10 | 6 |
| 9. Wood | 76 | 10 | 11 | 4 | 45 | 24 | 25 | 6 |
| 10. Furniture and Fixtures | 56 | 15 | 21 | 7 | 42 | 22 | 25 | 11 |
| 11. Paper and Allied Products | 55 | 26 | 18 | 1 | 50 | 28 | 17 | 3 |
| 12. Printing, Publishing and Allied Products | 91 | 4 | 4 | 2 | 68 | 14 | 12 | 6 |
| 13. Primary Metals | 62 | 21 | 16 | 1 | 47 | 26 | 26 | 2 |
| 14. Fabricated Metal Products | 56 | 23 | 16 | 4 | 49 | 23 | 22 | 5 |
| 15. Machinery (except Electrical) | 41 | 20 | 28 | 10 | 30 | 25 | 30 | 14 |
| 16. Transportation Equipment | 20 | 61 | 13 | 6 | 17 | 49 | 26 | 7 |
| 17. Electrical and Electronic Products | 56 | 8 | 25 | 10 | 64 | 6 | 17 | 12 |
| 18. Non-metallic Minerals | 76 | 12 | 10 | 2 | 63 | 20 | 13 | 4 |
| 19. Refined Petroleum and Coal | 87 | 6 | 5 | 2 | 78 | 5 | 13 | 1 |
| 20. Chemical Products | 50 | 19 | 26 | 3 | 43 | 21 | 29 | 5 |
| Total | 51 | 28 | 16 | 4 | 46 | 24 | 22 | 7 |

Note: Each row shows Canada's export share to the four U.S. regions, out of Canada's total exports to the United States, for each industry during the 1980s and 1990s. The sum of data columns one to four should add up to 100, as should the sum of data columns five to eight, for each industry. However, because of rounding, the sum might be slightly above or below 100. In the case of the last row (Total) the sum does not add up to 100 because "Other Manufacturing" is not included.

## TABLE A5

## ONTARIO'S EXPORT SHARE TO THE U.S. REGIONAL MARKETS, BY INDUSTRY, 1980-2000 (PERCENT)

| Industry | 1980–1989 | | | | 1990–2000 | | | |
|---|---|---|---|---|---|---|---|---|
| | NE | MW | South | NW | NE | MW | South | NW |
| 1. Agriculture, Fishing and Forestry | 42 | 45 | 11 | 2 | 36 | 45 | 14 | 4 |
| 2. Mining | 27 | 50 | 14 | 9 | 65 | 25 | 4 | 6 |
| 3. Food and Beverages | 41 | 43 | 11 | 4 | 42 | 33 | 16 | 8 |
| 4. Tobacco Products | 6 | 5 | 88 | 1 | 26 | 9 | 60 | 4 |
| 5. Rubber and Plastics | 28 | 42 | 23 | 8 | 23 | 46 | 24 | 7 |
| 6. Leather and Allied Products | 57 | 22 | 13 | 8 | 60 | 23 | 7 | 10 |
| 7. Textile Products | 26 | 22 | 48 | 4 | 20 | 20 | 55 | 6 |
| 8. Clothing | 48 | 30 | 14 | 8 | 45 | 26 | 14 | 16 |
| 9. Wood | 35 | 47 | 15 | 3 | 22 | 49 | 21 | 8 |
| 10. Furniture and Fixtures | 35 | 39 | 19 | 7 | 24 | 45 | 20 | 10 |
| 11. Paper and Allied Products | 26 | 60 | 9 | 5 | 29 | 50 | 16 | 5 |
| 12. Printing, Publishing and Allied Products | 73 | 17 | 7 | 3 | 48 | 26 | 17 | 9 |
| 13. Primary Metals | 57 | 31 | 8 | 4 | 52 | 35 | 10 | 3 |
| 14. Fabricated Metal Products | 31 | 47 | 16 | 6 | 22 | 50 | 22 | 6 |
| 15. Machinery (except Electrical) | 24 | 43 | 25 | 8 | 21 | 46 | 26 | 7 |
| 16. Transportation Equipment | 20 | 71 | 5 | 4 | 10 | 76 | 5 | 9 |
| 17. Electrical and Electronic Products | 38 | 22 | 29 | 11 | 38 | 19 | 23 | 20 |
| 18. Non-metallic Minerals | 48 | 40 | 9 | 2 | 27 | 56 | 14 | 3 |
| 19. Refined Petroleum and Coal | 40 | 53 | 6 | 0 | 41 | 38 | 16 | 3 |
| 20. Chemical Products | 22 | 45 | 32 | 2 | 27 | 43 | 26 | 4 |
| Total | 29 | 56 | 10 | 5 | 21 | 56 | 12 | 9 |

Note:    Each row shows Canada's export share to the four U.S. regions, out of Canada's total exports to the United States, for each industry during the 1980s and 1990s. The sum of data columns one to four should add up to 100, as should the sum of data columns five to eight, for each industry. However, because of rounding, the sum might be slightly above or below 100. In the case of the last row (Total) the sum does not add up to 100 because "Other Manufacturing" is not included.

## TABLE A6

## THE PRAIRIE REGION'S EXPORT SHARE TO THE U.S. REGIONAL MARKETS, BY INDUSTRY, 1980-2000 (PERCENT)

| Industry | 1980–1989 | | | | 1990–2000 | | | |
|---|---|---|---|---|---|---|---|---|
| | NE | MW | South | NW | NE | MW | South | NW |
| 1. Agriculture, Fishing and Forestry | 6 | 59 | 2 | 32 | 5 | 54 | 4 | 37 |
| 2. Mining | 8 | 56 | 3 | 33 | 15 | 50 | 15 | 20 |
| 3. Food and Beverages | 12 | 35 | 9 | 45 | 11 | 31 | 18 | 38 |
| 4. Tobacco Products | 15 | 66 | 9 | 10 | 9 | 87 | 3 | 1 |
| 5. Rubber and Plastics | 12 | 38 | 21 | 29 | 9 | 49 | 18 | 24 |
| 6. Leather and Allied Products | 20 | 32 | 14 | 35 | 16 | 32 | 31 | 21 |
| 7. Textile Products | 37 | 16 | 36 | 11 | 12 | 32 | 43 | 13 |
| 8. Clothing | 15 | 58 | 7 | 20 | 10 | 47 | 19 | 25 |
| 9. Wood | 5 | 49 | 27 | 19 | 5 | 41 | 19 | 35 |
| 10. Furniture and Fixtures | 12 | 56 | 14 | 18 | 18 | 42 | 24 | 16 |
| 11. Paper and Allied Products | 21 | 50 | 16 | 13 | 13 | 55 | 14 | 18 |
| 12. Printing, Publishing and Allied Products | 43 | 30 | 9 | 19 | 18 | 39 | 22 | 20 |
| 13. Primary Metals | 14 | 45 | 22 | 18 | 11 | 69 | 12 | 8 |
| 14. Fabricated Metal Products | 10 | 36 | 26 | 29 | 21 | 22 | 21 | 36 |
| 15. Machinery (except Electrical) | 4 | 38 | 30 | 28 | 6 | 46 | 26 | 21 |
| 16. Transportation Equipment | 9 | 40 | 18 | 33 | 5 | 54 | 10 | 31 |
| 17. Electrical and Electronic Products | 7 | 47 | 32 | 14 | 40 | 13 | 33 | 15 |
| 18. Non-metallic Minerals | 10 | 45 | 11 | 34 | 6 | 52 | 11 | 31 |
| 19. Refined Petroleum and Coal | 2 | 70 | 2 | 26 | 4 | 69 | 6 | 21 |
| 20. Chemical Products | 9 | 45 | 19 | 26 | 10 | 40 | 20 | 30 |
| Total | 8 | 54 | 8 | 30 | 13 | 48 | 15 | 23 |

Note:   Each row shows Canada's export share to the four U.S. regions, out of Canada's total exports to the United States, for each industry during the 1980s and 1990s. The sum of data columns one to four should add up to 100, as should the sum of data columns five to eight, for each industry. However, because of rounding, the sum might be slightly above or below 100. In the case of the last row (Total) the sum does not add up to 100 because "Other Manufacturing" is not included.

## TABLE A7

## BRITISH COLUMBIA AND THE TERRITORIES' EXPORT SHARE TO THE U.S. REGIONAL MARKETS, BY INDUSTRY, 1980-2000 (PERCENT)

| Industry | 1980–1989 | | | | 1990–2000 | | | |
|---|---|---|---|---|---|---|---|---|
| | NE | MW | South | NW | NE | MW | South | NW |
| 1. Agriculture, Fishing and Forestry | 4 | 6 | 3 | 87 | 10 | 3 | 2 | 84 |
| 2. Mining | 10 | 5 | 4 | 81 | 1 | 3 | 1 | 94 |
| 3. Food and Beverages | 10 | 5 | 3 | 82 | 11 | 8 | 5 | 75 |
| 4. Tobacco Products | 1 | 3 | 0 | 96 | 7 | 0 | 0 | 92 |
| 5. Rubber and Plastics | 3 | 7 | 7 | 84 | 4 | 12 | 13 | 70 |
| 6. Leather and Allied Products | 10 | 3 | 11 | 77 | 16 | 5 | 6 | 72 |
| 7. Textile Products | 8 | 8 | 12 | 72 | 10 | 5 | 16 | 69 |
| 8. Clothing | 14 | 4 | 7 | 74 | 18 | 17 | 15 | 50 |
| 9. Wood | 20 | 19 | 33 | 28 | 14 | 25 | 25 | 35 |
| 10. Furniture and Fixtures | 12 | 8 | 12 | 68 | 12 | 14 | 12 | 62 |
| 11. Paper and Allied Products | 10 | 26 | 7 | 56 | 9 | 29 | 8 | 53 |
| 12. Printing, Publishing and Allied Products | 6 | 5 | 8 | 80 | 6 | 5 | 5 | 83 |
| 13. Primary Metals | 34 | 23 | 12 | 30 | 15 | 29 | 13 | 43 |
| 14. Fabricated Metal Products | 4 | 10 | 10 | 76 | 5 | 11 | 13 | 71 |
| 15. Machinery (except Electrical) | 8 | 13 | 23 | 57 | 8 | 17 | 27 | 47 |
| 16. Transportation Equipment | 10 | 15 | 18 | 58 | 9 | 19 | 28 | 43 |
| 17. Electrical and Electronic Products | 9 | 15 | 19 | 57 | 13 | 15 | 17 | 55 |
| 18. Non-metallic Minerals | 2 | 1 | 3 | 95 | 1 | 5 | 11 | 77 |
| 19. Refined Petroleum and Coal | 2 | 3 | 0 | 95 | 6 | 3 | 4 | 87 |
| 20. Chemical Products | 2 | 7 | 15 | 75 | 4 | 14 | 26 | 56 |
| **Total** | **14** | **17** | **18** | **51** | **10** | **20** | **16** | **52** |

Note: Each row shows Canada's export share to the four U.S. regions, out of Canada's total exports to the United States, for each industry during the 1980s and 1990s. The sum of data columns one to four should add up to 100, as should the sum of data columns five to eight, for each industry. However, because of rounding, the sum might be slightly above or below 100. In the case of the last row (Total) the sum does not add up to 100 because "Other Manufacturing" is not included.

## TABLE A8

## ESTIMATION OF EQUATIONS FOR CANADA'S EXPORTS TO THE UNITED STATES (ANNUAL DATA, 1980-99)

| Dependent Variable | Independent Variables | | | | | |
|---|---|---|---|---|---|---|
| Canada's Real Export Growth to the U.S. Market | U.S. Real GDP Growth | Log of Real Exchange Rate | Capacity | FTA | $R^2$ | D-W |
| Food and Beverages | 0.652 (0.89) | −0.342 (−2.86) | −0.002 (−2.55)[b] | 0.113 (3.72)[a] | 0.55 | 1.78 |
| Tobacco Products | −8.997 (−1.01) | 0.596 (0.68) | −0.001 (−0.08) | 0.183 (0.40) | 0.14 | 2.00 |
| Rubber and Plastics | 0.733 (0.76) | −0.700 (3.42)[a] | −0.003 (−2.28)[b] | 0.193 (2.72)[b] | 0.41 | 1.89 |
| Leather and Allied Products | 0.423 (0.238) | −0.520 (−0.97) | −0.001 (−0.66) | 0.000 (0.000) | 0.08 | 2.11 |
| Textile Products | 1.851 (1.59) | −0.058 (−0.21) | 0.001 (0.59) | 0.024 (0.54) | 0.18 | 1.63 |
| Clothing | 1.206 (0.63) | −0.840 (−2.12)[b] | −0.002 (−1.25) | 0.121 (1.49) | 0.26 | 1.15 |
| Wood | 2.304 (1.88)[c] | −0.480 (−1.65) | −0.001 (−1.15) | 0.044 (0.96) | 0.27 | 1.35 |
| Furniture and Fixtures | 3.236 (2.69)[b] | −0.201 (−1.00) | 0.000 (−0.28) | 0.000 (0.012) | 0.42 | 2.11 |
| Paper and Allied Products | −0.008 (−0.01) | −0.312 (−2.81)[a] | 0.000 (0.81) | 0.014 (0.32) | 0.36 | 1.08 |
| Printing, Publishing and Allied Products | 1.108 (0.61) | −0.712 (−2.23)[b] | −0.002 (−1.79)[c] | 0.020 (0.33) | 0.33 | 1.12 |
| Primary Metals | 3.569 (1.21) | 0.174 (0.37) | −0.001 (−0.88) | 0.069 (0.57) | 0.11 | 2.79 |
| Fabricated Metal Products | 4.865 (2.93)[a] | −0.845 (−2.38)[b] | −0.004 (−3.28)[a] | 0.153 (2.39)[b] | 0.54 | 1.56 |
| Machinery (except Electrical) | 4.116 (2.42)[b] | 0.084 (0.57) | 0.000 (−0.23) | 0.002 (0.02) | 0.42 | 1.14 |
| Transportation Equipment | 1.606 (1.38) | −0.36 (−1.94)[c] | −0.000 (−0.54) | −0.024 (−0.58) | 0.31 | 1.33 |
| Electrical and Electronic Products | −1.356 (−0.59) | −0.165 (−1.17) | 0.001 (0.70) | 0.086 (1.22) | 0.20 | 2.48 |
| Non-metallic Minerals | 4.951 (4.36)[a] | −0.262 (−1.47) | −0.003 (−2.88)[a] | 0.102 (2.22)[b] | 0.63 | 2.38 |
| Refined Petroleum and Coal | 12.34 (1.97)[c] | −1.146 (−4.83)[a] | 0.002 (0.68) | −0.734 (−2.46) | 0.62 | 2.12 |
| Chemical Products | 0.648 (0.53) | −0.108 (−0.70) | 0.000 (−0.36) | 0.081 (1.83)[c] | 0.24 | 2.29 |
| Other Manufacturing | −0.015 (0.00) | −0.930 (−1.44) | −0.004 (−1.24) | 0.302 (1.87)[c] | 0.20 | 3.03 |

Note: The number in parentheses below each coefficient is a t-ratio. The dependent variable is measured as a percentage.

[a]Significantly different from zero at the 1 percent level, on the basis of a two-tailed test.
[b]Significantly different from zero at the 5 percent level, on the basis of a two-tailed test.
[c]Significantly different from zero at the 10 percent level, on the basis of a two-tailed test.

## TABLE A9

## ESTIMATION OF EQUATIONS FOR CANADA'S IMPORTS FROM THE UNITED STATES (ANNUAL DATA, 1980-99)

| Dependent Variable | Independent Variables | | | | |
|---|---|---|---|---|---|
| Canada's Real Import Growth from the U.S. Market | Canadian Real GDP Growth | Log of Real Exchange Rate | FTA | $R^2$ | D-W |
| Food and Beverages | 1.813 (2.48)[b] | 0.119 (1.38) | 0.063 (2.49)[c] | 0.24 | 1.89 |
| Tobacco Products | −4.704 (−1.58) | −0.218 (−1.01) | 0.132 (1.08) | 0.17 | 2.14 |
| Rubber and Plastics | 4.062 (4.11)[a] | 0.017 (0.20) | 0.019 (0.57) | 0.50 | 1.73 |
| Leather and Allied Products | 3.376 (2.48)[b] | 0.27 (1.13) | 0.005 (0.10) | 0.29 | 1.36 |
| Textile Products | 2.812 (3.46)[a] | 0.262 (2.35)[b] | 0.093 (3.39)[a] | 0.51 | 1.78 |
| Clothing | 3.939 (2.61)[b] | 0.418 (2.25)[b] | 0.157 (3.11)[a] | 0.40 | 0.96 |
| Wood | 3.752 (3.19)[a] | 0.400 (1.06) | −0.029 (−0.55) | 0.35 | 2.49 |
| Furniture and Fixtures | 7.669 (2.58)[b] | 0.666 (2.58)[a] | 0.085 (1.16) | 0.42 | 1.83 |
| Paper and Allied Products | 2.342 (2.28)[b] | 0.024 (0.16) | 0.034 (0.76) | 0.15 | 2.31 |
| Printing, Publishing and Allied Products | 0.885 (1.36) | 0.132 (1.43) | 0.025 (1.20) | 0.10 | 1.74 |
| Primary Metals | 3.282 (2.21)[b] | −0.314 (−0.80) | −0.032 (−0.42) | 0.27 | 2.24 |
| Fabricated Metal Products | 4.191 (5.62)[a] | 0.283 (2.47)[b] | 0.042 (1.57) | 0.66 | 2.20 |
| Machinery (except Electrical) | 5.718 (8.42)[a] | 0.144 (3.93)[a] | 0.015 (0.57) | 0.81 | 1.92 |
| Transportation Equipment | 3.478 (3.90)[a] | 0.152 (0.87) | −0.012 (−0.34) | 0.54 | 0.87 |
| Electrical and Electronic Products | 4.411 (6.59)[a] | −0.091 (−1.27) | 0.053 (2.34)[b] | 0.56 | 2.48 |
| Non-metallic Minerals | 4.575 (6.34)[a] | 0.300 (3.64)[a] | 0.024 (1.02) | 0.70 | 1.46 |
| Refined Petroleum and Coal | 6.435 (2.14)[b] | −0.185 (−1.18) | −0.176 (−1.27) | 0.14 | 1.29 |
| Chemical Products | 1.597 (2.40)[b] | −0.023 (−0.19) | 0.038 (1.24) | 0.20 | 1.99 |
| Other Manufacturing | 2.363 (4.24)[a] | 0.039 (0.60) | 0.032 (1.78)[c] | 0.53 | 1.36 |

Note:  The number in parentheses below each coefficient is a t-ratio.
[a]Significantly different from zero at the 1 percent level, on the basis of a two-tailed test.
[b]Significantly different from zero at the 5 percent level, on the basis of a two-tailed test.
[c]Significantly different from zero at the 10 percent level, on the basis of a two-tailed test.

# APPENDIX B

## THE INPUT-OUTPUT MODEL

IN THE INPUT-OUTPUT ANALYSIS, the following accounting balance between total supply and total demand (disposition) must hold for each industry $i$:

(B1) $g + m + v_w = Bg + c + i + v_a + x_d + x_r$,

where $g$ = gross value of output produced by industry,

$m$ = imports of goods and services (defined as positive),

$v_w$ = inventory withdrawals,

$B$ = intermediate input coefficient, technology matrix; $Bg$ yields the total use of industry $i$'s output as intermediate input by all industries in the economy,

$c$ = total consumption of goods and services, both personal and government,

$i$ = total capital formation, business and government,

$v_a$ = inventory additions,

$x_d$ = value of domestic exports of goods and services, and

$x_r$ = value of re-exports of goods and services.

In equation (B1), the left-hand side is the total supply and the right-hand side is the total demand of goods and services. By solving equation (B1) for $g$, we could obtain an expression that shows the linear transformation of final demand categories into industry outputs. It would show that industry output could be obtained if $(1 - B)^{-1}$ is post-multiplied by the exogenously given final demand. This expression, however, would not account for any leakage from the domestic industries. To the extent that imports and/or withdrawals from inventories share the supply of a commodity with the domestic industries, the impact of an increase in final demand on domestic industries will be reduced. To measure the impact of a change in final demand in domestic output, therefore, one should net out the leakage due to imports and inventory depletion.

Imports must be used to satisfy re-exports, final demand (excluding domestic exports) and intermediate input demand. Re-exports should be subtracted from total imports when computing the import leakage parameter, as re-exports should not be allocated to any other demand categories. If net imports are denoted by $m_n$, equation (B1) can be written as

(B2) $g = Bg + c + i + x_d - m_n + v_a - v_w$,

where $m_n = m - x_r$. The net imports must be allocated to $c$, $i$ and $v_a - v_w$ (if the net vector is positive). Then import leakage is specified as follows:

(B3) $m_n = \hat{\mu} \left( Bg + c + i + v_a \right),$

where $\hat{\mu}$ is a diagonal matrix of coefficients whose elements are calculated as the ratios of imports to use, where use is defined as $Bg + c + i + v_a$. This import share assumption implies that the domestic exports of a commodity are supplied by domestic industries producing the commodity. Of course, domestic exports may have imports indirectly embodied in them to the extent that producing industries import their intermediate inputs.

Next, we have to discount for leakage due to inventory depletion. It is given by

(B4) $v_w = \hat{v} \left( Bg + c + i + v_a + x_d \right),$

where $\hat{v}$ is a diagonal matrix of coefficients whose elements are calculated as the ratio of withdrawal of inventory to use, where use is defined as $Bg + c + i + v_a + x_d$. Note that inventory leakages are assumed to be linearly proportional to total demand (export included), which was not the case for the import leakage parameter because of the assumption that imports do not support domestic exports.

Statistics Canada does not provide separate data on inventory additions and withdrawals in the standard input-output table, so we have no way of knowing the value of vectors $v_a$ and $v_w$. The data is available only on changes, or the difference between them. We thus cannot discount inventory leakage from the model. As the magnitude of the net leakage vector is relatively small, it is not expected to change the result.

Substituting equation (B3) into equation (B1) and simplifying it, we have

(B5) $g = \left[ 1 - (1 - \hat{\mu}) B \right]^{-1} \left[ (1 - \hat{\mu})(c + i + v_a - v_w) + x_d \right].$

Equation (B5) states that domestic gross output, $g$, can be obtained by adding the intermediate and final demand expenditure net of leakage (imports). Equation (B5) allows us to calculate the direct and indirect effects of exogenous change in any demand component of total production $g$. It also gives us the output required to satisfy the total demand in the economy, net of all leakage.

Now, the sum of direct and indirect output required to produce domestic exports, $g_x$, is given by

(B6) $g_x = \left[ 1 - \left( 1 - \hat{\mu} \right) B \right]^{-1} x_d$.

We will use variations of equation (B6) to compute factor content and imported input content.

## CALCULATING CAPITAL CONTENT IN EXPORTS

To compute capital embodied in export, let the ratio of capital stock (k) and gross output (g) be denoted by $\kappa = k/g$. Then we have $k_x = \kappa g_x$, where $k_x$ denotes the level of capital embodied in the production of $g_x$.

Substituting this ratio into (B6) and diagonalizing the net export vectors, we have

(B7) $k_x = \kappa_x \left[ 1 - \left( 1 - \hat{\mu} \right) B \right]^{-1} \hat{x}_d$.

Equation (B7) estimates the direct and indirect capital embodied in domestic exports.

## CALCULATING SKILL CONTENT IN EXPORTS

For skill content of exports, we aggregated Statistics Canada Labour Force Survey data into four types of labour skill: (i) 0 to 8 years of schooling, (ii) high school graduation, (iii) post-secondary certificate or diploma and (iv) university graduation. We define the skill labour to output ratio as follows:

$\lambda_i = l_i / g$, where $i$ = indicates the four different types of labour skills. Therefore, $\lambda_{xi} = l_{xi} / g_x$.

Substituting this expression into (B6), we have

(B8) $l_{xi} = \lambda_{xi} \left[ 1 - \left( 1 - \hat{\mu} \right) B \right]^{-1} \hat{x}_d$.

Equation (B8) calculates total (direct and indirect) labour embodied in domestic exports by four skill levels.

## CALCULATING IMPORTED INPUT CONTENT

The level of intermediate input required to produce $g_x$ is given by

$$(B9) \quad u_x = B\left[1-(1-\hat{\mu})B\right]^{-1}\hat{x}_d .$$

The level of imported intermediate input embodied in this total intermediate input is given by

$$(B10) \quad m_x = \mu^T B\left[1-(1-\hat{\mu})B\right]^{-1}\hat{x}_d ,$$

where $\hat{x}_d$ is a diagonal matrix of vector $x_d$, and $\mu^T$ is the transposition of vector $\mu$, which in turn is obtained from the diagonal matrix $\hat{\mu}$ as defined in equation (B3). Once we have determined the level of imported input content given by equation (B10), we can calculate the percentage share of import content in total exports $\lambda_x$ as follows:

$$\lambda_x = m_x / x_d , \text{ where } 0 \leq \lambda_x \leq 1 .$$

# APPENDIX C

# REVEALED COMPARATIVE ADVANTAGE

## TABLE C1

## CANADIAN INDUSTRIES WITH RCA VIS-À-VIS U.S. INDUSTRIES IN 1985 AND 1997

| | Industries with RCA in 1985 | | Loss in RCA between 1985 and 1997 |
|---|---|---|---|
| 1 | Fish Products | 1 | Asphalt Roofing |
| 2 | Dairy Products | 2 | Steel Pipes and Tubes |
| 3 | Biscuits, Breads and Other Bakery Products | 3 | Iron Foundries |
| 4 | Rubber Products | 4 | Copper and Alloy Rolling, Casting and Extruding Products |
| 5 | Sawmill, Planing Mill and Shingle Mill Products | 5 | Wire and Wire Products |
| 6 | Veneer and Plywood | 6 | Record Players, Radios and TV Receivers |
| 7 | Sash, Door and Other Millwork | 7 | Ready-mix Concrete |
| 8 | Wooden Boxes and Coffins | | |
| 9 | Other Wood | | |
| 10 | Household Furniture | | **Gain in RCA between 1985 and 1997** |
| 11 | Office Furniture | 1 | Poultry, Meat and Meat Products |
| 12 | Other Furniture and Fixtures | 2 | Soft Drinks |
| 13 | Pulp and Paper | 3 | Brewery Products |
| 14 | Asphalt Roofing | 4 | Plastic Products |
| 15 | Primary Steel | 5 | Broad Knitted Fabric |
| 16 | Steel Pipes and Tubes | 6 | Other Converted Paper Products |
| 17 | Iron Foundries | 7 | Platemaking, Typesetting and Bindery |
| 18 | Non-ferrous Metal Smelting and Refining | 8 | Other Rolling, Casting and Extruding Non-ferrous Metallic Products |
| 19 | Copper and Alloy Rolling, Casting and Extruding Products | 9 | Power Boilers and Structural Metal |
| 20 | Wire and Wire Products | 10 | Hardware, Tools and Cutlery |
| 21 | Motor Vehicles | 11 | Truck and Bus Bodies and Trailers |
| 22 | Motor Vehicle Parts and Accessories | 12 | Railroad Rolling Stock |
| 23 | Shipbuilding and Repair | 13 | Miscellaneous Transportation Equipment |
| 24 | Record Players, Radios and TV Receivers | | |
| 25 | Communications and Energy Wire and Cable | | |
| 26 | Hydraulic Cement | | |
| 27 | Concrete Products | | |
| 28 | Ready-mix Concrete | | |
| 29 | Miscellaneous Non-metallic Minerals | | |
| 30 | Refined Petroleum and Coal | | |
| 31 | Signs and Displays | | |

# APPENDIX D

# INTRAINDUSTRY TRADE

## TABLE D1

## AVERAGE ANNUAL INTRAINDUSTRY TRADE BETWEEN CANADA AND THE UNITED STATES IN THE MANUFACTURING INDUSTRIES

| Industry | 1983–89 | 1990–97 | Growth or Loss (–) |
|---|---|---|---|
| Poultry, Meat and Meat Products | 7.11 | 14.32 | 101.21 |
| Fish Products | 22.07 | 30.95 | 40.21 |
| Fruit and Vegetables | 6.88 | 14.69 | 113.43 |
| Dairy Products | 0.51 | 1.30 | 155.97 |
| Feeds<br>Cane and Beet Sugar<br>Miscellaneous Food Products | 9.67 | 22.78 | 135.60 |
| Vegetable Oil Mills (except Corn Oil) | 11.69 | 29.94 | 156.07 |
| Biscuits<br>Bread and Other Bakery Products | 5.27 | 17.39 | 229.61 |
| Soft Drinks | 0.80 | 1.09 | 36.48 |
| Distillery Products | 5.42 | 18.57 | 242.37 |
| Brewery Products | 1.04 | 2.32 | 124.19 |
| Wines | 1.00 | 1.90 | 90.26 |
| Tobacco Products | 2.71 | 2.16 | –20.06 |
| Rubber Products | 80.50 | 103.17 | 28.10 |
| Plastic Products | 23.67 | 45.84 | 93.70 |
| Leather Tanneries<br>Footwear<br>Miscellaneous Leather and Allied Products | 15.24 | 40.57 | 166.16 |
| Man-made Fibres, Yarn and Woven Cloth<br>Wool, Yarn and Woven Cloth | 12.54 | 51.06 | 307.26 |
| Broad Knitted Fabric | 1.90 | 26.11 | 1272.85 |
| Miscellaneous Textile Products | 9.43 | 20.07 | 112.79 |
| Carpets, Mats and Rugs | 7.71 | 24.71 | 220.32 |
| Clothing and Hosiery | 3.78 | 17.10 | 352.06 |
| Sawmill, Planing Mill and Shingle Mill Products | 18.29 | 15.33 | –16.21 |
| Veneer and Plywood | 15.12 | 23.45 | 55.12 |
| Sash, Door and Other Millwork | 8.24 | 16.92 | 105.44 |
| Wooden Boxes and Coffins | 6.54 | 13.37 | 104.29 |

## TABLE D1 (CONT'D)

| Industry | 1983–89 | 1990–97 | Growth or Loss (–) |
|---|---|---|---|
| Other Wood | 16.31 | 26.22 | 60.74 |
| Household Furniture | 14.59 | 46.13 | 216.16 |
| Office Furniture | 10.82 | 37.12 | 242.96 |
| Other Furniture and Fixtures | 25.19 | 100.25 | 297.96 |
| Pulp and Paper | 14.46 | 17.06 | 17.96 |
| Asphalt Roofing | 4.63 | 19.69 | 325.46 |
| Paper Boxes and Bags | 4.21 | 14.63 | 247.31 |
| Other Converted Paper Products | 25.60 | 129.78 | 407.04 |
| Printing and Publishing | 9.43 | 9.74 | 3.30 |
| Platemaking, Typesetting and Bindery | 1.10 | 10.58 | 859.06 |
| Primary Steel | 14.80 | 33.69 | 127.63 |
| Steel Pipes and Tubes | 31.22 | 48.74 | 56.14 |
| Iron Foundries | 18.89 | 6.01 | –68.18 |
| Non-ferrous Metal Smelting and Refining | 89.21 | 627.12 | 602.98 |
| Aluminum Rolling, Casting and Extruding Products | 34.11 | 77.62 | 127.54 |
| Copper and Alloy Rolling, Casting and Extruding Products | 36.10 | 70.93 | 96.48 |
| Other Rolling, Casting and Extruding Non-ferrous Metal Products | 17.33 | 34.44 | 98.74 |
| Power Boilers and Structural Metal | 7.54 | 18.35 | 143.30 |
| Ornamental and Architectural Metal Products | 6.01 | 10.02 | 66.81 |
| Stamped, Pressed and Coated Metal Products | 4.09 | 9.02 | 120.74 |
| Wire and Wire Products | 49.27 | 84.81 | 72.13 |
| Hardware, Tools and Cutlery | 51.00 | 80.04 | 56.93 |
| Heating Equipment | 25.08 | 45.62 | 81.87 |
| Machine Shops | 0.00 | 0.00 | 0.00 |
| Other Fabricated Metals | 46.74 | 38.51 | –17.61 |
| Agricultural Implements | 70.37 | 80.62 | 14.57 |
| Commercial Refrigeration and Air Conditioning Equipment | 26.65 | 31.32 | 17.50 |
| Other Machinery and Equipment | 49.50 | 64.94 | 31.18 |
| Aircraft and Aircraft Parts | 107.50 | 96.31 | –10.41 |
| Motor Vehicles | 162.36 | 157.89 | –2.75 |
| Truck and Bus Bodies and Trailers | 8.97 | 27.55 | 207.18 |
| Motor Vehicle Parts and Accessories | 111.07 | 81.45 | –26.67 |
| Railroad Rolling Stock | 39.65 | 69.39 | 75.03 |

## TABLE D1 (CONT'D)

| Industry | 1983–89 | 1990–97 | Growth or Loss (–) |
|---|---|---|---|
| Shipbuilding and Repair | 15.40 | 38.15 | 147.73 |
| Miscellaneous Transportation Equipment | 71.26 | 478.78 | 571.89 |
| Small Electrical Appliances | 14.76 | 53.75 | 264.22 |
| Major Appliances (Electric and Non-electric) | 96.63 | 75.58 | –21.78 |
| Other Electrical and Electronic Products Batteries | 18.55 | 35.30 | 90.31 |
| Record Players, Radios and Television Receivers | 45.36 | 28.45 | –37.28 |
| Communications and Other Electronic Equipment | 72.98 | 367.47 | 403.51 |
| Office, Store and Business Machines | 0.00 | 166.51 | 0.00 |
| Communications and Energy Wire and Cable | 17.81 | 39.09 | 119.47 |
| Clay Products | 11.95 | 16.26 | 36.11 |
| Hydraulic Cement | 6.78 | 12.67 | 86.96 |
| Concrete Products | 1.75 | 6.11 | 249.32 |
| Ready-mix Concrete | 0.00 | 0.00 | 0.00 |
| Glass and Glass Products | 30.33 | 67.52 | 122.63 |
| Miscellaneous Non-metallic Minerals | 43.15 | 60.65 | 40.54 |
| Refined Petroleum and Coal | 10.14 | 14.27 | 40.71 |
| Industrial Chemicals | 48.24 | 81.21 | 68.33 |
| Chemical Products | 17.75 | 36.79 | 107.24 |
| Plastics and Synthetic Resins | 37.57 | 72.25 | 92.31 |
| Pharmaceuticals and Medicines | 3.94 | 14.33 | 263.60 |
| Paint and Varnish | 3.19 | 16.15 | 405.77 |
| Soap and Cleaning Compounds | 3.48 | 16.58 | 375.67 |
| Toilet Preparations | 8.54 | 34.47 | 303.42 |
| Floor Tile, Linoleum and Coated Fabrics Other Manufacturing | 39.01 | 52.79 | 35.32 |
| Jewellery and Precious Metals | 14.60 | 102.34 | 601.04 |
| Sporting Goods and Toys | 35.28 | 76.76 | 117.58 |
| Signs and Displays | 9.04 | 12.21 | 35.04 |
| **Total Manufacturing** | **35.11** | **49.56** | **41.16** |

# APPENDIX E

## COMPETITORS IN THE U.S. MARKET

### TABLE E1

### EXPORT SHARE TRENDS FOR THE MAJOR SUPPLIERS TO THE U.S. MARKET, 1980-2000

| Industry | | Import Share Percentage for Competing Countries, by Industry | | | | | |
|---|---|---|---|---|---|---|---|
| | | Canada | EU | Japan | Mexico | China | Other East Asia |
| Food and Beverages | Constant | 8.72 | 32.57 | 2.25 | 1.67 | 0.44 | 11.57 |
| | Time | 0.75 | −0.01 | −0.06 | 0.31 | 0.08 | −0.06 |
| | | $(15.49)^a$ | $(−0.21)$ | $(−1.15)$ | $(6.35)^a$ | $(1.58)$ | $(−1.18)$ |
| Tobacco Products | Constant | 3.04 | 26.61 | −0.01 | 7.26 | −0.87 | 10.43 |
| | Time | 1.09 | −0.31 | 0.18 | −0.14 | 0.26 | 0.60 |
| | | $(5.95)^a$ | $(−1.71)^c$ | $(0.96)$ | $(−0.76)$ | $(1.42)$ | $(3.27)^a$ |
| Rubber and Plastic Products | Constant | 17.43 | 28.96 | 20.24 | 1.12 | −5.84 | 33.58 |
| | Time | 0.16 | −0.86 | −0.46 | 0.19 | 1.61 | −0.74 |
| | | $(2.16)^b$ | $(−11.53)^a$ | $(−6.21)^a$ | $(2.62)^a$ | $(21.67)^a$ | $(−9.96)^a$ |
| Leather and Allied Products | Constant | 1.38 | 26.11 | 1.36 | 1.41 | −11.71 | 61.96 |
| | Time | −0.03 | −0.53 | −0.08 | 0.11 | 2.98 | 2.35 |
| | | $(−0.24)$ | $(−4.37)^a$ | $(−0.64)$ | $(0.88)$ | $(24.42)^a$ | $(−19.26)^a$ |
| Textile Products | Constant | −1.49 | 23.41 | 15.76 | −0.33 | 7.05 | 36.23 |
| | Time | 0.75 | 0.00 | −0.50 | 0.35 | −0.01 | −0.85 |
| | | $(10.13)^a$ | $(0.01)$ | $(−6.69)^a$ | $(4.71)^a$ | $(−0.17)$ | $(−11.49)^a$ |
| Clothing | Constant | 0.73 | 8.53 | 3.72 | −0.93 | 6.03 | 72.83 |
| | Time | 0.10 | −0.18 | −0.20 | 0.66 | 0.56 | −2.38 |
| | | $(1.81)^c$ | $(−3.28)^a$ | $(−3.60)^a$ | $(11.68)^a$ | $(9.96)^a$ | $(−42.36)^a$ |
| Wood | Constant | 62.76 | 4.86 | 2.40 | 2.71 | 0.40 | 23.08 |
| | Time | 0.39 | 0.00 | −0.14 | 0.03 | 0.21 | −0.73 |
| | | $(7.39)^a$ | $(−0.02)$ | $(−2.60)^a$ | $(0.59)$ | $(3.94)^a$ | $(−13.80)^a$ |
| Furniture and Fixtures | Constant | 27.40 | 27.32 | 3.46 | 2.43 | −4.89 | 35.24 |
| | Time | −0.13 | −0.71 | −0.10 | 0.79 | 1.04 | −0.61 |
| | | $(−1.40)$ | $(−7.60)^a$ | $(−1.02)$ | $(8.36)^a$ | $(11.02)^a$ | $(−6.48)^a$ |
| Paper and Allied Products | Constant | 87.12 | 8.95 | 0.84 | 1.56 | −1.15 | 0.99 |
| | Time | −0.97 | 0.31 | 0.10 | 0.02 | 0.24 | 0.12 |
| | | $(−19.69)^a$ | $(6.17)^a$ | $(2.00)^a$ | $(0.36)$ | $(4.76)^b$ | $(2.44)^b$ |
| Printing, Publishing and Allied | Constant | 23.18 | 44.76 | 15.08 | 3.09 | −3.67 | 11.02 |
| | Time | 0.11 | −0.82 | −0.53 | 0.13 | 0.77 | 0.47 |
| | | $(1.44)$ | $(−10.39)^a$ | $(−6.71)^a$ | $(1.70)^c$ | $(9.79)^a$ | $(5.90)^a$ |
| Primary Metal | Constant | 24.55 | 27.01 | 20.65 | 2.02 | −0.60 | 6.91 |
| | Time | 0.32 | −0.46 | −0.77 | 0.29 | 0.18 | −0.103 |
| | | $(5.49)^a$ | $(−8.01)^a$ | $(−13.24)^a$ | $(5.03)^a$ | $(3.04)^a$ | $(−1.77)^c$ |
| Fabricated Metal | Constant | 16.34 | 27.46 | 29.90 | 0.44 | −2.18 | 22.13 |
| | Time | 0.11 | −0.26 | −1.03 | 0.54 | 0.63 | −0.05 |
| | | $(1.85)^c$ | $(−4.48)^a$ | $(−17.49)^a$ | $(9.20)^a$ | $(10.62)^a$ | $(−0.83)$ |
| Machinery (except Electrical) | Constant | 14.78 | 41.14 | 32.50 | 0.43 | −1.91 | 6.79 |
| | Time | −0.37 | −1.11 | −0.35 | 0.27 | 0.36 | 1.32 |
| | | $(−4.68)^a$ | $(−14.22)^a$ | $(−4.54)^a$ | $(3.50)^a$ | $(4.63)^a$ | $(16.83)^a$ |

87

## TABLE E1 (CONT'D)

| Industry | | Import Share Percentage for Competing Countries, by Industry | | | | | |
|---|---|---|---|---|---|---|---|
| | | Canada | EU | Japan | Mexico | China | Other East Asia |
| Transportation Equipment | Constant | 33.54 | 23.14 | 42.80 | −1.71 | −0.20 | 1.10 |
| | Time | 0.10 | −0.15 | −0.83 | 0.69 | 0.04 | 0.11 |
| | | $(1.69)^c$ | $(−2.50)^b$ | $(−14.23)^a$ | $(11.73)^a$ | (0.64) | $(1.92)^c$ |
| Electrical and Electronic Products | Constant | 6.06 | 9.37 | 43.99 | 5.47 | −2.95 | 34.90 |
| | Time | 0.01 | 0.05 | −1.25 | 0.69 | 0.68 | −0.05 |
| | | (0.14) | (0.69) | $(−18.80)^a$ | $(10.31)^a$ | $(10.23)^a$ | (−0.76) |
| Non-Metallic Minerals | Constant | 16.64 | 41.84 | 22.26 | 5.12 | −3.17 | 13.05 |
| | Time | −0.15 | −0.41 | −0.75 | 0.32 | 0.85 | −0.20 |
| | | $(−3.17)^a$ | $(−8.47)^a$ | $(−15.46)^a$ | $(6.59)^a$ | $(17.45)^a$ | $(−4.18)^a$ |
| Refined Petroleum and Coal | Constant | 16.10 | 12.99 | 0.48 | 2.33 | 1.66 | 4.03 |
| | Time | −0.09 | 0.23 | −0.01 | 0.08 | −0.07 | −0.06 |
| | | (−0.89) | $(2.23)^b$ | (−0.06) | (0.80) | (−0.70) | (−0.54) |
| Chemical and Chemical Products | Constant | 16.84 | 39.89 | 9.52 | 3.05 | 1.11 | 1.87 |
| | Time | 0.03 | 0.34 | 0.06 | 0.00 | 0.06 | 0.13 |
| | | (0.58) | $(6.48)^a$ | (1.19) | (0.08) | (1.10) | $(2.57)^a$ |
| Other Manufacturing | Constant | 3.90 | 26.48 | 30.11 | 2.94 | −4.97 | 28.92 |
| | Time | 0.01 | −0.26 | −0.54 | 0.15 | 1.31 | −0.85 |
| | | (0.13) | $(−5.77)^a$ | $(−12.09)^a$ | $(3.37)^a$ | $(28.99)^a$ | $(−18.82)^a$ |

Note: The dependent variable is measured as a percentage. The constant term for each country and industry could be read as the U.S. import share of that country for that industry in 1980. The second row of numbers for each industry is the time coefficient, which measures a country's change in annual U.S. import share for that industry. The number in parentheses is the t-ratio for the time-trend coefficient.
[a]Significantly different from zero at the 1 percent level, on the basis of a two-tailed test.
[b]Significantly different from zero at the 5 percent level, on the basis of a two-tailed test.
[c]Significantly different from zero at the 10 percent level, on the basis of a two-tailed test.

Lawrence L. Schembri*  &  Mykyta Vesselovsky
Bank of Canada  Carleton University

2

# Comparative Advantage and Trade in North America: A Sectoral Analysis

## INTRODUCTION

THE EXPANSION OF TRADE AND INVESTMENT FLOWS among Canada, Mexico and the United States reflects the growing economic integration of North America. This upward trend, however, may facilitate even greater integration as the pressure to reduce trade and investment barriers rises. Developing policies to manage this growing integration will require a thorough understanding of the factors that govern these flows.

The purpose of this study is to explore trade in manufactured products among these three countries theoretically and empirically at a disaggregated sectoral level. Although this trade represents approximately 60 percent of North America's total international trade in goods and services, international competitiveness in this area is often seen as vital to achieving higher standards of living. These products have relatively high levels of value-added and productivity growth, and often exhibit increasing relative prices.

Clearly, several forces have contributed to the dramatic recent increase in trade flows among these countries (Tables 1-3 and Figures 1-3), the most prominent being the 1989 Canada-U.S. Free Trade Agreement (FTA) of 1989 and the 1994 North American Free Trade Agreement (NAFTA), which extended the FTA to Mexico. Yet the trade flows had begun their upward surge well before these agreements had come into effect, and have continued to rise since — by much more than expected originally (Helliwell 2001). This trade increase has therefore been caused by other factors. Improvements in communications and transportation technologies have undoubtedly played a role: first, by reducing the cost of international transactions directly; second, by making it much easier to manage and operate multinational firms with specialized production. In Mexico, for example, the profound economic reforms implemented since the debt crisis of 1982,[1] together with the country's sizeable difference in relative factor prices, have had a positive impact on trade.

* Formerly Associate Professor, Carleton University.

Explaining international trade flows is an important theoretical and empirical exercise because international trade can produce large welfare gains by specializing production in countries with a comparative advantage and expanding consumption opportunities. Consequently, it has created a large body of empirical research. Early work focussed on testing explanations suggested by the Ricardian and Heckscher-Ohlin theories of comparative advantage: the first is based on differences in technology, which would manifest themselves in different levels of productivity; the second on differences in relative factor endowments, which could cause disparities in factor prices. These tests of the traditional models of comparative advantage, however, failed to provide unambiguous answers.[2]

Recently, however, a number of studies (Trefler 1995; Davis and Weinstein 1998) have been successful in improving the empirical performance of the Heckscher-Ohlin model by incorporating general differences in production techniques between countries. Although these differences are typically uniform (Hicks-neutral) across industries and thus not Ricardian, they do move in the direction of marrying the two models. Other papers, such as Hakura (2001) and Harrigan (1997), go one step further by introducing unequal factor prices and Ricardian-type non-uniform technology differences across sectors. They find that these differences are important in explaining cross-country variations in the shares of total output across sectors.

The above evidence speaks in favour of a generalized Heckscher-Ohlin framework with international differences in technology as well as unequal factor prices between countries. The ability of such a framework to explain international trade in goods rather than factor content, however, remains largely unexplored.[3] One key difficulty in addressing this question is that both the Heckscher-Ohlin and Ricardian models assume perfect competition, which makes it difficult to derive clear predictions about trade flows in individual sectors. In contrast, new trade models allow for product differentiation and imperfect (often monopolistic) competition so that these factors can be merged with traditional models to obtain testable implications for trade in goods.[4]

The theoretical model used in this paper borrows from recent work by Choudhri and Schembri (2002) and Choudhri and Hakura (2001). Choudhri and Schembri use their model to derive an empirical relation for relative market shares of imports and domestic production, which they apply to Canada-U.S. trade in domestic consumption. They find that relative productivity differences are a significant determinant of these two countries' relative shares in each other's markets. This study adapts the Choudhri-Schembri approach to explore how well a model that combines both the Ricardian and Heckscher-Ohlin effects and incorporates monopolistic competition can explain North American trade in manufactured goods. The paper empirically implements a relation implied by the model, which (like the MacDougall relation) explains relative sectoral exports of two countries to a third country (or a group of countries). This relation includes variables that capture not only the Ricardian and Heckscher-Ohlin effects but also the influences of product differentiation and monopolistic competition.

One of the important contributions of this analysis is the construction of a unique two-digit industry-level data set for North America. The data set combines and concords data from a number of different sources, including the Organisation for Economic Co-operation and Development (OECD) and the Banco de Mexico. This difficult and time-consuming exercise proved fruitful in the end because the data set is used successfully to estimate the export relation derived from the theoretical model. Given the quality of the data, the empirical results are good: the key variables normally have the expected sign and are statistically significant, especially in the important case of Canadian and Mexican exports going to the U.S. market.

A brief overview of recent trends in manufacturing trade flows among the three countries is provided in the second section. The third discusses the basic theory underlying the export relation. More technical details on the derivation of the theoretical model are set out in Appendix A. We examine the methodology for empirical implementation of the export relation on the basis of various data sources, including the OECD, in the fourth section. Additional information on the construction of data and data sources is given in Appendices B and C. The fifth section describes key features of the data used to estimate the export relations for the Canadian, Mexican and U.S. markets. The key regression results are discussed in the sixth section, which is followed by some concluding remarks.

## NORTH AMERICAN TRADE IN MANUFACTURED GOODS: AN OVERVIEW

TRADE IN MANUFACTURED GOODS among Canada, Mexico and the United States has been growing very rapidly in recent years. Figures 1-3 display the total exports of manufactured goods to each of the three markets, measured in U.S. dollars. Interestingly, the take-off point for North American trade flows in all three markets begins in about 1988 — one year before the 1989 FTA and six years before the 1994 NAFTA. Moreover, the removal of tariffs was not immediate for all goods but phased in over five or ten years, and the trade barriers that were removed (tariffs, quotas and other non-tariff barriers) were relatively modest, especially in the Canada-U.S. case. As a result, it is difficult to explain the enormous increase in trade among these countries with traditional models based solely on the reduction in trade barriers mandated by these trade agreements. And while the transportation and communications cost reductions were very important, other forces, like the spread of multinationals (facilitated by the Maquiladora program[5] in Mexico) and resultant increases in intrafirm trade, also contributed significantly to higher trade flows.

Tables 1A, 1B and 2 provide useful decompositions of manufacturing exports at the two-digit International Standard Industrial Classification (ISIC) sector level for the three countries. Export data are also broken down by destination and source country. Several important observations can be drawn from Tables 1A and 1B, which provide decompositions in levels for 1998. First, Canada-Mexico two-way trade in manufactured goods is much smaller than trade between these two countries and the United States. Canadian exports to the United States are more than 250 times greater than Canadian exports to Mexico. Conversely, Mexican exports to the United States are 17 times greater than Mexican exports to Canada. Second, Mexico has large trade surpluses with both Canada and the United States in these goods, while the United States has a trade deficit with the other two countries. Third, the bulk of the trade among these countries is in fabricated metal products, ranging from a low of 58 percent for Canadian exports to the United States to a high of 82 percent for Mexican exports to Canada. Fabricated metal products encompass a wide range of goods, including autos and auto parts, and machinery and equipment. Canada's three next most important manufactured exports are chemical products (primarily oil production), followed by paper and wood products and manufactured food products. Canada is perhaps the most balanced of the three countries in its distribution of exports. By contrast, Mexico's exports are the most concentrated, primarily in fabricated metal products and, to a much smaller extent, in textiles and chemical products. As for the United States, fabricated metal and chemical products account for roughly 80 percent of their North American exports.

Table 2 displays data on annual growth rates for manufactured goods, by industrial sector, for the five years before and after the NAFTA. The most striking observations here are the consistently high growth rates for total manufactured exports over the entire period, ranging from 6.5 percent to 13 percent per annum, with Mexican exports to Canada and the United States growing at the highest rates. These export growth rates are approximately double the output growth rates for the same period. In general, export growth rates are not higher during the five years after the NAFTA (1994-98). The main exceptions are the growth rate increases for Canadian and Mexican exports to the United States. These increases, however, may have more to do with the strong U.S. economic expansion over this period than NAFTA-based trade barrier reductions. For Mexican exports to both Canada and the United States, growth rates are very high, exceeding 10 percent per annum on average during the 1988-98 period. Across industrial sectors, there is more variance in export growth rates, especially for exports from Canada to Mexico and vice versa. This observation undoubtedly reflects the rapidly changing structure of trade between the two countries and its relatively low volumes, especially at the sectoral level. Consequently, moderate shifts in sectoral export volumes can produce large percentage changes.

## Figure 1

## Manufacturing Exports To Canada, US$'000

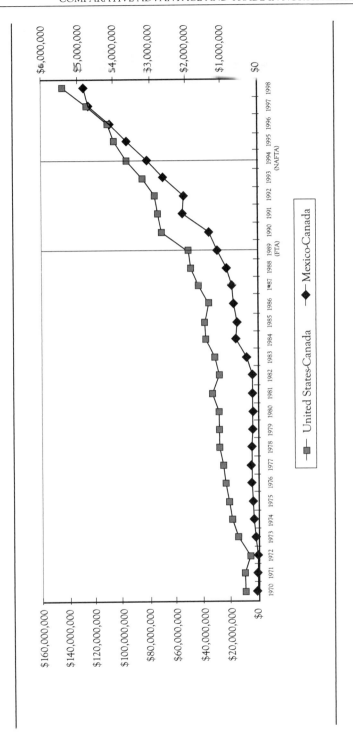

FIGURE 2

MANUFACTURING EXPORTS TO MEXICO, US$'000

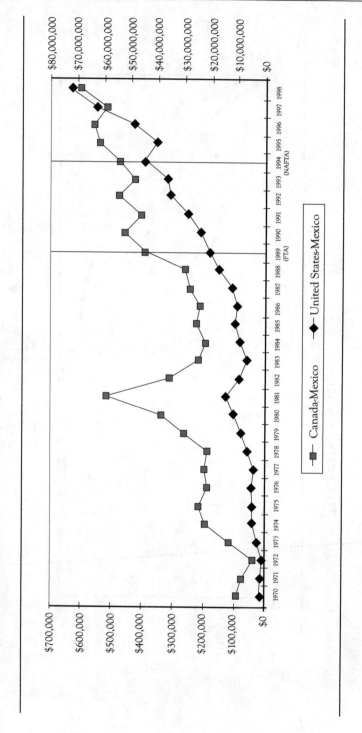

FIGURE 3

MANUFACTURING EXPORTS TO THE UNITED STATES, US$'000

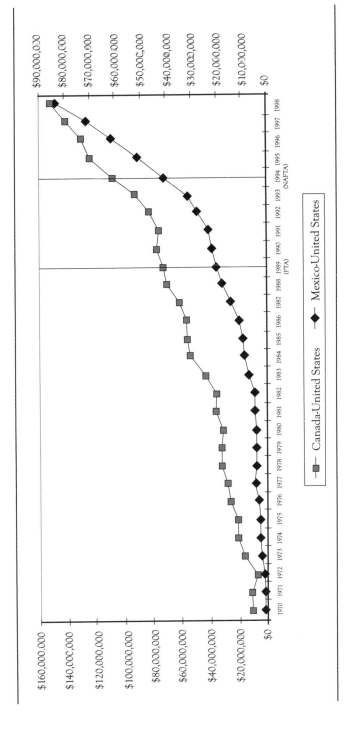

These figures and tables provide clear evidence of high rates of export growth for manufactured goods in North America. This growth is broadly based across sectors and countries, and is likely to continue into the future as these economies become even more integrated.

## TABLE 1A

### DECOMPOSITION OF MANUFACTURING EXPORTS IN 1998 (US$'000)

| | Canada | | Mexico | | United States | |
|---|---|---|---|---|---|---|
| | Mexico | U.S. | Canada | U.S. | Canada | Mexico |
| Food, Beverages and Tobacco | $81,926 | $5,266,090 | $58,927 | $2,818,140 | $6,660,615 | $2,128,141 |
| Textiles | $178,399 | $3,607,083 | $24,999 | $5,379,897 | $3,172,540 | $8,588,344 |
| Wood Products and Furniture | $232,257 | $2,905,159 | $2,554 | $1,197,406 | $13,022,031 | $2,501,501 |
| Paper, Paper Products and Printing | $24,137 | $5,439,886 | $27,527 | $2,490,603 | $12,134,123 | $601,787 |
| Chemical Products | $151,092 | $20,178,605 | $70,173 | $12,518,925 | $17,534,300 | $3,652,512 |
| Non-metallic Mineral Products | $80,518 | $1,874,525 | $475 | $610,839 | $1,618,086 | $1,291,280 |
| Basic Metals | $88,608 | $5,331,374 | $22,950 | $2,329,012 | $8,918,300 | $2,339,049 |
| Fabricated Metal Products | $3,942,181 | $97,406,321 | $391,293 | $44,131,480 | $87,481,381 | $60,367,879 |
| Other Manufacturing | $40,252 | $1,752,457 | $997 | $691,339 | $922,490 | $1,196,119 |
| Total Manufacturing | $4,819,370 | $143,761,500 | $599,895 | $72,167,641 | $151,463,866 | $82,666,612 |

Destination ■     Source ■     Industry ■

## TABLE 1B

### DECOMPOSITION OF MANUFACTURING EXPORTS IN 1998 (% OF TOTAL)

| | Canada | | Mexico | | United States | |
|---|---|---|---|---|---|---|
| | Mexico | U.S. | Canada | U.S. | Canada | Mexico |
| Food, Beverages and Tobacco | 2% | 4% | 10% | 4% | 4% | 3% |
| Textiles | 4% | 3% | 4% | 7% | 2% | 10% |
| Wood Products and Furniture | 5% | 2% | 0% | 2% | 9% | 3% |
| Paper, Paper Products and Printing | 1% | 4% | 5% | 3% | 8% | 1% |
| Chemical Products | 3% | 14% | 12% | 17% | 12% | 4% |
| Non-metallic Mineral Products | 2% | 1% | 0% | 1% | 1% | 2% |
| Basic Metals | 2% | 4% | 4% | 3% | 6% | 3% |
| Fabricated Metal Products | 82% | 68% | 65% | 61% | 58% | 73% |
| Other Manufacturing | 1% | 1% | 0% | 1% | 1% | 1% |
| Total Manufacturing | 100% | 100% | 100% | 100% | 100% | 100% |

Destination ■     Source ■     Industry ■

## TABLE 2

## AVERAGE ANNUAL EXPORT GROWTH RATES BEFORE AND AFTER THE NAFTA

AFTER THE NAFTA, 1994-98 (BEFORE THE NAFTA 1988-93)

| | Canada | | Mexico | | United States | |
|---|---|---|---|---|---|---|
| | Mexico | U.S. | Canada | U.S. | Canada | Mexico |
| Food, Beverages and Tobacco | 15% (1%) | 8% (15%) | 7% (–4%) | 6% (12%) | 7% (8%) | 12% (4%) |
| Textiles | 19% (8%) | 10% (13%) | 25% (2%) | 15% (14%) | 15% (9%) | 19% (13%) |
| Wood Products and Furniture | 3% (35%) | 8% (15%) | –30% (23%) | 3% (16%) | 9% (9%) | 13% (9%) |
| Paper, Paper Products and Printing | 17% (12%) | 7% (12%) | –10% (2%) | 8% (10%) | 6% (0%) | 17% (–21%) |
| Chemical Products | 12% (13%) | 8% (13%) | 17% (–5%) | 12% (12%) | 8% (7%) | 8% (7%) |
| Non-metallic Mineral Products | 10% (14%) | 6% (8%) | –188% (17%) | 7% (17%) | 11% (4%) | 13% (3%) |
| Basic Metals | 24% (–22%) | 10% (9%) | –34% (7%) | 9% (11%) | 7% (0%) | 15% (–2%) |
| Fabricated Metal Products | 10% (16%) | 9% (8%) | 7% (13%) | 11% (11%) | 8% (5%) | 14% (11%) |
| Other Manufacturing | 13% (12%) | 11% (16%) | 25% (–17%) | 10% (13%) | 13% (10%) | 12% (13%) |
| **Total Manufacturing** | 10% (16%) | 9% (9%) | 6% (8%) | 11% (12%) | 8% (5%) | 14% (10%) |

Destination ■     Source ■     Industry ▨

## THEORY

THIS SECTION OUTLINES A THEORETICAL MODEL that incorporates monopolistic competition into the Ricardo-Heckscher-Ohlin framework (for technical details, see Appendix A). This model is used to derive a relation explaining the relative exports of two countries to a third country.

Each country is assumed to contain the same set of monopolistically competitive industries. Each firm in these industries produces a single differentiated product. These firms are identical except that their product is slightly different from those of other domestic and foreign firms in the industry; hence each firm faces a downward-sloping demand curve. In addition, each firm has a downward-sloping marginal cost function based on a fixed production cost (e.g., headquarters services) and constant variable costs. Profit maximization implies that firms will produce output at the point when marginal revenue equals marginal cost. The number of firms in each industry is determined by the zero-profit condition. As entry is free, firms will enter the industry until profits are driven to zero.

The demand curve facing each firm can be derived from the Dixit and Stiglitz (1977) love-of-variety utility function, which assumes that consumers will spread their expenditure for a given industry over all firms in that industry. This utility function also treats all products symmetrically; hence the price of each product in the industry should be the same, in the absence of any frictions, because of the symmetry of demand and similarity of cost structure across firms.

To introduce some simple notation, let $P_i^j$ be the home price of each variety produced in country $j$'s industry $I$; $B_i^{jm} > 1$ represents an index of industry trade barriers for country $j$'s exports to country $m$ (so that $P_i^j B_i^{jm}$ represents the price of country $j$'s variety in country $m$'s market); $n_i^j$ is the number of varieties in country $j$'s industry; and $X_i^{jm}$ is the value of exports of sector $i$ from country $j$ to country $m$.

On the basis of this cost and demand structure, the basic building block of the theoretical model can be derived to express the relative exports of a country pair $(j, k)$ to country $m$'s market as

$$(1) \quad X_i^{jm} / X_i^{km} = (n_i^j / n_i^k)(B_i^{jm} / B_i^{km})^{-\sigma} (P_i^j / P_i^k)^{1-\sigma},$$

where $\sigma$ is the elasticity of substitution in demand across varieties (assumed to be the same for all industries). Factors emphasized by Ricardian and Heckscher-Ohlin models can be introduced into Equation (1) by linking the price ratio to relative productivity and relative factor prices.

The next step is to transform the relation given by Equation (1) into a regression model that incorporates the variables of interest and can be estimated empirically with the available data. First, the number of firms in each industry is difficult to measure empirically: no data are available. However, given the monopolistically competitive structure of the model under which each firm in the industry is identical, the number of firms in industry $i$ in country $j$ can be represented by the total employment of a composite factor in the industry, $F_i^j$, holding other factors constant. Note that this composite factor is an aggregate of the primary factors (capital, labour and intermediate goods) employed in industry $i$ in country $j$. Second, the price of a product is related to the cost of using one unit of the composite factor. This unit cost can be expressed as $C_i^j = \chi_i(\mathbf{W}^j)$, where $\mathbf{W}^j$ is the price vector for primary factors. Finally, we can incorporate productivity differences into the production function by allowing for only Hicks-neutral technology differences between countries. In particular, let $A_i^j$ denote the industry total factor productivity (TFP) for country $j$. Note that $A_i^j = n_i^j Q_i^j / F_i^j$, where $Q_i^j$ is the output of an individual firm in industry $i$.

Given these relationships between the number of firms, productivity and employment of the composite factor on the one hand, and prices and costs on the other, we can restate Equation (1) as

$$(2) \quad X_i^{jm} / X_i^{km} = (F_i^j / F_i^k)(B_i^{jm} / B_i^{km})^{-\sigma} (C_i^j / C_i^k)^{-(\sigma-1)}(A_i^j / A_i^k)^{\sigma-1}.$$

In this expression, Ricardian effects are represented by the ratio of TFPs in the two countries $j$ and $k$ in industry $i$. Note that TFP is assumed to be determined exogenously. The ratio of unit composite-factor costs captures the Heckscher-Ohlin effects because this ratio depends on relative factor prices and sectoral factor intensities (via the $\chi_i(.)$ function). This ratio of unit composite-factor costs is assumed to be exogenous because individual industries are assumed to be sufficiently small in relation to the entire economy that they take factor prices as given.[6] The influence of the new trade theory is reflected in the composite-factor quantity ratio, which is a proxy for the ratio of the number of varieties to firms in industry $i$ in country $j$. Note this ratio is determined endogenously even at the industry level and should be positively related to the relative size of the two countries: for example, larger countries will have larger industries with more varieties and firms of a given size.[7]

Two interesting special cases of the general model can be identified. The first assumes Hicks-neutral technical differences to be uniform across industries. In this case, the TFP ratio would not vary across countries and the Ricardian effects would be absent. The second assumes that the function defining the composite factor is the same for all industries [i.e., $\phi_i(.) = \phi(.)$] and thus there are no factor-intensity differences between industries. The cost ratio in this case would be identical in all industries and the Heckscher-Ohlin influences would be absent.[8]

## EMPIRICAL IMPLEMENTATION

THIS SECTION DISCUSSES THE EMPIRICAL IMPLEMENTATION of the theoretical model given by Equation (2) for explaining North America's international trade in manufactured products. The regression model for the ratio of exports in log-linear form is given by

(3)
$$\ln(X_{it}^{jm} / X_{it}^{km}) =$$
$$\beta_0 \ln(B_{it}^{jm} / B_{it}^{km}) + \beta_1 \ln(F_{it}^j / F_{it}^k) + \beta_2 \ln(A_{it}^j / A_{it}^k) + \beta_3 \ln(C_{it}^j / C_{it}^k) + e_{it}^{jkm},$$

where $\beta_0 = -\sigma$, $\beta_1 = 1$, $\beta_2 = \sigma - 1$, $\beta_3 = -(\sigma - 1)$, and $e_{it}^{jkm}$ is a mean-zero disturbance term that captures random departures from the theoretical model. Time subscripts have also been added. The regression model given by Equation (3) explains relative exports of industry $i$ of any country pair $(j, k)$ to a particular market $m$ in time period $t$. Apart from trade barriers, the explanatory variables in this model are industry-level variables for countries $j$ and $k$ only.

To define the composite factor, a Cobb-Douglas functional form is used. With additional assumptions, this specification allows for intermediate goods in the estimation based on OECD data (supplemented by some data from other sources).

An index of trade barriers ($B_{it}^{jm}$) that captures all types of trade costs and border effects adequately is difficult to construct. To get around this problem, relative trade barriers for an exporting pair of countries (in a specific market at a given time) are assumed to be the same across sectors. Relative barriers, however, are allowed to vary across markets, country pairs and time periods, and time fixed-effect variables are used to capture this variation.

To explain the measurement of other variables, we first define the industry use of the composite factor in country $j$ in the presence of $M$ intermediate goods as

$$(4) \quad \ln F_{it}^{j} = \theta_i^K \ln K_{it}^{j} + \theta_i^L \ln L_{it}^{j} + \sum_{r \in M} \theta_i^{zr} \ln Z_{it}^{jr},$$

where $K_{it}^{j}$ and $L_{it}^{j}$ represent amounts of capital and labour used in industry $i$; $Z_{it}^{jr}$ is an index for the amounts of industry $r$'s intermediate goods used in industry $i$; and $\theta_i^K$, $\theta_i^L$ and $\theta_i^{zr}$ are the shares of capital, labour and industry $r$'s intermediate goods in the value of output (i.e., the sum of the shares equals one). TFP is given by

$$(5) \quad \ln A_{it}^{j} = \ln Q_{it}^{j} - \ln F_{it}^{j}.$$

The cost of one unit of the composite factor can be derived from Equation (5) as

$$(6) \quad \ln C_{it}^{j} = \theta_i^K \ln R_t^{j} + \theta_i^L \ln W_t^{j} + \sum_{r \in M} \theta_i^{zr} \ln P_{it}^{jr},$$

where $R_t^{j}$ and $W_t^{j}$ represent the country's rental and wage rates (which are assumed to be the same across sectors because factors are assumed to be mobile), and $P_{it}^{jr}$ is the price index for $Z_{it}^{jr}$. In the estimation of the basic regression given by Equation (3), all intermediate goods are produced in monopolistically-competitive industries and are traded. Hence intercountry differences in the intermediate-goods price index are assumed to be relatively small. This assumption simplifies the estimation of the composite-factor cost ratio by letting $P_{it}^{jr}$ be the same for all $j$.

## THE DATA

THIS SECTION BRIEFLY DESCRIBES THE ANNUAL DATA (1970-96) used in the estimation. Further details on the construction and sources of the data are provided in Appendices B and C.

Most of the export and industry data for Canada, the United States and Mexico, which are members of the OECD, were taken from that organization's International Sector Database (ISDB) 1998 and the STAN Database for Industrial

Analysis which replaced the ISDB in 1998. These databases provide comparable industry-level sectoral data for a number of manufacturing sectors (generally at the 2-digit ISIC level), but cover only the value-added activity and two factors (capital and labour).

Some of the data for Mexico had to be found elsewhere because Mexico only became a member of the OECD in 1990; as a result, a sufficiently long time series was not available for several variables. Mexican industry-level capital stock data were kindly provided to us by the Banco de Mexico. Sectoral OECD data are available only up to 1996; this prevented us from extending the sample to more recent years. We also carried out a careful concordance of the data from the various sources to ensure matching across industries and countries. Finally, TFP and composite-factor cost data had to be constructed from the raw data on outputs, inputs and input prices. Because these data problems have been difficult to solve in the past, this study breaks new ground as one of the first to analyse trade flows at the sectoral level in North America.

Figures 4 and 5 display the interindustry variation in comparative productivity and costs for the three countries. Figure 4 shows each country's average TFP in relation to the United States [i.e., the 1970-96 average of $\ln(\tilde{A}_{it}^j / \tilde{A}_{it}^k)$, where $k$ = the United States] across the nine industries or sectors. If international differences in TFP were uniform across sectors, these measures of TFP would be flat and parallel to each other. As Figure 4 shows, however, each country's relative productivity varies considerably from one sector to another. Mexico's TFP index is below that of the other two countries for all industries. Canada's TFP index is below that of the United States for all industries except food, beverages and tobacco, and wood and wood products.

Figure 5 shows the average cost of the composite factor for each country in relation to the United States [i.e., the 1970-96 average of $\ln(\tilde{C}_{it}^j / \tilde{C}_{it}^k)$, where $k$ = the United States] across industries. The relative cost of the composite factor is much lower in Mexico, whereas the Canadian composite factor cost is similar to the U.S. one.

In the next section, the relative exports of a pair of North American countries to the third country are investigated through the use of these data in a regression model.

## FIGURE 4

## TOTAL FACTOR PRODUCTIVITY INDEXES ACROSS SECTORS

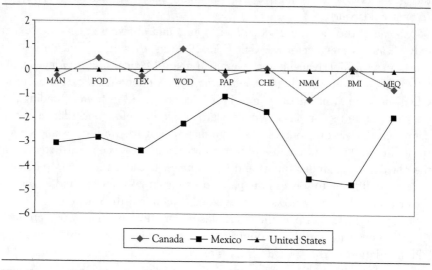

Note: For sector codes, see Appendix D.

## FIGURE 5

## COMPOSITE FACTOR COST INDEXES ACROSS SECTORS

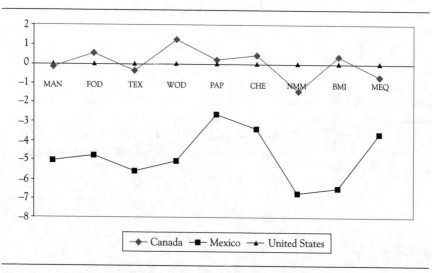

Note: For sector codes, see Appendix D.

# REGRESSION RESULTS

## BASIC MODEL

ANNUAL DATA FROM THE 1970-96 PERIOD are used to estimate the regression model for relative exports given by Equation (3) for the three markets. The United States is the reference country for the Canadian and Mexican markets (i.e., it is in the denominator). Mexico is the reference country for the U.S. market.

If we simplify the notation, the regression model given by Equation (3) can be written in the following form:

$$(7) \quad x_{it}^{jm} = \delta^{jm} + \delta_t^m + \beta_1 f_{it}^j + \beta_2 a_{it}^j + \beta_3 c_{it}^j + e_{it}^{jm},$$

where $x_{it}^{jm} \equiv \ln(X_{it}^{jm} / X_{it}^{km})$, $f_{it}^j \equiv \ln(F_{it}^j / F_{it}^k)$, $a_{it}^j \equiv \ln(A_{it}^j / A_{it}^k)$, and $c_{it}^j \equiv \ln(C_{it}^j / C_{it}^k)$; for $m$ = Canada, $j$ = Mexico and $k$ = United States; for $m$ = United States, $j$ = Canada and $k$ = Mexico; for $m$ = Mexico, $j$ = Canada and $k$ = United States; $i = 1,9$; and $t = 1970,1996$.

For each market, the data are pooled across industries and time periods to estimate Equation (7). Note that $\delta_t^m$ is the time fixed-effect term in market $m$: its purpose is to account for the influence of the omitted trade barriers term, $\ln(B_{it}^{jm} / B_{it}^{jk})$, which is assumed to be the same for all industries, but which changes over time. Also, $\delta^{jm}$ is the market fixed-effect term for exports from country $j$ to market $m$, which is designed to capture influences, such as distance, that do not vary over time but across markets.

The first three rows in Table 3 (the "Ricardo-Heckscher-Ohlin" table) present the results of estimating Equation (7), the basic regression model, with ordinary least squares.[9] The theoretical model implies that the coefficients on the relative market size variable, $f_{it}^j \equiv \ln(F_{it}^j / F_{it}^k)$, and the relative productivity variable, $a_{it}^j \equiv \ln(A_{it}^j / A_{it}^k)$, are positive, and that the coefficient on the relative cost variable, $c_{it}^j \equiv \ln(C_{it}^j / C_{it}^k)$, is negative. The results in the first three rows are generally consistent with these predictions. Seven of the nine coefficients have the expected signs and all three for the important U.S. market have the predicted signs and are statistically significant. The U.S. market results show that relative productivity, relative factor costs and relative economic size are important determinants of competitiveness and export penetration into the U.S. market by Canadian and Mexican firms.

## TABLE 3

## BASIC REGRESSIONS AND VARIATIONS FOR THREE EXPORT MARKETS

| Export Markets | Canada | | | Mexico | | | United States | | |
|---|---|---|---|---|---|---|---|---|---|
| **Ricardo-Heckscher-Ohlin** | | | | | | | | | |
| Relative Size ($f^j_{it}$) | 1.60* | | | 5.17* | | | 1.92* | | |
| | (0.25) | | | (0.69) | | | (0.17) | | |
| Relative Productivity ($a^j_{it}$) | 4.08* | | | –1.19 | | | 2.13* | | |
| | (1.82) | | | (2.07) | | | (0.82) | | |
| Relative Cost ($c^j_{it}$) | 1.44* | | | –48.3* | | | –1.36* | | |
| | (0.45) | | | (7.49) | | | (0.53) | | |
| **Heckscher-Ohlin** | | | | | | | | | |
| Relative Size ($f^j_{it}$) | | 1.60* | | | 1.86* | | | 1.83* | |
| | | (0.30) | | | (0.77) | | | (0.16) | |
| Relative Productivity ($a^j_{it}$) | | 9.96* | | | 110.3* | | | 2.89 | |
| | | (4.55) | | | (54.46) | | | (2.92) | |
| Relative Cost ($c^j_{it}$) | | 0.21 | | | –32.5* | | | –0.87 | |
| | | (1.29) | | | (8.91) | | | (0.96) | |
| **Ricardian** | | | | | | | | | |
| Relative Size ($f^j_{it}$) | | | 1.77* | | | 1.35 | | | 1.75* |
| | | | (0.27) | | | (0.81) | | | (0.16) |
| Relative Productivity ($a^j_{it}$) | | | 3.93* | | | –7.82* | | | 1.49 |
| | | | (1.87) | | | (1.72) | | | (0.80) |
| Relative Cost ($c^j_{it}$) | | | 0.81 | | | –68.9 | | | –0.84 |
| | | | (3.02) | | | (62.7) | | | (1.41) |
| Observations | 216 | 216 | 216 | 216 | 216 | 216 | 216 | 216 | 216 |
| $R^2$ | 0.62 | 0.62 | 0.60 | 0.56 | 0.26 | 0.29 | 0.81 | 0.72 | 0.78 |

Note:  The dependent variable is an index of relative exports ($x^j_{mit}$).
Standard errors are shown in parentheses. * denotes significance at the 5 percent level.
All standard errors are Newey-West corrected for heteroskedasticity and autocorrelation.
The industry "Other Manufacturing" was omitted from the estimation; thus there were only eight industries. Time and market fixed-effect terms are included in the regressions.

The results for the Canadian and Mexican markets are good, as most coefficients have the expected sign and are statistically significant, but they are not as strong as the ones for the U.S. market. The departures from the theoretical model are the following: the relative cost variable is positive (not negative) and statistically significant for the Canadian market, while the relative productivity variable is negative (not positive) but not statistically significant for the Mexican market. These minor inconsistencies are not surprising, given that the level of bilateral trade between Canada and Mexico is much smaller than each country's bilateral trade with the United States. As a result, the trade flows between these two countries may be driven by idiosyncratic factors, like the supply of a particular natural resource, or historical links that cannot be captured adequately by a fairly general model based on relative productivities, costs and economic size.

## VARIATIONS

TWO VARIATIONS OF THE BASIC REGRESSION NUMBER were estimated, and the results are shown in Table 3 under the headings "Heckscher-Ohlin" and "Ricardian."

Recall that the first case eliminates the Ricardian effects due to differences in technology across industries by assuming a Heckscher-Ohlin model with *uniform* Hicks-neutral technical differences. In this version of the Heckscher-Ohlin model, $a_{it}^j$ in Equation (7) is replaced by its average value over all of the industries in country $j$.[10] The second case suppresses the Heckscher-Ohlin effects due to differences in factor endowments by assuming a multi-factor Ricardian model with the same composite-factor function for all sectors. Shares of capital and labour in this version of the model are set at their average value across industries in country $j$, and these average shares are used to calculate $c_{it}^j$ in Equation (7).[11]

The results for the Heckscher-Ohlin and Ricardian models are shown in rows 4-6 and 7-9 in Table 3. In general, there is not much difference between the coefficient estimates for these two special cases and the basic regression model. Most of the estimated coefficients have their signs predicted by the theoretical model, although not as many are statistically significant. Also, these regression models fit the data less well than the basic regression because the $R^2$ for these regressions is generally lower.[12]

## TIME FIXED EFFECTS

FIGURE 6 DISPLAYS THE ESTIMATES of the time fixed-effects term for the U.S. market. This term represents the effect of relative tariff and non-tariff barriers on Canadian and Mexican exports to the U.S. market.[13] The graph shows a downward trend for this term over the sample period, with most of the reduction in the latter half of the sample, which represents the late 1980s and early 1990s. This decline implies that Mexican firms are gaining U.S. market share for their exports at their Canadian competitors' expense, over and above their relative gains through productivity improvements and cost reduction. This pattern is also true for Mexican exports to Canada. Given the scope and magnitude of economic reforms in Mexico, including the widespread liberalization of trade that preceded and, in fact, exceeded that of the NAFTA, this result is not unexpected, especially as many of these reforms took place over roughly the same period as the decline in the time fixed-effects term.

# FIGURE 6

## BEHAVIOUR OF TIME DUMMIES IN THE U.S. MARKET

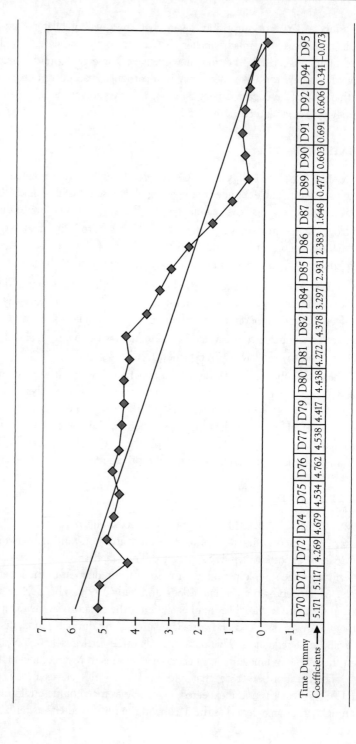

| Time Dummy | D70 | D71 | D72 | D74 | D75 | D76 | D77 | D79 | D80 | D81 | D82 | D84 | D85 | D86 | D87 | D89 | D90 | D91 | D92 | D94 | D95 |
|---|---|---|---|---|---|---|---|---|---|---|---|---|---|---|---|---|---|---|---|---|---|
| Coefficients | 5.171 | 5.117 | 4.269 | 4.679 | 4.534 | 4.762 | 4.538 | 4.417 | 4.438 | 4.272 | 4.378 | 3.297 | 2.931 | 2.383 | 1.648 | 0.477 | 0.603 | 0.691 | 0.606 | 0.341 | -0.073 |

In contrast to Mexico, the estimated time fixed-effects terms for Canada trend upward (these are not shown), indicating that Canada's barriers to trade are falling more gradually than those of its North American neighbours. Again, this is not surprising in a comparison with the U.S. market because Mexican barriers to trade and export were very high at the beginning of the sample period, while those facing Canadian exporters were relatively low. For Mexico's economy, however, integration with the U.S. market appears to be moving faster than for Canada's. Again, this is not unexpected, given the geographic proximity of the United States and Mexico, as well as the closer cultural and linguistic ties developing between them. There are almost 20 million Mexican-Americans in the United States, the vast majority of whom live close to the Mexican border.

## CONCLUDING REMARKS

THIS STUDY INVESTIGATES TRADE IN MANUFACTURED GOODS among Canada, Mexico and the United States at the sectoral (2-digit ISIC) level by first developing a theoretical model of sectoral trade flows to derive a relation determining the relative exports from two countries to a third, and then estimating this relation by means of a carefully constructed North American trade and industry database for the 1970-96 time period. The theoretical model incorporates traditional Ricardian and Heckscher-Ohlin channels of compa-rative advantage; consequently, differences in technology (productivity) and factor endowments (factor costs) are included in the derived relation as determinants of relative exports. In addition, the model integrates elements of more recent trade theories based on product differentiation and monopolistic competition, which imply that relative domestic market size should also be a determinant of relative export performance. The model also allows for time-varying trade barriers.

The regression results strongly support the theoretical model. The empirical evidence implies that differences in productivity, factor costs and domestic market size play important roles in explaining the North American international trade in manufactured goods. In addition, the results indicate that trade barriers facing the exports of Mexican goods seem to be falling faster than those for the other two countries. This result is not surprising given that the barriers facing Mexican exports were relatively high over the first half of the 1970-96 sample period, and that the Mexican government has pursued a program of vigorous trade liberalization over the past 15 years that includes the NAFTA and a host of other efforts.

These results also suggest that trade flows in North America will continue to increase as trade barriers fall because of ongoing reductions in communications and transportation costs, and as Canada and Mexico close the productivity gap with the United States through increases in human and physical capital and the adoption of new technologies. Policy makers will have to deal with the increasing trade flows and greater economic integration, as well as the resulting pressure on governments to reduce official barriers to trade. Calls for greater harmonization of product standards, more labour mobility, better North-South transportation links and even a common currency can only get louder.

# Endnotes

1 Lustig (2001) provides a useful survey of the recent economic reforms in Mexico.

2 For example, MacDougall (1951, 1952) provides a test of the single-factor (labour) Ricardian model; he finds a positive cross-industry association between the ratio of U.S. to U.K. labour productivity and the U.S.-U.K. export ratio. Although this evidence is still widely cited, the theoretical basis for the empirical model is suspect. The multi-factor Heckscher-Ohlin model has run into a string of empirical rejections, starting with Leontief's (1953) paradoxical findings that U.S. exports were less capital intensive than U.S. import-competing products.

3 A number of studies regress some measure of export performance (e.g., net exports) on industry characteristics such as capital and skill intensities (for a review of earlier literature, see Deardorff 1984). The theoretical basis for these regressions, however, is not clear: Leamer and Bowen (1981), for example, make this argument.

4 Helpman and Krugman (1985) is the standard reference for new trade models that incorporate monopolistic competition.

5 The Maquiladora program was started by the Mexican government in 1989 as a means of attracting foreign direct investment and promoting exports. Restrictions on foreign ownership were relaxed and duty-free treatment of intermediate imports were allowed in return for firms exporting the resulting products abroad.

6 Note that relative factor endowments do not enter Equation (2) directly but they would exert an indirect influence by means of relative factor prices.

7 Such a relation would potentially represent the home market effect discussed by Krugman (1980).

8 Note that in this case, $\mathbf{W}^j$ could still differ from $\mathbf{W}^k$ because of international differences in factor endowments, factor intensities and productivity. The cost ratio $[=\chi_i(\mathbf{W}^j)/\chi_i(\mathbf{W}^k)]$, however, would not vary across industries, as $\chi_i(.)$ would be the same for all $i$;.

9 Note that the estimates of the 81 time fixed-effect terms and the six market fixed-effect terms are not reported individually to conserve space, but are available on request from the authors.

10 Observed differences in this index are viewed as measurement errors (with a zero mean).

11 This index is the same for all sectors and equals $\theta^Y[\tilde{\theta}^K \ln(R_t^j/R_t^k) + \tilde{\theta}^L \ln(W_t^j/W_t^k)]$, where $\theta^Y$, $\tilde{\theta}^K$ and $\tilde{\theta}^L$ are the average values of $\theta_i^Y$, $\tilde{\theta}_i^K$ and $\tilde{\theta}_i^L$, respectively. Observed

differences in shares are now considered measurement errors, and estimates of $a_{it}^j$ and $f_{it}^j$ are based on the average values of the shares. See Appendix B for more details.

12  Instrumental variable techniques were also used to estimate the model to control for the endogeneity of the relative market size variable. The regression results do not change significantly. They are available on request from the authors.

13  These non-tariff barriers would include quotas and other non-tariff commercial policies, as well as other transportation and transaction costs.

14  This theory appendix is based on Section II of Choudhri and Hakura (2001).

15  For the sake of simplicity, headquarters technology is assumed to be the same for all countries. Allowing $\overline{F}_i^h$ to vary across countries, however, would not substantively affect the export relation.

16  Given that $\theta_i^K = \theta_i^Y \tilde{\theta}_i^K$ and $\theta_i^L = \theta_i^Y \tilde{\theta}_i^L$, Equations (4) and (6) can be used to express $\ln Q_{it}^j = \theta_i^Y \ln Y_{it}^j + \sum_r \theta_i^{zr} \ln Z_{it}^r = \theta_i^Y \ln \tilde{A}_{it}^j + \ln F_{it}^j$. The link between the two measures of TFP can be derived using Equation (5).

17  See Choudhri and Hakura for more details.

## ACKNOWLEDGMENTS

THE AUTHORS WOULD LIKE TO THANK Someshwar Rao, Prakash Sharma and Aaron Sydor of Industry Canada, and the Banco de Mexico for their kind assistance in assembling the data, as well as Ehsan Choudhri, Richard Harris and Daniel Schwanen for helpful advice.

## BIBLIOGRAPHY

Caballero, Ricardo, and Richard Lyons. "Internal versus External Economies in European Industry." *European Economic Review* 34 (1990): 805-30.

Choudhri, Ehsan, and Dalia S. Hakura. "International Trade in Manufactured Products: A Ricardo-Heckscher-Ohlin Explanation with Monopolistic Competition." International Monetary Fund Working Paper WP/01/41, April 2001.

Choudhri, Ehsan, and Lawrence Schembri. "Productivity Performance and International Competitiveness: An Old Test Reconsidered." *Canadian Journal of Economics* 35 (2002): 341-62.

Davis, Donald, and David Weinstein. "An Account of Global Factor Trade." *National Bureau of Economic Research Working Paper No. 6785* Massachusetts: NBER, 1998.

Deardorff, Alan. "Testing Trade Theories and Predicting Trade Flows." In *Handbook of International Economics*, Vol. 1. Edited by Ronald W. Jones and Peter B. Kenen. Amsterdam: North-Holland, 1984.

Dixit, Avinash, and Joseph E. Stiglitz. "Monopolistic Competition and Optimum Product Diversity." *American Economic Review* 67 (1977): 297-308.

Hakura, Dalia S. "Why Does HOV Fail? The Role of Technological Differences within the EC." *Journal of International Economics* 54 (2001): 361-82.

Hall, Robert E., and Dale Jorgenson. "Tax Policy and Investment Behavior." *American Economic Review* 57 (1967): 391-414.

Harrigan, James. "Technology Factor Supplies, and International Specialization: Estimating the Neoclassical Model." *American Economic Review* 87 (1997): 475-494.

Helliwell, John, F. "Canada: Life Beyond the Looking Glass." *Journal of Economic Perspectives* 15 (2001): 107-24.

Helpman, Elhanan, and Paul R. Krugman. *Market Structure and Foreign Trade: Increasing Returns, Imperfect Competition and the International Economy.* Cambridge: The MIT Press, 1985.

*IMF International Financial Statistics Yearbook,* 1999.

Krugman, Paul. "Scale Economies, Product Differentiation and the Pattern of Trade." *American Economic Review* 70 (1980): 950-9.

Leamer, Edward, and Harry Bowen. "Cross-section tests of the Heckscher-Ohlin Theorem: Comment." *American Economic Review* 71 (1981): 1040-1043.

Leontief, Wassily. "Domestic Production and Foreign Trade: The American Capital Position Re-examined." *Proceedings of the American Philosophical Society* 97 (1953): 332-49.

Lustig, Nora. "Life is Not Easy: Mexico's Quest for Stability and Growth." *Journal of Economic Perspectives* 15 (2001): 85-106.

MacDougall, G.D.A. "British and American Exports: A Study Suggested by the Theory of Comparative Costs, Part I." *Economic Journal* 61 (1951): 697-724.

_____. "British and American Exports: A Study Suggested by the Theory of Comparative Costs, Part II." *Economic Journal* 62 (1952): 487-521.

OECD, *Bilateral Trade Database 1998.*

Trefler, Daniel. "The Case of the Missing Trade and Other HOV Mysteries." *American Economic Review* 85 (1995): 1029-46.

# APPENDIX A

# THEORY[14]

ASSUME THERE ARE $I$ monopolistically competitive industries in $J$ countries and that consumer demand for each industry's varieties is based on the Dixit and Stiglitz (1977) model of the utility function. To simplify the exposition, assume initially that no intermediate goods are produced. The demand in country $m$ for a variety produced in country $j$ can then be expressed as

(A1) $D_i^{jm} = E_i^m (P_i^j B_i^{jm})^{-\sigma} / \sum_{k \in J} n_i^k (P_i^k B_i^{km})^{1-\sigma}$,

where $i-1$  $I$ indexes industries; $E_i^m$ is the total expenditure in country $m$ on all (domestic and foreign) varieties in the industry; $P_i^j$ denotes the home price of each variety produced in country $j$'s industry; $B_i^{jm}$ represents an index of industry trade barriers for country $j$'s exports to country $m$; $n_i^j$ stands for the number of varieties in country $j$'s industry; and $\sigma$ is the elasticity of substitution (assumed to be the same for all industries).

Letting $X_i^{jm} \equiv n_i^j P_i^j D_i^{jm}$ denote industry exports from country $j$ to country $m$, the relative exports of a country pair $(j, k)$ to country $m$'s market are determined by Equation (A1) as

(A2) $X_i^{jm} / X_i^{km} = (n_i^j / n_i^k)(B_i^{jm} / B_i^{km})^{-\sigma} (P_i^j / P_i^k)^{1-\sigma}$.

Assume that each firm requires a fixed amount of headquarters services and is manufactured at a plant under constant returns to scale. For country $j$, we express the plant production function as

(A3) $Q_i^j = \alpha_i^j F_i^{pj}$,

where $Q_i^j$ is the plant output, and $\alpha_i^j$ and $F_i^{pj}$ are the productivity and the quantity of the composite factor used in the plant. Letting $\mathbf{V}_i^{pj}$ represent a vector of primary factors employed at each plant, define $F_i^{pj} \equiv \phi_i(\mathbf{V}_i^{pj})$. The function $\phi_i(.)$ is assumed to be homogeneous of degree one and the same for all countries. (A3) allows only for Hicks-neutral technology differences between countries. The cost of using one unit of the composite factor can be expressed as $C_i^j = \chi_i(\mathbf{W}^j)$, where $\mathbf{W}^j$ is the price vector for primary factors. In view of Equation (A3), the unit variable cost equals $C_i^j / \alpha_i^j$. Profit maximization by the firm then implies that

(A4) $C_i^j / \alpha_i^j = (1 - 1/\sigma)P_i^j$.

Assume that headquarters operations require a fixed amount of the composite factor given by $\overline{F}_i^h \equiv \phi_i(\mathbf{V}_i^{hj})$, where $\mathbf{V}_i^{hj}$ represents the primary factors vector for headquarters.[15] Fixed headquarter costs thus equal $\overline{F}_i^h C_i^j$. The zero-profit condition can be stated as $\overline{F}_i^h C_i^j / Q_i^j + C_i^j / \alpha_i^j = P_i^j$. This condition, along with (A3) and (A4), can be used to determine

(A5) $F_i^{pj} = (\sigma - 1)\overline{F}_i^h$.

Let $A_i^j$ denote the industry TFP for country $j$. Note that $A_i^j = n_i^j Q_i^j / F_i^j$, where $F_i^j \equiv n_i^j (F_i^{pj} + \overline{F}_i^h)$ represents the total employment of the composite factor in the industry (since each firm uses the amount $F_i^{pj}$ at the plant and $\overline{F}_i^h$ at headquarters). By using Equations (A3) and (A5), we can link the plant technology index to TFP as

(A6) $\alpha_i^j = A_i^j \sigma / (\sigma - 1)$.

Equation (A5) can be employed to relate the industry employment of the composite factor to the number of varieties (firms) in the industry as

(A7) $F_i^j = n_i^j \sigma \overline{F}_i^h$.

Thus, $F_i^j$ can be used as a proxy for (difficult-to-measure) $n_i^j$.

Equations (A4), (A6) and (A7) can be used to express Equation (A2) as

(A8) $X_i^{jm} / X_i^{km} = (F_i^j / F_i^k)(B_i^{jm} / B_i^{km})^{-\sigma} (C_i^j / C_i^k)^{-(\sigma-1)} (A_i^j / A_i^k)^{\sigma-1}$.

Equation (A8) is Equation (2) in the text.

# APPENDIX B

# DATA CONSTRUCTION – FURTHER DETAILS

BECAUSE DATA ON INTERMEDIATE INPUTS, $Z_{it}^{jr}$, are not available, the factor usage (the economic size) and productivity variables, $F_{it}^j$ and $A_{it}^j$, cannot be directly estimated from Equations (4) and (5). The Cobb-Douglas functional form in Equation (4), however, can be utilized to estimate these variables using the following value-added function:

(A9) $\ln Y_{it}^j = \ln \tilde{A}_{it}^j + \tilde{\theta}_i^K \ln K_{it}^j + \tilde{\theta}_i^L \ln L_{it}^j$,

where $Y_{it}^j$ is value-added output; $\tilde{\theta}_i^K$ and $\tilde{\theta}_i^L$ are shares of capital and labour in value-added; and $\tilde{A}_{it}^j$ is TFP in the value-added activity, which can be estimated from the available data. Letting $\theta_i^Y$ denote the share of value-added in the value of output, Equations (5) and (A9) can be used to link the two measures of TFP as $\ln A_{it}^j = \theta_i^Y \ln \tilde{A}_{it}^j$.[16] This expression can be used to estimate $A_{it}^j$; then an estimate for the composite factor, $F_{it}^j$, can be obtained from (5) by means of data on $Q_{it}^j$. Note also that the TFP ratio is given by $\ln(A_{it}^j / A_{it}^k) = \theta_i^Y \ln(\tilde{A}_{it}^j / \tilde{A}_{it}^k)$.

Note that the cost of the composite factor in value-added is given by

(A10)    $\ln \tilde{C}_{it}^j = \tilde{\theta}_i^K \ln R_t^j + \tilde{\theta}_i^L \ln W_t^j$ .

Under the assumption that $P_{it}^{jr} = P_{it}^{kr}$, Equations (7) and (8) imply that

(A11)    $\ln(C_{it}^j / C_{it}^k) = \theta_i^Y \ln(\tilde{C}_{it}^j / \tilde{C}_{it}^k)$.

The cost ratio can thus be estimated through the use of data on value-added.

With annual data (mostly from the OECD) for nine ISIC 2-digit manufacturing sectors, each sector's shares of capital and labour in value-added were averaged over the three countries and the 1970-96 sample period to obtain estimates of $\tilde{\theta}_i^K$ and $\tilde{\theta}_i^L$, which were in turn employed to calculate $\ln \tilde{A}_{it}^j$ and $\ln \tilde{C}_{it}^j$. The three-country 1970-96 averages of sectoral shares of value-added in output were used to estimate $\theta_i^Y$. This estimate was employed to measure $\ln(A_{it}^j / A_{it}^k)$ and $\ln(C_{it}^j / C_{it}^k)$ under the assumption that prices of intermediate goods are the same in all countries.

The OECD does not provide data on real (gross) output by sector ($Q_{it}^j$). Without such data, the composite factor in value-added (i.e., $\ln \tilde{F}_{it}^j \equiv \ln Y_{it}^j - \ln \tilde{A}_{it}^j$) is used to measure $F_{it}^j$. This measure would be a good approximation for the relative quantity of the composite factor if the ratio of the intermediate goods to the value-added composite factor does not vary much across countries.[17] Another limitation of the OECD data is that they convert real industry (value-added) outputs to internationally comparable units by means of GDP purchasing power parities. This procedure does not allow for international differences in relative prices across sectors, which could introduce errors in the measures of $\ln \tilde{A}_{it}^j$ as well as $\ln \tilde{F}_{it}^j$.

# APPENDIX C

## DATA SOURCES

THIS APPENDIX PROVIDES DEFINITIONS for the variables used in the text and gives the sources of data for each variable. The bulk of the data was obtained from two OECD databases: the International Sector Database (ISDB) 1998 and the STAN Database for Industrial Analysis that replaced the ISDB in 1998.

1. $X_{it}^{jm}$ is the value of exports of sector $i$ from country $j$ to country $m$ in thousands of U.S. dollars. Source: OECD's *Bilateral Trade Database 1998*. Note: Mexican export data have been replaced by Canadian and U.S. import data because of restrictions on Mexican data during the 1990-96 period, as well as large discrepancies between Canadian and U.S. data over the period.

2. $Y_{it}^{j}$ is the value added at 1990 prices in U.S. dollars using the 1990 purchasing power parities (PPP) rate. For Canada and the United States, the source is the ISDB, variable code GDPD. Mexican data at 1990 prices were obtained from the STAN database and converted into U.S. dollars at the PPP rate provided with the STAN database.

3. $K_{it}^{j}$ is the gross capital stock at 1990 prices in U.S. dollars using the 1990 PPP rate. For Canada and the United States, the source is the ISDB, variable code KTVD. Mexican data on gross fixed capital formation were provided by the Banco de Mexico; these were used to construct Mexican capital stock assuming a depreciation rate of 10 percent and converted to 1990 prices in U.S. dollars using the PPP rate provided with the STAN database.

4. $L_{it}^{j}$ is total employment in sector $i$. For Canada and the United States, the source is the ISDB, variable code ET. For Mexico, the data come from the STAN database.

5. $\tilde{\theta}_{i}^{L}$ is the share of labour in value-added for each sector. This was calculated as the total compensation of employees (ISDB, variable code WSSS; the STAN database was used for Mexico) divided by value-added in current prices and national currency. This yearly index was then averaged over the 1970-96 period to obtain $\tilde{\theta}_{i}^{L}$.

6. $\tilde{\theta}_{i}^{K}$ is the share of capital in value-added for each sector. This was calculated as

$$\tilde{\theta}_{i}^{K} = (1 - \tilde{\theta}_{i}^{L}).$$

7. $\theta_{i}^{Y}$ is the ratio of value-added in current prices to gross output in current prices for each sector (the average for each sector over the 1970-96 period). The STAN database was the source for gross output.

8. $W_{t}^{j}$ is the manufacturing wage rate in country $j$ at time $t$. This was calculated as the ratio of labour compensation and total employment.

9. $R_t^j$ is the rental rate in country $j$ at time $t$. This was calculated with the Hall-Jorgenson method (Hall and Jorgenson 1967) as follows:

$$R_t^j = (r + \delta)P_I,$$

where $r$ is the real interest rate, calculated by taking the difference between government medium-term bond yield and the inflation rate as measured by the Consumer Price Index, as in Caballero and Lyons (1990) (Source: IMF 1999); $\delta$ is the depreciation rate of capital, assumed to equal 10 percent, as in Caballero and Lyons; and $P_I$ is the U.S. dollar price of a comparable investment good worth one U.S. dollar in 1990 prices. This was constructed as follows:

$$P_I = (IT*PPP) / (ITV*ER),$$

where $IT$ represents gross fixed capital formation in current prices and national currency; $ITV$ represents gross fixed capital formation in 1990 prices and national currency; $ER$ is the exchange rate in national currency units per U.S. dollar (from the STAN database); and $PPP$ represents the purchasing power parities (from the STAN database).

As data on IT were not available for Mexico, a proxy was constructed where value-added replaces gross fixed capital formation in the above equation.

# APPENDIX D

| SECTOR CODES FOR FIGURES 4 AND 5 | |
|---|---|
| **ISDB CODES** | **Industry** |
| MAN | Manufacturing |
| FOD | Food, Beverages and Tobacco |
| TEX | Textiles, Wearing Apparel and Leather |
| WOD | Wood and Wood Products, including Furniture |
| PAP | Paper and Paper Products, Printing and Publishing |
| CHE | Chemicals and Chemical Petroleum, Coal, Rubber and Plastic Products |
| NMM | Non-metallic Mineral Products except Products of Petroleum and Coal |
| BMI | Basic Metals |
| MEQ | Fabricated Metal Products, Machinery and Equipment |
| MOT | Other Manufacturing |

Gary Sawchuk & Aaron Sydor[*]
Industry Canada

**3**

# Mexico and Canada: Changing Specializations in Trade with the United States

## INTRODUCTION

THIS STUDY EXPLORES THE CHANGING SPECIALIZATION of Mexican and Canadian exports to the United States. The Canada-U.S. Free Trade Agreement (FTA) and the North American Free Trade Agreement (NAFTA) were expected to cause some gradual adjustment in the specialization of both countries' exports to the United States. It also seemed reasonable to expect that Mexico and Canada would specialize in different exports — with Mexico having an advantage in manufactured goods that benefit from more labour-intensive activities.

## A FEW KEY QUESTIONS

THIS STUDY WILL ADDRESS four main questions:

- Are we seeing a gradual adjustment in the specialization of Mexican and Canadian exports to the United States?

- Are there different factors behind each country's increased exports to the United States?

- Have recent trends brought Mexico and Canada into greater export competition with one another?

- Is export competition between Mexico and Canada for U.S. market share likely to increase?

Why are these questions important? Shifting trade patterns are inevitably linked to industry growth and the transformation of especially small open economies. Particular export specializations are often associated with economic change, including that to higher value-added activities. For Mexico and Canada, the answers to these questions can shed important light on their future growth.

---

*\* Now at the Department of Foreign Affairs and International Trade.* 117

To answer such questions, however, it is necessary to identify the key drivers behind U.S.-bound exports from Mexico and Canada and consider the changing nature of their comparative advantages. Within the past 15 years, Mexico has seen considerable and accelerating change in many directions. Canada, too, continues to evolve; and whether trying to build on its relatively abundant natural resources or seeking greater participation in the knowledge-based economy, what is usually at stake is more value-added activities.

This leads to additional questions. Although Canada may be producing export goods of generally higher value, are Mexican exports beginning to move up the value chain? If so, what impact might this have for future U.S. export competition between Mexico and Canada? Also, are the two countries becoming increasingly competitive and pursuing new or stronger comparative advantages in similar industries? Finally, will there always be room for both Mexico and Canada in the large U.S. import market?

The answers to these questions have important consequences.

## ORGANIZATION OF THE STUDY

AFTER THE INTRODUCTION, the second section reviews key facts associated with Mexican and Canadian exports to the United States, documenting recent changes in trade patterns and exports, and focussing on the industries in each country that are contributing most to recent export gains. The next two sections examine the principal factors contributing to the recent growth in exports to the United States from both countries: the third focusses on strong U.S. import demand, the fourth on several competitiveness factors. In the fifth section, we address several issues that might affect the levels and specializations of future Mexican and Canadian exports to the United States. We finish with a review of key messages and some concluding thoughts.

# SOME INTERESTING FACTS

## MEXICO AND CANADA: FAST GROWTH IN TRADE WITH THE UNITED STATES

BOTH MEXICO AND CANADA have seen a dramatic increase in their trade in manufactured goods[1] with the United States (Figure 1A). While Canada trades considerably more with the United States in absolute terms, the growth of Canada's trade in manufactured goods with the United States falls far short of Mexico's spectacular growth (390 and more than 800 percent, respectively, between 1980 and 1998). Since 1990, Mexico's manufactured goods trade with the United States rose from US$46 to US$155 billion for an average annual increase of 16.4 percent. The comparable figures for Canada moved from US$149 to US$292 billion for an average annual increase of only 8.8 percent.[2]

## FIGURE 1A

## MEXICO AND CANADA:
## TRADE IN MANUFACTURED GOODS WITH THE UNITED STATES

### MEXICO

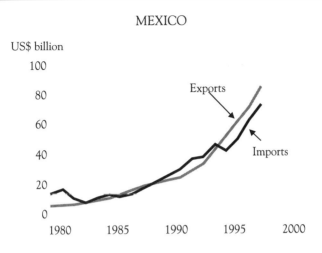

### CANADA

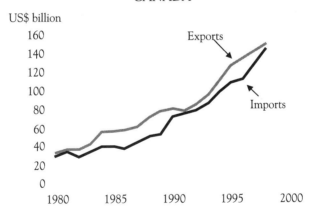

Source: OECD.

# FIGURE 1B

## THE COMMERCIAL SERVICES TRADE SHARE OF MERCHANDISE TRADE

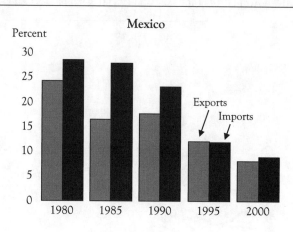

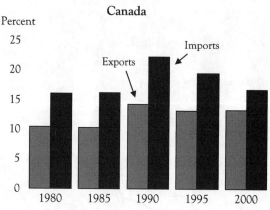

Source: WTO.

# FIGURE 2

## DIRECTION OF TRADE, 1998

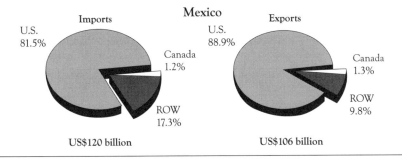

### Mexico

Imports

U.S.
81.5%

Canada
1.2%

ROW
17.3%

US$120 billion

Exports

U.S.
88.9%

Canada
1.3%

ROW
9.8%

US$106 billion

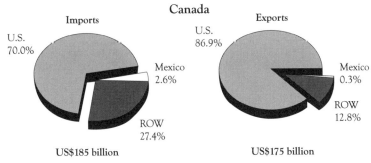

### Canada

Imports

U.S.
70.0%

Mexico
2.6%

ROW
27.4%

US$185 billion

Exports

U.S.
86.9%

Mexico
0.3%

ROW
12.8%

US$175 billion

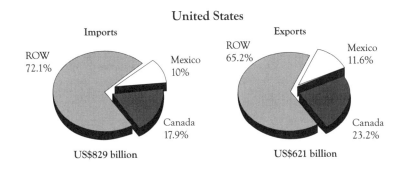

### United States

Imports

ROW
72.1%

Mexico
10%

Canada
17.9%

US$829 billion

Exports

ROW
65.2%

Mexico
11.6%

Canada
23.2%

US$621 billion

Source: OECD.

TABLE 1

MEXICO AND CANADA: RANKING BY SHARE OF THE U.S. IMPORT
MARKET

| | Mexico | | Canada | |
|---|---|---|---|---|
| | Rank 1990 | Rank 1998 | Rank 1990 | Rank 1998 |
| **All Manufacturing** | 5 | 3 | 2 | 1 |
| Food, Beverages and Tobacco | 5 | 2 | 1 | 1 |
| Textiles, Apparel and Leather | 8 | 2 | 13 | 7 |
| Wood Products and Furniture | 3 | 3 | 1 | 1 |
| Paper, Paper Products and Printing | 6 | 6 | 1 | 1 |
| Chemicals (excluding Drugs) | 5 | 7 | 1 | 1 |
| Drugs and Medicines | 16 | 16 | 9 | 6 |
| Petroleum Refineries and Products | 6 | 3 | 1 | 1 |
| Rubber and Plastic Products | 8 | 5 | 3 | 2 |
| Non-metallic Mineral Products | 4 | 4 | 3 | 2 |
| Iron and Steel | 7 | 3 | 2 | 2 |
| Non-ferrous Metals | 3 | 2 | 1 | 1 |
| Metal Products | 5 | 5 | 3 | 1 |
| Machinery (including Computers) | 8 | 2 | 3 | 3 |
| Electrical and Electronic Products | 6 | 1 | 3 | 4 |
| Shipbuilding and Repair | 20 | 24 | 2 | 2 |
| Motor Vehicles | 4 | 3 | 2 | 1 |
| Aircraft | 16 | 17 | 2 | 2 |
| Other Transport Equipment | 9 | 5 | 3 | 1 |
| Professional Goods | 6 | 2 | 5 | 6 |
| Other Manufacturing | 10 | 6 | 12 | 9 |

Source: Based on OECD, *Bilateral Trade Database, 2000*.

Trade with the United States accounts for the vast majority of all manufacturing trade for both countries. Figure 2 shows that the United States now accounts for almost 90 percent of Mexico's total manufacturing exports. The figure for Canada is only slightly lower. (By comparison, only 1.3 percent of Mexico's exports go to Canada and a minuscule 0.3 percent of Canada's exports go to Mexico.)[3] Consequently, the United States is the key trading partner for both Mexico and Canada *by far*.

Table 1 shows the interesting fact that while Canada was among the top three exporters in 16 (of 20) industry-defined U.S. import markets in 1990 and 15 in 1998, Mexico had just two third-place rankings in 1990, but by 1998 ranked among the top three exporters in 11 industry-defined U.S. import markets. The two countries' exports still appear complementary because they are not among the top in all the same U.S. markets. However, both Mexico and Canada were ranked among the top three exporters in 8 of the same industry-defined U.S. markets in 1998 — including motor vehicles and machinery — and among the top five exporters in 12 markets.

## TABLE 2

## MEXICO AND CANADA: INDUSTRY EXPORTS, EXPORT GROWTH AND EXPORT INTENSITIES

| | Mexico | | | Canada | | |
|---|---|---|---|---|---|---|
| | Level 1996 US$ billion | Growth 1990-96 (percent) | Export Intensity 1996 | Level 1996 US$ billion | Growth 1990-96 (percent) | Export Intensity 1996 |
| **All Manufacturing** | 61.1 | 18.2 | 106.6 | 131.8 | 8.3 | 73.4 |
| Food, Beverages and Tobacco | 1.6 | 10.8 | 9.9 | 5.3 | 9.4 | 38.2 |
| Textiles, Apparel and Leather | 5.2 | 27.5 | 101.4 | 2.2 | 20.7 | 52.8 |
| Wood Products and Furniture | 1.8 | 16.8 | 110.9 | 11.2 | 13.4 | 148.4 |
| Paper, Paper Products and Printing | 0.4 | 12.4 | 15.7 | 11.8 | 3.0 | 94.6 |
| Chemicals (excluding Drugs) | 1.9 | 10.6 | 34.4 | 9.2 | 9.2 | 152.6 |
| Drugs and Medicines | 0.0 | 19.9 | 2.5 | 0.4 | 28.2 | 18.6 |
| Petroleum Refineries and Products | 0.5 | –4.3 | 38.2 | 3.9 | –0.3 | 420.7 |
| Rubber and Plastic Products | 0.9 | 16.3 | 43.2 | 3.1 | 12.5 | 77.5 |
| Non-metallic Mineral Products | 1.0 | 12.6 | 23.1 | 1.4 | 10.8 | 60.5 |
| Iron and Steel | 1.4 | 15.8 | 49.9 | 3.5 | 6.7 | 122.8 |
| Non-ferrous Metals | 0.7 | 8.5 | 60.4 | 6.0 | 5.0 | 218.1 |
| Metal Products | 1.7 | 18.6 | 69.8 | 4.0 | 13.3 | 65.5 |
| Machinery (including Computers) | 5.7 | 23.9 | 196.8 | 10.7 | 10.9 | 166.4 |
| Electrical and Electronic Products | 18.7 | 16.4 | 482.1 | 8.6 | 9.9 | 127.5 |
| Shipbuilding and Repair | 0.0 | 5.6 | 116.2 | 0.7 | 15.9 | 138.8 |
| Motor Vehicles | 16.1 | 20.3 | 182.6 | 43.7 | 7.3 | 389.5 |
| Aircraft | 0.0 | 9.1 | 19.8 | 3.2 | 8.7 | 108.1 |
| Other Transport Equipment | 0.1 | 40.2 | 51.7 | 0.9 | 14.0 | 110.6 |
| Professional Goods | 2.3 | 22.7 | 397.1 | 1.4 | 11.9 | 73.7 |
| Other Manufacturing | 1.0 | 16.7 | 102.2 | 0.6 | 14.3 | 72.8 |

Notes:  Export intensity is U.S.-bound exports divided by value-added. It is a measure of how much individual industries depend on U.S. import markets.

Source: Based on OECD, *Bilateral Trade Database.*

## STRONG EXPORT PERFORMANCES

BOTH COUNTRIES HAVE BEEN RUNNING significant surpluses in their manufactured goods trade with the United States. Canada has maintained an annual trade surplus of about US$4.0 billion. Mexico had a large 1998 trade surplus of US$10.8 billion.

## FIGURE 3

## MEXICO AND CANADA: AVERAGE ANNUAL GROWTH IN EXPORTS TO THE UNITED STATES, 1990-98

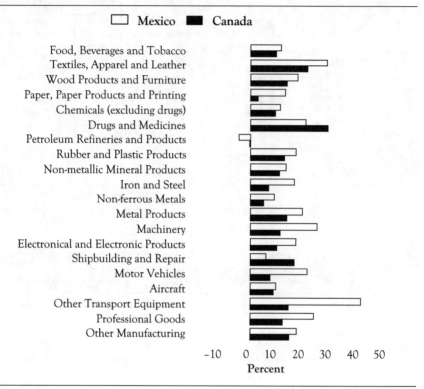

Source: OECD.

Figure 3 illustrates export growth rates for both Mexico and Canada by industry.[4] It bears repeating that Mexico's trade with the United States is starting from a smaller footing. However, what immediately becomes apparent is that Mexico's overall growth in exports to the United States is *not only* much faster than Canada's, but it is faster in *nearly all* manufacturing industries — including more technologically-based and knowledge-intensive industries like machinery (which includes computers), motor vehicles, and other transport equipment. In fact, Mexico's exports are growing much more quickly in these industries. The growth of Canada's exports to the United States was superior to Mexico's in only three manufacturing industries: drugs and medicines, ship-building and repair, and petroleum refineries and products (exports in the latter declined for both countries, but Canada's decline was slower).

124

## MEXICO AND CANADA: WHAT ARE THEIR EXPORT SPECIALIZATIONS?

FIGURE 4 SHOWS THE TOP FIVE U.S.-bound exports from Mexico and Canada. One point stands out: the surprising similarity between these exports. Canada's are motor vehicles, machinery, and electrical and electronic products, as well as two traditional natural resource-based industries: wood products, and paper and paper products. Mexico's top five are electrical and electronic products, motor vehicles, and machinery,[5] followed by textiles and apparel, and professional goods. It is also significant that three of Mexico's top five exports are held by "high tech" industries (the OECD definition of the term): electrical and electronic products, machinery and professional goods.

Figure 4 also reveals that Mexico is becoming increasingly specialized in its exports to the United States. Its top five exports made up 79 percent of its total U.S.-bound exports in 1998, *up* more than 8 percentage points from 70.9 percent in 1990. By contrast, Canada's top five U.S.-bound exports contributed a smaller 65.1 percent of total 1998 exports, *down* slightly from 67.2 percent in 1990 (see Table 3).[6]

## TABLE 3

### MEXICO AND CANADA: EXPORT SPECIALIZATIONS AND U.S. IMPORTS

| | Mexico | | | Canada | | | U.S. Imports | | |
|---|---|---|---|---|---|---|---|---|---|
| | Share of Total Manufacturing Exports, % | | Change in Share | Share of Total Manufacturing Exports, % | | Change in Share | Share of Total Manufacturing Exports, % | | Change in Share |
| | 1990 | 1998 | 1990-98 | 1990 | 1998 | 1990-98 | 1990 | 1998 | 1990-98 |
| All Manufacturing | 100.0 | 100.0 | | 100.0 | 100.0 | | 100.0 | 100.0 | |
| Food, Beverages and Tobacco | 4.3 | 2.6 | −1.7 | 4.0 | 4.4 | 0.3 | 4.7 | 3.6 | −1.1 |
| Textiles, Apparel and Leather | 5.6 | 10.3 | 4.7 | 0.9 | 2.0 | 1.2 | 10.3 | 10.1 | −0.2 |
| Wood Products and Furniture | 3.3 | 3.0 | −0.3 | 6.0 | 8.7 | 2.7 | 2.4 | 3.1 | 0.7 |
| Paper, Paper Products and Printing | 1.1 | 0.7 | −0.4 | 12.2 | 8.2 | −4.1 | 3.2 | 2.3 | −0.9 |
| Chemicals (excluding Drugs) | 4.3 | 2.5 | −1.8 | 6.3 | 6.7 | 0.4 | 5.9 | 6.3 | 0.4 |
| Drugs and Medicines | 0.1 | 0.1 | 0.0 | 0.1 | 0.4 | 0.3 | 0.6 | 1.3 | 0.7 |
| Petroleum Refineries and Products | 2.1 | 0.4 | −1.7 | 3.8 | 1.9 | −1.8 | 4.4 | 1.8 | −2.7 |
| Rubber and Plastic Products | 1.6 | 1.4 | −0.2 | 1.9 | 2.6 | 0.7 | 2.8 | 3.0 | 0.2 |
| Non-metallic Mineral Products | 2.3 | 1.6 | −0.7 | 0.9 | 1.1 | 0.2 | 1.4 | 1.4 | 0.0 |
| Iron and Steel | 2.1 | 1.8 | −0.3 | 2.7 | 2.4 | −0.3 | 2.6 | 2.6 | 0.0 |
| Non-ferrous Metals | 2.4 | 1.2 | −1.2 | 5.2 | 4.1 | −1.2 | 2.7 | 2.1 | −0.5 |
| Metal Products | 3.2 | 3.3 | 0.1 | 2.4 | 3.4 | 1.0 | 2.8 | 3.0 | 0.2 |
| Machinery (including Computers) | 7.4 | 10.8 | 3.4 | 6.9 | 8.3 | 1.4 | 13.4 | 16.5 | 3.1 |
| Electrical and Electronic Products | 35.2 | 31.2 | −4.0 | 6.1 | 6.9 | 0.8 | 13.9 | 15.7 | 1.8 |
| Shipbuilding and Repair | 0.0 | 0.0 | 0.0 | 0.1 | 0.2 | 0.1 | 0.1 | 0.2 | 0.1 |
| Motor Vehicles | 19.7 | 22.7 | 3.0 | 35.7 | 33.0 | −2.6 | 18.3 | 15.9 | −2.4 |
| Aircraft | 0.1 | 0.1 | −0.1 | 2.9 | 3.0 | 0.1 | 2.5 | 2.7 | 0.2 |
| Other Transport Equipment | 0.1 | 0.4 | 0.3 | 0.6 | 1.0 | 0.3 | 0.5 | 0.6 | 0.1 |
| Professional Goods | 3.0 | 4.0 | 1.0 | 0.9 | 1.1 | 0.3 | 3.2 | 3.6 | 0.4 |
| Other Manufacturing | 1.6 | 1.4 | −0.2 | 0.3 | 0.5 | 0.2 | 4.1 | 4.0 | −0.1 |

Source: Based on OECD, *Bilateral Trade Database.*

FIGURE 4

## MEXICO AND CANADA: TOP FIVE EXPORTS TO THE UNITED STATES, 1998

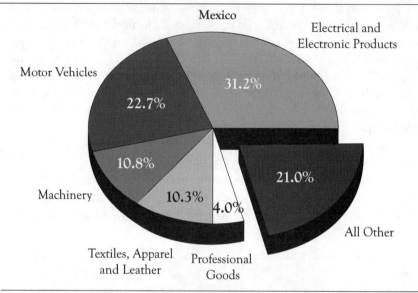

Mexico

Electrical and
Electronic Products

Motor Vehicles

31.2%

22.7%

10.8%

21.0%

Machinery

10.3%

4.0%

All Other

Textiles, Apparel
and Leather

Professional
Goods

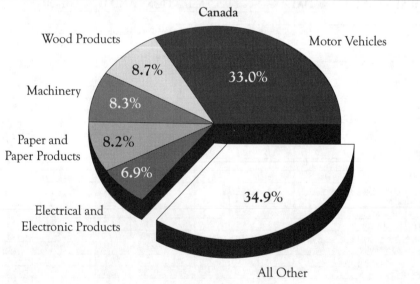

Canada

Wood Products

Motor Vehicles

8.7%

33.0%

Machinery

8.3%

Paper and
Paper Products

8.2%

6.9%

34.9%

Electrical and
Electronic Products

All Other

Note:   In Canada's case, top exports in terms of their contribution to export growth over the period
        1990-98 are slightly different from the top exports in terms of value: chemicals (excluding
        drugs) replace paper and paper products in the top five.

Source: Based on OECD, *Bilateral Trade Flows.*

Another way of examining export specialization is with the help of revealed comparative advantage (RCA).[7] The RCA is useful as a measure of how well a specific export is doing in capturing foreign markets. Here, it measures the competitiveness of a Mexican or Canadian product exported to the United States against the country's total U.S.-bound exports, as well as global U.S.-bound exports. So if a Mexican or Canadian industry has an RCA greater than 1.0, it has shown export specialization in that industry. The RCAs for industries in Mexico and Canada are shown in Figure 5.

It is interesting that not all of the two countries' top exports have high RCAs; in fact, the machinery exports of both countries have a low value, as do exports of Canadian electrical and electronic products. This means that global U.S.-bound exports in these areas are also very large. In only one industry do Mexico and Canada share a strongly positive RCA: motor vehicles.

It is also significant to note that Mexico has only two-thirds the number of industries with RCAs in the plus-one range as Canada — demonstrating, again, the more focussed and concentrated nature of Mexican exports. Mexico's strong RCAs are in electrical and electronic products, and motor vehicles; it has somewhat weaker RCAs in professional goods, textiles, non-metallic mineral products, and metal products. By comparison, Canada has generally high RCAs in transportation, resource-based industries, and chemicals.

## MEXICO AND CANADA: ARE THEIR EXPORT SPECIALIZATIONS BECOMING MORE SIMILAR?

ONE WAY TO LOOK FURTHER into whether Mexican and Canadian export specializations to the United States are adjusting gradually is to examine changes in the two countries' RCAs. Figure 5 shows that 1998 RCAs for Mexico and Canada are fairly complementary. They are above 1.0 in both countries for only two industries (metal products and motor vehicles).

However, Figure 6 clearly reveals that Mexico and Canada are increasing their RCAs in many of the same industries. Both show strong and growing RCAs in motor vehicles: this suggests some competition for the U.S. market in this industry. Both also show rising RCAs in textiles, professional goods and other transport equipment. In line with our previous findings, Canada has increasing RCAs in many more industries than Mexico. However, these are almost entirely confined to resource-based industries.

# FIGURE 5

## MEXICO AND CANADA: RCA

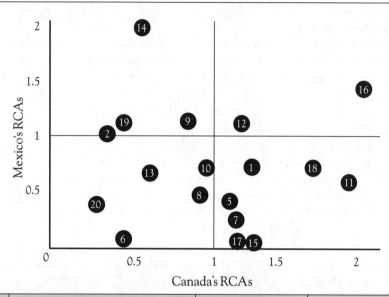

| | | Mexico | Canada |
|---|---|---|---|
| 1 | Food, Beverages and Tobacco | –0.21 | 0.35 |
| 2 | Textiles, Apparel and Leather | 0.48 | 0.21 |
| 3 | Wood Products and Furniture | –0.41 | 0.31 |
| 4 | Paper, Paper Products and Printing | –0.003 | –0.35 |
| 5 | Chemicals (excluding Drugs) | –0.33 | –0.01 |
| 6 | Drugs and Medicines | –0.06 | 0.13 |
| 7 | Petroleum Refineries and Products | –0.026 | 0.25 |
| 8 | Rubber and Plastic Products | –0.10 | 0.19 |
| 9 | Non-metallic Mineral Products | –0.54 | 0.12 |
| 10 | Iron and Steel | –0.13 | –0.13 |
| 11 | Non-ferrous Metals | –0.34 | –0.06 |
| 12 | Metal Products | –0.04 | 0.30 |
| 13 | Machinery (including Computers) | 0.10 | –0.01 |
| 14 | Electrical and Electronic Products | –0.55 | 0 |
| 15 | Shipbuilding and Repair | –0.05 | 0.09 |
| 16 | Motor Vehicles | 0.36 | 0.13 |
| 17 | Aircraft | –0.03 | –0.04 |
| 18 | Other Transport Equipment | 0.48 | 0.30 |
| 19 | Professional Goods | 0.18 | 0.04 |
| 20 | Other Manufacturing | –0.03 | 0.05 |

Note: Two industries excluded: 3 and 4 both have very high RCAs for Canada
Source: Based on OECD, *Bilateral Trade Flows*

# FIGURE 6

## MEXICO AND CANADA: CHANGES IN RCA

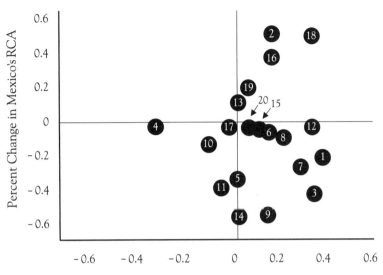

Percent Change in Canada's RCA

|    |                                    | Mexico | Canada |
|----|------------------------------------|--------|--------|
| 1  | Food, Beverages and Tobacco        | 0.35   | –0.21  |
| 2  | Textiles, Apparel and Leather      | 0.12   | 0.48   |
| 3  | Wood Products and Furniture        | 0.31   | –0.41  |
| 4  | Paper, Paper Products and Printing | –0.35  | –0.03  |
| 5  | Chemicals (excluding Drugs)        | –0.01  | –0.33  |
| 6  | Drugs and Medicines                | –0.13  | –0.06  |
| 7  | Petroleum Refineries and Products  | 0.25   | –0.26  |
| 8  | Rubber and Plastic Products        | 0.19   | –0.10  |
| 9  | Non-metallic Mineral Products      | 0.12   | –0.54  |
| 10 | Iron and Steel                     | –0.13  | –0.13  |
| 11 | Non-ferrous Metals                 | –0.06  | –0.34  |
| 12 | Metal Products                     | 0.30   | –0.04  |
| 13 | Machinery (including Computers)    | –0.01  | 0.10   |
| 14 | Electrical and Electronic Products | 0      | –0.55  |
| 15 | Shipbuilding and Repair            | 0.09   | –0.05  |
| 16 | Motor Vehicles                     | 0.13   | 0.36   |
| 17 | Aircraft                           | –0.04  | –0.03  |
| 18 | Other Transport Equipment          | 0.30   | 0.48   |
| 19 | Professional Goods                 | 0.04   | 0.18   |
| 20 | Other Manufacturing                | 0.05   | –0.03  |

Source: Based on OECD, *Bilateral Trade Flows*.

129

## ADDITIONAL FEATURES

### Export Intensities

Table 4 divides changes in the overall export intensities for Mexico and Canada into *within*-industry changes (individual industries are becoming more export-intensive) and *between*-industry changes (a shift in exports toward industries with higher export intensities). Plainly, the overall rise in U.S. export intensities for the two countries is largely due to an increase in the export intensities for individual industries. The Mexican results are much more extreme — Mexico actually saw a slight shift in its exports toward relatively less export-intensive industries, but it was more than compensated for by an increase in the export intensities of its individual industries. For example, the electrical and electronic products industry contributed almost half of the country's rise in export growth.

### TABLE 4

### MEXICO AND CANADA: CHANGES IN EXPORTS TO THE UNITED STATES AND THE CONTRIBUTION OF CHANGES TO INDUSTRY EXPORT INTENSITIES AND GROWTH

| All Manufacturing | Mexico | | | Canada | | |
|---|---|---|---|---|---|---|
| | Percent due to: | | | Percent due to: | | |
| | Export Growth | Changes in Industry Export Intensities | Shifts in Industry Output | Export Growth | Changes in Industry Export Intensities | Shifts in Industry Output |
| | 181.6% | 101.7% | 29.6% | 68.4% | 46.3% | 15.1% |
| Individual Industry Data, 1990-96 | Export Growth | Change in Export Intensity | Industry Growth | Export Growth | Change in Export Intensity | Industry Growth |
| Food, Beverages and Tobacco | 75.9 | 35.7 | 29.6 | 68.8 | 57.2 | 7.3 |
| Textiles, Apparel and Leather | 322.8 | 243.7 | 23.0 | 232.4 | 285.5 | −13.8 |
| Wood Products and Furniture | 143.5 | 141.5 | 0.8 | 137.4 | 79.1 | 32.6 |
| Paper, Paper Products and Printing | 86.6 | 75.1 | 6.6 | 23.2 | 19.4 | 3.1 |
| Chemicals (excluding Drugs) | 108.0 | 80.2 | 15.5 | 88.5 | 86.0 | 1.4 |
| Drugs and Medicines | 203.1 | 94.0 | 56.2 | 389.7 | 267.3 | 33.3 |
| Petroleum Refineries and Products | −1.9 | −2.5 | 0.5 | 32.3 | 37.2 | −3.5 |
| Rubber and Plastic Products | 147.2 | 88.1 | 31.4 | 107.5 | 68.0 | 23.6 |
| Non-metallic Mineral Products | 96.8 | 64.1 | 19.9 | 99.7 | 133.4 | −14.4 |
| Iron and Steel | 201.8 | 149.3 | 21.0 | 65.6 | 35.1 | 22.6 |
| Non-ferrous Metals | 29.8 | 6.9 | 21.4 | 46.4 | 38.5 | 5.7 |
| Metal Products | 151.9 | 113.3 | 18.1 | 114.0 | 126.0 | −5.3 |
| Machinery (including Computers) | 256.2 | 86.5 | 91.0 | 98.2 | 54.4 | 28.4 |
| Electrical and Electronic Products | 143.6 | 16.0 | 109.9 | 79.8 | 55.2 | 15.9 |
| Shipbuilding and Repair | 1,300.1 | 442.1 | 158.3 | 503.2 | 640.5 | −18.5 |
| Motor Vehicles | 274.1 | 94.9 | 91.9 | 56.3 | −0.9 | 57.8 |
| Aircraft | 9.8 | N/A | N/A | 38.9 | 14.3 | 21.5 |
| Other Transport Equipment | 330.2 | 433.4 | −19.4 | 87.9 | 44.5 | 30.1 |
| Professional Goods | 255.9 | 102.6 | 75.7 | 99.4 | 82.4 | 9.3 |
| Other Manufacturing | 180.6 | 103.3 | 38.0 | 140.7 | 105.1 | 17.4 |

Note: This breakdown of Mexico's and Canada's overall exports shows the relative importance of (1) the increased export intensity of the individual industries, and (2) shifts in national growth towards industries with high export intensities.

Source: Based on OECD, *Bilateral Trade Database* and *Structural Analysis Database*.

For Canada, *within*-industry improvements in export intensities were more muted, accounting for three-quarters of the overall increase in Canada's export orientation to the United States, while shifts to more export intensive industries accounted for the remaining quarter. The shift toward the more export intensive industries of motor vehicles, wood products and furniture, machinery and chemicals was also much more even.

## Moving Up the Value Chain

In Table 1, we described the rapid rise of Mexico's ranking within industry-defined U.S. import markets (by 1998, Mexico had advanced dramatically to be among the top three rankings in 11 industry-defined U.S. import markets; both Mexico and Canada were among the top three exporters in eight of those markets).

Does Mexico's climb to the top rungs of several U.S. import markets move it up the value chain, and will this change affect Canada's sector exports to the United States? Generally speaking, all countries would like to produce and export more value-laden and processed products, especially if their production requires higher amounts of domestic inputs involving more advanced activities requiring higher skills, or provides spin-off benefits that will accelerate the modernization and advancement of other industries and the overall economy.

Table 5 contrasts, in a very rudimentary way, the 1990 and 1996 levels of two key industry characteristics: average wage and capital intensity. (Rising values for these measures, and growing export shares in industries with high values for these measures, can be used to proxy the movement of exports up the quality spectrum of products offered on international markets.) These will be discussed at greater length in the fourth section. Here, we will address just one issue: are Mexico and Canada producing dissimilar goods in common industries, or at the very least, are they using very different mixes of capital and labour?

Table 5 shows that Mexican industries tend to have lower wages and capital/employee ratios[8] (exceptions for capital/employee ratios are in energy and in minerals and primary metals: the capital intensity of Mexico's machinery industry has risen quickly and has now slightly surpassed Canada's). Wages and the capital/employee ratio are also growing more slowly in Mexico. These industry characteristics underscore the general appropriateness of more labour-intensive techniques and manufacturing activities in Mexico, and the likely dissimilarity between manufactured goods from Mexico and Canada.

## TABLE 5

## CANADA AND MEXICO: INDUSTRY CHARACTERISTICS

| | Mexico | | | | Canada | | | |
|---|---|---|---|---|---|---|---|---|
| | Capital Expenditure per Employee* $'000 | | Wage Rates US$ | | Capital Expenditure per Employee* $'000 | | Wage Rates US$ | |
| | 1990 | 1996 | 1990 | 1996 | 1990 | 1996 | 1990 | 1996 |
| All Manufacturing | 10.3 | 14.7 | 5,006.2 | 5,058.6 | 15.9 | 22.0 | 31,872.9 | 33,396.7 |
| Food, Beverages and Tobacco | 14.4 | 20.6 | 4,031.0 | 4,551.4 | 27.4 | 33.3 | 29,600.7 | 29,617.3 |
| Textiles, Apparel and Leather | 5.7 | 6.3 | 3,489.5 | 3,011.8 | 7.1 | 7.5 | 20,279.3 | 21,925.1 |
| Wood Products and Furniture | 8.4 | 8.1 | 2,838.0 | 2,709.7 | 5.5 | 15.6 | 27,870.6 | 30,337.6 |
| Paper, Paper Products and Printing | 8.7 | 10.9 | 5,511.8 | 5,573.6 | 18.3 | 19.7 | 35,612.2 | 37,023.9 |
| Chemicals (excluding Drugs) | 20.8 | 31.4 | 8,937.2 | 10,786.1 | 44.5 | 58.3 | 38,408.9 | 39,735.0 |
| Drugs and Medicines | 18.3 | 33.7 | 9,702.1 | 13,356.0 | 57.3 | 57.0 | 36,064.0 | 38,229.3 |
| Petroleum Refineries and Products | 18.7 | 24.8 | 8,173.5 | 9,824.0 | 7.1 | 18.8 | 52,280.9 | 51,232.9 |
| Rubber and Plastic Products | 6.7 | 7.2 | 5,061.8 | 4,962.9 | 10.7 | 19.0 | 29,166.7 | 28,294.2 |
| Non-metallic Mineral Products | 14.6 | 23.5 | 5,419.7 | 5,437.4 | 19.3 | 18.7 | 32,501.2 | 33,116.3 |
| Iron and Steel | 26.7 | 72.3 | 10,307.9 | 10,423.9 | 3.4 | 17.0 | 45,836.3 | 48,058.3 |
| Non-ferrous Metals | 30.9 | 45.8 | 7,253.1 | 6,565.4 | 15.1 | 23.3 | 45,909.9 | 48,532.2 |
| Metal Products | 7.3 | 9.6 | 4,125.8 | 4,474.5 | 11.7 | 14.0 | 29,762.7 | 27,907.8 |
| Machinery (including Computers) | 6.2 | 16.1 | 5,443.7 | 6,076.2 | 11.6 | 16.0 | 31,136.3 | 32,677.5 |
| Electrical and Electronic Products | 4.1 | 4.7 | 4,993.2 | 5,047.4 | 16.2 | 24.4 | 32,426.7 | 40,223.4 |
| Shipbuilding and Repair | 2.3 | N/A | 8,493.3 | N/A | 2.1 | 13.2 | 36,838.0 | 35,748.0 |
| Motor Vehicles | 8.3 | 20.6 | 6,457.5 | 5,925.1 | 16.7 | 26.2 | 36,683.2 | 38,997.6 |
| Aircraft | N/A | N/A | N/A | N/A | 12.8 | 22.3 | 39,927.1 | 42,028.2 |
| Other Transport Equipment | 2.9 | 2.8 | 3,903.9 | 3,673.6 | 15.3 | 39.4 | 32,728.9 | 33,919.4 |
| Professional Goods | 3.3 | 5.2 | 4,748.9 | 4,785.2 | 9.3 | 17.1 | 25,638.0 | 27,966.7 |
| Other Manufacturing | 13.9 | 11.7 | 3,351.6 | 3,744.3 | 8.0 | 10.7 | 23,000.4 | 22,232.1 |

Note: *Estimated as value-added minus labour compensation.

Source: Based on OECD, *Structural Analysis Database*.

## Comparative Advantages: Build on the Traditional or Create New Ones?

Are Mexico and Canada increasing their exports on the basis of traditional comparative advantages or developing new ones? Table 6 shows the two countries' trade with the United States in terms of intraindustry and interindustry trade. There has been a rapid rise in intraindustry trade, especially in Mexico. In some ways, this rise reflects the increased integration of the three North American economies.

The large and growing importance of intraindustry trade in both Mexico and Canada suggests that the ability to exploit advantages like economies of scale, product differentiation, product mandates, and the development of new and better process and product features will figure prominently in the futures of both of these countries. Substantial intraindustry trade is also consistent with the transfer of technology between firms within an industry. Interindustry trade, however, is often associated with existing comparative advantages — plenty of natural resources, abundant relative labour or capital, or better technology.

## TABLE 6

## MEXICO AND CANADA: INTRAINDUSTRY TRADE

| | Mexico | | | Canada | | |
|---|---|---|---|---|---|---|
| | 1990 | 1998 | Change In Ratio 1990-98 | 1990 | 1998 | Change in Ratio 1990-98 |
| **All Manufacturing** | | | | | | |
| Food, Beverages and Tobacco | 92.3 | 86.1 | –5.9 | 87.6 | 89.6 | 1.6 |
| Textiles, Apparel and Leather | 89.8 | 77.0 | –5.5 | 63.7 | 91.3 | 8.7 |
| Wood Products and Furniture | 85.3 | 64.7 | –4.0 | 43.0 | 36.6 | –0.2 |
| Paper, Paper Products and Printing | 36.1 | 38.9 | 0.1 | 48.6 | 61.9 | 0.7 |
| Chemicals (excluding Drugs) | 54.3 | 44.6 | –0.4 | 87.7 | 85.3 | –1.4 |
| Drugs and Medicines | 25.6 | 41.5 | 0.4 | 33.9 | 58.4 | 0.9 |
| Petroleum Refineries and Products | 77.6 | 32.3 | –3.0 | 48.9 | 59.9 | 0.5 |
| Rubber and Plastic Products | 61.7 | 52.7 | –0.5 | 90.5 | 96.5 | 18.0 |
| Non-metallic Mineral Products | 67.0 | 64.2 | –0.2 | 76.5 | 91.2 | 7.1 |
| Iron and Steel | 81.3 | 93.7 | 10.5 | 88.8 | 96.7 | 21.4 |
| Non-ferrous Metals | 87.7 | 92.7 | 5.6 | 57.0 | 58.7 | 0.1 |
| Metal Products | 78.6 | 89.0 | 4.4 | 80.8 | 89.5 | 4.3 |
| Machinery (including Computers) | 64.6 | 96.3 | 24.2 | 61.6 | 67.0 | 0.4 |
| Electrical and Electronic Products | 80.8 | 83.8 | 1.0 | 70.8 | 66.4 | –0.5 |
| Shipbuilding and Repair | 14.7 | 7.6 | –0.1 | 74.2 | 94.4 | 13.8 |
| Motor Vehicles | 89.9 | 63.9 | –7.1 | 82.5 | 84.4 | 0.7 |
| Aircraft | N/A | N/A | N/A | 92.4 | 81.7 | –7.8 |
| Other Transport Equipment | 26.0 | 79.4 | 3.5 | 69.9 | 87.7 | 4.8 |
| Professional Goods | 80.3 | 81.5 | 0.3 | 42.6 | 48.1 | 0.2 |
| Other Manufacturing | 91.5 | 73.3 | –8.0 | 61.9 | 61.7 | 0.0 |

Note:   We begin by defining gross trade as the sum of exports and imports. Interindustry trade is the difference between exports and imports. Intraindustry trade is the difference between gross trade and interindustry trade (see Grubel and Lloyd, 1975).

Source: Based on OECD, *Bilateral Trade Database*.

Table 6 also shows that for Canada, intraindustry trade accounts for most of the trade in all but two industries (wood products and furniture, and professional goods). In addition, the importance of intraindustry trade has increased for most industries.

- Canadian industries with a high volume of intraindustry trade also have generally high export intensities: they include chemicals, metals (iron and steel, non-metallic minerals and metal products), motor vehicles, aircraft and other transport equipment. The export intensity of food and textiles is not high but is growing as producers increasingly turn to international markets, including the United States.

- Canadian industries that exhibit a high proportion of interindustry trade include a mixture of traditional export industries (wood, petroleum, and non-ferrous metals) and high tech or new economy industries (drugs and medicines, and professional goods). Canada's petroleum and wood industries are extremely strong exporters. Rising export intensities account for much of the export growth, especially for petroleum and non-ferrous metals.

While Mexico also demonstrates a high degree of intraindustry trade, there is a much wider variation between industries — from a low of 7.6 percent in ship-building to a high of 96.3 percent in machinery. Many with high export growth rates during the 1990s carry on a good deal of intraindustry trade; for many more, however, interindustry trade is increasing.

- In Mexico, the industries with a high proportion of intraindustry trade comprise a mixture of relatively high tech industries (electrical and electronic products, machinery and professional goods) plus metals (iron and steel, non-ferrous metals, and metal products) and food. With the exception of food, these industries exhibit above-average export intensities and above-average value-added growth rates.

- Mexican industries with high interindustry trade (except for the small but fast-growing drugs and medicines industry) can be characterized as low-export-intensity, low-growth industries.

## TABLE 7

## MEXICO AND CANADA: MANUFACTURING TRADE BALANCES WITH THE UNITED STATES

| | Mexico | | Canada | |
|---|---|---|---|---|
| | 1998 US$ Billion | Percent Change | 1998 US$ Billion | Percent Change |
| All Manufacturing | 10.5 | –517.6 | 4.6 | –37.6 |
| Food, Beverages and Tobacco | –0.7 | 344.2 | 1.2 | 74.1 |
| Textiles, Apparel and Leather | 3.2 | 1,313.8 | –0.6 | –24.5 |
| Wood Products and Furniture | 1.3 | 603.0 | 10.1 | 193.1 |
| Paper, Paper Products and Printing | –1.9 | 125.5 | 6.7 | 2.8 |
| Chemicals (excluding Drugs) | –5.2 | 231.8 | –3.4 | 149.9 |
| Drugs and Medicines | –0.2 | 107.8 | –0.9 | 166.5 |
| Petroleum Refineries and Products | –1.4 | 410.8 | 1.7 | –17.3 |
| Rubber and Plastic Products | –2.1 | 384.6 | –0.3 | –11.4 |
| Non-metallic Mineral Products | 0.7 | 175.3 | –0.3 | –28.9 |
| Iron and Steel | 0.2 | –183.2 | 0.2 | –46.7 |
| Non-ferrous Metals | –0.2 | –237.5 | 3.5 | 43.4 |
| Metal Products | –0.7 | 77.8 | –1.2 | 35.1 |
| Machinery (including computers) | –0.7 | –61.1 | –12.1 | 81.2 |
| Electrical and Electronic Products | 7.2 | 192.3 | –10.3 | 161.2 |
| Shipbuilding and Repair | –0.1 | 227.9 | 0.0 | –150.1 |
| Motor Vehicles | 10.0 | 1,171.4 | 13.2 | 59.3 |
| Aircraft | –0.7 | 62.3 | 1.4 | 328.2 |
| Other Transport Equipment | 0.1 | –189.6 | 0.3 | 34.6 |
| Professional Goods | 1.0 | –427.7 | –3.6 | 96.3 |
| Other Manufacturing | 0.5 | 826.9 | –1.0 | 193.6 |

Source: Based on OECD, *Bilateral Trade Database*.

Table 7 reveals that Mexico's largest positive trade balances are in industries characterized by intraindustry trade (motor vehicles, electrical and electronic products, and textiles and apparel). Such industries rely on considerable imports of parts and, in the case of apparel, textiles from the United States. By contrast, Canada's largest positive trade balances in manufacturing involve resource-based industries characterized by interindustry trade. A major exception is motor vehicles, which demonstrates a considerable volume of intraindustry trade (bilateral flows in parts and vehicles).

A number of facts in this section have demonstrated that there is major growth in exports from both Mexico and Canada to the United States. What is behind this growth?

## FACTORS DRIVING EXPORTS FROM MEXICO AND CANADA: THE CONTRIBUTION OF RISING U.S. IMPORT DEMAND

WHAT ARE THE KEY FACTORS BEHIND THE INCREASE in exports from Mexico and Canada to the United States? The next two sections examine the specific drivers behind this growth. This section examines the importance of rising U.S. import demand (and, for Canada, the importance of U.S. *regional* import demand.)[9] It also considers the *structure* of U.S. import demand and improvements in the export competitiveness of both Mexico and Canada, demonstrated when the export growth of either country outperforms U.S. import growth and gives that country a larger share of the U.S. import market. The following section takes a more detailed look at some *specific* factors related to the export competitiveness of the two countries.

### RISING U.S. IMPORT DEMAND

THE 1990S WERE A PERIOD OF unprecedented prosperity in the United States. This was reflected in rising import demand, especially for electrical and electronic products, and machinery. U.S. demand for automobiles has also been very robust over the last 10 years. This has benefited exports not only from Mexico and Canada, but from the rest of the world (ROW) as well (Table 8). While rising U.S. import demand is not the whole story, it provides an important starting point for understanding the growth of Mexican and Canadian exports to the United States.

We begin with a simple shift-share decomposition of U.S.-based exports for the two countries at the industry level which will underscore its significance.[10]

## TABLE 8

## U.S. IMPORTS FROM MEXICO, CANADA AND THE ROW (US$ BILLIONS, 1998)

| | Total | Mexico | Canada | ROW |
|---|---|---|---|---|
| **All Manufacturing** | 826.0 | 82.7 | 148.3 | 595.0 |
| Food, Beverages and Tobacco | 29.7 | 2.1 | 6.5 | 21.1 |
| Textiles, Apparel and Leather | 83.7 | 8.6 | 3.0 | 72.1 |
| Wood Products and Furniture | 25.6 | 2.5 | 13.0 | 10.2 |
| Paper, Paper Products and Printing | 19.5 | 0.6 | 12.1 | 6.7 |
| Chemicals (excluding Drugs) | 52.2 | 2.1 | 9.9 | 40.1 |
| Drugs and Medicines | 10.8 | 0.1 | 0.6 | 10.1 |
| Petroleum Refineries and Products | 14.6 | 0.3 | 2.9 | 11.4 |
| Rubber and Plastic Products | 24.9 | 1.2 | 3.8 | 19.9 |
| Non-metallic Mineral Products | 11.4 | 1.3 | 1.6 | 8.6 |
| Iron and Steel | 21.7 | 1.5 | 3.5 | 16.7 |
| Non-ferrous Metals | 17.7 | 1.0 | 6.0 | 10.7 |
| Metal Products | 24.5 | 2.7 | 5.1 | 16.7 |
| Machinery (including computers) | 136.6 | 9.0 | 12.3 | 115.3 |
| Electrical and Electronic Products | 129.8 | 25.9 | 10.2 | 93.7 |
| Shipbuilding and Repair | 1.7 | 0.0 | 0.4 | 1.3 |
| Motor Vehicles | 131.4 | 18.9 | 49.1 | 63.5 |
| Aircraft | 22.1 | 0.1 | 4.4 | 17.6 |
| Other Transport Equipment | 4.9 | 0.3 | 1.4 | 3.1 |
| Professional Goods | 30.0 | 3.3 | 1.7 | 25.0 |
| Other Manufacturing | 33.2 | 1.2 | 0.8 | 31.2 |

Source: Based on OECD, *Bilateral Trade Database*.

### A Simple Shift-share Decomposition

The growth in manufacturing exports from Mexico and Canada to the United States can be examined for individual industries in terms of the following expression:

$$\Delta E_{i,\text{Mexico or Canada}} = s_i \left( \Delta E_{i,\text{World}} \right) + \left( \Delta s_i \right) E_{i,\text{World}}$$

where $\Delta E_i$ is the growth in either Mexico's or Canada's exports to the United States from industry $i$, $E_{i,\text{World}}$ is total exports for industry $i$ from all countries to the United States, and $s_i$ is a share coefficient on U.S.-bound Mexican or Canadian exports for industry $i$ in relation to those from the ROW. The first term, often called the demand or share effect, shows Mexico's or Canada's exports in relation to the growth in U.S. import demand (the U.S. demand for world exports). The second term captures the change in performance between Mexico's or Canada's U.S.-bound exports in relation to those from the ROW: that is, a shift or change-in-share effect.[11] For this analysis, we draw on U.S. *import* data in order to provide consistent cross-country measures of exports to the United States from Mexico, Canada and the ROW. The data are from the OECD Bilateral Trade Database (OECD 2000) which uses the same 20 industries as those examined in the second section above. The results are shown in Table 9.

TABLE 9

MEXICO AND CANADA: DECOMPOSITION OF GAINS IN EXPORTS TO
THE UNITES STATES, 1990-98 (PERCENT)

| | Mexico | | | Canada | | |
|---|---|---|---|---|---|---|
| | U.S. Import Demand (1) | Competitiveness (2) | (1)/(2)* | U.S. Import Demand (1) | Competitiveness (2) | (1)/(2)* |
| All Manufacturing | 32.7 | 67.3 | 0.5 | 102.7 | −2.7 | −37.9 |
| Food, Beverages and Tobacco | 46.2 | 53.8 | 0.9 | 54.7 | 45.3 | 1.2 |
| Textiles, Apparel and Leather | 14.9 | 85.1 | 0.2 | 25.5 | 74.5 | 0.3 |
| Wood Products and Furniture | 55.1 | 44.9 | 1.2 | 81.8 | 18.2 | 4.5 |
| Paper, Paper Products and Printing | 36.5 | 63.5 | 0.6 | 128.4 | −28.4 | −4.5 |
| Chemicals (excluding Drugs) | 84.5 | 15.5 | 5.4 | 104.0 | −4.0 | −26.2 |
| Drugs and Medicines | 102.9 | −2.9 | −35.6 | 42.3 | 57.7 | 0.7 |
| Petroleum Refineries and Products | −123.7 | 23.7 | −5.2 | −59.8 | −40.2 | 1.5 |
| Rubber and Plastic Products | 42.6 | 57.4 | 0.7 | 64.7 | 35.3 | 1.8 |
| Non-metallic Mineral Products | 58.0 | 42.0 | 1.4 | 73.0 | 27.0 | 2.7 |
| Iron and Steel | 41.6 | 58.4 | 0.7 | 138.4 | −38.4 | −3.6 |
| Non-ferrous Metals | 65.7 | 34.3 | 1.9 | 109.8 | −9.8 | −11.2 |
| Metal Products | 34.3 | 65.7 | 0.5 | 58.9 | 41.1 | 1.4 |
| Machinery (including Computers) | 26.3 | 73.7 | 0.4 | 106.4 | −6.4 | −16.6 |
| Electrical and Electronic Products | 46.5 | 53.5 | 0.9 | 104.0 | −4.0 | −25.7 |
| Shipbuilding and Repair | 30,688.3 | −30,588.3 | −1.0 | 88.8 | 11.2 | 8.0 |
| Motor Vehicles | 22.4 | 77.6 | 0.3 | 89.5 | 10.5 | 8.6 |
| Aircraft | 104.2 | −4.2 | −24.6 | 110.6 | −10.6 | −10.4 |
| Other Transport Equipment | 8.3 | 91.7 | 0.1 | 69.7 | 30.3 | 2.3 |
| Professional Goods | 26.0 | 74.0 | 0.4 | 78.6 | 21.4 | 3.7 |
| Other Manufacturing | 36.4 | 63.6 | 0.6 | 46.2 | 53.8 | 0.9 |

Note: * This shift-share breakdown of overall export gains shows the relative importance of 1) rising U.S. import demand and 2) a competitiveness effect. Note that the former represents
what the industry's growth in exports would have been for each country had it maintained
its export share, while the latter represents any additional export growth (+ or −).

Source: Based on OECD, *Bilateral Trade Database*.

A salient finding from Table 9 is that all of Canada's growth in exports to
the United States can be accounted for by rising U.S. import demand. In fact,
Canada's rapid export growth has barely kept up with U.S. import growth — a
conclusion substantiated by Figure 7, which shows how Canada's share of U.S.
imports has remained relatively constant over the past two decades, even falling off somewhat from the early 1980s. Canada's change-in-share for U.S.-
bound exports of electrical and electronic products, machinery, aircraft, chemicals and the two important resource-based exports, paper and petroleum, was
actually negative during the 1990-98 period. The only two industry exports
whose share of the U.S. import market rose were food and textiles.

FIGURE 7

MEXICO AND CANADA: SHARE OF U.S. MANUFACTURING IMPORTS

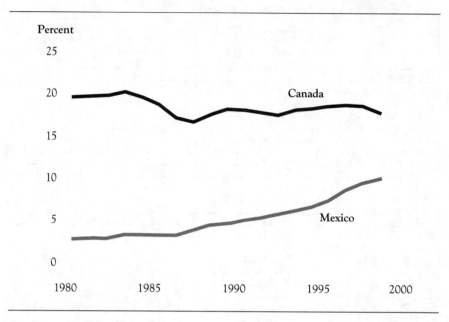

Source: Based on OECD, *Bilateral Trade Flows.*

Unlike Canada's, Mexico's exports have grown much faster than what can be accounted for by rising U.S. import demand alone — which was, nevertheless, a significant factor in the growth of exports like machinery, electrical and electronic products, and motor vehicles. These also benefited from greater export competitiveness, however, as their growth far exceeded that associated with rising U.S. import demand. The same was true for Mexican food, textiles, paper, rubber and plastics, and professional goods. The few industries where U.S. import demand was the predominant factor included wood, chemicals, drugs and medicines, and aircraft.

The bottom line for Canada is that there is nothing remarkable about the country's export growth, which has been *almost entirely* driven by increased U.S. demand. It appears that the exports of many Canadian industries that might be considered high tech, such as electrical and electronic products and machinery, are being carried along by the current buoyancy of U.S. import markets. Industries in which Canada has strong resource advantages are actually going through rather difficult times, once the growth in U.S. import demand is taken into account. That is, despite the growth in their U.S.-bound exports, their share of the U.S. import market has actually declined. Mexico enjoys precisely the opposite situation, one that saw the share of its major exports to U.S. markets increase substantially between 1990 and 1998. This finding underscores the need for the additional analysis of factors affecting competitiveness in the fourth section.

## Mexico and Canada: Dynamic Shift-share Analysis for the Top Five Exports

Most shift-share analyses are comparatively static in that they consider changes over the course of the whole time period under study.[12] However, we can also consider the annual changes in the size of U.S. markets and exports from Mexico and Canada for the purpose of identifying trends. The aim of this analysis is to discover whether there are any patterns in the profiles of the change in share effects over time.[13]

The results over time for all industries are shown in Tables 10A, B, C and D. The aggregate change-in-share effects are presented visually in Figure 8. Three key conclusions emerge:

1. Mexico's competitiveness effect is strong throughout the period; however, an upward trend begins in 1994, continues through to 1996, and then tapers off. This may reflect the one-time boost to competitiveness that resulted from the combined effects of the NAFTA and Mexico's peso crisis of 1994. This trend is reflected in the four high tech industries that have been important to Mexico's growth in exports to the United States: machinery, electronics, motor vehicles and professional goods.

2. Canada shows signs of greater competitiveness from 1991 to 1996, but then its competitiveness begins to decline again in 1997 and 1998. During that period, Canada saw a steady depreciation in its currency in relation to the United States, while it also moved slowly out of the recession of the early 1990s. The reduced competitiveness of 1997 and 1998 appears to have been driven largely by developments in Canada's resource-based industries and may be linked to reduced resource prices that resulted from economic difficulties in Asia during that time.

3. The size of the 1991 competitiveness effect stands out as positive for Mexico and negative for Canada. In large part this is a result of declining overall U.S. imports in that year, which exaggerate the impact of the shift-share analysis.

TABLE 10A

DECOMPOSITION OF MEXICO'S GAINS IN EXPORTS TO THE UNITED STATES:
ANNUAL CHANGES
SHARE OR INCOME EFFECT (PERCENT)

| | 1991 | 1992 | 1993 | 1994 | 1995 | 1996 | 1997 | 1998 |
|---|---|---|---|---|---|---|---|---|
| All Manufacturing | −6 | 53 | 60 | 56 | 49 | 25 | 41 | 63 |
| Food, Beverages and Tobacco | −33 | 324 | 10 | 29 | 25 | 73 | 35 | 55 |
| Textiles, Apparel and Leather | 11 | 56 | 48 | 36 | 15 | 14 | 29 | 51 |
| Wood Products and Furniture | −24 | 96 | 211 | 104 | 57 | 52 | 33 | 93 |
| Paper, Paper Products and Printing | −40 | 9 | 45 | 27 | 41 | −158 | −13 | 64 |
| Chemicals (excluding Drugs) | 84 | 90 | 2,794 | 42 | 72 | 200 | 112 | 257 |
| Drugs and Medicines | 65 | 38 | 114 | 81 | 188 | 91 | 143 | 122 |
| Petroleum Refineries and Products | −80 | −85 | −1 | 2 | −80 | 227 | −18 | −322 |
| Rubber and Plastic Products | 16 | 174 | 62 | 46 | 53 | 35 | 25 | 107 |
| Non-metallic Mineral Products | −252 | 71 | 104 | 70 | 114 | 30 | 50 | 85 |
| Iron and Steel | −53 | 65 | 31 | 63 | 6 | 70 | −6 | 383 |
| Non-ferrous Metals | −38 | 3 | 13 | 523 | 35 | −23 | 125 | 22 |
| Metal Products | −46 | 100 | 46 | 81 | 70 | 26 | 23 | 67 |
| Machinery (including Computers) | 9 | 50 | 133 | 44 | 110 | 14 | 28 | 44 |
| Electrical and Electronic Products | 74 | 66 | 85 | 72 | 143 | 3 | 29 | 36 |
| Shipbuilding and Repair | −2 | 25 | 603 | −128 | 61 | 305 | −225 | 30 |
| Motor Vehicles | −21 | 31 | 58 | 65 | 15 | 11 | 83 | 98 |
| Aircraft | 114 | 17 | −449 | 56 | −224 | 35 | 92 | 77 |
| Other Transport Equipment | 64 | 29 | 12 | 100 | 28 | −17 | 5 | 18 |
| Professional Goods | 49 | 38 | 33 | 40 | 87 | 44 | 64 | 34 |
| Other Manufacturing | −7 | 95 | 67 | 24 | 25 | 56 | 154 | 85 |

Source: Based on OECD, *Bilateral Trade Database.*

TABLE 10B

DECOMPOSITION OF CANADA'S GAINS IN EXPORTS TO THE UNITED STATES:
ANNUAL CHANGES
SHARE OR INCOME EFFECT (PERCENT)

| | 1991 | 1992 | 1993 | 1994 | 1995 | 1996 | 1997 | 1998 |
|---|---|---|---|---|---|---|---|---|
| All Manufacturing | −24 | 121 | −76 | 93 | 89 | 80 | 123 | 155 |
| Food, Beverages and Tobacco | −13 | 67 | 6 | −863 | 78 | −75 | 37 | 88 |
| Textiles, Apparel and Leather | 18 | 48 | 34 | 34 | 33 | −21 | 55 | 83 |
| Wood Products and Furniture | −70 | 68 | 68 | −89 | −1,599 | −70 | 97 | 215 |
| Paper, Paper Products and Printing | −98 | 103 | 191 | 115 | 89 | 89 | −60 | 169 |
| Chemicals (excluding Drugs) | 340 | 91 | 68 | 78 | 84 | −144 | 108 | 326 |
| Drugs and Medicines | 105 | 37 | 68 | 23 | 100 | −147 | 45 | −2,162 |
| Petroleum Refineries and Products | −688 | −69 | −7 | −27 | −60 | −116 | −109 | −50 |
| Rubber and Plastic Products | 99 | 89 | 63 | 52 | 83 | −61 | 48 | 123 |
| Non-metallic Mineral Products | −111 | 142 | 37 | 95 | 61 | −46 | 104 | 212 |
| Iron and Steel | −111 | 5 | 54 | 583 | 21 | −366 | −70 | 1,652 |
| Non-ferrous Metals | −168 | 20 | −2,945 | 95 | 93 | 146 | 127 | 162 |
| Metal Products | −65 | 132 | 61 | 60 | 72 | −39 | 72 | 86 |
| Machinery (including Computers) | 36 | 284 | 116 | 55 | 88 | −119 | 143 | 94 |
| Electrical and Electronic Products | 61 | 530 | 477 | 134 | 109 | −2 | 65 | 64 |
| Shipbuilding and Repair | −60 | 45 | 232 | −36 | 17 | −49 | −42 | 124 |
| Motor Vehicles | −98 | 62 | 63 | 108 | 98 | −94 | 100 | 155 |
| Aircraft | 228 | 76 | −103 | 27 | −53 | −78 | 188 | 149 |
| Other Transport Equipment | 31 | 355 | 63 | 23 | 142 | 98 | 76 | 63 |
| Professional Goods | 111 | 73 | 327 | 49 | 208 | −42 | 82 | 81 |
| Other Manufacturing | −12 | 86 | 66 | 30 | 36 | −53 | 162 | 92 |

Source: Based on OECD, *Bilateral Trade Database.*

## TABLE 10C
### DECOMPOSITION OF MEXICO'S GAINS IN EXPORTS TO THE UNITED STATES: ANNUAL CHANGES
SHIFT OR COMPETITIVENESS EFFECT (PERCENT)

| | 1991 | 1992 | 1993 | 1994 | 1995 | 1996 | 1997 | 1998 |
|---|---|---|---|---|---|---|---|---|
| **All Manufacturing** | 106 | 47 | 40 | 44 | 51 | 75 | 59 | 37 |
| Food, Beverages and Tobacco | −67 | −224 | 90 | 71 | 75 | 27 | 65 | 45 |
| Textiles, Apparel and Leather | 89 | 44 | 52 | 64 | 85 | 86 | 71 | 49 |
| Wood Products and Furniture | 124 | 4 | −111 | −4 | 43 | 48 | 67 | 7 |
| Paper, Paper Products and Printing | −60 | 91 | −145 | 73 | 59 | 58 | 113 | 36 |
| Chemicals (excluding Drugs) | 16 | 10 | −2,894 | 58 | 28 | −100 | −12 | −157 |
| Drugs and Medicines | 35 | 62 | −214 | 19 | −88 | 9 | −43 | −22 |
| Petroleum Refineries and Products | −20 | 185 | 101 | −102 | −20 | −127 | −82 | 422 |
| Rubber and Plastic Products | 84 | −74 | 38 | 54 | 47 | 65 | 75 | −7 |
| Non-metallic Mineral Products | 152 | 29 | −4 | 30 | −14 | 70 | 50 | 15 |
| Iron and Steel | −47 | 35 | 69 | 37 | 94 | 30 | 106 | −483 |
| Non-ferrous Metals | −62 | 97 | 87 | −423 | 65 | −77 | −25 | 78 |
| Metal Products | 146 | 0 | 54 | 19 | 30 | 74 | 77 | 33 |
| Machinery (including Computers) | 91 | 50 | −33 | 56 | −10 | 86 | 72 | 56 |
| Electrical and Electronic Products | 26 | 34 | 15 | 28 | −43 | 97 | 71 | 64 |
| Shipbuilding and Repair | 102 | 75 | −503 | 228 | 39 | −405 | 125 | −130 |
| Motor Vehicles | 121 | 69 | 42 | 35 | 85 | 89 | 17 | 2 |
| Aircraft | −14 | −117 | 549 | 44 | 124 | 65 | 8 | 23 |
| Other Transport Equipment | 36 | 71 | 88 | −200 | 72 | 117 | 95 | 82 |
| Professional Goods | 51 | 62 | 67 | 60 | 13 | 56 | 36 | 66 |
| Other Manufacturing | 107 | 5 | 33 | 76 | 75 | 44 | −54 | 15 |

Source: Based on OECD, *Bilateral Trade Database*.

## TABLE 10D
### DECOMPOSITION OF CANADA'S GAINS IN EXPORTS TO THE UNITED STATES: ANNUAL CHANGES
SHIFT OR COMPETITIVENESS EFFECT (PERCENT)

| | 1991 | 1992 | 1993 | 1994 | 1995 | 1996 | 1997 | 1998 |
|---|---|---|---|---|---|---|---|---|
| **All Manufacturing** | −76 | −21 | −24 | 7 | 11 | 20 | −23 | −55 |
| Food, Beverages and Tobacco | 113 | 33 | 94 | 963 | 22 | −25 | 63 | 12 |
| Textiles, Apparel and Leather | 82 | 52 | 66 | 66 | 67 | −79 | 45 | 17 |
| Wood Products and Furniture | −30 | 32 | 32 | −11 | 1,499 | −30 | 3 | −115 |
| Paper, Paper Products and Printing | −2 | −203 | −91 | −15 | 11 | 11 | −40 | −69 |
| Chemicals (excluding Drugs) | −240 | 9 | 32 | 22 | 16 | 44 | −8 | −226 |
| Drugs and Medicines | −5 | 63 | 32 | 77 | 0 | 47 | 55 | 2,262 |
| Petroleum Refineries and Products | 588 | −31 | 107 | 127 | 160 | 16 | 9 | −50 |
| Rubber and Plastic Products | 1 | 11 | 37 | 48 | 17 | −39 | 52 | −23 |
| Non-metallic Mineral Products | 11 | −42 | 63 | 5 | 39 | −54 | −4 | −112 |
| Iron and Steel | 11 | 95 | 46 | −483 | 79 | 266 | −30 | −1,552 |
| Non-ferrous Metals | 68 | 80 | 2,845 | 5 | 7 | −46 | −27 | −262 |
| Metal Products | −35 | −32 | 39 | 40 | 28 | −61 | 28 | 14 |
| Machinery (including Computers) | 64 | −184 | −16 | 45 | 12 | 219 | −43 | 6 |
| Electrical and Electronic Products | 39 | −430 | −577 | −34 | −9 | −98 | 35 | 36 |
| Shipbuilding and Repair | −40 | 55 | −132 | 136 | 83 | −51 | −58 | −224 |
| Motor Vehicles | −2 | 38 | 37 | −8 | 2 | −6 | 0 | −55 |
| Aircraft | −128 | −176 | 3 | 73 | 153 | −22 | −88 | −49 |
| Other Transport Equipment | −131 | −455 | 37 | 77 | −42 | −198 | −176 | 37 |
| Professional Goods | −11 | 27 | −227 | 51 | −108 | −58 | 18 | 19 |
| Other Manufacturing | 112 | 14 | 34 | 70 | 64 | −47 | −62 | 8 |

Source: Based on OECD, *Bilateral Trade Database*.

## A Further Shift-share Decomposition: Export Structure

How important is the "structure" of the two countries' exports? The notion that the structure of a country's exports affects its total export growth alludes to the "favourability" of a country's export specializations: for example, whether its export concentration is in areas where U.S. import demand is fast-growing (not to any dynamic changes in the country's export structure, which was discussed briefly in the second section).

### FIGURE 8

### MEXICO AND CANADA: EXPORT COMPETITIVENESS OR SHIFT EFFECT, 1991-98

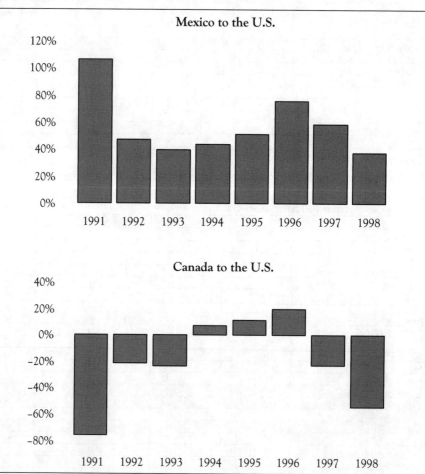

Source: Based on OECD, *Bilateral Trade Flows.*

To isolate the importance of export structure, we will perform a further decomposition of export growth for Mexico and Canada. First, we will use an additional notation:

$a_i$,                   Proportion of U.S. imports accounted for by imports of industry i

Then, using the Mexican example, instead of our earlier expression $\Delta E_{i,Mexico} = S_{i,Mexico} (\Delta E_{i,World}) + (\Delta S_{i,Mexico}) E_{i,World}$, we will have

$$E_{i,Mexico} = \quad S_{i,Mexico}\, a_i,\, \Delta E_{i,World} \qquad \text{U.S. import demand (or share) effect}$$

$$+ \; S_{i,Mexico}\, a_i\, E_{i,World} \qquad \text{Export structure effect}$$

$$+ \; \Delta S_{i,Mexico}\, a_i\, E_{i,World} \qquad \text{Competitiveness effect}$$

Where:

- *Export structure effect*: On the one hand, if Mexico or Canada has a favourable proportion of its industry exports in fast-growing U.S. industry-defined import markets, and a smaller proportion of industry exports in slower-growing markets, its export structure will have a positive impact on export growth. On the other hand, if the country's exports are dominated by relatively slow-growing industries or if it has a dearth of fast-growing ones, the export structure of either Mexico or Canada will have an unfavourable impact on export growth.

- *Competitiveness effect*: As before, if either country's rate of export growth exceeds that of the U.S. import market, the effect is positive and will denote that Mexico or Canada has a competitive advantage in that industry-defined U.S. import market. In other words, the effect is positive if Mexico or Canada specializes in exports from industries where the particular country enjoys an export competitive advantage, or produces few of the exports for which it has no such advantage.

This analysis drew on data from the OECD Bilateral Trade Database (OECD 2000). The results are shown in Tables 11A and B.

## TABLE 11A

### SHIFT-SHARE SUMMARY OF MEXICO'S GAINS IN EXPORTS TO THE UNITED STATES, 1990-98 (PERCENT)

|  | U.S. Import Demand Effect (1) | Export Structure Effect (2) | Competitiveness Effect (3) |
|---|---|---|---|
| All Manufacturing | 61.7 | –15.4 | 53.8 |
| Food, Beverages and Tobacco | 15.3 | –0.4 | 85.1 |
| Textiles, Apparel and Leather | 41.9 | 13.2 | 44.9 |
| Wood Products and Furniture | 51.4 | –14.8 | 63.5 |
| Paper, Paper Products and Printing | 78.1 | 6.4 | 15.5 |
| Chemicals (excluding Drugs) | 43.4 | 59.5 | –2.9 |
| Drugs and Medicines | 358.3 | –234.6 | –23.7 |
| Petroleum Refineries and Products | 40.1 | 2.5 | 57.4 |
| Rubber and Plastic Products | 57.9 | 0.2 | 42.0 |
| Non-metallic Mineral Products | 41.2 | 0.4 | 58.4 |
| Iron and Steel | 83.7 | –18.1 | 34.3 |
| Non-ferrous Metals | 32.2 | 2.2 | 65.7 |
| Metal Products | 21.1 | 5.3 | 73.7 |
| Machinery (including Computers) | 40.7 | 5.8 | 53.5 |
| Electrical and Electronic Products | 18,624.7 | 12,063.6 | –30,588.3 |
| Shipbuilding and Repair | 26.1 | –3.8 | 77.6 |
| Motor Vehicles | 97.5 | 6.7 | –4.2 |
| Aircraft | 6.7 | 1.6 | 91.7 |
| Other Transport Equipment | 22.8 | 3.2 | 74.0 |
| Professional Goods | 37.4 | –1.0 | 63.6 |
| Other Manufacturing | 32.7 | 0.0 | 67.3 |

Note:   A breakdown of overall export gains to show the relative importance of 1) rising U.S. import demand, 2) export structure effect and 3) competitiveness effect. Rising import demand is measured differently from that in Tables 10A to D, insofar as it shows how exports from Mexico's or Canada's 'i' industries would change if they grew at the same rate and represented the same percentage of total exports in the U.S. import market.

Source: Based on OECD, *Bilateral Trade Database*.

Canada does benefit from a fairly favourable export structure. Industry exports that are assisted include all three transportation exports (motor vehicles, aircraft and other transport equipment), as well as chemicals and certain resource-based industry exports (wood products and furniture, paper and paper products, iron and steel, and non-ferrous metals). However, the demand effect remains by far the most important one, even in key export industries. The results underline the weaker role played by the competitiveness effect — indeed, for many industries, including machinery, electrical and electronic products, and paper and paper products, this effect is negative.

TABLE 11B

SHIFT-SHARE SUMMARY OF CANADA'S GAINS IN EXPORTS TO THE
UNITED STATES, 1990-98 (PERCENT)

| | U.S. Import Demand Effect (1) | Export Structure Effect (2) | Competitiveness Effect (3) |
|---|---|---|---|
| All Manufacturing | 102.7 | 0.0 | –2.7 |
| Food, Beverages and Tobacco | 73.0 | –18.3 | 45.3 |
| Textiles, Apparel and Leather | 26.2 | –0.6 | 74.5 |
| Wood Products and Furniture | 62.2 | 19.6 | 18.2 |
| Paper, Paper Products and Printing | 180.5 | –52.1 | –28.4 |
| Chemicals (excluding Drugs) | 96.1 | 7.9 | -4.0 |
| Drugs and Medicines | 17.8 | 24.5 | 57.7 |
| Petroleum Refineries and Products | 173.2 | –113.4 | 40.2 |
| Rubber and Plastic Products | 60.9 | 3.8 | 35.3 |
| Non-metallic Mineral Products | 72.8 | 0.2 | 27.0 |
| Iron and Steel | 137.1 | 1.3 | –38.4 |
| Non-ferrous Metals | 140.1 | –30.2 | –9.8 |
| Metal Products | 55.2 | 3.7 | 41.1 |
| Machinery (including Computers) | 85.2 | 21.2 | –6.4 |
| Electrical and Electronic Products | 91.1 | 13.0 | –4.0 |
| Shipbuilding and Repair | 53.9 | 34.9 | 11.2 |
| Motor Vehicles | 104.6 | –15.1 | 10.5 |
| Aircraft | 103.5 | 7.2 | –10.6 |
| Other Transport Equipment | 56.0 | 13.7 | 30.3 |
| Professional Goods | 68.9 | 9.7 | 21.4 |
| Other Manufacturing | 47.5 | –1.3 | 53.8 |

Note: A breakdown of overall export gains to show the relative importance of 1) rising U.S. import demand, 2) export structure effect, and 3) competitiveness effect. Rising import demand is measured differently from that in Tables 10A to D, insofar as it shows how exports from Mexico's or Canada's 'i' industries would change if they grew at the same rate and represented the same percentage of total exports in the U.S. import market.

Source: Based on OECD, *Bilateral Trade Database*.

For Mexico, the competitiveness effect is still the major one — generally much greater than the demand effect. This is particularly true for Mexico's key exports of textiles and apparel, machinery, motor vehicles, professional goods, and electrical and electronic products. But it is also true for food and beverages, paper and paper products, rubber and plastics, iron and steel, metal products and other transport equipment. Mexico does not benefit from a favourable export structure effect, but its competitiveness effect more than compensates for this negative factor.

## FIGURE 9

## GROWTH IN GROSS STATE PRODUCT BY U.S. REGION, 1994-99

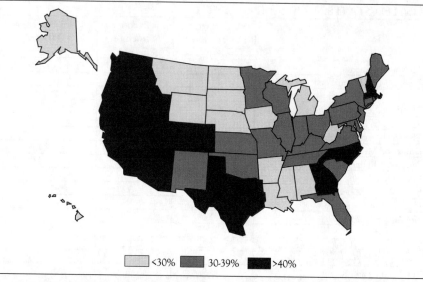

<30%   30-39%   >40%

Source: United States Bureau of Economic Analysis.

### The Changing Regional Dimension of Canadian Exports to the United States

The United States is a diverse economy, with significant regional differences in growth and income demand. It is interesting to see which regional markets are of growing significance to Canadian exports, by industry. Throughout the 1990s, the U.S. South and Southwest grew more quickly than other regions (Figure 9). These were also the regions where there was a more rapid growth in imports from Canada, although the level of Canadian exports was below that of the northern regions.[14] Consequently, it would also be beneficial to use shift-share analysis to extend our understanding of Canada's export patterns with respect to U.S. regions. For example, does U.S. demand play a strong role in explaining Canadian export growth to all U.S. regions?

Here, for the sake of brevity, is a shift-share equation for Canadian exports to an individual U.S. region j. This analysis is for Canada only, as data for Mexico are limited. We need one additional notation:

$\beta_{ij}$,  Proportion of U.S. imports of industry i accounted for by U.S. region j (we will focus on the eight United States Bureau of Economic Analysis regions)

then,

$$\Delta E_{ij,Canada} = \beta_{ij}, \Delta E_{i,Canada} \qquad \text{National import demand effect}$$
$$+ \Delta \beta_{ij} E_{i,Canada}, \qquad \text{Regional import demand effect}$$

where:

- *Regional import demand effect*: If the rates of export growth for various industries to a U.S. region are higher than the overall U.S. import growth for these industries, its regional import demand effect will show a positive impact on export growth.

In Table 12, we show the ratio of the regional import demand effect relative to the national. A value in excess of 100 indicates that the regional demand effect is larger than the economy-wide demand effect for that region and industry. A negative value indicates that the region underperformed the national average.

While the economy-wide demand effect continues to dominate in all regions, the importance of the regional import demand effect is relatively stronger in the U.S. Southeast, Southwest and Rocky Mountains. To illustrate this point, in 13 out of the 20 industries examined, New England underperformed the national average indicated by negative values in Table 12; for the Mideast it was 15 and for the Great Lakes 14, as compared to only 2 industries for the Southwest and none for the Southeast. Looking again at our key high technology industries, we observe that the regional demand effect is often highest in the Southeast and Southwest.

## TABLE 12
### CANADA'S EXPORT SHIFT OR COMPETITIVENESS EFFECT WITH U.S. REGIONS (IN PERCENT)

| | New England | Mideast | Great Lakes | Plains | Southeast | Southwest | Rocky Mountains | Far West |
|---|---|---|---|---|---|---|---|---|
| Food, Beverages and Tobacco | −15.4 | −9.2 | 16.7 | 25.3 | 31.4 | 79.9 | 76.1 | 9.9 |
| Textiles, Apparel and Leather | −1.1 | −3.2 | −5.8 | 27.9 | 7.5 | 15.4 | 5.6 | 4.4 |
| Wood Products and Furniture | 1.3 | 2.8 | −3.5 | −1.6 | 6.4 | 22.8 | 7.6 | −6.7 |
| Paper, Paper Products and Printing | −7.8 | −16.1 | −7.0 | 18.6 | 51.4 | 121.5 | 132.1 | −13.1 |
| Chemicals (excluding Drugs) | −18.8 | −8.7 | 7.7 | 20.7 | 2.8 | −13.9 | 17.5 | 30.4 |
| Drugs and Medicines | 6.8 | −1.9 | −4.7 | 7.8 | 24.4 | 13.3 | −4.1 | 7.2 |
| Petroleum Refineries and Products | −5.9 | −23.9 | −5.2 | 50.2 | 23.7 | 22.4 | 12.7 | 1.8 |
| Rubber and Plastic Products | −1.9 | 6.7 | −10.1 | 4.8 | 5.2 | 13.7 | 39.0 | 16.0 |
| Non-metallic Mineral Products | −14.1 | −10.1 | 2.2 | 15.2 | 13.3 | 2.7 | 11.9 | 10.7 |
| Iron and Steel | −22.3 | −19.4 | 18.3 | −20.1 | 12.9 | 8.6 | −16.2 | 18.6 |
| Non-ferrous Metals | −31.0 | −26.7 | 32.5 | 144.3 | 67.4 | 93.3 | 340.3 | 8.8 |
| Metal Products | 0.4 | −1.6 | −8.5 | 10.2 | 13.0 | 13.9 | 206.5 | −5.2 |
| Machinery (including Computers) | −10.2 | −4.6 | −8.7 | 7.3 | 17.6 | 40.3 | 21.5 | −1.4 |
| Electrical and Electronic Products | 65.6 | 13.1 | −4.6 | 15.2 | 37.8 | 42.3 | −28.0 | 41.9 |
| Shipbuilding and Repair | −1.2 | −19.3 | 247.4 | 79.6 | 49.6 | 111.5 | 61.9 | 0.8 |
| Motor Vehicles | 157.4 | 15.2 | −8.9 | 103.6 | 90.0 | 245.1 | 445.9 | 58.3 |
| Aircraft | −25.5 | −15.7 | −3.7 | 9.7 | 63.0 | 133.7 | 90.8 | −28.2 |
| Other Transport Equipment | 125.7 | 234.0 | −80.9 | −76.5 | 886.7 | −24.8 | 17,467.2 | 150.4 |
| Professional Goods | 38.3 | −4.8 | −12.4 | 31.0 | 17.1 | 32.6 | 3.0 | −5.7 |
| Other Manufacturing | −8.9 | −0.2 | −5.1 | 17.8 | 13.4 | 25.9 | −1.8 | −3.8 |

Source: Based on Strategis Trade Data Online.

## FIGURE 10

## PERCENTAGE OF HISPANIC POPULATION PER STATE, 2000

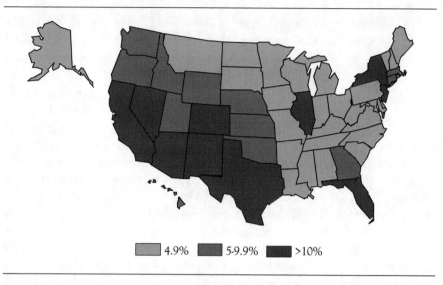

4.9%　　5-9.9%　　>10%

Source: United States Department of Commerce, Economics and Statistics Administration, United States Census Bureau, 2000.

## THE GROWING IMPORTANCE OF THE HISPANIC POPULATION IN THE UNITED STATES

ALTHOUGH DATA FOR A REGIONAL DIMENSIONS ANALYSIS of Mexico's exports to the United States were not available, the growing importance of the Hispanic population of the U.S. South and Southwest, in particular, can be considered (Figure 10).

The Hispanic population in the United States is rising rapidly, but it is growing especially fast within the South and Southwest. This should help build stronger economic links between the United States and Mexico, especially the border states of California, New Mexico, Texas and Florida, and facilitate even stronger growth in Mexican exports.

While U.S. import demand plays a critical role in explaining the increase in Mexican and Canadian exports, it is clearly not the whole story. Heightened competitiveness also plays a big role, especially in Mexico. What has propelled Mexico's improved competitiveness, and what particular factors or combination of factors are behind the rise in competitiveness of its U.S.-bound exports? Is it mostly Heckscher-Ohlin-type factor advantages related to Mexico's abundant labour force, or are Ricardian forces also at play, raising the relative competitiveness of individual Mexican industries? This is the subject of the next section.

# ADDITIONAL FACTORS BEHIND RISING EXPORTS FROM MEXICO AND CANADA

## THE NAFTA

THE PROMINENT ROLE PLAYED by the NAFTA must again be underscored. Focussing just on tariffs, the NAFTA greatly reduced those between Mexico and its two North American partners. Considerable reductions in tariffs had already occurred between Canada and the United States after the FTA, which was implemented on January 1, 1989. At the start of the NAFTA in 1994, Mexico's tariffs were still significant. Substantial reductions took place during the last half of the 1990s (Figure 11A) and boosted Mexican exports.[15]

FIGURE 11A

NAFTA TARIFF ELIMINATION SCHEDULE FOR U.S.-MEXICAN TRADE (SHARE OF TRADE COVERED*)

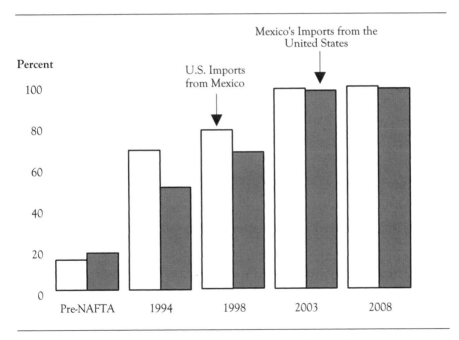

Note:   *Actual reductions have been higher than formally stated in the NAFTA agreement.
Source: Federal Reserve Bank of Dallas (1999).

## FIGURE 11B

## MEXICO AND CANADA: AVERAGE TARIFF RATES INTO THE UNITED STATES*

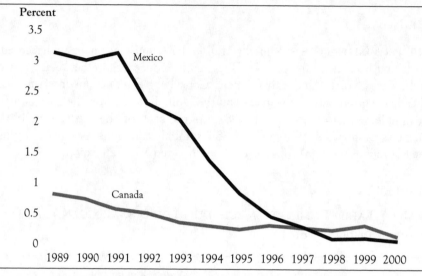

Note: *Calculated as collected duties as a share of total imports.
Source: United States International Trade Commission.

## FIGURE 12

## VALUE OF THE NATIONAL CURRENCY IN RELATION TO THE U.S. DOLLAR

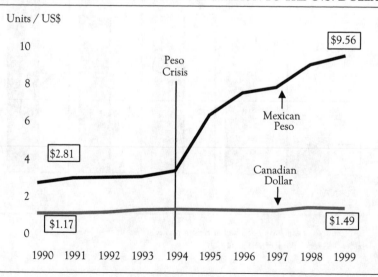

Source: IMF.

It is noteworthy that tariff reductions under the NAFTA are not yet fully implemented. The agreement specified a 15-year tariff elimination schedule on trilateral trade. However, the major benefits for Mexico's exports have already taken place. It was during the NAFTA's first five years that 76.2 percent of U.S. imports from Mexico (and 66.3 percent of U.S. exports to Mexico) were slated to become duty-free. However, Figure 11B shows that the average tariff rate on Mexican exports to the United States is now close to zero.

At the outset of this research, the expectation was that the Mexican and Canadian economies would gradually see some adjustment in their specialization of exports, and that Mexico and Canada would specialize in different exports — with Mexico enjoying an advantage in exports of manufactured goods benefiting from more labour-intensive activities. Table 6 shows that this is true: Mexico's industries are in general more labour-intensive than Canada's. But what is the nature of Mexico's labour advantage? Is it simply lower wages?

To investigate this, we need to compare the labour costs of the two countries in terms of their common currency equivalents and take their labour productivity into account: in other words, compare the relative unit labour costs (ULCs) of Mexico and Canada. In order to get a clear picture of relative labour compensation, this section will focus first, on three contributing factors to ULCs: currency movements, wages and productivity. It will then consider Mexico's and Canada's deteriorating terms of trade with the United States and finally, explore the importance of investment and the prominent role played by affiliates in an increasingly integrated North American economy.

## EXCHANGE RATE MOVEMENTS

IT IS NOT POSSIBLE TO DISCUSS Mexican and Canadian exports in the 1990s without mentioning the currency devaluations, and for Mexico, the peso crisis (Figure 12). Canada's dollar slid substantially in relation to the value of the U.S. dollar throughout the 1990s, a decline which helped spur Canadian exports to the United States. Mexico's peso, however, was affected by a much larger currency development. December of 1994, the first year of the NAFTA, saw Mexico's peso in crisis. Prior to 1994, Mexico had undertaken an aggressive program of structural reform. Massive amounts of foreign capital had entered the country, resulting in capital account deficits equal to 7 percent of gross domestic product (GDP). What triggered the crisis is unclear: what is known, however, is that in the extremely short period of December 1994, the peso lost nearly half of its value and foreign capital hemorrhaged out of the country. The International Monetary Fund (IMF) and the United States provided a financial bailout package that was combined with effective domestic stabilization policies. Mexico recovered quickly. However, the value of the peso, which had dropped from 3.38 pesos per US$ to 6.42 pesos per US$ during the crisis, continued to fall. In recent months, the peso has been one of the few currencies to appreciate in relation to the dollar; by some measures it is still considered over-valued.[16]

## LOWER LABOUR COSTS

TABLE 13 SHOWS THE AVERAGE ANNUAL LABOUR compensation per employee in the two countries, in common currency units. Mexico's average wages are much lower than Canada's in all industries. In addition, Canadian wage rates are rising more quickly in slightly more than half of the industries. However, average Mexican wages in drugs and medicines, and chemicals are climbing extremely fast, while in machinery, and food and beverages they are rising at rates significantly higher than those for Canadian wages. In textiles and motor vehicles, Mexican wages (in U.S. dollars) are actually declining.

## TABLE 13
## MEXICO AND CANADA: WAGE RATES PER PERSON (US$)

|  | Mexico | | | Canada | | |
|---|---|---|---|---|---|---|
|  | Level 1990 $ | Level 1996 $ | Growth % | Level 1990 $ | Level 1996 $ | Growth % |
| All Manufacturing | 5,006 | 5,059 | 1 | 31,873 | 33,397 | 5 |
| Food, Beverages and Tobacco | 4,031 | 4,551 | 13 | 29,601 | 29,617 | 0 |
| Textiles, Apparel and Leather | 3,489 | 3,012 | –14 | 20,279 | 21,925 | 8 |
| Wood Products and Furniture | 2,838 | 2,710 | –5 | 27,871 | 30,338 | 9 |
| Paper, Paper Products and Printing | 5,512 | 5,574 | 1 | 35,612 | 37,024 | 4 |
| Chemicals (excluding Drugs) | 8,937 | 10,786 | 21 | 38,409 | 39,735 | 3 |
| Drugs and Medicines | 9,702 | 13,356 | 38 | 36,064 | 38,229 | 6 |
| Petroleum Refineries and Products | 8,174 | 9,824 | 20 | 52,281 | 51,233 | –2 |
| Rubber and Plastic Products | 5,062 | 4,963 | –2 | 29,167 | 28,294 | –3 |
| Non-metallic Mineral Products | 5,420 | 5,437 | 0 | 32,501 | 33,116 | 2 |
| Iron and Steel | 10,308 | 10,424 | 1 | 45,836 | 48,058 | 5 |
| Non-ferrous Metals | 7,253 | 6,565 | –9 | 45,910 | 48,532 | 6 |
| Metal Products | 4,126 | 4,475 | 8 | 29,763 | 27,908 | –6 |
| Machinery (including Computers) | 5,444 | 6,076 | 12 | 31,136 | 32,678 | 5 |
| Electrical and Electronic Products | 4,993 | 5,047 | 1 | 32,427 | 40,223 | 24 |
| Shipbuilding and Repair | 8,493 | N/A | N/A | 36,838 | 35,748 | –3 |
| Motor Vehicles | 6,458 | 5,925 | –8 | 36,683 | 38,998 | 6 |
| Aircraft | N/A | N/A | N/A | 39,927 | 42,028 | 5 |
| Other Transport Equipment | 3,904 | 3,674 | –6 | 32,729 | 33,919 | 4 |
| Professional Goods | 4,749 | 4,785 | 1 | 25,638 | 27,967 | 9 |
| Other Manufacturing | 3,352 | 3,744 | 12 | 23,000 | 22,232 | –3 |

Source: Based on OECD, *Structural Analysis Database*.

## RISING PRODUCTIVITY

TABLE 14 COMPARES LABOUR PRODUCTIVITY and growth levels for Mexico and Canada in 1990 and 1998. As expected, Canada holds a labour productivity advantage (the levels) in most industries, but not in chemicals, petroleum or the metal sector (non-metallic mineral products, iron and steel, and non-ferrous metals).

Mexico lags behind Canada considerably in some key industries where its export growth has been strongest, such as electrical and electronic products, professional goods and textiles. These are industries where low wages really are important, however, and more than compensate for lower productivity. Overall, in manufacturing and in many industries, Mexico's labour productivity is growing more quickly than Canada's.[17]

## TABLE 14

### MEXICO AND CANADA: LABOUR PRODUCTIVITY (US$, PPPS)

| | Mexico | | | Canada | | |
|---|---|---|---|---|---|---|
| | Level 1990 $ | Level 1996 $ | Growth % | Level 1990 $ | Level 1996 $ | Growth % |
| **All Manufacturing** | 28,005 | 32,744 | 17 | 42,776 | 49,248 | 15 |
| Food, Beverages and Tobacco | 33,809 | 38,761 | 15 | 51,062 | 55,738 | 9 |
| Textiles, Apparel and Leather | 16,838 | 17,700 | 5 | 24,504 | 27,418 | 12 |
| Wood Products and Furniture | 20,616 | 23,373 | 13 | 29,845 | 31,951 | 7 |
| Paper, Paper Products and Printing | 26,045 | 28,949 | 11 | 48,243 | 48,739 | 1 |
| Chemicals (excluding Drugs) | 54,551 | 77,652 | 42 | 74,273 | 54,936 | −26 |
| Drugs and Medicines | 51,326 | 62,098 | 21 | 83,575 | 95,467 | 14 |
| Petroleum Refineries and Products | 49,341 | 71,807 | 46 | 53,211 | 69,830 | 31 |
| Rubber and Plastic Products | 21,645 | 21,001 | −3 | 35,696 | 44,282 | 24 |
| Non-metallic Mineral Products | 36,733 | 50,458 | 37 | 46,391 | 50,365 | 9 |
| Iron and Steel | 67,823 | 177,988 | 162 | 44,080 | 57,554 | 31 |
| Non-ferrous Metals | 69,975 | 84,501 | 21 | 54,599 | 76,308 | 40 |
| Metal Products | 21,043 | 24,203 | 15 | 37,154 | 38,261 | 3 |
| Machinery (including Computers) | 21,364 | 35,765 | 67 | 38,271 | 50,257 | 31 |
| Electrical and Electronic Products | 16,641 | 16,367 | −2 | 43,524 | 68,113 | 56 |
| Shipbuilding and Repair | 19,749 | N/A | N/A | 34,834 | 48,393 | 39 |
| Motor Vehicles | 27,039 | 33,125 | 23 | 47,829 | 56,999 | 19 |
| Aircraft | N/A | N/A | N/A | 47,222 | 40,647 | −14 |
| Other Transport Equipment | 12,472 | 16,264 | 30 | 42,990 | 63,367 | 47 |
| Professional Goods | 14,844 | 15,752 | 6 | 31,291 | 40,001 | 28 |
| Other Manufacturing | 31,645 | 28,778 | −9 | 27,799 | 30,562 | 10 |

Source: Based on OECD, *Structural Analysis Database*.

## TABLE 15

### MEXICO AND CANADA: LABOUR PRODUCTIVITY AND WAGES (US$)

| | Mexico | | Canada | | Level Comparison (1)/(2) |
|---|---|---|---|---|---|
| | 1996 Level $ (1) | Growth % | 1996 Level $ (2) | Growth % | |
| **Wages** | | | | | |
| Machinery | 6,057 | 12 | 50,257 | 31 | 830 |
| Electrical and Electronic Products | 5,047 | 1 | 68,113 | 56 | 1,350 |
| Motor Vehicles | 5,925 | −8 | 56,999 | 19 | 962 |
| **Productivity** | | | | | |
| Machinery | 35,765 | 67 | 44,555 | 3 | 125 |
| Electrical and Electronic Products | 16,367 | −2 | 54,843 | 6 | 335 |
| Motor Vehicles | 33,125 | 23 | 53,172 | 4 | 161 |

Source: Based on OECD, *Structural Analysis Database*.

Table 15 summarizes the results from previous tables for three industries of particular interest in this discussion: motor vehicles, electrical and electronic products, and machinery. In all three, Mexico's productivity and wages are rising faster. The table also shows that, in common currency units, the differences in labour productivity between Mexico and Canada are *not* fully compensated for by wage rate differences. Canada therefore holds a ULC advantage in these three industries. Furthermore the ULC, measured in common currency units (US$), has widened in Canada's favour.

## RELATIVE UNIT LABOUR COSTS

FIGURE 13 COMPARES 1996 ULCs for Mexico and Canada. What is clear is that the three ULC components contribute differently to each country's labour compensation. Overall, ULCs are much lower in Mexico, and falling — largely because of the depreciating exchange rate. Although Mexican wages (in pesos) have been rising quickly, this has been more than offset by the declining currency and has greatly enhanced Mexico's already strong labour competitiveness (and the Heckscher-Ohlin-type labour advantage that contributes to its export competitiveness).

On an industry basis, however, there is considerable variation in the ULCs of the two countries. Shipbuilding, for example, is a small industry with high ULCs in both. Mexican industries with high ULCs include other transport equipment, professional goods, rubber and plastics, and textiles and apparel. (In addition, a quick look ahead to Figure 14A shows that Mexico's ULCs for other transport equipment, textiles and apparel, and professional goods are among the fastest-growing, while those for machinery and motor vehicles are rising).

Canada's ULCs are high in textiles and apparel, petroleum, and iron and steel. Textiles and apparel, and drugs and medicines are the two Canadian industries where labour costs are rising fastest.

We examine the impact of relative ULCs on exports by comparing the relationship between changes in ULCs and changes in exports for both Mexico and Canada. In particular, we consider the responsiveness of exports (and export success in U.S. import markets) to overall labour costs, and identify the more sensitive exports in Figures 14A and B.

Most of Mexico's industries exhibit falling ULCs and rising exports. While other transport equipment has the fastest export growth, it shows little change in its ULC. Among the next fastest-growing exports, textiles and apparel, machinery, professional goods, and motor vehicles form a continuum in terms of declining ULCs. Motor vehicle and machinery exports may be the most sensitive to ULCs. However, while industries generally benefit from declining ULCs in Mexico, there does not appear to be a strong trend relating export growth to changes in labour costs.

## FIGURE 13

## MEXICO AND CANADA: UNIT LABOUR COSTS
### OVERALL GROWTH* (1990-96) AND INDUSTRY LEVELS (1996)

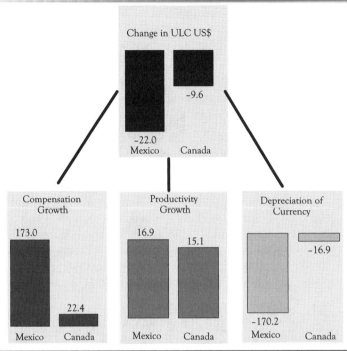

| Industry Levels (1996) | Mexico | Canada | (1)/(2) |
|---|---|---|---|
| Food, Beverages and Tobacco | 0.18 | 0.47 | 0.38 |
| Textiles, Apparel and Leather | 0.32 | 0.74 | 0.43 |
| Wood Products and Furniture | 0.25 | 0.66 | 0.38 |
| Paper, Paper Products and Printing | 0.34 | 0.65 | 0.52 |
| Chemicals (excluding Drugs) | 0.26 | 0.41 | 0.63 |
| Drugs and Medicines | 0.28 | 0.40 | 0.71 |
| Petroleum Refineries and Products | 0.28 | 0.73 | 0.39 |
| Rubber and Plastic Products | 0.41 | 0.60 | 0.68 |
| Non-metallic Mineral Products | 0.19 | 0.64 | 0.29 |
| Iron and Steel | 0.13 | 0.74 | 0.17 |
| Non-ferrous metals | 0.13 | 0.68 | 0.19 |
| Metal Products | 0.32 | 0.67 | 0.48 |
| Machinery (including Computers) | 0.27 | 0.67 | 0.41 |
| Electrical and Electronics | 0.52 | 0.62 | 0.83 |
| Shipbuilding and Repair | 0.84 | 0.73 | 1.14 |
| Motor Vehicles | 0.22 | 0.60 | 0.37 |
| Aircraft | N/A | 0.65 | N/A |
| Other Transportation | 0.57 | 0.46 | 1.23 |
| Professional Goods | 0.48 | 0.62 | 0.77 |
| Other Manufacturing | 0.24 | 0.68 | 0.36 |

* Cumulative percentage growth.
Source: Based on data from the United States Bureau of Labor Statistics.

## FIGURE 14A

## MEXICO: CHANGE IN EXPORTS TO THE UNITED STATES AND IN ULC

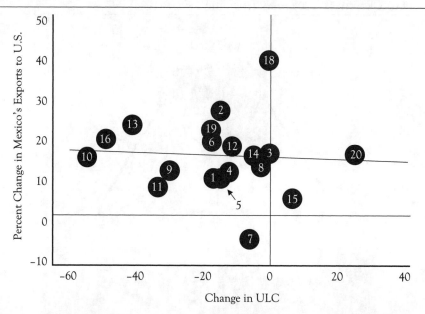

| | | Change in U.S.-bound Exports | Change in ULC |
|---|---|---|---|
| 1 | Food, Beverages and Tobacco | –17.1 | 10.8 |
| 2 | Textiles, Apparel and Leather | –15.3 | 27.5 |
| 3 | Wood Products and Furniture | –0.8 | 16.8 |
| 4 | Paper, Paper Products and Printing | –12.8 | 12.4 |
| 5 | Chemicals (excluding Drugs) | –15.0 | 10.6 |
| 6 | Drugs and Medicines | –18.1 | 19.9 |
| 7 | Petroleum Refineries and Products | –6.7 | –4.3 |
| 8 | Rubber and Plastic Products | –5.0 | 16.3 |
| 9 | Non-metallic Mineral Products | –30.5 | 12.6 |
| 10 | Iron and Steel | –54.8 | 15.8 |
| 11 | Non-ferrous Metals | –34.1 | 8.5 |
| 12 | Metal Products | –11.9 | 18.6 |
| 13 | Machinery (including Computers) | –41.5 | 23.9 |
| 14 | Electrical and Electronic Products | –5.7 | 16.4 |
| 15 | Shipbuilding and Repair | 5.9 | 5.6 |
| 16 | Motor Vehicles | –49.1 | 20.3 |
| 17 | Aircraft | | 9.1 |
| 18 | Other Transport Equipment | –1.1 | 40.2 |
| 19 | Professional Goods | –18.4 | 22.7 |
| 20 | Other Manufacturing | 24.6 | 16.7 |

Source: Based on OECD, *Bilateral Trade Flows*.

## FIGURE 14B

## CANADA: CHANGE IN EXPORTS TO THE UNITED STATES AND IN ULC

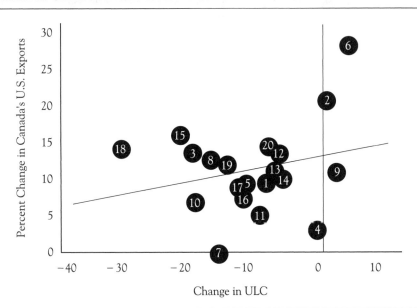

Change in ULC

|    |                                        | Change in U.S.-bound Exports | Change in ULC |
|----|----------------------------------------|------------------------------|---------------|
| 1  | Food, Beverages and Tobacco            | –9.3                         | 9.4           |
| 2  | Textiles, Apparel and Leather          | 0.4                          | 20.7          |
| 3  | Wood Products and Furniture            | –21.0                        | 13.4          |
| 4  | Paper, Paper Products and Printing     | –1.2                         | 3.0           |
| 5  | Chemicals (excluding Drugs)            | –12.5                        | 9.2           |
| 6  | Drugs and Medicines                    | 3.8                          | 28.2          |
| 7  | Petroleum Refineries and Products      | –16.8                        | –0.3          |
| 8  | Rubber and Plastic Products            | –18.2                        | 12.5          |
| 9  | Non-metallic Mineral Products          | 1.9                          | 10.8          |
| 10 | Iron and Steel                         | –20.6                        | 6.7           |
| 11 | Non-ferrous Metals                     | –10.3                        | 5.0           |
| 12 | Metal Products                         | –7.3                         | 13.3          |
| 13 | Machinery (including Computers)        | –7.9                         | 10.9          |
| 14 | Electrical and Electronic Products     | –6.7                         | 9.9           |
| 15 | Shipbuilding and Repair                | –22.8                        | 15.9          |
| 16 | Motor Vehicles                         | –12.9                        | 7.3           |
| 17 | Aircraft                               | –13.7                        | 8.7           |
| 18 | Other Transport Equipment              | –32.2                        | 14.0          |
| 19 | Professional Goods                     | –15.5                        | 11.9          |
| 20 | Other Manufacturing                    | –8.8                         | 14.3          |

Source: Based on OECD, *Bilateral Trade Flows.*

Canada's two fastest-growing exports are among those experiencing the largest increases in ULCs: namely, (the relatively small) drugs and medicines, and textiles and apparel. Interestingly, the industries that benefit most from declining ULCs include other transport equipment, iron and steel, wood and wood products, and petroleum: on the whole, however, these have experienced average and below-average export growth.

## DETERIORATING TERMS OF TRADE

THIS STUDY HAS SHOWN THAT the value of exports from Canada (and especially Mexico) to the United States has increased dramatically. It has also shown that Canada's share of the U.S. import market has remained stable, while Mexico's is rising. How do prices, and particularly export prices, affect this situation?

Figures 15A and B present information on the movement in export prices and quantities of (real) exports. Overall, export prices rose in both countries, but especially in Mexico. However, there were also some price declines. The big price drops for Mexico were in motor vehicles, and machinery. Canada experienced price declines in electrical and electronic products and an eclectic group including other transport equipment and several mining and metal-related industries (non-ferrous metals, iron and steel, and non-metallic minerals), as well as energy, rubber and plastics, and drugs and medicines. Resource-based industries such as wood products, and paper and paper products, saw their Canadian prices rise.

In Figure 15A, most of Mexico's industries are in the upper-right quadrant. Their experience (rising prices and quantity) is consistent with a positive shift in demand, positive demand effects that outweigh positive shifts in supply, or both. Mexico also has a few industries in the lower-right quadrant. This denotes positive supply shifts, supply effects that outweigh positive demand effects, or both. Canada's export price and real export changes are less dramatic, but they follow Mexico's pattern.

In the two key industries of motor vehicles and machinery, the Mexican and Canadian experiences were very different: Mexico's export prices dropped, Canada's rose. While demand is an important driver for both, Mexico benefited from supportive supply conditions which were reflected in export price declines. The electrical and electronic products industry of both countries benefited from positive price and quantity changes (as did professional goods, other manufacturing, textiles and apparel, wood and wood products and metal products).

## FIGURE 15A

## MEXICO: CHANGE IN EXPORT PRICE AND EXPORT QUANTITY, 1990-98

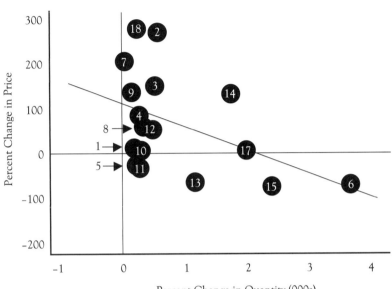

Percent Change in Quantity (000s)

|    |                                       | Change in :<br>Price of Exports | Change in:<br>Quantity of Exports |
|----|---------------------------------------|---------------------------------|-----------------------------------|
| 1  | Food, Beverages and Tobacco           | 12.1                            | 80.2                              |
| 2  | Textiles, Apparel and Leather         | 271.0                           | 453.0                             |
| 3  | Wood Products and Furniture           | 151.3                           | 416.0                             |
| 4  | Paper, Paper Products and Printing    | 85.3                            | 157.8                             |
| 5  | Chemicals (excluding Drugs)           | -24.6                           | 122.1                             |
| 6  | Drugs and Medicines                   | -69.1                           | 3,567.9                           |
| 7  | Energy                                | 206.7                           | -69.9                             |
| 8  | Rubber and Plastic Products           | 61.1                            | 217.7                             |
| 9  | Non-metallic Mineral Products         | 138.7                           | 41.2                              |
| 10 | Iron and Steel                        | 8.2                             | 179.6                             |
| 11 | Non-ferrous Metals                    | -31.7                           | 164.5                             |
| 12 | Metal Products                        | 56.8                            | 356.8                             |
| 13 | Machinery (including Computers)       | -64.3                           | 1,049.6                           |
| 14 | Electrical and Electronic Products    | 134.8                           | 1,621.5                           |
| 15 | Motor Vehicles                        | -73.8                           | 2,292.8                           |
| 16 | Other Transport Equipment*            | 1,621.7                         | -45.9                             |
| 17 | Professional Goods                    | 8.4                             | 1,867.2                           |
| 18 | Other Manufacturing                   | 279.8                           | 130.6                             |

Note:    * "Other Transport Equipment" is not included in the graph.
Source: Based on OECD, *Bilateral Trade Database*.

**FIGURE 15B**

CANADA: CHANGE IN EXPORT PRICE AND EXPORT QUANTITY, 1990-98

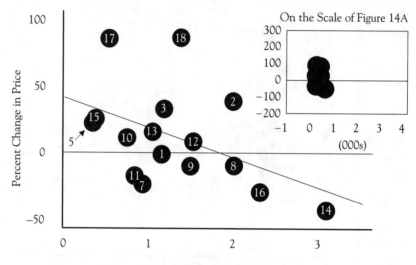

Percent Change in Quantity (00s)

|  |  | Change in Price of Exports | Change in Quantity of Exports |
|---|---|---|---|
| 1 | Food, Beverages and Tobacco | –1.5 | 113.7 |
| 2 | Textiles, Apparel and Leather | 38.8 | 198.4 |
| 3 | Wood Products and Furniture | 33.1 | 117.2 |
| 4 | Paper, Paper Products and Printing* | 40,191.3 | –99.7 |
| 5 | Chemicals (excluding Drugs) | 22.6 | 34.4 |
| 6 | Drugs and Medicines* | –31.9 | 885.4 |
| 7 | Energy | –24.0 | 91.7 |
| 8 | Rubber and Plastic Products | –9.4 | 199.9 |
| 9 | Non-metallic Mineral Products | –9.3 | 148.7 |
| 10 | Iron and Steel | 11.9 | 72.9 |
| 11 | Non-ferrous Metals | –17.2 | 81.5 |
| 12 | Metal Products | 8.8 | 151.8 |
| 13 | Machinery (including Computers) | 15.8 | 103.2 |
| 14 | Electrical and Electronic Products | –43.0 | 307.0 |
| 15 | Motor Vehicles | 25.5 | 36.9 |
| 16 | Other Transport Equipment | –29.5 | 231.0 |
| 17 | Professional Goods | 86.5 | 51.9 |
| 18 | Other Manufacturing | 87.3 | 136.5 |

Note: * "Paper, Paper Products and Printing" and "Drugs and Medicines" are not included in the graph.
Source: Based on OECD, *Bilateral Trade Database*.

160

## AFFILIATES AND NORTH AMERICAN TRADE

THE 1990S SHOWCASED A SINGULARLY IMPORTANT DEVELOPMENT in production: trade and export patterns. Increasingly, firms went offshore to source components and cross-border to manufacture and assemble. Trade and export patterns created a more integrated and interdependent North American production system that linked the national economies (Arndt and Huemer 2001a, 2001b) as evidenced by the expansion of auto and auto parts trade under the much earlier Canada-U.S. auto pact, and the further rapid development of the maquiladora operations[18] of U.S. firms in northern Mexico. This development has had several implications.

First, it resulted in a considerable increase in intraindustry trade, which made possible more export and import of both parts and components and finished products. This is illustrated in Figure 16, which shows the two-way trade in finished products and components for the motor vehicle, computer and apparel industries. In the case of motor vehicles, both Mexico and Canada are net importers of parts, add value in the form of assembly and then export the completed vehicle. However, specialization in the industry dictates that a specific model of car may be produced only at one location to serve the entire North American market. This results in an increased flow of both parts and completed vehicles in both directions across the border. The textile and apparel industry is organized in a similar fashion. Canada, for example, has specialized in one 'model' (men's suits), while Mexico has specialized in a wide array of textile products, from shirts to undergarments.

Second, and a closely related point, was the rise in intrafirm trade (Figure 17). Both Mexico and Canada rely heavily on trade between U.S. affiliates and their parent in the United States. For Mexico, more than a quarter of all trade is simply the movement of goods between parent and affiliate. For Canada, the figure is one-third.

Third, because of the role played by U.S.-based multinational corporations (MNCs) in both Mexico and Canada, the two countries have potential access to similar technologies. Of course, capital and infrastructure are important keys to the effective use of any technology, and these depend on ongoing investments. As Figure 18 shows, MNCs have made sizeable investments in Mexico centered on motor vehicles, food and beverages, machinery, and drugs and medicines.

# FIGURE 16

## TRADE IN RELATED PRODUCTS

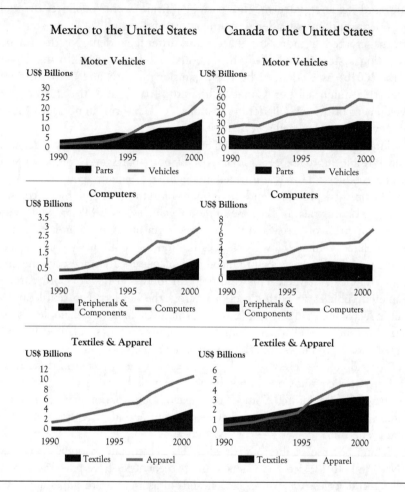

Source: United States International Trade Commission.

## FIGURE 17

### MEXICO AND CANADA : INTRAFIRM TRADE AS A SHARE OF TOTAL TRADE WITH THE UNITED STATES,* 1998

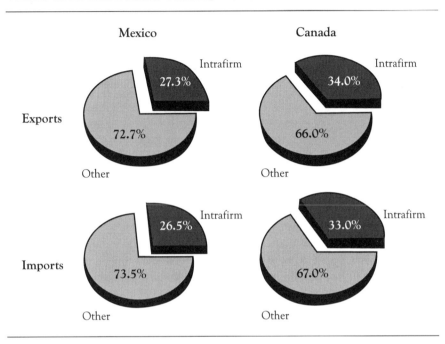

Note:   * U.S. MNCs only.
Source: U.S. Bureau of Analysis.

Finally, recent advances in information technology, communications and transportation should help make foreign sourcing and production even easier. These advances will allow companies to coordinate cross-border manufacturing activities better and to take greater advantage of international cost differences, and therefore will encourage more intraindustry and intrafirm trade. As capital intensity in Mexico rises and the country pursues more value-added activities, it will become more competitive across a range of production. This will bring Mexico and Canada into greater export competition with one another.

## FIGURE 18
## INVESTMENT BY MNCS IN MEXICO
## (MILLIONS OF DOLLARS, 1993)

| | MEXICO | | |
|---|---|---|---|
| | Gross Fixed Capital Formation | Stock of FDI | Capital Under Foreign Influence |
| **All Manufacturing** | 7,735 | 27,864 | 52,446 |
| Food, Beverages and Tobacco | 1,684 | 5,462 | 8,379 |
| Textile, Apparel and Leather | 82 | 543 | 761 |
| Wood and Paper Products | 99 | 578 | 1,214 |
| Chemicals (excluding Drugs) | 457 | 3,120 | 5,234 |
| Drugs and Medicines | 212 | 2,027 | 3,122 |
| Petroleum Refineries and Products | 8 | 60 | 142 |
| Rubber and Plastic Products | 362 | 637 | 1,181 |
| Non-metallic Mineral Products | 18 | 815 | 1,099 |
| Metal Products | 835 | 1,952 | 3,398 |
| Machinery (including Computers) | 195 | 3,703 | 7,182 |
| Electrical and Electronic Products | 183 | 1,572 | 3,370 |
| Motor Vehicles | 3,552 | 6,750 | 16,116 |
| Other Transportation Equipment | 5 | 95 | 300 |
| Scientific Instruments | 5 | 222 | 322 |
| Other Manufacturing | 36 | 329 | 628 |

Source: OECD (1999c).

# SOME ISSUES

IN THIS SECTION, WE EXPLORE A FEW PIVOTAL ISSUES that will have a significant impact on future exports from Mexico and Canada to the United States.

## SLOWDOWN IN U.S. IMPORT DEMAND

THROUGHOUT MUCH OF THE 1990S, the U.S. economy experienced a remarkable period of growth and prosperity, which created a growing demand for imports. Now, however, U.S. import demand is showing signs of slowing down (Figure 19). What does this mean for Mexican and Canadian exports? If U.S. demand slows, Canada will not be able to maintain its export growth without becoming more competitive with the exports of other countries, which, increasingly, will include Mexico.

FIGURE 19

U.S. ECONOMIC GROWTH

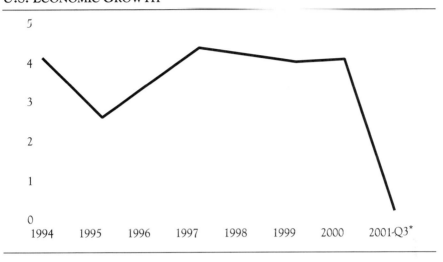

* Change from 2000-Q3.
Source: United States Bureau of Economic Analysis.

## Mexico is Adapting to U.S. Demand

Earlier, we observed that the export composition of the two countries is changing (Table 2). But how well are Mexican and Canadian exports "adapting" to U.S. import demand? In particular, are they expanding in areas where U.S. import demand is rising?

A brief look back at Table 2 reminds us that Canada's exports to the United States exceed Mexico's across most industries (except for textiles and apparel, electrical and electronic products, machinery and professional goods). Table 16 shows us that Canada's export profile is closer to the U.S. import demand profile than Mexico's (as illustrated in a comparison of the industry share make-up of Canada's exports and U.S. import markets).

However, Table 16 also establishes the fact that Mexico's export profile is *coming closer* to the U.S. import demand profile. Mexico's exports are growing faster than Canada's, both in relative absolute amount and share, where U.S. import demand is largest. Table 5 shows this in more detail. In this sense, Mexico's exports are adapting to U.S. import demand.

## TABLE 16

## U.S. IMPORT PROFILE AND THE SIMILARITY OF MEXICO'S AND CANADA'S EXPORT PROFILES

| | Unites States | | | Mexico | | | Canada | | |
|---|---|---|---|---|---|---|---|---|---|
| | Imports 1998 US$ billion | Share 100% | Change in Share | Exports to United States 1998 US$ billion | Share 100% | Change in Share | Exports to United States 1998 US$ billion | Share 100% | Change in Share |
| All Manufacturing | 826.0 | 100.0 | 0.0 | 82.7 | 100.0 | 0.0 | 148.3 | 100.0 | 0.0 |
| Food, Beverages and Tobacco | 29.7 | 3.6 | −1.1 | 2.1 | 2.6 | −1.7 | 6.5 | 4.4 | 0.3 |
| Textiles, Apparel and Leather | 83.7 | 10.1 | −0.2 | 8.6 | 10.4 | 4.7 | 3.0 | 2.0 | 1.2 |
| Wood Products and Furniture | 25.6 | 3.1 | 0.7 | 2.5 | 3.0 | −0.3 | 13.0 | 8.8 | 2.7 |
| Paper, Paper Products and Printing | 19.5 | 2.4 | −0.9 | 0.6 | 0.7 | −0.4 | 12.1 | 8.2 | −4.1 |
| Chemicals (excluding Drugs) | 52.2 | 6.3 | 0.4 | 2.1 | 2.5 | −1.8 | 9.9 | 6.7 | 0.4 |
| Drugs and Medicines | 10.8 | 1.3 | 0.7 | 0.1 | 0.1 | 0.0 | 0.6 | 0.4 | 0.3 |
| Petroleum Refineries and Products | 14.6 | 1.8 | −2.7 | 0.3 | 0.4 | −1.8 | 2.9 | 2.0 | −1.8 |
| Rubber and Plastic Products | 24.9 | 3.0 | 0.2 | 1.2 | 1.4 | −0.2 | 3.8 | 2.6 | 0.7 |
| Non-metallic Mineral Products | 11.4 | 1.4 | 0.0 | 1.3 | 1.6 | −0.7 | 1.6 | 1.1 | 0.2 |
| Iron and Steel | 21.7 | 2.6 | 0.0 | 1.5 | 1.8 | −0.3 | 3.5 | 2.4 | −0.3 |
| Non-ferrous Metals | 17.7 | 2.1 | −0.5 | 1.0 | 1.2 | −1.2 | 6.0 | 4.1 | −1.2 |
| Metal Products | 24.5 | 3.0 | 0.2 | 2.7 | 3.3 | 0.1 | 5.1 | 3.4 | 1.0 |
| Machinery (including Computers) | 136.6 | 16.5 | 3.1 | 9.0 | 10.8 | 3.4 | 12.3 | 8.3 | 1.4 |
| Electrical and Electronic Equipment | 129.8 | 15.7 | 1.8 | 25.9 | 31.3 | −4.0 | 10.2 | 6.9 | 0.8 |
| Shipbuilding and Repair | 1.7 | 0.2 | 0.1 | 0.0 | 0.0 | 0.0 | 0.4 | 0.3 | 0.1 |
| Motor Vehicles | 131.4 | 15.9 | −2.4 | 18.9 | 22.8 | 3.0 | 49.1 | 33.1 | −2.6 |
| Aircraft | 22.1 | 2.7 | 0.2 | 0.1 | 0.1 | −0.1 | 4.5 | 3.0 | 0.1 |
| Other Transport Equipment | 4.9 | 0.6 | 0.1 | 0.3 | 0.4 | 0.3 | 1.4 | 1.0 | 0.3 |
| Professional Goods | 30.0 | 3.6 | 0.4 | 3.3 | 4.0 | 1.1 | 1.7 | 1.1 | 0.3 |
| Other Manufacturing | 33.20 | 4.02 | −0.10 | 1.20 | 1.45 | −0.16 | 0.78 | 0.53 | 0.18 |

Source: Based on OECD, *Structural Analysis Database*.

## Will Export Competition between Mexico and Canada in U.S Markets Rise?

Greater *direct* competition with Canadian exporters is a possibility, especially in the key industries of motor vehicles, electrical and electronic products and machinery, which are characterized by much intraindustry trade. As well, they are better-paying and depend on higher productivity than the domestic average for both countries. As productivity and wage levels in these industries rise in Mexico, the products of the two countries could become more aligned and see competition between them increase. Moreover, these industries do not rely on natural resource advantages. The mechanism for improving export growth will involve greater competitiveness on the basis of cost and, preferably, improved productivity.

This raises two questions: Where should Canada be transforming its competitive advantage? And what is the role played by U.S. import markets?

## Mexico, Canada and their Exports: Industrial Structure and Adjustment

U.S. import markets perform an important role in the industrial makeup of Mexico and Canada and the direction in which their economies are heading in that they encourage the growth of particular industries that are important for the future well-being of both countries. This is significant because the global knowledge-based economy is very much about meeting competitiveness challenges while expanding into new activities and industries with higher future payoff. These include machinery, and electrical and electronic products, as well as higher-end activities related to transportation, manufacturing, drugs and medicines, etc. The viability of these Mexican and Canadian industries will depend largely on the performance of their exports to the United States, as their smaller domestic markets cannot provide enough demand to sustain them. Their exports, therefore, are significantly dependent on the U.S. import market.

Even slight shifts in North American trade patterns and export specialization would have implications for the industrial structure of both countries, as well as the direction of their future economic growth.[19] One significant measure discussed in the second section was the U.S.-bound export intensity, which is rising for most industries in both Mexico and Canada. This measure also highlights the extent to which an individual industry depends on U.S. import markets as a mainstay for its growth and vitality. The higher its U.S. export intensity, the more its growth and development depend on its success in the U.S. import market; and the greater its export growth, the more significant the effect on output growth.

Table 2 reveals that many of the industries with high U.S.-bound export intensities are important to their countries' economic future. For Mexico, these include electrical and electronic products, machinery, and motor vehicles. Figure 4 shows that these three industries comprise almost two-thirds (64.7 percent) of Mexico's 1998 exports to the United States, provide above-average wages and are among the more productive of the Mexican economy. They would never have grown to their present size without their ability to export to the United States. These industries also play an important role in the Canadian economy. The U.S. import markets are just as crucial to the strength and ebullience of traditional Canadian industries like wood, chemicals, petroleum, non-ferrous metals, and aircraft. Without access to U.S. import markets, these Canadian industries might not be as successful and would have a more limited future.

Table 17 examines the contribution of exports to the United States to the growth of individual industries in Mexico and Canada.

## TABLE 17

### DEPENDENCE OF INDUSTRY-DEFINED EXPORTS AND INDUSTRIAL OUTPUT ON U.S. IMPORT MARKETS

| | Mexico | | Canada | |
|---|---|---|---|---|
| | Level* 1996 % | Change 1990-96 % | Level* 1996 % | Change 1990-96 % |
| All Manufacturing | 30 | 102 | 42 | 46 |
| Food, Beverages and Tobacco | 3 | 36 | 12 | 57 |
| Textiles, Apparel and Leather | 33 | 244 | 21 | 285 |
| Wood Products and Furniture | 37 | 142 | 53 | 79 |
| Paper, Paper Products and Printing | 6 | 75 | 35 | 19 |
| Chemicals (excluding Drugs) | 13 | 80 | 52 | 86 |
| Drugs and Medicines | 1 | 94 | 9 | 267 |
| Petroleum Refineries and Products | 10 | -2 | 24 | 37 |
| Rubber and Plastic Products | 15 | 88 | 31 | 68 |
| Non-metallic Mineral Products | 12 | 64 | 25 | 133 |
| Iron and Steel | 17 | 149 | 39 | 35 |
| Non-ferrous Metals | 18 | 7 | 48 | 39 |
| Metal Products | 26 | 113 | 26 | 126 |
| Machinery (including Computers) | 74 | 87 | 61 | 54 |
| Electrical and Electronic Products | 78 | 16 | 48 | 55 |
| Shipbuilding and Repair | 10 | 442 | 61 | 641 |
| Motor Vehicles | 48 | 95 | 73 | -1 |
| Aircraft | N/A | N/A | 51 | 14 |
| Other Transport Equipment | 17 | 433 | 42 | 45 |
| Professional Goods | 96 | 103 | 36 | 82 |
| Other Manufacturing | 39 | 103 | 24 | 105 |

Note: *Exports to the United States as a share of shipments.
Source: Based on OECD, *Structural Analysis Database*.

- Several of the largest industries in the Mexican and Canadian economies (represented by their large percentage of total output) show a significant reliance on U.S. import markets. But smaller industries, perhaps critical to future economic activity, also have relatively high rates of export intensity in both countries.

- For example, many of Mexico's relatively high tech industries (e.g., electrical and electronic products, professional goods, machinery, and motor vehicles) reap enormous benefits from U.S. import markets — these are the Mexican industries with the highest export intensities. Others with high export intensities include textiles, and wood. For Canada, electrical and electronic products, motor vehicles, and machinery are three of five industries with the highest export intensities which rely on exports to the United States for their growth. The other two are petroleum and non-ferrous metals (they comprise an important 4 percent of the economy).

- In 1996, these three Canadian industries made up about one-quarter (27.7 percent real value-added) of the manufacturing sector, up 24.9 percent from 1990. These are also among the fastest-growing parts of the Mexican economy. Their total share is smaller than Canada's at only 20.6 percent of manufacturing value-added in 1996. However, this is an improvement of 16.1 percent from 1990, and in the future their share should be higher. Canadian industries with lower export intensities (e.g., food, textiles, and drugs and medicines) are among the slower-growing segments of the economy.

## TRADE IN THE WIDER CONTEXT: THE IMPACT OF TRADE DIVERSION AND CREATION

IT IS IMPORTANT TO CONSIDER EXPORTS from Mexico and Canada and trade flows to the United States in the wider context of trade with the ROW and possible future developments (e.g., the movement toward a free trade area of the Americas (FTAA) and possible further multilateral reductions in trade impediments). For instance, it is assumed that the NAFTA has contributed to the growth in trade among its North American partners. Some of this increase might properly be described as trade creation, but some, too, as trade diversion — the NAFTA may have deflected trade internally that would otherwise have taken place between individual North American countries and the ROW (the NAFTA dealt Mexico and Canada a price advantage over other countries and produced incentives for U.S. customers not only to shift from domestic goods to imports, but to substitute imports from Mexico and Canada for imports from elsewhere).

It would be helpful to know whether the NAFTA resulted in new trade opportunities within North America or if it simply diverted manufacturing export trade from the ROW to North America. If it is the latter, and if world trade impediments continue to decline, what will happen to existing trade and export patterns (i.e., will growing interest lead to the opening up of the NAFTA trade liberalization plans to participation by other countries)? If the NAFTA is simply contributing to more vigorous trade competition and growth, however, it may lead to higher income-induced import demand that will be large enough to overcome any relative price-induced trade diversion effects of manufactured goods exports from the ROW to North America.

Here we examine some key evidence, namely the change in distribution of trade flows. Figure 20 builds on the 1998 trade share information presented earlier in Figure 4 by including information for 1990 (three years before the NAFTA was implemented). Figure 20 shows that the trade flow distribution between the NAFTA countries and the ROW changed somewhat between 1990 and 1998. Mexico's trade share with the ROW fell dramatically, from

169

FIGURE 20

TRADE SHARES OF THE NAFTA COUNTRIES

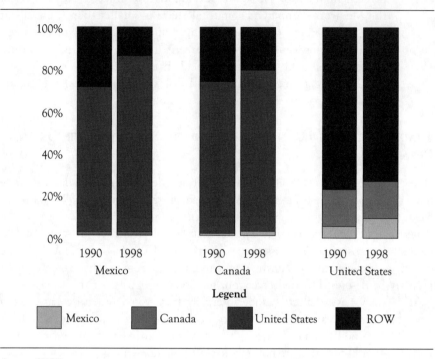

Source: OECD.

28.5 to 13.8 percent. Canadian trade with the ROW also decreased, from a share of 25.7 to 20.3 percent.[20] Meanwhile, the share of U.S. trade with the ROW decreased from 77.1 to 73.1 percent, with most of that decrease attributed to an expansion in U.S. trade with Mexico.

The fact that the share of total trade between the North American countries increased rather noticeably certainly suggests that there is the possibility of trade diversion. However, the NAFTA could have simply resulted in an expansion of trade within North America at a faster rate than with the ROW (for instance, Mexico's trade in manufactured goods with the United States grew by 18.2 percent, Canada's by 8.3 percent and the ROW's by 7.6 percent between 1990 and 1998). Indeed, Figure 21 shows that trade with countries outside North America still grew as a share of GDP for both Canada and the United States. Although far from providing conclusive evidence that there is no trade diversion, we nevertheless can conclude that, on the aggregate, any trade diversion may still be modest. This finding is compatible with that from the shift-share analysis in the third section, in that it shows U.S. import demand as driving Canada's export growth to the United States. For Mexico, the story clearly is different: not only did Mexico's trade with the ROW as a share of its GDP fall, but Mexico's increased trade with the United States was found to be largely a result of competitive factors. As a result, we cannot rule out the distinct influence that might be played by trade diversion in the case of Mexico's export growth with the United States.

### Particular Industries

Table 18 documents that between 1990 and 1998, U.S. trade grew across all industries, not only with Mexico and Canada, but also with the ROW. The sole exception was in petroleum for Canada and the ROW (which exhibited minor decreases). However, it is notable that Mexico's trade with the United States grew consistently faster than that for Canada and the ROW. Canada's U.S. trade grew slightly faster than that for the ROW.

FIGURE 21

TRADE WITH THE WORLD AS A SHARE OF GDP
(EXCLUDING TRADE BETWEEN NAFTA COUNTRIES)

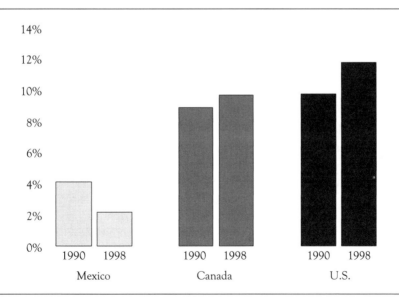

Source: OECD.

171

## TABLE 18

### TRADE WITH THE UNITED STATES

| | US$ billion, 1990 | | | Growth, 1990-98, % | | |
|---|---|---|---|---|---|---|
| | Mexico | Canada | ROW | Mexico | Canada | ROW |
| **All Manufacturing** | 21.7 | 78.3 | 330.5 | 18.2 | 8.3 | 7.6 |
| Food, Beverages and Tobacco | 0.9 | 3.2 | 16.0 | 10.9 | 9.4 | 3.5 |
| Textiles, Apparel and Leather | 1.2 | 0.7 | 42.7 | 27.5 | 20.7 | 6.8 |
| Wood Products and Furniture | 0.7 | 4.7 | 4.9 | 16.8 | 13.4 | 9.5 |
| Paper, Paper Products and Printing | 0.2 | 9.6 | 4.0 | 12.4 | 3.0 | 6.8 |
| Chemicals (excluding Drugs) | 0.9 | 4.9 | 19.4 | 10.7 | 9.2 | 9.5 |
| Drugs and Medicines | 0.0 | 0.1 | 2.4 | 19.9 | 28.2 | 19.8 |
| Petroleum Refineries and Products | 0.5 | 3.0 | 15.7 | –4.3 | –0.3 | –3.9 |
| Rubber and Plastic Products | 0.4 | 1.5 | 10.4 | 16.3 | 12.5 | 8.4 |
| Non-metallic Mineral Products | 0.5 | 0.7 | 4.8 | 12.6 | 10.8 | 7.7 |
| Iron and Steel | 0.5 | 2.1 | 8.6 | 15.8 | 6.7 | 8.6 |
| Non-ferrous Metals | 0.5 | 4.1 | 6.9 | 8.5 | 5.0 | 5.6 |
| Metal Products | 0.7 | 1.9 | 9.5 | 18.6 | 13.3 | 7.4 |
| Machinery (including Computers) | 1.6 | 5.4 | 50.9 | 23.9 | 10.9 | 10.8 |
| Electrical and Electronic Products | 7.7 | 4.8 | 47.4 | 16.4 | 9.9 | 8.9 |
| Shipbuilding and Repair | 0.0 | 0.1 | 0.4 | 5.7 | 15.9 | 14.8 |
| Motor Vehicles | 4.3 | 27.9 | 46.7 | 20.3 | 7.3 | 3.9 |
| Aircraft | 0.0 | 2.3 | 8.5 | 9.1 | 8.7 | 9.5 |
| Other Transport Equipment | 0.0 | 0.5 | 1.6 | 40.2 | 14.0 | 9.1 |
| Professional Goods | 0.7 | 0.7 | 12.5 | 22.8 | 11.9 | 9.0 |
| Other Manufacturing | 0.4 | 0.3 | 17.12 | 16.68 | 14.29 | 7.8 |

Source: Based on OECD, *Structural Analysis Database*.

In the three key industries of motor vehicles, electrical and electronic products, and machinery, the trade performance of both countries was quite impressive — especially in motor vehicles. Table 18 shows that the growth in the Mexican motor vehicle trade with the United States was 20.3 percent, or more than four times faster than the comparable growth in the ROW (3.9 percent). The Canada-U.S. motor vehicle trade grew 7.3 percent. In machinery, Mexico's trade with the United States grew twice as fast (23.9 percent, versus 10.9 and 10.8 percent for Canada and the ROW). Similarly, in electrical and electronic products, Mexico's growth was 16.4, as opposed to 9.9 and 8.9 percent for Canada and the ROW.

Another important sector for Mexico was the trade in textiles to the United States, which grew at a hefty 27.5 percent. Canada's textiles trade with the United States also had a significant growth of 20.7 percent. The comparable growth for the ROW was 6.8 percent. Figure 22 shows that this growth appears to have been at Hong Kong's expense: Mexico's share of U.S. apparel imports between 1990 and 2000 rose from 4.5 to 14.5 percent, while Hong Kong's fell by a similar amount.

FIGURE 22

## SHARE OF U.S. IMPORTS, TOP THREE EXPORTING COUNTRIES

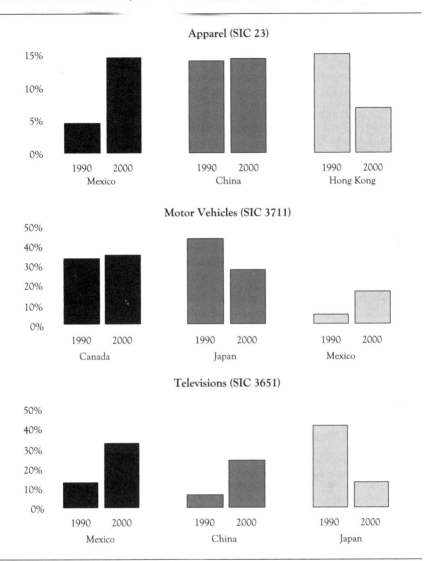

Source: United States International Trade Commission.

A similar story is found in the television (TVs) component of electrical and electronic products and in motor vehicles. The U.S. import market for TVs grew strongly in the 1990s, and while Mexico's share increased dramatically, Japan's declined. This could be a consequence of the NAFTA; however, over the same period China also managed to increase its share of the U.S. import market. For motor vehicles, the two NAFTA partners increased their share at the expense of Japan.

# THE RESEARCH IN BRIEF

## SUMMARY OF KEY MESSAGES

IN SPITE OF CANADA'S STRONG GROWTH in exports to the United States, Mexico's U.S.-bound exports have grown twice as fast. Mexico has benefited from strong U.S. import demand and greater export competitiveness, while Canada has relied mainly on strong U.S. import demand. Moreover, Canada's share of the U.S. import market is not rising, whereas Mexico's share is rising quickly.

### Mexican and Canadian Exports Are Concentrated in Similar Industries

Perhaps surprising to many is the fact that, at an aggregate industry level, the strong areas of U.S.-bound exports for both countries are in similar industries: motor vehicles, electrical and electronic products, and machinery. In all three, Mexico's U.S. export trade growth performance was superior to Canada's. Mexico's export intensity in motor vehicles, and machinery is also growing quite strongly. These are among the industries in each country that are associated with higher productivity and wages than other domestic industries.

### The Exports of Mexico and Canada Are Complementary,
### Not Competing, and Reflect Their Respective Comparative Advantages

The evidence from industry characteristics like capital-labour ratios and wage levels suggests that Mexican and Canadian exports may not always be alike, and are actually dissimilar in many industries. However, dynamic change is widespread, and certainly in Mexico. Although manufacturing for export is more labour-intensive in Mexico than in Canada, there is some evidence that Mexico is moving up the value chain: export industries are increasing their capital-labour ratios relatively quickly and exports appear to be shifting to industries with relatively higher or faster-growing capital-to-labour requirements, like motor vehicles and machinery.

As well, Mexico and Canada are not export leaders in all the same U.S. import markets. For instance, Mexico is strengthening its trade linkages with the

United States most quickly in textiles, while wood resource products remain important for Canada. At the same time, Mexico is making its export presence felt in a widening number of U.S. import markets. In 1998, Mexico and Canada were both ranked among the top three exporters in the same six (of 20) industry groups; in 12 groups, they were both in the top five. This is a dramatic increase from a few years ago, and reflects the rising importance of exports from Mexico. One key point: in its shift toward openness, Mexico underwent considerable liberalization in its trade with the United States, which contributed to its recent rapid growth in U.S.-bound exports. Now that most of the effects of this liberalization are in place, can Mexico continue its rapid U.S. export growth? Can it develop new export markets? We will have to wait and see.

Further inroads into the U.S. marketplace, especially into more sophisticated product lines and upgrades, will likely depend on Mexico's ability to complement its low-cost labour advantages with additional competitive advantages through improved productivity and quality (i.e., further develop its competitiveness along Ricardian lines, to round out the benefits from low-cost, Heckscher-Ohlin-type labour advantages).

## Does Mexico's Rise as an Exporter to the United States Pose Problems for Canada's U.S.-bound Export Interests?

Is there room for both Mexico and Canada in the large U.S. import market? While the review of capital and labour intensity supports the contention that Mexico's exports reflect more labour-intensive activities, it is equally accurate to say that as Mexican wages and productivity rise, especially in their key industries, there is the possibility for greater *direct* competition with Canadian exporters. That is, the nature of individual Mexican exports could become more closely aligned with individual Canadian manufacturing exports. As well, the rise in Canadian exports has been based primarily on growing U.S. import demand. As U.S. demand slows, it will be more difficult for Canada to maintain its share of U.S. import markets without becoming more competitive with the ROW, and increasingly with Mexico, in all industries. The best way for Canada to improve its competitiveness and bring benefits to its workers and consumers is through improved productivity. This means that Canadian industry will have to become more innovative.

Mexico and Canada were both fortunate to be located so near the fast-growing U.S. import markets of the 1990s. For much of its modern history, Canada has benefited from having a population stretched out along the U.S. border in close proximity to the many major centres of the U.S. economy, like New York, Chicago and Detroit. A common shared heritage and language have also helped to cement this economic relationship. Mexico, however, is even closer to important and fast-growing markets in the U.S. South and Southwest.

The United States is also witnessing the strong emergence of an Hispanic population, again, especially in the South. This can only enhance Mexico's economic links with the United States.

## The Mexican, Canadian and U.S. Economies Have Become More Integrated

There are signs that export competition between Mexico and Canada may become a more serious challenge. For example, intraindustry trade with the United States is growing for both Mexico and Canada. A great deal of this involves intrafirm trade. Intraindustry trade is associated with more product differentiation, competition in designing and incorporating process and product features, as well as economies of scale and the related improvements in cost and productivity. Intrafirm allocations of activity do depend on cost considerations, but they also depend on the ability to create and compete in new product niches. At present, Mexico compares favourably in terms of many cost considerations. As the country's ability to attract investment and technology grows, it will be able to compete more strongly in a wider range of intra-(multinational) corporation economic activities.

This is most important in the key industries of motor vehicles, electrical and electronic products, and machinery, which already have a considerable amount of intraindustry and intrafirm trade — the latter involving affiliates of the same U.S.-based multinationals. This means that Mexican and Canadian affiliates will be privileged to the same technologies, and while cost factors will play a role in the assignment of production activities, so too will the infrastructure available to take advantage of newer technologies. As the Mexican economy advances, it will be able to put in place the support systems to compete for production facilities on these grounds as well. As productivity and wage levels rise in Mexico, these better-paying industries will become more attractive, and competition with Canada will escalate.

## Mexico and Canada: U.S. Exports in the Context of U.S. Trade with the Rest of the World

Finally, we should consider these two countries' exports and trade flows to the United States against the background of the continuing interest on the part of many for a larger FTAA, or multilateral reductions in international protection. Our basic finding is that the growth in exports from Mexico and Canada is unlikely to represent any significant trade diversion effects from the NAFTA. U.S. trade with countries outside North America also grew, although not as fast as total U.S. trade with Mexico and Canada. Trade diversion is a possibility, but it is unlikely to be a major problem, except perhaps in specific industries. These industries could also change as

Mexico advances economically and is able to take advantage of the NAFTA with a wider range of products. Currently, however, Mexican exports like electrical and electronic products (TVs), and textiles are rising at the expense of foreign — in these cases Asian — suppliers.

Overall, however, the possible extension of the NAFTA to a larger FTAA and the further liberalization of world trade through the World Trade Organization are not expected to have a significant effect on Mexican and Canadian exports to the United States. Of course, particular industries in Mexico and Canada may be vulnerable. For Mexico, these could include some labour-intensive activities in electrical and electronic products as well as textiles, machinery and professional goods. Mexico's proximity to U.S. markets and U.S. corporate facilities (in the case of intrafirm trade), however, will likely still provide the country with considerable advantages.

## CONCLUDING THOUGHTS

ONE INTERESTING PUZZLE THAT REMAINS to be studied more fully has to do with the increased linkages between the three North American economies that have resulted from the greater movement of goods back and forth across the borders at various stages of processing.

There is also a need for more detailed industry analysis to improve our understanding of individual industry adjustments. This would be particularly useful in determining the overall contribution of the FTA and NAFTA tariff reductions to the restructuring of Mexico's and Canada's domestic industries.

Finally, it has become clear that in today's global environment, the future prosperity of individual nations increasingly depends on their ability to lever advantages from continual productivity and quality improvements. It will be important, therefore, to study further the impact of enhanced productivity and quality improvements on the export competitiveness of both Mexico and Canada, and the export benefits to be derived from each country's labour and natural resource advantages. And as Ricardian forces play a larger role in the future growth of exports from Mexico and Canada to the United States, it will be necessary to monitor the effects of this growth and see whether it is making the two countries' trade specialization more similar.

## ENDNOTES

1   In the following, unless otherwise noted, trade and exports will refer to trade and exports in manufactured goods.

2   Trade in services is an important component of international trade for both countries. In 2000, the commercial service trade was about one-tenth the value of

merchandise trade for Mexico and about 15 percent for Canada (Figure 1B). Given the lack of comparable industry-level data for the trade in services, however, this study will focus entirely on merchandise trade.

3   The importance of the United States to the merchandise trade of both Mexico and Canada may be somewhat overstated because of the transshipment problem.

4   The growth rates of manufacturing industry exports for Mexico and Canada are shown in Table 2. The individual industry shares of total manufacturing exports and their recent changes for both Mexico and Canada are shown in Table 3.

5   Given the importance of motor vehicles, machinery, and electrical and electronic products to the exports of each of the two countries, they will receive special attention in the forthcoming analysis. Another reason for special interest in these industries is that they have higher productivity and wages in relation to other domestic industries in both Mexico and Canada. Consequently, they comprise industrial activity that both countries would like to see prosper.

6   Mexico's biggest increases were in textiles and apparel, machinery, and motor vehicles. In Canada, however, motor vehicles, and paper and paper products saw their shares of exports to the United States drop in 1998, while those of wood products, machinery, and electrical and electronic products rose.

7   The RCA that Mexico has in a particular product sold in the United States is calculated as Mexico's share of U.S. imports of the product divided by Mexico's share of total U.S. imports. A measure of less than 1.0 suggests that Mexico does not have a comparative advantage for that product in the U.S. market. A country's RCA for all its exports in a foreign market always averages out to 1.0.

8   We use data on capital expenditures because there are no data on capital stock for Mexico.

9   Unfortunately, a current lack of data does not permit a similar assessment for Mexico.

10  Shift-share methodology is well established. Recent examples of its use to study exports include Herschede (1991), Khalifah (1996) and Peh and Wong (1999). Shift-share analysis is closely related to the literature on constant market shares. See Leamer and Stern (1969) and Richardson (1971).

11  Another way of looking at the second term is that it shows the difference between the actual change in the amount of exports in industry i and the amount if exports had simply grown in proportion to U.S. import demand — and, as noted above, a positive difference implies an improvement in export performance or competitiveness in relation to world exports to the United States in the industry-defined market.

12  The shift-share technique is used in a study of the export competitiveness of the Association of South East Asia Nations economies by Wilson and Wong (1999).

13  It is important to look at trends because focussing on individual years may actually give a somewhat myopic picture of a country's export performance, as results may be unduly influenced by exceptional years in the data.

14  There is difficulty in assessing the importance and implications of trans-shipments, especially for an analysis of the regional dimension of Canadian exports to U.S. regions.

15  A discussion of the impacts of trade diversion and creation on Mexico's and Canada's exports to the United States will be provided in the fifth section, entitled "Some Issues."

16    Consensus Forecast, December 19, 2001.

17    Interestingly, Mexico's average productivity has grown much more rapidly than wage rate per person over the 1990s. However, there is a correlation between relative wage rates and labour productivity levels (48.7 percent), but a much smaller one between wage rates and productivity growth (9.5 percent). For Canada, the reverse is true: the equivalent Canadian correlation figures are 32.3 and – 0.7 percent, respectively.

18    For more on maquiladora operations, please see Sydor (2001, 19).

19    Does rapid economic growth lead to rapid trade expansion, or is it the other way around? Anecdotal evidence suggests that countries with strong export performance have strong growth performance, and vice versa. Models by Grossman and Helpman (1991) and Riviera-Batiz and Romer (1991) posit that expanded international trade increases growth rates. Several empirical researchers, including Kunst and Marin (1989), Marin (1992) and Serletis (1992), find that developed or industrialized economies exporting a large share of their output seem to grow faster than others. In contrast, others have noted that an increase in GDP generally leads to a corresponding expansion of trade. Neoclassical trade theory typically stresses the causality that runs from home-factor endowments and productivity to export growth. Henriques and Sadorsky (1996) find empirical evidence in Canada that changes in growth precede changes in exports. (This affirms the theoretical development of a small open economy, i.e., a small economy developing efficiently in line with its comparative advantages will specialize and hence turn to foreign markets for the export of goods that use its most abundant factor of production most intensively).

20    Clausing (2001) investigates changes in trade patterns introduced by the FTA. Results indicate that there were substantial trade creation effects with little evidence of trade diversion.

# BIBLIOGRAPHY

Arndt, Sven W., and Alex Huemer. "North American Trade After NAFTA: Part 1." *Claremont Policy Briefs* (April 2001a): 1-4.

_____. "North American Trade After NAFTA: Part 2." *Claremont Policy Briefs* (July 2001b): 1-4.

Clausing, Kimberly A. "Trade Creation and Trade Diversion in the Canada-United States Free Trade Agreement." *Canadian Journal of Economics* (August 2001).

Consensus Forecast. London UK: Consensus Economics Inc, December 19, 2001.

Federal Reserve Bank of Dallas. *El Paso Business Frontier*, Issue 2, 1999.

Grossman, Gene M., and Elhanan Helpman. *Innovation and Growth in the Global Economy*. Cambridge MA: The MIT Press, 1991.

Grubel, Herbert G., and P. J. Lloyd. *Intra-Industry Trade: The Theory and Measurement of International Trade in Differentiated Products*. London and Basingstoke: The MacMillan Press, 1975.

Henriques, Irene, and Perry Sadorsky. "Export-led Growth or Growth-driven Exports? The Canadian Case." *Canadian Journal of Economics* 29, 3 (1996): 540-55.

Herschede, Fred. "Competition Among ASEAN, China, and the East Asian NICs: A Shift-share Analysis." *ASEAN Economic Bulletin* 7, 3 (1991): 290-306.

International Monetary Fund. *International Financial Statistics Yearbook.* Washington DC: International Monetary Fund, 2001.

_____. *Mexico: Recent Economic Developments.* Washington: Western Hemisphere Department, June 1995.

Khalifah, N. Aini. "Identifying Malaysia's Export Market Growth: A Shift-share Analysis." *Asia-Pacific Development Journal* 3, 1 (1996): 73-92.

Kunst, R., and D. Marin. "On Exports and Productivity: A Causal Analysis." *Review of Economics and Statistics* 71 (1989): 699-703.

Leamer, E. F., and R. M. Stern. *Quantitative International Economics.* Chicago: Allyn and Bacon Inc., 1970, pp. 171-83.

Marin, D. "Is the Export-led Growth Hypothesis Valid for Industrialized Countries?" *Review of Economics and Statistics* 74 (1992): 678-88.

OECD. *Regulatory Reform in Mexico.* Paris: OECD, 1999a.

_____. *OECD Economic Surveys 1998-99, Mexico.* Paris: OECD, 1999b.

_____. *Measuring Globalization: The Role of Multinationals in OECD Economies.* Paris: OECD, 1999c.

_____. *Structural Analysis Database (STAN), 1978-97.* Paris: OECD, 1999d.

_____. *Bilateral Trade Database 1980-98.* Paris: OECD, 2000.

Peh, Kian-Heng, and Fot-Chyi Wong. "Growth in Singapore's Export Markets, 1991-96: A Shift-share Analysis." *Asian Economic Journal* 13, 3 (1999): 321-44.

Richardson, J. David. "Constant-market-shares Analysis of Export Growth." *Journal of International Economics* I, 2 (1971): 227-39.

Riviera-Batiz, Luis A., and Paul M. Romer. "International Trade with Endogenous Technological change." *European Economic Review* 35, 4 (1991): 971-1001.

Sydor, Aaron. "Mexico: A Country in Transition." *Micro-Economic Monitor.* Ottawa: Industry Canada, October 2001.

Serletis, A. "Export Growth and Canadian Economic Development." *Journal of Development Economics* 38 (1992): 133-45.

United States International Trade Commission. *Impact of the North American Free Trade Agreement on the U.S. Economy and Industries: A Three-year Review.* Washington, D.C.: USITC, 1997.

United States Trade Representative. *Study on the Operation and Effect of the North American Free Trade Agreement.* Washington, D.C., 1997. Available at: http://www.ustr.gov/reports/naftareport/contents.pdf.

Wilson, Peter, and Wong Yin Mei. "The Export Competitiveness of ASEAN Economies, 1968-95." *ASEAN Economic Bulletin* 16, 2(1999): 208-29.

*Keith Head & John Ries*
*University of British Columbia*

4

# Free Trade and Canadian Economic Performance: Which Theories Does the Evidence Support?

## INTRODUCTION

OVER THE PAST TWO DECADES, Canada has made major commitments to free trade. Free trade agreements (FTAs) were negotiated successfully with the United States (1988), Mexico (1993), Chile (1997) and Costa Rica (2001). The 2001 Summit of the Americas in Quebec City brought the Free Trade Area of the Americas proposal into the sphere of public discussion again. Despite the protests that marked the last World Trade Organization (WTO) meeting in Seattle, we can reasonably expect that a new Millennium Round of multilateral trade negotiations will eventually start to move forward. In addition, the 1994 Bogor Declaration of the Asia Pacific Economic Cooperation forum has called for its industrialized members (such as Canada) to achieve "free and open trade and investment no later than the year 2010."

In light of this full plate of trade liberalization initiatives, it is important to determine what lessons can be drawn from Canada's experience with North American FTAs. The issue of free trade with the United States caused considerable controversy in the 1980s, leading to a 1988 election that many saw as a referendum on the issue. Canadian economists offered theoretical arguments for and against further liberalization with their large neighbour. At the time, there was relatively little empirical ground for these positions, as many of the ex-ante arguments drew upon then-recent innovations in international trade theory.

A reasonably large body of ex-post empirical analyses has since emerged. This study synthesizes the new research with a view to determining which theories receive support from the evidence. In addition to guiding future Canadian trade policy, we hope that our analysis will be useful for students of international trade theory. Canada's experience provides a valuable "natural laboratory" for understanding how trade liberalization affects the economic performance of a small, high-income economy trading with a much larger country.

This study assesses the impact of free trade on three aspects of the Canadian economy. First, we examine the trade creation effects of Canada's North American FTAs. Common across theories is the notion that the removal of barriers impeding trade will lead to an increase in trade. The magnitude of the trade creation effects due to FTAs is uncertain, and therefore we summarize the estimates provided by recent studies of Canada-U.S. trade. We also discuss negative aspects of FTAs: trade diversion and increased dependence on a single trading partner.

The second area we investigate is intersectoral resource allocations across manufacturing sectors. The Heckscher-Ohlin theorem predicts the expansion of industries producing goods intensive in a county's abundant factors. ccording to this traditional theory, a key component of gains from trade is the shift of resources toward the production of goods that Canada is relatively efficient at producing. Also, we discuss the "new" trade theory developed by Krugman (1980), which predicts that the country with the larger market size will be the net exporter in increasing-returns industries. Both the Heckscher-Ohlin theorem and Krugman predict that trade liberalization will lead to greater specialization within an economy.

Finally, we consider whether free trade has enhanced productivity. Theory suggests three mechanisms through which trade liberalization leads to greater efficiency. One is better access to foreign markets, which can increase plant output: if there are plant-level economies of scale, higher output translates into lower average costs and greater efficiency. A second is greater technological innovation, which may occur either because trade facilitates the flow of knowledge or because open markets increase the incentives for innovation. A third is increased competition. "Market selection," a concept analogous to the Darwinian "natural selection," implies that less efficient firms will be forced out of the market, restructuring industry toward more efficient operations. We assess the productivity performance of Canadian manufacturing in the context of these three theories.

We have organized the study into sections on trade creation, intersectoral resource allocation and industry efficiency. In each section, we discuss theory and relevant empirical evidence for each of these three aspects of Canada's manufacturing performance. Our conclusion draws lessons from Canada's experience with freer trade and discusses the likely effects of additional liberalization.

## TRADE CREATION AND DIVERSION

TARIFFS PUT FOREIGN FIRMS at a competitive disadvantage in relation to domestic firms, as they create a wedge between the price that foreign firms receive for their products and the price that domestic consumers pay for them. The removal of tariffs in an FTA eliminates this wedge and lowers the prices consumers pay for imports from FTA partner countries.

Tariff reductions have a variety of welfare effects. Consumers benefit when the prices of imports fall. Not only do they pay less for a given amount of imports from FTA partners, they expand imports in response to falling import prices. The expansion of trade between trade agreement members is known as *trade creation* and reflects gains to consumers. Domestic producers and third-country (non-FTA country) producers, however, may lose sales as consumers shift consumption toward the goods of FTA partner countries. This process is called *trade diversion* and may lead to welfare losses. In this section, we evaluate the evidence to gauge the extent of trade creation and trade diversion in Canada's FTAs. We also provide an estimate of the dollar value of consumer gains resulting from the removal of tariffs on U.S. goods.

## TRADE CREATION

HERE WE EXAMINE THE EVIDENCE on the trade-creating effects of Canada's FTAs with the United States, Mexico and Chile, with the focus on the Canada-U.S. FTA. We also define the costs associated with FTAs that occur when domestic purchases are diverted toward firms in FTA partner countries and away from efficient third-country firms.

The Canada-U.S. FTA called for a phasing out of tariffs on manufactured goods between the two countries. Across 93 industry classifications in 1988, Canadian tariffs averaged 6.1 percent and U.S. tariffs 3.7 percent (Lester and Morehen 1987). Some industries had very high Canadian tariffs: leather footwear, clothing and household furniture rates stood at 20.7, 19.7 and 13.1 percent, respectively. By contrast, the tariff rates in other industries were lower: for example, motor vehicle levies averaged just 1.8 percent, as the 1965 Canada-U.S auto pact had eliminated tariffs on most auto trade.

Figures 1 and 2 provide evidence that the Canada-U.S. FTA led to increased trade intensity between the two countries. Figure 1 shows Canadian merchandise exports to the rest of the world (ROW) and to the United States in relation to manufacturing shipments. It shows a steady increase in the share of Canadian manufacturing shipments exported to the United States, ultimately reaching almost 50 percent in 1998. Figure 1 reveals that most Canadian exports go to the United States (87 percent in 1998). Figure 2 compares Canadian imports to Canadian domestic absorption (shipments minus exports plus imports), showing that the United States provides a large portion of the goods consumed by Canadians and that this share has risen over the post-FTA period (to 40 percent in 1998).

## FIGURE 1

### TRENDS IN CANADIAN MERCHANDISE EXPORTS AS A SHARE OF MANUFACTURING SHIPMENTS

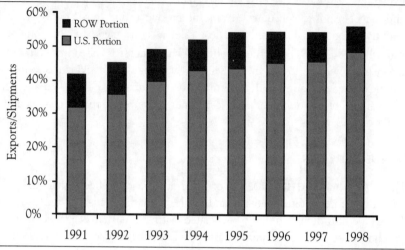

Source: Canadian Trade, by Industry (strategis.ic.gc.ca).

## FIGURE 2

### TRENDS IN CANADIAN MERCHANDISE IMPORTS AS A SHARE OF DOMESTIC ABSORPTION

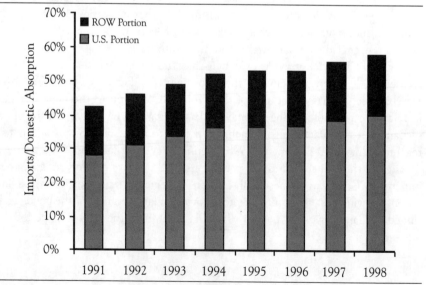

Source: Canadian Trade, by Industry (strategis.ic.gc.ca).

# FIGURE 3

## CANADIAN EXPORTS TO MEXICO, BRAZIL AND CHILE

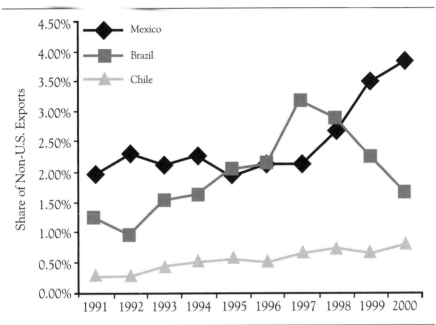

Source: strategis.ic.gc.ca.

There is also evidence that the North American Free Trade Agreement has generated increased trade with Mexico. Figure 3 shows trends in Canada's exports to Mexico, Brazil and Chile as a share of non-U.S. exports, while Figure 4 shows their shares of Canada's non-U.S. imports. Canada's FTAs with Mexico and Chile became effective in 1994 and 1997, respectively, with bilateral tariffs gradually being phased out. We add Brazil, a country that currently has no FTA with Canada, for comparison purposes. Figure 3 reveals that Canada's exports to Mexico increased rapidly from 1997 to 2000 and now comprise about 4 percent of Canada's total non-U.S. exports. Exports to Chile are small but growing, with steady growth even before the 1997 FTA. Interestingly, exports to Brazil have dropped over the same time period that exports to Mexico have grown, suggesting that Canadian exporters have shifted their attention toward the Mexican market. Figure 4 highlights the rise in Canada's imports from Mexico to 11 percent of total non-U.S. imports by 2000, while showing that Canadian imports from Chile and Brazil have changed little over the same period.

## FIGURE 4

### CANADIAN IMPORTS FROM BRAZIL, CHILE AND MEXICO

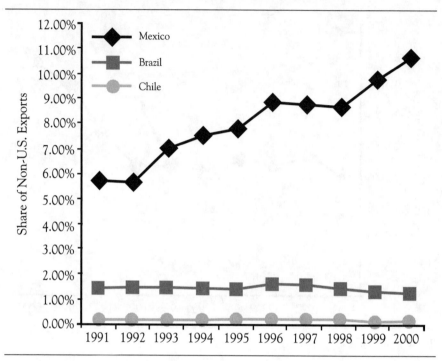

Source: strategis.ic.gc.ca.

Of course, one has to be careful about interpreting rising trade with FTA partners like the United States and Mexico throughout the period as being caused by the phasing out of bilateral tariffs. Figures 5 and 6 indicate that trade growth is positively related to the size of tariff reductions. In these figures, we group Canadian Standard Industrial Classification (SIC) 3-digit manufacturing industries into quintiles by their 1988 tariff levels. Then we sum imports and exports to the United States and the ROW and calculate the percentage change from 1988 to1998 for each quintile.

Figures 5 and 6 show a clear positive relationship between the size of tariff reductions (equal to the tariff level in 1988) and the growth of trade with the United States. Export growth is highest in industries with the largest U.S. tariff reductions (Figure 5). Likewise, import growth corresponds to Canadian tariff reductions (Figure 6). Interestingly, there is no apparent relationship between trade with the ROW and tariff changes.

## FIGURE 5

### EXPORT GROWTH, 1988-98

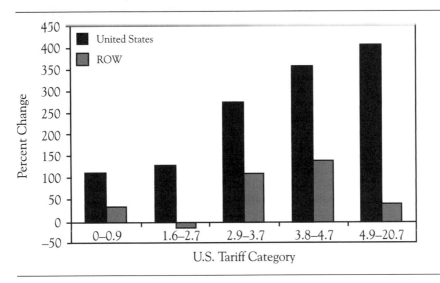

Source: strategis.ic.gc.ca, Lester and Morehen (1987).

## FIGURE 6

### IMPORT GROWTH, 1988-98

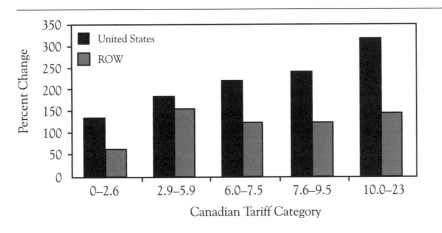

Source: strategis.ic.gc.ca, Lester and Morehen (1987).

Three research studies also link trade growth to tariff reductions. Trefler (1999) investigates the effect of the Canada-U.S. FTA on various performance measures of 213 4-digit SIC manufacturing industries in Canada. He examines the change in the growth rate of Canadian imports from the United States across two time periods, one before and one after the implementation of the FTA. He finds that Canadian tariff reductions explain roughly one-half of the observed increase in Canadian imports from the United States.

Clausing (2001) conducts a similar exercise but focusses on U.S. imports at the 10-digit harmonized system level. Using a gravity specification, she finds that U.S. tariff reductions mandated by the Canada-U.S. FTA significantly increased Canadian imports. She finds extremely large effects, concluding that the FTA was responsible for more than one-half of the $42 billion increase in U.S. imports from Canada over the 1989-94 period.

Schwanen (1997) compares the growth in trade between Canada's liberalized and non-liberalized sectors as well as the country's increase in trade with the United States against that with other countries. His premise is that growth in trade should be most pronounced in liberalized sectors and in trade between the United States and Canada. He finds that over the 1988-95 period, Canadian exports to the United States grew 139 percent in liberalized sectors and 64 percent in non-liberalized sectors. Exports to non-U.S. destinations in liberalized sectors grew only 34.7 percent, whereas exports to non-U.S. destinations in non-liberalized sectors increased 53.6 percent. Imports show a similar pattern, with growth highest for Canadian imports from the United States in liberalized sectors. It is worth noting, however, that Schwanen excludes motor vehicles from the analysis, an industry that realized significant changes in trade and one that had enjoyed free trade before the FTA. The results would be different if motor vehicles were included as a non-liberalized sector.

Figures 5 and 6 and the results of Trefler, Clausing and Schwanen indicate that the rise in trade with the United States that occurred after the Canada-U.S. FTA was not simply coincidental, but that trade increases are systematically related to tariff reductions. What is surprising is the magnitude of the measured effects. Two of the studies indicate that roughly half of the trade increase exhibited in the years after the FTA was attributable to tariff reductions.

More trade can translate into a higher standard of living through a number of mechanisms, many of which will be discussed in subsequent sections. Here we will consider the most basic gain economists point to when considering tariff reductions: the benefits enjoyed by consumers who can buy imports at a lower cost. Consumers receive a "surplus" whenever the value they obtain from a good exceeds the price they have to pay for it. On a graph, consumer surplus would be the area underneath the demand curve but above the price. Figure 7 shows the demand for U.S. goods. Eliminating tariffs from their most-favoured-nation (MFN) levels lowers prices and increases consumer surplus by the amount of the shaded area in the figure.

FIGURE 7

CONSUMER SURPLUS FROM TARIFF REDUCTIONS

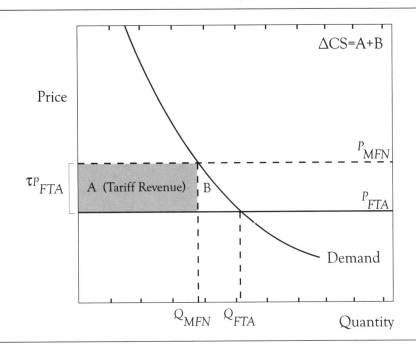

To calculate that area, we need to know the shape of the demand curve for imported products from the United States. A fairly reliable approximation is to assume a constant elasticity of demand with respect to price. This means that a reduction of 1 percent in price increases demand by $\eta$ percent. In mathematical terms, we say that import demand is given by $\alpha P^{-\eta}$. Using this functional form and calculating the area between tariff-free and tariff-inclusive prices, we get a change in the consumer surplus formula of

$$\Delta CS = V(1-(1+\tau)^{1-\eta})/(\eta-1),$$

where $V$ is the value of expenditures on goods from the United States in the absence of any tariffs and $\tau$ is the ad valorem tariff to be removed.

In order to use the above formula, we need to plug in a value for the price elasticity of demand for U.S. manufactured goods ($\eta$). Relating the change in imports to changes in tariffs across 109 industries, we estimate the value for the price elasticity to be approximately five. Details of the estimation procedure are available from the authors on request.

We use this elasticity value, combined with actual tariff and import data, to calculate the ΔCS associated with imposing 1988-level tariffs on U.S. imports in 1998 (when all such tariffs had, in fact, been removed) for each 3-digit SIC industry. Summing across all manufacturing industries, we find tariff imposition would cost Canadian consumers C$7.86 billion in lost surplus. This is 4.1 percent of 1998 expenditures on U.S.-made manufactured goods. The loss would be partially offset by increases in government duty revenue of C$6.56 billion. Thus, the net benefit to Canadians of implementing the FTA tariff reductions appears to be C$1.29 billion, or about $40 per person per year.

This "back-of-the envelope" calculation is incomplete in two ways. First, it omits the loss in profits for Canadian producers when Canadian consumers switch to buying imported U.S. goods after the tariff reduction. Second, it omits possible improvements to productive efficiency that are encouraged by competing in open markets. The first effect can reduce the net gain from free trade still further but will not eliminate it. The second effect might dramatically increase the benefits of a free trade regime. We will discuss the effects of tariff changes on productive efficiency in the next section.

## TRADE DIVERSION

AS WE NOTED IN THE INTRODUCTION, Canada has been busily signing FTAs since 1988. Some economists, most notably Bhagwati (1998), have strongly criticized regional agreements of the kind Canada has been actively pursuing. The critics refer to the bilateral agreements as "preferential" agreements rather than "free trade" agreements. There is a potential welfare-reducing aspect of preferential agreements, in that they may divert trade away from efficient trading partners.

To demonstrate the potential welfare costs of trade diversion, let us consider two trading partners — Mexico and Brazil — offering Canadians a good at two different prices. Suppose Brazilian firms are more efficient and willing to sell this good at a price, $P_B=\$10$, that is lower than the price offered by Mexican firms, $P_M=\$11$. With a tariff of, say, 20 percent, the Brazilian and Mexican goods will cost $12 and $13.20 in Canada, respectively. Under these circumstances, Canadian consumers would rather import from Brazil than pay more for the Mexican good. But suppose Canada enters into an FTA with Mexico and eliminates tariffs on Mexican goods. Now, the $12 cost of the Brazilian good in Canada is higher than the $11 free-trade price of the one from Mexico. Some Canadian consumers will now begin to purchase the Mexican good. The shift of Canadian purchases away from Brazil and toward Mexico due to preferential tariff treatment is trade diversion.

Canada might be worse off because of this trade diversion. Canadian consumers who shift consumption toward the Mexican good gain as the price they pay falls by $1. However, the Canadian government loses $2 per unit on the goods that were purchased initially from Brazil and are being purchased now from Mexico duty-free. On net, there is a loss in Canadian surplus for that good. However, lower prices mean that Canadians will buy more of the good in total. The consumer surplus associated with those additional purchases is a source of welfare gain. The overall effect is ambiguous, but could well be negative.

Is there evidence of trade diversion in Canada's FTAs? The data provided earlier suggest the answer is no. Figure 4 shows a rapid increase in the purchase of Mexican goods but no corresponding decreases in purchases of Brazilian and Chilean goods. Figure 6 does not portray a negative relationship between the growth of Canadian imports from the United States and the growth of imports from the ROW across tariff categories. Growing Canadian imports from FTA partner countries, therefore, do not appear to have caused a discernible decrease in imports from non-partner countries. Hence, possible negative effects of trade diversion, while theoretically plausible, are not evident in Canada's experience with FTAs.

## HOLD-UP EFFECTS

MCLAREN (1997) FORMALIZED what he calls the "Judge Bowker" argument against free trade. The idea is that countries have the option of making irreversible investments that lower the costs of trading with each other. Anticipating tariff liberalization with the United States, Canadian firms make investments that will facilitate exports to that market. This is fine as long as there are complete, enforceable contracts between the two countries. In practice, however, the United States may be able to renegotiate or circumvent the signed agreement. The more Canadian exporters commit themselves to trade with the United States, the less bargaining power the Canadian government has with its trading partner.

McLaren cites Hawaii's experience with trade liberalization with the United States in 1876 as an example of hold-up. Hawaii invested heavily in sugar production in response to the removal of a large U.S. tariff. This investment was U.S.-specific, as the United States was the only major market for Hawaiian sugar. Later threats by the United States to abrogate the tariff treaty resulted in Hawaii's agreement to allow the U.S. naval facility at Pearl Harbor. The logic is that the "side payment" was less costly to Hawaii than forfeiting relationship-specific investment in the U.S. export market.

So far, there does not seem to be any empirical work confirming the importance of hold-up effects in trade. In light of Canadian dependence on the American market, some might interpret U.S. harassment of Canadian softwood lumber exports as a tactic aimed at extracting side-payments. However, this dispute precedes the Canada-U.S. FTA by six years. Moreover, U.S. tariffs on sawmill products were nearly zero before the FTA. Thus it seems unlikely that the FTA caused a major increase in U.S.-specific investments in that industry.

Figure 1 shows that Canada now sells almost 90 percent of its exports to the United States, which is the destination for 50 percent of our manufacturing shipments. The Schwanen and Clausing analyses suggest the increased dependency is a consequence of the FTA. Also, a key component of McLaren's argument is that an increase in bilateral trade dependence seems to have been a consequence of the FTA. Although the treaty gave both countries the right to be relieved of the treaty obligations with six months' advance notice, neither side has attempted to use that threat to encourage a renegotiation. We have not found any clear cases where the United States took advantage of increased Canadian export dependence to extract side payments from Canada. Moreover, the FTA establishes rules and institutions (dispute resolution panels) aimed at restricting this type of opportunistic behaviour. Finally, even if the United States were to opt out of the FTA, the damage it could impose on Canada would be quite limited because the United States has obligations to the WTO that would prevent it from raising trade barriers arbitrarily on another member (such as Canada).

The lesson to draw from this section is that Canada's FTAs have created substantial new trade with the United States and possibly Mexico. We see no evidence that this new trade with these two countries partly constitutes trade diverted from third countries. Finally, although Canada is now quite dependent on the United States as a destination for exports, there is little evidence, so far, of a serious threat to Canadian sovereignty.

## INTERINDUSTRY RESOURCE REALLOCATION

TRADE LIBERALIZATION MAKES IT LESS COSTLY for economies to specialize in the activities they do best. Two centuries of research on the benefits of trade are based on this simple idea. To gain real insight, one needs to be very careful in defining what an economy "does best." Trade theorists have devoted the most attention to the opportunity costs of producing goods in different industries. Countries that have low opportunity costs in one industry have a comparative advantage in that industry and will respond to trade liberalization by reallocating scarce resources away from industries in which they have a comparative disadvantage. A second source of advantage flows from the demand side. Recent work has suggested that there are plausible circumstances in which having relatively large demand in an industry confers what might be called a comparative home-market advantage. As with traditional comparative advantages, the existence of home-market effects will lead to resource reallocations across industries following trade liberalization.

Traditional trade theory, as embodied in the Heckscher-Ohlin theorem, predicts the expansion of industries producing goods intensive in a country's abundant factors. The specification developed by Vanek (1968) predicts that a country's pattern of net exports of factor services will be given by its share of the world supply of a given factor minus its share of world demand. Assuming homothetic preferences, world demand is given by its share of world gross national product. In the case of Canada, we would expect greater exports of resource-intensive goods.

The Canadian economy is composed of the agriculture, logging, mining, manufacturing, services and government sectors. The first three sectors are resource-intensive, and we might expect trade liberalization to promote those sectors at the expense of manufacturing. Within manufacturing, however, there are resource-intensive sectors like pulp and paper, food and metals. Thus, the Heckscher-Ohlin theorem would predict the expansion of these sectors within manufacturing and the contraction of others.

The traditional trade models focussed on the production side to show how country differences might influence the pattern of trade. Another natural possibility is to consider the importance of differences in demand structures. The role of demand was stressed in Linder (1961). His hypothesis primarily revolved around who would trade with whom. Linder argued that internal demand would stimulate new product development and that the pioneering country, after developing a new product, would then begin to export it to countries with similar levels of per-capita income. Two decades later, the Krugman (1980) model of a two-sector economy (an increasing returns-to-scale sector and a constant returns-to-scale sector) showed that relatively high domestic demand in the increasing-returns sector implies a trade surplus in that sector. Krugman referred to this possibility as the "home-market effect." The basic idea is that there is a trade-off between serving small markets with local production and thereby avoiding tariffs, and serving them from a single plant in the large country and thereby achieving economies of scale. A reduction in tariffs reduces the benefit of local presence. Krugman showed that trade liberalization will cause industries (manufacturing) with increasing returns to concentrate in large markets and thereby increase large-country net exports in these industries.

Krugman's model is highly specialized. Davis (1998) shows that the home-market effect may disappear when there are trade costs in the constant returns-to-scale sector. Moreover, his assumptions of ad valorem tariffs, Dixit-Stiglitz preferences and atomistic firms imply that free on board prices are independent of the number and location of firms, as well as transportation costs. The later work of Feenstra, Markusen and Rose (2001), Head and Ries (2001), and Head, Mayer and Ries (2002) show that home-market effects occur in other models characterized by economies of scale and product variety linked to mobile firms. However, all three studies develop cases where small-country manufacturing grows in response to trade liberalization. These "reverse" home-market effects occur when varieties are tied to nation of production and trade liberalization gives small-country producers better access to large-country consumers.

The home-market effect predicts that trade liberalization will shift manufacturing toward the larger country. As U.S. manufacturing industries are on average 10 times larger than those in Canada, this raises the concern that the Canada-U.S. FTA will have served to reduce the size of Canadian manufacturing. A further elaboration of the theory predicts differential impacts across manufacturing. Weder (1995) assumes balanced trade in manufacturing. (In the Krugman model, the perfectly competitive, constant returns-to-scale sector absorbs any trade imbalances arising in the manufacturing sector.) According to Weder, exchange rate adjustment implies that industries with a relatively large share of demand will expand and firms with a relatively small share of demand will contract. Head and Ries (2001) provide a model that generates the opposite result: when varieties are linked to country of production, relatively small demand industries in the small country benefit from trade liberalization.

### EMPIRICAL EVIDENCE

CLEARLY, THEORY DOES NOT RESTRICT THE TYPE of interindustry restructuring that may occur as a result of trade liberalization. Observing what has occurred in Canadian manufacturing will shed light on the practical importance of the alternative theories.

### FIGURE 8

### EMPLOYMENT IN MANUFACTURING

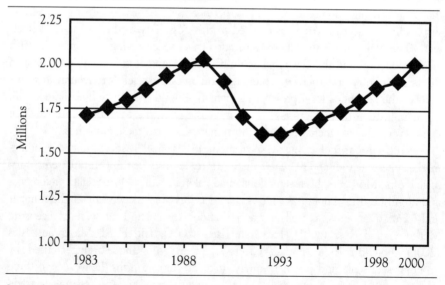

Source: CANSIM Matrix#4285 (Employment).

Figure 8 shows employment in manufacturing from 1983 to 2000. The 1991-92 Canadian recession and the subsequent recovery are apparent. Manufacturing employment fell from a peak of 2.03 million in 1989 to 1.62 million in 1993. This led many critics of the Canada-U.S. FTA to claim that the massive job losses resulted from the agreement. By 2000, however, manufacturing employment had recovered to 2.01 million.

Head and Ries (2001) test whether it is home-market or reverse home-market effects that characterize North American manufacturing by examining differential impacts of tariff reductions across 3-digit SIC manufacturing industries. We examine whether the effect of tariff reductions on changes in a Canadian industry's share of North American (Canada and the United States) output depended on its initial (1988) output share. We find that Canadian industries with small shares benefited more than those with large shares. This finding supports models that predict reverse home-market effects where trade liberalization benefits the smaller industries by giving them better market access.

As we mention at the outset of this section, trade liberalization should allow countries to specialize production in activities that they do best, whether their best is due to supply or demand factors. We should therefore look for an increase in Canadian manufacturing specialization after the FTA. We would consider manufacturing to be specialized if a few sectors constitute a majority of total manufacturing employment or output. It would be considered non-specialized if all sectors had similar output. A natural way to measure manufacturing specialization is to construct a Herfindahl index. We use 2-digit SIC manufacturing data for the years 1983 to 2000 to calculate real gross domestic product (GDP) and employment Herfindahl indexes for Canadian manufacturing. These are calculated as the sum of each industry's squared share of the variable in question:

$$H = \sum_i (shr_i)^2,$$

where $shr_i$ is industry $i$'s share of real GDP or employment, in manufacturing.

Figure 9 displays the two Herfindahl indexes. They behave very differently in the post-FTA period. The employment Herfindahl is remarkably flat, whereas the real GDP Herfindahl increases, especially in 1999 and 2000. Thus while the distribution of employment in manufacturing has hardly changed at all, the distribution of GDP has become more concentrated. The GDP in an industry rises when capital, labour or factor productivity increases. As employment did not become more concentrated, it must be either capital or productivity that caused the increased concentration of Canadian industry in terms of GDP.

# FIGURE 9

## IS CANADIAN MANUFACTURING BECOMING MORE SPECIALIZED?

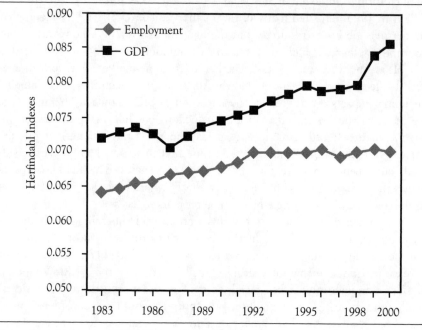

Source: Statistics Canada, CANSIM Matrix #4285 (Employment), #4677 (real GDP).

Overall, the figure provides no evidence that the FTA increased speciali-zation in Canadian manufacturing through an intersectoral reallocation of labour. While there does appear to be more concentration of capital or pro-ductivity (or both) in large industries, no studies have linked this reallocation *across* industries to trade liberalization. However, there are studies that link tariff reductions to increased productivity *within* industries. The next section discusses this topic.

## EFFICIENCY GAINS WITHIN INDUSTRIES

WHILE TRADITIONAL TRADE THEORY EMPHASIZES efficiency gains that arise from interindustry reallocations of resources, the "newer" trade theory developed in the early 1980s shows how gains from trade could arise from rationalization within industries. Later research added dynamic effects and modelled the effects of trade on endogenous technological progress. More recent research explores the implications of the considerable amount of hetero-geneity in business performance between firms in the same industry.

FIGURE 10

MFP IN LOW- AND HIGH-TARIFF INDUSTRIES

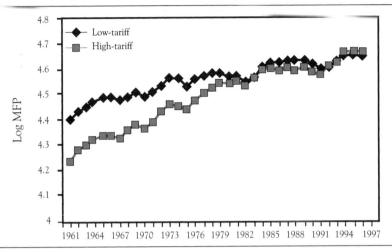

Source: Statistics Canada, CANSIM Matrix #9456.

There are two pieces of information to suggest that trade liberalization has increased productivity within Canadian manufacturing. Trefler relates changes in 4-digit SIC value-added per worker to Canadian tariff reductions under the Canada-U.S. FTA. He identifies substantial effects. In his preferred specification, he finds that Canadian tariff reductions increased value-added per worker by 0.6 percent per year from 1988 to 1996. For highly impacted industries — those with tariff reductions exceeding eight percentage points — the annual effect was 3.2 percent!

Greater value-added per worker could reflect a deepening of capital rather than an increase in multifactor productivity (MFP). To examine whether large tariff reductions are related to higher MFP, we divide the 22 2-digit SIC manufacturing industries in Canada into two equal groups of 11 on the basis of 1988 tariff levels. We calculate the average of tariff reductions and log MFP for each group. The results for 1961-97 are displayed in Figure 10. High-tariff industries lagged in productivity until the early 1980s, then fell behind again until 1988. After the 1989 implementation of the Canada-U.S. FTA, the high-tariff industries rapidly caught up to low-tariff ones in terms of MFP, and even surpassed them for a few years. Figure 10, therefore, suggests that MFP growth is accelerated by tariff reductions. We should introduce a note of caution regarding this interpretation, however. We were unable to generate a robust, statistically significant difference between the MFP of the two groups when we conducted regression analysis. Nevertheless, coupled with the Trefler results, there is evidence that the FTA has promoted industry efficiency. Next, we consider the theoretical underpinnings for this result.

## SCALE EFFECTS

CANADIAN TRADE ECONOMISTS HAVE SPENT A LOT OF TIME and attention on finding out whether trade liberalization moves manufacturing firms down their average cost curves. The process of achieving greater economies of scale through concentrating production at a smaller number of factories is sometimes referred to as rationalization. Early work on this subject gave rise to the East-man-Stykolt hypothesis, according to which high tariffs cause excess entry and inefficient scale in Canadian manufacturing (Eastman and Stykolt 1967).

There are two distinct reasons why trade liberalization might boost scale effects. The first involves a domestic industry that competes with imports but does not export. It is "sheltered" by an import tariff of $t$ dollars per unit. Assume that imports are supplied elastically from the United States or the ROW at a pre-duty price of $p^*$. In that case, it is reasoned that domestic prices can be no higher than $p^*+t$. If entry of domestic firms continues until there are no economic profits, the domestic average costs will be set to equal the tariff-inclusive import price. Thus

$$AC(q) = p^* + t,$$

where $AC(q)$ is a domestic firm's average cost of producing a given amount of output and is assumed to be decreasing. Given all these assumptions, the lowering of domestic tariffs will force down price, reduce average costs and raise output per firm.

This mechanism is illustrated in frame (A) of Figure 11. The average cost per firm is given by

$$AC(q) = F/q + c,$$

where $F$ is a fixed cost. Solving for output per firm, we find

$$q = F/(p^* + t - c).$$

Hence, scale is inversely proportionate to ad valorem tariffs. Removal of a 10 percent domestic tariff should cause domestic firms to expand by 10 percent! Cox and Harris (1985) built similar effects into their computable general equilibrium analysis of the effects of Canadian trade liberalization, and predicted substantial gains in scale and correspondingly much larger gains in economic welfare than conventional constant-returns analyses had predicted. The Cox-Harris results may have been influential in encouraging the Mulroney government to pursue the FTA even though it was going to mean much larger tariff reductions for Canada than for its trade partner.

# FIGURE 11

## SCALE EFFECTS OF TARIFF REDUCTIONS

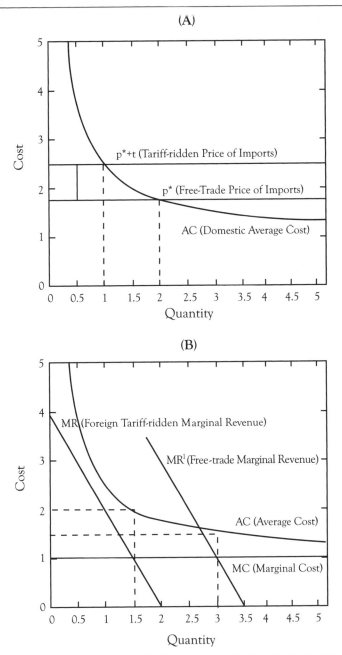

The second reason why trade liberalization might boost scale effects applies to reductions in *foreign* tariffs. Better access to foreign markets gives domestic firms more customers and therefore allows them to spread their fixed costs over more units, and results in lower average costs per unit. This is illustrated in frame (B) of Figure 11, where lower foreign tariffs shift out the representative exporter's marginal revenue curve. The firm's new profit maximizing quantity rises from 1.5 to 3.0, so that it moves down the average cost curve as it achieves economies of scale.

This exporter's experience suggests that tariff reductions by trading partners benefit Canadian firms by allowing them to expand output. One might also expect, however, that Canadian tariff reductions would have the opposite effect. The Eastman-Stykolt hypothesis showing scale increase resulting from Canadian tariff reductions is predicated on the notion that Canadian manufacturers are pricing to eliminate imports (tariff-limit pricing). There are reasons to be suspicious of this proposition. First, from a practical standpoint, Canada imports in every manufacturing industry and thus tariff-limit pricing does not appear to be empirically relevant. Moreover, even though Muller and Rawana (1990) establish that tariff-limit pricing is consistent with game theory and does not require explicit collusion by domestic firms, their analysis assumes that foreign supply does not respond to tariff reductions. Head and Ries (1999) present an imperfect competition model with Cournot oligopolists in both the home and foreign markets. In this model, foreign firms expand output in response to home tariff reductions. It shows that home tariff reductions reduce scale of firms in the home market, which contradicts the Eastman-Stykolt prediction. Thus, once again, different models generate opposing predictions, and the practical relevance of the models becomes an empirical question.

Figure 12 is a slightly updated version of a figure which appears in Head and Ries (1999) showing shipments, establishments and average scale (shipments divided by establishments) in Canadian manufacturing. The dramatic increase in scale after 1988 is *prima facie* evidence of the positive scale effect of trade liberalization. However, we note in our study that part of this increase is attributable to changes in the way Statistics Canada measures establishments, which result in the omission of small establishments. We relate average shipments in Canadian industry to both Canadian and U.S. tariff levels. We find that U.S. tariff reductions caused a 9.8 percent increase in scale, but this was largely offset by an 8.5 percent decline due to Canadian tariff reductions. Undercounting, industry composition changes and the depreciation of the Canadian dollar explain the increase of shipments per establishments depicted in Figure 12.

Trefler (1999) and Gu, Sawchuk and Whewell (2001) also find that Canadian tariff reductions lowered output per firm in Canadian manufacturing. Their results and ours constitute strong evidence against the Eastman-Stykolt hypothesis that Canadian tariff reductions raise scale. However, coupled with gains in scale associated with U.S. tariff reductions, we observe that tariff reductions under the Canada-U.S. FTA had no net effect on scale.

## FIGURE 12

## SCALE OF CANADIAN MANUFACTURING

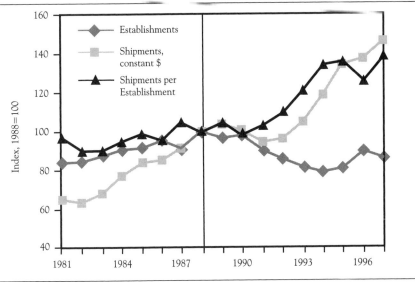

Source: Statistics Canada, CANSIM.

## DYNAMIC GAINS FROM TRADE

THE SO-CALLED "TRADE AND GROWTH" LITERATURE focusses on how productivity growth is influenced by trade. Dynamic gains from trade occur when liberalization increases the returns associated with innovation, thereby inducing greater investment in knowledge creation. In addition, there is an extensive empirical literature estimating the relationship between trade and growth.

Grossman and Helpman (1995) describe two mechanisms through which trade increases productivity and enhances economic growth. One mechanism is knowledge spillovers that are by-products of trade. Through the process of importing and exporting, firms learn of new technologies that can increase their output. A second mechanism involves the provision of intermediate inputs. Trade increases a firm's access to intermediate inputs and gives it incentives to create these inputs. Productivity is enhanced when firms have access to a larger range of intermediate inputs or state-of-the-art intermediates. These different models indicate that trade liberalization can increase welfare by increasing productivity.

The most common way to estimate MFP is to employ growth accounting to relate growth in output to growth in factor inputs (labour, capital, etc.). A large body of literature adds trade, or measures of openness to trade, as covariates in cross-country growth accounting regressions. The idea is to explain growth that is not accounted for by increased factor usage. While early literature finds both positive and negative relationships, more recent studies obtain positive ones. Levine and Renelt (1992) estimate growth equations using a large panel of countries and find a robust positive relationship between country income and the ratio of trade to GDP. Frankel and Romer (1999) consider an important econometric issue inherent in relating trade to income: unobservable factors that cause a country to have a high income are also likely to result in high values of trade. Using distance between trading partners to instrument for trade, they also find that the trade to GDP ratio has a strong effect on income. Finally, Frankel and Rose (2000) show that currency unions stimulate trade and trade stimulates output. This literature indicates that by promoting trade, Canada's FTAs could underlie the recent MFP increases in Canadian manufacturing.

## SELECTION EFFECTS

TRADE ADVOCATES HAVE LONG ARGUED THAT trade liberalization benefits countries by increasing competition, which induces greater efficiency within the domestic economy. It is only recently, however, that a theory has been developed to demonstrate the mechanisms through which a reduction in trade barriers results in higher productivity. Melitz (1999) develops a trade model of firms with heterogeneous levels of productivity. Increased competition caused by the lowering of trade barriers generates a selection effect: high-productivity firms increase output by exporting more, while low-productivity firms are forced to exit the market.

His model allows firms to enter the market if they pay a non-recoverable (sunk) cost. Before entering, a firm does not know its productivity as reflected by its marginal cost of production. In equilibrium, both high- and low-cost firms exist in the market. Trade liberalization increases imports and forces out marginal producers. While no individual firm is more productive in the new equilibrium, the industry as a whole is more productive, as the composition of industry output has shifted toward the more productive firms.

Melitz's theory may explain productivity increases in Canada. The closest test of this theory is contained in Gu, Sawchuk and Whewell, who relate Canadian tariff cuts under the FTA to industry turnover rates. They find that tariff reductions promote both entry and exit in Canadian manufacturing, and that the increase in exit rates due to tariff reductions is more pronounced in large firms. This is somewhat at odds with Melitz's theory that if large firms are the ones with low marginal costs, they are the least likely to be in jeopardy when trade barriers fall.

Productivity appears to have increased in liberalized manufacturing sectors in Canada. Current theory identifies increased scale, dynamic gains from trade and selection effects as sources of efficiency gains stemming from trade liberalization. Our review of the empirical literature, however, indicates that increased scale was not an outcome of the Canada-U.S. FTA. Moreover, while Gu, Sawchuk and Whewell show that tariff reductions had selection effects on Canadian industry (by inducing turnover), the selection was not consistent with the Melitz theory prediction. This leaves dynamic gains from trade as the means by which efficiency in Canada improved after the FTA. We do not know of any research, however, that confirms dynamic gains from trade as the source of observed productivity increases in Canada.

## Conclusion

IN LIGHT OF THE FTAs Canada has already signed, and given the prospect of more in the future, this study presents a synthesis of the theoretical and empirical literature on trade liberalization as it relates to Canada. We find that the literature indicates a substantial increase in trade, and see no evidence of welfare losses associated with trade diversion and increased trade dependence. We find only limited evidence that the Canada-U.S. FTA has increased specialization within Canadian manufacturing. Finally, we consider the manufacturing productivity growth that occurred in Canada during the 1990s and conclude that this increase in industrial efficiency was not the result of greater scale in Canadian manufacturing induced by the elimination of tariffs. Nor does it appear that tariff reductions "naturally" selected away from small, inefficient firms toward larger, more productive firms. The trade and growth literature identifying spillovers and greater incentives to invest in knowledge capital therefore remains the theoretical explanation for the increased efficiency, although empirical research has not yet explicitly tested this proposition.

The Canada-U.S. FTA stimulated a large increase in trade. Increased trade is the prerequisite for the various gains from trade espoused by economists. Consumers clearly have benefited from the ability to purchase goods supplied by foreign producers at lower prices. Moreover, if trade liberalization has stimulated MFP in Canada, this is strong evidence in favour of FTAs, as productivity increases translate directly into higher incomes and an improved standard of living. As the critics of free trade have not yet presented any serious evidence of a link between more trade and lower welfare in Canada — even employment in manufacturing has rebounded to its pre-FTA levels — we see no reason that Canada should deviate from its commitment to open market policies.

# BIBLIOGRAPHY

Bhagwati, Jagdish. "Preferential Trade Agreements: The Wrong Road." In *A Stream of Windows: Unsettling Reflections on Trade, Immigration and Democracy*. Cambridge MA: The MIT Press, 1998, pp. 289-97.

Clausing, Kimberly A. "Trade Creation and Trade Diversion in the Canada-United States Free Trade Agreement." *Canadian Journal of Economics*, 34, 3 (2001): 677-96.

Cox, David, and Richard Harris. "Trade Liberalization and Industrial Organization: Some Estimates for Canada." *Journal of Political Economy* 93 (1985): 115-45.

Davis, Donald R. "The Home Market, Trade, and Industry Structure," *American Economic Review* 88, 5 (1998): 1264-76.

Eastman, H., and S. Stykolt. *The Tariff and Competition in Canada*. Toronto: MacMillan, 1967.

Feenstra, Robert C., James R. Markusen and Andrew K.Rose. "Using the Gravity Equation to Differentiate Among Alternative Theories of Trade. *Canadian Journal of Economics* 32, 2 (2001): 430-47.

Frankel, Jeffrey A., and David Romer. "Does Trade Cause Growth?" *American Economic Review* 89, 3 (1999): 379-99.

Frankel, Jeffrey A., and Andrew K. Rose. *Estimating the Effect of Currency Unions on Trade and Output*. NBER Working Paper No. 7857. Cambridge: National Bureau of Economic Research, August 2000.

Grossman, Gene M, and Elhanan Helpman. "Technology and Trade," in *Handbook of International Economics*, Volume 3. Edited by Gene M. Grossman and Kenneth Rogoff. Amsterdam: Elsevier Science, 1995, pp. 1279-1337.

Gu, Wulong, Gary Sawchuk and Lori Whewell."The Effects of the FTA on Firm Size and Firm Turnover in Canadian Manufacturing." Ottawa: Industry Canada, 2001. Manuscript.

Head, Keith, Thierry Mayer and John Ries. "On the Pervasiveness of Home Market Effects." *Economica* 69, 275 (2002): 371-90.

Head, Keith, and John Ries. "Increasing Returns versus National Product Differentiation as an Explanation for the Pattern of U.S.-Canada Trade." *American Economic Review* 91, 4 (2001): 858-76.

_____. "Rationalization Effects of Tariff Reductions." *Journal of International Economics* 47 (1999): 295-320.

Krugman, Paul R. "Scale Economies, Product Differentiation, and the Pattern of Trade." *American Economic Review* 70 (1980): 950-59.

Lester, John, and Thomas Morehen. *New Estimates of Canadian Tariff Rates by Industry and Commodity*. Working Paper No. 88-2. Ottawa: Department of Finance, 1987.

Levine, R., and D. Renelt. "A Sensitivity Analysis of Cross-Country Growth Regressions." *American Economic Review* 82, 4 (1992): 942-63.

Linder, Staffan B. *An Essay on Trade and Transformation*. Uppsala: Almqvst and Wiksells, 1961.

McLaren, John. "Size, Sunk Costs, and Judge Bowker's Objection to Free Trade." *American Economic Review* 87, 3 (1997): 400-20.

Melitz, Marc J. "The Impact of Trade on Intra-Industry Reallocations and Aggregate Industry Productivity." Economics Department, Harvard University, 1999. Manuscript.

Muller, A., and D. Rawana. "Tariff-Limit Pricing, Relative Plant Scale, and the Eastman-Stykolt Hypothesis." *Canadian Journal of Economics* 21 (1990): 237-331.

Schwanen, Daniel. "Trading Up," C.D. Howe Institute Commentary 89. Toronto: C.D Howe Institute, 1997.

Trefler, Daniel. *The Long and the Short of the Canada-U.S. Free Trade Agreement*. Perspectives on North American Free Trade, Paper Number 6. Ottawa: Industry Canada Research Publications Program, 1999.

Vanek, Jaroslav. "The Factor-Proportions Theory: The N-Factor Case." *Kyklos* 4 (1968): 749-56.

Weder, Rolf. "Linking Absolute and Comparative Advantage to Intra-Industry Trade Theory." *Review of International Economics* 3, 3 (1995): 342-54.

# Comment on:

## FREE TRADE AND CANADIAN ECONOMIC PERFORMANCE: WHICH THEORIES DOES THE EVIDENCE SUPPORT?

*Comment by Eugene Beaulieu*
*University of Calgary*

ALMOST 20 YEARS AGO Richard Harris challenged Canadians to pursue closer North American (NA) integration. At the time, he applied "new" trade theory to the question of NA integration and found that Canada stood to realize large welfare gains from signing a free trade agreement (FTA) with the United States (Harris 1985; Cox and Harris 1985). The research was an important contribution to the debate in Canada and to modeling trade policy in general. Although Harris's work in the 1980s was influential, the empirical veracity of the model has not been explored until recently. Head and Ries (1999) have provided important empirical evidence on the underlying theoretical model in past collaborations. In this study, they provide a very useful overview of the evidence on the effects of North American integration in Canada and examine the empirical evidence on different economic models underlying the NA economy.

## WHICH THEORY?

HEAD AND RIES EXAMINE A CRUCIALLY important topic, as academics, policy makers and others debate the future course of Canadian trade policy. They examine the lessons to be drawn from Canada's existing set of experiences with NA FTAs and assess the impact of free trade on three aspects of Canadian manufacturing performance.

First, they examine the extent of trade creation, trade diversion and the increased dependence of Canada on a single trading partner. They show that tariff reductions included in the trade agreements can explain only approximately one half of the enormous increase in the volume of trade among NA free trade partners. To the extent that some of the new trade among these countries represents trade diverted from third countries, there is an associated loss. Head and Ries argue that trade diversion has been small.

Second, they analyse the impact of NA integration on the intersectoral resource allocations across manufacturing sectors and on the degree of specialization within Canada. There is mixed evidence on whether Canada has become more specialized following the Canada-U.S. FTA and the NAFTA. On the one hand, the distribution of GDP has become more concentrated. On the other hand, there is no evidence that the Canada-U.S. FTA increased specialization in Canadian manufacturing through an intersectoral reallocation of labour. There does appear to be greater concentration of capital and/or productivity in large industries, although no studies have linked this reallocation *across* industries to trade liberalization. Head and Ries conclude that there is no evidence that the Canada-U.S. FTA increased specialization in Canadian manufacturing through an intersectoral reallocation of labour.

Finally, they examine whether free trade has enhanced productivity. Free trade can enhance productivity through better access to foreign markets as increased plant output with plant-level economies of scale yields lower average costs or through increased technological innovation from increased competition. Again the evidence is mixed. There was a dramatic increase in scale after 1988; however, U.S. tariff reductions caused a 9.8 percent increase in scale, which was largely offset by an 8.5 percent decline due to Canadian tariff reductions. Head and Ries attribute the productivity gains to undercounting, industry composition changes and the depreciation of the Canadian dollar.

There are studies that link tariff reductions to increased productivity *within* industries. Recent research explores the implications of the enormous amount of heterogeneity in business performance between firms in the same industry. This type of analysis requires micro-economic data that is not generally available from Statistics Canada. Firm- and establishment-level micro-data are disseminated in the United States through Census data centres. These data have been important pieces of this research agenda in the United States. Statistics Canada has started opening data centres throughout Canada, but does not include firm or establishment data. A clear and strong message from Head and Ries is that the status quo in terms of data dissemination must change.

## COMMENTS

I HAVE A NUMBER OF GENERAL COMMENTS. First, there is a lack of consensus on the correct underlying trade model. Head and Ries conclude that more research is required and correctly point out that micro-data are required. There is ample theoretical support for the proposition that trade liberalization promotes industry efficiency, and efficiency did appear to increase in liberalizing manufacturing sectors in Canada. However, the lack of micro-economic data available in Canada has constrained research efforts in this direction. A recent attempt to overcome the problem was to employ administrative data from the government of Ontario on plant closures in that province (Beaulieu 2001). The table below shows that the incidence of plant closures in Ontario was proportionately higher within high-tariff industries during the immediate post-FTA period compared to subsequent periods. This is consistent with the results from Head and Ries but leaves most of the same questions unanswered.

Another recent attempt to overcome data limitations was to analyse historical micro-data (Keay 1999). Keay employs micro-economic data to examine the performance of 39 Canadian and 39 U.S. firms from 1907 to 1990. He finds that Canadian firms are smaller (on average) and they are on the increasing returns portion of their low-run average cost (LRAC) curve (increased output/lower AC). He also finds, accordingly, that AC tends to be higher for Canadian firms when compared to U.S. firms. These empirical results are necessary, but not sufficient conditions for Canadian firms to reap large gains by moving down their AC curve. The problem, according to Keay, is that there are very small elasticities of AC with respect to output. This result can explain why the empirical evidence suggests that rationalization occurred but there were no commensurate productivity improvements.

Again, improved access to Canadian micro-data is required to analyse alternative explanations for the conflicting evidence and to understand the impact of deeper integration. The recent move by Statistics Canada to open data centres at different locations across Canada is a step in the right direction. However, access to confidential data must be extended to include enterprise data to bring the level of Canadian research employing micro-economic data up to the standards of other OECD countries.

## INCIDENCE OF ACTUAL MANUFACTURING PLANT CLOSURES IN ONTARIO, 1988-95

| | 1988-95 | Canada-U.S. FTA Implementation 1988-90 | | Recession 1991-92 | | Recovery 1988-95 | |
|---|---|---|---|---|---|---|---|
| High Tariffs | 55 | 32 | 18% | 19 | 13% | 4 | 6% |
| Medium Tariffs | 195 | 69 | 39% | 83 | 58% | 43 | 61% |
| Low Tariffs | 140 | 75 | 43% | 42 | 29% | 23 | 33% |
| All Manufacturing | 390 | 176 | | 144 | | 70 | |

# BIBLIOGRAPHY

Beaulieu, Eugene. "North American Integration and Plant Closures in Ontario." *Canadian Foreign Policy* 8, 2 (2001): 23-38.

Cox, David, and Richard Harris. "Trade Liberalization and Industrial Organization: Some Estimates for Canada." *Journal of Political Economy* 93, 1 (1985): 115-45.

Harris, Richard G. *Trade, Industrial Policy and International Competition.* Report of the Royal Commission on the Economic Union and Development Prospects for Canada, Volume 13. Toronto: University of Toronto Press, 1985.

Head, K., and J. Ries. "Rationalization of Trade Reductions." *Journal of International Economics* 47, 2 (1999): 295-320.

Keay, Ian. "Average Cost Savings Following Liberalized Trade and the Exploitation of Scale Economies: Canadian and American Manufacturers, 1910-1990." Kingston: Queen's University, 1999. Mimeograph.

*Pierre-Paul Proulx*
*Université de Montréal*

5

# Cities, Regions and Economic Integration
# in North America

## INTRODUCTION

ECONOMIC INTEGRATION IS ACCOMPANIED by a spatial and sectoral reorganization of economic activity and an increase in the share carried on in urban centres. The roles of the various stakeholders change — including those of national and city governments and businesses. Globalization influences the factors that determine economic growth as well. This study focusses on the causes of the urbanization process and its effects, including those that regionalize and *metropolize* a growing share of economic activity.

The agglomeration process is at work — even without a North American monetary union. It is undoubtedly creating increasingly specialized concentrations of activity in U.S. cities and regions.

In this study, we examine some indicators that highlight the importance of cities in the new economy. We also list the main features of the globalization process now under way; discuss causes of *metropolization*, a term to describe the rising concentration of economic activity in urban centres; examine some data on the specialization of Canadian and American cities; and present our empirical analysis of growth indicators in the major North American cities. In the process, we examine a number of current theories on the economic growth of cities, and in particular, one of our own theories on the formation of regions (some of them cross-border) in North America.

## THE IMPORTANCE OF CITIES

IN 1999, THERE WERE 219 U.S. METROPOLITAN REGIONS with a population of at least 100,000. The 291 million persons living there represent 80 percent of the U.S. population. These regions accounted for 84 percent of total employment (108 out of 129 million), 85 percent of gross domestic product (GDP), 90 percent of financial services, 87 percent of transportation and public service activity, 93 percent of high tech jobs and 93 percent of business services. In a 1999 list of countries and cities, New York City ranked 16th in GDP, just behind Australia and ahead of Los Angeles-Long Beach, which preceded Argentina. After New York City came Chicago, and then Taiwan.[1]

The most recent U.S. Census shows that the population of the largest American cities grew twice as fast in the 1990s as it did in the 1980s, and that the population of three out of four urban centres increased.[2]

The Canadian data show a similar phenomenon of metropolization because they reflect the rising population densities, GDP and employment, etc. of the urban centres. In 1996, 61.9 percent of Canada's population was living in metropolitan regions (more than 100,000 inhabitants). Between 1991 and 1996, the populations of the metropolitan regions, towns and rural areas rose 6.4, 5.3 and 3.9 percent, respectively.

We are at the point where, as Linda McCarthy says in her recent review of written materials on urban growth for the United States Economic Development Administration,

> ...America's economy should now be seen as a common market of metropolitan-based local economic regions. These regions are indeed strongly interdependent, but they also compete with each other and with the rest of the world....The new leadership coalitions and networks recognize that the geographic focus of their efforts has to be the metropolitan region as a whole, not just the central city or suburbs independently...The big city mayors concur: The American economy, in reality, comprises regional economies centered in America's cities, within which the fates of central cities, suburbs and rural areas are entwined...[3]

This metropolization process is occurring within the overall economic integration of the western hemisphere. This prompts us to posit that the major cities of Canada, the United States and Latin America make up an increasingly significant network of large cities with growing mutual international trade relations.

In a Standard and Poor's and DRI/McGraw-Hill (2000) report to the United States Conference of Mayors and the National Association of Counties, we read that

> ...as the focal points of economic activity, cities and counties within metropolitan regions are essential to the nation's economic development. The geographic concentration of business and people in metro areas creates unique economic conditions that generate new industries, speed the diffusion of knowledge, spur technological innovation and increase productivity. Metro areas have larger markets for goods and services, more specialized labor pools and more extensive and sophisticated transportation and telecommunications networks than non-metro areas. These competitive advantages make metro areas engines of U.S. economic growth and global competitiveness. (p.1)

As we know, this is the theme of many U.S. studies, including one by Michael Porter (2001) for the United States Competitiveness Council on some 50 U.S. regional "clusters." Ottawa appears to be following suit: on May 11, 2000, the Minister of Industry Canada announced a $2.5-million grant "for a major national study that will investigate, in communities across Canada, how local networks of firms and institutions, businesses and people, interact to spark economic growth."

## FEATURES OF ECONOMIC INTEGRATION: THE CONTEXT IN WHICH OUR CITIES AND REGIONS OPERATE

THE FOLLOWING QUOTATION highlights in an interesting way the main features and the scope of the changes our cities can expect in the new context of economic integration.

> Rapid progress is expected in the fields of information technology, materials, genetic engineering, environmental protection and energy. In the longer term, people will become used to networks which connect everything. The interaction between technological progress and economic and social development will change when, where and how people work, play and rest; how, where and what they produce and consume; and when, where and how they interact with other people, businesses, social organisations or the government. (Organisation for Economic Cooperation and Development 1999)

This is the new environment in which individuals, companies and institutions, as well as national, metropolitan and municipal governments must operate and which we need to understand as clearly as possible to guide our own development. It includes the opening up of the economy; the role of technological change; the interaction between technology, the economy and society; and changes in the activities of stakeholders in the private and public sectors and "civil society."

Let us list some of its main features at the start of this new millennium. Our challenge is to identify the causes and effects of these phenomena accurately. (We make no claim to have determined either causes or effects, as we have not developed a quantifiable model for the globalization process.) Let us nevertheless try to list the causes in order to derive maximum benefit from their positive effects, to avoid their negative effects as much as possible, and to create the institutions, policies, programs and behaviours that will help us direct the effects of economic integration toward the pursuit of our social, economic and cultural objectives. The new economy of information, knowledge, high technology and high-grade services is emerging in many interrelated ways, just as the steel, printing and electrical technologies did when they first appeared. Here is a selective and necessarily partial list:

- an increasing use of information technologies, microprocessors, digital technologies, information highways, artificial intelligence, robotics, information networks and virtual reality interfaces, and e-commerce — business to business (B2B) and business to consumer (B2C);
- an increasing number of biotechnological applications in production, distribution and management activities;
- a convergence of information and communications technologies (ICTs), biotechnology (biochips and the human genome) and nanotechnology;
- the rising importance of information, knowledge and training;
- liberalization, deregulation, privatization, internationalization, multinationalization, globalization;
- greater income disparity between countries, cities, regions and individuals;
- metropolitan regions that become separated from their hinterlands;
- peripheral regions that fall behind;
- a relative decline in the production of goods and a growth in the production of services, with a large proportion of activities now in a tertiary-level industrial world;
- a spatial reorganization of economic activity and a relative decline in the Northeast region of the North American continent (our empirical findings below lead us to conclude that the long decline of the continent's Northeast, documented by many writers, continues: the gradual movement of economic activity toward the West and South of the continent explains slower growth rates in population, personal income, manufacturing employment and competitiveness in a cross-border Northeast region of North America);
- the rising importance of exports and imports as well as intrafirm and intraindustry transactions, and hence specialization, economies of scale and the centralization of economic activity;
- the redirection of our external trade flows toward a North-South axis, hence the challenge of accelerating our penetration of western hemisphere markets in order to compete with the stepped-up South-North competition;
- a major increase in foreign direct investment (FDI), and particularly in alliances and partnerships for rapid penetration of markets, access to new technologies and sharing of the high cost of research and development (R&D) and activities in the new industrial sectors;
- the rising importance of multinational corporations (MNCs), hence the need to ensure that our small- and medium-sized businesses (SMEs) find niche markets and participate in the proliferating e-platforms;
- mobility of capital, increased financial flows and instability in capital markets;
- a decline in the Canadian share of European FDI in North America (3 percent in 1992, 1 percent in 1999);

- a decline in the Canadian share of U.S. FDI (at original cost) from 16.7 percent in 1989 to 9.9 percent in 1999 (the U.S. share of total Canadian FDI remains at 70 percent or more);

- displacement of the tax base to lower tax countries, hence obvious constraints on the tax levels our governments can levy, especially on mobile factors;

- increased competition in national, regional and local markets, hence the importance of innovation and productivity;

- reduced inflation, apparently largely due to the effects of the increasingly widespread introduction of information technologies;

- a greater interdependence among countries, regions and cities, with a growing percentage of trade flows going through cities;

- Americanization;

- the key role of media and advertising;

- the expanding importance of sports and recreational activities as consumer goods and decision factors for the location of individuals and, consequently, companies with intensive human resource needs, which locate according to labour force availability, (e.g., the consumer city of Glaeser [1991]);

- the establishment of monetary zones;[4]

- trade liberalization agreements like the World Trade Organization (WTO), the Canada-U.S. Free Trade Agreement (FTA), the North American Free Trade Agreement (NAFTA) and, potentially, the Free Trade Area of the Americas (FTAA);

- the weakness of the Canadian dollar (in part a reflection of our low productivity vis-à-vis our American neighbours), hence a very low per capita income in Canadian cities when compared to that of U.S. cities; and

- the increasing importance of action from a distance, hence (although it may appear counter-intuitive) the importance of local and regional synergies, action from nearby and the level at which economic regions function — an important determinant of a region's power to compete in the new, increasingly continental and global economic space.

We note, following E. Costello, that globalization now simultaneously affects finance, production, R&D, technology, consumption and culture (hence the battles for cultural influence, culture being an important determinant in consumer spending), while the previous stages in globalization affected only some of these factors.

It follows from this new context that there is a search for a new model of governance and management of states. The increased interdependence induced by globalization encourages governments to pool skills and competencies in order to address transborder problems and decentralize other functions: this is the source of our interest in what determines the economic growth of cities.

# AGGLOMERATION OF ECONOMIC ACTIVITY, METROPOLIZATION AND ECONOMIC GROWTH

> Scholars and policymakers have increasingly come to suspect that the specific spatial arrangement of economic activities into geographical agglomerations or clusters might also in itself somehow influence the creation of knowledge and, consequentially, economic growth. (Maskell 2001)

A common theme in the writings of a growing number of economists attempting to explain economic growth is that rising earnings due to economies of scale (internal to businesses, or external, such as those originating from knowledge spillovers), together with transportation costs, create urbanization economies that are specific to certain locations (Hanson 2000).

A growing number of U.S. states and cities are abandoning economic development policies and programs aimed at particular industries and sectors and adopting an approach focussed on industrial clusters. There is increasing recognition that to be competitive we should not only make national policies and investments but also strengthen innovative clusters in various regions. Clusters, according to Porter, involve a geographical concentration of 1) firms that collaborate (e.g., in pre-competitive R&D) and compete with each other; 2) suppliers; 3) firms that service other firms; and 4) university research centres. These clusters are usually primary-resource-based in rural areas and either local or open (exporting) types in more urbanized regions. In dynamic high tech regions (like Silicon Valley, for example) we find dense and flexible networks of tight relationships between entrepreneurs, venture capitalists, university researchers, lawyers and consultants, highly skilled workers and other stakeholders who know how to transform new ideas into new products, services, processes and management methods fast enough to stay at the leading edge of the innovation curve.

In its 2001 report, the United States Competitiveness Council proposes that the U.S. government concentrate its efforts on innovation (R&D), education and training, and the strengthening of regional technology clusters. Industrial clusters, together with the convergence of basic technologies and their application, result in the birth and development of economic activities located in increasingly specialized cities and regions of the United States.

A clear understanding of what gives rise to the birth of clusters is crucial, for it will help us see more clearly why cities and regions have an expanding role in the North American economic integration process. Let us briefly review some of the literature on the subject.

In this section of our study, we group together phenomena that more closely resemble causes than effects of the agglomeration and metropolization processes. We have discussed the many causes that have given rise to (and still

216

explain) the globalization process, which entails a sectoral and spatial reorganization of economic activity. An increasing share of this activity is carried on in the major urban agglomerations. As noted above, technological change and trade liberalization agreements like the FTA, the NAFTA and, potentially, the FTAA are among the important factors in this process.

The innovation that accompanies technological change is an activity increasingly found in urban agglomerations. According to Gertler (1995), sophisticated production facilities are not only more successful but are also set up more easily when purchaser and vendor are near to and able to interact with each other. He stresses how important it is to be able to assess the credibility of the vendor and the producer, and to convey the purchaser's technological needs to the producer easily. He notes the effect of "organizational distance" on innovation, by which he means similarity of institutional culture, training practices and attitudes toward technology. He finds that there is less organizational distance in metropolitan regions.

In their study of industry clusters in the United States, Feldman and Audretsch (1999) also underline the importance of the metropolitan region as a cradle of innovation and technological change. They point out that 3,819 of the 3,969 new manufactured products they studied came from metropolitan regions. Their results show that only 14 U.S. cities are more innovative than the national average. Innovation, they say, is a metropolitan phenomenon.

For Storper (1996), interdependences based on full trust are another significant reason for the development of metropolitan regions. This concept looks to knowledge and "mutual confidence" between people as foundations on which to establish projects, exchanges of information about markets, technologies and "implied knowledge," which in turn create a collective learning process and economic activities that would be impossible without such full-trust interdependences.

Research by the Groupe européen de recherches sur les milieux innovateurs [Translation: European Research Group on Innovative Milieux] (GREMI 1991, 1993)[5] points to the importance of synergies as well as physical proximity to explain economic growth. Much of the literature on regional clusters emphasizes the importance of the latter factor.

The studies we find most persuasive consider information technologies and face-to-face meetings in a metropolitan setting to be complementary. Gaspar and Glaeser (1998) believe cities will cease to be places for production, and become places for interaction where direct contacts are very important.

Hall (1999) agrees when he notes that much information is still exchanged "face to face," hence the growth in air and high-speed rail transportation, the hotel industry and the number of conventions. He quotes John Goddard, a British researcher, who finds, like Gaspar and Glaeser, that "telecommunications are used much of the time for preliminary routine encounters, leading to a positive need for the more complex kind of exchange for which face-to-face contact is deemed essential."

Metropolization is also influenced in varying degrees by the decisions of competing cities, as well as those of national and foreign business managers, and regional leaders; by the policies and programs of governments at various levels; and by foreign countries. The decisions of international agencies like the WTO and the International Monetary Fund also have a significant influence on the operations of a number of businesses and institutions.[6]

This study underlines the crucial influence of business leaders and MNCs on the competitiveness and growth of metropolitan regions.

The specific location where companies, including MNCs and the private sector, decide to do business in a metropolitan region is an important determining factor for its growth. In a variety of ways, this has contributed to the design and implementation of a number of major city strategies. The econometric findings of this study and previous ones (Proulx, Kresl and Langlois 1999; Proulx 2001) show that cooperation between the public and private sectors improves the competitiveness of major North American cities.

Location decisions by large companies in particular (and decisions on the location of their head offices) are another important determinant of the pace of metropolization. The major contract originators are increasingly important with the establishment of purchase platforms like B2B and the Internet.

According to the most recent available estimates, MNCs account for 46 percent of exports and 44 percent of imports between Canada and the United States (Cameron 1998). The location of the head offices of these companies is still a determinant in the location of their suppliers, although the rapid growth of e-commerce modifies the strategies that small businesses must use to penetrate these networks.

A recent study on factors influencing economic development in Montreal (Kresl and Proulx 2000) found that the available market (i.e., of the metropolitan region to which a company is planning to move), the quality of the labour force, and the availability and costs of transportation were important factors for the location decisions of MNCs. Other factors important to the competitiveness of cities included innovative activity, synergies and networking (within and outside the metropolitan region), the level of information about outside markets, multimodal infrastructures and the quality of life, as indicated by cultural activities (Proulx 1998).[7] These studies also indicate that some specific local factors such as taxation of firms, and increasingly, taxation of individuals, are considered in the final decisions, but that taxation is a significant variable only where the tax burden differs significantly from the average in competing locations.

The research is virtually unanimous that metropolization is accompanied by synergies, collaboration between the private and public sectors, and exchanges of information and knowledge among scientists, researchers, universities and private laboratories — in short, the city is an innovative milieu.

Kherdjemil (1999) examines the strong points, convergences and peculiarities of the different explanatory models for the development of metropolitan regions. He reviews the notion of industrial district, a concept developed in the late nineteenth century by Alfred Marshall (1890), that singles out the improved performance brought on by economies of scale and agglomeration. He also cites the importance of various factors, including the industrial environment, which help facilitate contacts between people. There are also savings in transaction costs, because exchanges are personalized and the positive externalities inherent in the skill-sharing process are brought about by the dynamic of fluidity of work among the various firms.

For Pecqueur (1992), the capacity of a metropolitan region to secure its development is based on its ability to produce a set of rules that perpetuate a social and cultural solidarity among stakeholders. In his view, a territory may innovate, adapt and regulate itself, in short be what he calls a localized productive system, which he defines as a configuration of firms organized within a convenient space around a particular trade or even a number of industrial trades. Businesses maintain relationships between themselves and with the social and cultural milieu in which they are placed. These are trading relationships, which are also informal, and produce some positive externalities for all of the companies.

Our colleagues at the GREMI, including Maillat (1995), assert that the relative strength of technological production in a territory is a function of its logic of interaction and its learning dynamic. The mobility and exchange of engineering scientists and technicians between metropolitan region firms is one of the important factors in this collective learning process.

In his overview of metropolitan region approaches to local development, Kherdjemil notes that "[Translation] whether one is referring to the industrial district, the localized productive system or the innovative milieu, it appears that the innovation process… is an essential feature of the territory…. It is the territory, and geographical proximity between the stakeholders, that will allow a more effective coordination as well as absorption of collective learning among them."

We must not forget the importance of outside recruitment of scientists, and networking within firms or industrial networks to promote this access to knowledge, which is so essential to the creation of new knowledge. Camagni (1995) writes that the various stakeholders need to network to create a synergetic milieu for mutually beneficial interaction. Van Geenhuizen and Nijkamp (1998) also highlight the importance of synergies and networking.

Storper shows that technological districts, which generate a production-based technology learning, create rents similar to those generated by the steel and auto industries in the past. These industrial districts (for example, the growing multimedia and e-commerce cities and Montreal's garment district on Chabanel Street) feature a very significant combination of flexibility and specialization.

Maskell defines two types of agglomeration economy: the urbanization economy, which emerges because of the geographical proximity of industries and services, and the localization economy, which arises from the geographical agglomeration of related economic activity.

Conventional cluster analysis has focussed on the agglomeration effects originating in cost advantages due to the reduction of interfirm transaction costs, the presence of a dedicated infrastructure, the availability of a specialized and highly skilled labour force, and an educational system adapted to the needs of companies. The major cities contain the highly skilled human resources, multimodal infrastructures, information, knowledge and synergies to create what economists call agglomeration economies, which come about first, because of economies of scale and second, because of urbanization savings due to the availability of qualified human resources, venture capital, etc.

Some more recent explanations have pointed to the decrease in transaction costs like the costs of information and search, negotiation and decision, and monitoring and implementation of contracts as a reason for the agglomeration of economic activities in metropolitan regions (e.g., analyses of the Coase [1996] type). Proximity makes any business activity outside the community expensive — plus everyone benefits from the atmosphere of mutual confidence in the clusters. The clusters exist, therefore, because they reduce the costs to businesses of identifying, assessing and exchanging products, services or skills.

Maskell notes, however, that this reasoning could lead to the existence of a single company per cluster, and suggests an additional explanation for the existence of clusters. He makes the distinction between "the horizontal dimension of the cluster" — firms with similar capabilities performing similar activities — and "the vertical dimension" — firms with dissimilar but complementary capabilities carrying out complementary activities. The firms in the vertical dimension of the cluster are often business partners and collaborators, while the firms in the horizontal dimension are mainly rivals and competitors.

Maskell emphasizes the importance of the experimentation by some independent companies conducting complementary activities in the clusters. By mutual self-analysis and discussion of differing approaches, they initiate an ongoing process of continuous learning and improvement that would not work in a big company or outside the geographical cluster. The Boston model initially focussed much more on the internalization of activities within major companies, while the Silicon Valley model was closer to what Maskell describes. Saxenian (1994) discusses these models in detail. One can therefore imitate and profit from the experience of the other companies in the cluster, a process that is all the more productive if there is a common social culture, a common language, etc. Co-localization thus allows externalities and learning between similar companies; this is the cluster's horizontal dimension.

The cluster also attracts specialized suppliers and discriminating purchasers — the cluster's vertical dimension, according to Porter. Cluster agglomeration reduces transaction costs, eases the problem of asymmetrical information and makes specialization possible. This allows vertical differentiation, which strengthens the cluster.

Thus new companies are attracted from outside. In addition, new companies can arise from existing ones, creating the spinoff process.

## REGIONAL AND METROPOLITAN SPECIALIZATION: A MUST IN THE WESTERN HEMISPHERE

THE METROPOLIZATION AND GEOGRAPHIC AGGLOMERATION of economic activities are accompanied by increasing specialization in the cities and regions of North America. The *Cybercities* report of the American Electronics Association (AEA 2000), published jointly with the NASDAQ, presents some data on high tech industries with at least 15,000 employees in 60 U.S. metropolitan regions. According to the authors, factors contributing to the success of these industries include the availability of highly skilled labour and the presence of universities heavily involved in research. Another factor they emphasize is critical mass.

Additional factors include the availability of venture capital, an efficient transportation infrastructure and widespread use of new technology (computers and the Internet), as well as quality of life, a factor difficult to define, as for some it means a good climate, for others few transportation problems, and for still others an active cultural scene (Florida 2000). The proximity between San Jose, San Francisco and Oakland, for example, allows these cities to take advantage of a common manpower and capital pool (Marshall). The San Jose high tech industry is said to have created 40 percent of all Silicon Valley jobs since 1993.

Boston was the leading city for high tech job creation until 1996. Colorado Springs was the cybercity with the highest growth rate between 1993 and 1998, followed by Dallas and Houston. Washington DC is a leader in software employment. Minneapolis-St. Paul is one of the top 10 cybercities. San Jose, an extremely diversified high tech city, is the U.S. leader in computers, electronic components, semiconductors and the production of industrial electronics.

According to the AEA-NASDAQ data, high tech employment in the following cities chosen for examination by the Montreal TechnoVision report (2000) was:[8]

| San Jose | 252,900 |
|---|---|
| Boston | 234,822 |
| Chicago | 180,425 |
| Dallas | 176,600 |
| Los Angeles | 160,544 |
| Atlanta | 117,279 |
| Philadelphia | 88,647 |
| Seattle | 75,565 |
| Detroit | 59,310 |

The data show that the cities reviewed in the Montreal TechnoVision report increased their high tech employment by the following number of workers:

| Houston | 27,900 |
|---|---|
| Seattle | 25,900 |
| Atlanta | 38,500 |
| Washington | 46,400 |
| New York | 5,500 |
| Chicago | 38,200 |
| Detroit | 11,200 |
| Philadelphia | 11,600 |
| Miami | 2,800 |
| Boston | 21,800 |
| Los Angeles | 9,900 |

The Montreal TechnoVision study reports that 160,000 persons work in Montreal's new economy. The definitions of the high tech sectors are not directly comparable; however, we can conclude that Montreal is a respectable player in the North American high tech field.

In the most recent E&B Data survey (October 4, 2001) on the topic, the Montreal Census Metropolitan Area ranked ninth among the 15 largest North American metropolitan regions in information technology, with 70,000 jobs. San Francisco led with 305,000, while Toronto, Chicago and Atlanta had 95,000, 75,000 and 55,000, respectively. Montreal was eighth in biopharmaceuticals, with 11,000 jobs, behind Toronto with 15,500 and ahead of Washington with 8,000. Montreal was fifth in aerospace, with 26,000 jobs, behind New York's 28,500 and ahead of Dallas's 24,500. The leaders were Los Angeles (92,500), Seattle (92,000) and Washington (35,000).

A recent study of 14 U.S. high tech metropolitan regions, published by the Brookings Institution, reveals a great deal about their specialization process (Cortright and Mayer 2001). One of the most relevant findings is that *they tend to specialize in few products and technologies*. The authors examined employment concentration, patent activity and venture capital flows. Their results show that employment is concentrated in a few sectors: for example, workers in Washington, Denver and Atlanta make software, but little hardware. For others, like those in Phoenix, the reverse is true.

Innovation is also characteristic of a small number of specialized companies in a particular technology. San Jose, Phoenix, Portland and Austin innovate in electronics and software, but not in biomedical technology. Washington, Raleigh-Durham, San Diego, Boston and Seattle innovate in biotechnology but not in electronics and software.

Venture capital flows are also specialized: software and biotechnology in Boston; communications and data storage in Denver; medical industries in San Diego.

The major city specializations are set out below.

| | |
|---|---|
| Atlanta | data bases and telecommunications |
| Austin | semiconductors, computers and production of manufactured equipment |
| Boston | computers, medical equipment, software and biotechnology |
| Denver | data storage, telecommunications equipment and software |
| Minneapolis-St.Paul | computers, peripherals and medical instruments |
| Phoenix | semiconductors and aerospace |
| Portland | semiconductors, display technology screens, production of manufacturing equipment, automation and electronic design software |
| Raleigh-Durham | computers, data bases and pharmaceuticals |
| Sacramento | computers and semiconductors |
| Salt Lake City | software and medical equipment |
| San Diego | communications equipment and biotechnology |
| San Jose | semiconductors, computers, software, communications equipment, production of manufacturing equipment, electronic design and automation software, and data storage |
| Seattle | aerospace software and biotechnology |
| Washington | data bases, Internet service, telecommunications and biotechnology |

According to Cortright and Mayer, 1997 total employment in high technology — computers and electronic products (NACI 334), software (NACI 5112), information and data processing systems (NACI 514), and computer design systems and related services (NACI 5415) [9] — was as follows:

| | | | |
|---|---|---|---|
| San Jose | 212,249 | Austin | 49,521 |
| Washington | 138,662 | San Diego | 47,296 |
| Boston | 133,745 | Portland | 45,155 |
| Minneapolis | 66,738 | Raleigh-Durham | 40,153 |
| Atlanta | 57,837 | Denver | 33,288 |
| Phoenix | 56,051 | Sacramento | 23,993 |
| Seattle | 55,897 | Salt Lake City | 22,404 |

Cortright and Mayer also estimated the location quotients, and examined patent activity and venture capital investments between 1995 and 1999.

The Milken Institute studies (see Web site), which provide estimates of location coefficients for U.S. cities by industry, together with our ongoing studies with the Corptech data base (2001), contribute to the knowledge of U.S. city and regional specializations (Figure 1).

In part, our 1999 empirical study (Proulx et al.) on the competitiveness of cities contributes to a debate involving Jacobs, Porter, Marshall, Romer and Arrow described in an NBER working paper (Glaeser 1991). Jacobs favours a strategy of economic diversification and competition between businesses to promote urban growth, while Porter and others favour competition and specialization. Still others favour monopolies and concentration (Shumpeter's thesis) as a means of increasing urban growth. Glaeser and his colleagues obtain results showing that the concentration of certain urban industries in fields like insurance and automobiles reduces urban growth. Hanson concludes that long-term sectoral growth is higher in relatively diversified cities. He also identifies some effects of agglomeration for specific externalities in certain industries and locations on the demand side.

Our 1999 results lead us to conclude that the creation of firms (and thus of increased competition) and specialization is to be encouraged. The competition variable is positive and significant in our multiple regression equations. Specialization is positive and concentration negative for competitiveness, although these two variables are not statistically significant.

## FIGURE 1

### RANKING OF STATES AND CITIES IN THE BIOTECHNOLOGY INDUSTRY: PERCENTAGE OF ESTABLISHMENTS, BY STATE

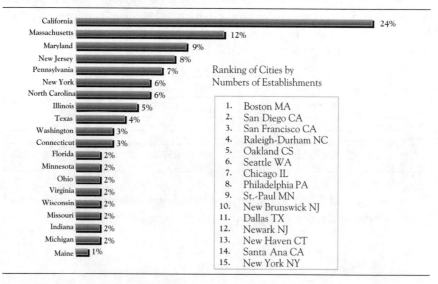

Source: The Corptech data base (2001).

A Moody's investors report (2000) identifies and measures concentration by industrial sector and calculates an index of metropolitan diversity for Canadian cities. The report is essentially trying to determine to what degree the industrial structure of each of Canada's 25 Census Metropolitan Areas resembles the national structure. The study is designed to determine how much a particular industry is over- or under-represented in a given city by comparison with the same industry nationally. Employment data up to 1999 are used in doing the calculations. Thirty-four industries grouped in seven major industrial groups were studied.

An examination of the location quotients (a sector's share in metropolitan employment divided by that sector's share in national employment) of five cities — Calgary, Montreal, Ottawa, Toronto and Vancouver — indicates that:

- Montreal has no particular concentration in banking or finance. In the latter industry, its location quotient is 1.08, Toronto's 2.14 and Vancouver's 1.74.
- In the insurance industry, Montreal's location quotient is 1.19, Toronto's 1.25 and Vancouver's 1.14.
- Montreal wins in the aerospace industry, with a location quotient of 4.35, while Toronto's is 1.26.
- Montreal has the highest location coefficient in the food, tobacco and beverage sectors.
- Montreal has a coefficient of 1.50 (Toronto's is 1.48) in the area of consumer durable goods.
- Montreal's location quotient of 1.40 in consumer non-durable goods indicates an industry worth scrutinizing in the context of the CMM economic development strategy.
- Ottawa, with a quotient of 3.09, stands out in the electronics field. Montreal has a coefficient of 1.82, Toronto 1.33.
- Montreal's specialization is evident in the field of textiles and clothing, with a coefficient of 3.14.
- The location coefficients also indicate that Montreal is relatively specialized in publishing and radio and television broadcasting (1.53) and in telecommunications (1.78).

There is a concentration of employment in certain Montreal sectors: aerospace, computers and software, consumer durable and non-durable goods, electronics, finance, recreation, media, printing, oil and gas, telecommunications, textiles, leather and clothing, and the personal transportation industry.

This brief overview shows that the Canadian and U.S. cities and regions are characterized by specialization that is destined to become even more pronounced in the future, which allows the establishment and reinforcement of industrial clusters.

# Competitiveness and Growth in a Sample of North American Cities

WE CARRIED OUT a classic linear multiple regression analysis of economic growth determinants in the metropolitan regions in 1999 and again in 2001.[10]

## The Sample

OUR SAMPLE INCLUDES ALL 1999 urban agglomerations with a population of more than 850,000 (plus Quebec City): 56 U.S. Metropolitan Statistical Areas (MSAs) or Central MSAs (CMSAs) and seven major metropolitan regions as defined by Statistics Canada: Vancouver, Edmonton, Calgary, Toronto, Montreal, Quebec City and Ottawa-Hull. Table 1 lists the cities studied and their location, by region and boundary (northern and southern).

## Table 1

### Sample of Cities Studied in 1999 and 2001: Classification, by Region

| City | Partner | Northern Boundary | Southern Boundary | Region |
|------|---------|-------------------|-------------------|--------|
| New York | | | | Northeast |
| Los Angeles | | | X | Pacific |
| Chicago | | | | East Central |
| Washington-Baltimore | | | | Northeast |
| San Francisco-Oakland | | | | Pacific |
| Philadelphia | | | | Northeast |
| Boston | | | | Northeast |
| Detroit | Windsor | X | | East Central |
| Dallas-Fort Worth | | | | West Central |
| Houston | | | | West Central |
| Atlanta | | | | South |
| Miami-Fort Lauderdale | | | | South |
| Seattle | Vancouver | X | | Pacific |
| Cleveland | | X | | East Central |
| Phoenix | | | X | West Central |
| Minneapolis-St. Paul | | | | East Central |
| San Diego | | | X | Pacific |
| St. Louis | | | | West Central |
| Pittsburgh | | | | Northeast |
| Denver | | | | West Central |
| Tampa-St. Petersburg | | | | South |
| Portland-Salem | | | | Pacific |

## TABLE 1 (CONT'D)

| City | Partner | Northern Boundary | Southern Boundary | Region |
|------|---------|-------------------|-------------------|--------|
| Cincinnati | | | | East Central |
| Kansas City | | | | West Central |
| Sacramento | | | | Pacific |
| Milwaukee | | | | East Central |
| Norfolk | | | | South |
| San Antonio | | | X | West Central |
| Indianapolis | | | | East Central |
| Orlando | | | | South |
| Columbus | | | | East Central |
| Charlotte | | | | South |
| New Orleans | | | | South |
| Las Vegas | | | | West Central |
| Salt Lake City | | | | West Central |
| Buffalo | Toronto | X | | Northeast |
| Greensboro | | | | South |
| Nashville | | | | South |
| Hartford | | | | Northeast |
| Rochester | | X | | Northeast |
| Memphis | | | | South |
| Austin | | | | West Central |
| Raleigh-Durham | | | | South |
| Jacksonville | | | | South |
| Oklahoma City | | | | West Central |
| Grand Rapids | | | | East Central |
| West Palm Beach | | | | South |
| Louisville | | | | South |
| Dayton | | | | East Central |
| Richmond | | | | South |
| Providence | | | | Northeast |
| Greensville | | | | South |
| Birmingham | | | | South |
| Albany | | | | Northeast |
| Honolulu | | | | Pacific |
| Fresno | | | | Pacific |
| Calgary | | | | West Central |
| Edmonton | | | | West Central |
| Vancouver | Seattle | X | | Pacific |
| Toronto | Buffalo | X | | East Central |
| Ottawa | | X | | Northeast |
| Quebec | | X | | Northeast |
| Montreal | | X | | Northeast |

## THE 1999 STUDY: DEPENDENT VARIABLES AND FINDINGS

THE ONLY DEPENDENT VARIABLE USED in the 1999 study is an index of competitiveness (IND) inspired by Kresl's research on cities. It is made up of three indicators (weighted in terms of their share of the total for the middle year or at the end of each of the periods studied): manufacturing value-added, retail sales and GDP in business services.

The increase in retail sales captures the changes in population and income, and the metropolitan region's drawing power in terms of leisure and cultural activities and restaurants. The change in manufacturing value-added reflects expenditures on investment in human capital, machinery and equipment, and structures. The change in GDP for services indicates to what degree the metropolitan region serves as a location for services within its economic space and the extent of its conversion to services. High rates of change for these variables indicate that the metropolitan region in question is competitive and is a good place for the production and purchase of goods and services.

In our 1999 study, the equation defining our competitiveness variable was *Competitiveness = 0.3683 * (change in manufacturing value-added) + 0.5002 * (change in retail sales) + 0.1314 * (change in revenues from certain activities in the business services sector).*

We used 1987 as the weight for the 1977-92 IND; and the last year for the subperiods (i.e. 1982 for the 1977-82 subperiod, 1987 for the 1982-87 subperiod and 1992 for the 1987-92 subperiod). We used 1997 as the weight in calculating the IND for the 1987-97 period, estimated in the context of the 2001 study.

*By some estimates, there is a fairly tight statistical correlation between the variations in GDP and the IND, both of which are dependent* variables *in our study. The relation is 0.88 percent, according to a Spearman rank correlation coefficient.*[11]

## OUR DICHOTOMOUS VARIABLES: WHERE ARE THESE REGIONS IN NORTH AMERICA?

Our *dichotomous variables* capture three phenomena of a metropolitan region:

1. its *location* in the various regions, some of which are cross-border;

2. its *size*, measured in terms of population; and

3. its proximity to the Canadian *border* or to the southern border of the United States.[12]

The metropolitan regions are characterized by location as the Northeastern (NE), East Central (EC), West Central (WC), Southern (SO) or Pacific (PA) region of the continent. We wanted to test our assumption that the NE region (in which Montreal, Boston, etc. are located) is in relative competitive decline in North America. As we show below, *our 1999 and 2001 study results are compatible and confirm our assumption of a relative decline for the NE region of the continent.*

We omit the NE variable in the equations, which means that in the equations where we regress the dependent variables one by one against four dichotomous variables to capture the presence of the metropolitan regions in the EC, WC, SO and PA regions, the examination of these coefficients allows us to infer the coefficient for the NE region.

As shown in Table 1, we situate Montreal, Quebec City and Ottawa-Hull in the NE region; Toronto in the EC region; Calgary and Edmonton in the WC region; and Vancouver in the PA region.

We also wanted to address the issue of the *effects of the city's size on its economic performance* (economies of scale) by using either the dichotomous variable POPP (cities of less than 1.5 million inhabitants) or POPM (medium-sized cities of 1.5 to 5 million inhabitants).[13]

Our last dichotomous variable captures the city's location as either close to the Canada-U.S. border (NOB) or the southern border of the United States (SOB), to test whether being close to a border affects its growth, other things being equal. Hanson has found that Mexican cities have benefited from nearness to the U.S. border.

We begin with regressions intended to capture the effects of structural variables, i.e. location and size. We then add some explanatory variables, some of which may be influenced by policies.

## THE 1999 STUDY: EMPIRICAL RESULTS

OUR REGRESSION ANALYSIS IS CONVENTIONAL and lacking in refinements to reflect non-linearities obviously present in the relationships examined.

All equations are adjusted for heteroskedasticity (maximum likelihood). The dependent variable, IND, is a linear function of a series of independent variables plus an error term. Because cross-section and time-series data were involved, we pooled the data to do our regression analysis.

The regressions are run for (a) the total sample of 63 metropolitan areas, or the North American sample and (b) for the U.S. cities. The degrees of freedom preclude separate analysis for the Canadian cities, although a comparison of the results obtained in regressions (a) and (b) suggests comments on the Canadian cities. The regressions cover the following time periods: 1977-82, 1982-87, 1987-92 and 1977-92.

**TABLE 2**

**THE 1999 STUDY: BASE EQUATION FOR 1977-92 (1.3)
NORTH AMERICAN SAMPLE RESULTS, AFTER CORRECTION FOR
HETEROSKEDASTICITY (MAXIMUM LIKELIHOOD)**

| Variable | Coefficient | t-ratio | |
|---|---|---|---|
| EC | 1.2654 | 1.3450 | Non-significant positive |
| WC | 1.3850 | 2.9440 | Significant positive |
| SO | 0.9857 | 1.9854 | Significant positive |
| PA | 1.5453 | 2.4879 | Significant positive |
| | | | |
| POPP | 0.2459 | 1.5475 | Non-significant positive |
| POPM | 0.7548 | 1.9854 | Significant positive |
| NOB | 0.8956 | 2.3450 | Significant positive |
| SOB | −0.2145 | −1.0570 | Non-significant negative |
| CONSTANT | 0.5568 | 2.1240 | |
| LIKELIHOOD | −102.5600 | | |

Lack of U.S. data made study of the IND beyond 1992 impossible; as a result, the regressions are for the 1977-92 time period. Our more recent 2001 study covers the period through 1997.

As indicated above, we omit the NE region and metropolitan regions with more than five million inhabitants in dealing with our proxy variables representing the regions and cities. Coefficients of the regional and size variables are thus to be interpreted with reference to the NE and large metropolitan areas.

Our initial base equation experiments with more structural and permanent variables (i.e., region, proximity to NOB or SOB and size, as determined by population), leaving more policy-relevant variables to be added in subsequent equations.

In our base equation, we regress the IND against

1. the regional variables EC, WC, SO, and PA;

2. the population size variables POPP and POPM; and

3. the border variables NOB and SOB.

Let us examine regression 1.3 (the North American sample), estimated for the 1977-92 time period (see Table 2 for the empirical results).

The coefficient for each regional variable is positive and (except for EC) statistically significant in terms of the t-ratio. This confirms our previous conclusion that *Montreal and Boston are located in a Northeast region which is in relative decline when compared to other North American regions.*

NOB is positive and significant for competitiveness, while SOB is non-significant and negative.

POPP and POPM are both positive for competitiveness: the former is statistically non-significant, while the latter meets the significance test. The positive signs show that growth in competitiveness for small- and medium-sized metropolitan regions has been stronger than for large metropolitan regions (the omitted variable).

The discriminant analysis we examine later shows that POPP and POPM are significant variables. The probability of finding small- and medium-sized metropolitan regions among competitive cities grows from quartile to quartile for cities ranked by competitiveness.

The population density variable (DEN) is positive but not significant, which allows us to conclude that the larger metropolitan regions are not at a competitive disadvantage when compared to small- and medium-sized ones.

In Equation (2.0), we start with Equation (1.3) and add a variable to capture initial average wage (INIWAGE) and another to capture initial productivity (INIPROD). INIWAGE is negative but not statistically significant for competitiveness, while INIPROD is positive and highly significant, a result confirmed by our discriminant analysis. High INIWAGE values in a metropolitan region are not a significant determinant for its subsequent competitiveness, but high INIPROD values certainly give it a head start in its relative competitiveness among similar areas.

Equation (2.0) is slightly "better" than Equation (1.3) because the coefficients for the log likelihood estimate are higher in absolute value: $-102.54$ versus $-102.56$, respectively (see the appendix to the 1999 study).

We will comment no further on these results, except to note that Equation (9.0) is our best equation, with an absolute maximum likelihood value of $-95.34$. As we show below, Equation (9.0), appropriate to U.S. metropolitan regions only, involves regressing IND against the regional, population and border variables, to which we add CSI, SERV, CONC, TECH and FISC. The next-best are Equations (8.0), (6.0) and (5.0), respectively.

## THE 1999 STUDY: REGRESSION ANALYSIS EQUATIONS

(1.3)  $IND = a + EC + WC + SO + PA + POPP + POPM$
$\qquad\quad$ +ns $\quad$ +s $\quad$ +s $\quad$ +s $\quad$ +ns $\quad$ +s
$\quad$ +NOB −SOB,
$\quad$ +s $\quad$ −ns

where +ns = statistically non-significant variable with a positive sign, +s = significant variable with a positive sign, and −ns = non-significant variable with a negative sign.

(2.0)  Same as Equation (1.3), but add −INIWAGE + INIPROD.
$\qquad\qquad\qquad\qquad\qquad\qquad\qquad\quad$ −ns $\qquad\quad$ +s

(2.1)    Same as Equation (2.0), except that DIFFPROD replaces INIPROD,
                                                           +s
         where DIFFPROD = change in PRO.

(3.0)    Same as Equation (2.0), except that INIPOP replaces INIPROD.
                                          +ns                        +s

As a result, we also exclude POPP and POPM from this equation.

As INIPOP is non-significant, there is no indication of strong agglomeration economies by this measure.

(4.0)    Same as Equation (1.3), but add
         + SPEC (77) + CONC (90) – CONCE (77),
             +ns           +ns              –ns
where
SPEC = Ei\Et, by city, divided by Ei\Et for the United States (a localization index in which Ei = employment, by industry, and Et = total employment);
CONC = number of firms per employee, by city; and
CONCE = share of total employment in the top three industries, by city.

The results of this equation are relevant to the debate between Jacobs and Marshall, Arrow, Romer and Porter noted above.

We conclude that support for the creation of companies (and hence competition) is a good strategy; that specialization should be encouraged, but concentration and monopoly powers should not. The analyses of specialization, competition and concentration should, however, be done at the North American level or higher, not at the national, given the growing importance of North-South integration. These conclusions are subject to additional testing.

(5.0)    IND = Same as Equation (1.3), but add
               +TECH  + SERV  +  EXP,
                 +s      +s(NA)  +ns (NA)
                 +ns(US)    +s (US)
where

TECH = the share of total city employment in 21 high tech industries;
SERV = the ratio of service employment to total employment in the city; and
EXP = total exports of the city.
NA = North American sample; and
US = U.S. sample.

The EXP coefficient is the highest in this equation but is only statistically significant for the U.S. city sample.

The TECH variable is a positive and significant determinant of competitiveness, and includes industries such as pharmaceuticals, computers, office equipment, industrial electrical equipment, medical and ophthalmic equipment, communications equipment, missiles, measuring devices, engineering and architectural services. Despite its positive effect on competitiveness, it is not a significant variable in the regression equation for American cities alone.

(6.0)    Same as Equation (1.3), but add the following variables:

$$IND = a + IT + HT + SOFT + COMMUNIC.$$
$$\phantom{IND = a + }{+s} \quad {+ns} \quad {+s} \qquad\qquad {+ns}$$

Competitiveness is positively related to the share of total metropolitan employment in information technology (IT), high technology (HT), software (SOFT) and computers and communications (COMMUNIC). Our analysis of variance indicates that IT is a significant explanatory factor, as its coefficient increases from quartile to quartile when cities are ranked by competitiveness.

(7.0)    Same as Equation (1.3), but add the following variables:

$$IND = a + CSI - HQ,$$
$$\phantom{IND = a + }{+s} \quad {-ns}$$

where CSI = the percentage of total metropolitan employment in administrative and scientific jobs (i.e., scientists and engineers). Discriminant analysis shows that CSI is a very significant determinant of metropolitan competitiveness.

The HQ variable (number of head offices weighted by value of sales) is negative and non-significant in this equation, presumably because of multicollinearity problems (i.e., scientists and engineers at head offices, reflected in CSI).

(7.1) Same as Equation (7.0), except for the HQ variable. The coefficients of CSI are positive and statistically significant in these equations, an indication of the importance of highly qualified human resources to metropolitan competitiveness.

(8.0)    Same as Equation (1.3), but add the following variables:

$$IND = CSI + SERV + CONC + TECH.$$
$$\phantom{IND = }{+s} \qquad {+s} \qquad {+s} \qquad {+s}$$

Equation (8) is our second-best equation (maximum likelihood –99.34), and our best equation for the North American sample, as Equation (9.0) is estimated for U.S. metropolitan regions only.

*The regression equations that follow add variables that are more influenced by government policies than those above.*

We drop the POPP and POPM variables from Equations (9.0) to (11.0), as their coefficients are not significant in previous equations.

Equation (9.0) keeps the border and regional variables that figured in Equation (1.3) but without the POPP and POPM variables, as noted above. It is estimated only for the sample of U.S. cities because of the lack of comparable Internet-usage data for all of North America. **Equation (9.0) is our best equation** — the one with the highest maximum log likelihood estimate of −95.34.

(9.0)  IND = a + CSI + SERV + CONC + TECH − FISC +
         +s      +s      +s       +s      −ns
       INTERNET/97 (work and home).
         +ns

The CSI variable remains a significant determinant of competitiveness.

We also experimented with a fiscal variable FISC (total public revenues per $1,000 of personal income) which is of the expected sign but not statistically significant. Our earlier study (Proulx 1998) indicates that taxes have a significant effect on location *only if tax loads in the jurisdiction in question are significantly different from the average.* We did not formulate conclusions on the FISC variable in 1998, as we would have needed to take into account public revenues and expenditures to gauge adequately the effects of taxes and public expenditures on metropolitan competitiveness. An estimate of simple correlation coefficients between IND and FISC was −0.78, and one between IND and public expenditures was +0.66.

Of course, both personal and corporate income tax rates, as well as public expenditures, should be taken into account to assess the effects of taxation adequately. These effects may well have a significant influence on the location decisions of both highly qualified manpower and companies, as the latter are attracted to metropolitan regions with a pool of highly qualified human resources.

The INTERNET (at work and at home [U.S. Census Bureau 1997]) variable has a positive but non-significant effect on competitiveness.

(10.0)  Same as Equation (1.3), except for the absence of POPP and POPM:
        IND = a + CSI + CULT/92 + UNI/per capita/ 99 + DEST/92.
              +s      +ns                  +ns              +s

Our CULT variable represents cultural assets (i.e., orchestras, opera and ballet companies, theatres, museums, art galleries and libraries) per capita.

Universities (UNI) per capita are a necessary factor for metropolitan competitiveness but not sufficient by themselves. We have observed, however, the great significance of CSI, most of whom are university graduates. This is shown in Equation (10.1), where we substitute the percentage of the metropolitan population with B.A. degrees in 1990 for the university per capita count, and are left with a positive but still non-significant variable. *We conclude that this finding highlights the high geographic mobility of university graduates, hence the importance of attracting, training and retaining them in metropolitan development strategies.*

DEST is the number of direct (non-stop) air destination routes flying out of the metropolitan region in 1992. It is a positive and significant determinant of competitiveness but does not reach the significance cutoff point (1.745) in our discriminant analysis.

(10.1)   Same as Equation (10.0), except for the substitution of a BA/90 variable (positive but not significant) for the UNI variable.

All results remain unchanged.

(11.0)   (U.S. data only).
$$IND = a - FISC + INTERNET + DEST$$
$$\quad\quad\quad -ns \quad\quad\quad\quad +s \quad\quad +s$$

The results are the same as those obtained in previous equations.

## THE 1999 STUDY: DISCRIMINANT ANALYSIS

IN THE 1999 STUDY, we describe the composition of the PROBIT and LOGIT formulations used to estimate the probabilities of metropolitan regions being in different quartiles of the IND, as well as the assumptions and method used to obtain the log likelihood and the optimization procedures.

The discriminant analysis allows us to identify and measure the characteristics of metropolitan regions and classify them from least to most competitive. We chose the variables in terms of their significance to the regression analysis. The coefficients in Table 3 give the probability for a variable to be in a particular quartile. Thus the coefficient for the PA variable rises from 0.08 for the least competitive metropolitan region quartile to 0.14 for the most competitive one: this shows that a city in the PA region is likelier to be in the more, rather than less competitive quartile of cities.

Each of the four quartiles of cities is regressed on the variables shown in the first column of Table 3.

**TABLE 3**

**THE 1999 STUDY: COMPETITIVE DISCRIMINANT ANALYSIS**

| Variable | (prob y = 0) | (prob y = 1) | (prob y = 2) | (prob y = 3) | t-ratio |
|----------|--------------|--------------|--------------|--------------|---------|
| EC | 0.05 | 0.08 | 0.10 | 0.11 | 1.874 |
| WC | 0.09 | 0.10 | 0.15 | 0.16 | 2.254 |
| SO | 0.06 | 0.08 | 0.12 | 0.12 | 2.157 |
| INIPROD | 0.005 | 0.007 | 0.289 | 0.454 | 4.425 |
| POPP | 0.06 | 0.154 | 0.298 | 0.319 | 2.754 |
| POPM | 0.08 | 0.1875 | 0.287 | 0.312 | 2.954 |
| IT | 0.004 | 0.021 | 0.186 | 0.253 | 4.594 |
| SOFT | 0.03 | 0.08 | 0.256 | 0.289 | 1.854 |
| DEST | 0.10 | 0.15 | 0.18 | 0.19 | 1.745 |
| CSI | 0.08 | 0.11 | 0.13 | 0.16 | 2.014 |
| CONC | 0.04 | 0.08 | 0.09 | 0.19 | 1.421 |
| SERV | 0.16 | 0.18 | 0.22 | 0.25 | 1.321 |

Note: For Canada, the regression does not respect the fifth Gauss-Markov point listed above.

The PA, WC, and SO regions are statistically significant in terms of the t-ratio, while the EC variable is not.

These results show that the two most significant variables in explaining competitiveness for the 1977-92 time period are INIPROD and IT.

## THE 2001 STUDY: DESCRIPTIVE DATA

THE CITY DATA IN THE 2001 study are arranged in descending IND order for the 1987-97 period (Table 4).[14] We used 1997 as the reference point in our IND calculations for the period.

In this ranking, we find Vancouver (ninth), Toronto (fifteenth), Calgary (twenty-third), Montreal (thirty-fourth), Edmonton (thirty-fifth), Ottawa-Hull (sixtieth) and Quebec City (sixty-third) among the 63 metropolitan regions (Table 4).

We observe the following increases (in Canadian constant dollars) in IND components over the course of the 1987-97 period:

- Retail sales: Montreal, 24%; Vancouver, 96%; Calgary, 71%; Toronto, 48%; Edmonton and Ottawa, 45%; and Quebec City, 16%.

- Manufacturing value-added: Montreal, 92%; Vancouver, 128%; Toronto, 110%; Edmonton, 93%; Calgary, 79%; Ottawa, 26%; and Quebec City, 22%. Montreal therefore ranks fourth among the seven Canadian cities.

- GDP in business services: Montreal, 78%; Calgary, 161%; Vancouver, 160%; Edmonton, 142%; Toronto, 119%; Ottawa, 108%; and Quebec City, 82%. Montreal therefore ranks last among Canadian cities.

## TABLE 4

## COMPETITIVENESS INDEX, 1987-97

| | | | | | |
|---|---|---|---|---|---|
| 1 | Austin | 3.4835 | 32 | Grand Rapids | 0.9278 |
| 2 | Washington-Baltimore | 2.2878 | 33 | Birmingham | 0.9128 |
| 3 | Greenville | 2.2729 | 34 | Montreal | 0.8995 |
| 4 | Las Vegas | 2.1088 | 35 | Edmonton | 0.8814 |
| 5 | Salt Lake City | 1.5248 | 36 | San Diego | 0.8741 |
| 6 | Portland | 1.5035 | 37 | Chicago | 0.8686 |
| 7 | Houston | 1.4818 | 38 | San Antonio | 0.8284 |
| 8 | Denver | 1.4063 | 39 | Philadelphia | 0.8221 |
| 9 | Vancouver | 1.3655 | 40 | Miami | 0.8132 |
| 10 | Raleigh | 1.3198 | 41 | Dayton | 0.8107 |
| 11 | Dallas-Fort Worth | 1.2392 | 42 | New Orleans | 0.8020 |
| 12 | Charlotte | 1.2352 | 43 | Detroit | 0.7874 |
| 13 | Phoenix | 1.1761 | 44 | Oklahoma City | 0.7787 |
| 14 | Sacramento | 1.1476 | 45 | Milwaukee | 0.7515 |
| 15 | Toronto | 1.1468 | 46 | Cincinnati | 0.7395 |
| 16 | Tampa | 1.1425 | 47 | St. Louis | 0.7159 |
| 17 | West Palm Beach | 1.1263 | 48 | Fresno | 0.6963 |
| 18 | Seattle | 1.007 | 49 | Jacksonville | 0.6808 |
| 19 | Louisville | 1.0705 | 50 | Cleveland | 0.6784 |
| 20 | Atlanta | 1.0378 | 51 | Memphis | 0.6491 |
| 21 | Columbus | 1.0253 | 52 | New York | 0.6329 |
| 22 | Kansas City | 1.0209 | 53 | Greensboro | 0.5943 |
| 23 | Calgary | 1.0077 | 54 | Los Angeles | 0.5878 |
| 24 | San Francisco | 0.9857 | 55 | Providence | 0.5864 |
| 25 | Indianapolis | 0.9749 | 56 | Boston | 0.5831 |
| 26 | Richmond | 0.9618 | 57 | Honolulu | 0.5249 |
| 27 | Minneapolis | 0.9547 | 58 | Albany | 0.5084 |
| 28 | Orlando | 0.9544 | 59 | Buffalo | 0.5026 |
| 29 | Pittsburgh | 0.9423 | 60 | Ottawa | 0.4782 |
| 30 | Nashville | 0.9329 | 61 | Rochester | 0.3626 |
| 31 | Norfolk | 0.9296 | 62 | Hartford | 0.3490 |
| | | | 63 | Quebec | 0.3436 |

During the 1992-97 period, we observe the following increases in the components of the IND:

- Retail sales: Vancouver, 35%; Calgary, 32%; Toronto, 30%; Ottawa, 28%; Montreal, 25%; Edmonton, 21%; and Quebec City, 2%.

- Manufacturing value-added: Vancouver, 52%; Toronto, 40%; Edmonton, 29%; Calgary, 26%; Montreal, 19%; Ottawa, 11%; and Quebec City, 10%.

- GDP in business services: Calgary, 90%; Edmonton, 76%; Toronto, 59%; Vancouver, 48%; Ottawa, 41%; Montreal, 28%; and Quebec City, 23%.

We have analogous information for each of the 56 U.S. cities in our samples for the 1977-87 and 1987-97 periods. For the latter period:

- Retail sales increased by 265% in Austin, 125% in Salt Lake City, 85% in Seattle, 55% in Chicago, 47% in Philadelphia, 38% in Buffalo, 48% in New York, 31% in Albany, 28% in Boston and 24% in Hartford.

- Manufacturing value-added increased by 422% in Austin, 176% in Portland, 174% in Sacramento, 172% in Phoenix, 160% in Dallas-Fort Worth, 142% in Salt Lake City, 103% in Houston, 100% in Raleigh, 95% in Indianapolis, 80% in Seattle, 71% in San Diego, 55% in Atlanta, 43% in Chicago, 33% in Washington-Baltimore, 28% in Philadelphia, 23% in Boston, 15% in Rochester, 9% in Albany, 7% in Hartford and 1% in New York.

- GDP in business services increased by 1,051% in Greenville, 543% in Washington-Baltimore, 478% in Austin, 421% in Houston, 417% in West Palm Beach, 393% in Denver, 356% in Raleigh, 269% in Seattle, 262% in Sacramento, 255% in San Diego, 242% in Atlanta, 205% in Boston, 203% in Dallas-Fort Worth, 194% in New York, 186% in Phoenix and 168% in Providence.

## THE 2001 STUDY: VARIABLES, HYPOTHESES AND INTERPRETATION

HERE ARE SOME BRIEF COMMENTS on the hypotheses and reasons that led us to introduce the various explanatory variables into our 2000 regression analysis, and its interpretation.

We introduce the DEN variable to capture the effect of population density on our dependent variables. DEN is related to the POPM and POPP variables, although there are some cities that are similar in size but unequal in density. However, we do not introduce these variables in the same equation.

The 1997 initial population POPI variable is intended to measure the economies of scale effect. If it is significant, we can show that the large urban agglomerations are on a winning streak because they have reached critical masses and thresholds that enable them to be competitive.

We use PRO, the productivity measurement variable (manufacturing value-added divided by manufacturing employment in 1997), because it is a key explanatory factor for living standards, per capita GDP and competitiveness of cities.[15]

Our study of the industrial structure effect (STR) is brief. We wanted to confirm the effect of service sector growth (the reorientation of the metropolitan economy toward the services sector) on our dependent variables. We know that the specializations of cities can differ, with some (including Montreal) opting for the production of goods, others tending toward services. We know, however, that we are moving toward an industrial-service economy, with the production of both goods and services figuring in many sectors of the economy.

The 1999 REC variable allows us to test the impact of the presence of research centres on our dependent variables. Future work should focus on the various fields of research, as metropolitan regions are increasingly specializing in specific research niches.

The CDB variable is designed to capture the various 1999 costs of doing business in the metropolitan regions. It combines a number of costs, which should be broken down in future studies. We can expect that higher costs would have a negative effect on the growth of cities.

Professional and managerial employment in a city as a percentage of the total 1999 U.S. national metro area workforce, PM, can be expected to show a positive effect on urban growth.[16] The data for this variable and those we discuss below come from the on-line data base of Arthur Andersen, who compiled and used it to select the business cities for *Fortune* magazine.

The presence of university and college graduates should have a positive effect on urban growth. The variable EDU for 1999 represents the ratio of college and university enrolment to total population.

The variables for the percentage of the population with a bachelor's degree, BAC, or a college diploma COL should have a positive effect on urban growth. The empirical findings of the earlier 1999 study do not show a statistically significant relationship between the number of university graduates and urban competitiveness, although the employment of university graduates is a significant variable. We have reconciled these apparently contradictory results, noting the substantial mobility of the university-trained labour force, especially between American metropolitan areas, hence the lack of a relationship. One may study in Boston or Los Angeles but not necessarily work in either. As a critical mass of university graduates is positive for urban competitiveness, we conclude that it is desirable not only to train graduates but also to find ways to attract and retain them.

The RS variable represents the 1999 availability of recreation and entertainment activities in the metropolitan regions, while the CS is the comparable variable for cultural activities. These data draw on *Places Rated Almanac* (1999) research.

The spirit of entrepreneurship is also said to be a determinant of economic growth, and some firms will choose to locate in dynamic cities almost exclusively because of this variable. We derived an index of business start-ups, BS, in order to capture this spirit of entrepreneurship. Because the variable may also reflect the presence of venture capital, we use the variable VC to capture venture capital activity in the various metropolitan regions.

The presence of company head offices, HQ, represents the decision-making power that is found in the major metropolitan regions. The available studies suggest that the presence of head offices should be positive for city competitiveness. Could it be that organizational change (i.e, MNCs dispersed and split up into independent units) and technological change (management from a distance using intranets, etc.) break up the positive relationship between the presence of head offices and certain city growth indicators? Our 1999 study shows that the number of direct flight national destinations (DEST) goes hand in hand with major city competitiveness.

## THE 2001 STUDY: EMPIRICAL RESULTS

THE RESULTS OF THE ECONOMETRIC ANALYSIS (Proulx 2001) are available at the Quebec Ministère des Affaires municipales et de la Métropole. We made estimates on the basis of two samples: the first, totalling 63 metropolitan regions (Table 1) and the second comprising 27 cities that replied to a questionnaire, which enabled us to measure the scope of the relationship between city governments and the private sector, our governance variable (GOV) in certain regression equations (Table 5).

As the data compiled for the variation in GDP and change in total employment cover only year-to-year change, we dispense with detailed comments on the equations designed to explain these two dependent variables. Future studies might examine the determinants for the variation in GDP and employment over longer periods, as in the case of the IND (the dependent variable on which we focus our attention).

We used the E-VIEWS program to perform the regressions. We examine the statistics t, $R^2$ and $R,^2$ adjusted for degrees of freedom, as well as the F variable, in our analysis of the econometric results.

We examine, equation by equation, the sign of the coefficients of the explanatory (positive or negative) variables and the meaning of the explanatory variables (in terms of the t variable, where the variable in question is significant when the value of t is greater than 1.00, meaning that there is a 66.6 percent probability that the actual value of the coefficient is not zero).

We confine ourselves to some general conclusions on the main hypotheses in the comments that follow. The reader can find a more detailed analysis of our results by consulting the work sheets filed in our study (Proulx 2001).

## TABLE 5

### THE GOVERNANCE VARIABLE: COOPERATION BETWEEN CITIES AND THE PRIVATE SECTOR

| | |
|---|---|
| Atlanta | 2.0 |
| Austin | 2.7 |
| Calgary | 2.3 |
| Chicago | 3.7 |
| Columbus | 1.0 |
| Dallas | 2.0 |
| Edmonton | 2.3 |
| Greensboro | 2.7 |
| Houston | 3.0 |
| Indianapolis | 3.0 |
| Kansas City | 2.7 |
| Las Vegas | 2.3 |
| Louisville | 3.0 |
| Memphis | 2.7 |
| Milwaukee | 2.3 |
| Minneapolis | 1.3 |
| Montreal | 1.3 |
| Nashville | 1.7 |
| New Orleans | 2.7 |
| Orlando | 2.7 |
| Ottawa | 1.3 |
| Portland | 3.0 |
| San Antonio | 1.3 |
| Seattle | 3.0 |
| Toronto | 3.0 |
| Vancouver | 2.0 |
| Washington | 2.3 |

## THE 2001 AND 1999 STUDIES COMPARED: RESULTS FOR THE NORTH AMERICAN SAMPLE

OUR INITIAL INTEREST WAS IN THE PROCESS of territorial reconstitution of the North American economy under the effects of technological change, public policies such as the WTO, the FTA and the NAFTA, and corporate repositioning strategies. Then the 1999 study determined that the competitiveness of the cross-border NE region was in relative decline. This led us to re-examine the performance of the North American regions in terms of per capita GDP, growth in per capita GDP, growth in employment and changes in competitiveness in our 2001 study.

Consequently, the 2001 study begins with an estimate of the base equation (Table 6).

TABLE 6

THE 2001 STUDY: BASE EQUATION FOR 1987-97 RESULTS FOR THE
NORTH AMERICAN SAMPLE

| Variable | Coefficent | t-ratio |
|---|---|---|
| EC | 0.163420 | Positive non-significant |
| WC | 0.635268 | Positive significant |
| SO | 0.338326 | Positive significant |
| PA | 0.279448 | Positive significant |
| | | |
| POPP | –0.240000 | Negative significant |
| POPM | –0.203900 | Negative non-significant |
| NOB | –0.308281 | Negative significant |
| SOB | –0.354628 | Negative significant |
| CONSTANT | 0.916716 | |
| $R^2$ | 0.128900 | |

Now let us examine the major findings of the 2001 empirical study.

## IS THE NORTHEAST REGION IN RELATIVE DECLINE?

FIGURES FROM THE 63-CITY SAMPLE suggest that in 1999, metropolitan areas of the EC region had a lower income per capita than the cities located in the NE region. Their GDP and total employment growth between 1997 and 1998 confirm this conclusion.

Our findings on the basis of the IND, however, show that the competitiveness of EC region cities improved in comparison with that of NE region cities, in line with the 1999 study. At first sight, these findings are hard to reconcile with the results we obtained for the dependent variables of per capita GDP, change in GDP and change in metropolitan employment.[17] The economic recovery of the "rust belt" may explain this result in terms of competitiveness, as IND captures the growth in the manufacturing value-added, retail sales and GDP in services. It is also likely that the effects of lower competitiveness in the NE region are felt only in the longer run, which may explain the difference in some data for one or two years at the end of the 1990s.

Our findings (level of GDP, change in GDP and change in total employment) make it impossible to reach any conclusions on a comparison between the cities of the WC and NE regions. The coefficients of the WC variable are, however, systematically positive in equations where IND is the dependent variable: this would indicate that the competitiveness of the cities in the NE region has deteriorated against their WC region counterparts.

The results for the last three regressions, in which per capita income appears as a dependent variable, prevent us from concluding that the metropolitan regions in the SO region have a per capita income lower than those in the

NE, all things being equal. The SO coefficient sign is systematically negative in the equations where GDP change is a dependent variable, showing some improvement for NE cities. No conclusion is possible on the change in employment, while the results for the IND indicate that city competitiveness in the SO region has probably improved against that of the NE region (15 positive and significant, one positive and non-significant, and three negative but non-significant coefficients).

The PA variable coefficients in equations with per capita GDP as a dependent variable are all negative, indicating a negative effect derived from location in that region. The change in GDP between 1997 and 1998 displays a similar pattern, which shows decreased income growth for the PA region when compared to the NE region. The PA variable coefficients in the equations with change in employment as a dependent variable are all positive, showing relative employment decline for the NE cities. The PA coefficients in equations with IND as a dependent variable are all positive, showing a competitive decline for the NE.

*The 2001 findings on the growth of competitiveness are therefore systematic and in agreement with those of the 1999 study: the metropolitan areas of the NE region became less competitive in relation to other regions during the 1987-97 period.*

This deterioration is not demonstrated by other variables in the study. The EC coefficient is systematically negative in the estimated equations, but is statistically significant in only eight out of 19 equations.

We begin our study on the effect of city size (measured by population) by examining equations with IND as the dependent variable. The POPP and POPM coefficients are systematically negative, demonstrating that the major cities benefit from economies of scale when compared to the small- and medium-sized cities. These findings do not agree with those of the 1999 study, where the POPP and POPM variables had positive coefficients.

Next, we turn to our econometric findings on the border effect. The SOB coefficients are all positive in equations with GDP level, change in GDP or change in employment as a dependent variable, which would suggest that a U.S. city benefits from being close to the southern border of the United States. In the 1999 study, the SOB was non-significant and negative for competitiveness. Furthermore, NOB was positive and significant for competitiveness in 1999, while it is negative and significant in 2001.

The 2001 findings are clear and in agreement on the effect of location near the Canadian border for both U.S. and Canadian cities: negative for GDP, and changes in GDP, employment and competitiveness. The findings of the 1999 study (Table 2) prevent us, however, from reaching any conclusion on the topic.

The effect of DEN is clear only for GDP change, which is positive, and the IND, which is negative. In the 1999 study, DEN was positive and non-significant for equations where IND was the dependent variable.

The POPI, which is used to identify economies of scale (from our findings with POPP and POPM we know that the larger cities achieve economies of scale), has a statistically systematic effect only for employment changes, and it is positive. Admittedly, this is a limited measure of both economies of scale and employment changes. However, it is our only systematic result with the POPI variable.

We assumed that productivity (PRO) would have a positive effect on the dependent variables. The empirical findings between 1998 and 1999 are negative for both GDP change and competitiveness, counter-intuitive results that we are unable to explain. The INIPROD variable was positive and significant for competitiveness in 1999.

The STR, added to the base equation, Equation (1.3), produces negative coefficients for all dependent variables. Cities that specialize in the production of goods do not benefit. This finding should be examined in greater detail, as the Montreal Census Metropolitan Area specializes in the production of high technology goods.

As expected, REC is positive for GDP level and IND. These findings confirm the importance of R&D for metropolitan growth.

The CDB variable is negative for city competitiveness. Our only systematic finding is that per capita GDP is positive for the CDB variable.[18] We did not do any work with the KPMG (1999) cost data to verify whether our findings were in agreement with our expectations of a negative effect.

The PM variable is positive for competitiveness, as expected. This result confirms that the stronger the city is as a control centre, the more competitive it is. The statistical equation results for the other dependent variables — per capita GDP, change in per capita GDP and total employment — are inconclusive and therefore passed on without comment. We note, however, that the CSI variable in the 1999 study (Equation [5.0]) was positive and significant for competitiveness, as in the 2001 study.

The EDU variable coefficients are positive in equations to determine change in per capita GDP and IND, as expected. However, they are non-significant.

The findings of the 2001 study confirm the importance of a labour force with university degrees in an economy of information, knowledge and high technology. All of the dependent variables are positive for the BAC variable. Seven of the twelve coefficients are significant, five non-significant, a result analogous to that of the 1999 study.

The COL variable is positive for GDP change and negative for the IND, according to our results. The coefficients of this variable are all non-significant, however, so no conclusion is possible on this relationship.

The RS variable is positive for per capita GDP and the IND. Recreational activities can be considered consumer expenditures, but the importance of human resources as a factor in business location means that we can consider RS as an investment that has positive effects on urban growth. Against expectations, CS is negative for change in employment and the IND.

As expected, the BS variable, which reflects entrepreneurship and the availability of venture capital, among other factors, is positive and significant for the IND. Sign changes in the equations make it impossible to draw any conclusions on the effects of this variable for per capita GDP, change in per capita GDP and change in employment. We confine ourselves to the conclusion derived from the equation where the IND for business start-ups appeared (it is positive), as the other dependent variables measured only changes over a short period.

The VC variable is positive for city competitiveness, as expected. Our findings, however, show it as negative for GDP change, but we are inclined to let the conclusion stand: namely, that the VC effect is positive, given that the study only takes into account GDP change for a single year.

The HQ variable is positive for city per capita GDP (two significant and two non-significant coefficients), as expected. We note that HQ had a non-significant negative effect on competitiveness in the 1999 study, as it does in 2001. However, we concluded that the CSI variable captured the effects of the presence of head offices to which it was correlated.

The DEST variable is positive for GDP change. Our econometric findings do not allow any conclusions on the effects of this variable on our other dependent variables.

## THE EFFECTS OF GOVERNANCE IN SAMPLE TWO

WE CONTINUE OUR ANALYSIS by examining the findings for the sample of 27 cities that replied to our questionnaire, which allowed us to assign a GOV variable value for each city (Table 5).

*The sample of 27 cities replying to our questionnaire was not a random sample,* so we do not comment on the study's findings except on our results for the GOV variable.

The signs of the GOV variable coefficients are systematically negative in the equations with change in employment as a dependent variable. This finding is counter-intuitive, but of little importance, as it refers to employment change from 1997 to 1998 — too short a period for any conclusions.

The coefficients of the GOV variable are all positive in the equations with the IND as a dependent variable; however, they are non-significant in three out of four equations. *It is therefore impossible to draw any firm statistical conclusion that public-private sector collaboration has beneficial effects on the competitiveness of cities, although we have some indications that it does.*

## Concluding Comments

WE HAVE EXAMINED at some length the causes of the agglomeration effects observed in the context of globalization and North-South as well as South-North integration in the western hemisphere. They are due to factors that include information technologies, synergies, reduced transaction costs, internal and external economies of scale and the ability of companies to compare their performance. The result is the *metropolization* process on which we have focussed.

We find that U.S. cities and regions are becoming specialized as they increasingly interact with each other.

The 1999 and 2001 empirical studies also show that the ongoing process of sectoral and spatial reconstitution has not halted the declining trend for the cross-border NE region of North America. Some cities and regions there are dynamic, but the process of slow relative decline continues.

Our findings do not allow us to conclude, however, that the large metropolitan areas are at an advantage (or disadvantage) of scale in relation to the smaller ones. Nor do they show that the competitiveness performance of cities near the Canada-U.S. border is different from that of cities elsewhere on the continent. This is also true for cities close to the Mexican border. This finding should be studied in more detail together with data on GDP growth, employment, etc., for individual American states and Canadian provinces.

Our findings do not determine the effect on city competitiveness of an initial high level of productivity (INIPROD), or the presence of cultural and recreational activities.

The discriminant analysis done as part of the 1999 study of North American cities helped identify the major determinants of competitiveness for the period ending in 1992 (Table 3): variables included specialization, competition, jobs in high tech and services, export activity, jobs in ICTs (highly significant), software and communications, a highly skilled labour force (significant in both the 1999 and 2001 studies), universities and the number of direct flights.

A high degree of industrial concentration in a city, however, appears to reduce its competitiveness, at least until 1992. Our 1999 findings for the specialization variable and our study of the new economic integration environment suggest that competitiveness is impossible without specialization.

Our limited study of taxation nevertheless allows us to confirm the expected conclusion that both above- and below-average tax burdens harm city competitiveness.

Our 2001 empirical study confirms the following variables as positive for city competitiveness: a highly skilled labour force, universities, direct flights, greater emphasis on services than goods, research centres and business start-ups.

Our 2001 findings do not allow us to conclude that the presence of cultural activities (the 1999 study found they were positive but not statistically significant), head offices (negative in 1999, positive in 2001) or venture capital enhance metropolitan competitiveness — despite the fact that business start-ups and competition (in the 1999 study) had some positive effects on competitiveness.

Our brief look at the links between the public and private sectors suggests that they contribute to the competitiveness of North American cities. A negative finding would have been surprising, given the importance assigned to synergies among stakeholders in this study's theoretical analysis of the causes of agglomeration and economic growth.

Let us conclude then by saying that the increasingly specialized cities and regions of North America are expected to play an important role in the economic integration process now under way on this continent. To make our study more useful for economic policy purposes, additional work is obviously needed in a number of areas. They include studying city specializations and metropolitan economic dynamics; learning about the rising competition from China, as well as Mexico and other Latin American countries; understanding a city's influence on its economic hinterland; developing a more conclusive analysis of North American economic regions; and examining the competitiveness and specialties of Canadian and U.S. regional clusters.

# ENDNOTES

1   We cite data from a report prepared for the United States Conference of Mayors and the National Association of Counties (Standard and Poor's and DRI/McGraw Hill 2000). The definition of metropolitan regions is that of the United States Office of Management and Budget, which classifies a region as metropolitan if it contains a city with a population of at least 50,000 and comprises an area with a total metropolitan population of at least 100,000 (75,000 in New England). See http://www.whitehouse.gov/omb/inforeg/msa99.pdf for the 1999 list of U.S. metropolitan regions and their counties.

2   *New York Times*, May 7, 2001.

3   Linda McCarthy (2000) draws on the following sources, among others: Barnes, W.R., and L.C Ledebur, *Local Economies: The U.S. Common Market of Local Economic Regions*, Washington D. C., National League of Cities, 1994; Wallis, A.D., "The Third Wave: Current Trends in Regional Governance," *National Civic Review*, 83, 3 (1994): 290-309; Cisneros, H. G., *Urban entrepreneurialism and national economic growth*, Washington, DC: United States Department of Housing and Urban Development, 1995; and *In the National Interest: The 1990 Urban Summit*, edited by Berkman, R. et al., New York: The Twentieth Century Fund Press, 1992.

4   According to Frankel and Rose (2001), Canada's per capita GDP would increase by 37 percent in a North American monetary union. They use a gravity model and a two-stage estimation method by which they estimate first, the effects of monetary union on trade flows and second, the effects of these flows on per capita GDP. Such results are subject to further analysis, given the effects of the FTA and the NAFTA and the fact that the Frankel and Rose estimates are drawn from a sample that includes a fair number of developing countries.

5   See the *Revue d'Économie Régionale et Urbaine* for literature on the topic: No. 4 in 1993 presents some new analyses on localization; Nos. 3 and 4 in 1991 discuss innovative settings and innovation networks.

6   The location of headquarters of international organizations also has a great influence on the growth of metropolitan regions.

7   Proulx (1998) reviews the academic literature and examines the site locator's methods; it also contains the results of a summary investigation on U.S. firms that have moved to Montreal recently.

8   The AEA-NASDAQ report (AEA 2000) provides information and files on more cities than those on the list below.

9   The data are available by NACI sector in the report (Cortright and Mayer 2001).

10   The complete results are available in Proulx (2001).

11   These results were obtained by Pierre Langlois in a report prepared as an M.A. thesis in economics at the Université de Montréal (Langlois 1999).

12   See Table 1 for the details on each city.

13   There are probably some non-linearities in the analysis which do not concern us.

14   Many of our data (Proulx 2001, Appendices 2 and 3) are from the Arthur Andersen on-line data bank. The rest were extracted from the data banks of Statistics Canada, the United States Bureau of Economic Analysis and the United States Census Bureau.

15   We used the PRO variable in our 1999 DIFFPROD study, but because of the limited scope of our project, our inclination was not to undertake this analysis in the 2001 study.

16   In the United States, the proportion of "current metro area population employed in executive, administrative, managerial and professional specialties" stands at 25.2 percent, according to the Arthur Andersen on-line data base. It lists the difference between this and the percentage for each city. We have added (or subtracted) this percentage difference from the U.S. average to arrive at our PM variable.

17   The only exception is in Equation (1.4.15), when we add the BS variable to the base equation. BS has a significant and positive coefficient on competitiveness in this regression equation, while the coefficient for EC is negative, albeit non-significant.

18   The CDB variable reflects the per-unit labour cost, energy costs, state and local taxes and office rents. See Markey and Burt, *Dismal Sciences*, for the weighting factors and definitions.

# BIBLIOGRAPHY

AEA. "Cybercities." *Cyber Report Series*. American Electronics Association, with NASDAQ, 2000.

Arthur Andersen. On-line data base. Available at: http://www.arthurandersen.com/.

Camagni, Roberto. "The Concept of Innovative Milieu and its Relevance for Public Policies in European Lagging Regions." *Papers in Regional Science*, 74, 4 (1995): 317-340.

Cameron, Richard A. *Intrafirm Trade of Canadian-based Foreign Transnational Companies*. Ottawa: Industry Canada Working Paper No. 26, December 1998.

Coase, R. *The Information Age: Economy, Society and Culture. Volume 1: The Rise of Network Society*. Oxford and Malden MA: Blackwell Publishers, 1996.

Corptech data base, 2001.

County Business Patterns, U.S. Department of Commerce.

Cortright, J., and H. Mayer. *High Tech Specialization: A Comparison of High Technology Centers*. Institute of Portland Metropolitan Studies, Portland State University and Brookings Institution, Survey Series, January 2001.

E&B Data, High Technologies Benchmark Survey, 2001, Major North American Metropolitan Regions. Available at: http://www.ebdata.com.

Feldman, M. P., and D. B. Audretsch. "Innovation in Cities: Science-Based Diversity, Specialization and Localized Competition." *European Economic Review* 43 (1999): 421-427.

Florida, Richard. *The Rise of the Creative Class*. Basic Books, 2002.

Frankel, J.A., and A. K Rose. *An Estimate of the Effect of Common Currrencies on Trade and Income*, April 12, 2001. Mimeograph.

Geenhuizen, M.S. van, and P. Nijkamp. *The Local Environment as a Supportive Operator in Learning and Innovation*. Delft University of Technology, October 1998.

Gaspar, Jess, and E. Glaeser. "Information Technology and the Future of Cities." *Journal of Urban Economics* 43 (1998): 136-56.

Gertler, Meric S. "Being There: Proximity, Organization and Culture in the Development and Adoption of Advanced Manufacturing Technologies." *Economic Geography* 71, 1 (January 1995): 3.

Glaeser, E. *Growth in Cities*. NBER Working Paper No. 3787, 1991.

GREMI. *Revue d'Économie Régionale et Urbaine* 3 and 4 (1991).

_____. *Revue d'Économie Régionale et Urbaine* 4 (1993).

Hall, Peter. "Great Cities in the 21st Century: Infrastructure Planning and Development." Duplicated, lecture in Madrid, 1999, p. 5.

Hanson, Gordon H. *Scale Economies and the Geographic Concentration of Industry*. NBER Working Paper No. 8013, November 2000.

Kherdjemil, Boukhalfa. "Territoires, mondialisation et redéveloppement." *Revue d'économie régionale et urbaine* 2 (1999): 267-281.

KPMG. *Une comparaison des coûts des entreprises dans les grandes villes nord-américaines*. September 1999.

Kresl, P.K., and P. P. Proulx. "Montreal's Place in the North American Economy." *The American Review of Canadian Studies* 30, 3 (Autumn 2000): 283-314.

Langlois, Pierre. "Croissance économique : Dynamique des métropoles américaines." Master's thesis in economics, Université de Montréal, 1999.

McCarthy, Linda. *Competitive Regionalism: Beyond Individual Competition*, U.S. Economic Development Administration, Review of Economic Development Literature and Practice, No. 2, (October 2000), pp. 1-2.

Maillat, Denis. "Milieux innovateurs et dynamique territoriale." In *Économie industrielle et économie spatiale*. Edited by A. Rallié and A. Torres. Paris : Économisa, 1995.

Markey and Burt. *Dismal Sciences*. Available at http://www.economy.com/dismal.

Marshall, Alfred. *Principles of Economics*. 1890.

Maskell, Peter. "Growth and the territorial configuration of economic activity." Danish Research Unit for Industrial Dynamics, Summer Conference, June 12-15, 2001, p. 4.

Milken Institute Web site. Available at http://www.milkeninstitute.org.

Montreal TechnoVision. *Annual Report*, 2000.

Moody's. *Investors Report*, 2000.

Organisation for Economic Co-operation and Development. "21$^{st}$ Century Technologies: A Future of Promise." *OECD Observer* 217-218 (Summer 1999): 56-58.

Pecqueur, Bernard. *Le développement local*. Paris : Syros, Alternatives, 1992.

*Places Rated Almanac*, 1999.

Porter, Michael. United States Competitiveness Council, 2001.

Proulx, Pierre-Paul. "Critères de localisation d'activités économiques à Montreal, vers un modèle opérationnel pour favoriser la rétention et l'attraction d'entreprises à Montreal." *Montreal International* (January 1998). Mimeograph.

_____. "La région métropolitaine de Montreal: son positionnement en Amérique du Nord et des éléments de réflexion pour une stratégie de développement économique." Quebec: Report to the Ministère des Affaires municipales et de la Métropole, March 2001.

Proulx, P.-P., P. Kresl and P. Langlois. "La région métropolitaine de Montreal et les métropoles de l'Amérique du Nord: compétitivité et politiques." Report to the Ministère des Finances du Québec, July 1999.

Saxenian, Annalee. *Regional Advantage, Culture and Competition in Silicon Valley and Route 128*. Cambridge: Harvard University Press, 1994.

Standard and Poor's and DRI/McGraw Hill. *U.S. Metro Economies, The Engines of America's Growth*. Report prepared for the U.S. Conference of Mayors and the National Association of Counties, May 2000.

Storper, Michael. "Regional Economies as Relational Assets." *Revue d'économie régionale et urbaine* 4 (1996).

United States Census Bureau. *A 1997 Survey*. Available at: http://www.census.gov/.

# APPENDIX A

## THE 2001 STUDY: VARIABLES AND DATA

### TABLE A1

### DATA AND REGRESSION ANALYSIS

| 1 | SAMPLE: America 1997 (1997.wfl) |
|---|---|
| 2 | SAMPLE: Governance 1997 (gouv1997.wfl) |

**Dependent Variables**

| 1 | GDP | = | GDP per capita at 1999 level |
|---|---|---|---|
| 2 | Δ GDP | = | Variation in GDP per capita 1998-99 |
| 3 | Δ TE | = | Variation in total employment 1997-98 |
| 4 | IND | = | Index of competitiveness 1987-97 |

**Dichotomous Variables**

| | EC | = | **East Central region** |
|---|---|---|---|
| | **WC** | = | **West Central region** |
| | SO | = | Southern region |
| | PA | = | Pacific region |
| | POPP | = | Small population classification (less than 1.5 million) |
| | POPM | = | Medium-sized population classification (from 1.5 to 5 million) |
| | SOB | = | Southern border effect |
| | NOB | = | Northern border effect |

**Independent Variables**

| | DEN | = | Density |
|---|---|---|---|
| | POPI | = | Initial population |
| | PRO | = | Productivity |
| | STR | = | Industrial structure |
| | REC | = | Research centres |
| | CDB | = | Cost of doing business |
| | PM | = | Professional or management employment (Arthur Andersen [AA] data) |
| | EDU | = | Registration in colleges and universities — total population (AA) |
| | BAC | = | Percent of the population with a university degree (AA) |
| | COL | = | Percent of the population with a college degree (AA) |
| | RS | = | Recreation score (results) (AA) |
| | CS | = | Culture score (results) (AA) |
| | BS | = | Business start-ups (AA) |
| | VC | = | Venture capital (AA) |
| | HQ | = | Headquarters according to FORTUNE 500 (AA) |
| | DEST | = | Number of destinations for direct flights (AA) |
| | GOV | = | Governance effect |

The dependent variables we used (by subset of regressions) are 1) a snap-shot cross-section (i.e., 1999) for GDP; 2) the variation in GDP between 1998 and 1999; 3) the variation in total employment (including employment in the public sector) between 1997 and 1998;* or 4) an IND whose construction for the 1987-97 period we have explained.

Table A2 lists information on the years for which data was available for the 2001 study.

## TABLE A2
### THE 2001 STUDY: DATA AVAILABILITY

| Variables | United States | Canada |
|-----------|---------------|--------|
| DEPENDENT | | |
| TE | 1976–99 | 1987–99 |
| GDP | 1997–99 | 1987–99 |
| IND | 1977–87, 1987–97, 1992–97 | 1987–97, 1992–97 |
| INDEPENDENT | | |
| DEN | 1977,1987, 1992, 1997–99 | 1987–92,1997–99 |
| POPI | 1977, 1987, 1992 | 1987, 1992 |
| PRO | 1977, 1987, 1992, 1997 | 1987–97 |
| STR | 1977–96 | 1987–97 |
| REC | 1999 | 1999 |
| CDB | 1999 | 1999 |
| PM | 1999 | 1999 |
| EDU | 1999 | 1999 |
| BAC | 1999 | 1999 |
| COL | 1999 | 1999 |
| RS | 1999 | 1999 |
| CS | 1999 | 1999 |
| BS | 1999 | 1999 |
| VC | 1999 | 1999 |
| HQ | 1999 | 1999 |
| FLT | 1999 | 1999 |
| GOV | 1999 | 1999 |

Note: In our 2001 data bank, the Canadian data for total full-time and part-time employment for all sectors (including the public sector) are from Statistics Canada. The U.S. data, similarly defined, are from the United States Bureau of Economic Analysis. In 1999, we subtracted public sector employment from Canadian city employment data to make them comparable to the U.S. data, which, because they were derived from the U.S. Department of Commerce's *County Business Patterns*, did not include the public sector.

Paul Beaudry      &      *David A. Green*
*University of British Columbia*      *University of British Columbia*
*and Canadian Institute*
*for Advanced Research*

**6**

# Canada-U.S. Integration and Labour Market Outcomes: A Perspective Within the General Context of Globalization

## INTRODUCTION

ANY DISCUSSION OF greater economic integration between Canada and the United States must start by examining the implications of integration more broadly. In particular, we should rephrase a standard set of questions. For example: What would be the margins most likely affected by the economic integration of two advanced industrialized countries? Would the integration process favour mainly the equalization of the price of goods (and therefore country specialization) or the reallocation of factors across borders? Alternatively, would it favour the transmission of knowledge? Although the answers to these questions are highly controversial, we believe that it is necessary to take a stance on these issues.

In our view, developed from studies of labour market outcomes, the most relevant aspect of the current economic integration between the two countries is the entire process that facilitates the allocation of physical investment (and thus the allocation of production) across borders. Accordingly, in this study, we address the link between Canada-U.S. integration and labour market outcomes by emphasizing how the facilitation of investment flows (i.e., flows of physical capital) between Canada and the United States is likely to affect labour market outcomes. We address this issue in three steps. First, we review theory and evidence about how movements in physical capital likely affect labour market outcomes in the current technological environment. Second, we examine the forces that affect the direction of physical capital movements across countries. Finally, we discuss whether or not further economic integration with the United States is likely to favour Canada in terms of investment flows.

Before we proceed, a brief note on why we believe physical capital flows are so important to a proper understanding of the current process of economic integration. First, at least among advanced industrialized countries, relative prices among traded goods are rather similar; hence, it is unlikely that further economic integration will have significant effects along this margin. Second, much of the international finance literature (e.g., as reviewed in Obstfeld and Rogoff 2000) suggests that capital mobility across countries is still far from perfect. In particular, domestic savings and investment rates still appear tightly linked, even among industrialized countries; hence, this is a margin on which further integration can potentially have large effects. Third, in our own work (Beaudry and Green 1998, 2000a, 2000b), which examines in substantial detail labour market outcomes in Canada, the United States, the United Kingdom and Germany, we have found that differences in physical capital accumulation across these countries has affected labour market outcomes greatly over the last 20 years. Hence, we think that capital flows are, conceptually and empirically, the most likely venue by which further economic integration among industrialized countries is likely to affect labour market outcomes.

The remaining sections of the study are structured as follows. In the second section, we present a simple theoretical model to illustrate how capital flows can affect labour market outcomes. We take special care to discuss the effects of capital flows both in terms of the overall effect on wage levels as well as the distributional effect between more- and less-educated workers; furthermore, we highlight how recent technological change may affect this relationship. In the third section, we present international evidence regarding the effects of increases in physical capital on the wage structure. In the fourth section, we review the main determinants of international capital flows, and relate these to the particular case of Canada-U.S. integration. This last section is more speculative, as it is based mainly on conjectures and extrapolations from our research. It is followed by a short concluding section.

## CAPITAL FLOWS AND LABOUR MARKET OUTCOMES: A SIMPLE THEORETICAL FRAMEWORK

THE OBJECT OF THIS SECTION is to illustrate how physical capital flows likely affect labour market outcomes in a world with workers of different skill levels, and where technological choice is endogenous. To this end, let us consider a situation where only one good is produced, denoted by $Y$.[1] Furthermore, let there be three inputs: high-skilled labour, denoted by $H$; low-skilled labour, denoted by $L$; and physical capital, denoted by $K$. Since (for now) we are interested only in understanding the effects of exogenous change in $K$, we can adopt a simple static framework.

The labour supply decisions of workers are assumed to be given by the upward-sloping functions $\psi^H(w^H)$ and $\psi^L(w^L)$, where $w^H$ and $w^L$ represent the wages paid to high- and low-skilled workers, respectively. Without loss of generality, we can interpret these labour supply curves as wage bargaining curves, and thereby alternatively interpret movements along them as generating either changes in participation or changes in involuntary unemployment. Without imposing any additional structure on the functioning of such an economy, a capital inflow can have one of four effects. It can

1) increase the wage and employment of high-skilled workers, while reducing it for low-skilled workers;

2) increase the wage and employment of low-skilled workers, while reducing it for high-skilled workers;

3) increase the wage and employment of both types of workers, with the effect on wages being greatest for the high-skilled workers; or

4) increase the wage and employment of both types of workers, with the effect on wages being greatest for the low-skilled workers.

To clarify which of these effects is most likely in the current technological environment, it is useful to consider an environment where there are two competing means of producing Y.[2] By using this framework, we can highlight an important link between the nature of technological change and the effects of capital inflows on labour market outcomes. In particular, we argue that the conditions under which capital inflows are especially good in terms of labour market outcomes conform surprisingly well to many casual observations on the nature of recent technological change.

Let us begin with the extreme case where firms can produce Y using either a traditional technology, which requires only low-skilled labour and capital, or a modern technology, which requires high-skilled labour and capital. These two production functions will be denoted by $F^T(L,K^T)$ and $F^M(H,K^M)$, where $K^T$ and $K^M$ are the amount of physical capital used in the traditional and modern modes of production, respectively. Both of these production functions are assumed to be convex and to satisfy constant returns to scale. If we further assume that firms are price takers, then the general equilibrium determination of wages and employment for this economy is given by the solution to the following set of six equations, where we assume that capital is mobile in the sense of being allocated efficiently between the two different modes of production:[3]

(1) $\quad w^L = \dfrac{\partial F^T(L,K^T)}{\partial L}$ ;

(2)  $w^H = \dfrac{\partial F^M (H, K^M)}{\partial H}$ ;

(3)  $\dfrac{\partial F^T (H, K^T)}{\partial K} = \dfrac{\partial F^M (H, K^M)}{\partial K}$ ;

(4)  $K^T + K^M = K$ ;

(5)  $H = \psi^H (w^H)$ ; and

(6)  $L = \psi^L (w^L)$.

Equations (1) and (2) represent the marginal product conditions that implicitly define demand for high- and low-skilled workers. Equation (3) represents the marginal product condition which determines the allocation of capital between the modes of production. Finally, Equations (4) to (6) guarantee that the total demand of factors is equal to the total supply.

On the basis of this simple set-up, we can ask how an inflow of physical capital affects wages and employment; in other words, we can perform the comparative static exercise associated with increasing $K$. Note that an increase in $K$ is meant to capture the idea of a reduction in a barrier to the free international movement of capital. As can be verified easily by using Equations (1) to (6), an increase in total capital will unambiguously cause an increase in both wages and employment levels, regardless of the precise forms of $F^T(\cdot)$ and $F^M(\cdot)$. In particular, this implies that in this case, an increase in physical capital does not cause either type of labour to be displaced by physical capital, and thus would be highly desirable.

An obvious question that emerges from this simple exercise relates to the generality of the result that an increase in physical capital is likely to improve labour market outcomes of both high- and low-skilled workers. The analyses in Beaudry and Green (1998, 2000a) provide insight into this issue: they illustrate the simple conditions under which an increase in physical capital will cause such beneficial effects. The first condition is that the economy is in a state of technological transition, which means that it is in the process of adopting a new production method but has not yet entirely abandoned the more traditional one. The second is that the new method of production is skill-biased in relation to the more traditional mode of production; in other words, the main characteristic of the new method of production must be that it uses high-skilled labour more intensively than the traditional mode. Under these two conditions, an inflow of physical capital will necessarily cause wages and employment of both types of labour to rise. Obviously, the above example satisfies the latter condition, as it corresponds to an extreme case of skill bias where the modern form of production does not use any low-skilled labour.

The reason we consider this theoretical discussion useful is that it links the discussion of technological change to that of the effects of capital flows on labour market outcomes. In particular, the two conditions which assure that an increase in physical capital will have very desirable labour market outcomes conform surprisingly well to the type of technological transition that many believe has been taking place in industrialized economies. For example, there is an extensive literature which suggests that over the last 20 to 25 years, the economy has been moving away from the traditional forms of work organization, based on a hierarchical and centralized system, toward a more decentralized and autonomous system. Moreover, one of the main properties of this new form of work organization has been its emphasis on, and need for, highly educated workers. Hence, at least on a priori grounds, it appears reasonable to think that an inflow of physical capital is likely to generate desirable labour market outcomes in our current technological environment.

One additional element that is important to discuss within this framework is the effect of an increase in physical capital on wage inequality (i.e., the effect of an inflow of physical capital on the ratio of low- to high-skilled wages). In particular, the previous discussion argues that in the current technological environment, an inflow of physical capital is likely to increase both $w^H$ and $w^L$; however, it does not tell us how it affects the ratio of the two. To derive conditions associated with this question, it is helpful to maintain the view that the economy is in a state of technological transition. This allows the derivation of simple conditions to show whether an inflow of physical capital likely generates a decrease, or an increase, in wage inequality. As it turns out, the relevant condition relates to whether the new mode of production uses physical capital more or less efficiently than the more traditional mode (Beaudry and Green 1998, 2000a). In particular, if the new mode of production uses less physical capital per unit of output, an inflow of physical capital will cause a drop in the ratio of high- to low-skilled wages.

To see this more clearly, let us consider a specific example. For this case, let us maintain the assumption that the modern mode of production uses only high-skilled labour and capital, while the traditional mode uses only low-skilled labour and capital. Furthermore, to assure that wages can be expressed as an explicit function of aggregate capital, let us choose particular functional forms for these production functions, and let us assume that labour supply is inelastic. In particular, the production function for the traditional mode of production can be set as a Leontief, with $F^T(L,K^T) = Min[L,K^t]$, while the modern form of production can be set as a Cobb-Douglas, with $F^M(L,K^M) = (HK^M)^{.5}$. Finally, we will assume that the capital labour ratio in the economy, $\dfrac{K}{H+L}$, is greater than 1, to assure that factor prices are always positive. Under these assumptions, the wages of high- and low-skilled labour can be solved explicitly as

(7) $\quad w^H = (\dfrac{K-L}{H})^{.5}$ and

(8) $\quad w^L = 1 - (\dfrac{H}{K-L})^{.5}.$

Equations (7) and (8) show that both $w^H$ and $w^L$ are increasing functions of capital. Moreover, it can be easily verified that an increase in $K$ can simultaneously lead to a decrease in the ratio of high- to low-skilled wages, as long as the stock of capital is not too great ($K < 4H + L$). Our interest in this example is that it illustrates a clear case where, during a technological transition, an increase in physical capital is desirable for both wage growth and inequality. Hence, in this example, an inflow of capital could be viewed as a silver bullet in terms of labour market outcomes. Obviously, we do not think that the real economy is as simple as this example. Nevertheless, the example illustrates why capital inflows may be particularly desirable when an economy is witnessing a technological transition toward a skill-biased and capital-efficient production process. It should not come as a great surprise, therefore, if such a pattern is observed. In fact, it may be reasonably interpreted as suggesting that the economy has been witnessing a technological transition toward a skill-biased and capital-efficient technology.

## THE EFFECT OF PHYSICAL CAPITAL ACCUMULATION ON WAGE STRUCTURE: INTERNATIONAL EVIDENCE

### EMPIRICAL FRAMEWORK

THE MODEL DESCRIBED IN THE SECOND SECTION sets out the theoretical result that in an economy in transition between two competing technologies, an increased supply of physical capital leads to higher wages and employment for both low- and high-skilled workers. Furthermore, under certain conditions having to do with the relative efficiency of capital use in the competing technologies, an increased supply of physical capital will generate a reduction in the differential between high- and low-skilled wages. Our goal in this section is to examine whether this model provides a useful depiction of the recent evolution of developed economies. To the extent that it does, it can be used as a basis for discussing the implications of North American integration for the labour market. First, we summarize our previous investigations of the implications of this theoretical model, carried out with Canadian, American and German data. Second, we provide new evidence on long-term movements in capital use, wages and employment, incorporating combined data from these three countries, as well as the United Kingdom. It is worth emphasizing that in our earlier studies, as well as in this one, we focus on international comparisons to examine the theory. This stems from our belief that cross-country variation is essential in investigating macro-level issues like the impacts of technical change and aggregate capital movements on wage and employment levels.

## FRAMEWORK WITH INELASTIC LABOUR SUPPLY

WE BEGIN BY DERIVING AN EMPIRICAL SPECIFICATION that allows for an exploration of the theoretical results of the previous section. As a first step, we will assume that both high- and low-skilled labour is inelastically supplied. This makes the intuition clearer, and provides a direct link to our earlier studies, where results were derived in that context.

In order to understand the empirical implications of the theoretical framework from the previous section, it is useful to define the economy's aggregate production function, denoted by $F(L,H,K)$, as

$$F(L,H,K) = \max_{L^T,L^M,H^T,H^M,K^T,K^M} F^T(L^T,H^T,K^T) + F^M(L^M,H^M,K^M) ,$$

subject to

$$L^T + L^M = L, \ \ H^T + H^M = H, \ \ K^T + K^M = K,$$

where $L$, $H$ and $K$ are the total amounts of low-skilled labour, high-skilled labour and physical capital in use in the economy, respectively. In the previous section, we considered a special case where

$$F^T(L^T,H^T,K^T) = F^T(L,K^T)$$

and

$$F^T(L^M,H^M,K^M) = F^M(H,K^M);$$

that is, where the traditional technology uses only low-skilled labour and capital, while the modern technology uses only high-skilled labour and capital. This specification is useful for gaining intuition, but we do not need to be as restricted to obtain our results.

By means of this aggregate production function, we can derive expressions for the wages in a competitive equilibrium, assuming for the moment that the supplies of $L$ and $H$ are inelastic. These are simply the marginal product conditions associated with $L$ and $H$. If we use a log-linear approximation, these can be expressed as

(9) $\quad \log(w_t^H) \approx \alpha_0 + \alpha_1 \log\left(\dfrac{H_t}{K_t}\right) + \alpha_2 \log\left(\dfrac{L_t}{K_t}\right)$ and

(10) $\log(w_t^L) \approx \beta_0 + \beta_1 \log\left(\dfrac{L_t}{K_t}\right) + \beta_2 \log\left(\dfrac{H_t}{K_t}\right),$

where we exploit the property of homogeneity of degree zero implied by the assumption that the underlying production functions, and hence the aggregate production function, exhibit constant returns to scale. We can easily extend this framework to allow for the ongoing, exogenous technical change. To do this, we rewrite the aggregate production function as

$$Y_t = F(\theta_t^L L_t, \theta_t^H H_t, K_t),$$

Where $\theta^L$ and $\theta^H$ are low- and high-skilled factor augmenting terms, respectively. In this framework, exogenous technological change appears as movements in $\theta^L$ and $\theta^H$. Earlier work on movements in skill differentials in earnings assume that growth in $\theta^H$ has been greater than growth in $\theta^L$, resulting in an increase in demand for high-skilled, in relation to low-skilled, workers (Katz and Murphy 1992; Murphy, Riddell and Romer 1998). In Beaudry and Green (2000a), we argue that this model does not in fact fit the Canadian data. Nonetheless, we would like to allow for the possibility of ongoing technical change. In the context of our model, we assume that the main features of technical change and labour market outcomes can be explained by firms endogenously choosing between modern and traditional technologies. However, there may also be ongoing, incremental technical change within each of the two dominant technologies. In empirical investigations of our model, we would like to control any such incremental change in order to isolate the larger movements related to choices among technologies.

In Beaudry and Green (1998), we incorporate a control for ongoing technical change by relating the $\theta^L$ and $\theta^H$ terms to movements in measured total factor productivity (TFP). We then derive equations for high- and low-skilled wages as follows:

(11) $\log(w_t^H) = \alpha_0 + \alpha_1 \log\left(\dfrac{H_t}{K_t}\right) + \alpha_2 \log\left(\dfrac{L_t}{K_t}\right) + \alpha_3 \text{TFP}_t + e_t^H$ and

(12) $\log(w_t^L) = \beta_0 + \beta_1 \log\left(\dfrac{L_t}{K_t}\right) + \beta_2 \log\left(\dfrac{H_t}{K_t}\right) + \beta_3 \text{TFP}_t + e_t^L,$

where $e_t^L$ and $e_t^H$ are approximation errors that are assumed not to be correlated with other variables, and $\text{TFP}_t$ is the log of TFP.[4]

Recall from the discussion in the previous section that we focus on an economy where there are two competing technologies currently in use; the production functions use some combination of the three factors $H$, $L$ and $K$; and the main feature defining the difference between the two technologies is that one is skill-biased in relation to the other. We argued that this is a plausible representation of the way the current economy has been described by other investigators. However, whether or not this is an accurate depiction of the actual economy ultimately must be determined by comparing predictions from the model to the data. We are particularly interested in the prediction — given this structure for the economy — that an increase in $K$ will lead to increases in both $w^H$ and $w^L$. In terms of the estimating equations derived above, we can state this in the form of an hypothesis about the values of the parameters:

Hypothesis 1:    An increase in $K$ will lead to increases in both $w^H$ and $w^L$, which implies that $\alpha_1 + \alpha_2 < 0$ and $\beta_1 + \beta_2 < 0$.

With this set of assumptions, the model also implies that $L$ and $H$ are q-substitutes, which means that an increase in the price of one of the two factors leads to a decrease in the price of the other. This, too, can be stated in terms of an explicit hypothesis about values of wage equation parameters:

Hypothesis 2:    $L$ and $H$ are q-substitutes, implying that $\alpha_2 < 0$ and $\beta_2 < 0$.

If we go further and add the assumption discussed in the previous section, that the modern technology is more capital-efficient, then we get the further implication that an increase in $K$ leads to a decrease in the difference between high- and low-skilled wages:

Hypothesis 3:    An increase in capital leads to a decrease in the skill-wage differential, implying $\alpha_1 + \alpha_2 - \beta_1 - \beta_2 > 0$.

Note that by framing the discussion in terms of the aggregate production function, both the wage equation estimation and the hypotheses are written in terms of the aggregate factor usage in the economy, not in terms of the amounts of each factor used explicitly with each technology. This is important because we view the competing technologies as general-purpose technologies applicable to a wide variety of production processes. This in turn means that the different technologies are being applied within the same industries, and that identifying factor allocation across technologies in standard data sets is difficult.

## Previous Empirical Work with this Framework

HERE WE CONSIDER EVIDENCE from our previous studies using this framework. This is not to imply that there have been no other insightful studies on the issues we are considering; however, we know of few other recent studies that consider the impact of $K$ on the wage structure.

In Beaudry and Green (1998), we use data from the Canadian Survey of Consumer Finances (SCF) and the U.S. Current Population Survey (CPS) for available years between 1971 and 1995, in combination with capital and TFP series, to test Hypotheses 1 to 3, along with other implications of the endogenous technological choice model. In our preferred specification, with the degree of skill bias of any exogenous technical change being estimated from the data, we obtained estimates of $\alpha_1$, $\alpha_2$, $\beta_1$ and $\beta_2$, all of which are negative, and, statistically speaking, (except for $\beta_1$) significantly different from zero at conventional significance levels. This implies that Hypotheses 1 and 2 cannot be rejected using U.S. and Canadian data over an extended time period. In testing Hypothesis 3, we find that the sum of coefficients as set out is indeed positive, but not well-defined in relation to its standard error. These results stand up to a barrage of robustness checks, including instrumental variables estimation and using Canadian data on its own. The instrumental variables estimation is particularly important in our context, as we explicitly assume in the previous section that supplies of $L$ and $H$ are functions of wages in the economy, making them endogenous variables. In Beaudry and Green (1998), we use demographic variables as instruments, taking advantage of the fact that much of the increase in $H$ observed in the data occurs because of the entry into the labour force of the large and relatively well-educated baby boom generation, and not because the entry of successive generations into the labour force during our sample period increased the education levels.

The results of our 1998 analysis have several important implications for our current discussion. First, the results that $K$ increases the wages of both high- and low-skilled workers, and that $H$ and $L$ are q-substitutes, are ratifications of important implications of our two-technology, endogenous choice model. The fact that they cannot be rejected in North American data supports our claim that this model provides a useful lens for examining issues related to capital movements, technical change and the labour market. Second, their estimates point to quite substantial impacts from increased capital flows on wages. A 1 percent increase in $K$, holding all else constant, would generate a 1.2 percent increase in low-skilled wages and a 0.7 percent increase in high-skilled wages. The relative sizes of these impacts is, then, the source of the result that increases in $K$ lead to a reduction in the skill differential. Therefore, increases in $K$ generate both high wage levels and lower skill differentials, as claimed in our theoretical derivation in the previous section.

A third interesting implication of our 1998 results is that increases in $H$ and $K$ have offsetting impacts on the wage structure. $H$ and $L$ are q-substitutes: thus an increase in $H$ will lead to a decrease in the wages of low-skilled workers. It will also lead to a decrease in the wages of high-skilled workers because of a standard own-price effect. Given the assumptions stated to this point (both technologies are in use, there are three factors of production, the modern technology is defined as being relatively skill-biased and more capital-efficient), plus the assumption that the modern technology exhibits capital skill complementarity in relation to the traditional technology,[5] we also show that educational policies that increase $H$ while decreasing $L$ lead to an increase in the wage-skill differential. Therefore, the impacts of increases in $H$ (i.e., falling wages and increasing skill differentials) are the opposite of those from increases in $K$ (i.e., rising wages and decreasing skill differentials). This raises the possibility of the existence of a balanced path for the joint accumulation of $H$ and $K$, along which both wage levels and skill differentials would not change. In Beaudry and Green (2000a), using a somewhat different though strongly related model to the one presented here, we show that in a model with two competing technologies and three factors of production, such a balanced path must exist. In addition, we show that the existence of a balanced path implies very tight restrictions on parameters in wage regressions (the counterparts of the $\alpha$'s and $\beta$'s above). We test these restrictions with data from the United States and Germany, and cannot reject them in any specification of our estimating equations. This work provides strong support for the appropriateness of the model we use as the basis of our discussion in this study.

We also use this model as the basis for explaining the radically different evolutions of U.S. and European wages over the last two decades. The U.S. wage distribution has been characterized by large declines in real wages for the least skilled, virtually unchanged real wages for the most skilled, and sharply rising wage differentials. In contrast, the German wage distribution over the last two decades has been characterized by rising real wages for workers at all skill levels and no increase in skill differentials. We explain this difference as arising from the different accumulation paths for K/L and H/L in the two countries. In particular, we argue that Germany has accumulated K/L and H/L in balance, while the United States has accumulated H/L at the same rate as Germany, but has greatly underaccumulated K/L. In the model developed here, the underaccumulation of K/L in the United States means that there is not enough capital per worker to both service the expansion of the modern sector generated by the increased human capital and provide capital to maintain the marginal product (and hence, wages) for the low-skilled workers in the traditional sector. Therefore, the accumulation of H/L without a large enough accumulation of K/L to match, has implied an increase in capital scarcity in the United States that has meant both falling real wages for most workers and increases in the skill differentials. In Beaudry and Green (2000a), we show that this explanation has strong support in the U.S. and German data. This characterization of the United States as an essentially capital-starved economy, and the consequences in terms of falling real wages and increased inequality, will be important for our discussion on the implications of North American integration in the next section.

## FRAMEWORK WITH ELASTIC LABOUR SUPPLY

WE NOW TURN TO OUR MORE GENERAL FRAMEWORK, which allows labour supply responses to wage movements. The results in the subsection above allow us to consider the impact of increased capital flows on wages, but not on employment, which is assumed to be fixed. For the purposes of our empirical work, we will consider revised versions of Equations (5) and (6), which include population and wages as determinants of labour supplies. This will allow us to normalize for country size in the ensuing regressions. With elastic labour supply and these adjustments, the only exogenous variables in our system are $K$ and population $P$. Thus, we can derive reduced form equations expressing the wages of high- and low-skilled workers and employment as functions of $K$ and $P$. To do this, first let us create log-linear approximations to the labour supply equations, (5) and (6):

(13) $\log(H_t) \approx \phi_0^H + \phi_1^H \log(w_t^H) + \phi_2^H \log(P_t)$ and

(14) $\log(L_t) \approx \phi_0^L + \phi_1^L \log(w_t^L) + \phi_2^L \log(P_t)$.

We can then substitute Equations (13) and (14) into the marginal product conditions, expressed in Equations (9) and (10). Rationalizing terms leads to reduced form equations for $w_t^H$ and $w_t^L$:

(15) $\log(w_t^H) = \gamma_0^H + \gamma_1^H \log(K_t) + \gamma_2^H \log(P_t) + u_t^H$, and

(16) $\log(w_t^L) = \gamma_0^L + \gamma_1^L \log(K_t) + \gamma_2^L \log(P_t) + u_t^L$,

where $u_t^H$ and $u_t^L$ are approximation errors that are assumed to be independent of $K_t$. The parameters $\gamma_0^H$, $\gamma_1^H$, $\gamma_2^H$, $\gamma_0^L$, $\gamma_1^L$ and $\gamma_2^L$ are functions of the parameters in Equations (9), (10), (13) and (14). When we examine these functions, we find that $\gamma_1^H$ and $\gamma_1^L$ are both positive if: 1) $\phi_1^H$ and $\phi_1^L$ are positive; 2) the aggregate production function satisfies concavity (i.e., $\alpha_1 * \beta_1 - \alpha_2 * \beta_2 > 0$);

and 3) the assumptions of the last section hold, implying that $\alpha_1$, $\alpha_2$, $\beta_1$ and $\beta_2$ are all negative. Therefore, as long as the assumptions of the last section hold (the economy does not operate on backward-bending portions of the aggregate labour supply curves and the aggregate production function is well-behaved), an increase in $K_t$ causes an increase in the equilibrium wages for both low- and high-skilled workers.

Whether these assumptions match reality must be determined by examining the data. In particular, we are unsure whether it is reasonable to assume that the economies we study are not on a backward-bending portion of the relevant aggregate labour supply curves. The claim that our earlier assumptions hold is supported in Beaudry and Green (1998, 2000b). Our results in those studies were obtained by means of instrumental variables methods and are particularly interesting because they are consistent, even under the assumption of elastic labour supply made in this section. In particular, viewed in light of the more general model discussed here, the estimating equations in those studies are structural equations with endogenous variables on the right-hand side.

To obtain reduced form expressions for employment, we can substitute Equations (15) and (16) into Equations (13) and (14). This yields:

(17) $\log(H_t) = \delta_0^H + \delta_1^H \log(K_t) + \delta_2^H \log(P_t) + v_t^H$, and

(18) $\log(L_t) = \delta_0^L + \delta_1^L \log(K_t) + \delta_2^L \log(P_t) + v_t^L$.

Given the assumptions that $\phi^H$ and $\phi^L$ are positive, the assumptions implying that increases in $K_t$ lead to increases in wages will also imply that increases in $K_t$ lead to increases in employment levels for both types of workers.

Next, we will estimate versions of Equations (15) to (18) with data from Canada, the United States, the United Kingdom and Germany. We assume that all four countries are in the course of transition from the traditional to the modern technology during our sample period, and that all face similar underlying production functions. More specifically, we assume that all face the same values for $\alpha_1$, $\alpha_2$, $\beta_1$, $\beta_2$, $\phi_1^H$ and $\phi_1^L$. This implies that we can pool the data from the four countries and estimate common values for $\gamma_1^H$, $\gamma_1^L$, $\gamma_2^H$, $\gamma_2^L$, $\delta_1^H$, $\delta_2^H$, $\delta_1^L$ and $\delta_2^L$. However, we will allow the wage and employment levels ($\gamma_0^H$, $\gamma_0^L$, $\delta_0^H$ and $\delta_0^L$) to differ across countries. This allows for the possibility of persistent differences not only in wage and employment levels across countries, but also in the returns to skill both in terms of wages and employment across countries. We believe that the types of forces we are studying (the impacts of capital movements and technological change on the labour market) are long-term phenomena. For this reason, we believe that the right variation to estimate these effects is low-frequency or long-term variation. Therefore, we will estimate the equations in difference form, using data from the beginning and end of the available data periods for each country. Differencing in this way will eliminate the country-specific intercept terms. We will effectively identify the parameters of interest (the coefficients on $K_t$) in each equation by comparing differences in capital growth rates to differences in growth rates in wages and employment across countries. As in Beaudry and Green (1998, 2000a), we are concerned that we not confuse estimated capital effects with effects of incremental technical change. One can derive reduced form expressions similar to those given above by incorporating terms representing exogenous technical change. We allow for the impacts of such technical change in our estimation in two ways: first, we can assume that it takes the form of an arbitrary time effect, which will be captured by the intercept coefficient in our differenced estimation framework (note that without such a time effect, there would not be an intercept term); second, we include differenced, country-specific TFP in the differenced regressions, using observed TFP as an additional control for how much incremental technical change any given country has experienced.

## DATA

HERE, WE EXAMINE THE IMPLICATIONS of our theory by using data from Canada, the United States, the United Kingdom and Germany. These countries have exhibited widely different patterns in wage and employment outcomes, as well as growth in the capital stock. In this sense, they provide useful variations for identifying the key parameters in the equations above. For all four countries, our time span runs from the late 1970s to the latest data to which we have access. For Canada, our data runs from 1979 to 1995; for the United States and the United Kingdom, from 1979 to 1996; and for Germany, from 1983 to 1996.

We obtained relevant data (hourly wages, education levels, gender, etc.) for the United States from the Panel Study on Income Dynamics (PSID) and for Germany from the German Socio-Economic Panel (GSOEP). Both are panel data sets that follow a set of families and their offshoots across time. We use an Equivalence File constructed by GSOEP researchers that provides comparable data constructs from the PSID and the GSOEP.[6] In all our samples, we use weights presented in the publicly available data to overcome the fact that the sampling schemes are not completely representative. When we refer to Germany, we actually mean the former West Germany; the panel data we use follows a sample of families from that area. We use capital stocks and TFP figures that are relevant only for the former West Germany.

The U.K. data we use comes from the General Household Survey (GHS), which represents individuals in England, Scotland and Wales.[7] It is based on an annual survey of between 10,000 and 12,000 households conducted continuously throughout the year. Information is collected on a respondent's personal demographic and labour market data, with some added information on the head of household and spouse. However, education data, which is central to our analysis, is collected only for the main respondents and so we focus on their data. For Canada, we use SCF data; like the GHS, this is a large, cross-sectional survey with no panel component.

For all four countries, we use data for all individuals between the ages of 16 and 65. Our wage measure for the United States, the United Kingdom and Germany is the hourly wage. This is constructed by dividing total annual labour earnings by annual hours of work, as reported in the Equivalence File for the United States and Germany. For the United Kingdom, it is constructed using annual earnings, weeks worked and usual hours-per-week variables.[8] The Canadian data do not include information on hours worked per week that can be matched consistently with the weeks worked in the survey year, so in this case we are forced to use weekly wages. We assume that the overtime patterns in real weekly-wage growth will mirror those in real hourly wages for Canada. The fact that we use weekly wages for Canada, but hourly wages for the other countries, means that, by definition, average wages will be larger in Canada. This difference will be absorbed in the country-specific intercepts in the wage equations, which in turn are eliminated in the differencing. All the constructed wages are deflated by means of country-specific gross domestic product (GDP) deflators. We also use data from the U.S. CPS, a relatively close match to the SCF, in that it is a representative cross-sectional survey to construct a weekly wage measure and employment measures in weeks to match the SCF. We estimate separate regressions with the CPS and PSID data for the United States, to see whether bringing in weeks-based data for Canada is likely to create problems.

A potential concern in discussing wage-education profiles for these four countries is the comparability of years-of-education measures across data sets. For the United States, the years-of-education measure is based on the highest number of years of schooling completed. For West Germany, years-of-education is a constructed variable based on norms for various reported completed levels of education. The years-of-schooling variable in the Equivalence File attempts to generate a measure that is comparable to the U.S. measure, and to account for educational contributions from apprenticeship programs. For the United Kingdom, we use a generated variable (Schmitt 1995) that essentially equals the age at which the individual left full-time education, minus five. For Canada, education is reported in categories for the highest level of education attained (e.g., public school, some high school, completed high school, etc.). We assume that the "some high school" or "completed high school" category that is available in most years for the SCF is equivalent to 12 years of education in the other data sets, and that completing a bachelor of arts (B.A.) degree is equivalent to 16 years of education. While these are attempts to generate comparable education measures, the results are undoubtedly not perfectly comparable. However, we analyse within-country patterns separately, effectively allowing for different wage levels and education differentials across countries. Our key assumption is that we can compare time patterns in wage levels and wage-education differentials meaningfully across countries even if we do not consider comparisons of the levels in a given year as necessarily informative.

We divide the labour force into the low- and the high-skilled in a way originated by Katz and Murphy, but now quite common in the larger literature examining movements in wage structures. The low-skilled are defined as workers with 12 or fewer years of education (or those that have completed high school or less, where education is not reported in years), while the high-skilled are workers with 16 or more years of education (or with a B.A. or more, where education is not reported in years). Hours or weeks of work for workers with an intermediate number of years of education are partitioned between the low- and high-skilled categories, under the Katz and Murphy division rule (i.e., 0.69 of the sample is assigned to low-skilled categories, 0.29 to high-skilled categories). In Beaudry and Green (1998), we experimented with various other divisions of this middle category for the United States and Canada, but found that within a limited, reasonable range, these variations have limited effects on conclusions. While we use all workers to compute total hours or weeks of employment within each skill group, we use only average annual wages for males with less than five years of experience to construct our wage series, with the low-skilled and high-skilled wage groups defined as those with 12 or fewer and 16 or more years of education, respectively. All wages are deflated with country-specific GDP price deflators. We focus on younger workers because we believe that movements related to technological impacts are hidden by institutional impacts for older workers. In a study examining the Canadian wage-age relationship, we argue that wages for older workers follow patterns that suggest that an implicit contract-type framework is relevant (Green and Townsend 2001). We focus on males in order to avoid difficulties related to compositional changes associated with changes in female labour force participation. We view the resulting wage series as wage indices for the economy.

Finally, our TFP and capital series are all taken from Jorgensen and Yip (1999) and cover the time period from 1975 to 1995. The attractive feature of the Jorgensen and Yip data is that they have been constructed to provide internationally comparable capital stocks for the G7 countries, with special attention given to quality improvements in physical capital and labour.

## ESTIMATION RESULTS

IN TABLE 1 WE PRESENT THE LONG DIFFERENCES for important variables from our data. The table reveals some striking differences and similarities across countries. For example, the first row shows the annualized growth rate of the capital stock by country. The capital stocks grow at remarkably similar rates across the four countries in our time period. However, population grows quite differently across the countries, with the result that $K/P$ grows substantially faster in the United Kingdom and Germany than in Canada and the United States. According to our model, this means there is more capital per worker available in the United Kingdom and Germany to support the expansion of the modern sector without taking capital out of the hands of low-skilled workers in the traditional sector. The wage series show patterns familiar to students of international movements in wage structure. Both Canada and the United States experienced substantial declines in the real wages of low-skilled workers during this period, while high-skilled workers in those countries faced rather flat real wage trends. In contrast, both high- and low-skilled wages rose in the United Kingdom and Germany, and at nearly equal rates in each case. It is these stark differences that make comparisons across the four countries interesting. We argue that technological forces as large as those being proposed here ought to operate in essentially the same manner across developed countries. Confronting the model with data from countries with such different experiences puts this claim and the model to a tough test. Finally, all four countries are characterized by very high rates of growth in high-skilled employment, with essentially unchanged low-skilled employment.

## TABLE 1

### ANNUALIZED GROWTH RATES IN KEY VARIABLES

|  | United Kingdom 1979–96 | United States – PSID 1979–96 | United States – CPS 1979–95 | Germany 1983–96 | Canada 1979–95 |
|---|---|---|---|---|---|
| $K$ | 0.02800 | 0.0250 | 0.0240 | 0.0290 | 0.0260 |
| $\dfrac{K}{P}$ | 0.02600 | 0.0150 | 0.0150 | 0.0230 | 0.0140 |
| $w^H$ | 0.00680 | 0.0047 | 0.0067 | 0.0100 | –0.0027 |
| $w^L$ | 0.00460 | –0.0140 | –0.0090 | 0.0130 | –0.0180 |
| $H$ | 0.00470 | 0.0340 | 0.0410 | 0.0350 | 0.0540 |
| $L$ | –0.00086 | 0.0084 | 0.0090 | 0.0016 | –0.0022 |

We begin our analysis of the data in Table 1 by recreating the basic wage equations from our earlier work. That is, we implement Equations (9) and (10) with the data described in the earlier section. We report results using both the PSID- and the CPS-based U.S. data in Table 2, columns 1 and 2. We should emphasize that we have chosen intentionally to focus only on long-term differences in this study. We have assembled data on each year for each of the four countries, but have deliberately chosen not to use the data, because we believe that the issues under study are essentially long-term phenomena. Estimation based on annual data (or, more to the point, on first differenced annual data, as is commonly done in the wage structure literature) emphasizes high-frequency variation. That means, for example, that it identifies effects of capital movements on the basis of very short-term fluctuations, which we do not believe tell the true story of how relative capital movements shift the wage structure. What this means for the results we are presenting is that we have very few degrees of freedom. This affects the way we interpret the entries in the following tables, where we attempt to portray the long-term relationships among the variables of interest as simply as possible. If the measure we wished to examine were just a ratio of differences in variables, then we would just plot that ratio. However, we are interested in partial derivative effects, which require some extra calculation. If we had only two countries in our sample, we would simply calculate the partial derivative effects of interest from Equations (9) and (10), which would yield a unique set of effects. With three countries, we could bring in TFP measures and calculate the partial derivatives from Equations (11) and (12), again obtaining a unique set of partial derivatives. With four countries, there are multiple ways to make the same calculations and we view the ordinary least squares (OLS) approach we take as one way of constructing single calculated derivatives. We highlight this interpretation by not presenting standard errors associated with the derivatives.

The first column of Table 2 reports the effects of long-term movements in $H/K$ and $L/K$ on the long-term movements in the average wages of high- and low-skilled workers. The results mirror those from Beaudry and Green (1998), with all four partial derivatives being negative. As discussed earlier, this implies that Hypothesis 1 (increases in $K$ lead to increases in both $w^H$ and $w^L$) cannot be rejected. The fact that the effects of $H/K$ on $w^L$ and of $L/K$ on $w^H$ are both negative means that $L$ and $H$ are q-substitutes (Hypothesis 2), a key implication of the assumed form of the theoretical model we have been discussing. In addition, the condition spelled out in Hypothesis 3 ($K$ effects are larger for $w^L$ than for $w^H$) is met, implying that increasing $K$ decreases skill differentials. Overall, the results show that long-term patterns in four quite different developed countries fit with the implications of the theoretical model set out earlier. In particular, these results imply that increasing $K$ both increases wage levels for workers of different skill types and decreases skill differentials. Furthermore, as we argue in Beaudry and Green (2000a), they suggest that accumulations of $H$ without balancing accumulations of $K$ will lead to falling real wages for all skill types and increasing skill differentials.

In Table 2, columns 2 and 3, we perform two robustness checks on the column 1 results. In column 2, we re-estimate Equations (9) and (10), but substitute the U.S. CPS-based data for the U.S. PSID-based data. As described earlier, the CPS data is similar in form to the Canadian SCF data, while the PSID data is similar to the German GSOEP data. However, Table 1 suggests that the basic patterns in the CPS and PSID data are very similar. Thus, it is no surprise that using CPS data instead of PSID data does not change the conclusions in column 1: the calculated derivatives are again all negative and of a similar order of magnitude to those in column 1. In column 3, we return to using the data set that includes the PSID data, and introduce country-specific changes in TFP as a proxy for ongoing technical change. The coefficient on the TFP variable is negative and quite small in both equations, which suggests that ongoing skill-biased technical change plays only a minor role in descriptions of the evolution of the wage structure. The coefficients on $H/K$ and $L/K$ maintain the same sign pattern as in column 1. Thus, our main conclusions are not altered by the introduction of TFP.

In columns 4 to 6 of Table 2, we present the results from our reduced form estimations. In all cases, we use the PSID data for the United States, but the nature of the results does not change if we use the CPS data. Column 4 corresponds to a regression of wages on $K$ and $P$ separately, with no intercept included — see Equations (15) and (16). The results are as predicted from the theory if the economy is operating on the upward-sloping part of both the high- and low-skilled labour supply curves. The effect of capital is positive and the effect of population growth negative on wages of high- as well as low-skilled workers; and both effects are larger on the wages of low-skilled workers. In column 5, we augment the specification by including a constant term. This effectively allows for a general technical change that affects all countries equally, but does not alter the sign pattern of the $K$ and $P$ effects. The intercepts are positive for the wages of high-skilled workers, but negative for those of low-skilled workers. As a result, even though these results may indicate a skill bias to technical change, it is still a small effect in relation to the $K$ and $P$ effects. Finally, in column 6, we remove the intercept and include the change in TFP as a more direct measure of technical change. This measure also allows for the ongoing technical change to differ in the four countries in a way directly related to measured TFP growth. Again, the coefficients indicate positive impacts for $K$ and negative impacts for $P$.

## TABLE 2

### CALCULATED PARTIAL DERIVATIVE EFFECTS: WAGE EQUATIONS

|  | 1 | 2 | 3 | 4 | 5 | 6 |
|---|---|---|---|---|---|---|
| **High-Wage** | | | | | | |
| $\dfrac{H}{K}$ | −0.58 | −0.28 | −0.280 | − | − | − |
| $\dfrac{L}{K}$ | −0.53 | −0.37 | −0.420 | − | − | − |
| K | − | − | − | 0.41 | 0.300 | 0.310 |
| P | − | − | − | −0.84 | −0.870 | −0.170 |
| Int | − | − | − | − | 0.003 | − |
| TFP | − | − | −0.027 | − | − | −0.032 |
| **Low-Wage** | | | | | | |
| $\dfrac{L}{K}$ | −0.74 | −0.77 | −0.620 | − | − | − |
| $\dfrac{H}{K}$ | −1.37 | −1.25 | −1.020 | − | − | − |
| K | − | − | − | 0.66 | 4.240 | 0.610 |
| P | − | − | − | −2.74 | −1.530 | −2.410 |
| Int | − | − | − | − | −0.110 | − |
| TFP | − | − | −0.031 | − | − | −0.015 |

Notes: Column 1 corresponds to Equations (9) and (10) and uses data from all four countries, with PSID-based data for the United States. Column 2 is the same, but with CPS-based U.S. data. Column 3 corresponds to Equations (11) and (12), implemented with data from all four countries, with PSID-based data for the United States. Column 4 is a reduced form specification corresponding to Equations (15) and (16). Column 5 is the same as 4 but includes an intercept. Column 6 is the same as 4 but includes growth in TFP.

The regressions are run on a panel of five countries: Canada, the United States, Germany, France and the United Kingdom. Country fixed effects are included in all regressions.

Overall, the combination of the different types of wage regressions performed here, and the results of our earlier work, support our claim that the theoretical structure set out in the first sections of the study fits the data. It is remarkable that it fits data drawn from countries with such different experiences. The key implication of these results here is that increases in K, with either the workforce or the population constant, have positive impacts on the wages of both low- and high-skilled workers. Furthermore, the impact on the wages of low-skilled workers is larger, with the resulting implication that increases in K also reduce skill differentials and thus help reduce inequality.

**TABLE 3**

**CALCULATED PARTIAL DERIVATIVE EFFECTS: EMPLOYMENT EQUATIONS**

|  | 1 | 2 | 3 | 4 |
|---|---|---|---|---|
| High-Skilled Employment |  |  |  |  |
| $\dfrac{K}{P}$ | 1.77 | 0.520 | – | – |
| K | – | – | 1.3300 | 1.600 |
| P | – | – | 0.8100 | –0.950 |
| Int | – | 0.025 | – | – |
| TFP | – | – | – | 0.084 |
| Low-Skilled Employment |  |  |  |  |
| $\dfrac{K}{P}$ | –0.26 | 0.460 | – | – |
| K | – | – | –0.0038 | –0.160 |
| P | – | – | 0.2200 | 1.250 |
| Int | – | –0.014 | – | – |
| TFP | – | – | – | –0.049 |

Notes:  All specifications (columns 1-4) use PSID-based data for the United States. In column 1, population growth rates are subtracted from employment growth rates to form the dependent variable, and from capital growth rates to form the independent variable. Column 2 is the same, but includes an intercept. In column 3, employment growth rates are regressed on K and P growth rates separately. Column 4 is the same but includes growth in TFP. The regressions are run on a panel of five countries: Canada, the United States, Germany, France and the United Kingdom. Country fixed effects are included in all regressions.

Table 3 contains the reduced-form estimation results related to employment. The implications from the employment regressions are somewhat less clear-cut than those from the wage regressions. In Table 3, column 1, we adopt a restricted specification in which the dependent variable is either high- or low-wage employment growth in relation to population growth. We regress this on the difference between capital growth and population growth. Putting everything in per capita terms in this way allows us to focus on the way capital affects the employment rate. The results indicate that increases in capital per capita increase employment rates for high-skilled workers but reduce them for the low-skilled. The specification in column 2 is the same as that in column 1, but includes an intercept to pick up general effects of technological change. Once this intercept is added, $K$ has nearly identical, positive impacts on $H$ and $L$. In column 3, we implement Equations (17) and (18) in long difference form. Here, the results show that increases in $K$ with $P$ constant lead to increases in $H$, but very small decreases in $L$. The latter outcome would arise in the framework set out earlier if low-skilled employment is on the backward-bending portion of its labour supply curve. Notice, though, that we derived these implications from a model in which the supplies of $H$ and $L$ depended only on their own wages, plus population; in other words, we assumed there was a set pool of each type of worker and that any labour supply effects were related to the extent to which that pool participated in the labour market. Alternatively, we could consider a model in which the supplies of $H$ and $L$ also respond to the ratio of high- to low-skilled wages, as some individuals alter their education plans in response to long-term movements in the wage differential. Plots of graduation rates by cohort in Beaudry and Green (1998) suggest that this type of adjustment plays only a minor role for Canada and the United States over this period. Nonetheless, to the extent that adjustment occurs on this margin, our conclusions from before do not hold for the estimated coefficients in column 2. Finally, in column 3, we repeat the specification in column 2, but add changes in TFP as an extra factor. Again, the results show that growth in $K$ generates large positive effects for $H$ but small negative effects for $L$. Population and TFP effects have opposing impacts for the two types of labour. Overall, the results for employment indicate that increases in $K$, and particularly $K$ per capita, lead to strong increases in $H$ but much smaller and possibly negative impacts on $L$. Thus, increasing $K$ is good for employment, but may not lead to reductions in employment skill differentials.

## DISCUSSION OF THE ROLE OF CANADA-U.S. INTEGRATION IN INCREASING CAPITAL FLOWS TO CANADA

OUR DISCUSSION SO FAR SUGGESTS that in the current environment, for both theoretical and empirical reasons, positive capital inflows into a country are likely to induce desirable labour-market outcomes. Hence, given our focus on North American linkages in this volume, the key remaining question is whether further economic integration between Canada and the United States is likely to generate increased capital flows to Canada. It is useful to begin by reviewing the main determinants of capital flows between countries, and then discuss them within the context of Canada-U.S. integration.

### THE DETERMINANTS OF INTERNATIONAL CAPITAL FLOWS

OPEN ECONOMY MACRO-ECONOMIC THEORY identifies many factors that influence international capital flows. For example, if we adopt the standard neoclassical growth model as our point of reference, there are at least three elements that may affect international capital flows: differences in savings rates, population growth rates or initial levels of income per capita. These elements affect capital flows because each affects the returns on capital in the absence of economic integration. Hence, if a country has a low propensity for saving, a high population growth or a low initial capital stock, it can be expected to attract capital from other countries, as the returns on capital are likely to be high in the domestic country. Obviously, such movements in capital respond to financial returns, net of tax, so that differences in the taxation of business income also will influence international capital flows.

One element not emphasized in the traditional international finance literature is how skill, or education, affects capital flows. Because of our emphasis on the importance of taking the skill levels of the population into account, we need to clarify the way skill, or education, may affect capital flows. In general, it is difficult to say whether a more educated population is likely to attract a greater inflow of capital (given a fixed national savings rate), as education could be, in principle, either a complement or a substitute to physical capital. A great deal of evidence, however, suggests that education is likely to complement physical capital (e.g., Goldin and Katz 1998), and therefore it is probably more reasonable to think that, other things being equal, an increase in education likely favours capital inflows.[9]

In brief, there are many elements specific to a country that would lead it to want a high degree of international integration to attract international capital. In particular, if the country has a relatively low savings rate, a highly educated population or a high rate of population growth, it has an incentive to facilitate international capital flows as a means of improving labour-market outcomes within its domestic economy.

## Canada-U.S. Integration and the Global Context

IF WE LOOK AT CANADA AND THE UNITED STATES in isolation, it is difficult to predict how greater Canada-U.S. integration is likely to affect capital flows. Both countries have rather high and similar rates of population growth and low levels of savings, and have almost converged in terms of education patterns among new cohorts. Both countries are likely net demanders of capital on the world market; but which is the strongest demander between the two is unclear. In effect, the slightly higher rates of population growth in Canada may at first suggest that Canada is more in need of increased capital inflows, but differences in savings rates could easily offset this.

Notwithstanding these macro-economic aspects, there are nevertheless margins where integration may help capital flow from the United States into Canada more freely. A standard claim in the popular press is that Canada has an underdeveloped venture capital market in relation to the United States. In general, Canada's difficulty arises because of economy-of-scale conditions; in the United States, with a much larger flow of new investment each year, venture capital firms can afford to specialize in one market niche. This includes keeping their own stable of experts who can evaluate new applications. Conversely, in Canada, firms need to diversify their efforts and, it is argued, have difficulty in identifying new opportunities. In this context, better access to American venture capital markets may bring more capital funds to Canadian start-up firms. For this argument to hold true, of course, one needs to provide an explanation for why U.S. venture capital firms do not currently take advantage of the plums arguably being left un-picked in Canada. Knowing what barriers exist is a necessary first step to deter-mining whether any particular integration scheme will yield benefits. Even if po-tential benefits do exist, however, it is unclear whether they are sufficiently large to have a very big impact on total capital formation in Canada. This is particularly true if one acknowledges that integration may improve Canadian access to U.S. venture capital funds, but is unlikely to generate perfect access by itself.

Instead of looking at Canada and the United States in isolation, we need to consider how Canada-U.S. integration is likely to affect capital flows from the rest of the world (i.e., Japan and Europe). Note that in relation to Europe and Japan, North America is likely to continue to be a net demander of international capital, as it has a higher rate of population growth and a lower rate of savings. As dis-cussed earlier, our work on Germany and the United States supports a claim that the main source of difference in the evolution of wage structures between the two countries is the difference in accumulation of capital per worker. The two coun-tries have accumulated human capital at similar rates over the last 20 years, al-though the United States has lagged well behind Germany in terms of accumula-tion of capital per unit of labour. Then, in our model, as both economies move toward larger shares of production in the modern sector, Germany will be able to achieve technological transition while taking less capital out of the hands of low-skilled workers. Thus, the German wage structure is characterized by rising real wages, while the opposite is true in the United States, particularly for the least skilled. The key question about integration then becomes whether or not focus-sing on ties with an economy which appears to need more capital itself will help Canada in its attempt to avoid a falling real wage and the rising inequality out-comes of the United States. Is it reasonable to expect that by reducing investment barriers between Canada and the United States, Canada will end up with a larger share of the total investment pie in North America? Alternatively, is there a rea-son to believe that such integration will lead to greater investment in Canada from economies other than the United States? Could further integration of the goods market generate a desire on the part of foreign investors to build plants in Canada in order to access the U.S. market? If so, why would these same foreign investors not just invest directly in the United States? We have no answers to these ques-tions, but we do know where to look for them. Integration may be useful if Canada can figure out a way to use it to increase investment in Canada from non-U.S. investors. Whether or not there is a way to design integration measures to accomplish this is beyond the scope of this study.

An interesting perspective on these issues is gained from Globerman and Shapiro (2003), who present evidence on foreign direct investment (FDI) flows in and out of Canada and the United States. They show that Canada was a modest net exporter of capital during the 1990s, while the United States became a substantial net importer, particularly in the latter part of the decade. Moreover, Canada has seen less and less FDI from the large European countries (i.e., Germany and the United Kingdom), while the United States has seen substantial increases in FDI from these countries. Globerman and Shapiro issue a clear warning against reading too much into the short-term fluctuations in these numbers. Nonetheless, the longer-term patterns appear to indicate that if Canada and the United States have undergone a period of increasing integration over the past 10 to 15 years, the outcome has been the opposite of what our results suggest as a goal. In particular, while Canada has continued to be a small net exporter, the relative size of the net export during the 1990s has declined in relation to the 1980s. Moreover, if Europe is one key place to look for the capital flows that we argue are so beneficial, then it is the United States, not Canada, that has obtained increasing access to them. Thus, the initial, rough evidence suggests that increased integration has not brought about increased access to European capital. At the very least, it suggests that clear arguments must be made to justify claims that further integration will lead to improved capital formation outcomes in Canada.

## CONCLUSION

IN THIS STUDY, we examine the ramifications of further North American integration by focussing on the implications of increased capital flows for labour market outcomes in Canada. We argue that integration may be able to make the greatest difference in the area of capital flows. To consider the question, we first describe, and then attempt to establish the credibility of, a model of labour market outcomes in an era of technological change. We argue that in such an era, capital growth is particularly important. In our model, technological change occurs endogenously through firms choosing between two existing technologies, a traditional and a modern one. We argue that the data confirm the claim that the last 20 years can be characterized as a period of transition from a traditional, hierarchical type of production technology toward a modern, more flexible one. In that context, greater capital flows make it possible to move capital into the expanding modern sector without taking as much out of the hands of lower-skilled workers in the traditional sector. As a result, increased capital flows lead to high real wages and smaller increases in the wage-skill differential. We argue, further, that Canada and the United States have both underaccumulated capital per worker in relation to European economies and have paid the price in terms of falling real wages and increased inequality. North American integration would be a process of further tying one economy with high net capital demands (and the ensuing troublesome labour market outcomes) to another. It is unclear why we should expect greater integration of Canadian and American capital markets to lead to an increase in the amount of capital flowing from the United States to Canada. The flow could just as easily go the other way. In other words, can we hope to avoid problems of falling real wages and increased inequality by integrating with an economy that itself is having those problems? The answer may be yes, if greater North American integration can lead to increased investment flows into Canada from non-U.S. sources. The challenge is to decide whether integration will have that effect.

## ENDNOTES

1   The presence of only one produced good should be interpreted as the reduced form of a more general production structure where there is already perfect integration in the goods market.

2   There is a growing literature which uses models of endogenous technological choice as a means of understanding recent technological change. For example, see Basu and Weil (1998), Caselli (1999) and Zeira (1998).

3   It is simple to extend our analysis to the case where the two modes of production use the different types of physical capital. For example, if one dollar of capital inflow can buy either one unit of traditional capital or $\theta$ units of the new capital, then our analysis carries through by replacing Equation (4) with $K^T + K^M/\theta = K$.

4   In the Beaudry and Green (1998) derivation, $\alpha_3$ is a function of $\alpha_1$, $\alpha_2$, a parameter that captures the degree of skill bias of technical change and factor income shares. The coefficient $\beta_3$ is similarly defined. The equation is estimated by non-linear least squares. Here we consider the less efficient (though still consistent) approach in which we do not impose the restrictions on $\alpha_3$ and $\beta_3$ derived in our earlier study.

5   In this context, capital skill complementarity refers to relative factor intensities in the competing technologies. In particular, it means that the modern technology is more intensive in its use of both $K$ and $H$ than the traditional technology.

6   These files are constructed and maintained by the German Institute for Economic Research, the Department of Policy Analysis and Management at Cornell University, and the University of Michigan.

7   We thank David Card for helping us get access to the GHS data.

8   In the GHS before 1982, usual hours are divided into regular and overtime hours. Plots of the data suggest to us that the best match to the post-1982 GHS data is created by using only regular-time hours before 1982.

9   As we demonstrated in Beaudry and Green (1998, 2000a), empirical observations of the type presented in the third section of this study support the view that an increase in skill increases the return in capital and hence would favour a capital inflow in an open economy context.

# BIBLIOGRAPHY

Basu, Susanto, and David Weil. "Appropriate Technology and Growth." *Quarterly Journal of Economics* 113, 4 (November 1998): 1025-54.

Beaudry, Paul, and David Green. *What is Driving U.S. and Canadian Wages: Endogenous Technical Change or Endogenous Choice of Technique?* NBER Working Paper No. 6853, December 1998.

_____. *The Changing Structure of Wages in the U.S. and Germany: What Explains the Difference?* NBER Working Paper No. 7697, May 2000a.

_____. "Cohort Patterns in Canadian Earnings: Assessing the Role of Skill Premia in Inequality Trends." *Canadian Journal of Economics* (November 2000b): 907-36.

Caselli, Francesco. "Technological Revolutions." *American Economic Review* (March 1999): 78-102.

Globerman, Steven, and Daniel Shapiro. "Assessing Recent Patterns of Foreign Direct Investment in Canada and the United States." In *North American Linkages: Opportunities and Challenges for Canada.* Edited by Richard G. Harris. The Industry Canada Research Series. Calgary: University of Calgary Press, 2003. Chapter 7.

Goldin, Claudia, and Laurence Katz. "The Origins of Technology-Skill Complementarity." *Quarterly Journal of Economics* 113 (1998): 693-732.

Green, David, and James Townsend. "Age Differences and Cohort Effects: An Examination of the Age Dimension of Increases in Wage Inequality." Vancouver: University of British Columbia, Department of Economics, 2001. Mimeograph.

Jorgenson, Dale W., and Eric Yip. "Whatever Happened to Productivity Growth?" Cambridge MA: Harvard University, June 1999. Mimeograph.

Katz, Lawrence F., and Kevin M. Murphy. "Changes in Relative Wages, 1963-1987: Supply and Demand Factors." *Quarterly Journal of Economics* 107 (1992): 35-78.

Murphy, Kevin M., W. Craig Riddell and Paul M. Romer. *Wages, Skills and Technology in the United States and Canada.* NBER Working Paper No. 6638, July 1998.

Obstfeld, Maurice, and Kenneth Rogoff. "The Six Major Puzzles in International Macroeconomics: Is There a Common Cause?" In *NBER Macroeconomics Annual 2000.* Edited by Ben Bernanke and Kenneth Rogoff. Cambridge MA: MIT Press, 2000.

Schmitt, John. "The Changing Nature of Male Earnings in Britain, 1974-1988." In *Changes and Differences in Wage Structures.* Edited by Richard Freeman and Lawrence F. Katz. Chicago: University of Chicago Press, 1995, pp. 177-204.

Zeira, Joseph. "Workers, Machines and Economic Growth." *Quarterly Journal of Economics* 113, 4 (November 1998): 1091-1118.

Steven Globerman     &     Daniel Shapiro

Western Washington University     Simon Fraser University

7

# Assessing Recent Patterns of Foreign Direct Investment in Canada and the United States

## INTRODUCTION

POLICY MAKERS HAVE EXPRESSED CONCERNS about the ability of the Canadian economy to compete effectively for foreign direct investment (FDI) against the U.S. economy, notably, for example, when Canada was negotiating the Canada-U.S. Free Trade Agreement (FTA), and the North American Free Trade Agreement (NAFTA). In both cases, opponents of the agreements argued that the associated trade and investment liberalization would lead to the closure of U.S. affiliates in Canada, with the subsequent repatriation of direct investment capital. It was also argued that Canadian multinational companies (MNCs) would relocate investment capacity to the U.S. market and serve the Canadian market primarily through exports.[1]

The primary basis for these concerns is the perception that the United States enjoys a strong location advantage due to its large domestic market, which gives rise to agglomeration economies that make it cheaper for MNCs to locate activities there. The components of agglomeration economies are positively related to the size and scope of economic activities in a region. Large concentrations of production capacity in urban U.S. regions are thus alleged to contribute to external efficiency benefits that are captured by manufacturing and service companies located in those regions.[2] Savings in transportation costs also are associated with a location near large concentrations of consumers in urban U.S. areas.

More recently, Canada's impaired ability to attract inward FDI has been linked to relatively high personal and corporate tax rates, excessive government regulation and barriers to interprovincial trade. In particular, Canada's relatively high personal tax rates are seen by many as contributing to an out-migration of highly skilled Canadian workers, and hence to an overall scarcity of scientific and technical talent in Canada when compared to the United States. As a consequence, firms in knowledge-intensive industries are unlikely to view Canada as enjoying a location advantage in the relevant activities (McCallum 1999).[3] By balkanizing an already small domestic market, government regulations and policies restricting competition within and across provincial boundaries dissipate potential agglomeration economies in Canada. This further discourages inward FDI since, as noted above, it is strongly and positively related to larger relevant geographic markets.[4]

Another factor allegedly discouraging FDI in Canada is the relatively small share of Canadian industrial activity concentrated in high technology industries.[5] Given the growth of FDI in "new economy" industries like telecommunications, software and financial services, a dearth of technological centres of excellence in Canada would presumably discourage MNCs from establishing affiliates in Canada to take advantage of technology spillovers and related benefits. Conversely, Canadian companies would presumably be encouraged to expand their presence abroad, especially in technologically dynamic U.S. locations.

The advantages of operating in Canada have also been identified, however. For example, Canada enjoys relatively low costs of doing business when compared to many other developed countries, including the United States. Moreover, free trade between Canada and the United States has been trade-creating (Head and Ries 1999). Since FDI and trade tend to be complementary, increased bilateral trade presumably enhances the benefits of bilateral FDI. According to Head and Ries, the fact that Canada has not suffered any significant overall deterioration of its relative cost position in relation to the United States is suggested by the fact that, as a percentage of bilateral trade, Canada's trade surplus is higher than it was in 1970 and about the same as it was immediately preceding the Canada-U.S. FTA. To be sure, the dramatic depreciation of the Canadian dollar against the U.S. dollar over the past three decades has been an important factor in maintaining relative costs. It also attests to a decline in Canadian productivity as compared to its U.S. counterpart in trade-related sectors.[6]

Whether a depreciating currency mitigates or exacerbates domestic productivity problems in the long run may be debatable. What the trade data suggest, however, is that the depreciation of the Canadian dollar has offset Canada's relatively poor productivity performance against that of the United States. The dramatic decrease in the value of the Canadian dollar — along with decreasing relative real wage rates in Canada — has also presumably mitigated any productivity-related deterioration in Canada's relative attractiveness as a location for FDI.[7] The broad purpose of this study is to assess whether there has been any recent systemic deterioration in Canada's location advantage for FDI in relation to the United States. A specific objective is to identify the reasons for any substantial differences in recent patterns of FDI between Canada and the United States.

Our study proceeds as follows. The section below sets out and discusses data on aggregate FDI flows in Canada and the United States for the post-1960 period. We pay special attention to FDI patterns during the 1980s and 1990s. Next, we present and evaluate FDI data disaggregated by country of origin and industrial sector in order to identify the contributions of geographical and sectoral differences in FDI flows to observed differences in overall Canada-U.S. FDI patterns. We then consider various hypotheses on Canada's alleged location disadvantage in relation to the United States against the background of historical FDI patterns. We conclude with an assessment of Canada's future FDI prospects and a brief discussion of policy options.

## AGGREGATE FDI FLOWS

IN THIS SECTION, WE PRESENT AND CONSIDER various time series describing inward and outward FDI patterns for Canada and the United States. Here is a relevant conceptual issue: Is it preferable to use stock or flow measures of FDI for the comparison? In principle, changes in stock values over time should reflect accumulated retained earnings and net flows over time. In effect, long-run changes in the balance of payments definition of FDI, which is based on flows, will be reflected in the changes in FDI stocks over time. Nevertheless, a number of researchers have expressed a preference for using stock data to identify long-run FDI patterns where stock data are available over time (Lipsey 1993; Graham and Wada 2000).

In practice, FDI stocks are measured at book value, FDI flows at market value, and this may create differences in the series. In principle, it is desirable to measure FDI at market value, and this consideration suggests the use of flow data. As a practical matter, because flow data are measured for balance of payments purposes, they are often more readily available for comparative purposes across countries and over time. In addition, evaluation of hypotheses on factors influencing FDI patterns over time might require a focus on the balance of payments definition rather than on stocks. To the extent that a country is characterized by a relatively long history of inward and outward FDI flows, even relatively large recent changes in inward or outward FDI behaviour might be obscured by the use of stock measures. That is, changes in stocks on a year-to-year basis will be small when they take place against an absolutely large accumulated base value.

On the other hand, because direct investment flows in any year can be heavily influenced by specific transactions, flow figures can exhibit a fair amount of volatility. As a result, one must be cautious in drawing inferences from short-term flow data. Nevertheless, since much of the concern about Canada's diminishing location advantage is of relatively recent origin, it seems appropriate to focus on FDI flows, especially those over the past decade or two. In fact, the broad picture of FDI patterns in Canada and the United States is not notably different depending upon whether stock or flow data are used. In our opinion, however, focussing on flow data more readily allows an evaluation of the underlying reasons for the observed patterns. We therefore focus primarily on flow data.

If one were to rely on Canadian data alone, it would be hard to argue that Canada's position has deteriorated. Figure 1 provides time-series data on Canadian FDI inflows and outflows for the 1927-2000 period. It is readily seen that both series increase rapidly in the period after the FTAs, and particularly after 1993.[8] The increase in FDI inflows was particularly marked in the last two years of the 1990s so that a negative net position for most of the 1990s became positive during those years. The rapid increase in outflows (CDI) can be seen as an indication of relative weakness, but as we discuss below, it can also be seen as an indication of the competitive advantage of Canadian companies.

## FIGURE 1

## CANADA: FDI INFLOWS AND OUTFLOWS, 1927-2000

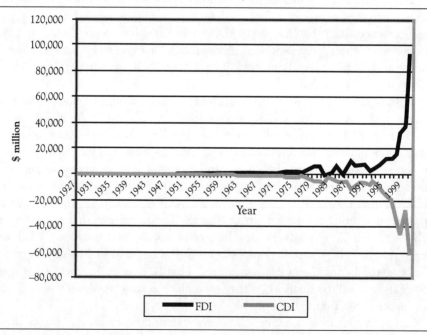

Source: CANSIM (D58062, D58052).

## TABLE 1

## CANADIAN SHARES OF U.S. DIRECT INVESTMENT FLOWS (PERCENT)

| | 1994 | 1995 | 1996 | 1997 | 1998 | 1999 |
|---|---|---|---|---|---|---|
| Canada's Share of Total U.S. Outflows | 8.3 | 9.3 | 8.5 | 8.0 | 6.8 | 10.3 |
| Canada's Share of U.S. Outflows to Canada and Mexico | 57.6 | 74.2 | 74.9 | 57.7 | 65.9 | 72.7 |

Source: Calculated from U.S. Bureau of Economic Analysis data, available at: http://www.bea.doc.gov/bea/di.

Similarly, an examination of Canada's share of U.S. FDI outflows in the post-NAFTA period (Table 1) shows little cause for concern. Notwithstanding short-run volatility, Canada's share of total U.S. FDI outflows remained roughly constant over the 1994-99 period, as did Canada's share of U.S. flows going to Canada and Mexico. Thus, the evidence suggests that recent FDI inflows to Canada have increased rapidly and that our share of U.S. FDI outflows has remained constant. Of course, the issue is whether Canada's position relative to the United States has deteriorated, and that requires direct comparison with the United States.

The International Monetary Fund (IMF) reports net direct FDI flows (in nominal U.S. dollars) from 1961 to 1999. Separate estimates for direct investment inflows and outflows that provide perspective on the observed pattern of net FDI are also available. Globerman and Shapiro (2001) discuss and empirically document the fact that countries that attract relatively large inflows of FDI are also likely to be characterized by relatively large FDI outflows. This is because the factors that make a country attractive to foreign-owned MNCs will also encourage and support the emergence and growth of domestically owned MNCs. The latter, in turn, will engage in outward FDI. As a consequence, relatively small negative values of net FDI should not necessarily be interpreted as evidence of a location disadvantage with respect to MNC activities. However, a trend of large negative net FDI flows might signal a growing location disadvantage that, in turn, is encouraging less inward FDI by foreign firms and more outward FDI by domestic firms.

## NET FDI FLOWS

TABLE 2 SUMMARIZES AVERAGE NET FDI FLOWS for Canada and the United States over five-year periods from 1961 to 1999. The data in the table highlight differences in the behaviour of the two time series. In particular, from 1961 to 1975, Canada experienced net inflows of FDI, whereas the United States experienced net outflows. However, that pattern is reversed in 1976, as Canada is characterized by net FDI outflows from 1976 to 1999 and the United States generally by net inflows. Note, however, that the IMF data do not extend to 2000, when Canada experienced net FDI inflows (Figure 1). Moreover, as a percentage of gross domestic product (GDP), Canada's net position actually improved in the 1990s. Nevertheless, there are broad differences in the two time series, as illustrated by the simple correlation coefficient between Canadian and U.S. net FDI flows. The latter equals –.468 for annual values of net FDI over the 1976-99 period.[9]

While the Canadian and U.S. net FDI patterns differ in their signs over most of the subperiods shown in Table 2, the differences are largely tempered by the fact that the net FDI flows are relatively small in most subperiods. For example, the net outflows for Canada over the 1990s are generally less than 10 percent of the value of gross FDI inflows over that period. Thus, it seems fair to say that inward and outward FDI flows for Canada were relatively balanced over that period, as were flows for both countries in the 1960s and 1970s. In this context, 1986-90 and 1996-99 appear to be subperiods in which relatively large net FDI inflows to the United States contrast sharply with relatively balanced FDI flows to Canada.

## TABLE 2

## CANADA AND THE UNITED STATES: NET FDI FLOWS, AVERAGE ANNUAL VALUES

|  | Canada | United States | Canada | United States |
|---|---|---|---|---|
|  | (US$ million) | (US$ million) | Percent of GDP | Percent of GDP |
| 1961-65 | 300 | –3,236 | 0.62 | 0.56 |
| 1966-70 | 484 | –4,884 | 0.63 | 0.59 |
| 1971-75 | 107 | –7,704 | 0.08 | 0.62 |
| 1976-80 | –1,373 | –7,912 | 0.55 | 0.40 |
| 1981-85 | –4,083 | 10,694 | 0.99 | 0.32 |
| 1986-90 | –2,734 | 22,874 | 0.45 | 0.47 |
| 1991-95 | –618 | –29,668 | 0.10 | 0.55 |
| 1996-99 | –772 | 40,138 | 0.08 | 0.57 |

Source: Calculated from data in International Monetary Fund, *International Financial Statistics Yearbook*, various years.

## GROSS FDI FLOWS

DATA REPORTED IN TABLE 3 document recent gross FDI inflows and outflows for the two countries. In this regard, we focus on the latter part of the 1980s and the 1990s. This is because it is generally agreed that the large inflows of FDI to the United States in the latter part of the 1970s and early 1980s represented a "catching-up" phenomenon. That is, accelerated inflows of FDI to the United States did not necessarily reflect improving locational advantage for the United States as much as an adjustment to longer-run locational attributes. For example, Caves and Mehra (1986) suggest that the rapid increase in FDI in the United States in the 1970s resulted from "the convergence of income and productivity levels among most industrial countries, the rapid growth of foreign MNCs and the end, in the early 1970s, of the previous decade's overvaluation of the U.S. dollar."

It is obvious from the data in Table 3 that both countries experienced relatively large and consistent increases in both FDI inflows and outflows throughout the 1990s. However, the increase in inflows is relatively larger in the United States. For example, the value of gross FDI inflows in 1999 is about six times the value of FDI inflows in 1990 to the United States, whereas gross FDI inflows to Canada in 1999 are only about three times the 1990 value. On the other hand, gross outflows increased at much more comparable rates. Thus, gross outflows in 1999 are approximately five times the value of gross outflows in 1990 for the United States. For Canada, gross outflows in 1999 are slightly less than four times the value of gross outflows in 1990.

It is also obvious from Table 3 that the absolutely and relatively faster growth of inward FDI to the United States during the 1990s is heavily conditioned by the 1999 data. For example, gross inflows of FDI to the United States in 1998 are approximately four times higher than the 1990 value. Gross inflows to Canada in 1998 are slightly less than three times higher than the 1990 value. Inward FDI flows are even more similar if we consider the 1990-97 period, when gross FDI inflows are approximately doubled in the United States, and increased by a factor of about 1.5 in Canada.

An examination of the ratio of U.S.-Canada inflows leads us to the same conclusion. The ratio increased over the 1994-99 period, reaching its peak in 1999. However, while the ratio rose over that period, it is not higher than its average value for 1988-93. Clearly, care must be exercised when asserting that Canada has suffered from a declining share of inward FDI to North America in recent years, as differences in the inward FDI experiences of Canada and the United States are sensitive to the inclusion or exclusion of specific years that, in fact, may represent anomalies.

## TABLE 3

### GROSS FDI FLOWS BETWEEN CANADA AND THE UNITED STATES

| | 1988-93 (annual average) | 1994 | 1995 | 1996 | 1997 | 1998 | 1999 |
|---|---|---|---|---|---|---|---|
| Canada | | | | | | | |
| Inflows (dollars) | 5,336 | 8,207 | 9,257 | 9,636 | 11,761 | 21,705 | 25,061 |
| Inflows (percent) | 4.7 | 8.1 | 9.4 | 9.2 | 9.9 | 18.8 | N/A |
| Outflows (dollars) | 5,309 | 9,296 | 11,464 | 13,098 | 22,515 | 31,286 | 17,816 |
| Outflows (percent) | 4.7 | 9.2 | 11.7 | 12.5 | 18.9 | 27.1 | N/A |
| United States | | | | | | | |
| Inflows (dollars) | 44,781 | 45,095 | 58,772 | 84,455 | 105,488 | 186,316 | 275,533 |
| Inflows (percent) | 5.3 | 4.4 | 5.3 | 7.0 | 8.0 | 12.8 | N/A |
| Outflows (dollars) | 39,323 | 73,252 | 92,074 | 84,426 | 99,517 | 146,052 | 150,901 |
| Outflows (percent) | 4.6 | 7.1 | 8.3 | 7.0 | 7.6 | 10.0 | N/A |
| United States-Canada | | | | | | | |
| Inflows | 8.39 | 5.49 | 6.34 | 8.76 | 8.71 | 8.58 | 10.99 |
| Outflows | 7.41 | 7.87 | 8.03 | 6.44 | 4.42 | 4.66 | 8.46 |

Notes: Dollar amounts are in millions of U.S. dollars. Percentage amounts are of gross fixed capital formation. N/A = not available.
Source: UNCTAD (2000).

Table 3 also reports gross FDI flows as a percentage of gross fixed capital formation for the two countries. It shows that gross FDI flows as a percentage of fixed capital formation increased over the 1990s in both countries. Moreover, for both countries, there is an accelerated increase in the relevant percentages for both inflows and outflows in the latter half of the 1990s. Especially marked increases are apparent in 1998, and even larger increases would presumably be reported for 1999 were data on fixed capital formation available for that year at the time of writing.

What is especially interesting to note in Table 3 is that gross FDI inflows as a percentage of fixed capital formation are higher in Canada than in the United States over the latter part of the 1990s. It is perhaps relevant that gross FDI outflows as a share of fixed capital formation were higher in Canada than in the United States over the 1990s, with the difference being more marked than in the case of FDI inflows. Nevertheless, the relatively high ratio for gross FDI flows suggests that overall macro-economic conditions in the United States may have been more favourable for both foreign and domestic investment compared to Canada.

In short, FDI flow data suggest that the United States attracted relatively more inward FDI than Canada from the mid-1980s through the 1990s, with the differences being most notable in the late 1980s and late 1990s. This assessment is basically supported by data on FDI stocks summarized in Table 4.

## TABLE 4

## CANADA AND THE UNITED STATES: FDI STOCKS

| | 1980 | 1985 | 1990 | 1995 | 1998 | 1999 |
|---|---|---|---|---|---|---|
| Canada | | | | | | |
| Inward (dollars) | 54,149 | 64,634 | 112,872 | 123,181 | 143,234 | 166,266 |
| Inward (percent change) | | 19.3 | 74.6 | 9.1 | 16.3 | 16.1 |
| Inward (percent of GDP) | 20.6 | 18.6 | 19.7 | 21.5 | 23.9 | N/A |
| Outward (dollars) | 23,777 | 43,127 | 84,829 | 118,105 | 160,936 | 178,347 |
| Outward (percent change) | | 81.4 | 96.6 | 39.2 | 36.3 | 10.8 |
| Outward (percent of GDP) | 9.0 | 12.4 | 14.8 | 20.6 | 26.9 | N/A |
| United States | | | | | | |
| Inward (dollars) | 83,046 | 184,615 | 394,911 | 535,553 | 811,756 | 1,087,289 |
| Inward (percent change) | | 122.3 | 113.9 | 39.9 | 51.5 | 33.9 |
| Inward (percent of GDP) | 3.1 | 4.6 | 7.1 | 7.6 | 9.5 | N/A |
| Outward (dollars) | 220,178 | 251,034 | 430,521 | 699,015 | 980,565 | 1,131,466 |
| Outward (percent change) | | 14.0 | 71.4 | 62.3 | 40.2 | 15.3 |
| Outward (percent of GDP) | 8.1 | 6.2 | 7.8 | 9.9 | 11.5 | N/A |
| United States-Canada | | | | | | |
| Inward | 1.53 | 2.86 | 3.50 | 4.35 | 5.66 | 6.54 |
| Outward | 9.26 | 5.82 | 5.07 | 5.92 | 6.09 | 6.34 |

Note: Dollar amounts are in millions of U.S. dollars. N/A = not available.
Source: UNCTAD (2000).

Table 4 shows a persistent increase in the ratio of inward U.S. FDI stocks to Canadian FDI stocks over the decades of the 1980s and 1990s. The increase is especially marked in the 1980s.[10] Canada's relative stock of outflows increased rapidly in the early 1980s and was relatively stable thereafter, a result consistent with the flow data.

Additional evidence highlighting differences between the United States and Canada in recent FDI experiences is provided in Table 5, which provides data on shares of Organisation for Economic Co-operation and Development (OECD) inflows and outflows accounted for by Canada and the United States. The data in Table 5 support broad inferences drawn from the preceding tables. The U.S. share of inflows increased markedly in the 1980s and rose again in the late 1990s. The relative increase in FDI inflows to the United States towards the end of the 1990s is distinctly different from the Canadian experience. Specifically, while Canada's share of total OECD inflows of FDI is relatively constant over the 1996-99 period, it did fall somewhat in 1998-99, and this decline coincided with an increase in the U.S. share. Thus, the ratio of the Canada-U.S. share rose to a peak in 1998-99. Again, the important influence of very recent FDI inflow experiences in the United States is highlighted. With regard to FDI outflows, the U.S. share has tended to decrease over the sample period, whereas Canada's share is relatively stable. It therefore appears that a large increase of U.S.-bound OECD investment in 1998-99, combined with a relative reduction in outflows of FDI from the United States, resulted in relatively larger net inflows to the United States.

## TABLE 5

### CANADIAN AND U.S. SHARES OF OECD DIRECT INVESTMENT FLOWS (PERCENT)

| | 1971 –80 | 1981 –90 | 1988 –93 | 1994 | 1995 | 1996 | 1997 | 1998 | 1999 (P) |
|---|---|---|---|---|---|---|---|---|---|
| Canada | | | | | | | | | |
| Inflows (percent) | 2.8 | 3.8 | 3.5 | 5.0 | 4.0 | 3.8 | 3.8 | 3.2 | 3.5 |
| Outflows (percent) | 3.6 | 3.9 | 2.5 | 3.9 | 3.7 | 3.8 | 5.3 | 4.2 | 2.3 |
| United States | | | | | | | | | |
| Inflows (percent) | 29.4 | 41.9 | 30.6 | 27.7 | 25.5 | 35.8 | 36.5 | 38.0 | 41.3 |
| Outflows (percent) | 43.7 | 16.6 | 20.5 | 30.6 | 29.8 | 27.2 | 26.6 | 20.9 | 19.8 |
| United States-Canada | | | | | | | | | |
| Inflows | 10.5 | 11.0 | 8.7 | 5.5 | 6.4 | 9.4 | 9.6 | 11.8 | 11.8 |
| Outflows | 15.6 | 4.3 | 8.2 | 7.8 | 8.1 | 7.1 | 5.0 | 5.0 | 8.6 |

Source: Calculated from data in OECD (2000a).

## SUMMARY

BOTH FDI FLOW AND STOCK DATA POINT to the growth of inward FDI to the United States relative to Canada over the past few decades. However, the pattern is somewhat variable over time. For example, inward FDI to Canada increases relative to inward FDI to the United States in the early 1990s. Indeed, the most notable recent increases in the U.S. share of inward FDI occur in the latter part of the 1980s and the 1990s. To the extent that developments surrounding the FDI process in those time periods were idiosyncratic, it would be potentially misleading to draw general conclusions from them about Canada's long-run locational attractiveness.

Swimmer (2000) and others have pointed to Canada's declining share of inward FDI to North America as evidence of Canada's decreasing attractiveness to MNC investors. The data presented in this section serve as a caution against drawing this conclusion based primarily upon gross and net FDI flows. In particular, the surge in inward FDI to the United States in 1998 and 1999 heavily influences any bilateral comparisons covering the past decade or two. In addition, there is evidence that inflows into Canada increased significantly in 2000, a year for which we do not have comparative data.

Moreover, conclusions about Canada's decreasing attractiveness to foreign investors are arguably best viewed within the context of capital investment more generally. That is, capital investment, in general, proceeded more rapidly in the United States than in Canada in the latter part of the 1980s and 1990s, arguably the result of stronger economic growth in the United States. Indeed, FDI, specifically, accounted for a relatively larger share of capital formation in Canada than in the United States, suggesting that MNCs may have found Canada a more attractive place to invest than the United States, "holding constant" cyclical economic conditions in the two countries.

## FDI FLOWS, BY COUNTRY OF ORIGIN AND INDUSTRIAL SECTOR

THE DATA PRESENTED IN THE PRECEDING SECTION documented that FDI inflows to the United States increased at a more rapid rate in the latter half of the 1990s than did FDI inflows to Canada. In this section, we consider whether and to what extent this difference is specific to individual investing countries or to particular industries. To the extent that MNCs from a specific country have historically favoured investing in the United States rather than Canada, an increase in the propensity of that country to invest abroad would presumably contribute to an increase in FDI flows to the United States relative to Canada, all other things constant. This is more likely when agglomeration economies are stronger for national groups of investors. Duffield and Munday

(2000), among others, document the role that agglomeration economies play in encouraging a geographical concentration of FDI by investors located in specific countries. To the extent that increased FDI inflows to the United States primarily reflect the behaviour of investors from one or a few countries, one might hesitate to draw the inference that there has been any deterioration in Canada's location advantages relative to the United States. Rather, it might reflect episodic changes in country sources of FDI that are characterized by location preferences tied to accumulated past investments.

To the extent that FDI is becoming increasingly concentrated in specific industries, in particular new economy industries, differences in Canadian and U.S. patterns of FDI might be seen to be a function of differences in the mix of industries in the two countries. Specifically, to the extent that FDI is increasingly attracted to new economy businesses, the concentration of such businesses in the United States would place Canada at an increasing location disadvantage compared to the United States. Any such finding would focus policy attention on the issue of how to encourage a faster transformation of Canada's industrial structure toward a greater representation of faster growing, technology-intensive industries.

## LOCATIONAL PATTERNS

SOME PERSPECTIVE ON THE FIRST ISSUE can be gained by identifying those countries whose FDI outflows increased relatively rapidly over the 1990s. In this regard, Table 6 reports the percentage increases in FDI outflows over the 1996-99 period for leading OECD countries, as well as the share of total OECD outward FDI accounted for by each country. As can be seen, among the major OECD countries, the percentage increases in FDI outflows are especially noteworthy for the United Kingdom, France and Germany. This development could be expected to contribute to faster inward FDI growth in the United States than in Canada, since European FDI in the United States has been absolutely and relatively greater than European FDI in Canada.

The importance of European location preferences is illustrated by data in Table 7. It reports the share of inward direct investment to Canada and the United States originating in different regions. Noteworthy of emphasis is the virtual disappearance of European investors as sources of inward FDI to Canada in the latter part of the 1990s. Indeed, investors based in the "NAFTA zone", essentially meaning the United States, became increasingly dominant sources of inward FDI to Canada in the 1990s. At the same time, European investors became essentially the dominant source of inward FDI to the United States, with a major concomitant decline in the share of inward FDI coming from outside of Europe and North America. Furthermore, the stock of total inward direct investment to the

United States owned by French, German and U.K. investors amounts to about 40 percent of the total stock of FDI in the United States.[11] In contrast, the entire stock of direct investment in Canada from the European Union (EU) amounts to only about 20 percent of the total stock of FDI in Canada.

## TABLE 6

### SHARE AND PERCENTAGE INCREASE IN FDI OUTFLOWS, 1996-99

| Country | Share of Total OECD Outflows (percent) | Percentage Change |
|---|---|---|
| United States | 22.6 | 64 |
| United Kingdom | 19.2 | 484 |
| Germany | 13.0 | 94 |
| France | 9.1 | 141 |
| Netherlands | 7.3 | 46 |
| Japan | 4.4 | –12 |
| Canada | 3.7 | 35 |
| Spain | 3.4 | 534 |
| Switzerland | 3.2 | 11 |
| Sweden | 2.8 | 306 |

Source: Calculated from data in OECD (2000b).

## TABLE 7

### DIRECT INVESTMENT FROM ABROAD IN CANADA AND THE UNITED STATES: INFLOWS BY ZONE PERCENTAGE OF TOTAL COUNTRY INFLOWS

| | 1987-92 (annual average) | 1993 | 1994 | 1995 | 1996 | 1997 | 1998 |
|---|---|---|---|---|---|---|---|
| Canada | | | | | | | |
| Europe | 26 | 9 | –11 | –2 | 1 | 6 | 2 |
| NAFTA | 46 | 83 | 98 | 63 | 69 | 74 | 86 |
| Other | 28 | 8 | 13 | 39 | 30 | 19 | 12 |
| United States | | | | | | | |
| Europe | 55 | 78 | 65 | 68 | 66 | 67 | 89 |
| NAFTA | 5 | 7 | 13 | 8 | 10 | 15 | 7 |
| Other | 40 | 13 | 34 | 24 | 38 | 26 | 8 |

Source: Calculated from data in OECD (2000b).

The relatively rapid growth of outward FDI from the large EU countries, combined with the latter's overrepresentation in U.S. FDI stocks, could be expected to contribute to a faster growth of inward FDI to the United States than to Canada for reasons discussed above. To be sure, this observation does not explain the historical preference of large European-based companies to invest in the United States. An identification of the source of this preference is presumably a prerequisite to mitigating or reversing the preference. On the basis of other persuasive evidence, we would argue that the preference largely derives from the larger U.S. domestic market combined with sector and nationality-specific agglomeration economies (Globerman 2001; Globerman and Shapiro). An implication is that Canadian government policies promoting faster real economic growth will also indirectly encourage inflows of FDI from European and other developed countries by promoting a larger overall domestic market in Canada. We shall have more to say about this in the concluding section of the paper.

## INTERNATIONAL MERGERS AND ACQUISITIONS

A POTENTIALLY IMPORTANT DEVELOPMENT for FDI location patterns is the disproportionate share of mergers and acquisitions (M&As) in total FDI flows in recent years. The dramatic increase in international M&A activity in the latter half of the 1990s is illustrated in Figures 2 and 3, although there was also an upswing in such activity in the late 1980s.[12] Worth highlighting is the surge of acquisitions made by EU-based investors in the late 1990s and the growing prominence of U.S.-based acquired companies in that period. The importance of M&As as a vehicle for FDI is illustrated by the fact that, by 1999, cross-border M&As (valued at US$720 billion) accounted for the vast majority of the total value of global FDI flows (valued at US$865 billion).[13]

The relevance of the growth in international M&A activity to recent differences in Canada-U.S. patterns of FDI is suggested by the observation that over the period from 1986 to 1998 there was an almost perfect correlation between total recorded FDI in the United States and total acquisitions of U.S. companies by foreign investors (Thomsen 2000). Moreover, about 80 percent of FDI in the United States was accounted for by cross-border M&As, whereas the latter accounted for only about 60 percent of the total value of global direct investments. Thomsen infers that the absolutely and relatively robust U.S. economy, combined with the highly liquid and relatively deregulated U.S. equity markets, was a special impetus to increased foreign M&A activity in the United States.

To the extent that the United States was an especially attractive location for foreign M&A activity, the growth of such activity in the 1990s would have contributed further to increased inward FDI to the United States compared to

Canada. A related and supporting development is the emergence of Western European investors, and especially those in the United Kingdom, as increasingly important participants in international M&A activity. Table 8 reports the sources of inward and outward international M&A deals for select countries. It is seen that the United Kingdom displaces the United States as the single most important acquiring country in international M&A deals in 1999. By the same token, the United States is an increasingly favoured location for international acquisitions compared to Canada in 1998 and 1999.[14]

In summary, recent differences in the inward FDI experiences of Canada and the United States arguably reflect strongly the growing importance of Western European investors, especially those located in the United Kingdom, in international M&A activity combined with a dominant preference on the part of those investors for making acquisitions in the United States. As a consequence of Canada's increasing reliance on the United States as a source of FDI inflows and the relative decline in U.S.-originated M&A purchases (Table 8), Canada's relative position as an FDI recipient declined during the latter half of the 1990s.

---

TABLE 8

INTERNATIONAL M&A DEALS IN OECD COUNTRIES: BILLIONS OF U.S. DOLLARS AND PERCENT OF OECD TOTAL

| | Inward | | | | Outward | | | |
|---|---|---|---|---|---|---|---|---|
| | 1996 | 1997 | 1998 | 1999 | 1996 | 1997 | 1998 | 1999 |
| United States | 70.6 (37.8%) | 64.3 (26.4%) | 190.8 (38.4%) | 293 (40.8%) | 65.5 (27.1%) | 80.8 (26.7%) | 132.8 (25.8%) | 145.7 (18.9%) |
| United Kingdom | 39.2 (21.0%) | 55.4 (22.7%) | 85.6 (17.2%) | 123 (17.1%) | 34.8 (14.4%) | 32.6 (10.8%) | 117.1 (22.7%) | 246.2 (32.1%) |
| Germany | 6.7 (3.5%) | 19.3 (7.9%) | 37.9 (7.6%) | 42.4 (5.9%) | 27.4 (11.3%) | 15.7 (5.2%) | 60.4 (11.7%) | 93 (12.1%) |
| Canada | 10.4 (5.5%) | 12 (4.9%) | 15.4 (3.1%) | 29 (4.0%) | 22.1 (9.2%) | 24.7 (8.2%) | 42.3 (8.2%) | 16.3 (2.1%) |
| Total OECD | 186.6 | 243.2 | 496.4 | 717.8 | 240.9 | 301.6 | 515.4 | 767.3 |

Source: KPMG Corporate Finance, Dealwatch Database, 2000, reported in OECD (2000b).

## FIGURE 2

### CROSS-BORDER M&AS: PURCHASES, 1987-99

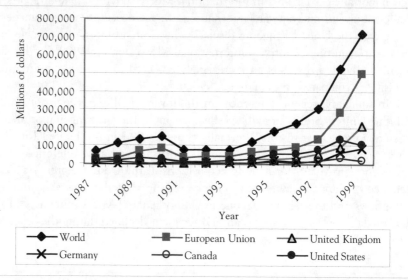

Source: UNCTAD (2000).

## FIGURE 3

### CROSS-BORDER M&AS: SALES, 1987-99

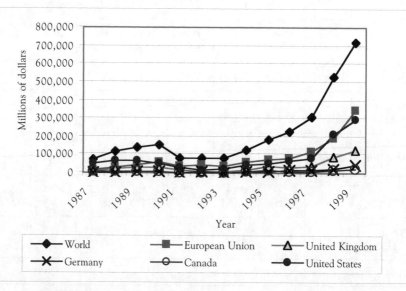

Source: UNCTAD (2000).

## SECTORAL PATTERNS

AN OBVIOUS QUESTION RAISED by the data presented in the preceding section is why European investors engaging in M&A activity exhibited such a marked preference for the United States, rather than Canada, as the location for their takeover activities during the latter part of the 1990s. One possible reason is that favoured industrial sectors are more heavily represented in the United States. In particular, European investors preferring acquisitions in new economy sectors might have found that acquisition targets were disproportionately located in the United States.

### TABLE 9

### CROSS-BORDER M&A ACTIVITY, BY SECTOR AND INDUSTRY OF SELLER (PERCENT OF TOTAL)

| Sector and Industry | World | | | United States | | |
|---|---|---|---|---|---|---|
| | 1997 | 1998 | 1999 | 1997 | 1998 | 1999 |
| Primary | 2.9 | 2.0 | 1.3 | 2.6 | 0.5 | 1.6 |
| Secondary | 39.8 | 49.5 | 38.2 | 34.1 | 71.0 | 26.8 |
| Food, Beverages | 7.2 | 3.2 | 3.7 | 1.8 | 0.5 | 0.6 |
| Wood | 2.2 | 1.4 | 1.5 | 2.5 | 0.5 | 0.0 |
| Publishing | 0.8 | 2.4 | 1.3 | 1.7 | 5.0 | 3.0 |
| Petroleum | 3.7 | 12.6 | 4.1 | 2.5 | 25.7 | 0.2 |
| Chemicals | 11.6 | 6.0 | 12.0 | 13.9 | 2.9 | 5.3 |
| Minerals/Metals | 5.2 | 3.1 | 2.8 | 2.3 | 1.8 | 2.4 |
| Machinery | 2.4 | 1.7 | 2.9 | 2.2 | 2.5 | 6.3 |
| Electrical | 2.5 | 6.7 | 5.3 | 3.7 | 8.6 | 5.9 |
| Motor vehicles | 1.3 | 9.5 | 2.5 | 1.7 | 20.9 | 1.0 |
| Tertiary | 57.3 | 48.5 | 60.5 | 63.2 | 28.5 | 71.6 |
| Utilities | 9.7 | 6.0 | 6.7 | 0.1 | 1.4 | 6.2 |
| Trade | 7.1 | 5.1 | 5.0 | 11.0 | 5.5 | 3.8 |
| Communications | 5.8 | 9.7 | 23.3 | 2.6 | 5.2 | 33.4 |
| Finance | 16.6 | 15.6 | 15.5 | 21.4 | 6.7 | 18.2 |
| Business Services | 8.6 | 8.0 | 6.6 | 10.3 | 8.0 | 6.2 |
| Total (billions of dollars) | 305 | 532 | 720 | 82 | 210 | 233 |

Source: Calculated from UNCTAD (2000). Only selected industries are reported.

Table 9 reports cross-border M&A activity, by sector, of the selling firm. On a worldwide basis, the tertiary sector (the broad industrial sector) accounts for the majority of the value of cross-border acquisitions and the primary sector accounts for the lowest percentage. Within the tertiary sector, communications and finance account for the majority of acquisitions. Indeed, in 1999, the communications sector accounted for almost one-quarter of all acquisition activity. The share of acquisitions in the tertiary sector has been increasing over time. The share of M&A activity accounted for by the tertiary sector was 28.6 percent in 1987 and averaged 44.7 percent for the period 1987-96.

In comparison to worldwide patterns, M&A activity in the United States was even more disproportionately concentrated in the tertiary sector and in communications and finance specifically, at least in 1999. For example, in that year, over half of all foreign acquisitions in the United States were concentrated in the latter two sectors. However, in 1998, over 70 percent of foreign acquisitions in the United States were in the secondary sector, whereas less than 30 percent were in the tertiary sector. Indeed, in 1998, acquisitions in the petroleum and motor vehicle sectors accounted for almost half of all foreign acquisitions in the United States for that year. The point that might be made here is that the sectoral pattern of acquisitions in the United States varies substantially from year to year and there is no dominant pattern of new economy acquisitions, at least in recent years. Rather, it would appear that foreign acquisitions are motivated by the strategic imperatives of specific acquirers, and those imperatives vary from year to year as the identities of acquiring companies and sectors change.

The extent to which Canada has been at a disadvantage in terms of attracting corporate acquisitions of domestic companies is further considered with attention to Table 10. It shows the percentage inflows of FDI into Canada and the United States by broad industrial sector. One basic point that is underscored by the information in Table 10 is that sectoral concentrations of FDI inflows vary considerably from year to year. This observation makes it difficult to argue that the absolutely and relatively larger flows of inward FDI to the United States in the latter part of the 1990s are the consequence of new economy businesses being more heavily represented in the United States than in Canada. Moreover, for the time period covered in Table 10, there is no evidence that Canada has had relatively less inward FDI in the tertiary sector than the United States, at least on any systematic basis, including the important and increasingly technology-intensive financial sector.

One notable difference in Table 10 is the significantly larger proportion of inward FDI in the secondary sector for the United States compared to Canada for the years 1996-98. However, as Table 9 suggests, foreign acquisitions made in U.S. secondary industries during 1997 and 1998 were not concentrated in obvious new economy sectors such as electrical products or machinery.

## TABLE 10

## FDI INFLOWS, BY INDUSTRIAL SECTOR

|  | 1987-92 | 1993 | 1994 | 1995 | 1996 | 1997 | 1998 |
|---|---|---|---|---|---|---|---|
| **Canada** **Percentage of Canadian Inflows (classified)** | | | | | | | |
| Primary | 19.2 | 29.5 | −1.5 | −8.6 | 35.9 | 30.5 | 36.4 |
| Secondary | 19.5 | 45.7 | 63.4 | 47.7 | 8.2 | 21.0 | 28.0 |
| Tertiary | 61.3 | 24.7 | 38.1 | 60.8 | 55.9 | 48.5 | 35.6 |
| Financial | 45.1 | 8.0 | −6.3 | 21.1 | 27.4 | 33.5 | 26.0 |
| **United States** **Percentage of U.S. Inflows** | | | | | | | |
| Primary | 4.4 | 2.0 | 3.4 | 7.5 | 6.1 | 3.4 | 30.8 |
| Secondary | 45.9 | 27.4 | 46.6 | 49.6 | 48.9 | 35.5 | 46.3 |
| Tertiary | 49.5 | 70.6 | 49.9 | 42.9 | 44.9 | 61.1 | 22.8 |
| Financial | 21.1 | 53.5 | 18.4 | 25.0 | 15.5 | 24.7 | 9.7 |
| **Canada** **Percentage of Canadian + U.S. Inflows** | | | | | | | |
| Primary | 28.4 | 55.6 | −1.0 | −11.1 | 38.8 | 50.7 | 10.9 |
| Secondary | 3.8 | 11.8 | 16.6 | 7.7 | 1.8 | 6.3 | 5.8 |
| Tertiary | 10.1 | 2.7 | 10.0 | 11.0 | 11.8 | 8.4 | 13.9 |
| Financial | 16.4 | 1.2 | −5.0 | 6.9 | 16.1 | 13.5 | 21.7 |

Note:   For Canada, substantial amounts of FDI were classified as "unallocated," and so percentages are based on classified allocations. For the United States, the 1998 data are the result of the apparent classification of the BP-Amoco merger under the primary sector.

Source: Calculated from data in OECD (2000a).

## SUMMARY

A CONSIDERATION OF SOURCES OF ORIGIN of inward FDI to North America in the latter part of the 1990s reveals certain strong patterns. One is that major Western European companies increased their outward FDI disproportionately in the latter part of the 1990s. In particular, outward FDI from the United Kingdom accelerated substantially in 1998 and 1999. The large Western European countries, particularly the United Kingdom, had relatively large accumulated stocks of FDI in the United States and relatively small accumulated stocks of FDI in Canada. All other things constant, agglomeration economies associated with relatively large historical investments in the United States would have predisposed European investors to concentrate their more recent outward FDI in the United States.

Another operative factor in the latter part of the 1990s was the prominence of M&As as the dominant mode of FDI. All else constant, the more liquid U.S. securities markets were more favourable venues for corporate acquisitions than Canadian securities markets, although this still begs the question as

299

to why U.S. companies were so attractive to foreign acquirers.[15] The hypothesis that U.S. companies are attractive acquisition targets because they are concentrated in new economy activities and that European companies need to acquire U.S. companies in order to obtain needed technological expertise, is contradicted by data that show no concentration of inward FDI to the United States in the late 1990s in conventionally defined technology-intensive sectors. Indeed, sectoral patterns of foreign acquisitions in North America are fairly volatile on a year-to-year basis.

It would seem, therefore, that FDI patterns in North America in the 1990s strongly reflect strategic corporate acquisitions made by European MNCs, pursuant to motives that are relatively specific to the individual acquisitions. In this context, it is unclear that the acquisition pattern has very much to say about Canada's general location advantage compared to the United States. As such, policy concerns in Canada related to recent international M&A behaviour may be, at best, premature and, at worst, misplaced. In the following section, we expand upon these latter points.

## EVALUATING HYPOTHESES ABOUT CANADA'S DECLINING LOCATION ATTRACTIVENESS

IN THIS SECTION, WE ADDRESS IN MORE DETAIL the likelihood that differences between Canada and the United States in recent FDI patterns reflect location disadvantages for Canada.

### TAX DIFFERENCES

AS NOTED EARLIER, it is frequently argued that relatively high Canadian taxes have discouraged inward FDI and will continue to do so unless they are substantially reduced. Any detailed evaluation of this assertion is challenged by several complexities. One is how to measure the ex-ante tax burden facing potential foreign investors. In this regard, marginal tax rates are more appropriate than average tax rates. In addition, effective tax rates are conceptually more appropriate than nominal tax rates. Thus, the relevant tax burden is the rate of tax on the next dollar of income after all relevant tax deductions, tax credits and tax expenditures are taken into account. Obviously, this tax burden will vary by industry source, business location, and size of company, among other things. It will also be conditioned by the ability of investors to alter the reported geographic sources of income and expenses among tax jurisdictions.[16] As a consequence, even comparisons of marginal effective tax rates across broad industrial categories of foreign investors in different countries may be misleading, especially given differences across countries in the industrial distribution of economic activity.[17]

It is beyond the scope of this study to attempt any original empirical analysis of the linkages between tax differences among North American government jurisdictions and FDI patterns in North America. Rather, with the aforementioned caveats in mind, we briefly review and assess the available literature, focussing on two issues: 1) What are the differences in the fiscal regimes between Canada and the United States? 2) How important are tax differences to foreign investors?

## 1) Tax Regimes

THE RELEVANT EFFECTIVE TAX RATES to compare across countries are presumably not just at the corporate level, but at the individual level as well. Indeed, it is argued by some observers that high marginal personal tax rates are encouraging outward migration of highly educated Canadians to the United States, especially under the NAFTA visa provisions.[18] This emigration, in turn, contributes to a reduction in the stock of human capital in Canada, which makes FDI in Canada less profitable than it would otherwise be. Of course, comparisons of marginal personal tax rates are also complicated by a variety of considerations similar to those relevant to comparing corporate tax rates, including the domicile of the taxpayer and differing national treatments of earned versus unearned income.

Chen (2000) shows that marginal effective tax rates vary significantly across industry sectors in Canada as a result of differences in capital structures, statutory rates and relevant capital cost allowance rates. The marginal effective tax rate is lower for manufacturing than for service industries. Chen compares estimated marginal effective corporate tax rates between Canadian and U.S. manufacturing industries, as well as between Canadian and U.S. service industries. For manufacturing, the 21.2 percent rate in the United States is marginally below the 22.4 percent rate in Canada. However, while the marginal effective corporate tax rate on services in the United States is virtually identical to that for manufacturing, it is significantly higher (at about 26 percent) in Canada.[19] Chen's estimates therefore suggest that differences in the corporate tax regime are likely to have the most marked effects on the North American distribution of inward FDI in the service industries. However, as earlier reported data show, Canada's share of Canadian plus U.S. inward FDI in the tertiary sector, with some year-to-year variation, actually increased between the 1987-92 period and 1998. Moreover, Canada's share of inward FDI in the financial sector increased quite significantly over that period. This is especially noteworthy given regulatory restrictions that essentially prevent foreign takeovers of Canadian deposit-taking institutions.

## 2) Impact of Taxes on FDI and Migration

HINES (1996) OFFERS A COMPREHENSIVE REVIEW of studies examining the relationship between tax policy and the activities of MNCs. His review highlights the added complexity induced by considerations such as the home country's tax treatment of the unrepatriated portion of the profits earned by foreign subsidiaries of home country companies. Differences between home countries in their treatment of foreign-sourced income can bias the estimated impacts of host country tax differences on FDI flows if the former are ignored. Furthermore, home country tax provisions that allow domestic companies to claim, as tax credits, income taxes paid to foreign governments contribute to a potentially significant difference between an MNC's nominal and effective tax rate on foreign-sourced income. A failure to acknowledge explicitly such provisions can be expected to lead to errors-in-variables problems in regression models with associated estimation biases.

Hines concludes from the variety of studies examining the FDI-taxation relationship in different contexts that, despite all the other economic and political considerations that are clearly very important, taxation exerts a significant influence on the magnitude and location of FDI.[20] However, he cautions that existing studies are unsatisfactory in a number of respects, including their failure to incorporate general equilibrium effects of taxes, such as changes in factor and product prices, into the specified models.

As none of the studies reviewed by Hines focus specifically on MNC decisions to invest in the United States rather than Canada, extrapolation of his review to the distribution of FDI in North America might be inappropriate. Moreover, a cursory review of recent and major acquisitions of U.S. companies suggests the importance of strategic considerations rather than tax considerations as motives for the acquisitions. Table 11 reports eight transactions out of the largest 20 acquisitions in 1998 and 1999. All but one of the transactions reported are horizontal in nature, suggesting the prominence of motives such as geographic expansion and economies of scale.

A perusal of various press reports issued at the time of the mergers also fails to uncover any mention of taxation as a factor in the acquisition, although there are references to various types of synergies.[21] Moreover, it is worthy of note that most of the transactions listed in Table 11 occurred in industries where foreign ownership in Canada is restricted, either through regulations (telecommunications and banking) or state-ownership (utilities). Absent such restrictions, it is conceivable that some large Canadian companies might have appeared on the list of acquisitions.

## TABLE 11

### LARGEST CROSS-BORDER ACQUISITIONS OF U.S. COMPANIES, 1998-99

| Year | Value ($ billions) | Acquiring Firm (home economy) | Industry of Acquiring Firm | Acquired U.S. Firm | Industry of Acquired Firm |
|------|------|------|------|------|------|
| 1999 | 60.3 | Vodafone (U.K.) | Telecommunications | AirTouch | Telecommunications |
| 1998 | 48.2 | BP (U.K.) | Oil and Gas | Amoco | Oil and Gas |
| 1998 | 40.5 | Daimler-Benz (Germany) | Transportation Equipment | Chrysler | Transportation Equipment |
| 1999 | 12.6 | Scottish Power (U.K.) | Electric, Gas and Water Distribution | PacifiCorp | Electric, Gas and Water Distribution |
| 1999 | 10.8 | Aegon (Netherlands) | Insurance | TransAmerica Corp. | Insurance |
| 1999 | 10.1 | Global Crossing (Bermuda) | Telecommunications | Frontier Corp. | Telecommunications |
| 1998 | 9.3 | Nortel Networks (Canada) | Communications Equipment | Bay Networks | Computer and Office Equipment |
| 1999 | 9.1 | Deutsche Bank (Germany) | Banking | Bankers Trust | Banking |

Source: Calculated from data in OECD (2000a).

There is very little evidence bearing upon the impacts of personal tax rates on the migration of managers and related professional workers. A recent survey for Canada, reported in Globerman (2000), casts doubt on the strength of Canada-U.S. tax differences as a motive for emigration from Canada. Specifically, the opportunity to work for leading companies in new economy industries is apparently a stronger motive for Canadian migration to the United States.

### INFRASTRUCTURE

MARTIN AND PORTER (2001) allege that specific factors in the "microeconomic business environment" have contributed to Canada's deteriorating competitiveness. One is a decline in Canada's investment in specialized human resources to support innovation and skill upgrading. A second is less competitive domestic markets compared to the United States. In a recent study, Globerman and Shapiro review various findings bearing upon the relationship between social infrastructure and FDI. The findings confirm the assertion that a "superior" educational infrastructure encourages inward FDI and that government regulations that raise costs and reduce competition discourage inward FDI. However, Globerman and Shapiro also estimate the impacts of broader measures of social and political infrastructure on FDI. One is a Human Development Index (HDI), constructed as a weighted aggregate value of three specific subindices (GDP per capita, education and life expectancy). A second is a Governance Index, constructed as a weighted aggregate value of six subindices that measure such phenomena as government effectiveness, regulatory burden on business, rule of law and government corruption. For specific years in the 1990s, Canada scores higher than the United States on both indices. In particular, Canada scores higher on the Governance Index, which is statistically more important than the HDI in the two countries' regression models to explain inward FDI.

An implication of the preceding finding is that, broadly defined, the micro-economic business environment for investment in Canada is not unambiguously less favourable than that in the United States, at least in terms of foreign investment.[22] This is not to say that Canada's location advantages cannot be improved by policies promoting additional skill upgrading and increased competition in domestic markets. Rather, it is to say the indices cited above are linked in no obvious way to the surge in foreign acquisitions of U.S. companies in the late 1990s. That is, broad international measures of infrastructure cannot explain the surge of foreign acquisitions in the United States rather than in Canada.

## SUMMARY

IN THIS SECTION, we briefly assessed two broad arguments that have been put forth to explain Canada's declining share of inward FDI to North America. Perhaps the most prominent argument is that higher taxes in Canada discourage investment by both domestic and foreign investors. Available evidence suggests that taxation is a relevant determinant of MNC location choices, other things constant. Certainly, we cannot dismiss the relevance of this consideration as an explanation of Canada's declining share of Canadian plus U.S. direct investment. Nevertheless, while relevant Canadian tax rates are higher than in the United States, recent differences in inward FDI behaviour between the two countries are not consistent with taxes being a major cause of those differences. For example, corporate tax rates for tertiary industries are especially unfavourable in Canada relative to the United States. Yet inward FDI to Canadian tertiary industries did not decline relative to inward FDI to U.S. tertiary industries.

Canada's declining capacity to innovate and support new economy activities has also been identified as a major component of Canada's less desirable micro-economic climate for investment. In our opinion, the evidence offers no obvious support for this assessment. For example, there is no identifiable trend for inward FDI to Canadian new economy industries to decline relative to inward FDI to counterpart U.S. industries. Furthermore, broader measures of the domestic business climates in both countries, specifically indices of social and political infrastructure, show that Canada has a relatively favourable environment compared to the United States.

We did not explicitly consider the impact of the two major regional free trade agreements that Canada implemented in the past two decades, i.e., the Canada-U.S. FTA and the NAFTA. Very few economists tie Canada's declining share of inward FDI relative to the United States to the trade agreements. It is at least plausible that the enhanced ability to ship goods into Canada at less cost, owing to lower tariffs, encouraged European and other foreign investors to invest less in Canada than they would otherwise have done. Specifically, the trade agreements made it more economical to centralize production facilities in the (much larger) U.S. domestic market. While we cannot reject the relevance of this possibility, the concentration of inward FDI from select European countries, most notably the United Kingdom in the late 1990s, seems somewhat idiosyncratic from the perspective of the trade liberalization explanation. Specifically, it is not clear why U.K. investors would be especially drawn by the NAFTA to invest in the United States. Nor is it clear why foreign investors would be motivated by regional free trade to accelerate their acquisition activities in the United States rather than increase the volume of "Greenfield" investments.

## OVERALL SUMMARY AND POLICY CONCLUSIONS

INWARD FDI TO CANADA CERTAINLY DECREASED when compared to inward FDI to the United States over the post-1975 period. Moreover, outward FDI from Canada increased when compared to outward FDI from the United States over the same period. The cause (or causes) of this decline is much more difficult to ascertain, in our opinion. Discounting the 1970s and early 1980s experience, for reasons discussed earlier, the FDI patterns are heavily influenced by international M&A waves over the latter half of the 1980s and 1990s. Our analysis shows that U.S. firms were particularly attractive to acquiring (European) companies in the 1990s, despite the fact that Canada also enjoyed a major increase in international M&A activity. While similar data on international M&A activity are unavailable for the 1980s, it would seem that such activity in Canada had reached a peak in 1987, whereas it continued to grow through the rest of that decade in the United States (Khemani 1991; Lipsey 1993). In short, it would seem that an understanding of Canada-U.S. FDI patterns over the past two decades requires an understanding of foreign, especially European, investors' preferences to acquire U.S. companies.

There is no obvious sectoral pattern to Canada's share of inward FDI. Combined with the concentrated (country) source of inward FDI to North America, the absence of an obvious sectoral pattern casts doubt on readily available explanations of Canada's location attraction for inward FDI and, in particular, the empirical relevance of differences in tax rates or Canada's underrepresentation in new economy industries. Indeed, it is tempting to conclude that the North American pattern of inward FDI, at least in the latter half of the 1990s, reflects a relative abundance of attractive takeover targets in the United States, which, when combined with the greater liquidity of U.S. capital markets, makes domestic takeovers easier to carry out in that country than elsewhere.[23] A relative abundance of attractive takeover targets in the United States might also be related to agglomeration economies deriving from the relatively large prior investments in the United States made by European investors, especially U.K. investors.[24] It might also reflect Canadian legal and regulatory restrictions on foreign control in sectors that attracted significant acquisition activity during the period, most notably communications and banking.[25]

The main point here is that one must be cautious in drawing conclusions about long-run trends in locational advantage from international M&A activity. Year-to-year changes in FDI values may be heavily influenced by a small number of very large acquisitions. For example, in the year 2000, two specific acquisitions (Vivendi's acquisition of Seagrams and Alcatel's purchase of Newbridge) accounted for virtually all of the inward FDI to Canada through the M&A channel. In effect, one should be cautious in inferring major policy conclusions from what may amount to a relatively small number of idiosyncratic observations.

The growth in Canadian outward FDI seems easier to explain. Specifically, Canada's outward FDI experience is consistent with the growing commercial and technological competence of Canadian MNCs that, in turn, allows them to compete more profitably in foreign markets. In this respect, the choice of FDI as the mode for competing in foreign markets is completely consistent with patterns of international business expansion exhibited in earlier periods by U.S., European and Japanese MNCs.

Our interpretation of the FDI data does not mean that Canadian policy makers should be sanguine about incentives for continued foreign and domestic investment in Canada. There is clear evidence that Canada's relative performance in terms of productivity and GDP per capita has been weak during the 1990s (Sharpe 2001; Martin and Porter 2001), and this does imply underinvestment in human and physical capital. In particular, we do not maintain that Canada's tax structure is "optimal" in any meaningful sense. High marginal tax rates are undoubtedly inflicting relatively large "dead-weight" costs on the domestic economy, even if they are not materially altering the location choices of foreign investors. As well, improved efficiency in the delivery of education, training and other programs to enhance human capital is desirable for economic and social reasons that extend well beyond any marginal impact it might have on inward FDI. The removal of regulations and foreign ownership restrictions that have the effect of reducing competition from both new domestic and foreign companies seems justified — without recourse to unfavourable comparisons with inward FDI flows to the United States.

The available evidence is unequivocal in identifying the overwhelming importance of a large and growing real domestic economy in attracting inward FDI over the long run. Indeed, even in the short run, the more robust U.S. economy in the late 1980s and most of the 1990s may have contributed, in part, to the preference of non-North American investors for acquisitions in the United States. To the extent that lower marginal tax rates and other manifestations of an improved micro-economic environment promote faster real economic growth in Canada, they will also promote increased inward FDI. The point to emphasize, it seems to us, is that real economic growth is the relevant policy goal, not increased foreign ownership of the Canadian economy. Indeed, the latter is desirable only insofar as it promotes the former. While it might be obvious, perhaps trivial, it nevertheless seems useful to caution against making public policy the handmaiden of FDI patterns.

## ENDNOTES

1   For discussions and evaluations of the debates surrounding continental investment patterns subsequent to trade integration agreements, see Rugman (1990) and Waverman (1991).

2   For an extensive discussion and assessment of agglomeration economies, see Krugman (1991). Globerman (2000) provides an overview of the empirical evidence surrounding the scope and magnitude of agglomeration economies.

3   A recent unpublished study (Swimmer 2000) identifies Canada-U.S. differences in the corporate capital gains tax rate as a primary factor encouraging increased FDI in the United States relative to Canada.

4   Some recent evidence on the relationship between domestic market size and FDI is reviewed in Globerman and Shapiro (2001).

5   See Reguly (2000). Any evaluation of this claim is obviously sensitive to the definition of technological intensity that is chosen. For a broad presentation of evidence that Canada is seriously lagging behind the United States in innovation and entrepreneurship, see Trajtenberg (2000).

6   By way of illustration, the Canadian dollar exchange rate in 1972 was C$0.9956/US$1. In 1985, it was C$1.3975/US$1. In 1998, it was C$1.5305/US$1.

7   Evidence on this point is provided in Martin and Porter (2001).

8   Figure 1 shows that there were decreases in inward FDI over the 1988-91 period that contrast with the positive growth thereafter. Given the pro-cyclical nature of FDI, the timing of the decrease is consistent with a significant economic slowdown in Canada over the 1989-91 period. The slowdown was more pronounced and longer-lasting in Canada than in the United States. See TD Bank Financial Group (2001).

9   The correlation coefficient is statistically significant at the 0.01 level.

10    Safarian and Hejazi (2001) also document a decrease in Canada's relative share of inward FDI extending back to the 1970s. As noted above, the late 1970s and early 1980s may have marked a period of "catch-up" for the United States as a destination for inward FDI.

11    The United Kingdom, by itself, accounts for about 23 percent of the total stock of inward FDI in the United States.

12    Khemani (1991) documents the growth in international M&As during the latter part of the 1980s as compared to earlier periods.

13    Acquisitions dominate mergers in terms of both number and aggregate value. For example, fewer than three percent of cross-border M&As are mergers.

14    This does not deny the fact that foreign takeovers in Canada increased during both the late 1980s (Khemani, 1991) and the late 1990s (Table 8). Indeed, foreign takeovers in Canada reached a record level in 1998 and represented more than 70 percent of FDI inflows for that year.

15    The United States was also a highly attractive location for international M&As during the 1980s. In this regard, Lipsey (1993) reports that over 80 percent of inflows of FDI to the United States from 1984 to 1987 were for acquisitions. This share was surpassed during the 1988-90 period when close to 90 percent of FDI inflows took the form of M&As.

16    For evidence on geographic income shifting by multinational companies through transfer pricing, see Klassen, Lang and Wolfson (1993).

17    For a discussion of the relevant caveats in calculating and comparing effective marginal tax rates across countries, see Chen (2000).

18    For a review and assessment of this argument, see Globerman (2000).

19    Mintz (1999) shows that cross-country differences in average effective tax rates are greater than differences in marginal effective tax rates.

20    More recent studies offering the same broad conclusion are discussed in Dahlby (Chapter 13 in this volume).

21    See, for example, the discussion of the Vodafone acquisition in Eccles, Lanes and Wilson(1999) and the discussion of Nortel's acquisition of Bay Networks in Karimkhany (1998).

22    Components of this environment, such as public health and education, may be tied to higher tax rates in Canada, which would further mitigate the negative impact of Canada's relative tax rates on Canada's share of inward FDI.

23    Evidence suggests that there is a strong positive correlation between aggregate merger activity and share prices, and that merger peaks often coincide with stock market booms (Haque, Harnhirun and Shapiro 1995). The stronger equity markets in the United States from the late 1980s through the 1990s might also, therefore, help explain the relative growth of inward FDI to the United States when compared to Canada.

24    Reports in the business literature suggest that Europeans continue to be attracted to the large U.S. domestic market despite the NAFTA (e.g., Baker 2001).

25    Andrade, Mitchell and Stafford (2001), argue that there is a tendency for mergers to cluster by industry during specific periods, suggesting that mergers are a response to random and exogenous industry shocks. These authors identify deregulation as the most important shock.

## ACKNOWLEDGMENTS

THE AUTHORS THANK Ken McKenzie and Someshwar Rao for helpful comments on an earlier draft.

## BIBLIOGRAPHY

Andrade, G., M. Mitchell and E. Stafford. "New Evidence and Perspectives on Mergers." *Journal of Economic Perspectives* 15, 2 (2001): 103-10.

Baker, S. "Why Europe Keeps Gobbling Up U.S. Companies." *Business Week*. June 18, 2001, p. 56.

Caves, R.E., and S.K. Mehra. "Entry of Foreign Multinationals into U.S. Manufacturing Industries." In *Competition in Global Industries*. Edited by M. Porter. Cambridge: Harvard Business School Press, 1986, pp. 449-83.

Chen, D. "The Marginal Effective Tax Rate: The Only Rate That Matters in Capital Allocation." Toronto: C.D. Howe Institute Backgrounder, 2000.

Dahlby, Bev. "Economic Integration: Implications for Business Taxation." In *North American Linkages: Opportunities and Challenges for Canada*. Edited by Richard G. Harris. Calgary: University of Calgary Press, 2003. Chapter 13.

Duffield, N., and M. Munday. "Industrial Performance, Agglomeration and Foreign Manufacturing Investment in the U.K." *Journal of International Business Studies* 31, 1 (2000): 21-38.

Eccles, R.G., K.L. Lanes and T.C. Wilson. "Are You Paying Too Much for That Acquisition?" *Harvard Business Review* July-August (1999):136-43.

Globerman, S. "Trade Liberalization and the Migration of Skilled Professionals and Managers: The North American Experience." *The World Economy* 23, 7 (2000): 901-22.

_____. *The Location of Higher Value-Added Activities*. Ottawa: Industry Canada, Occasional Paper No. 27, 2001.

Globerman, S., and D. Shapiro. *National Infrastructure and Foreign Direct Investment*. Report prepared for Industry Canada, 2001. Mimeograph.

Graham, E.M., and E. Wada. "Domestic Reform, Trade and Investment Liberalisation, Financial Crisis, and Foreign Direct Investment into Mexico." *The World Economy* 23, 6 (2000): 777-97.

Haque M., S. Harnhirun and D. M. Shapiro. "A Time Series Analysis of Causality between Aggregate Mergers and Stock Prices: The Case of Canada." *Applied Economics* 27, 4 (1995): 563-68.

Head, K., and J. Ries. *Can Small-Country Manufacturing Survive Trade Liberalization: Evidence From the Canada-U.S. Free Trade Agreement*. Perspectives on North American Free Trade Series No. 1. Ottawa: Industry Canada, 1999.

Hines, Jr., J.R. *Tax Policy and the Activities of Multinational Corporations*. Cambridge: National Bureau of Economic Research, Working Paper No. W5589, 1996.

Karimkhany, K. "Nortel Buys Bay Networks." *Wired News*, June 15, 1998. Available at: http://www.wired.com/news.

Klassen, K., M. Lang and M. Wolfson. "Geographic Income Shifting by Multinational Corporations in Response to Tax Rate Changes." *Journal of Accounting Research* 31, Supplement (1993):141-73.

Khemani, R.S. "Recent Trends in Merger and Acquisition Activity in Canada and Selected Countries." In *Corporate Globalization through Mergers and Acquisitions*. Edited by L. Waverman. Ottawa: Investment Canada, 1991, pp. 1-22.

Krugman, P. *Geography and Trade*. Cambridge: The MIT Press, 1991.

Lipsey, R.E. "Foreign Direct Investment in the United States: Changes Over Three Decades." In *Foreign Direct Investment*. Edited by K.A. Froot. Chicago: University of Chicago Press, 1993, pp.113-70.

Martin, R.L., and M.E. Porter. *Canadian Competitiveness: A Decade After the Crossroads*. Toronto: C.D. Howe Institute, 2001. Mimeograph.

McCallum, J. *Two Cheers for the FTA*. Toronto: Royal Bank of Canada, Economics Department, 1999. Mimeograph.

Mintz, J. *Why Canada Must Undertake Business Tax Reform Soon*. Toronto: C.D. Howe Institute Backgrounder 36, 1999.

OECD. *International Direct Investment Statistics Yearbook*. Paris: OECD, 2000a.

_____. *Recent Trends in Foreign Direct Investment*. Paris: OECD, 2000b.

Reguly, E. "Canada Must Innovate or Become a Forgotten Backwater." *The Globe and Mail*. January 10, 2000, p. B15.

Rugman, A.M. *Multinationals and Canada-U.S. Free Trade*. Columbia: University of South Carolina Press, 1990.

Safarian, A.E., and W. Hejazi. "Canada and Foreign Direct Investment: A Study of Determinants." Toronto: University of Toronto, 2001. Mimeograph.

Sharpe, A. "Determinants of Trends in Living Standards in Canada and the United States, 1989-2000." *International Productivity Monitor 2* (2001): 3-10.

Swimmer, D. "Investment Framework Policies and Canada's Declining Share of Inward Foreign Direct Investment." Ottawa: Industry Canada, 2000. Unpublished mimeograph.

TD Bank Financial Group. "The Penny Drops." April 24, 2001. Available at: http://www.td.com/economics/

Thomsen, S. *Investment Patterns in a Longer-Term Perspective*. Paris: OECD, Working Papers On International Investment, 2000.

Trajtenberg, M. *Is Canada Missing the Technology Boat? Evidence From Patent Data*. Discussion Paper No. 9. Ottawa: Industry Canada, 2000.

UNCTAD. *World Investment Report 2000*. Geneva: United Nations, 2000.

Waverman, L. "A Canadian Vision of North American Integration." In *Continental Accord: North American Economic Integration*. Edited by S. Globerman. Vancouver: The Fraser Institute, 1991, pp. 31-64.

*Part II*
*The NAFTA Countries as a Common Market*

Richard G. Harris*    &    Nicolas Schmitt
Simon Fraser University    Simon Fraser University and
Université de Genève

*8*

# The Consequences of Increased Labour Mobility within an Integrating North America

## INTRODUCTION

ONE HALLMARK OF A TRUE COMMON MARKET is labour mobility. The North American Free Trade Agreement (NAFTA) has some provisions on labour mobility — in particular, the temporary migration of business people and professionals under the TN visa program, which has been extremely successful. However, migration within the NAFTA is limited, and traditional immigration controls are viewed as instruments of national social and economic policy within all three member countries. Much of the discussion on migration within the NAFTA has been focussed on the movement of Mexicans northward across the U.S.-Mexico border. In Canada, the discussion has revolved around the movement of highly skilled individuals to the United States. There has been almost no discussion of movement toward a common continental labour market, with mobility rights for all NAFTA workers. In contrast, mobility of labour is one of the central features of the single market program and the entire integration program of the European Union (EU). This has led to a new and growing literature on the consequences of increased labour mobility for labour markets, economic growth, trade, investment and social policy. Given that labour mobility is not currently high on the policy agendas of the NAFTA countries, why produce a study on this subject now? Our position is that this question is likely to move up on the policy agenda for a number of reasons.

### WHY IS LABOUR MOBILITY LIKELY TO BECOME A BIGGER ISSUE IN THE FUTURE?

THERE ARE A NUMBER OF SPECIFIC REASONS why labour mobility within the NAFTA is likely to become more important as North American integration deepens, with or without the help of governments:

* During the period in which the research program of this volume was carried out, Richard G. Harris was a fellow of the Canadian Institute for Advanced Research. Their generous support is gratefully acknowledged.

1. Growth in the service trade is expanding rapidly between the three countries, particularly in business services. Given the potential size of this market, it is reasonable to assume the after-market and complementary aspects of most service activity are often both firm and place-specific. Customers want to be serviced in their home location. The existing TN visa program helps in part, but reducing border frictions for these types of labour flows completely would facilitate better integration of the service markets and facilitate growth of Canadian service exports to the United States.

2. Multinational enterprises (MNEs) routinely move staff across borders, and the ease with which this is accomplished can affect foreign direct investment (FDI) decisions. Reducing the barriers for MNEs to move staff easily between Canada and the United States may help to remove the bias against Canadian locations for North American-based FDI. This would help Canada attract its share of North American destined FDI, and at the same time discourage Canadian firms from moving south of the border.

3. Telemobility is likely to increase in importance. Virtual labour mobility is already a substitute for physical labour mobility in many areas. Call centres in various Canadian cities that serve the entire NAFTA market provide, in essence, a form of mobile labour service. The Internet has enhanced dramatically the ability of firms and individuals to deliver labour services via digitally based telecommunication networks, giving rise to the vision of a continental e-labour market. Doctors located in one city who perform surgery in another and university professors who deliver courses via distance learning technology are two common examples — but there are many others.

4. The "brain drain" debate in Canada highlights serious concerns about the country's loss of highly skilled workers to the United States, particularly in high technology. The mobility of high tech workers is a reality as long as shortages of such workers persist in the U.S. economy. Initiatives to further ease the extent to which workers can move between Canada and the United States may encounter public resistance in Canada, given the concerns about a brain drain to the United States. To be fair, this issue is as much about other policies, like taxation and currency depreciation, as it is about labour markets. The current degree of mobility, however, is a function of current circumstances and not a permanent institutional characteristic of the North American labour market.

5. Border controls are becoming increasingly difficult to enforce without impeding other forms of commerce. At both the Mexico-U.S. and Canada-U.S. borders there have been increased demands by business to expedite the flow of cross-border business visits and the movement of goods and services. Reducing border costs, however, comes at the cost of a diminished ability to control immigration. The call for formal mechanisms to reduce border impediments to trade in goods may therefore have implications for the degree of labour mobility within the NAFTA and the means by which it is regulated.

6. The increase in the average age of the Canadian population has not only well-known implications for the funding of social programs like pensions and health care, but it also implies that the flow of workers entering into retirement will increase relative to the number of first-time entrants into the workforce. Although extra-NAFTA immigration helps to fill the gap, pressure to improve labour mobility within the NAFTA will grow as the demand for younger workers increases. These pressures will be greater if adjustment costs for both firms and individuals are lower for NAFTA migration than for extra-NAFTA migration.

## WELFARE AND TRADE

A PREOCCUPATION OF THE TRADITIONAL ECONOMIC ANALYSIS of a move toward a common market is the trade and welfare consequences of the assumed increase in factor mobility. Full labour mobility is not absolutely essential for a common market, but the consensus view is that the greater the mobility, the larger the efficiency gains. Different theories give rise to quite different predictions as to the welfare gains. In some instances countries can lose by increasing factor mobility. In almost all cases there are distributional consequences that are negative for some groups and positive for others. Then there is the classic Mundell (1957) question: "What happens to trade and welfare as labour mobility increases?" One defense of strong restrictions on labour mobility is the prediction of Heckscher-Ohlin theory that most of the efficiency gains from integration can be realized through free trade in goods and services. The NAFTA has certainly moved us a long way toward free trade. Does this mean that the efficiency gains from increased labour mobility are negligible? This study seeks to address this and other related questions.

An important caveat is that we do not explore the social and fiscal policy implications of formal labour market integration. Within a true common market there is labour mobility but not necessarily citizenship mobility, which only comes with more formal political integration. In a common market, but in the absence of political union, an individual's right to social and transfer programs

315

can be defined by citizenship and is not available unless one resides in one's home country. In practice, however, in both Canada and the United States, most citizenship rights currently depend more or less on residency. Increasing labour mobility, therefore, may imply increasing access to local social programs and public goods for non-citizen workers, like, for example, workers moving between cantons within the Swiss federation. However, this topic is too complex to explore here, and this study has a distinctive Canada-U.S. focus, although there are some references to Mexico-U.S. migration issues. Deeper Canada-U.S. integration could, of course, involve a variety of formal and informal mechanisms which would enhance Canada-U.S. labour mobility without the creation of a fully integrated continental labour market.

The study proceeds as follows. After the introduction, the second section discusses some recent trends in international labour flows and some historical data. The third reviews theories on international factor movements, and amendments to deal with a number of medium-term considerations like uncertainty, labour market rigidities and short-run factor specificity. It also draws out the implications of these theories, should a Canada-U.S. labour market integration proceed. The fourth section deals with the regional and industrial structure implications of labour mobility. In particular, it asks the question: Could increased labour mobility lead to a core-periphery pattern of economic development in North America that is biased against Canada, given the existence of continental free trade? The fifth section discusses some dynamic factors, including those surrounding the recent brain drain debate in Canada. The next section discusses novel types of labour relocation, including temporary workers and virtual labour mobility. The seventh section discusses the macro-economic adjustment implications of labour mobility and the lessons that can be drawn from the European and U.S. experiences. The last section provides some conclusions and some possible policy implications of these developments for future Canada-U.S. integration and the NAFTA.

## HISTORICAL AND RECENT TRENDS IN MIGRATION

HISTORICAL CENSUS DATA SHOW that rates of permanent outmigration are currently near an all-time low, and also that Canada has enjoyed a net inflow of permanent migrants for a very long time. For many years, immigration rates have been between 0.5 and 1 percent of the population, while rates of emigration have been in the 0.2 to 0.3 percent range. Historically, there have been large flows out of Canada and into the United States. The classic Dales model of Canadian post-Confederation economic development was predicated on the assumption of highly mobile flows of labour into and out of Canada. From 1870 to 1901 there were, in fact, very large rates of emigration from

Canada, most of it to the United States (Table 2.1). Except during the period of the Great Depression, immigration has usually exceeded emigration in Canada, although there were large flows from Canada to the United States in the period immediately after World War II, with relatively little reverse migration (Tables 2.2A, 2.2B and 2.3).

## TABLE 2.1

## CANADIAN POPULATION AND GROWTH COMPONENTS

| Period | Net Natural Increase | Immigration | Emigration | Emigration / Immigration | Census Population at End of Period |
|---|---|---|---|---|---|
| 1851–1861 | 611 | 352 | 170 | 0.48 | 3,230 |
| 1861–1871 | 610 | 260 | 411 | 1.58 | 3,689 |
| 1871–1881 | 690 | 350 | 404 | 1.15 | 4,325 |
| 1881–1891 | 654 | 680 | 826 | 1.21 | 4,833 |
| 1891–1901 | 668 | 250 | 380 | 1.52 | 5,371 |
| 1901–1911 | 1,025 | 1,550 | 739 | 0.48 | 7,207 |
| 1911–1921 | 1,270 | 1,400 | 1,089 | 0.78 | 8,788 |
| 1921–1931 | 1,360 | 1,200 | 971 | 0.81 | 10,377 |
| 1931–1941 | 1,222 | 149 | 241 | 1.62 | 11,507 |
| 1941–1951 | 1,972 | 548 | 379 | 0.69 | 13,648 |
| 1951–1956 | 1,473 | 783 | 184 | 0.24 | 16,081 |
| 1956–1961 | 1,675 | 760 | 278 | 0.37 | 18,238 |
| 1961–1966 | 1,518 | 539 | 280 | 0.52 | 20,015 |
| 1966–1971 | 1,090 | 890 | 427 | 0.48 | 21,568 |
| 1971–1976 | 931 | 1,053 | 492 | 0.47 | 23,518 |
| 1976–1981 | 977 | 771 | 366 | 0.47 | 24,900 |
| 1981–1986 | 987 | 677 | 360 | 0.53 | 26,204 |
| 1986–1991 | 987 | 1,199 | 279 | 0.23 | 28,111 |
| 1991–1996 | 908 | 1,170 | 230 | 0.20 | 29,959 |

Source: Helliwell (1999), Table 2.

## TABLE 2.2A

## CANADIAN-BORN IMMIGRANTS TO THE UNITED STATES, 1951-98

| Years | Average Annual Flows (thousand) |
|---|---|
| 1951–1960 | N/A |
| 1961–1970 | 41.30 |
| 1971–1980 | 17.00 |
| 1981–1990 | 15.70 |
| 1991–1996 | 16.20 |
| 1991–1998 | 14.06 |

### TABLE 2.2B

### U.S. IMMIGRATION TO CANADA, 1961-2000

| Years | Average Annual Flows (thousand) |
|---|---|
| 1951–1960 | 10.10 |
| 1961–1970 | 16.70 |
| 1971–1980 | 17.90 |
| 1981–1990 | 7.90 |
| 1991–1994 | 7.10 |
| 1991–2000 | 6.05 |

### TABLE 2.3

### FLOW OF NON-IMMIGRANT PROFESSIONAL WORKERS AND THEIR FAMILIES TO THE UNITED STATES

| | 1989 | 1990 | 1991 | 1992 | 1993 | 1994 | 1995 | 1996 | 1997 | 1998 |
|---|---|---|---|---|---|---|---|---|---|---|
| | Canada-U.S. Free Trade Agreement (FTA) | | | | | | | | | |
| Professional Workers under FTA (TC) | 2,677 | 5,293 | 8,123 | 12,531 | 16,610 | | | | | |
| Spouses and Children of FTA Workers | 140 | 594 | 777 | 1,271 | 2,386 | North American Free Trade Agreement (NAFTA) | | | | |
| Professional Workers under the NAFTA (TN) | | | | | | 19,806 | 23,904 | 26,987 | N/A | 59,061 |
| Spouses and Children of NAFTA Workers (TD) | | | | | | 5,535 | 7,202 | 7,694 | N/A | 17,816 |

The most recent brain drain debate on Canadian migration to the United States attracted a great deal of media attention, and a number of efforts have been made to estimate these flows more accurately. Finnie (2001) is the most recent study, based on tax filer, census and U.S. Current Population Survey data. Finnie suggests the tax filer data indicate that the number of tax filers leaving Canada to all destinations has increased steadily in recent years, from about 15,360 in 1991 to 28,870 in 1997, with an average of about 21,700 per year over this period. He summarizes his evidence on the 1990s as follows:

> They suggest that 178,000 people left Canada to go to the United States between 1991 and 1996, and past experiences indicate that 126,000 of these would be expected to remain permanently in the United States and 52,000 to return to Canada. Emigration to the United States was, furthermore, 30 percent higher in this period than from 1986 to 1991, permanent migration increasing by 15 percent and temporary migration doubling. (Finnie 2001, p. 3)

## TABLE 2.4

## FLOW OF TEMPORARY WORKERS UNDER THE CANADA-U.S. FTA AND THE NAFTA

| Categories* | 1989 | 1990 | 1991 | 1992 | 1993 | 1994 | 1995 | 1996 | 1997 | 1998 | 1999 |
|---|---|---|---|---|---|---|---|---|---|---|---|
| Traders | 24 | 18 | 11 | 3 | 5 | 6 (0) | 7 (0) | 5 (0) | 6 (1) | 5 (1) | 11 (4) |
| Investors | 27 | 27 | 28 | 29 | 16 | 12 (0) | 22 (0) | 11 (3) | 18 (2) | 22 (0) | 14 (2) |
| Intracompany Transferees | 867 | 1,297 | 1,139 | 1,101 | 1,090 | 1,474 (7) | 1,333 (15) | 1,299 (15) | 1,633 (25) | 1,922 (42) | 1,734 (44) |
| Professionals | 1,741 | 2,756 | 3,466 | 3,673 | 4,348 | 5,109 (19) | 5,082 (66) | 6,240 (88) | 7,572 (69) | 8,502 (96) | 7,331 (77) |
| Total | 2,659 | 4,098 | 4,644 | 4,806 | 5,459 | 6,601 | 6,444 | 7,555 | 9,229 | 10,451 | 9,090 |

Notes: * Temporary workers who qualify in these categories are business persons who require an employment authorization but are exempt from labour market assessment (employment validation). Business visitors are not included since an employment authorization is not required.

The numbers are based on persons not on employment authorization documents. The numbers in parentheses indicate workers coming to Canada from Mexico.

Source: Unpublished data provided by Citizenship and Immigration Canada.

One of the interesting trends of the last decade has been the shift toward temporary forms of migration. The extent of this shift is indicated in Table 2.4. Of particular interest is the dramatic increase in the number of people using the NAFTA TN visa. For a number of reasons, the TN data are thought to be unreliable as indicators of permanent migration flows. Nevertheless, the dramatic increase in their use undoubtedly indicates some form of increased labour market participation by Canadians in the U.S. market. Likewise, the figures on MNE employee transfers have been rising rapidly (Table 2.4). These represent both the increased importance of FDI to the economy and the shift toward shorter-term MNE employee assignments.

## TRADE AND MIGRATION: TRADITIONAL THEORIES AND IMPLICATIONS

A S NOTED IN THE INTRODUCTION, liberalization over the last two decades has been mainly in the areas of trade and investment. If anything, mobility of people has probably decreased over the same period. This is clearly the case by comparison to earlier periods in history. Recent historical research by O'Rourke and Williamson (1999) documents the importance of large-scale migration in the first great era of globalization before World War I. While trade was an important part of globalization, they conclude that migration had a far bigger impact. Around 60 million Europeans set sail for the resource-rich and labour-scarce Americas in the century following 1820, three-fifths of them to the United

States. People were also on the move within Europe. Indeed, in the 1890s, more Italians emigrated to France and Germany than to America. This migration had profound effects. Between 1870 and 1910, it swelled the U.S. labour force by 24 percent and cut Ireland's by 45 percent. O'Rourke and Williamson emphasize the strong convergence effects of these factor movements. They conclude that just as trade caused global commodity prices to converge, so mass migration contributed to the convergence of wage levels. In the new post-1980 era of globalization, we know that trade has been growing about twice as fast as economic output, yet migration flows have been relatively stable.

Economists have been concerned with both the positive and normative implications of labour migrations, policy-induced or not, as well as changes in the labour mobility regime, like a shift to more open borders. A large part of the international trade literature presumes that most economic benefits of integration can be obtained through goods market integration and without labour mobility. Is this perspective relevant to the NAFTA? For the purposes of this study, we assume that the NAFTA approximates a classic free trade area, including free movement of capital, even if it also contains few provisions facilitating the international mobility of some categories of workers. Will greater trade flows within the NAFTA increase or decease migration pressures within the NAFTA countries? This question can be addressed in a number of ways. One familiar approach is to ask whether labour migration and international trade are substitutes or complements in achieving a given pattern of economic output and welfare. If they are substitutes, for example, freer trade ought to reduce migration pressures. An alternative approach is to focus specifically on the wage impacts of reduced barriers to trade and lower barriers to labour mobility. We turn now to the answers provided by alternative mainstream international trade theories.

## NEOCLASSICAL TRADE THEORY

THE HECKSCHER-OHLIN MODEL, which explains trade as a reflection of differences across countries in factor abundance, provides a very clear picture of the link between trade and migration: the pressure of international labour migration decreases with freer trade and it disappears completely with free trade. In other words, trade and international labour migration are substitutes (Mundell). This result is the intellectual basis for one of the main motivations behind the U.S. desire to negotiate the NAFTA with Mexico — that the systemic illegal migration from Mexico was viewed as politically unsustainable. According to this theory, free trade should eliminate (or at least reduce) illegal migration from Mexico to the United States.

The reason why the Heckscher-Ohlin approach yields this result is simple. The United States has a relative abundance of capital, while Mexico has a relative abundance of labour. In free trade, a country will export (or import) the good that uses the relatively more (or less) abundant factor in that country more intensively. Hence, Mexico exports its labour-intensive product to the United States and imports the U.S. capital-intensive product. As long as the pattern of trade remains unchanged, freer trade increases the wage rate in Mexico while it decreases wages in the United States. Consequently, the pressure within Mexico for labour to migrate to the United States decreases. With complete free trade, wages are equalized and the pressure to migrate disappears.

Another standard model of international economics is the specific factor model. Factors of production, like capital or natural resources, are often specific to the sector in which they are employed. Consider a trade liberalization where the price of the importable good falls, but the price of the exportable good remains unchanged. By lowering the price of the importable good, trade liberalization depresses the demand for labour in the Mexican import sector. If labour is mobile (or not specific) in this economy, the nominal wage must fall. The effects of trade liberalization on real wages, however, are ambiguous, because the real wage expressed in terms of the exportable good falls, but the real wage expressed in terms of the importable good increases. Hence, with migration pressure responding to real wages, a fundamental ambiguity exists around the direction of the migration as a response to freer trade, as individual preferences determine whether real wages in Mexico to fall or rise.[1]

The assumptions underlying the neoclassical approach are quite stringent. In recent years, many arguments have been put forward showing that, on theoretical grounds, when these assumptions are relaxed, pressures to migrate can easily increase with freer trade. What could cause an increase in migration pressure with freer trade? We review a number of potential explanations below.[2] They correspond to relaxing at least one of the key assumptions of the standard neoclassical approach: identical production technologies, the use of the same factors of production, constant returns to scale technologies, instantaneous adjustments to policy changes, perfect competition, homogeneous product, full employment and complete markets.

## DEPARTURES FROM THE NEOCLASSICAL TRADE MODEL

### Technological Differences and Increasing Returns

Consider a situation in which the technology of production is not the same across countries. The factor price differences might be due to specialization effects or extreme factor endowment differences. Suppose, for instance, that pre-NAFTA

Mexico produces a good with a labour-intensive technology, while the United States produces the same good with a capital-intensive technology. If the NAFTA gives the United States a comparative advantage in producing this good, this forces Mexico to shift out of producing this labour-intensive product. This in turn drives the Mexican wage down and increases migration pressure into the United States — as long as Mexico does not expand the production of other goods that use labour intensively or adopt the same technology as the United States.

Technological differences between countries may imply that one country has a very large absolute productivity advantage in a given sector. Such differences may exist because of limitations on technological transfer or differences in complementary public inputs (whether through public services, infrastructure, transportation, communication or education) and thus make wage differences alone insufficient to create a comparative advantage for a country. Hence, the opening up of trade causes the United States to expand production in the sector where it has a large absolute advantage but is also labour-intensive. This in turn could lead to more pressures on migration from Mexico to the United States.

The introduction of increasing returns to scale at the sector level can also reverse the standard result. Suppose, for instance, that the technology used in the labour-intensive sector exhibits increasing returns to scale. The expansion of production in the United States through trade liberalization could encourage immigration to staff a growing and a more efficient industry. In general, when trade is based on economies of scale, migration and trade are complements (Markusen 1983; Markusen and Melvin 1981).[3]

## Adjustment Lags, Migration Costs, Risk and Migration Networks

The theories discussed above implicitly assume that adjustments are instantaneous or, if they are not, that they do not affect comparative static results. Of course, adjustments can take time. In particular, while investments and the creation of new jobs usually take some time to respond to trade reforms, increased migration pressure might be an obvious short-term response to these adjustment lags.

One form of adjustment cost is the real cost of migration associated with the relocation of workers and their families. The existence of these costs can lead to increased migration pressure in response to trade liberalization through the following channel. Suppose the cost of migration is high in relation to income, thereby limiting the number of potential migrants. If trade liberalization raises incomes, it may increase migration pressure as this constraint is being relaxed. Similarly, if migration involves some risk and there is no insurance against this risk, higher income through trade liberalization may reduce risk aversion, thereby increasing migration pressure. Finally, when trade liberalization increases income inequality, those who are deprived might decide to migrate to maintain their family income (Stark and Taylor 1991). Of course, these forces tend to disappear with more job opportunities at home.

Migration pressures that follow freer trade may be compounded by the existence of migration networks. A migration network is a series of formal or informal links among groups of people with similar source country background. In the majority of cases, migration networks emerge when there are significant language and cultural differences between countries. Their main characteristic is that, once established, they can keep migration flows going. If trade liberalization tends to increase pressure on migration, the existence of migration networks may magnify this effect, as networks lower the cost of migrating by providing information, jobs, insurance, etc. Limits to this effect exist if there are diminishing returns to migration networks and, of course, increasing job opportunities in the source country of migration. Improved international mobility of labour expands trade through these networks, because not only do the countries of origin often have products that the migrants wish to consume in their country of immigration (hence affecting mainly imports), but there might also be implicit costs to trade with these countries (hence affecting both imports and exports). Positive and significant relationships have been found between trade and immigration in the United States by Gould (1994), and in Canada by Head and Ries (1998) and Head, Ries and Wagner (1998). Head and Ries calculate that a 10 percent increase in immigrants leads to an increase of 1 percent in exports and 3 percent in imports, while Head, Ries and Wagner find that immigration-creating trade networks might explain as much of 10 percent of Canadian trade over the first half of the 1990s.

**Foreign Direct Investment**

Finally, we turn to the FDI effect. It is well known that market dealings often involve transaction costs. The more complex a product or a service, the higher the transaction cost, because such a product or service needs before- and/or after-sale services, specialized management, quality control or other specialized service. An exporting firm might find local specialized individuals to carry out these services in the foreign country through licensing or other arms-length market-based arrangements. Alternatively, it might prefer to invest abroad (FDI) and send its own personnel to provide the services. In this case, the firm chooses to internalize the provision of such services. By doing so, it often reduces its transaction costs by avoiding opportunistic behaviour associated with market transactions. Trade liberalization is commonly thought to be a major factor driving new FDI.[4] The more important FDI is to an economy, the more likely it is that demand for highly specialized workers who provide these trans-action services within the firm will rise. Trade liberalization may therefore in-duce more migration of specialized workers, insofar as FDI requires them (Globerman 2000).

## SHORT-RUN SPECIFICITY

IT MAY BE IMPORTANT TO DISTINGUISH FACTORS that persist in the long run from those that are viewed as part of a dynamic adjustment process. An im-portant characteristic of modern economies like Canada and the United States is the importance of sector-specific factors of production in either physical or human capital. In fact, one aspect of globalization is probably an overall in-crease in factor specificity through specialization. When a particular type of la-bour is specific to an import-competing sector, trade liberalization lowers its real return, contributing to pressure on outmigration. In short, whether labour is a specific factor or not (but used jointly with other specific factors), freer trade can easily contribute to increased migration pressure in an otherwise standard environment.[5] In addition, when the firm's motive for migration is internalization, we must conclude that countries like Canada and the United States are not immune to migration pressures in the wake of freer trade, even if it is not always easy to predict the sectors in which such pressure might occur. The most likely outcome is that migration pressure will occur in a different di-rection for each sector unless other forces (like taxes) make the pressure more systematically asymmetric between the two countries.

## Unemployment

There is a substantial labour market and macro-economic literature that iden-tifies unemployment as both a push and pull factor in the migration decision. A wide range of unemployment theories can be used to explain migration. These include rigid wage theories, efficiency wage models or rural-urban migration models. These theories are usually not focussed on the issue of economic inte-gration but do have integration implications.[6] The unemployment issue figures prominently in virtually all discussions of North-South migration and the mi-gration of illegal Mexican workers into the United States, for example. Be-tween Canada and the United States, low U.S. unemployment rates and higher ones in Canada ought to lead to outmigration from Canada. Improving factor mobility, then, ought to lead to an increase in the rate at which regional cross-border differences in unemployment are reduced by cross-border migration. This is all fairly standard.

There is remarkably little literature on the implications for trade or economic integration of most theories of unemployment, with the notable exception of the Brecher-Srinivasan model of trade with rigid wages. In this model there are two factors: skilled and unskilled labour. If there is a rigid wage in the unskilled labour sector, equilibrium is achieved by having the quantity of unskilled employment adjust so all firms are on their demand curves. The flexible wage for skilled labour adjusts to clear the market for skilled labour at all times. In general, shocks to technology or prices will impact on both the quantity of unskilled unemployment and the skilled wage. An interesting implication of this type of analysis occurs if we start with free trade and consider an outmigration of skilled labour. This has two impacts: first, the usual neoclassical effect of raising the real wage of the skilled labour that remains; and second, raising the unemployment rate for unskilled labour, for which demand has fallen, given that there are fewer skilled workers available. This type of argument certainly voices one of the concerns driving the debate on the brain drain.[7] The loss of skilled workers in Canada could contribute to job losses and rising unemployment among the less skilled.

What does relaxing migration restrictions within the NAFTA countries imply? The case concerning migration between Mexico and "the United States-Canada" is clear and fairly easy to explain in terms of the traditional theories of comparative advantage. Whatever model one uses, the large differences in income levels and the relative supply of unskilled to skilled labour between Mexico and the other NAFTA countries are sufficiently important that we can expect (along with the different causes of migration pressure reviewed in the previous section) significant emigration from Mexico in response to relaxed migration restrictions. This will be the case for at least the next 10 to 15 years, as it will be only after significant income and development convergence with the other two NAFTA countries that such migration pressure can be expected to subside. How would trade and wages be affected? As most migrating Mexicans are probably not working in the Mexican manufacturing industry but rather in the subsistence sector of the economy, Mexican exports on the supply side would not be affected. However, United States. trade would be affected, as a large inflow of low-skilled (and legal) migrants would depress U.S. and Canadian low-skill wages and favour sectors that use low-skilled labour (importables) intensively. Canada-United States migration, however, is not easily accommodated within this framework.

## CANADA-U.S. LABOUR MOBILITY UNDER THE NAFTA

### Some Stylized Facts

The main message of the last section is that regional trade liberalization under the NAFTA may actually increase migration pressure in Mexico and Canada. In Mexico, it comes mainly from low-skilled workers, because technological or other differences do not guarantee that sectors intensively using low-skilled workers will expand, at least in the short and medium term. In Canada, this migration pressure is generally much less intense, although it may exist in some sectors and for some categories of individuals. It is mainly associated with FDI activity and especially with industry-specific labour. To derive more explicit implications from the theory requires stronger assumptions on the relevant starting point. Any attempt to address the potential implications of either introducing reduced barriers to labour mobility or opening up a common market in labour within North America will require some quantitative assessment of the current state of trade and wages across the Canada-U.S. regions. In addition, specific predictions require limiting the range of relevant theories. The "facts" on Canada-U.S. comparisons are the subject of a large body of research within Canada and a number of other studies in this volume. Generally speaking, the literature falls into three areas: 1) explanations for the observed increase in wage inequality across skill groups in both Canada and the United States; 2) explanations of the Canada-U.S. productivity gap; and 3) explanations for the large growth in trade and investment after the Canada-U.S. Free Trade Agreement (FTA) in 1988 and the NAFTA in 1993. From this literature, one can take five important stylized facts that any analysis of increased Canada-U.S. labour mobility must accommodate:

1.  Wage level differences between Canada and the United States remain significant. While there are many serious measurement problems, the average gap in real incomes is in the 20 to 30 percent range. Perhaps more relevant to the issue of skilled labour mobility are the starting salaries for recent university graduates. According to a Statistics Canada report, after taking inflation and purchasing power parity into account, the median annual earnings of bachelor's graduates working in applied and natural sciences jobs upon arrival in the United States was $47,400, considerably higher than the $38,400 earned by their counterparts in Canada. The gap in salaries between bachelor's graduates in health occupations upon arrival in the United States and those who remained in Canada was similar. (Human Resources Development Canada and Statistics Canada 1999, p. 10)

2. Overall earnings inequality has increased in both countries. In 1971, a worker at the 90th percentile of wage distribution earned 266 percent more than a worker at the 10th percentile. By 1995, this number had risen to 366 percent (Acemoglu 2000). A substantial part of this growth in inequality is not explained by education. When one controls for education, experience and other variables, there has been a remarkable increase in measured *within-group* or *residual wage inequality*. Many studies point to as much as 60 percent of the observed increase in wage inequality has been within groups that have the same education and age levels.

3. The Canada-U.S. productivity gap, both in the total economy and in manufacturing, remains substantial and appears to have widened in the latter part of the 1990s. Most explanations have focussed on the superior performance of the U.S. economy in the new economy sectors.

4. Trade and FDI have grown dramatically within the NAFTA countries since 1988. Canada's export-to-GDP ratio has gone from about 26 percent of GDP in the mid-1980s to 42 percent, according to 2001 data. Most of the growth in exports was in old economy sectors. The United States now accounts for almost 85 percent (2000 data) of Canada's merchandise exports. Two-way flows FDI into and out of Canada have grown dramatically. In 2000, the United States accounted for 63.9 percent of inward FDI stocks in Canada.

5. The relative price of capital equipment to labour has diverged substantially between Canada and the United States over the 1990s, a period during which the machinery and equipment investment intensity of Canadian industry fell. A rough order of magnitude is that that the relative price of machinery and equipment to labour in Canada rose by 30 percent as compared to the same relative price in the United States (Harris 2001b; Lafrance and Schembri 2000).

### An Explanation: General-purpose Technologies and the New Economy

Accommodating these facts is largely impossible within the static-oriented theories discussed in the last section. The trends identified above are inconsistent with the basic Heckscher-Ohlin model of trade, as it predicts absolute factor price convergence. They are also inconsistent with most other neoclassical models that usually predict relative factor price convergence. At the very least, one needs to append to the basic international trade framework a dynamic theory which helps to explain the Canada-U.S. divergences during the

327

1990s. That decade was, of course, characterized by a number of other events that one may want to factor into a broader explanation of these trends and in choosing among competing trade theories. These would include macro-policy developments, the Asia crisis in 1997-98, and the emergence of the new economy in the United States. A very promising theoretical approach has emerged which adds a significant dynamic element to the otherwise static theories discussed previously, and in particular helps to explain the major divergences between the U.S. and Canadian economies over the 1990s (Harris 2002).

This line of research comes from those models focussed around skill-biased technological change or the new general-purpose technology (GPT).[8] In both these cases, a basic assumption is made that an economy-wide acceleration of technological change rooted in the information technology (IT) sectors has taken place, which in turn has given rise to an increase in the wages of skilled labour in the United States and to the strong increase of within-group inequality. Work by Industry Canada and others has identified the same forces at work in Canada, but with a lag in relation to the United States. Canada's weak productivity performance, together with the fact that most IT capital is imported jointly, explains the real wage gap, particularly for skilled workers in the two countries. The fact that relative supplies of highly educated labour grew much faster in Canada than in the United States also helps to explain why the increase in the skill premium was less dramatic in Canada than in the United States. More importantly, however, this theory suggests that returns to learning and highly specialized skills that complement the information and communications technology (ICT)-based GPT will persist for some time. This has a number of implications for both labour markets and the globalization process, including labour migration.

The facts dictate a starting point at which the average level of labour productivity in Canada is lower than that in the United States, but perhaps converging toward U.S. levels. With growth driven by an ICT-based GPT, however, the demand for skills is highly selective, with some skills in high demand and others less so. Certain types of skilled labour continue to be in short supply in the United States, so their wages remain high there. As Canada is both close to the United States and relatively abundant in skilled labour over the medium term, migration pressure on skilled labour remains high. Longer-term implications for the brain drain are discussed below.

What about Canadian unskilled labour? When one considers that Canadian unskilled workers are mid-skilled in relation to Mexican unskilled workers, once can see that they do not really compete — simply because manufacturing sectors which are very intensive in the use of low-skilled workers no longer exist in Canada. Goods that require unskilled labour are now all imported from developing countries, including Mexico. In addition, the wage gap between U.S. and

Canadian mid-skilled labour is much lower than that for skilled workers, thanks in part to the NAFTA. Hence, the introduction of continental free labour mobility would probably not have much effect on the Canadian patterns of comparative advantage (including outsourcing), nor would it bring much pressure from low-skilled Mexican or mid-skilled U.S. migrants, because the NAFTA already has in-duced most of the adjustments in sectors using intensively low- or mid-skilled la-bour. The only remaining issue is whether, with free mobility, Canada would absorb some low-skilled Mexican workers and start to build labour-intensive in-dustries like those observed in the southern U.S. states. Without detailed quanti-tative modelling one cannot be sure. A common sense guess, however (except possibly for agriculture), is that the answer is probably negative, as there are no labour-intensive industries in the northern U.S. states.

A forward-looking issue has to do with the aging of the Canadian popula-tion is the extent to which immigration may be viewed as part of a "solution" to the problem of growing dependency ratios. Certainly, opening the Canadian border to unskilled labour from the United States, and in particular Mexico, might be part of the solution. Even with complete continental free mobility of labour, however, there is no guarantee that the resulting inflows would be suffi-cient to make a great deal of difference to the larger macro-problem posed by an aging population.

## Productivity Effects

Would increased migration of skilled workers from Canada to the United States tend to reduce or increase the labour productivity gap between the two countries? The static theories we have outlined have little to say about this question other than through indirect effects on factor accumulation. In general, we expect out-migration of skilled labour to reduce the average labour productivity of unskilled labour if skilled labour and capital substitute for unskilled labour — which cer-tainly seems to be the case empirically.[9] A potentially more damaging channel would be via the reduced adoption and use of IT technology, which is comple-mentary to particular types of skilled labour. If increased North American labour mobility implied a loss of skilled labour supply in Canada, this could potentially slow the rate at which productivity grows in Canada and lead to an increase in the Canada-U.S. productivity gap.

## Unemployment

Lowering barriers to migration may alter structural conditions in regional labour markets and thus affect the unemployment rate. Canada has had a significantly higher permanent unemployment rate than the United States for some time now, for which differences in measurement cannot entirely account. Lowering barriers to international mobility should produce some migration of relatively low-skilled workers from Canada to the United States (assuming that there is a large proportion of low-skilled workers among the unemployed). Will the unemployment rates between the two countries be equalized as a result? Probably not, as preferences, even language, make international labour mobility lower than its interprovincial counterpart. Even under the most liberal labour mobility regime, unemployment rates across regions will not be equalized. Interprovincial and interstate labour mobility has not equalized unemployment rates either across Canadian provinces across American states. Still, the introduction of the option to move to another country necessarily implies that there will be some increase in migration and thus some convergence of wages and unemployment rates.

### Complements or Substitutes? The European Experience

The EU is probably the most interesting recent case relevant to the NAFTA, as it is an example in which migration rules were relaxed once free trade had been reached. Indeed, the 1992 Single Market Program, which introduced free labour mobility within the EU, came at the end of a long process of trade liberalization. By all accounts, the 1992 changes have produced very little movement of people within the EU, suggesting that within the EU, trade and migration are substitutes. Table 3.1 illustrates this point for six EU countries for which data on intra-EU migration exists. It indicates the share of all the migrants coming from other EU countries between 1988 and 1997. The last row shows the share of migrants coming from other EU countries with respect to the total population of these six countries between 1988 and 1995. Although migration may take time to adjust to the elimination of restrictions, it has been very stable within the EU: the proportion of EU migrants since 1992 is comparable to the figure for the pre-1992 period, and its share with respect to total population has been very low.[10] Straubhaar (1988), using econometric techniques, found that trade and migration are substitutes within the EU.[11] An important reason for this is that culture and "distance" restrict the scope for migration within Europe. Krueger (2000) does not expect this picture to change much in the future. The best proof of this is that the low level of migration *within* EU countries that is estimated to be half the rate found within the United States. Indeed, Krueger reports that 2.8 percent of Americans moved between state boundaries in 1987, but only 1.1 percent of Germans, 1.1 percent of Britons and 0.5 percent of Italians moved across regions within their respective countries. This means that to date, the gains from integration within Europe have been through international trade, not free mobility of labour.

## TABLE 3.1

## INFLOWS OF FOREIGN POPULATION IN SELECTED EUROPEAN UNION COUNTRIES (IN THOUSANDS)

| Years | 1988 | 1989 | 1990 | 1991 | 1992 | 1993 | 1994 | 1995 | 1996 | 1997 |
|---|---|---|---|---|---|---|---|---|---|---|
| Belgium | | | | | | | | | | |
| Total | 38.2 | 43.5 | 50.5 | 54.1 | 55.1 | 53 | 56 | 53.1 | 51.9 | 49.2 |
| EU (percent) | 52 | 52 | 49 | 46 | 49 | 50 | 48 | 50 | 55 | 56 |
| Denmark | | | | | | | | | | |
| Total | N/A | N/A | 15.1 | 17.5 | 16.9 | 15.4 | 15.6 | 33 | 24.7 | N/A |
| EU (percent)* | | | 15 | 15 | 16 | 20 | 24 | 13 | 16 | |
| France | | | | | | | | | | |
| Total** | 44 | 53.2 | 102.4 | 109.9 | 116.6 | 99.2 | 69.3 | 56.7 | 55.6 | 80.9 |
| EU (percent) | N/A | N/A | 11 | 11 | 22 | 15 | 16 | 14 | 13 | 8 |
| Germany | | | | | | | | | | |
| Total | 648.6 | 770.8 | 842.4 | 920.5 | 1,207.6 | 986.9 | 774 | 788.3 | 708 | 615.3 |
| EU (percent) | 22 | 18 | 17 | 16 | 12 | 14 | 20 | 23 | 24 | 25 |
| Luxemburg | | | | | | | | | | |
| Total | 8.2 | 8.4 | 9.3 | 10 | 9.8 | 9.2 | 9.2 | 9.6 | 9.2 | 9.7 |
| EU (percent) | 85 | 82 | 82 | 78 | 72 | 77 | 77 | 73 | N/A | N/A |
| Netherlands | | | | | | | | | | |
| Total | 58.3 | 65.4 | 81.3 | 84.3 | 83 | 87.6 | 68.4 | 67 | 77 | 76.7 |
| EU (percent) | 27 | 24 | 23 | 25 | 27 | 23 | 23 | 22 | 25 | 27 |
| EU-6 | | | | | | | | | | |
| Total (percent of population) | 0.65 | 0.8 | 0.6 | 0.59 | 0.75 | 0.62 | 0.45 | 0.45 | N/A | N/A |
| EU Migration (percent of population) | 0.2 | 0.21 | 0.13 | 0.12 | 0.13 | 0.11 | 0.12 | 0.13 | N/A | N/A |

Notes:   * Includes Finland and Sweden from 1995.
** From 1990, spouses of French nationals, parents of French children, refugees, the self-employed and others eligible for a residence permit are also included.
N/A = Not available.
Source:   OECD (1998) and Krueger (2000).

# Agglomeration, Convergence and Regional Development

A CENTRAL ISSUE WHEN WE ADDRESS both the positive and normative effects of increased labour mobility is its potential impact on the pattern of regional economic activity within a more integrated North American market. Traditional trade theory has little to say on this subject, but it has become the central question in the new theories of trade and geography initiated by Krugman (1991). These theories predict that, in some circumstances, increased factor mobility will lead to divergence in regional income levels and the concentration of economic activity in some regions at the expense of others. However, there is also a considerable body of theory and evidence that suggests increased integration leads to convergence of regional income levels. Which of these is more relevant in explaining what might happen in North America if labour mobility between countries increases?

## Agglomeration and Divergence

THE NEW ECONOMIC GEOGRAPHY MODELS are characterized by the joint presence of economies of scale and costs to trade. The latter can include transport costs, border costs and other transaction costs associated with interregional trade in goods, or more formal barriers to trade such as tariffs and quotas. With or without factor mobility, these models are subject to cumulative causation effects. In particular, factor mobility reinforces the gains to regions that tend to attract industries characterized by economies of scale due to their size advantage. This advantage translates into higher productivity and higher real incomes, and thus attracts additional factors by migration. Manufacturing production (assumed to exhibit economies of scale) tends to concentrate where there is a large market, and a market is large where manufacturing production is concentrated (backward linkages). This is reinforced by the fact that the cost of living is lower in the region with the larger manufacturing sector, because local consumers rely less on imports that are subject to transport costs (forward linkage). Both forces tend to favour agglomeration at the core, leaving other regions (or countries) a rural hinterland. Large regions become larger and a core-periphery pattern of economic development emerges.

The predicted outcome is sensitive to the specification of trade costs. With free trade and no trade costs, this asymmetric pattern of development cannot occur. The fact that trade costs are unlikely to be zero, however, gives credence to the view that by opening up labour mobility, some regions of a free trade area (especially the smaller regions) may be hollowed out through the loss of industry and skilled people. In the absence of factor mobility, the cumulative causation effect is reduced and de-industrialization is less likely. The models still predict the possible emergence of permanent income and productivity differences, but without a migration channel the de-industrialization effects are much less pronounced. For small regions within existing common markets, the policy issue is clear: free movement of labour may lead to lower incomes. For existing free trade areas that are contemplating the reduction of the barriers to labour mobility, the possibility of becoming a peripheral region in a large integrated economic area is obviously worrisome. The applicability of this question to the European Single Market is obvious and has generated a great deal of research on regional development patterns within Europe. At this point, the evidence is not clear. The early evidence comparing U.S. states to EU countries suggested that actual outcomes were different from those predicted by the model. In the United States, where labour mobility is high, it appears that incomes were levelled but industrial development was relatively uneven. These models can explain this outcome, provided trade costs are sufficiently low. In Europe, however, where labour mobility has been historically low, income levels across countries exhibited a great deal of variability but industrialization patterns were more balanced.

The early models only worked with the polar cases of perfect mobility or complete immobility. The more realistic case of imperfect mobility leads to some important differences, highlighted by Ludema and Wooton (1999). They show that with imperfect labour mobility and an appropriate choice in the sequence of trade versus labour market integration, it is possible to avoid the potentially negative effects of agglomeration on some regions.

Consider a typical geography and trade model in the Krugman tradition with two sectors: agriculture and manufacturing. The agriculture sector produces a homogeneous product under constant returns to scale with sector-specific immobile labour. The manufacturing sector produces differentiated products with increasing returns to scale at the plant level and employs workers who are internationally mobile. Only the differentiated products face barriers to trade. As a result, the production of differentiated products tends to be concentrated in the country where the demand for them is greater, so as to minimize trade costs. Real wages may thus be higher in the larger country, providing an incentive for skilled workers to move to the industrialized core, which in turn reinforces the decisions of firms to locate at the core.

Suppose now that internationally mobile workers have a preference to live and work in their home country. A higher real wage than the one at home would induce them to move, with the size of this wage premium dependent on the intensity of their preference. This scenario produces a labour supply characterized by the willingness of workers to take employment in one country as a function of the real wage as well as specific preferences about "home." The equilibrium can be stable (or not) and can produce complete agglomeration (or not). Accordingly, if workers have strong preferences toward staying in their home country, it is more difficult to get complete agglomeration as an equilibrium, as only very high compensation will induce some workers to move to the other country. Ludema and Wooton show that strong preferences for home are not needed to produce such a result. In other words, with imperfect international mobility of labour, it is difficult to produce complete agglomeration (one region has all the manufacturing activity). They look at two policies: first, trade integration (lower trade costs) and second, factor market integration, which allows for reduced migration costs. Given home locational preferences, there is never complete migration from one region to another. Not surprisingly, trade liberalization never leads to complete agglomeration if home preferences are strong enough. But of particular interest is the result that *for a given level of trade costs, an increase in factor mobility tends to level the agglomeration effect.* One could imagine that the NAFTA area, now characterized by relatively free (but not costless) trade, may have been subject to agglomeration forces. At the regional level, this is even clearer, given the uneven growth rates across U.S. states. If we look at Canada and the United States, Canada, as the smaller country, may have been pushed in part toward specialization in sectors where the agglomeration effects under free trade do not occur. The Ludema-Wooton model would then predict that increased mobility, holding the trade regime constant, tends to lead to more even patterns of industrial development.

Suppose the NAFTA partners were to move toward a common market in labour: how would more labour mobility across the Canada-U.S. border affect the pattern of regional development in Canada? It would not be unreasonable to assume, for example, that the income variability (before tax and transfers) and industrial specialization observed in U.S. states would also be observed in Canada. Theory provides no precise answer to this question. Clearly, however, the impact of opening up the U.S. labour market to Canadian labour would have a much greater impact on regional development within Canada than the converse. The local demand linkages for a number of the smaller Canadian regions are not likely to be important (even with some trade costs), because exports of manufactured goods from these regions will tend to matter more than production for local use. If we assume that skilled labour is the main target of mobility-enhancing policies, then Canadian regions where the geographically proximate border wage gap is largest and the markets are smallest would be impacted the most visibly in the short term. Reduction in trade costs and the benefits of specialization may lead to a levelling of income levels over the longer term. It is interesting to note that border state-province comparisons indicate there is already a tendency for proximate border regions to look somewhat similar. Lowering the costs of labour mobility may therefore not have a large effect on the smaller Canadian regions if the relevant migration margin is between adjacent border regions.

## CONVERGENCE

THERE IS AN ALTERNATIVE EMPIRICAL APPROACH to regional development based on the convergence hypothesis. It posits that increased integration leads to faster rates of income and productivity level convergence. If economic growth is being driven by spillovers of knowledge and human capital, which are common rationales for expecting convergence, then it stands to reason that increased labour mobility ought to have some positive effects on these forces. The evidence for this hypothesis has been mixed. Generally, most of the evidence presented has been for trade integration, and studies like Ben-David (1993) find strong effects of trade integration on convergence (Harris 1996). Some studies claim to find strong convergence effects on U.S. states and Canadian provinces (Barro and Sala-i-Martin 1995; Coulombe and Lee 1995; Coulombe and Day 1999). Generally, however, there appears to be no strong case that greater labour mobility leads to faster rates of convergence in productivity. Hulten and Schwab (1993) use total factor productivity (TFP) levels as their indicator to find that in fact the opposite is true for U.S. states.

# THE BRAIN DRAIN AND KNOWLEDGE TRANSFERS

THE CANADIAN POLICY DEBATE ON North American labour migration has been focussed almost exclusively on the brain drain — of medical professionals, high tech professionals, business managers, scientists and engineers — from Canada to the United States. It is well-known that the numbers were initially small but have been growing. The extent to which the rapid increase in TN visas issued represents a more permanent flow remains unresolved. The major concern is that the current flow represents the best and brightest of Canadians, and there is some evidence to support this view. The brain drain debate raises three questions on common market-like arrangements for labour. First: To what extent is one country in a regional economic grouping likely to be the location of most human capital-intensive activities? Second: Will a common labour market significantly reduce real barriers to skilled labour mobility? Third: What are the broader growth consequences of these movements?

## HUMAN CAPITAL SPECIALIZATION AND NORTH AMERICAN INTEGRATION

AT THE ROOT OF THE BRAIN DRAIN DEBATE lies the fear that, given high mobility of highly skilled labour or human capital, Canada could conceivably lose most of its human capital intensive employment. In effect, the worry is that Canada could become specialized in sectors where human capital requirements are low. This may not lead to lower incomes but it might lead to substantially reduced employment opportunities for highly educated Canadians. The situation in North America sees the United States continue to attract large numbers of high-ability individuals to study and pursue careers in science and engineering. Many of these choose to stay in the United States. A National Science Foundation study notes that

> ... between 1988 and 1996, foreign students from major Asian and European countries, Canada, and Mexico earned over 55,000 U.S. S&E doctoral degrees ... During this period, about 63 percent of these doctoral recipients planned to remain in the United States after completion of their studies, and about 39 percent had firm plans to do so. (Johnson and Regets 1998)

The same study reported that 43 percent of Canadians studying in the United States intended to stay there.

The earlier discussion on agglomeration and core-periphery development is relevant to these arguments. There are a number of theoretical arguments which counter the hypothesis that Canada could become marginalized in terms of economic agglomeration activity. Nevertheless, the commonly cited agglomeration benefits associated with labour networking, and the success of regional agglomerations like Silicon Valley, raise legitimate concerns. It is useful to recall that at least three forces are at work in the agglomeration models: first, the strength of the agglomeration effect (through increasing returns to scale effects); second, the rapidity at which human capital (people) moves in relation to firms or capital relocation; and third, the attachment of labour to its home location. With respect to the first, we have evidence that a number of Canadian high technology centres like Kanata are succeeding. In addition, Canadian cities are of sufficient economic diversity that their prospects for de-industrialization are slight. Increasingly, new forms of knowledge transfers via digital networks are replacing face-to-face contact. To that extent, the "stickiness" of the people's locational preference may be more relevant than higher wages abroad. On the second issue, the worry is whether firms lead or follow human capital. If the firms move first, they create a positive dynamic which tends to provide additional pull to human capital seeking to migrate. If firms are less likely to move, the scope for a destabilizing outmigration of people and capital is less likely. The attachment of people to their home locations depends on a host of economic, social and cultural factors. Canada is certainly not disadvantaged in this respect — any more than an average U.S. state seeking to attract or keep people.

## HOW MOBILE IS HIGHLY SKILLED LABOUR IN NORTH AMERICA?

THERE IS A GENERAL VIEW that skilled labour is already very mobile across the Canada-U.S. border, and thus any further changes in labour mobility provisions are likely to have little incremental effect. Perhaps the analogy most frequently made is between highly skilled workers and FDI. Both are regarded as highly desirable and in short supply. Competition for both these factors has created a seller's market, and both can pick their location of choice. Moreover, since both skilled workers and FDI are viewed as engines of economic growth and employment, there is considerable international tax competition to keep and attract these highly mobile factors. The analogy is instructive and contains a lot of truth. Recent surveys report that a very high proportion of science, engineering and business students are willing to move to a job in the United States.

> The majority of respondents (78 percent) indicate that they are willing to relocate to the United States, and 88 percent are willing to relocate within Canada. Overall, only 12 percent of respondents indicate that they would NOT consider relocation. (Personnel Systems 1999, p. 3)

It is useful to remember that this perception in Canada follows a decade-long economic boom in the United States together with some critical skilled-labour shortages there. The expansion of the TN and H1-B visa program has to a considerable extent been an endogenous response to this boom. Tax competition between jurisdictions lowers effective marginal rates on income earned by human capital and can be viewed as an efficiency-enhancing outcome of this process. But is it permanent?

A more cynical view of the situation is one of scientists and engineers as "guest workers." If there is a prolonged slump or oversupply of labour in these areas, cross-border mobility may dissipate quickly. It is interesting historically, for example, that in some engineering areas there was little cross-border mobility between Canada and the United States during the 1970s and 1980s. Using immigration regulations as a means of controlling labour supply is, of course, one of the conventional rationales behind immigration policy. A government's commitment to increase labour mobility within a common market permanently is essentially another example of giving up some national sovereignty in favour of a more liberal regime — exactly the same argument used in the case of removing the power to tax trade under the FTA. Canada has a similar reason to favour a more permanent mobility regime for human capital. The increasingly specialized nature of human capital means that such a regime would substantially decrease the risk of unemployment by expanding the relevant job market for any Canadian resident undertaking the lengthy training in one of these areas. This would benefit not only Canadian suppliers of labour but also the sectors that provide the training, as well as the economy at large. There is always the risk, however, that immigration controls, like tariffs, would be used as political devices for rent sharing and in other unpredictable ways, which could be detrimental to the smaller country.

## GROWTH AND KNOWLEDGE TRANSFERS

THE TRADITIONAL ARGUMENT about the brain drain is that it leads to a transfer of scarce resources from one country to another, which leads to a higher growth rate in the country gaining these talents compared to the country losing them. Part of the Canadian concern about allowing increased mobility of skilled labour is that the growth rate might fall in response to an outmigration of "brains." This argument, which is commonplace, has not gone unchallenged. There are arguments that a brain drain could lead to faster growth in the country losing talented individuals — it could in fact attenuate or even reverse the negative brain drain effect on growth. Two arguments in the literature are relevant here. First, a brain drain may foster investments in human capital (Stark, Helmenstein and Prskawetz 1998); second, a brain drain could lead to higher growth rates through the transfer, or spillover, of knowledge generated by highly skilled labour.

Consider the first argument. Assume that individuals in a country are differentiated by skill. For any one of them, contemplating whether or not to migrate, income abroad is uncertain. Whatever their skill level, they will either be highly successful abroad or not. Their expected income abroad increases with their skill level. Suppose now that the skill level people choose to acquire is a positive function of training and investments in human capital. An individual considering the possibility of migrating (in an uncertain environment) will want to invest more in human capital than someone not contemplating migration. Simply put, such an investment will improve the probability of success abroad. Of course, this additional investment in human capital also raises the probability that an individual will actually migrate. However, not everyone will migrate; and of those who do, some will not succeed and may return to their country of origin. As a result, the average human capital level may increase in the source country even in the presence of a brain drain. In addition, if these effects are strong enough, the growth rate may increase, not decrease (a "beneficial brain drain"). In a recent empirical study using cross section data for 37 developing countries, Beine, Docquier and Rapoport (2001) find that the possibility of a beneficial brain drain growth effect may be more than a theoretical curiosity.

This effect applies to developed countries as well, at least insofar as investments in human capital are seen as a form of insurance (rather than an income effect, as in less developed countries). Simply put, individuals are investing in human capital to keep their options open if they decide to move abroad.[17]

Consider now the second argument and ignore the possible connection between individual skill and investment in human capital. Skilled individuals may simply not be able to use their skills in one country and have to migrate to another to do so. In particular, skilled individuals involved in innovation may need inputs not readily available in their country of origin — whether with respect to new products, new production processes or new knowledge. It is thus only by migrating that they can create these new products, services or knowledge. In other words, it is efficient for the world if skilled individuals migrate to the country where they find the inputs to complement their skill. If imitation or knowledge spillovers are important, the country subjected to brain drain may benefit from a higher growth rate than it would have if the brain drain had not taken place. In fact, this means that both countries (the country of emigration and immigration) benefit from growth rates that are higher than they would be without the brain drain.

The country of emigration may benefit further in relation to other countries as a result of network effects. The skilled individuals who migrated know their country of origin better than outsiders. They are thus better able to channel the necessary FDI and other resources to take advantage of untapped human resources there. Recently, it has been proposed, on the basis of this argument, that the term "brain drain" should be replaced by the phrase "brain circulation," in reference to scientists in particular. The general idea that the creation of knowledge is increasingly a global industry with relatively rapid international spillovers is contrary to the conventional proprietary view of knowledge. Evidence like that in Coe and Helpman (1995) on international research and development (R&D) spillovers gives considerable validation to this view of knowledge for a highly open economy such as Canada. They find that most TFP growth in Canada is, in fact, accounted for by world R&D spillovers and not domestically generated R&D.

## NEW FORMS OF LABOUR MOBILITY

THE TN VISA PROGRAM was a case of policy ahead of theory. The original motivation for the program was to allow businesses to provide the customer and related technical support essential to the modern economy. Highly firm-specific, tacit knowledge can often only be transferred in close physical proximity to the customer. In addition, activities like sales, advertising and management of MNE subsidiaries often require repeated visits to the foreign market. The TN program was explicitly designed to facilitate these types of activities across the NAFTA borders. It evolved into much more than that: it became a form of temporary mobility for certain types of professionals, but it stands as an important example of a successful policy designed to facilitate modern international business. The traditional economic approach to labour mobility has been to treat it in a comparative statics framework in which an individual's migration decision reflects a relatively permanent relocation of that person, and thus of the location from which that person delivers the labour services. But we can imagine other forms of labour service delivery across borders that do not involve a migration decision. In the section below, we outline four types of "delivery mechanisms" based on a type of labour mobility that does not involve a permanent migration. Each of them has been made possible by new forms of technology in transport and communications. They also reflect the judgment that the close proximity of most Canadians to the Canada-U.S. border makes these types of delivery mechanisms more relevant to this particular case than for many other regional trade groupings.

## TEMPORARY VISITS ASSOCIATED WITH RELATED BUSINESS SERVICE TRADE

AS WE HAVE NOTED, this type of mechanism already exists in the form of the TN visa program. The motivation is to facilitate the type of trade where close interaction with the customer at the point of delivery, follow-up service related to previous sales or preliminary interaction with customers prior to sale are an important aspect of the job. For many types of modern goods and services these activities are an essential part of business. In general, the NAFTA already provides for a fairly high degree of mobility with regard to these activities. However, improvements are possible — especially in border procedures. One area where these impediments are currently binding is in border communities, where there is the potential for cross-border trade in services that is not feasible between communities located beyond a normal commuting distance. With some imaginative approaches, integration at the border could be enhanced in areas like Vancouver-Seattle and Windsor-Detroit.

Currently, the actual barriers often lie in labour market regulations and entry barriers that are not covered by trade agreements. Certain occupations — often unionized — are subject to entry restrictions which prohibit full temporary mobility. For example, certain jobs in the film industry, which is important in most Canadian cities, are subject to union membership restrictions. Similar restrictions also apply to Canadians who wish to work in California or New York. Deeper integration, which would facilitate temporary labour mobility, will require fairly major changes in the way in which some occupations are both organized and regulated. Other examples include pilots, certain types of health professionals, engineers, technicians and the construction trades.

There has been relatively little economic theory or measurement with respect to these types of labour movements. A major issue is the quantification of the welfare effects of facilitating this type of mobility. The general argument usually made is that these type of visits are complementary to trade and FDI. However, there are other possibilities. In many cases, the service delivered is non-traded and sold by a foreign-based subsidiary of an MNE. In these cases, by facilitating this type of mobility, the decision to produce and sell in the foreign market rather than export is made easier. At the margin, therefore, it is possible that trade and this form of labour mobility are substitutes in some sectors.

## VIRTUAL MOBILITY AND E-LABOUR MARKETS

INNOVATION IN COMMUNICATIONS TECHNOLOGY, such as the Internet and similar private data networks, has given firms and individuals the ability to transmit large volumes of data instantly, and at close to zero marginal cost to other related parties, anywhere in the world. It has already affected many types of business, and may soon begin to affect labour markets in a similar way. There are indications this is already happening in areas like the delivery of software coding and call service centres. Its economic effects are many, but one of relevance here is its ability to remove the barriers to delivery of particular types of services. In the international trade literature, a common distinction is drawn between services and goods. For commodities with a sufficient degree of durability and transportability, production can be divorced from consumption. Trade is realized by the transport of goods from the location of production to the location of consumption. Service transactions, on the other hand, are often characterized by the requirement for a coincidence in time and space for buyers and sellers to meet. Traditionally, delivery of labour services has also been characterized by this requirement. As with some business services, there are labour services which could, in principle, be delivered electronically. This raises the prospect of a continental e-labour market for some types of labour services. Examples include software engineering, data entry, translation services and distance teaching.

As in the definition of any market, the key issue is the degree of substitutability between alternative sources of supply — in this case the virtual versus the physical supply. Firms may seek to source labour via the Internet when it is technically possible and cost-effective.

There is not yet a large economic literature on this subject, but it is certain to grow with the emerging field of Internet economics. One issue related to the earlier discussion of agglomeration and regional development is how e-labour markets within the NAFTA would affect various regions. This problem has been treated theoretically in Harris (1998). The general fear that agglomeration might be biased against the smaller country is shown not to occur in this case. On the contrary, according to the Harris model, the emergence of the Internet for business labour services results in greater specialization by skilled labour in the integrating region as a whole, but with a dramatic increase in market size for the specialized labour services provided by the smaller region. The smaller region sells more specialized labour services, but to a much larger market with virtual labour market integration. The net welfare effect is positive and proportionately larger for the smaller region.

In a fully integrated virtual labour market, the location of the country where the labour services are performed should not, in principle, be a barrier to sourcing. Reducing the regulatory and trade barriers for firms and individuals in these types of virtual employment arrangements is necessary if a North American e-labour market is to evolve. Most worker-firm contractual relationships are heavily conditioned by local labour laws and various tax policies. It would be advantageous to create new forms of cross-border worker-firm contractual relationships to make the telemobility of labour services easier. This would expand the North American market for virtual labour services and potentially increase employment of skilled labour in regions where job growth has been slow but labour supply has been ample.

At the moment, there are few restrictions beyond the general labour market regulations on the development of an e-labour market. However, that situation could change. If the telemobility of labour services grows, we can expect workers who are affected adversely to seek restrictions on this type of competition. A North American integration program should, at a minimum, seek to preserve the rights of labour originating anywhere in North America to deliver services digitally to any other North American location when this is technically possible and economically desirable.

## CROSS-BORDER LABOUR DEMAND VARIATIONS

REGIONAL LABOUR MARKETS and particular regional industries are subject to shocks in supply and demand which are not correlated across regions or industries. This type of idiosyncratic risk has two implications. First, there is the potential demand for insurance to reduce the resulting income risk. Second, there are efficiency gains in moving labour from locations where its productivity is temporarily low to locations where it is high. Movement toward both objectives is possible if at least some labour is locationally mobile. Greater labour specialization has compounded the potential severity of this problem. Highly specialized talents are often in very inelastic supply over the short term. Greater mobility for these types of people is particularly beneficial, and in some cases critical. Regions that lose people with highly specialized skills to foreign-based demand obviously incur short-term costs. Over the longer term, however, other things being equal, the larger market available to specialized labour tends to reduce income variability and employment risks in these occupations and thus increase the long-term supply of individuals with these talents.

Regional mobility of labour, however, even within existing common markets, is quite low. The actual extent to which region-specific variations in labour demand could be facilitated by moving workers is an unresolved empirical question. Historically, however, Canada has had some large interprovincial labour flows in response to specific regional booms and busts. In principle, there is no reason why this could not occur across borders. Canadian labour flows have historically moved from East to West; the existence of a North-South option might change this pattern significantly. The closer proximity of northern U.S. states rather than distant Canadian provinces might lead Canadians responding to local employment shocks to move from North to South. Likewise, province-specific booms could well give rise to northward inflows of nearby U.S. labour.

To the extent the workers' choice set expands this type of labour mobility, it would be an unambiguous welfare improvement, and moreover would tend to improve expected output for the integrated industry. In modern terms, the existence of labour mobility essentially gives workers a put option on local employment conditions. The option is only exercised if local employment conditions become sufficiently bad in relation to conditions elsewhere. Competition among workers would raise the pattern of wages so that, at the margin, mobile workers would have the same levels of expected real income (net of all expected costs of moving) as immobile workers over the course of their working lives. Note that the total welfare benefits of greater labour mobility are particularly important for non-traded goods (construction or health care, for example), where imports cannot provide an alternative source of supply. These benefits include a more secure source of supply with more stable prices than would otherwise be the case, and these benefits accrue to local consumers, not just mobile labour.

Historically, the workers who exhibit this type of temporary mobility within countries are younger and both skilled and unskilled. The costs of a temporary move are much lower for them than for older workers, or those with working spouses or dependents who are not mobile. The aging Canadian population means that the potential supply of younger workers available for interprovincial and intercity migrations is falling. While increased immigration targeted at young workers is one obvious response, another is to increase the temporary cross-border mobility of both skilled and unskilled workers from the United States. A significant extension of the TN visa program to a wider range of occupations would be one possible response to this growing problem.

## SEASONAL LABOUR DEMAND AND SUPPLY

ONE OF THE MOST IMPORTANT DIFFERENCES between Canada and the United States is weather. The Canadian winter is a reality many of us would like to forget in January and February. It affects both the supply of labour and demand in a large number of sectors. Currently, there is little in the way of seasonal North-South labour flows outside of professions like golf instruction and professional hockey. There are, however, many climate-motivated permanent moves. More than two million Canadians by birth are currently living in California. There is a very significant fraction of retired Canadians who winter in the southern United States, but they do not work, and from a macro-economic perspective contribute significantly to a tourism deficit in the current account. The full extent of the snowbird migration seems to be unknown, but one estimate put the number at about 1.5 million in 1997 and growing rapidly.[13] A full common market in labour services between Canada and the United States could change both of these situations, although the magnitude remains unclear. Canadian winters would certainly induce a larger number of people with transportable skills to make this seasonal move to southern U.S. locations. Most of us in the education business, for example, already know of people who do this. Other occupations, like the building trades, tourism, consultants of all types, and health and agricultural workers could potentially benefit from this type of mobility. The issue of cross-border labour mobility for retired Canadians is now almost never discussed. But an aging population and its implications for pension and health programs may put the issue higher on the agenda. If one policy response to aging is part-time or temporary work by the aged, its availability to retired Canadians spending the winter in the United States would be a highly significant and valuable option both to them and to Canada. Specific arrangements for these types of employment arrangements could be made in both countries, so that unemployment or pension benefits, for example, were portable across borders for workers past a certain age. This provision would both increase the attractiveness of these people to potential employers, and increase the likelihood of a positive decision by them to stay in the labour force after the normal age of retirement. For both countries, the fiscal and real output benefits would be favourable.

## PERSONNEL OF MULTINATIONAL ENTERPRISES

THE LAST FORM OF UNCONVENTIONAL MOBILITY deals with MNE personnel. Their mobility is already very high, and the number of transfers significant, as discussed above in the second section. In many ways, the MNE market for professionals is global in scope, and the mobility of management is on par with the mobility of the investment itself. One distinguishing characteristic of MNE personnel is the relatively short tenure of their foreign postings and the frequency with which they are required to relocate. One study (Solomon 1998) found there had been a substantial increase in short-term overseas assignments among MNEs, largely to save costs but also because of the reluctance of people to move for longer periods and the need to accommodate project-specific tasks.

Specialization of tasks within large organizations is a common theme in the current human resources literature. A common North American labour market would have little incremental impact on this type of specialization, as the mobility of MNE employees is already very high. The TN visa program, together with continental free trade, undoubtedly has contributed toward greater task specialization within large MNEs. As the organizational form of business shifts toward more contracting out, however, more formal arrangements to facilitate the temporary movement of personnel who are not at arm's-length with the previous MNE, will be increasingly useful and important.

## MOBILITY AND ADJUSTMENT

A N ALTERNATIVE PERSPECTIVE ON LABOUR MOBILITY is provided by the macro-economic literature on regional adjustment mechanisms and the related literature on the costs and benefits of optimal currency areas.[14] Factor flows in an integrated economic area with high factor mobility are an important adjustment mechanism for asymmetric shocks across regions. Macro-economists, as well as labour market economists, are often concerned with how wages, labour force participation, unemployment rates and migration flows adjust to these shocks. In a cost-benefit analysis of more formal mechanisms for labour mobility, a principal benefit would be the greater capacity of labour markets to adjust to regional macro-economic shocks.

In principle, such adjustment is presumed to be more efficient and flexible the greater the response of wages and migration to a shock, as opposed to changes in unemployment or participation rates. This is a central question in the empirical literature on adjustment mechanisms in Europe. With substantial wage and other forms of labour regulation in Europe, the loss of exchange rate movements as an adjustment mechanism puts all the weight on the alternatives noted above. The general worry is that Europe's labour markets are relatively poor at adjusting and, in particular, that labour mobility is quite low within Europe. The usual benchmark for comparison is the interregional migration of labour within the United States. We review some of the basic findings of this literature next. It is important to note that this question is of interest apart from whether the NAFTA countries are on a flexible or some form of fixed exchange rate regime. Even under flexible exchange rates, increased cross-border labour mobility would be a valuable adjustment mechanism.

As a benchmark, we review what is known about interprovincial Canadian migration. Rosenbluth (1987) finds that interprovincial migration within Canada accounts for approximately 1 percent of the Canadian population each year. This is a large proportion in relation to the annual change in population. In general, increases in provincial demand for labour have meant an increase of inmigration and a decrease of outmigration. Gunderson (1994) claims that regional migration is more important to Canada than immigration: at the country level, two-thirds of all migration is regional, and it ranges from 40 percent (Quebec) to 94 percent (Northwest and Yukon Territories) at the provincial level. He cites two types of barriers to labour mobility in Canada: natural or economic barriers (distance and culture or language) and artificial barriers (professional or trade licensing and education or language requirements). Global competition, free trade, technical change and industrial restructuring have increased the need to reduce these barriers in order to achieve efficient allocations of labour so that Canada can be strong and competitive. Data for 1994 to 2000 are presented in Table 7.1 below.

Migration tends to occur from low-wage regions with high unemployment to higher-wage regions with low unemployment and is negatively affected by distance. Mobility also tends to be higher among young people because they enjoy a longer benefit period from the move, cause less family disruption, and, typically, lose less in forgone wages. The Atlantic and Prairie provinces are the main sources of outmigration, while Ontario and British Columbia are the main destinations. Quebec mobility (in and out) is lower than in most provinces, probably because of linguistic and cultural differences.

Finnie (1999) updates some of these data in his empirical analysis of interprovincial migration from 1982 to 1995. Consistent with the previous studies, the author finds that the largest number of people (measured as a percentage of the provincial population) move from the Atlantic and Prairie provinces to the larger, and nearby, provinces of Ontario, Quebec and British Columbia. Overall, the annual outmigration rates for provinces were at a constant 1.5 percent of the population from 1982-83 to 1988-89, but this level dropped to 1.2 percent in 1994-95 — all provinces fell except Newfoundland. Though this drop appears to be small, Finnie claims that it represents a structural downward shift in interprovincial migration rates. Over the 1982-95 period, 7.4 percent of the Canadian population took part in interprovincial migration. These movers were classified into three groups: single movers (4.5 percent), multiple movers (1 percent) and returnees (1.9 percent). The Atlantic and Prairie provinces had the highest provincial rates in each of these three categories. There is no earnings pattern for men between the ages of 20 and 24. However, for older groups of men, multiple movers tended to have the highest initial incomes, followed by single movers and returnees. Unfortunately, there are no data available on education, occupation, etc. For women, movers are typically not concentrated among the high-income earners. In fact, women who move typically work in low-income jobs.

**TABLE 7.1**

**CANADIAN DOMESTIC AND INTERNATIONAL MIGRATION, 1994-2000**

| Province or Territory | Total Immigration | Numbers by Source | | Percent by Source | |
|---|---|---|---|---|---|
| | | Other Provinces | Other Countries | Other Provinces | Other Countries |
| Canada | 3,553,298 | 1,469,023 | 2,084,275 | 0.41 | 0.59 |
| British Columbia | 728,810 | 302,397 | 426,413 | 0.41 | 0.59 |
| Alberta | 557,437 | 97,133 | 460,304 | 0.17 | 0.83 |
| Saskatchewan | 135,428 | 12,926 | 122,502 | 0.10 | 0.90 |
| Manitoba | 134,632 | 26,686 | 107,946 | 0.20 | 0.80 |
| Ontario | 1,310,240 | 800,292 | 509,948 | 0.61 | 0.39 |
| Quebec | 355,242 | 200,364 | 154,878 | 0.56 | 0.44 |
| New Brunswick | 84,900 | 4,839 | 80,061 | 0.06 | 0.94 |
| Nova Scotia | 131,803 | 18,621 | 113,182 | 0.14 | 0.86 |
| Prince Edward Island | 20,372 | 1,084 | 19,288 | 0.05 | 0.95 |
| Newfoundland | 57,401 | 3,452 | 53,949 | 0.06 | 0.94 |
| Yukon Territory | 12,795 | 575 | 12,220 | 0.04 | 0.96 |

Source: Statistics Canada and the authors' calculations.

## EVIDENCE FROM EUROPE AND THE UNITED STATES

IN CONSIDERING HOW an integrated labour market in North America might adjust to macro-economic shocks, we might usefully examine the EU and the United States. Both have formal common labour markets with permanent labour mobility rights for all workers. If Canada were to have an integrated labour market with the United States, for example, an obvious question is whether or not the degree of North-South labour mobility would converge toward U.S. or European levels. The difference is significant. The general view of European labour mobility is that, in contrast to the United States, it is exceptionally low. Most studies find that migration within Europe is largely within European states. Migratory responses to labour market shocks are low and are accommodated mainly by changes in the labour force participation rate. The lagged responses of migration to changes in employment are exceptionally long. Decressin and Fatas (1995), for example, find that there is a zero percent response after the first year. Two, three and four years after the employment shock, the respective numbers are 27, 45 and 80 percent. In the United States, however, state data show that a 52 percent shock in labour demand is accommodated by migration. Barro and Sala-i-Martin (1995) find similarly qualitative results for the United States as a whole. Interestingly, they also find evidence that income differences seem to play a relatively minor role in explaining migration in Europe but are more important in the United States. A recent study by Puhani (2001) looks specifically at France, Germany and Italy. In the case of

Germany, he finds that for a given decrease in unemployment, 29.6 percent of that decrease would be accommodated by an increase in migration over 1.66 years. The numbers for France and Italy are much lower — 8.4 and 3.7 percent respectively. He concludes that labour mobility is an inconsequential adjustment mechanism within Europe.

The contrast between the U.S. and European experience carries mixed messages for the Canada-U.S. case. Most labour market specialists view Canada as lying somewhere between the United States and Europe in terms of labour market adjustment mechanisms and unemployment experience, for example. This perspective would suggest that full Canada-U.S. labour mobility might serve to increase the macro-economic adjustment capacity within Canada by more than what has been observed in the EU, but less than in the United States. An alternative perspective, however, is that these types of changes are very slow to evolve and involve fundamental changes in the life experience and outlook of workers. It is worth recalling that historically there have been very large flows across the Canada-U.S. border. Under a more liberal migration regime, in particular with the elimination of uncertainty as to access rights, it is quite possible that the U.S. benchmark would prove more relevant and that macro-economic adjustment would improve.

## CONCLUSION: POLICY AND RESEARCH IMPLICATIONS

THIS STUDY HAS EXAMINED the interactions between deeper North American economic integration and increased labour mobility between Canada and the United States. It has identified a number of potential channels through which increased labour mobility would affect the economy and some of the positive and normative implications. While the NAFTA is still a long way from a common market with permanently enshrined mobility rights for workers, we have identified a number of factors that are pushing it in that direction. These factors have implications for both future research and policy.[15]

### RESEARCH PRIORITIES

LABOUR MOBILITY STUDIES in both Canada and the United States remain largely national in scope. It is clear that we need additional quantitative work to identify the probable flows and their frequency in response to various shocks under a common labour market. In addition, we need more work on issues like firm location, patterns of comparative advantage and the productivity effects of a substantial liberalization of cross-border labour flows. The NAFTA studies that focussed on trade and investment liberalization did not identify the static or dynamic efficiency gains to internal North American labour mobility. This remains a largely uncompleted task for general equilibrium modellers. Given the human capital intensity of the new economy, this is potentially an important research issue, and some of the recent work in Europe could be a useful starting point. In addition, there is a need for research on the distributive consequences of greater labour mobility in Canada. Disaggregation by skill and/or occupation will be a necessary feature of this research program. A possible consequence of increased cross-border movement is knowledge spillover, and while an extensive literature on R&D spillover and aggregate human capital stock now exists, we know relatively little about how international labour flows contribute to knowledge spillover and consequent productivity gains. The quantification of this particular spillover channel is important if we are to assess the costs and benefits of greater labour market integration. On the human capital supply side, there are concerns about opening the markets for higher education in Canada under the NAFTA.[16] Many of these worries seem excessive, but research on human capital supply mechanisms and some estimates of how greater labour mobility might affect private and social rates of return on human capital acquisition in Canada would be very useful.

## POLICY

THERE IS ADMITTEDLY LITTLE FORMAL DISCUSSION on taking the NAFTA toward a common labour market. However, the ongoing bottom-up integration is giving rise to greater cross-border labour flows and demands to facilitate them.[17] Policy can be either ahead or behind in this process. If Canada were to enter a formal agreement to open its borders in some permanent way to free the movement of labour under the NAFTA, it would undoubtedly be seen as a sacrifice of national sovereignty. However, as in other policy areas, before rejecting this option, we should undertake a more realistic assessment of its long-term consequences. It is possible that, as in the case of freer trade in goods, the forces of integration and globalization will benefit most those who adapt successfully to the implied levels of greater mobility. For smaller countries in particular, failure to do so may imply a loss of both investment and human capital to jurisdictions that adapt more effectively.

Short of a common labour market, the issues raised in this study suggest a number of medium-term policy options for Canada and the United States that would serve to enhance labour mobility in the northern part of the continent. In each case, we would recommend a more serious examination of these options.

1.  The NAFTA TN visa program has led to increased mobility for professionals and basically anyone with a technical university degree. A useful approach would be to increase the scope of that program to other classes of labour by creating a negotiated schedule of dates for

liberalizing the movement of various occupations. Generally, one could imagine moving from the highest- to the lowest-skilled labour categories. It would certainly be relatively easy to extend the program to technical and trade workers, for example.

2. How can Canada-U.S. border procedures be amended to lower transactions costs for individuals seeking work in the other country? Would it be useful for Canada and the United States to coordinate border management with respect to non-NAFTA nationals?

3. With regard to e-labour markets, a reduction of labour barriers for firms that are (or might be) virtual employers should be considered. It would be advantageous to create new legal forms of cross-border worker-firm contractual relationships which would facilitate the telemobility of labour services across the border. This would expand the North American market for virtual labour services and potentially increase employment of skilled labour in regions with low job growth but ample labour supply. If telemobility of labour services grows, there is a danger that adversely affected workers will lobby for restrictions on this type of competition

4. Work on the harmonization of professional and occupational standards, and the elimination of entry barriers like residency prerequisites for licensing occupations currently subject to these restrictions, should be initiated by a joint Canada-U.S. task force. This will often require province-state cooperation. In some instances, the standards issue could be dealt with through a principle of mutual recognition, while in others, a common Canada-U.S. standard may be appropriate or necessary. These should be examined on a case-by-case basis.

## ENDNOTES

1   See Venables (1999) for other cases using the same model.
2   See Martin and Taylor (1996) and Venables (1999) for surveys on some of these links between trade and migration.
3   Economies of scale at the firm level are important ingredients in the more recent approach to geography and trade. This approach has something important to say about the links between trade and migration. We develop this approach in the fourth section of this study, on agglomeration, convergence and regional development.

4   Notice that FDI in this case is designed mainly for the provision of these services, not for production in another country. Hence, FDI and trade are complements here, an outcome often found in the empirical literature.

5   Hence, along with factor specificity, only differences in factor endowments can explain trade and increased migration pressure associated with trade liberalization.

6   They have also played a prominent role in optimal currency area theory. See the seventh section on the macro-economics of mobility.

7   Unemployment or underemployment is a large concern in the literature on North-South migration in North America and East-West migration in Europe. As this is not very relevant to the Canada-U.S. situation, it will not be covered here. See Faini, Grether and de Melo (1999) for an overview of this debate.

8   There is an extensive literature on this issue. See in particular the Beaudry and Green study in this volume and a recent survey by Acemoglu (2000).

9   The large literature on skill-based technical change (SBT) deals with this issue. The elasticity of substitution between skilled and unskilled labour is on the order of 0.5 to 1.0. See Murphy, Riddell and Romer (1998).

10  At the individual country level, the proportion of EU citizens migrating to other EU countries tends to be larger in smaller countries, but it remains very stable.

11  As Table 1 indicates, the same conclusion does not hold with respect to non-EU migrants, at least during the period 1990-94.

12  The choice of non-English speaking immigrants to Canada to locate in English Canada rather than Quebec is a very simple form of the same phenomenon: learning English allows more options and thus more potential mobility than learning French.

13  See "Canadian snowbirds face taxing plight," *Financial Post*, v. 10 (45) N, October 8, 1997, p. F7.

14  Most of the empirical literature on optimal currency areas and asymmetric shocks takes the state of labour mobility as fixed. The question in this section is: How would adjustment costs change if formal restrictions on cross-border flows were reduced? It is unclear whether such a measure would increase or decrease labour mobility.

15  As this study was written prior to the September 11, 2001 terrorist attacks in New York, Washington and Pennsylvania, it does not discuss the interaction between labour mobility and security issues. Clearly this is an issue which needs further attention in light of specific recommendations on improving cross-border labour mobility. However, the basic thrust of the recommendations here is not in conflict with the desire or requirement for increased border security.

16  A number of concerns have been expressed about the impact of the NAFTA on Canadian sovereignty in the areas of culture, water, health, environment, education and immigration.

17  For a discussion of bottom-up versus top-down integration, see Harris (2001a).

## ACKNOWLEDGMENTS

WE ARE GRATEFUL TO OUR DISCUSSANT, Eugene Beaulieu, for comments on the conference draft and to Martin Andressen for research assistance. The authors can be reached at rharris@sfu.ca and schmitt@sfu.ca.

## BIBLIOGRAPHY

Acemoglu, D. "Technical Change, Inequality and the Labour Market." NBER Working Paper No. 7800, July 2000, p. 63.

Barro, Robert J., and Xavier Sala-i-Martin. *Economic Growth.* New York, London and Montreal: McGraw-Hill, 1995, xviii, p. 539.

Beine, Michel, Frederic Docquier and Hillel Rapoport. "Brain Drain and Economic Growth: Theory and Evidence." *Journal of Development Economics* 64, 1 (2001): 275-89.

Ben-David, Dani. " Equalizing Exchange: Trade Liberalization and Income Convergence." *Quarterly Journal of Economics* 108, 3 (1993): 653-79.

Coe David T., and Elhanan Helpman. International R&D Spillovers." *European Economic Review* 39, 5 (1995): 859-87.

Coulombe, Serge, and Kathleen M. Day. "Economic Growth and Regional Income Disparities in Canada and the Northern United States." *Canadian Public Policy* 25, 2 (1999): 155-78.

Coulombe, Serge, and Frank C. Lee. "Convergence across Canadian Provinces, 1961 to 1991." *Canadian Journal of Economics* 28, 4a (1995): 886-98.

Decressin, Jorg, and Antonio Fatas. "Regional Labor Market Dynamics in Europe." *European Economic Review* 39, 9 (1995): 1627-55.

Faini, Ricardo, Jean-Marie Grether and Jaime de Melo. "Globalisation and Migration Pressures from Developing Countries: A Simulation Analysis." In *Migration: The Controversies and the Evidence.* Edited by Ricardo Faini, Jaime de Melo and Klaus Zimmermann. New York and Melbourne: Cambridge University Press and CEPR, 1999.

Finnie, Ross. "Inter-provincial Migration in Canada: A Longitudinal Analysis of Movers and Stayers and the Associated Income Dynamics." *Canadian Journal of Regional Science* 22, 3 (1999): 227-62.

_____. *The Brain Drain: Myth and Reality — What It Is and What Should Be Done.* Working Paper No.13. Kingston: School of Policy Studies, Queen's University, 2001.

Globerman, Steven. "Professionals and Managers: The North American Experience." *World Economy* 23, 7 (2000): 901-22.

Gould, David. "Immigration Links to the Home Country: Empirical Implications for U.S. Bilateral Trade Flows." *Review of Economics and Statistics* 76, 2 (1994): 302-16.

Gunderson, Morley. "Barriers to Interprovincial Labour Mobility." In *Provincial Trade Wars: Why the Blockade Must End*. Edited by Filip Palda. Vancouver: The Fraser Institute, 1994, pp. 131-54.

Harris, R.G. "Evidence and Debate on Economic Integration and Economic Growth." In *The Implications of Knowledge-Based Growth for Micro-Economic Policies*. Edited by Peter Howitt. Calgary: University of Calgary Press, 1996, pp. 119-55.

_____. "The Internet as a GPT: Factor Market Implications" In *General Purpose Technologies and Economic Growth*. Edited by Elhanan Helpman. Cambridge and London: MIT Press, 1998, pp. 145-66.

_____. "North American Economic Integration: Issues and a Research Agenda." Discussion Paper No. 10. Ottawa: Industry Canada, 2001a. Available at: http://www.strategis.ca/SSG/1/ra01809e.html

_____. "Is There A Case for Exchange Rate-Induced Productivity Changes?" In *Revisiting the Case for Flexible Exchange Rates*. Edited by L. Schembri. Ottawa, Bank of Canada, 2001b, pp. 277-309.

_____. "Social Policy and Productivity Growth: What are the Linkages?" In *Productivity Issues in Canada*. Edited by Someshwar Rao and Andrew Sharpe. The Industry Canada Research Series. Calgary: University of Calgary Press, 2002, pp. 789-841.

Head, Keith, and John Ries. "Immigration and Trade Creation: Econometric Evidence from Canada." *Canadian Journal of Economics* 31, 1 (1998): 47-62.

Head, Keith, John Ries and Don Wagner. "Immigrants and the Trade of Provinces." Working Study No.21. Vancouver: Research on Immigration and Integration in the Metropolis, December 1998.

Helliwell, John. "Checking the Brain Drain: Evidence and Implications." Vancouver: University of British Columbia, 1999. Mimeograph.

Hulten, Charles Reid, and Robert M. Schwab. "Endogenous Growth, Public Capital, and the Convergence of Regional Manufacturing Industry." NBER Working Paper No. 4538, November 1993, p. 25.

Human Resources Development Canada and Statistics Canada. *An Analysis of Results from the Survey of 1995 Graduates Who Moved to the United States*. Catalogue Number: 81-587-XIE. Ottawa: Statistics Canada, 1999, p. 10.

Johnson, Jean M., and Mark C. Regets. "International Mobility of Scientists and Engineers to the United States: Brain Drain or Brain Circulation?" Issue Brief No. 98316. Washington DC: National Science Foundation, 1998.

Krueger, Alan. "From Bismarck to Maastricht: The March to European Union and the Labour Compact. National Bureau for Economic Research (NBER) Working Paper No. 7456, January 2000.

Krugman, Paul. "Increasing Returns and Economic Geography." *Journal of Political Economy* 99 (1991): 483-99.

Lafrance, R., and L. Schembri. "The Exchange Rate, Productivity and the Standard of Living." *Bank of Canada Review* (2000): 17-28.

Ludema, Rodney, and Ian Wooton. "Regional Integration, Trade and Migration: Are Demand Linkages Relevant for Europe?" In *Migration: The Controversies and the Evidence*.

Edited by Ricardo Faini, Jaime de Melo and Klaus Zimmermann. New York and Melbourne: Cambridge University Press and CEPR, 1999, pp. 51-68.

Markusen, James. "Factor Movements and Commodity Trade as Complements." *Journal of International Economics* 14 (1983): 341-56.

Markusen, James, and Jim Melvin. "Trade, Factor Prices and Gains from Trade with Increasing Returns to Scale." *Canadian Journal of Economics* 14 (1981): 450-69.

Martin, Philip and J. Edward Taylor. "The Anatomy of a Migration Hump." In *Development Strategy, Employment and Migration: Insights from Models*. Edited by J.E. Taylor. Paris: Organisation for Economic Co-operation and Development (OECD), 1996, pp. 43-62.

Mundell, R.A. "International Factor and Factor Mobility." *American Economic Review* 47 (1957): 321-35.

Murphy, Kevin M., W. Craig Riddell and Paul M. Romer. "Wages, Skills and Technology in the United States and Canada." In *General Purpose Technologies and Economic Growth*. Edited by E. Elhanan. Cambridge and London: MIT Press, 1998, pp. 283-309.

OECD. *Trends in International Migration*. Annual Report. Paris: OECD, 1998.

O'Rourke, Kevin, and Jeffrey Williamson. *Globalisation and History: The Evolution of a Nineteenth-Century Atlantic Economy*. Cambridge and London: MIT Press, 1999; xii, 343.

Personnel Systems. "Today's Technology Graduate: Mobile, In Demand & Demanding!" Ottawa: Personnel Systems, 1999, p. 3.

Puhani, Patrick A. "Labour Mobility: An Adjustment Mechanism in Euroland? Empirical Evidence for Western Germany, France and Italy." *German Economic Review* 2, 2 (2001): 127-40.

Rosenbluth, G. "The Causes and Consequences of Interprovincial Migration." University of British Columbia Department of Economics Discussion Paper 87-29, August 1987, p. 18.

Solomon, C.M. "Today's Global Mobility – Short-term Assignments and Other Solutions." *Workforce* (Supplement, July 1998): 12-17.

Stark, Oded, and John E. Taylor. "Migration Incentives, Migration Types: The Role of Relative Deprivation." *The Economic Journal* 101 (1991): 1163-78.

Stark, Oded, Christian Helmenstein and Alexia Prskawetz. "Human Capital Depletion, Human Capital Formation, and Migration: A Blessing or a 'Curse'?" *Economics Letters* 60, 3 (1998): 363-67.

Straubhaar, T. "International Labour Migration within a Common Market: Some Aspects of EC Experience." *Journal of Common Market Studies* 27 (1988): 45-61.

Venables, Anthony. "Trade Liberalization and Factor Mobility: An Overview." In *Migration: The Controversies and the Evidence*. Edited by Ricardo Faini, Jaime de Melo and Klaus Zimmermann. New York, Cambridge and Melbourne: Cambridge University Press and CEPR, 1999, pp. 23-48.

# Comment on:

## THE CONSEQUENCES OF INCREASED LABOUR MOBILITY WITHIN AN INTEGRATING NORTH AMERICA

*Comment by Eugene Beaulieu*
*University of Calgary*

RICHARD HARRIS CHALLENGED CANADIANS to pursue closer North American (NA) integration almost 20 years ago. At the time, he applied "new" trade theory to the question of NA integration and found that Canada stood to realize large welfare gains from signing a free trade agreement (FTA) with the United States (Harris 1985; Cox and Harris 1985). The research was an important contribution to the debate in Canada and to modelling trade policy in general. Through this work, he became one of the architects of the intellectual argument supporting Canada's pursuit of a FTA for trade in goods with the United States in the early 1980s. Today, Harris and Schmitt are challenging us to consider closer economic integration with the United States, this time in labour markets. Harris and Schmitt explore the idea of closer labour market integration under several alternative underlying economic models and challenge us to take a closer look at the costs and benefits of an integrated NA labour market. Although Harris's work in the 1980s was influential, the empirical veracity of the model has not, until recently, been explored (Head and Ries 1999, 2003).

It is worth being reminded that the predicted economic gains of the Canada-U.S. FTA have varied considerably depending on the underlying assumptions of the models used (Hazledine 1988, 1990). Nonetheless, the Canadian pursuit of free trade in goods with the United States was based, in part, on these models. The MacDonald Commission concluded:

> The most important advantage to Canadians of a free-trade agreement with the United States would be its effect on productivity and thus, in particular, on the competitiveness of our manufacturing sector. Improved and more stable access would create opportunities for Canadian business and increase the tendency toward specialization and rationalization of Canadian production (vol. 1, p. 325).

And policy makers were listening:

> The economic models assumed free trade would narrow if not eliminate the gap in productivity between Canadian- and American-based firms. How? I was afraid we would see the less efficient Canadian firms simply going under, with the resulting losses of output and employment in Canada.... In the end, a new equilibrium might be reached, but not without substantial temporary and in some cases permanent dislocation for workers, firms, and communities most directly affected. (Ritchie 1997, p. 24)

Harris and Schmitt make an important contribution as we consider the policy options of NA integration.

## DEEPER LABOUR MARKET INTEGRATION

HARRIS AND SCHMITT CHALLENGE US to consider deeper integration with the United States. This is déjà vu, as the current challenge is reminiscent of Harris's earlier challenge for us to consider the large gains from liberalizing trade in goods. The difference in the current challenge is that Harris and Schmitt do not present a compelling argument that increased labour market integration will yield the large gains to Canada that were predicted for trade liberalization. The reason for this is simply that the consequences of NA labour market integration have not been studied carefully. In the conclusions, Harris and Schmitt challenge the research agenda to examine the potential static and dynamic gains in an integrated NA labour market.

They provide a provocative argument for further research on the consequences of a common NA labour market and map out an important direction for further research. Along the way, they provide an excellent survey of important issues to consider while pondering labour market integration, and they examine the theoretical and empirical evidence on these issues. In particular, they summarize historical and recent trends in migration and consider traditional theories and implications of international trade and migration. As expected, they present departures from the neoclassical trade model to consider issues such as technological differences, increasing returns, migration costs, risk and migration networks and unemployment. They consider the effects of increased NA labour market integration with respect to agglomeration, convergence and regional development. They summarize the literature on the "brain drain" and knowledge transfers and examine the degree of mobility of highly skilled labour in NA.

# WHERE DO WE GO FROM HERE?

I HAVE SOME GENERAL COMMENTS. First, there is a lack of consensus on the correct underlying trade model. Therefore, it is difficult to predict the magnitudes of the gains from NA labour integration. Harris and Schmitt suggest that there may be substantial gains from further and deeper economic integration within NA. They conclude that more research and CGE studies on labour market integration are required, but these types of studies also will require micro-studies to provide parameter estimates and help determine the correct underlying assumptions. There is ample theoretical support for the proposition that trade liberalization promotes industry efficiency, and efficiency did appear to increase in liberalizing manufacturing sectors in Canada. However, the lack of micro-economic data available in Canada has constrained research efforts in this direction. Improved access to Canadian micro-data is required to explain the conflicting evidence and to understand the impact of deeper integration. This point is discussed further in my comments on the study by Head and Ries (Chapter 4 in this volume).

The pursuit of deeper NA labour market integration faces institutional challenges that even affect provincial labour flows in this country. As Harris and Schmitt point out, there are a number of "natural" and "artificial" barriers to labour mobility *within* Canada. They remain significant and have not been reduced by the 1995 Agreement on Internal Trade. In fact, the federal and provincial governments continue to contribute institutional barriers to labour mobility. For example, the federal government continues to promote labour *immobility* through its hiring practices, as the job advertisement below indicates.

**Example: Public Service Commission Job Posting**

**POLICY ANALYST** Ottawa, ON
Department of Justice.
SALARY: $46,865 - $50,670 (PM-04)
LANGUAGE: English

**WHO CAN APPLY:** Persons residing or working in Eastern Ontario or Western Quebec, who have a home or business postal code beginning with: K1 to K7, K8A to K8H, K0A to K0J, J8L to J8Z, J9A to J9J, or J0X.

Source: Public Service Commission Web site.

To conclude on a cautionary note, Canadian trade policy must consider the effect that deeper NA integration may have on world trading and political relations. Moving toward deeper regional integration contributes to an increasingly

357

regional world economy that may ultimately lead to a tripolar world economy. The increased regionalism in world political and economic relations may derail the multilateralism approach of the early postwar period. A tripartite world economy increases the potential for protectionist action and trade wars.

## BIBLIOGRAPHY

Cox, David, and Richard Harris. "Trade Liberalization and Industrial Organization: Some Estimates for Canada." *Journal of Political Economy* 93, 1 (1985): 115-45.

Harris, Richard G. *Trade, Industrial Policy and International Competition.* Report of the Royal Commission on the Economic Union and Development Prospects for Canada, Volume 13. Toronto: University of Toronto Press, 1985.

Hazledine, Tim. "Review Article and Comment." *Canadian Public Policy* 14, 2 (1988): 204-13.

_____. "Why Do the Free Trade Gain Numbers Differ So Much? The Role of Industrial Organization in General Equilibrium." *Canadian Journal of Economics* 23, 4 (November 1990).

Head, K., and J. Ries. "Rationalization of Trade Reductions." *Journal of International Economics* 47, 2 (1999): 295-320.

_____. "Free Trade and Canadian Economic Performance: Which Theories Does the Evidence Support?" In *North American Linkages: Opportunities and Challenges for Canada.* Edited by Richard Harris. Calgary: University of Calgary Press, 2003. Chapter 4.

Ritchie, Gordon. *Wrestling With the Elephant: The Inside Story of the Canada-U.S. Trade Wars.* Toronto: Macfarlane, Walter & Ross, 1997.

Report of the Royal Commission on the Economic Union and Development Prospects for Canada ("The MacDonald Commission") Volume I. Toronto: University of Toronto Press, 1985.

Drusilla K. Brown  &  Alan V. Deardorff & Robert M. Stern
Tufts University        University of Michigan

*9*

# Impacts on NAFTA Members of Multilateral and Regional Trading Arrangements and Tariff Harmonization

## INTRODUCTION

THE PURPOSE OF OUR STUDY is to assess how the members of the North American Free Trade Agreement (NAFTA) — Canada, Mexico and the United States — may be affected by 1) the prospective Doha Round (DR) of multilateral trade negotiations to be carried out under the auspices of the World Trade Organization (WTO); 2) the variety of free trade agreements (FTAs) that NAFTA countries have actually negotiated, and others currently being considered; and 3) the adoption of a common external tariff that would replace each country's national tariffs and do away with rules of origin. In the foregoing assessments, we rely on the Michigan Model of World Production and Trade, which is a multicountry, multisector computational general equilibrium (CGE) model that we have used for more than 25 years to analyse changes in trade policies.

In the second section, we analyse first the potential economic effects of trade liberalization on agricultural products and services, currently in the early negotiation stages of the DR as part of the built-in agenda mandated by the Uruguay Round (UR). We then consider the liberalization of trade in industrial products, which is on the agenda for the DR. In the third section, we analyse regional negotiating options of interest to the present NAFTA countries. These options include the expansion of the NAFTA to include Chile and what we refer to as a Western Hemisphere FTA (WHFTA), an approximation of the Free Trade Area of the Americas (FTAA). In the fourth section, we analyse several bilateral FTAs that the NAFTA members have already signed or are currently considering. The fifth section presents our analysis of the economic effects of the harmonization of NAFTA external tariffs. The sixth and final section presents our overall conclusions and their policy implications.

# THE PROSPECTIVE DOHA ROUND

IN THIS SECTION we use CGE model-based simulation analysis to examine the economic effects of the trade liberalization that may occur in the DR. We begin by providing a brief overview of the Michigan CGE model.

## OVERVIEW OF THE MICHIGAN MODEL

THE DISTINGUISHING FEATURE OF THE MICHIGAN MODEL is that it incorporates some aspects of new trade theory (NTT), including increasing returns to scale, monopolistic competition and product heterogeneity.[1] A more complete description of the formal structure and equations of the model can be found on-line at http://www.fordschool.umich.edu/rsie/model/.

### Sectors and Market Structure

The version of the model used here consists of 20 countries or regions and the rest of the world (ROW), as well as 18 production sectors. The coverage of each country or region and sector is set out in the tables that follow. Agriculture is modelled as perfectly competitive, with product differentiation by country of origin. All other sectors are modelled as monopolistically competitive, with free entry and exit of differentiated-product firms.

### Expenditure

Consumers and producers are assumed to use a two-stage procedure to allocate expenditure across differentiated products. In the first stage, expenditure is allocated across goods without regard to country of origin or producing firm. At this stage, the utility function is Cobb-Douglas, and the production function requires intermediate inputs in fixed proportions. In the second stage, expenditure on monopolistically competitive goods is allocated across the competing varieties supplied by each firm from all countries. In the case of perfectly competitive sectors, since individual firm supply is indeterminate, expenditure is allocated over each country's industry as a whole, with imperfect substitution between products of different countries. The aggregation function in the second stage is a constant elasticity of substitution (CES) function.

### Production

The production function is separated into two stages. In the first stage, intermediate inputs and a primary composite of capital and labour are used in fixed proportion to output.[2] In the second stage, capital and labour are combined through a CES function to form the primary composite. In the monopolistically competitive sectors, additional fixed inputs of capital and labour are required. It is assumed that fixed capital and labour are used in the same proportion as variable capital and labour, so that production functions are homothetic.

## Supply Prices

To determine equilibrium prices, perfectly competitive firms operate such that price is equal to marginal cost, while monopolistically competitive firms maximize profits by setting price as an optimal markup over marginal cost. The number of firms in sectors under monopolistic competition is determined by the condition that there are zero profits.

## Capital and Labour Markets

Capital and labour are assumed to be perfectly mobile across sectors within each country. Returns to capital and labour are determined so as to equate factor demand to an exogenous supply of each factor. The aggregate supplies of capital and labour in each country are assumed to remain fixed so as to abstract from macro-economic considerations (e.g., the determination of investment), since our micro-economic focus is on the intersectoral allocation of resources.

## World Market and Trade Balance

The world market determines equilibrium prices such that all markets clear. Total demand for the product of each firm or sector must equal the total supply of that product. It is also assumed that trade remains balanced for each country and region (i.e., any initial trade imbalance remains constant as trade barriers are changed). This assumption reflects the reality of mostly flexible exchange rates among the countries involved. Moreover, this is a way of abstracting from the macro-economic forces and policies that are the main determinants of trade imbalances.

## Trade Policies, Rents and Revenues

We have incorporated import tariff rates and export taxes and subsidies into the model as policy inputs that are applicable to the bilateral trade of the various countries and regions. These have been computed by means of the GTAP 4 Data Base provided in McDougall, Elbehri and Truong (1998). The export barriers have been estimated as export-tax equivalents. We assume that revenues from both import tariffs and export taxes, as well as rents from non-tariff barriers (NTBs) on exports, are redistributed to consumers in the tariff- or tax-levying country and are spent like any other income. When tariffs are reduced, import prices fall, as does the income available to purchase them, and there is no bias toward expanding or contracting overall demand.

## Model Closure and Implementation

We assume in the model that aggregate expenditure varies endogenously to hold aggregate employment constant. This closure is analogous to the Johansen closure rule (Deardorff and Stern 1990). The Johansen closure rule keeps the requirement of full employment while dropping the consumption function. This means that consumption can be thought of as adjusting endogenously to ensure full employment. In the present model, however, we do not distinguish consumption from other sources of final demand. That is, we assume instead that total expenditure adjusts to maintain full employment.

The model is solved by means of GEMPACK (Harrison and Pearson 1996). When policy changes are introduced, the solution method yields percentage changes in sectoral employment and certain other variables of interest. Multiplying the percentage changes by the levels projected for 2005 (which is when the UR provisions will have been fully implemented) yields the absolute changes — positive or negative — that might result from the various liberalization scenarios.

## The Data

Needless to say, the data needs of this model are immense; apart from numerous share parameters, it requires various types of elasticity measures. Like other CGE models, most of our data come from published sources.

As mentioned above, the main data source is the GTAP 4 Data Base of the Purdue University Center for Global Trade Analysis Project (McDougall et al.). The reference year for this data base is 1995. From this source, we have extracted the following data, aggregated to our sectors and regions:

1. Bilateral trade flows among 20 countries and regions, broken down into 18 sectors. Trade with the ROW is included to close the model.

2. Input-output tables for the 20 countries and regions, excluding the ROW.

3. Components of final demand along with sectoral contributions for the 20 countries and regions, excluding the ROW.

4. Gross value of output and value-added at the sectoral level for the 20 countries and regions, excluding the ROW.

5. Bilateral import tariffs by sector among the 20 countries and regions.

6. Elasticity of substitution between capital and labour, by sector.

7. Bilateral export-tax equivalents among the 20 countries and regions, broken down into 18 sectors.

The monopolistically competitive market structure in the non-agricultural sectors of the model imposes an additional data requirement relating to the number of firms at the sectoral level. These data have been drawn from the United Nations Industrial Development Organization (UNIDO) 1998 *International Yearbook of Industrial Statistics*.[3]

We also need estimates of sectoral employment for the countries and regions of the model. These data have been drawn from the UNIDO 1995 *International Yearbook of Industrial Statistics* and the World Bank 1997 *World Development Report*. The employment data have been aggregated according to our sectoral and regional aggregation to obtain sectoral estimates of workers employed in manufacturing. The *World Development Report* was used to obtain data for the other sectors.[4]

We have projected the GTAP 4 Data Base to the year 2005 by extrapolating the labour availability in different countries and regions, through the use of an average weighted population growth rate of 1.2 percent per annum. This figure was computed from the 1997-2010 growth-rate forecasts provided for various countries in Table 2.3 of the World Bank's 1999 *World Development Indicators*. The other major variables also have been projected, through the use of an average weighted GDP growth rate of 2.5 percent per annum for all of the countries and regions of our model during 1990-97, as per Table 11 of the 1989-99 *World Development Report*.[5]

The projected data base provides us with an approximate picture of the world in 2005 if the UR negotiations had not occurred. The UR reductions in trade barriers were implemented in 1995 and will be completed by 2005. In Brown, Deardorff and Stern (2002), we have analysed the impact of the UR-induced changes that are expected to occur over the course of the 10-year implementation period as a consequence of the negotiated reductions in tariffs and NTBs. We then readjusted the scaled-up data base for 2005 to reflect how the world might look post-UR implementation. In what follows, we use these readjusted data as the starting point to carry out the liberalization scenarios for the prospective DR, involving possible reductions in tariffs on agricultural products and manufactures and reductions of barriers to trade in services.

## COMPUTATIONAL SCENARIOS

AS NOTED ABOVE, the built-in agenda of the UR mandated that multilateral negotiations under WTO auspices would commence for agricultural products and services in 2000. It had been expected that the agenda for a broader nego-tiating round would be approved at the December 1999 WTO Ministerial Meeting in Seattle. Because of a lack of consensus among the members,[6] how-ever, decisions on the details of the negotiating agenda for a new round were put off until the November 2001 WTO Ministerial Meeting in Doha. At that meeting, it was agreed that negotiations would be launched at the beginning of 2002, and it is anticipated that they will be completed in three years. It is in this context that we will use the Michigan model to assess the magnitude of the economic effects that may result from the DR negotiations. Accordingly, we have run what we refer to as the DR "liberalization scenarios." These scenarios assume 33 percent reductions in post-UR tariffs and service barriers, as follows:

**DR-1** *Agricultural liberalization is modelled as a 33 percent reduction in post-UR agricultural import tariffs.[7]*

**DR-2** *Liberalization of industrial products is modelled as a 33 percent re-duction in post-UR tariffs on mining and manufactured products.*

**DR-3** *Liberalization of services is modelled as a 33 percent reduction in estimated post-UR service barriers.*

**DR-4** *This combines DR-1, DR-2 and DR-3.*

In addition, we thought it would be of interest to run a fifth scenario of global free trade, as follows:

**DR-5** *Global free trade is modelled as complete removal of all post-UR tariffs on agricultural products and industrial products, as well as service barriers.*

With regard to DR-3, we note that while service issues were addressed, the main accomplishment of the UR was the creation of the General Agreement on Trade in Services (GATS). The GATS is an umbrella agreement that sets out the rules governing the four modes of international service transaction delivery. They are:

1. cross-border services (e.g., telecommunications);

2. services provided in the country of consumption (e.g., tourism);

3. services that require a domestic presence in the form of foreign direct investment (FDI); and

4. movement of natural persons.

## TABLE 1

## AVERAGE GROSS OPERATING MARGINS OF SERVICE FIRMS LISTED ON NATIONAL STOCK EXCHANGES, 1994-96 (PERCENT)

| | Construction | Trade and Transportation | Other Private Services | Government Services | Average |
|---|---|---|---|---|---|
| **NAFTA Countries** | | | | | |
| United States | 20 | 35 | 46 | 40 | 40 |
| Canada | 14 | 21 | 42 | 15* | 33 |
| Mexico | 26 | 35 | 47 | | 39 |
| **Industrialized Countries** | | | | | |
| Japan | 14 | 23 | 27 | 43 | 27 |
| Australia | 15 | 8* | 15* | | 13 |
| New Zealand | 15 | 21 | 27 | | 21 |
| EU/EFTA | 20 | 24 | 34 | 38 | 29 |
| **Developing Countries** | | | | | |
| **Asia** | | | | | |
| Hong Kong | 14 | 16 | 23 | | 19 |
| China | 42 | 36 | 72 | 75 | 49 |
| Korea | 15 | 24 | 41 | | 24 |
| Singapore | 11* | 13 | 21 | 26 | 18 |
| Taiwan | 21 | 28 | 50 | | 35 |
| Indonesia | 23 | 32 | 58 | | 44 |
| Malaysia | 19 | 17 | 22 | 26 | 18 |
| Philippines | 41 | 42 | 50 | | 45 |
| Thailand | 38 | 42 | 49 | 41 | 45 |
| Rest of Asia | 23 | 23 | 34 | | 27 |
| **Other** | | | | | |
| Chile | 69 | 32 | | | 41 |
| CCS | 29 | 40 | 49 | 32 | 38 |
| Middle East and North Africa | 40 | 35 | 48 | | 39 |
| ROW | 12 | 19 | 32 | 19 | 22 |
| **Average** | **22** | **27** | **35** | **36** | |

Note:   In this table and others that accompany this paper, EU is the European Union and EFTA is the European Free Trade Association, which includes Iceland, Norway and Switzerland. Rest of Asia is India, Sri Lanka and Vietnam. CCS is the Caribbean, Central and South America and includes Argentina, Brazil, Colombia, Uruguay, Venezuela and the rest of the Andean Pact. Middle East and North Africa includes Morocco, Turkey and the rest of North Africa.

   *Taken as benchmark country.

Source:   Adapted from Hoekman (2000).

In an earlier study, Brown and Stern (2001) developed a new version of the Michigan model for the purpose of analysing the behavior of multinational firms, which are major providers of services, both intrafirm and in the production and sale of foreign affiliates located in host countries.[8] To approximate existing service barriers, Brown and Stern used the Hoekman (2000) estimates of barriers to FDI, which are based on the gross operating margins of service firms listed on national stock exchanges for the 1994-96 time period. These margins, which were calculated as the difference between total revenues and total operating costs, are indicated in percentage form in Table 1 for construction, trade and transportation, other private services and government services.

Some of the differences between total revenues and costs are presumably attributable to fixed cost. Given that gross operating margins vary across countries, a portion of them can also be attributed to barriers to FDI. For this purpose, we have selected as a benchmark for each sector the country with the smallest gross operating margin, on the assumption that operations in that country can be considered to be freely open to foreign firms; thus, the excess in other countries is assumed to be due to barriers to establishment by foreign firms. That is, the barrier is modelled as the cost increase attributable to an increase in fixed cost borne by multinational corporations attempting to establish local enterprise in a host country. This abstracts from the possibility that fixed costs may differ among firms because of variations in market size, distance from headquarters and other factors. In this study, we further assume for purposes of analysis that we can interpret this cost increase as an ad valorem equivalent tariff on international service transactions generally. Our DR-3 scenario assumes, then, that these service barriers are to be reduced by 33 percent in a new trade round.

## COMPUTATIONAL RESULTS

TO HELP THE READER INTERPRET THE RESULTS, it is useful first to review the features of the model that serve to identify the various economic effects that are being captured in the different scenarios. Although the model includes the aforementioned features of NTT, it remains the case that markets respond to trade liberalization in much the same way that they would with perfect competition. That is, when tariffs or other trade barriers are reduced in a sector, domestic buyers (both final and intermediate) substitute toward imports, and the domestic competing industry contracts production, while foreign exporters expand. With multilateral liberalization reducing tariffs and other trade barriers simultaneously in most sectors and countries, each country's industries share in both of these effects, expanding or contracting primarily on the basis of whether they receive more or less protection than industries in other sectors and countries. At the same time, countries with larger average tariff reductions than their trading partners tend to experience a real depreciation of their currencies in order to maintain a constant trade balance, so that all countries therefore experience mixtures of both expanding and contracting sectors.

Worldwide, these changes cause increased international demand for all sectors, with world prices rising most for those sectors where trade barriers fall the most. This in turn causes changes in countries' terms of trade that can be positive or negative. Those countries that are net exporters of goods with the greatest degree of liberalization will experience increases in their terms of trade, as the world prices of their exports rise relative to their imports. The reverse occurs for net exporters in industries where liberalization is slight — perhaps because it had already happened in previous trade rounds.

The effects on the welfare of countries arise from a mixture of these terms-of-trade effects, together with the standard efficiency gains from trade, and also from additional benefits due to elements of NTT. Thus, we expect, on average, that the world will gain from multilateral liberalization as resources are reallocated to those sectors in each country where there is a comparative advantage. In the absence of terms-of-trade effects, these efficiency gains should raise national welfare (measured by the equivalent variation for every country), although some factor owners within a country may lose, as noted below. However, it is possible for a particular country — whose net imports are concentrated in sectors with the greatest liberalization — to lose overall if the worsening of its terms of trade swamps these efficiency gains.

Although NTT is perhaps best known for introducing new reasons why countries may lose from trade, in fact, its greatest contribution is to expand the list of reasons for gains from trade. This is the dominant contribution of NTT to our model. That is, trade liberalization permits all countries to expand their export sectors at the same time as all sectors compete more closely with a larger number of varieties from abroad. As a result, countries as a whole gain from lower costs due to increasing returns to scale, lower monopoly distortions due to greater competition, and reduced costs and/or increased utility due to greater product variety. All of these effects make it more likely that countries will gain from liberalization in ways that are shared across the entire population.

In perfectly competitive trade models such as the Heckscher-Ohlin model, one expects countries as a whole to gain from trade but owners of one factor — the "scarce factor" — to lose through the mechanism first explored by Stolper and Samuelson (1941). The additional sources of gain from trade due to increasing returns to scale, competition, and product variety, however, are shared across factors, and we routinely find in our CGE modelling that both labour and capital gain from liberalization.

In the real world, all of the above effects occur over time, some of them more quickly than others. Our model, however, is static, based on a single set of equilibrium conditions rather than relationships that vary over time. Our results, therefore, refer to a time horizon that is somewhat uncertain, depending on the assumptions that have been made about which variables do and do not adjust to changing market conditions, and on the short- or long-run nature of these adjustments. Because our elasticities of supply and demand reflect relatively long-run adjustments, and because we assume that markets for both labour and capital clear within countries, our results are appropriate for a relatively long time horizon of several years — perhaps two or three, at a minimum.

However, our model does not allow for the very long-run adjustments that could occur through capital accumulation, population growth and technological change. Our results should be thought of as being superimposed on longer-run growth paths of the economies involved. Our model does not capture the extent to which these growth paths themselves may be influenced by trade liberalization.

## Aggregate Results[9]

The aggregate effects on economic welfare of the individual DR scenarios (DR-1 to DR-4) and global free trade (DR-5) are presented in Table 2,[10] and the sectoral employment results of scenario DR-4 for Canada, Mexico and the United States are presented in Table 3.

## TABLE 2

### GLOBAL WELFARE EFFECTS OF MULTILATERAL TRADE LIBERALIZATION
#### (PERCENT OF GNP AND BILLIONS OF DOLLARS)

| | WTO Millennium Round – 33 Percent Reductions in: | | | | | | | | Global Free Trade | |
| --- | --- | --- | --- | --- | --- | --- | --- | --- | --- | --- |
| | Agricultural Tariffs—DR-1 | | Manufactures Tariffs—DR-2 | | Service Barriers—DR-3 | | Combined Liberalization— DR-4 | | All Barriers Removed—DR-5 | |
| | (1) | | (2) | | (3) | | (4) | | (5) | |
| | Percent of GNP | $ (billion) | Percent of GNP | $ (billion) | Percent of GNP | $ (billion) | Percent of GNP | $ (billion) | Percent of GNP | $ (billion) |
| **NAFTA Countries** | | | | | | | | | | |
| Canada | 0.01 | 0.1 | 0.38 | 2.8 | 1.46 | 10.6 | 1.85 | 13.5 | 5.62 | 40.9 |
| Mexico | 0.03 | 0.1 | 0.32 | 1.1 | 1.49 | 5.2 | 1.84 | 6.5 | 5.58 | 19.6 |
| United States | −0.04 | −4.1 | 0.34 | 31.3 | 1.65 | 150.0 | 1.95 | 177.3 | 5.92 | 537.2 |
| **Industrialized Countries** | | | | | | | | | | |
| Japan | 0.07 | 4.3 | 0.89 | 57.8 | 0.95 | 61.6 | 1.90 | 123.7 | 5.77 | 374.8 |
| Australia | −0.04 | −0.2 | 0.56 | 2.5 | 0.65 | 2.8 | 1.16 | 5.1 | 3.52 | 15.5 |
| New Zealand | −0.04 | 0.0 | 1.88 | 1.4 | 1.20 | 0.8 | 3.04 | 2.2 | 9.22 | 6.8 |
| EU/EFTA | 0.02 | 2.2 | 0.58 | 63.3 | 0.94 | 103.4 | 1.54 | 168.9 | 4.67 | 511.9 |
| **Developing Countries** | | | | | | | | | | |
| **Asia** | | | | | | | | | | |
| Hong Kong | 0.02 | 0.0 | 1.56 | 2.0 | 1.78 | 2.3 | 3.36 | 4.3 | 10.18 | 13.1 |
| China | 0.18 | 1.6 | 0.54 | 4.9 | 0.79 | 7.1 | 1.50 | 13.6 | 4.55 | 41.2 |
| Korea | 0.16 | 0.9 | 1.40 | 8.0 | 0.91 | 5.2 | 2.48 | 14.1 | 7.51 | 42.7 |
| Singapore | 0.12 | 0.1 | 2.85 | 2.1 | 2.62 | 1.9 | 5.60 | 4.2 | 16.96 | 12.6 |
| Taiwan | 0.71 | 2.5 | 1.58 | 5.6 | 0.49 | 1.7 | 2.78 | 9.8 | 8.44 | 29.6 |
| Indonesia | 0.06 | 0.1 | 0.06 | 0.1 | 0.79 | 2.0 | 1.65 | 4.2 | 5.00 | 12.7 |
| Malaysia | 0.28 | 0.3 | 1.99 | 2.4 | 0.54 | 0.6 | 2.81 | 3.4 | 8.51 | 10.2 |
| Philippines | 0.20 | 0.2 | 3.52 | 3.1 | 1.68 | 1.5 | 5.40 | 4.8 | 16.38 | 14.5 |
| Thailand | 0.03 | 0.1 | 1.47 | 3.0 | 1.12 | 2.3 | 2.62 | 5.4 | 7.94 | 16.4 |
| Rest of Asia | 0.40 | 2.3 | 0.90 | 5.2 | 0.47 | 2.7 | 1.78 | 10.2 | 5.38 | 30.8 |
| **Other** | | | | | | | | | | |
| Chile | −0.05 | 0.0 | 1.29 | 1.0 | 1.17 | 0.9 | 2.40 | 1.9 | 7.28 | 5.9 |
| CCS | −0.03 | −0.5 | 0.31 | 5.1 | 1.13 | 18.9 | 1.41 | 23.6 | 4.28 | 71.4 |
| Middle East and North Africa | 0.09 | 0.8 | 0.92 | 8.0 | 0.88 | 7.6 | 1.90 | 16.4 | 5.75 | 49.7 |
| **Total** | | 10.8 | | 210.7 | | 389.6 | | 613.0 | | 1,857.4 |

Note: These numbers have been rounded.

TABLE 3

SECTORAL EMPLOYMENT EFFECTS FOR CANADA, MEXICO AND
THE UNITED STATES OF 33 PERCENT REDUCTIONS IN POST-UR
AGRICULTURAL AND MANUFACTURES TARIFFS AND SERVICE BARRIERS
(PERCENT OF EMPLOYMENT AND NUMBER OF WORKERS)

| Sector | Canada (1) | | Mexico (2) | | United States (3) | |
|---|---|---|---|---|---|---|
| | Percent of Employment | Number of Workers | Percent of Employment | Number of Workers | Percent of Employment | Number of Workers |
| Agriculture | 2.96 | 18,705 | 0.33 | 31,653 | 3.23 | 132,608 |
| Mining | −0.44 | −834 | 0.26 | 438 | 0.08 | 577 |
| Food, Beverages and Tobacco | 1.05 | 5208 | 0.05 | 270 | 0.29 | 9,113 |
| Textiles | −3.71 | −1,275 | −0.31 | -858 | −1.55 | −18,826 |
| Wearing Apparel | −7.86 | −11,324 | −1.71 | −3,241 | −4.37 | −47,605 |
| Leather Products and Footwear | −9.36 | −702 | −1.56 | −2,023 | −6.21 | −9,042 |
| Wood and Wood Products | 1.08 | 5,256 | 0.04 | 156 | 0.13 | 5,765 |
| Chemicals | 0.53 | 2,129 | 0.21 | 523 | 0.27 | 7,792 |
| Non-metallic Mineral Products | 0.17 | 135 | 0.06 | 1,895 | −0.13 | −1,019 |
| Metal Products | 0.75 | 2,108 | 1.02 | 2,968 | 0.17 | 4,792 |
| Transportation Equipment | 0.41 | 779 | 0.76 | 993 | 0.18 | 3,496 |
| Machinery and Equipment | 1.03 | 1,459 | 1.05 | 2,187 | 0.63 | 18,216 |
| Other Manufactures | −0.48 | −279 | −1.74 | −436 | 0.47 | 8,534 |
| Electricity, Gas and Water | 0.21 | 1,599 | 0.08 | 651 | 0.19 | 8,919 |
| Construction | 0.13 | 2,122 | −0.13 | −2,340 | 0.10 | 13,049 |
| Trade and Transport | 0.10 | 4,284 | 0.22 | 26,328 | −0.14 | −43,127 |
| Other Private Services | −0.86 | −28,571 | −0.98 | −52,116 | −0.25 | −92,052 |
| Government Services | −0.04 | −800 | −0.24 | −7,050 | 0.00 | −1,191 |
| **Total** | | 0.0 | | 0.0 | | 0.0 |

Note: The total labour force is assumed to be fixed, so the intersectoral employment shifts sum to zero.

**DR-1: Agricultural Liberalization** — The assumed 33 percent reduction in post-UR agricultural-import tariffs is shown in Table 2 to increase global welfare by $10.8 billion.[11] The welfare increases for Canada ($67 million) and Mexico ($111 million) are relatively small, whereas the United States records a welfare decline of $4.1 billion. The expansion of U.S. agriculture apparently has the effect of drawing resources away from the monopolistically competitive, non-agricultural sectors, thereby producing negative scale effects in these sectors. Similar negative welfare effects are also noted for Australia and New Zealand, both of which are net exporters of agricultural products.

**DR-2: Liberalization of Industrial Products** — The assumed 33 percent reduction of post-UR manufacturing tariffs results in an increase in global welfare of $210.7 billion, which is considerably greater than the $90.3 billion welfare gain from the UR liberalization of manufacturing tariffs noted in Brown, Deardorff and Stern (2002). Liberalization of manufactures in a new trade round is seen to increase welfare in all of the countries and regions listed.

While not noted in the table, there are positive effects as well on real wages and the return to capital. There are welfare gains of $63.3 billion for the EU/EFTA, $57.8 billion for Japan, $31.3 billion for the United States, $2.8 billion for Canada and $1.1 billion for Mexico. While the welfare gains for the developing countries and regions are much smaller in absolute terms, the percentage gains tend to be larger, ranging from 0.5 percent for China to 3.5 percent for the Philippines.

**DR-3: Liberalization of Services** — As noted above, the UR negotiations on services resulted in the creation of the GATS, but no significant liberalization of service barriers occurred. Since the conclusion of the UR, there have been successful multilateral negotiations to liberalize telecommunications and financial services. While it would be desirable to assess the economic effects of these sectoral agreements, we cannot do so here because of lack of data. What we have done is to use the estimates of service barriers, based on the calculations of gross operating margins for service firms in the countries and regions in our model, as described above and shown in Table 1. It is important to emphasize that these estimates of service barriers are intended to be indirect approximations of what the actual barriers may be, and thus should not be taken literally. In any event, assuming that the ad valorem equivalents of these barriers are reduced by 33 percent, it can be seen in Table 2 that global economic welfare rises by $389.6 billion, which exceeds the $210.7-billion welfare increase for manufactures liberalization. All of the countries and regions listed experience positive welfare gains as well as increases in real wages and returns to capital. The United States has the largest welfare gain of $150.0 billion, compared to $103.4 billion for the EU/EFTA, and $61.6 billion for Japan. Canada's welfare gain is $10.6 billion and Mexico's gain is $5.2 billion. For several of the smaller industrialized and developing countries, the percentage increases in welfare are noteworthy.

**DR-4: Combined Liberalization Effects (DR-1 + DR-2 + DR-3)** — The results for DR-4 are the sum of the other three scenarios. Overall, in Table 2, global welfare rises by $613.0 billion. Canada's welfare gain is $13.5 billion and Mexico's gain is $6.5 billion. The United States has a welfare gain of $177.3 billion, the EU/EFTA a gain of $168.9 billion, and Japan a gain of $123.7 billion. The percentage welfare gains are sizable in most of the smaller industrialized countries and in the developing countries.

**DR-5: Global Free Trade** — Since our model is linear, the effects of the removal of all tariffs and service barriers would amount to some three times the results of DR-4. Thus, in Table 2, global free trade would increase global welfare by $1.9 trillion. The welfare gains for the United States are $537.2 billion (5.9 percent of GNP); the EU/EFTA, $511.9 billion (4.7 percent of GNP); Japan, $374.8 billion (5.8 percent of GNP); Canada, $40.9 billion (5.6 percent of GNP); and Mexico, $19.6 billion (5.6 percent of GNP). The gains as a percentage of

GNP for the other industrialized countries and the developing countries are also sizable, ranging from about 3.5 percent for Australia to 17 percent for Singapore.

## SECTORAL RESULTS

THE DR-4 SECTORAL EMPLOYMENT results for Canada, Mexico and the United States are presented in Table 3.[12] For all three NAFTA countries, there are notable employment declines in textiles, wearing apparel, leather products and footwear, and some service sectors, while there are employment increases in most of the remaining manufactures sectors, especially agriculture. The sectoral employment results for global free trade in DR-5, which are not shown here, are about three times the amounts shown in Table 3.

## CONCLUSION

THE ABOVE COMPUTATIONAL RESULTS suggest that for the NAFTA countries and the other industrialized and developing countries, there are substantial welfare gains to be realized from a new WTO multilateral negotiating round. The sectoral employment increases for the NAFTA countries are concentrated in agriculture and the relatively more capital-intensive industries, and there are sectoral employment decreases in the relatively labour-intensive industries. This is the case for the assumed 33 percent reductions in the post-UR tariffs and barriers to services – and even more so if there were global free trade.

We should note, as discussed above, that our computational model is based on a comparative static approach, meaning that we move from an initial position to a new equilibrium in which all of the liberalization, and the adjustment to it, is complete. That is, we abstract from a variety of dynamic and related effects that may occur through time, especially with the international mobility of real capital, increases in capital accumulation via real investment, and technological improvements. Our results should thus be interpreted as a lower limit to the economic benefits that may ultimately be realized from the prospective DR and, if it were possible, from a movement to global free trade.[13]

# REGIONAL NEGOTIATING OPTIONS

IN THIS SECTION, WE CONSIDER TWO REGIONAL NEGOTIATING OPTIONS that are being actively pursued by the NAFTA countries: an expansion of the NAFTA to include Chile and a WHFTA, an approximation of the FTAA. These two options are:

RA-1    NAFTA-Chile FTA — *elimination of all bilateral post-UR agricultural and manufactures tariffs and service barriers between NAFTA members and Chile.*

RA-2    WHFTA — *elimination of all bilateral post-UR agricultural and manufactures tariffs and service barriers among NAFTA members, Chile, and countries comprising the CCS aggregate.*

In each of these cases, our reference point is the post-UR 2005 data base described above, together with the post-UR tariff rates on agricultural products and manufactures, and the specially-constructed measures of service barriers used in the DR scenarios. Four scenarios have been carried out for each of the two arrangements noted above:

**(A)**    removal of agricultural tariffs;

**(M)**    removal of manufactures tariffs;

**(S)**    removal of service barriers; and

**(C)**    combined removal of agricultural and manufactures tariffs and service barriers.

Because of space constraints, we report only the latter combined results, denoted RA-1C and RA-2C.

**RA-1C: NAFTA-Chile FTA** — Table 4, column (1), indicates the results of an FTA involving the NAFTA countries and Chile.[14] The complete removal of all post-UR bilateral tariffs on agriculture and manufactures and service barriers vis-à-vis Chile increases global welfare by $5.5 billion. The welfare of the NAFTA members rises, with a gain of $4.2 billion for the United States, $290 million for Canada and $411 million for Mexico. Chile's welfare increases by $740 million (0.92 percent of GNP). There is some evidence of trade diversion for a number of countries, including the CCS aggregate. The sectoral employment effects for the NAFTA members and Chile are shown in Table 5, columns (1)-(4). The U.S. employment effects are negligible, as are those for Canada and Mexico. The employment effects for Chile are noticeably larger, with increases in agriculture, mining, metal products, and other private services, and reductions in textiles and wearing apparel, other manufactures, trade and transport and government services.

# TABLE 4

## GLOBAL WELFARE EFFECTS OF REGIONAL NEGOTIATING OPTIONS
### (PERCENT OF GNP AND BILLIONS OF DOLLARS)

| | NAFTA-Chile FTA (1) | | WHFTA (2) | |
|---|---|---|---|---|
| | Percent of GNP | $ (billion) | Percent of GNP | $ (billion) |
| **NAFTA Countries** | | | | |
| Canada | 0.040 | 0.3 | 0.383 | 2.8 |
| Mexico | 0.116 | 0.4 | 0.806 | 2.8 |
| United States | 0.046 | 4.2 | 0.581 | 52.7 |
| **Industrialized Countries** | | | | |
| Japan | 0.002 | 0.1 | 0.006 | 0.4 |
| Australia | −0.003 | 0.0 | −0.009 | 0.0 |
| New Zealand | −0.001 | 0.0 | −0.004 | 0.0 |
| EU/EFTA | −0.001 | −0.1 | −0.008 | −0.9 |
| **Developing Countries** | | | | |
| **Asia** | | | | |
| Hong Kong | 0.003 | 0.0 | −0.034 | 0.0 |
| China | −0.002 | 0.0 | −0.008 | −0.1 |
| Korea | −0.004 | 0.0 | −0.028 | −0.2 |
| Singapore | 0.004 | 0.0 | 0.036 | 0.0 |
| Taiwan | 0.003 | 0.0 | 0.015 | 0.1 |
| Indonesia | −0.001 | 0.0 | −0.002 | 0.0 |
| Malaysia | 0.005 | 0.0 | 0.069 | 0.1 |
| Philippines | 0.005 | 0.0 | 0.013 | 0.0 |
| Thailand | 0.002 | 0.0 | −0.003 | 0.0 |
| Rest of Asia | 0.001 | 0.0 | −0.001 | 0.0 |
| **Other** | | | | |
| Chile | 0.922 | 0.7 | 2.478 | 2.0 |
| CCS | −0.010 | −0.2 | 1.103 | 18.4 |
| Middle East and North Africa | −0.003 | 0.0 | −0.017 | −0.1 |
| **Total** | | **5.5** | | **77.9** |

Note: These numbers have been rounded.

# TABLE 5

## SECTORAL EMPLOYMENT EFFECTS OF A NAFTA-CHILE FTA AND A WHFTA

### (PERCENT OF EMPLOYMENT AND NUMBER OF WORKERS)

| | NAFTA-Chile FTA | | | | | | | |
|---|---|---|---|---|---|---|---|---|
| Sector | United States (1) | | Canada (2) | | Mexico (3) | | Chile (4) | |
| | Percent of Employment | Number of Workers | Percent of Employment | Number of Workers | Percent of Employment | Number of Workers | Percent of Employment | Number of Workers |
| Agriculture | −0.02 | −656 | −0.02 | −110 | −0.03 | −2,907 | 0.45 | 4,896 |
| Mining | 0.00 | 14 | 0.01 | 17 | −0.02 | −33 | 1.24 | 1,196 |
| Food, Beverages and Tobacco | −0.01 | −193 | −0.01 | −52 | −0.01 | −47 | −0.04 | −99 |
| Textiles | 0.02 | 198 | −0.01 | −2 | 0.13 | 364 | −1.28 | −467 |
| Wearing Apparel | −0.02 | −204 | −0.02 | −25 | −0.03 | −52 | 0.26 | 157 |
| Leather Products and Footwear | −0.03 | −42 | −0.07 | −5 | −0.01 | −11 | 0.62 | 27 |
| Wood and Wood Products | 0.00 | 187 | −0.02 | −86 | −0.03 | −118 | 0.21 | 89 |
| Chemicals | 0.02 | 511 | 0.00 | −15 | 0.04 | 98 | −1.97 | −1,577 |
| Non-metallic Mineral Products | 0.00 | 37 | 0.00 | −2 | 0.01 | 399 | −0.55 | −50 |
| Metal Products | 0.00 | −109 | −0.01 | −42 | 0.06 | 163 | 1.72 | 1,902 |
| Transportation Equipment | 0.02 | 340 | −0.02 | −29 | 0.25 | 322 | −2.89 | −296 |
| Machinery and Equipment | 0.02 | 468 | 0.06 | 86 | −0.05 | −105 | −5.27 | −760 |
| Other Manufactures | 0.00 | 68 | 0.00 | −1 | −0.04 | −11 | −1.92 | −20 |
| Electricity, Gas and Water | 0.01 | 268 | 0.00 | 17 | 0.01 | 94 | 0.04 | 101 |
| Construction | 0.00 | 488 | 0.00 | 70 | 0.01 | 256 | −0.05 | −284 |
| Trade and Transport | 0.00 | 323 | 0.01 | 240 | 0.01 | 1,340 | −0.54 | −7,756 |
| Other Private Services | 0.00 | −1,597 | 0.00 | −96 | 0.00 | 10 | 0.59 | 5,466 |
| Government Services | 0.00 | −100 | 0.00 | 36 | 0.01 | 238 | −0.42 | −2,525 |
| Total | | 0.0 | | 0.0 | | 0.0 | | 0.0 |

## TABLE 5 (CONT'D)

| Sector | WHFTA | | | | | | | | | |
|---|---|---|---|---|---|---|---|---|---|---|
| | United States (5) | | Canada (6) | | Mexico (7) | | Chile (8) | | CCS (9) | |
| | Percent of Employment | Number of Workers | Percent of Employment | Number of Workers | Percent of Employment | Number of Workers | Percent of Employment | Number of Workers | Percent of Employment | Number of Workers |
| Agriculture | −0.48 | −19,640 | −0.20 | −1,254 | −0.16 | −15,595 | 0.71 | 7,728 | 0.97 | 216,949 |
| Mining | −0.20 | −1,400 | −0.49 | −946 | −0.12 | −191 | −1.18 | −1,138 | 0.64 | 7,179 |
| Food, Beverages and Tobacco | −0.34 | −10,610 | −0.05 | −251 | 0.02 | 75 | −0.37 | −838 | 0.67 | 28,096 |
| Textiles | 0.47 | 5,685 | −0.40 | −137 | 0.61 | 1,660 | −1.21 | −439 | 0.14 | 1,746 |
| Wearing Apparel | 0.53 | 5,778 | −0.63 | −906 | −1.15 | −2,179 | 0.72 | 429 | 2.10 | 35,488 |
| Leather Products and Footwear | −0.41 | −604 | −1.52 | −114 | −0.33 | −426 | 0.08 | 4 | 2.92 | 9,996 |
| Wood and Wood Products | 0.09 | 3,884 | −0.08 | −385 | −0.32 | −1,384 | 0.28 | 120 | −0.91 | −12,007 |
| Chemicals | 0.13 | 3,784 | 0.18 | 730 | 0.31 | 772 | 1.36 | −1,087 | −0.42 | −10,756 |
| Non-metallic Mineral Products | 0.04 | 321 | 0.01 | 9 | 0.36 | 12,221 | −1.53 | −139 | −0.66 | −1,730 |
| Metal Products | 0.04 | 1,092 | −0.04 | −100 | −0.25 | −724 | 2.47 | 2,731 | −0.48 | −8,372 |
| Transportation Equipment | 0.15 | 2,995 | 0.52 | 986 | 1.25 | 1,638 | 4.89 | 501 | −1.45 | −13,332 |
| Machinery and Equipment | 0.38 | 11,145 | 0.19 | 273 | −0.46 | −954 | −3.33 | −480 | −3.00 | −34,525 |
| Other Manufactures | 0.68 | 12,358 | -0.27 | −159 | −0.46 | −114 | 0.66 | 7 | −1.33 | −1,394 |
| Electricity, Gas and Water | 0.07 | 3,137 | 0.02 | 163 | 0.02 | 134 | 0.01 | 20 | −0.22 | −11,475 |
| Construction | 0.04 | 5,444 | 0.05 | 846 | 0.10 | 1,809 | 0.19 | 1,086 | −0.27 | −26,865 |
| Trade and Transport | 0.00 | 1,066 | 0.05 | 1,917 | 0.05 | 6,231 | −0.71 | −10,226 | −0.49 | −105,770 |
| Other Private Services | −0.03 | −12,453 | −0.01 | −325 | −0.06 | −3,462 | 0.59 | 5,474 | −0.22 | −48,196 |
| Government Services | −0.04 | −11,983 | −0.02 | −348 | 0.02 | 490 | −0.62 | −3,752 | −0.16 | −25,030 |
| Total | | 0.0 | | 0.0 | | 0.0 | | 0.0 | | 0.0 |

Note: The total labour force is assumed to be fixed, so the intersectoral employment shifts sum to zero.

**RA-2C: WHFTA** — Discussions have been ongoing for several years to create an FTAA.[15] The most recent efforts to move forward in this were made at an April 2001 Summit of the Americas meeting of the 34 member nations in Quebec City. Since the country detail in our model does not include all the individual FTAA members, we have chosen to approximate it by combining the United States, Canada, Mexico and Chile with the CCS aggregate into what we refer to as a WHFTA. The complete removal of service barriers and all bilateral tariffs on agriculture and manufactures can be seen in Table 4, column (2), to increase global welfare by $77.9 billion. The welfare of the NAFTA members rises by $52.7 billion for the United States, $2.8 billion for Canada and $2.8 billion for Mexico. The welfare of Chile rises by $2.0 billion and the CCS aggregate by $18.4 billion. There is evidence of trade diversion for Australia, New Zealand, the EU/EFTA, some Asian developing countries, and the Middle East and North Africa. The sectoral employment effects are indicated in Table 5, columns (5)-(9). The United States shows relatively small employment declines in agriculture, mining, food, beverages and tobacco, and other private and government services, and increases in all other sectors. While the employment effects for Canada are also small, the absolute employment increases for Mexico, Chile and the CCS aggregate are noteworthy. This suggests that the smaller countries in a WHFTA would experience more employment adjustments than the larger ones.

## BILATERAL NEGOTIATING OPTIONS

A S MENTIONED ABOVE, the NAFTA countries are currently engaged in, or are considering, a number of bilateral trading arrangements. Canada has negotiated an FTA with Chile and considering one with the EU. Mexico has concluded FTAs with the EU, Chile and several other Latin American countries, and is considering an FTA with Japan. The United States has recently concluded a bilateral FTA with Jordan and is actively considering FTAs with Chile, Singapore and Korea.[16] In what follows, we analyse the effects on economic welfare and sectoral employment of the following bilateral arrangements:

| | |
|---|---|
| **C-ChFTA** | *Canada-Chile FTA* |
| **C-EUFTA** | *Canada-EU FTA*[17] |
| **M-ChFTA** | *Mexico-Chile FTA* |
| **M-EUFTA** | *Mexico-EU FTA* |
| **M-JFTA** | *Mexico-Japan FTA* |
| **US-ChFTA** | *U.S.-Chile FTA* |
| **US-SFTA** | *U.S.-Singapore FTA* |
| **US-KFTA** | *U.S.-Korea FTA* |

As with the regional scenarios, we report only the results of the combined removal of agricultural and manufactures tariffs and service barriers, denoted by C-ChFTA-C, etc. The results for the separate removal of the agricultural, manufactures, and service barriers are available on request. We should emphasize that our computational analysis does not take into account other features of the various

FTAs, such as the negotiation of explicit rules and the development of new institutional and cooperative arrangements (e.g., covering investment, labour standards
and the environment) that could be beneficial to the countries involved. These
factors do not lend themselves readily to quantification. By the same token, we
have not made allowance for rules of origin that may be negotiated as part of each
FTA and that could be designed with protectionist intentions.

C-ChFTA-C — The welfare effects of a C-ChFTA are noted in Table 6,
column (1). Global economic welfare rises by $354 million, Canada's by $257 million and Chile's by $124 million. The sectoral employment effects for both
countries (available on request) are negligible.

## TABLE 6

### GLOBAL WELFARE EFFECTS OF CANADIAN FTA INITIATIVES
(PERCENT OF GNP AND MILLIONS OF DOLLARS)

|  | Canada-Chile FTA (1) | | Canada-EU/EFTA (2) | |
|---|---|---|---|---|
|  | Percent of GNP | $ (million) | Percent of GNP | $ (million) |
| **NAFTA Countries** |  |  |  |  |
| Canada | 0.04 | 257 | 0.95 | 6,912 |
| Mexico | 0.00 | 0 | –0.03 | –96 |
| United States | 0.00 | 1 | –0.01 | –899 |
| **Other Industrialized Countries** |  |  |  |  |
| EU/EFTA | 0.00 | –6 | 0.15 | 16,937 |
| Japan | 0.00 | 1 | 0.00 | –165 |
| Australia | 0.00 | –1 | 0.00 | 0 |
| New Zealand | 0.00 | 0 | 0.00 | –2 |
| **Developing Countries** |  |  |  |  |
| **Western Hemisphere** |  |  |  |  |
| Chile | 0.15 | 124 | 0.01 | 8 |
| CCS | 0.00 | –16 | 0.00 | 2 |
| **Asia** |  |  |  |  |
| Hong Kong | 0.00 | 0 | 0.01 | 11 |
| China | 0.00 | –2 | –0.01 | –64 |
| Korea | 0.00 | –1 | 0.00 | –1 |
| Singapore | 0.00 | 0 | –0.01 | –6 |
| Taiwan | 0.00 | 0 | –0.01 | –44 |
| Indonesia | 0.00 | 0 | 0.00 | –12 |
| Malaysia | 0.00 | 0 | –0.02 | –28 |
| Philippines | 0.00 | 0 | 0.00 | –4 |
| Thailand | 0.00 | 0 | 0.01 | 14 |
| Rest of Asia | 0.00 | 0 | 0.00 | 25 |
| **Middle East and North Africa** | 0.00 | –2 | 0.00 | –29 |
| Total |  | 354 |  | 22,560 |

Note: These numbers have been rounded.

## TABLE 7
## SECTORAL EMPLOYMENT EFFECTS OF A CANADA-EU FTA
(PERCENT OF EMPLOYMENT AND NUMBER OF WORKERS)

| Sector | Canada (1) | | EU/EFTA (2) | |
|---|---|---|---|---|
| | Percent of Employment | Number of Workers | Percent of Employment | Number of Workers |
| Agriculture | 1.35 | 8,546 | -0.07 | -6,145 |
| Mining | -1.75 | -3,352 | 0.48 | 4,513 |
| Food, Beverages and Tobacco | 0.73 | 3,594 | -0.02 | -1,193 |
| Textiles | -0.18 | -63 | 0.04 | 619 |
| Wearing Apparel | -0.10 | -147 | 0.05 | 974 |
| Leather Products and Footwear | -2.14 | -160 | 0.23 | 876 |
| Wood and Wood Products | 0.87 | 4,212 | -0.07 | -2,608 |
| Chemicals | 0.59 | 2,352 | 0.01 | 676 |
| Non-metallic Mineral Products | 0.10 | 80 | -0.01 | -205 |
| Metal Products | 1.45 | 4,075 | -0.02 | -1,221 |
| Transportation Equipment | 1.87 | 3,517 | -0.04 | -1,018 |
| Machinery and Equipment | 2.36 | 3,341 | -0.08 | -3,523 |
| Other Manufactures | 1.37 | 800 | -0.04 | -686 |
| Electricity, Gas and Water | 0.13 | 975 | 0.01 | 570 |
| Construction | 0.06 | 919 | 0.01 | 820 |
| Trade and Transport | -0.09 | -3,615 | -0.01 | -1,568 |
| Other Private Services | -0.77 | -25,741 | 0.03 | 12,905 |
| Government Services | 0.03 | 668 | -0.01 | -3,786 |
| Total | | 0.0 | | 0.0 |

Note: The total labour force is assumed to be fixed, so the intersectoral employment shifts sum to zero.

**C-EUFTA-C** — As noted in Table 6, column (2), a C-EUFTA increases global welfare by $22.6 billion. Canada's welfare increases by $6.9 billion (0.95 percent of GNP) and that of the EU/EFTA by $16.9 billion (0.15 percent of GNP). There is some evidence of trade diversion for Mexico, the United States, Japan and several Asian countries. The sectoral employment effects are noted in Table 7, which shows employment increases for Canada, especially in agriculture, food, beverages and tobacco, and most manufactures sectors, and declines in mining, labour-intensive manufactures, trade and transport, and other private services. The employment changes for the EU/EFTA tend to be the obverse, but relatively very small.

**M-ChFTA-C** — In Table 8, column (1), it can be seen that a M-ChFTA increases global welfare by $466 million, with an increase of $416 million for Mexico and $138 million for Chile. Both the Mexican and Chilean gains are relatively small percentages of GNP. The sectoral employment changes (available on request) are negligible for both countries.

**M-EUFTA-C** — Table 8, column (2), shows that a M-EUFTA increases global welfare by $10.2 billion, Mexico's by $3.6 billion and that of the EU/EFTA by $7.3 billion. There is small evidence of trade diversion for a number of countries. The sectoral employment effects are indicated in Table 9, column (1). There are employment increases in Mexico in agriculture, labour-intensive and durable manufactures, and declines in the service sectors. The employment changes in the EU/EFTA are the obverse but relatively very small.

**M-JFTA-C** — Table 8, column (3), shows that a M-JFTA increases global welfare by $7.3 billion, Mexico's by $1.9 billion and Japan's by $6.3 billion. The sectoral employment results in Table 9, column (2), indicate employment increases for Mexico in trade and transport and other private services, and declines in all other sectors. While relatively very small, the sectoral employment effects for Japan are negative for agriculture and labour-intensive manufactures, and positive for durable manufactures and services, except for trade and transport.

## TABLE 8

### GLOBAL WELFARE EFFECTS OF MEXICAN FTA INITIATIVES
(PERCENT OF GNP AND MILLIONS OF DOLLARS)

| | Mexico-Chile FTA (1) | | Mexico-EU FTA (2) | | Mexico-Japan FTA (3) | |
|---|---|---|---|---|---|---|
| | Percent of GNP | $ (million) | Percent of GNP | $ (million) | Percent of GNP | $ (million) |
| **NAFTA Countries** | | | | | | |
| Canada | 0.00 | 0 | –0.01 | –65 | –0.01 | –33 |
| Mexico | 0.12 | 416 | 1.02 | 3,615 | 0.54 | 1,912 |
| United States | 0.00 | –30 | 0.00 | –476 | –0.01 | –750 |
| **Other Industrialized Countries** | | | | | | |
| EU/EFTA | 0.00 | –18 | 0.07 | 7,341 | 0.00 | –121 |
| Japan | 0.00 | –6 | 0.00 | –178 | 0.10 | 6,343 |
| Australia | 0.00 | –1 | 0.00 | 5 | 0.00 | 9 |
| New Zealand | 0.00 | 0 | 0.00 | –1 | 0.00 | 2 |
| **Developing Countries** | | | | | | |
| **Western Hemisphere** | | | | | | |
| Chile | 0.17 | 138 | 0.01 | 9 | 0.00 | –1 |
| CCS | 0.00 | –25 | 0.00 | 22 | 0.00 | –21 |
| **Asia** | | | | | | |
| Hong Kong | 0.00 | 0 | 0.00 | 5 | 0.00 | –4 |
| China | 0.00 | –2 | 0.00 | –18 | 0.00 | 0 |
| Korea | 0.00 | –4 | 0.00 | –17 | 0.00 | –13 |
| Singapore | 0.00 | 0 | –0.01 | –6 | 0.00 | –3 |
| Taiwan | 0.00 | 2 | –0.01 | –35 | –0.01 | –26 |
| Indonesia | 0.00 | –1 | 0.00 | –5 | 0.00 | 5 |
| Malaysia | 0.00 | 1 | –0.02 | –22 | –0.01 | –10 |
| Philippines | 0.00 | 0 | 0.00 | –4 | 0.00 | –1 |
| Thailand | 0.00 | 0 | 0.00 | 6 | 0.00 | 1 |
| Rest of Asia | 0.00 | 0 | 0.00 | 20 | 0.00 | –3 |
| **Middle East and North Africa** | 0.00 | –5 | 0.00 | 17 | 0.00 | 16 |
| Total | | 466 | | 10,211 | | 7,302 |

Note: These numbers have been rounded.

## TABLE 9

### SECTORAL EMPLOYMENT EFFECTS OF A MEXICO-EU FTA AND A MEXICO-JAPAN FTA

(PERCENT OF EMPLOYMENT AND NUMBER OF WORKERS)

| Sector | Mexico-EU FTA (1) | | | | Mexico-Japan FTA (2) | | | |
| | Mexico | | EU/EFTA | | Mexico | | Japan | |
| | Percent of Employment | Number of Workers | Percent of Employment | Number of Workers | Percent of Employment | Number of Workers | Percent of Employment | Number of Workers |
|---|---|---|---|---|---|---|---|---|
| Agriculture | 0.46 | 43,777 | -0.04 | -3,639 | -0.07 | -6,833 | -0.02 | -746 |
| Mining | 0.09 | 145 | -0.04 | -418 | -0.12 | -200 | -0.12 | -80 |
| Food, Beverages and Tobacco | 0.28 | 1,400 | -0.02 | -809 | -0.03 | -168 | -0.01 | -367 |
| Textiles | 0.29 | 785 | -0.02 | -356 | -0.40 | -1,080 | -0.01 | -41 |
| Wearing Apparel | 0.11 | 211 | -0.01 | -192 | -0.39 | -736 | -0.01 | -109 |
| Leather Products and Footwear | -0.03 | -41 | -0.04 | -162 | -0.20 | -264 | -0.02 | -20 |
| Wood and Wood Products | -0.03 | -146 | 0.00 | -42 | -0.26 | -1,157 | 0.00 | -32 |
| Chemicals | -0.09 | -237 | 0.01 | 544 | -0.34 | -848 | 0.01 | 200 |
| Non-metallic Mineral Products | -0.37 | -12,375 | 0.01 | 298 | -0.23 | -7,844 | 0.00 | 47 |
| Metal Products | 1.00 | 2,918 | 0.01 | 297 | -0.29 | -858 | 0.02 | 560 |
| Transportation Equipment | 0.83 | 1,089 | 0.02 | 594 | -0.61 | -793 | 0.05 | 318 |
| Machinery and Equipment | 1.99 | 4,156 | 0.01 | 295 | -0.07 | -136 | 0.06 | 1,397 |
| Other Manufactures | 0.95 | 238 | -0.01 | -248 | -1.22 | -305 | 0.05 | 277 |
| Electricity, Gas and Water | 0.10 | 852 | 0.00 | 176 | -0.05 | -414 | 0.01 | 262 |
| Construction | -0.34 | -6,044 | 0.01 | 1,328 | -0.03 | -531 | 0.01 | 607 |
| Trade and Transport | -0.10 | -11,756 | 0.00 | 566 | 0.21 | 24,374 | -0.02 | -2,730 |
| Other Private Services | -0.40 | -21,238 | 0.00 | 2,237 | 0.03 | 1,722 | 0.00 | 405 |
| Government Services | -0.13 | -3,735 | 0.00 | -467 | -0.13 | -3,930 | 0.00 | 53 |
| Total | | 0.0 | | 0.0 | | 0.0 | | 0.0 |

Note: These numbers have been rounded.

**US-ChFTA-C** — To supplement the regional scenario noted for the expansion of the NAFTA to include Chile, the results of a US-ChFTA are indicated in Table 10, column (1). Global welfare increases by $4.7 billion, U.S. welfare by $4.2 billion and Chile's by $479 million. The sectoral results for the United States are shown in Table 11, column (1), and indicate relatively small employment declines in U.S. agriculture, mining, food, beverages and tobacco, wearing apparel, leather products and footwear, and other private services, and employment increases in the other sectors. The sectoral employment effects for Chile show increases in agriculture, mining, metal products, and other private services, and declines in several manufacturing sectors and services. A number of these sectoral changes for Chile are relatively large and indicate the adjustments that may occur with a US-ChFTA.

**US-SFTA-C** — The welfare effects of a US-SFTA are noted in Table 10, column (2). Global welfare rises by $20.6 billion, U.S. welfare by $16.7 billion and Singapore's by $2.0 billion. The sectoral employment effects for the United States are indicated in Table 11, column (2). There are increases in employment, but relatively small ones, in all U.S. sectors, except for wearing apparel, trade and transport, and other private services. For Singapore, there are relatively large sectoral employment increases in wearing apparel and trade and transport services, and declines in most other sectors.

**US-KFTA-C** — The welfare effects of a US-KFTA are shown in Table 10, column (3). Global welfare rises by $38.8 billion, U.S. welfare by $29.2 billion and Korea's by $8.2 billion. A US-KFTA shows no evidence of trade diversion. The sectoral employment effects are indicated in Table 11, column (3). Employment for the United States increases notably in agriculture and food, beverages and tobacco, and declines in most of the manufacturing and service sectors. For Korea, there are noteworthy employment declines in agriculture, food, beverages and tobacco, non-metallic mineral products, construction, and other private services, and increases in most manufacturing sectors and trade and transport services.

## TABLE 10
### GLOBAL WELFARE EFFECTS OF U.S. FTA INITIATIVES
(PERCENT OF GNP AND MILLIONS OF DOLLARS)

| | U.S.-Chile FTA (1) | | U.S.-Singapore FTA (2) | | U.S.-Korea FTA (3) | |
|---|---|---|---|---|---|---|
| | % of GNP | $ (million) | % of GNP | $ (million) | % of GNP | $ (million) |
| **NAFTA Countries** | | | | | | |
| Canada | 0.005 | 34 | −0.012 | −90 | 0.035 | 252 |
| Mexico | −0.001 | −5 | −0.015 | −53 | 0.017 | 61 |
| United States | 0.046 | 4,215 | 0.184 | 16,724 | 0.322 | 29,226 |
| **Other Industrialized Countries** | | | | | | |
| EU/EFTA | 0.000 | −42 | 0.009 | 956 | 0.002 | 196 |
| Japan | 0.002 | 130 | 0.018 | 1,180 | 0.004 | 268 |
| Australia | −0.002 | −10 | 0.032 | 140 | 0.002 | 10 |
| New Zealand | −0.001 | −1 | 0.026 | 19 | 0.003 | 2 |
| **Developing Countries** | | | | | | |
| **Western Hemisphere** | | | | | | |
| Chile | 0.596 | 479 | 0.014 | 11 | 0.008 | 6 |
| CCS | −0.008 | −129 | −0.002 | −32 | 0.008 | 135 |
| **Asia** | | | | | | |
| Hong Kong | 0.003 | 4 | −0.021 | −27 | 0.061 | 78 |
| China | −0.001 | −11 | −0.006 | −57 | 0.005 | 42 |
| Korea | −0.003 | −17 | 0.017 | 96 | 1.436 | 8,172 |
| Singapore | 0.004 | 3 | 2.701 | 2,009 | 0.022 | 16 |
| Taiwan | 0.002 | 7 | −0.003 | −10 | 0.000 | 0 |
| Indonesia | −0.001 | −3 | 0.007 | 17 | 0.013 | 34 |
| Malaysia | 0.004 | 5 | −0.204 | −244 | 0.013 | 16 |
| Philippines | 0.004 | 4 | −0.035 | −31 | 0.014 | 12 |
| Thailand | 0.002 | 4 | 0.003 | 6 | 0.005 | 11 |
| Rest of Asia | 0.001 | 4 | −0.005 | −28 | 0.014 | 82 |
| **Middle East and North Africa** | −0.002 | −16 | 0.003 | 24 | 0.023 | 200 |
| Total | | 4,652 | | 20,612 | | 38,821 |

Note. These numbers have been rounded.

# TABLE 11
## SECTORAL EMPLOYMENT EFFECTS OF U.S. FTAS WITH CHILE, SINGAPORE, AND KOREA
(PERCENT OF EMPLOYMENT AND NUMBER OF WORKERS)

| Sector | U.S.-Chile FTA (1) | | | | U.S.-Singapore FTA (2) | | | | U.S.-Korea FTA (3) | | | |
|---|---|---|---|---|---|---|---|---|---|---|---|---|
| | United States | | Chile | | United States | | Singapore | | United States | | Korea | |
| | Percent of Employment | Number of Workers | Percent of Employment | Number of Workers | Percent of Employment | Number of Workers | Percent of Employment | Number of Workers | Percent of Employment | Number of Workers | Percent of Employment | Number of Workers |
| Agriculture | -0.02 | -730 | 0.30 | 3,258 | 0.09 | 3,794 | -2.71 | -127 | 1.28 | 52,508 | -3.93 | -111,888 |
| Mining | 0.00 | -10 | 1.14 | 1,094 | 0.08 | 586 | -2.97 | -18 | -0.10 | -707 | 0.67 | 207 |
| Food, Beverages and Tobacco | -0.01 | -206 | -0.11 | -251 | 0.04 | 1,118 | -5.23 | -2,796 | 0.12 | 3,958 | -0.92 | -4,836 |
| Textiles | 0.02 | 216 | -0.77 | -280 | 0.05 | 614 | -4.91 | -223 | -0.45 | -5,429 | 4.86 | 31,653 |
| Wearing Apparel | -0.02 | -203 | 0.24 | 144 | -0.03 | -372 | 15.28 | 8,411 | -0.68 | -7,452 | 8.68 | 50,828 |
| Leather Products and footwear | -0.03 | -40 | 0.36 | 16 | 0.18 | 263 | -5.40 | -139 | -0.78 | -1,131 | 7.03 | 7,398 |
| Wood and Wood Products | 0.00 | 49 | 0.08 | 35 | 0.03 | 1,145 | -4.63 | -1,944 | -0.03 | -1,317 | 0.08 | 298 |
| Chemicals | 0.02 | 507 | -1.74 | -1,395 | 0.06 | 1,649 | -5.87 | -8,483 | 0.01 | 223 | 0.24 | 1,540 |
| Non-metallic Mineral Products | 0.00 | 27 | -0.46 | -42 | 0.04 | 304 | -3.33 | -545 | -0.02 | -154 | -0.67 | -2,764 |
| Metal Products | 0.00 | -95 | 1.41 | 1,556 | 0.07 | 1,975 | -7.13 | -2,989 | -0.06 | -1,568 | 0.71 | 6,888 |
| Transportation Equipment | 0.02 | 373 | -2.15 | -220 | 0.06 | 1,151 | -5.43 | -202 | -0.08 | -1,546 | 0.24 | 376 |
| Machinery and Equipment | 0.02 | 515 | -5.20 | -749 | 0.15 | 4,296 | -4.42 | -3,067 | 0.01 | 194 | 1.37 | 6,708 |
| Other Manufacturers | 0.00 | 78 | -1.95 | -21 | 0.18 | 3,270 | -4.69 | -1,355 | -0.34 | -6,164 | 4.74 | 23,587 |
| Electricity, Gas and water | 0.01 | 269 | 0.03 | 89 | 0.02 | 694 | -0.79 | -298 | 0.01 | 294 | 0.24 | 2,310 |
| Construction | 0.00 | 514 | -0.05 | -263 | 0.00 | 482 | -0.05 | -98 | 0.00 | -218 | -0.08 | -2,812 |
| Trade and Transport | 0.00 | 341 | -0.41 | -5,927 | -0.07 | -21,804 | 1.89 | 14,225 | -0.06 | -17,633 | 0.61 | 22,198 |
| Other Private Services | 0.00 | -1,568 | 0.54 | 5,011 | 0.00 | -206 | 0.60 | 1,911 | 0.00 | -650 | -0.87 | -31,933 |
| Government Services | 0.00 | -38 | -0.34 | -2,055 | 0.00 | 1,041 | -1.60 | -2,265 | -0.05 | -13,210 | 0.01 | 241 |
| Total | 0.0 | 0.0 | 0.0 | 0.0 | 0.0 | 0.0 | 0.0 | 0.0 | 0.0 | 0.0 | 0.0 | 0.0 |

Note: The total force is assumed to be fixed, so the intersectoral employment shifts sum to zero.

# HARMONIZATION OF THE NAFTA'S EXTERNAL TARIFFS

IN THIS SECTION, we suppose that the NAFTA is turned into a customs union with a common external tariff and no rules of origin or other types of restrictions. Ideally, we should use the highly disaggregated tariff schedules of Canada, Mexico and the United States for this purpose; however, time and resource constraints prevent us from doing so. Instead, as an approximation, we will use the sectoral tariff averages contained in our model data base. The problem here is that these tariff rates, which have been calculated as part of the GTAP data base, are themselves import-weighted averages from lower levels of aggregation. In any event, we have calculated a vector of common external tariffs, by sector, for the three NAFTA countries on the following alternative assumptions:

- simple arithmetic average;
- import-weighted average; and
- production-weighted average.

We then use our model to calculate the effects of changing existing post-UR tariffs to these common external ones.

The existing post-UR average tariff rates for the NAFTA countries are given in Table 12, together with the calculated harmonized rates. It should be noted that these are the averages for all trading partners, whereas in the model there is one set of tariff rates for each trading partner. Nonetheless, these average rates provide some indication of the heights of the tariffs for the individual sectors in the NAFTA countries. We should note also that the estimated service barriers have not been included in the harmonization experiment, as these have been imputed from cost-price margins, and therefore should not be interpreted in the same manner as the statutory import tariffs on traded goods.

## COMPUTATIONAL RESULTS

THE AGGREGATE EFFECTS ON ECONOMIC WELFARE for the NAFTA countries and other countries and regions covered in our model are indicated in Table 13. With the simple average tariffs that are higher than each of the weighted schemes, it turns out that the United States would have to raise its tariffs. The end result is a rather large decline in the volume of trade for the United States and most non-NAFTA countries, whereas Canada's and Mexico's trade expands. As noted in Table 13, column (1), U.S. economic welfare rises by $13.5 billion, due in large measure to improved terms of trade. Canada's rises by $1.9 billion and Mexico's by $2.3 billion, due to the pervasive trade diversion.

## TABLE 12

## NAFTA POST-UR EXTERNAL TARIFF RATES AND CALCULATED HARMONIZED TARIFF RATES (PERCENT)

| Sector | Average Tariff Rates | | | Harmonized Rates | | |
|---|---|---|---|---|---|---|
| | United States | Canada | Mexico | Simple Average | Trade-weighted | Production-weighted |
| Agriculture | 4.5 | 1.2 | 2.8 | 2.8 | 4.1 | 3.9 |
| Mining | 0.3 | 13.5 | 8.3 | 7.3 | 1.5 | 3.2 |
| Food, Beverages and Tobacco | 18.8 | 6.8 | 5.0 | 10.2 | 17.2 | 17.3 |
| Textiles | 9.9 | 17.9 | 13.6 | 13.8 | 11.0 | 10.7 |
| Wearing Apparel | 11.3 | 22.2 | 17.0 | 16.8 | 12.1 | 12.2 |
| Leather Products and Footwear | 8.3 | 14.1 | 17.4 | 13.3 | 8.9 | 10.7 |
| Wood and Wood Products | 2.1 | 3.9 | 9.8 | 5.3 | 2.5 | 2.7 |
| Chemicals | 5.2 | 7.0 | 8.7 | 7.0 | 5.5 | 5.6 |
| Non-metallic Mineral Products | 8.2 | 5.7 | 15.1 | 9.7 | 8.2 | 8.5 |
| Metal Products | 3.8 | 6.0 | 9.3 | 6.3 | 4.2 | 4.2 |
| Transportation Equipment | 2.7 | 6.2 | 12.6 | 7.2 | 3.2 | 3.4 |
| Machinery and Equipment | 3.2 | 3.2 | 9.4 | 5.3 | 3.4 | 3.5 |
| Other Manufactures | 2.9 | 3.0 | 15.0 | 7.0 | 3.2 | 3.7 |

Tariff changes are smaller with the trade-weighted and production-weighted harmonized tariffs. Accordingly, there are larger tariff reductions for Canada and Mexico, and both experience a deterioration in the terms of trade. In Table 13, columns (2) and (3), it can be seen that Canada's welfare declines while Mexico's rises (insofar as the efficiency effects outweigh Mexico's worsened terms of trade). Global welfare increases by $134.5 million for the import-weighted tariffs and declines by $2.4 billion for the production-weighted tariffs. Thus, it appears that the adoption of a trade-weighted common external tariff is much less disruptive to trade and welfare than a simple average or production-weighted system.

The sectoral employment effects are shown in Table 14. For all three countries, the signs and magnitude of the effects for the simple-average tariffs in column (1) do not correspond well with the trade- and production-weighted tariff effects in columns (2) and (3). For Canada, there are decreases in employment with the trade- and production-weighted tariffs in mining, textiles, wearing apparel, leather products and footwear and services, and increases in the remaining sectors. The sectoral employment effects for Mexico with the trade- and production-weighted tariffs are relatively small, except for machinery and equipment and other manufactures. Finally, for the United States, the sectoral employment effects for the trade- and production-weighted tariffs appear relatively small. It can be concluded, therefore, that the adoption of a common external tariff based on trade or production weights would, by and large, have minimal employment impacts on the NAFTA countries.

## TABLE 13

### GLOBAL WELFARE EFFECTS OF NAFTA TARIFF HARMONIZATION
(PERCENT OF GNP AND MILLIONS OF DOLLARS)

| | Simple Average (1) | | Trade-weighted (2) | | Production-weighted (3) | |
|---|---|---|---|---|---|---|
| | Percent of GNP | $ (million) | Percent of GNP | $ (million) | Percent of GNP | $ (million) |
| **NAFTA Countries** | | | | | | |
| Canada | 0.261 | 1,899.1 | −0.108 | −789.4 | −0.084 | −612.7 |
| Mexico | 0.639 | 2,255.2 | 0.164 | 579.8 | 0.202 | 713.1 |
| United States | 0.148 | 13,468.9 | 0.008 | 764.0 | 0.017 | 1,567.5 |
| **Other Industrialized Countries** | | | | | | |
| EU/EFTA | −0.092 | −10,116.3 | −0.003 | −328.9 | 0.005 | 597.5 |
| Japan | −0.187 | −12,167.5 | −0.001 | −49.0 | −0.008 | −542.1 |
| Australia | −0.059 | −260.4 | −0.010 | −44.9 | −0.039 | −169.4 |
| New Zealand | −0.185 | −135.7 | −0.002 | −1.8 | −0.002 | −1.5 |
| **Developing Countries** | | | | | | |
| **Western Hemisphere** | | | | | | |
| Chile | −0.253 | −203.4 | −0.001 | −0.5 | −0.015 | −12.1 |
| CCS | −0.206 | −3,438.6 | 0.005 | 82.1 | −0.057 | −950.0 |
| **Asia** | | | | | | |
| Hong Kong | −0.491 | −632.3 | −0.006 | −7.6 | −0.011 | −14.0 |
| China | −0.283 | −2,565.7 | −0.003 | −30.5 | −0.048 | −435.6 |
| Korea | −0.339 | −1,927.9 | −0.005 | −27.1 | −0.018 | −103.5 |
| Singapore | −0.614 | −456.4 | −0.002 | −1.4 | −0.046 | −34.0 |
| Taiwan | −0.715 | −2,506.7 | −0.004 | −15.7 | −0.025 | −86.9 |
| Indonesia | −0.278 | −703.8 | 0.004 | 9.7 | −0.039 | −99.9 |
| Malaysia | −1.381 | −1,651.1 | −0.008 | −9.9 | −0.064 | −76.5 |
| Philippines | −1.267 | −1,118.1 | 0.005 | 4.5 | −0.119 | −104.9 |
| Thailand | −0.540 | −1,113.2 | 0.004 | 7.4 | −0.069 | −141.4 |
| Rest of Asia | −0.316 | −1,807.4 | −0.003 | −15.7 | −0.012 | −70.0 |
| **Middle East and North Africa** | −0.642 | −5,544.4 | 0.001 | 9.5 | −0.216 | −1,863.4 |
| Total | | −28,725.8 | | 134.5 | | 2,439.7 |

Note: These numbers have been rounded.

## TABLE 14

### SECTORAL EMPLOYMENT EFFECTS FOR CANADA, MEXICO AND THE UNITED STATES OF NAFTA TARIFF HARMONIZATION
(PERCENT OF EMPLOYMENT AND NUMBER OF WORKERS)

| | (1) Simple Average | | | | | |
|---|---|---|---|---|---|---|
| Sector | Canada | | Mexico | | United States | |
| | Percent of Employment | Number of Workers | Percent of Employment | Number of Workers | Percent of Employment | Number of Workers |
| Agriculture | −0.66 | −4,168 | −0.19 | −17,723 | −1.19 | −48,627 |
| Mining | −1.05 | −2,013 | −0.07 | −120 | 2.33 | 16,532 |
| Food, Beverages and Tobacco | 0.21 | 1,063 | 0.13 | 651 | −0.67 | −21,199 |
| Textiles | −2.41 | −828 | −0.05 | −146 | 1.15 | 13,946 |
| Wearing Apparel | −3.06 | −4,403 | 0.93 | 1,753 | 3.28 | 35,772 |
| Leather Products and Footwear | 0.52 | 39 | 0.24 | 309 | 5.14 | 7,486 |
| Wood and Wood Products | −0.47 | −2,302 | −0.15 | −678 | 0.10 | 4,408 |
| Chemicals | 0.61 | 2,420 | −0.28 | −700 | −0.11 | −3,066 |
| Non-metallic Mineral Products | 1.03 | 814 | −0.14 | −4,702 | −0.06 | −431 |
| Metal Products | 0.61 | 1,730 | 0.07 | 211 | 0.01 | 213 |
| Transportation Equipment | 1.85 | 3,476 | 1.08 | 1,408 | 0.46 | 9,078 |
| Machinery and Equipment | 0.59 | 843 | 2.09 | 4,356 | −0.54 | −15,545 |
| Other Manufactures | 3.09 | 1,808 | −1.15 | −288 | 2.04 | 37,049 |
| Electricity, Gas and Water | 0.10 | 747 | 0.12 | 979 | −0.03 | −1,595 |
| Construction | 0.11 | 1,848 | 0.12 | 2,165 | 0.03 | 3,558 |
| Trade and Transport | −0.05 | −2,049 | 0.06 | 7,062 | −0.09 | −27,877 |
| Other Private Services | −0.02 | −720 | 0.08 | 4,364 | −0.08 | −29,723 |
| Government Services | 0.08 | 1,693 | 0.04 | 1,099 | 0.07 | 20,021 |
| Total | | 0.0 | | 0.0 | | 0.0 |

| | (2) Trade-weighted | | | | | |
|---|---|---|---|---|---|---|
| Sector | Canada | | Mexico | | United States | |
| | Percent of Employment | Number of Workers | Percent of Employment | Number of Workers | Percent of Employment | Number of Workers |
| Agriculture | 0.59 | 3,711 | 0.02 | 1,747 | −0.08 | −3,474 |
| Mining | −2.11 | −4,029 | −0.08 | −138 | 0.50 | 3,564 |
| Food, Beverages and Tobacco | 1.24 | 6,135 | 0.20 | 1,004 | −0.11 | −3,329 |
| Textiles | −3.64 | −1,251 | −0.17 | −465 | 0.25 | 3,020 |
| Wearing Apparel | −6.09 | −8,770 | −0.01 | −19 | 0.46 | 5,013 |
| Leather Products and Footwear | −4.99 | −374 | −0.67 | −863 | 0.45 | 648 |
| Wood and Wood Products | 0.15 | 725 | −0.30 | −1,328 | −0.01 | −638 |
| Chemicals | 0.54 | 2,170 | −0.32 | −786 | −0.01 | −260 |
| Non-metallic Mineral Products | 0.92 | 727 | −0.16 | −5,423 | −0.05 | −398 |
| Metal Products | 0.66 | 1,859 | 0.35 | 1,023 | −0.07 | −1,789 |
| Transportation Equipment | 1.06 | 1,988 | 0.41 | 537 | −0.09 | −1,824 |
| Machinery and Equipment | 0.61 | 862 | 1.87 | 3,891 | −0.14 | −3,936 |
| Other Manufactures | 0.82 | 481 | 2.75 | 688 | 0.10 | 1,744 |
| Electricity, Gas and Water | 0.01 | 97 | 0.04 | 362 | −0.01 | −520 |
| Construction | 0.00 | −38 | 0.02 | 346 | 0.00 | 116 |
| Trade and Transport | 0.00 | 10 | 0.05 | 6,440 | 0.00 | −1,016 |
| Other Private Services | −0.04 | −1,167 | −0.02 | −999 | 0.00 | 124 |
| Government Services | −0.14 | −3,136 | −0.16 | −4,642 | 0.01 | 2,956 |
| Total | | 0.0 | | 0.0 | | 0.0 |

## TABLE 14 (CONT'D)

| Sector | (3) Production-weighted | | | | | |
| --- | --- | --- | --- | --- | --- | --- |
| | Canada | | Mexico | | United States | |
| | Percent of Employment | Number of Workers | Percent of Employment | Number of Workers | Percent of Employment | Number of Workers |
| Agriculture | 0.47 | 2,986 | 0.00 | −21 | −0.20 | −8,034 |
| Mining | −1.83 | −3,510 | 0.02 | 25 | 1.20 | 8,504 |
| Food, Beverages and Tobacco | 1.25 | 6,188 | 0.21 | 1,032 | −0.11 | −3,437 |
| Textiles | −3.93 | −1,350 | −0.21 | −580 | 0.11 | 1,320 |
| Wearing Apparel | −6.29 | −9,062 | 0.00 | −1 | 0.43 | 4,657 |
| Leather Products and Footwear | −2.01 | −151 | −0.23 | −294 | 3.28 | 4,772 |
| Wood and Wood Products | 0.07 | 339 | −0.31 | −1,345 | −0.02 | −715 |
| Chemicals | 0.58 | 2,318 | −0.29 | −726 | −0.05 | −1,485 |
| Non-metallic Mineral Products | 0.98 | 770 | −0.15 | −4,972 | −0.02 | −137 |
| Metal Products | 0.59 | 1,650 | 0.27 | 797 | −0.11 | −3,124 |
| Transportation Equipment | 1.06 | 1,993 | 0.44 | 579 | −0.07 | −1,333 |
| Machinery and Equipment | 0.50 | 714 | 1.81 | 3,764 | −0.26 | −7,403 |
| Other Manufactures | 1.16 | 682 | −2.48 | −620 | 0.42 | 7,721 |
| Electricity, Gas and Water | 0.02 | 188 | 0.05 | 414 | −0.02 | −984 |
| Construction | 0.01 | 144 | 0.03 | 546 | 0.00 | 161 |
| Trade and Transport | −0.01 | −254 | 0.05 | 6,210 | −0.01 | −3,991 |
| Other Private Services | −0.03 | −1,084 | −0.01 | −632 | 0.00 | −1,340 |
| Government Services | −0.11 | −2,561 | −0.14 | −4,177 | 0.02 | 4,848 |
| Total | | 0.0 | | 0.0 | | 0.0 |

Note: The total labour force is assumed to be fixed, so the intersectoral employment shifts sum to zero.

## CONCLUSIONS AND IMPLICATIONS FOR POLICY

WE HAVE USED THE MICHIGAN MODEL of World Production and Trade to simulate the economic effects of the trade liberalization that may be negotiated in the prospective DR, as well as a variety of regional and bilateral preferential trading arrangements. We have also analysed the economic effects of the harmonization of the NAFTA's external tariffs. The predominant conclusion that emerges from our model simulations of the DR is that multilateral trade liberalization has positive – and often sizable – impacts on the economic welfare of the NAFTA countries, as well as the other industrialized and developing countries and regions covered in the Michigan model.

A second conclusion is that while regional and bilateral FTAs may be welfare-enhancing for the member countries directly involved, these gains are considerably smaller than those resulting from multilateral trade liberalization, even when comparing the complete elimination of regional and bilateral tariffs to the reduction of multilateral tariffs by only one third. Thus, the benefits of FTAs to their developing country partners appear somewhat limited and, in some cases, could even prove disruptive because of intersectoral shifts in output and employment, depending on how rapidly the FTAs are implemented. It is also the case that most of the regional and bilateral FTAs involve elements of trade diversion and are therefore detrimental to some non-member countries.

Finally, the effects of adopting a common external tariff for NAFTA members will depend on the method of calculation. A trade-weighted harmonized tariff appears to be less disruptive to trade and welfare than a simple or production-weighted average. There would be relatively small sectoral employment impacts with both trade- and production-weighted tariffs.

# ENDNOTES

1　Readers not interested in the model details may proceed directly to the computational results.

2　Intermediate inputs include both domestic and imported varieties.

3　This source does not provide number-of-firms data for all countries. We have used the number-of-firms data for similar countries in these cases.

4　We also need data on supply elasticities from the ROW; these have been taken from the Michigan model data base.

5　Hertel and Martin (1999) and Hertel (2000) provide a more elaborate and detailed procedure for calculating 2005 projections.

6　Deardorff and Stern (2002) discuss the differences that prevented consensus in Seattle.

7　Reductions in post-UR agricultural export subsidies and in aggregate measures of support will presumably also be negotiated in a new trade round, but they are not included in this scenario.

8　Because of computer-capacity constraints, Brown and Stern (2001) used a three-sector aggregation consisting of agriculture, manufactures and services, and the same 20-country and region breakdown as is being used here. They also differ from the present analysis by making allowances for international flows of FDI and increases in capital stocks in response to the multilateral trade liberalization that they analyse.

9　The potential gains from a new WTO trade round are also analysed in Hertel, on the basis of the GTAP CGE model, which is a widely used modelling structure. The version used by Hertel assumes perfect competition in all sectors. It also assumes national product differentiation (i.e., the Armington assumption), which may tend to exaggerate terms-of-trade effects.

10　The aggregate results for the effects on exports, imports and the returns to capital and labour are available in Brown, Deardorff and Stern (2002).

11　All dollar amounts in this study are in U.S. dollars.

12　Sectoral results for percentage changes in exports, imports, output and scale economies are given in Brown, Deardorff and Stern (2002).

13　Brown and Stern have used their three-sector, 20-country CGE model, which incorporates the behaviour of multinational corporations (MNCs) and their foreign affiliates and international mobility of FDI-related capital, to assess the removal of post-UR tariffs and service barriers. If we make allowances for imperfect mobility of real international capital and an increase of 3 percent in the world capital stock in response to the increase in the real return on capital due to the assumed liberalization, global welfare would increase by $203.7 billion. The welfare increase for the United States is $222.5 billion; for Canada, $85.0 billion; and for Mexico, $0.5 billion. International capital mobility, combined with an increase in capital accumulation, may therefore generate welfare changes that are different in size and geographical distribution as compared to the results generated in the more disaggregated, sectoral version of the Michigan model used here, which abstracts from the behavior of MNCs in response to trade liberalization. Time and resource constraints have thus far prevented Brown and Stern from expanding the sectoral coverage of their FDI model to analyse the more detailed responses to trade liberalization for the world's major trading countries and regions.

14   For a more comprehensive analysis of the accession of Chile to the NAFTA, see Brown, Deardorff and Stern (2000).

15   See Office of the United States Trade Representative (2001a).

16   See Office of the United States Trade Representative (2001b, c) and United States International Trade Commission (2001) for information on the U.S. FTA initiatives.

17   Since in our model the EU is combined with the (much smaller) EFTA countries, this scenario, and others involving FTAs with the EU, is actually modelled to include the EFTA as well.

# BIBLIOGRAPHY

Brown, Drusilla K., Alan V. Deardorff, and Robert M. Stern. "Computational Analysis of the Accession of Chile to the NAFTA and Western Hemisphere Integration." *The World Economy* 23 (2000): 145-74.

_____. "CGE Modeling and Analysis of Multilateral and Regional Negotiating Options." In *Issues and Options for U.S.-Japan Trade Policies.* Edited by Robert M. Stern. University of Michigan Press, 2002, pp. 23-65.

Brown, Drusilla K., and Robert M. Stern. "Measurement and Modeling of the Economic Effects of Trade and Investment Barriers in Services." *Review of International Economics* 9 (2001): 262-86.

Deardorff, Alan V., and Robert M. Stern. *Computational Analysis of Global Trading Arrangements.* Ann Arbor MI: University of Michigan Press, 1990.

_____. "What You Should Know about Globalization and the World Trade Organization." *Review of International Economics* (2002): 404-423.

Harrison, W.J., and Ken Pearson. "Computing Solutions for Large General Equilibrium Models Using GEMPACK." *Computational Economics* 9 (1996): 83-127.

Hertel, Thomas W., and Will Martin. "Would Developing Countries Gain from Inclusion of Manufactures in the WTO Negotiations?" Presented at the Conference on the WTO and the Millennium Round, Geneva, September 1999.

Hertel, Thomas W. "Potential Gains from Reducing Trade Barriers in Manufacturing, Services and Agriculture." *Federal Reserve Bank of St. Louis Review* 82 (2000): 77-99.

Hoekman, Bernard. "The Next Round of Services Negotiations: Identifying Priorities and Options." *Federal Reserve Bank of St. Louis Review* 82 (2000): 31-47.

McDougall, Robert A., Aziz Elbehri and Truong P. Truong (eds.). *Global Trade, Assistance and Protection: The GTAP 4 Data Base.* W. Lafayette IN: Purdue University, 1998.

Office of the United States Trade Representative. "Accomplishments of the FTAA Ministerial." USTR Fact Sheet, April 7, 2001a.

_____. "Joint Declaration of the Proposed U.S.-Singapore Free Trade Agreement." USTR Press Release 00-08, January 17, 2001b.

_____. "United States and Chile Free Trade Agreement: Third Negotiating Round." Press Release 01-19, April 2, 2001c.

Stolper, Wolfgang, and Paul A. Samuelson. "Protection and Real Wages." *Review of Economic Studies* 9 (1941): 58-73.

United Nations. *International Yearbook of Industrial Statistics.* New York: United Nations Industrial Development Organization, 1995.

_____. *International Yearbook of Industrial Statistics.* New York: United Nations Industrial Development Organization, 1998.

United States International Trade Commission. "ITC to Analyze Impact of a U.S.-Korean Free Trade Agreement." USITC News 01-003, Inv. No. 332-425, January 11, 2001.

World Bank. *World Development Indicators, 1999,* Table 2.3.

_____. *World Development Report,1998-99,* Table 11.

Sven W. Arndt
*Claremont McKenna College*

# 10

# The Pros and Cons of North American
# Monetary Integration

## INTRODUCTION

QUESTIONS ARE ONCE AGAIN BEING RAISED about exchange rate arrangements in North America. The current discussion is a reaction in part to the arrival of the European Monetary Union (EMU) and its implications for the U.S. dollar and in part to monetary and financial turmoil around the globe. In Canada, concerns about the effects of floating rates on competitiveness add a new element to the debate.

The North American Free Trade Agreement (NAFTA) and various plans to promote regional integration in the western hemisphere raise questions not only about the costs and benefits of *widening* regional trade areas, but also about whether trade integration needs *deeper* cooperation — particularly in monetary and financial terms — in order to achieve its full potential. In Canada recently, deepening cooperation has been subject to renewed scrutiny by academic economists and policy analysts, with particular focus on monetary union. Mexicans, for their part, have pondered the pros and cons of deepening in terms of dollarization.

This study examines the major arguments for and against enhanced monetary integration in North America, with particular emphasis on the Canadian perspective. In this context, the question is whether the current floating rate regime should be replaced by greater fixity of exchange rates in relation to the U.S. dollar. While the choice among fixed rate systems is wide in principle, for practical purposes the Canadian debate centres on the pros and cons of monetary union. As other countries in the northern hemisphere may be reluctant to embrace monetary union, the following discussion also examines other potential candidate regimes, including currency boards and dollarization.

Although much of the debate focusses on traditional concerns of macroeconomic stability and policy management, some observers suspect that the floating rate system has retarded the development of high tech manufacturing in Canada. The depreciation of the Canadian dollar, possibly in response to deflation in world commodity prices, may have shielded Canadian manufacturing in ways that undermine incentives to innovate and modernize.

The next section of the study reviews the core arguments for and against fixed rates and currency union. The third section examines problems associated with nominal rigidities, while the fourth focusses on the role of exchange rate regimes in the evolution of economic structure. Then, the study addresses the question of causality: Do exchange rate movements give rise to internal adjustment problems or do internal adjustment problems give rise to exchange rate movements? The sixth section considers trade-offs among alternative exchange rate regimes, while the seventh takes up the political dimension of closer monetary cooperation and is followed by the conclusion.

## THE TRADITIONAL ARGUMENTS

THE LINE-UP OF KEY ARGUMENTS for and against fixed rates depends to some extent on the regime under consideration. Fixed rate regimes fall into two major categories: soft and hard pegs. The former are widely believed to be too fragile for the prevailing conditions in many countries. The class of hard pegs, which is the focus here, includes currency boards, dollarization and currency union. The following discussion focusses on currency union, with references to the other hard options, as needed. The basic arguments and insights pertaining to optimum currency areas hearken back to Mundell (1961), McKinnon (1963), Kenen (1969) and others (Tower and Willett 1976; Berg and Borensztein 2000b; Eichengreen 1997; Emerson et al. 1990; de Grauwe 1997). They are well-known, and hence will be sketched only briefly here.

### GREATER EFFICIENCY AND LOWER TRANSACTIONS COSTS

THE CHIEF ARGUMENT IN FAVOUR of a common currency is its contribution to efficiency and lower transaction costs. It allows individuals to engage in trade without the cost of currency conversion. Courchene and Harris (2000) estimate Canadian currency conversion costs at about 0.5 percent of gross domestic product (GDP), while Murray (2000) pegs annual transaction costs at approximately $3 billion, the discounted present value of which amounts to about one-tenth of current GDP. These savings are supplemented by cost reductions related to accounting, hedging, invoicing and other operations.

Unlike floating rates and pegged rate systems, a common currency eliminates uncertainties about future values of exchange rates and thereby improves the efficiency of decision-making. Grubel (2000) argues that the removal of exchange rate risk reduces interest rates, thereby cutting the cost of servicing the Canadian national debt, reducing the complexity of cross-border price comparisons and providing assorted other benefits.

FIGURE 1A

CONSUMER PRICES — INDEX NUMBERS (1995=100)

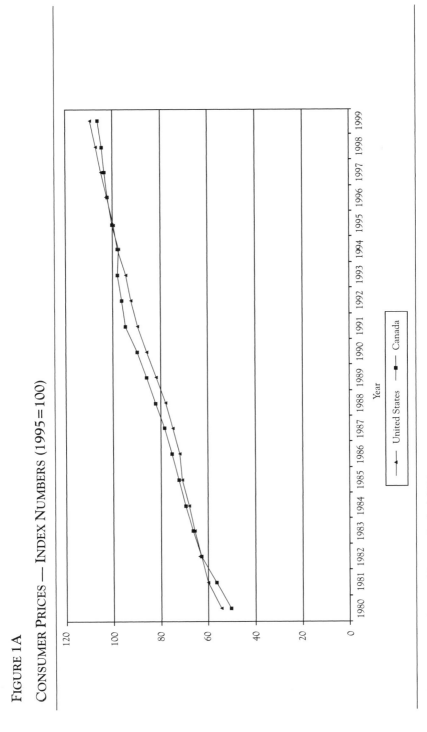

Source: *International Financial Statistics Yearbook 2000.*

FIGURE 1B

INDUSTRY-PRODUCER PRICES — INDEX NUMBERS (1995=100)

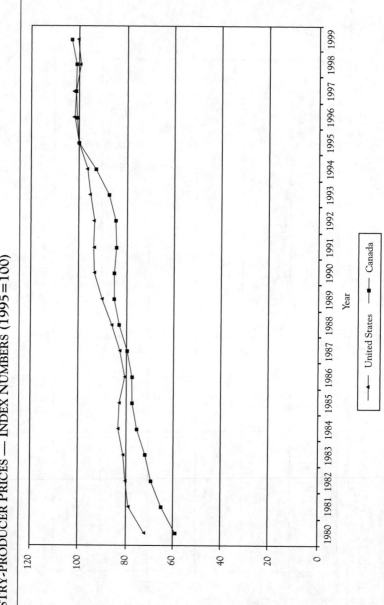

Year

United States       Canada

Source: *International Financial Statistics Yearbook 2000.*

It is important to note, however, that the exchange rate must be truly fixed. Regimes which allow for the periodic adjustment of exchange rate pegs, for example, do not eliminate all the costs and uncertainties associated with variable rates. This is one of several considerations which inclines many observers toward the "hard" pegs of currency boards and dollarization rather than the "soft" fixity of adjustable pegs.

## PRICE STABILITY

A SECOND ARGUMENT IN FAVOUR of fixed rates applies particularly to inflation-prone countries. Such countries can "import" price stability by pegging to a low-inflation country or joining low-inflation currency unions. While this consideration is relevant for many Latin American countries, and explains why Argentina and Ecuador would pursue currency board or dollarization schemes, it is not a decisive issue in Canada.

As Figures 1A and 1B suggest, U.S. and Canadian prices display very similar long-run patterns. On average, the U.S. track record is better over the last two decades of the twentieth century for consumer prices, but worse for producer prices. Thus, Canada would not gain much inflation control from joining a currency area with the United States. Indeed, Murray has argued that, recently, Canada's record on inflation has been better than the U.S. record. This may be due to the fact that unlike the Federal Reserve, Canada's central bank announces its inflation targets: this both provides more incentives for policy makers to deliver lower inflation and enhances policy credibility in financial markets.

## LOST SEIGNIORAGE AND IMPAIRED POLICY AUTONOMY

CURRENCY BOARDS, DOLLARIZATION AND CURRENCY UNIONS have their weaknesses, however. One is the partial or complete loss of seigniorage earnings, particularly in the case of dollarization. Another is the diminution or loss of macro policy independence. Grubel estimates Canada's seigniorage profits at about $2 billion per annum. They would be lost entirely under full dollarization and partially under formal monetary union. The constraints on macroeconomic policy independence are particularly severe in the realm of monetary policy, but, as the EMU has shown, they also impinge on fiscal policy.

Restraints on policy autonomy matter, particularly in the presence of asymmetric structures and shocks among member countries and imperfections in their respective goods and factor markets. Asymmetries reduce the extent to which adjustment and the demands on policy share common elements across countries and, therefore, raise the likelihood that countries will disagree on the desired stance of region-wide or system-wide macro policy. Asymmetries make shocks more country-specific and thus reduce common elements in adjustment patterns and policy needs.

If, for example, one country is a resource exporter while the other is not, a decline in world resource prices will have orthogonal implications for the two countries. As monetary policy now is either a region-wide instrument (under currency union) or has region-wide effects, policies that tilt in favour of one country will be inimical to the other. In a currency board and under dollarization, monetary policy will tend to be driven by the requirements of the centre country, implying that the presence of strong asymmetries will expose peripheral countries to harmful policy shocks. In the case of currency union, where policy makers must manage conflicting regional interests, monetary policy loses its suitability for targeting country-specific disturbances.

From the foregoing, it is clear that loss of monetary policy autonomy is a problem in all fixed rate regimes, particularly for smaller countries. Any tendency for national monetary conditions to deviate from the large country or from a group of dominant trading partners runs the risk of destabilizing markets. But whereas a small country has no formal influence over its partner's monetary policy under currency boards and dollarization, it participates in the formulation of monetary policy in a currency union. Thus, even a small country may have considerable clout in the conduct of area policy, particularly if it can influence its partner or partners through moral suasion or the soundness of its analysis.

## COMPENSATING FOR THE LOSS OF EXCHANGE RATE FLEXIBILITY

THE LOSS OF EXCHANGE RATE FLEXIBILITY does not necessarily impair an economy's ability to adjust to shocks and disturbances. The burden of adjustment borne by the exchange rate is simply shifted to other variables such as interest rates, wages, prices, employment and output. Adjustment capacity does suffer, however, if wages and prices are sticky, and if labour and other factors of production are immobile. Sticky prices and wages and labour immobility undermine an economy's ability to respond efficiently to shocks and disturbances, and shift the brunt of adjustment to employment and output.

In addition to their role in facilitating adjustment, floating rates have been valued for their apparent ability to shelter the economy from certain types of shocks and disturbances. As Murray describes it, "...movements in the nominal exchange rate can work to offset some of the effects of temporary shocks and facilitate the transition to a new steady state if the shock proves to be permanent." (p. 43) This buffer function, however, has come under critical scrutiny recently. It is discussed below.

## VOLATILITY AND MISALIGNMENT

E XCESSIVE VOLATILITY AND SUSTAINED MISALIGNMENT are frequent criticisms of Canada's floating rate regime. Fixed exchange rates are seen by many as a way of curtailing both. In building their case for greater fixity of exchange rates, Courchene and Harris observe that "...real exchange rates are substantially more volatile under a flexible rate regime than under a fixed one, and almost all of this volatility is due to movements in the nominal exchange rate." (p. 4) They also express concerns over what they see as large and sustained exchange rate misalignments.

### VOLATILITY

WHETHER EXCHANGE RATE VOLATILITY is excessive or not depends on what is driving the adjustment process and on how adjustment is distributed between the exchange rate and other variables in the system. Exchange rates behave much like asset prices, which tend to adjust faster than prices in goods and factor markets and tend to be more volatile than the underlying fundamentals. Asset prices and the exchange rate carry the brunt of adjustment in the short run, while the rest of the system struggles to overcome its inherent inertia and thus responds to shocks more gradually.

When goods prices are sticky in a floating-rate regime, the movement of the real exchange rate is dominated by the nominal rate. When prices eventually become unstuck, the real rate starts to revert toward its steady-state value. While this process may exhibit considerable exchange rate volatility, it would be a mistake to conclude that the observed volatility is necessarily disruptive. In fact, volatility may be beneficial in this case because it allows the rest of the economy to take its measured time in responding to the disturbance; stretching out the pace of adjustment may limit the extent of disruption. This is especially valuable when shocks are temporary.

Opponents of floating rates, however, often argue that gyrations in currency values unrelated to fundamentals may provoke unwarranted and uneconomic adjustments if they are interpreted as representing permanent shifts in relative prices. Such adjustments are inefficient, because they will have to be corrected when the exchange rate reverses its course. For this scenario to work, however, prices, wages, employment, capital formation and related variables would have to be highly flexible and responsive. There is virtually no evidence to support that view: this suggests that exchange rate volatility is more likely to act as an efficient buffer than a source of instability.

There are two issues here. The first pertains to the causes of exchange rate volatility, the second to the sensitivity of the real economy to exchange rate movements. If exchange rate volatility indicates the presence of disturbances from other sources and if the sensitivity of the real sector is sluggish, then exchange rate movements are important early shock absorbers that allow the rest of the system to avoid costly resource realignments. There is little evidence, as noted above, that exchange rate movements at high frequencies affect the allocation of resources; at lower frequencies, the debate continues on whether observed resource movements are necessarily inefficient. Hence, criticisms that exchange rates display "excess" volatility are still very much judgment calls.

In a system of fixed nominal exchange rates, the real exchange rate adjusts as long as prices are flexible, thus providing an important means of responding to shocks. When prices are sticky, however, there is no real rate response in the short run, and adjustment is shunted to interest rates and potentially to employment and output. It would thus be inappropriate to interpret the absence of exchange rate movement as a sign of systemic stability and therefore evidence of superior performance. The proper comparison is not between exchange rate volatility across regimes, but between exchange rate volatility and volatility in the variables which adjust when the exchange rate cannot.

When volatility is compared across exchange rate regimes, it is important to include exchange rate realignments that take place in fixed rate regimes during currency crises. These crisis realignments impose very heavy burdens in terms of lost output, employment, and economic and social instability. It is these extreme disruptions that have contributed to the widely-held belief that only the so-called "corner" solutions — of fully floating rates or hard pegs — represent viable options for most countries.

Figure 2 shows nominal and real effective exchange rates for the Canadian dollar, as well as the dollar's movement against the U.S. dollar. We note first how closely the nominal effective rate tracks the bilateral rate: this underscores the importance of the bilateral relationship. Overall, all three rates show considerable movement in both nominal and real terms: but was it excessive? The answer depends on the presumed causes, as we shall see below.

Would fixed rates have dampened volatility? Certainly in nominal rates, but what about real rates? Were there misalignments during the period? What would be the norm against which misalignment would be measured? Parity? But what if there are longer-run forces defining a downward trend, as the figure seems to suggest? What would be the implications of defending a peg? The debate over these issues continues.

## MISALIGNMENTS

IN ADDITION TO EXCESSIVE VOLATILITY, floating rate systems are often blamed for sustained exchange rate misalignments. These are typically expressed in terms of real exchange rates and may be defined as departures from purchasing power parity, as persistent incompatibilities with macro-economic fundamentals, or as incompatible with international competitiveness. Critics of the floating rate system believe misalignments are a particularly unattractive feature because they encourage inefficient resource allocation.

FIGURE 2

CANADA: EXCHANGE RATES (1995 = 100)

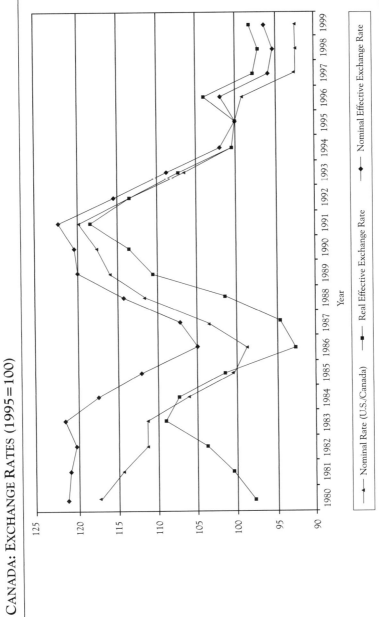

Source: *International Financial Statistics*, January 2002.

399

It is important to recall that misalignments in real terms also occur in fixed rate systems whenever relative prices change. Indeed, fixed rate regimes typically start to unravel after the real exchange rate has persistently deviated from the rate that is consistent with the peg. Put differently, movement of relative prices generates an equilibrium nominal exchange rate which persistently (and often increasingly) deviates from the peg. Under floating rates, changes in relative prices are accommodated continuously by nominal exchange rate adjustments. Under fixed rates, the pressures are allowed to accumulate until the system breaks. An imperfect analogy here might be the adjustment caused by moving tectonic plates in a series of frequent small tremors as opposed to the adjustment caused by large but infrequent earthquakes.

When critics attack volatility and misalignment, they imply that observed movements of exchange rates cannot be explained in terms of standard fundamentals and must thus be the result of irrational behaviour and market inefficiencies. An example might be the movement of Canada's nominal and real exchange rates relative to the price ratio, as shown in Figure 3. When the nominal exchange rate fluctuates so significantly relative to a stable price ratio, is this evidence of departures from fundamentals and speculative excess?

Recent work by economists at the Bank of Canada argues that the long-run behaviour of the real Canada-U.S. exchange rate can be largely explained by inflation differentials, the relative price of energy and the relative price of non-energy commodities (Amano and van Norden 1993; Murray 2000; and others). Speculation and other forms of "irrational" behaviour are apparently not important determinants. Thus, volatility in the exchange rate is due largely to volatility in the variables that drive it. This argument goes a step further to suggest that certain episodes of increased volatility in the exchange rate may have been due to stabilizing rather than destabilizing speculation (Murray, van Norden and Vigfusson 1996).

Movement of the Canadian dollar against the U.S. dollar is often matched by similar movement of many other currencies against the U.S. dollar, which appreciated strongly during the first half of the 1980s and depreciated strongly during the second. This development was driven by U.S. monetary and fiscal policies. The Reagan Administration's large budget deficits expanded demand for non-tradeables, which raised the relative price of non-tradeables to tradeables (i.e., caused a real appreciation).

This pattern is reflected in Figure 3, which shows the Canadian dollar falling in the first half of the 1980s and rising in the second, while the ratio of consumer prices fluctuates much less. If the Canadian dollar had been tied to its U.S. counterpart during the 1980s, it would still have fluctuated, except that the pattern would have been reversed.

This is just another example of how Canada is affected by the actions and policies of its dominant neighbor, regardless of the nature of the exchange rate regime. Canada has tried to deal with such problems in trade relations by embracing the Canada-U.S. Free Trade Agreement (FTA) and the NAFTA. The current interest in monetary union may be interpreted as an effort to bring similar discipline and control to continental monetary conditions. If the Canadian dollar is tied to the U.S. dollar, it would certainly provide a buffer against cross-border volatility and misalignment. The more integrated the two economies become in terms of trade and investment, the more that protection matters and the stronger the case for currency union becomes.

In sum, excessive volatility and misalignment can clearly complicate the effectiveness of floating rates, but misalignment in particular is also a problem that affects pegged rates and volatility asserts itself strongly during the financial crises that often end fixed rate regimes. Indeed, excessive volatility and sustained misalignment are apt descriptions of the recent performance of many fixed rate regimes. Until recently, however, currency boards, dollarization and currency union were widely believed to be immune to such criticisms. The Argentinian crisis of 2002 has raised new doubts about the stability of currency boards and, tangentially, of dollarization as well.

In the end, a key issue for Canadians will be the extent of their influence over regional monetary policies under various exchange rate regimes. From this perspective, the majority of fixed rate regimes do not offer much because Canada would have little influence over U.S. policies, even though those policies would have serious repercussions for Canada. For currency union to be of interest to Canada, it would have to offer meaningful influence over the union's monetary policies, which means significantly more than becoming an additional district in the U.S. Federal Reserve System.

In a sense, the problems Canada faces with monetary integration are opposite to the problems of trade integration. With the Canada-U.S. FTA and the NAFTA, minimalist arrangements were preferable for Canada and Mexico, because they limited the extent to which Washington could dictate trade policy toward third countries. With monetary cooperation, however, minimalist options do not allow much joint management.

## EXCHANGE RATES AND ECONOMIC STRUCTURE

THE NOVELTY IN THE CONTEMPORARY CANADIAN DEBATE over closer monetary cooperation is that it goes beyond traditional considerations by arguing that floating rates have inimical effects on Canada's long-run competitiveness. Sustained depreciation of the Canadian dollar, often attributed to deflation in world commodity prices, is believed to have retarded innovation and modernization in the Canadian manufacturing sector.

FIGURE 3

CANADA: NOMINAL AND REAL EXCHANGE RATES (1995 = 100)

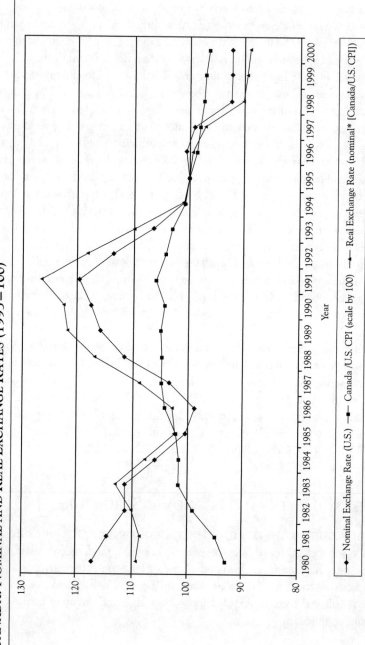

*Source: International Financial Statistics, January 2002.*

Critics, including Courchene and Harris, and Grubel, interpret the "float-ing-rate-as-buffer" argument not as a strength of flexible exchange rates but as a weakness. They worry that the value of the Canadian dollar has been dominated by developments in the commodity sector. While sustained depreciation may protect Canada's resource-based industries in the face of world commodity price deflation, it also shields other sectors from foreign competition, and that may not be good. Specifically, protection from foreign competition may have under-mined incentives to invest, innovate and modernize in the country's manufac-turing industries. Even a strong supporter of floating rates, like McCallum (1999, 2000), acknowledges the possibility of such a causal relationship.

This perspective introduces a new dimension into the debate on optimal exchange rate policy because it goes beyond the traditional preoccupation with macro-economic stability to the implications of floating rates for economic structure and long-run growth. Here, the buffering function of the floating rate is not the benign force described above and reflected in the earlier quotation from Murray, but a source of long-term decline. Currency depreciation shields one sector from the consequences of declining world commodity prices, but only at the expense of lost competitiveness in the rest of the economy. In this context, exchange rate buffering generates efficiency and welfare losses analo-gous to those attributed to tariffs and other forms of protection.

The effects of monetary integration on economic structure have received some attention in the literature. Frankel and Rose (1998), for example, have argued in evaluating the EMU that monetary integration promotes synchroni-zation of business cycles among member countries through increased trade linkages. Trade encourages similarity among industrial structures and thus re-duces the problems associated with asymmetric shocks. This view is shared by the European Union (EU) and may be particularly relevant to monetary unions among similar countries in which intraindustry trade dominates.

This view is challenged by Krugman (1993), for example, who argues that trade and monetary integration tend to encourage greater specialization among members, thereby sharpening differences among them and intensifying the problems created by asymmetric shocks (Soltwedel, Dohse and Krieger-Boden 2001). In the end, the outcome is likely to depend on the relative importance of interindustry and intraindustry trade in the integrated area. Where inter-industry trade dominates, as it would in currency unions between industrialized and industrializing countries, greater specialization and hence heightened asymmetry would be the likely result. Where intraindustry trade is dominant, as in the EU, greater specialization is compatible with a rising correlation among business cycles, especially if specialization along product-variety lines is preva-lent. Specialization in terms of intraindustry product variety ensures that in-dustry-specific shocks affect everybody.

Recent developments in offshore assembly, component trade and intra-product specialization add a new force that tends to increase cyclical linkage and thus reduce the problem of asymmetric shocks even in — or perhaps especially in — monetary unions between industrialized and industrializing economies. As major industries resort increasingly to offshore sourcing and production, industry-specific global demand and supply shocks affect every country which has a piece of the action. A demand shock in the motor vehicle industry, for example, affects producers in the United States, Canada and Mexico in similar ways, because the industry has been internationalized and production is shared among the three NAFTA members. Analogous considerations apply to aircraft, consumer electronics, apparel and many other industries (Arndt 1998, 2001; Arndt and Huemer 2000).

## PRICE DEFLATION IN THE WORLD RESOURCE SECTOR

AS NOTED ABOVE, the contemporary Canadian debate on the optimal exchange rate regime has been influenced strongly by the role of world prices of raw materials, natural resources and agricultural commodities. Under floating rates, a relative decline in commodity prices shifts world·demand away from Canadian products. The Canadian dollar depreciates to an extent that depends on the magnitude of the shock, the importance of commodity trade in Canada's total trade and the presence of nominal rigidities in the system.

The essence of the argument is as follows. Although the nominal exchange rate is a general price, it often moves as a result of changing conditions in particularly dominant sectors. The influence is more pronounced as the share of those sectors in total trade grows. Exchange rate changes generated in this manner have implications not only for the sectors in question, but for every part of the economy in which exchange rates matter.

Let us consider manufacturing, for example. In a fixed exchange rate system, global deflation of commodity prices would exert downward pressure on domestic commodity prices at the initial exchange rate. The decline in the relative price of commodities reduces profitability in the resource sector and creates incentives for labour and capital to relocate. As the domestic currency depreciates, however, the need for domestic commodity price reductions is eased. At the same time, and at given world prices for manufactured goods, this depreciation allows domestic manufacturing prices to rise. Here the change in internal relative prices is accomplished, at least in part, by a rise in manufacturing prices rather than a decline in resource sector prices. The change in relative prices still shifts profitability toward manufacturing and encourages reallocation of productive resources into that sector.

If factor prices are downwardly flexible, wages and capital rentals can be adjusted downward in the resource sector to help absorb the shock. If factor prices are rigid in the resource sector, the adjustment burden falls more fully on resource reallocation. In the presence of nominal rigidities, especially the downward rigidity of wages, currency depreciation eases the burden of adjustment in the resource sector because the required realignment of relative prices described above is accomplished in part by a rise in manufacturing prices.

To this point, the story is largely conventional. What distinguishes the Canadian debate, however, is the concern that adjustment under floating rates may have adverse effects on the modernization of the manufacturing sector. The currency depreciation protects domestic manufacturing industries from foreign competition and thereby undermines incentives to stay competitive and modernize. In the view of critics who believe that Canadian manufacturing is not moving fast enough toward high tech, knowledge-intensive industries, part of the blame belongs to the sustained depreciation of the Canadian dollar.

This is a subtle but important shift in emphasis and focus. It is no longer the relative price between domestic manufacturing and domestic resource industries, but the relative price between domestic and foreign (especially U.S.) manufacturing that causes concern. An increase in the former favours expansion of Canadian manufacturing; an increase in the latter biases the expansion against modernization. As a result, Canadian manufacturing may expand, but it will do so in the direction of older, more traditional types of manufacturing. From a long-run perspective, this is a recipe for trouble.

This possibility is at the heart of the call for monetary union by Courchene and Harris. It is acknowledged as potentially troublesome, even by opponents of monetary union like McCallum (1999, 2000). And it is relevant to resource-rich, advanced countries like Norway and Iceland (Gylfason 2000). The evidence, however, is far from clear, and a great deal more research is needed before any policy-related conclusions would be justified. Moreover, as McCallum (2000) notes, even if the evidence ultimately links the exchange rate to technical progress in manufacturing, it may be no more than an argument for a stronger Canadian dollar than it would be for currency union.

## THE ROLE OF WORLD COMMODITY PRICES

THE CASE CONSISTS OF TWO PROPOSITIONS: first, the sustained depreciation of the Canadian dollar is the result of a global slump in commodity prices; second, the sustained depreciation of a country's currency undermines industrial innovation and technical progress.

FIGURE 4

WORLD COMMODITY PRICE INDICES (1990 = 100)

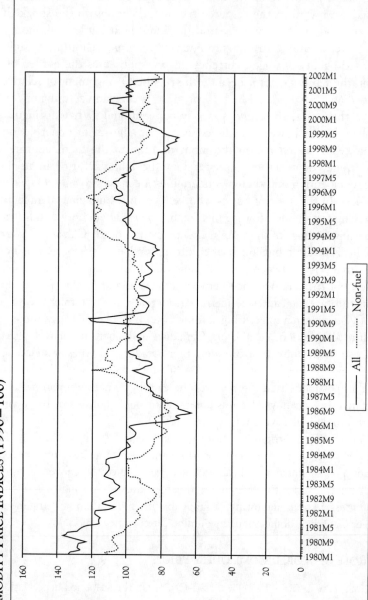

Source: International Monetary Fund.

With respect to the first proposition, the evolution of commodity prices is displayed in Figure 4. After a significant drop in the first half of the 1980s, commodity prices have fluctuated around a rather flat trend since then. A comparison of fluctuations in commodity prices with fluctuations in the exchange rate (Figure 3) suggests a rough correlation, especially in the earlier part of the period. Commodity prices decline between 1980 and 1986 and the Canadian dollar depreciates. Prices rise subsequently, with fuel-inclusive commodity prices peaking in 1991, and the dollar appreciates. After that, the relationship is much more questionable.

While it is certainly possible to see interaction between world commodity prices and the exchange rate, that relationship is not compelling in a causal sense, especially in view of competing explanations of exchange rate behaviour. It would thus be a mistake to base an argument for fixed rates on the presumed role of world commodity prices in depressing the value of the floating Canadian dollar.

## THE ROLE OF PRODUCTIVITY

IN RECENT WORK, Harris (1999, 2001) has focussed on technology shocks and productivity to explain the alleged lack of innovative vigour in Canadian manufacturing. He emphasizes the role of productivity under floating rates in economies with structurally diverse sectors. The framework is a two-sector model of a small open economy that relies on imported technology for industrial advancement. One of the two sectors consists of "old economy" industries (which include heavy manufacturing and, in Canada's case, natural resources), while the other contains "new economy" industries (like information-based, software, and high tech manufacturing). Labour markets serving the two sectors are structurally different: in the old economy, the nominal wage is inflexible, perhaps because of strong labour unions; in the new, wages are flexible and competition ensures full employment.

The system is shocked by the arrival of a general-purpose technology (GPT) in the new economy, together with a world price decline in the old economy. This double whammy is intended to mirror the stylized facts of the past decade, during which the information revolution coincided with depressed world commodity prices. The GPT shock boosts productivity in the new economy and encourages resource reallocation from the old to the new. At the initial exchange rate, the sector-specific productivity shock tends to cause output and employment to fall in the old economy and rise in the new.

This is the conventional result of sector-specific technological change. The depression in world commodity prices merely intensifies the pressures on the old economy. Currency depreciation, on the other hand, inhibits this process; by protecting the old economy, it stabilizes employment there and thus mutes pressure to re-allocate resources. In this set-up, depreciation inhibits the process of economic transformation regardless of its cause, which could run from depressed commodity prices to an asset bubble in the United States.

## NOMINAL RIGIDITIES

THE ROLE OF NOMINAL RIGIDITIES in the old economy is crucial in this scenario. If prices and wages in the old economy were flexible downward, the exchange rate would be relieved of much of the burden of adjustment. The combination of asymmetric shocks and nominal rigidities implies that the existing currency union between the old and the new economies is a mistake which should be replaced with floating rates. Dissolution is clearly not an option, which means that labour market reforms are needed to enable the country to deal more effectively with these types of asymmetric shocks.

If labour market and related structural reforms are politically unattainable, is enlarging the currency union to include the United States the answer? If labour markets remain rigid in the old economy, what exactly will fixed rates vis-à-vis the United States achieve — apart from reducing the importance of Canada's old sectors in the continent-wide economy and permanently fixing the exchange rate between Canada's manufacturing sector and its U.S. counterpart?

Harris does not say how labour market rigidities would affect adjustment in the context of a Canada-U.S. currency union. While deflation in world commodity prices would still exert downward pressure on commodity prices, this time throughout the currency union, the resultant pressure on the value of the union's currency in world exchange markets would be weaker in view of the reduced weight and importance of the continent-wide resource sector in the continent-wide economy. With currency depreciation carrying a smaller burden of adjustment to global price deflation, however, downward pressure on Canadian commodity prices would be commensurately greater. Labour market rigidities would then ensure depressed conditions in the sector.

While currency union would not do much to solve the problems of the old sector, this scenario implies that competitive pressure flowing from the adoption of GPT innovations in the United States would not be muted by depreciation and thus would be fully felt by Canadian manufacturers. Harris argues that this would stimulate technological progress in Canada. This leaves the question of whether and to what extent Canada has fallen behind technologically.

## TECHNOLOGICAL CHANGE

THE MODERNIZATION ARGUMENT turns on the impact of the exchange rate regime on industrial competitiveness. In this sense, it differs from traditional trade and exchange rate theory. When a new, cost-saving technology becomes available, it is adopted, relative goods and factor prices adjust, factors are reallocated and trade patterns reflect the new realities. While differential rates of growth in tradeables and non-tradeables may affect exchange rates, the causality runs from growth to the exchange rate.

In the Harris model, technologies are imported and their implementation is costly. Currency depreciation impedes their implementation: first, because its protective effect reduces the urgency of the competitiveness pressures; second, because it raises the cost of, and reduces the expected return on, imported technologies. To the extent that this helps explain the stylized facts, however, it is again more an argument for a strong dollar than for currency union.

There is considerable disagreement, however, over the stylized facts and over whether and by how much technical progress has lagged in Canada. While innovation may have been sluggish in computers and electronic equipment, there is no consensus that Canada has lagged in overall terms, especially in comparison with Europe's industrialized nations (Murray; McCallum 1999, 2000; Schreyer 2000). Evidence amassed in a recent study by the Organisation for Economic Co-operation and Development (OECD 2000) gives a mixed picture at best.

The study shows that Canada continues to have one of the smallest gaps in per capita GDP when compared to the United States; however, its growth rate of per capita GDP has been lower recently than most of the countries in the sample. The study attributes this in part to slower growth of labour productivity. Relatively speaking, human capital formation has played an important role in Canadian labour productivity growth. Much of the observed growth in productivity appears to be based on growth within sectors rather than on sectoral shifts.

In the mid-1990s, Canada did lag behind the United States and other countries in the share of value-added of information and communication technology industries (ICT) in total GDP. The OECD data confirm the aforementioned observation that productivity growth in office, accounting and computing equipment appears to have been comparatively anemic, especially toward the end of the decade. However, the contribution of ICT capital to output growth was higher in the 1990s than in the preceding decade, smaller than in the United States, but comparatively strong in relation to other countries in the sample.

It is difficult to make a strong case for technological backwardness on the basis of this kind of evidence.

## COLLECTING THE PIECES OF THE ARGUMENT

THERE IS A WIDELY HELD VIEW among economists that neither Canada nor the United States, as configured currently, represent optimal currency areas. Some, including Mundell, have argued in the past that if there were to be just two currency areas in North America, a North-South rather than an East-West division of the continent would be better. In assessing the extent to which Canada itself satisfies the optimum currency area criteria, most economists would give it a low or failing grade on labour-market flexibility and on symmetry of structure.

Monetary union advocates hope to reduce the problems associated with internal asymmetries between the resource sector and the rest of the Canadian economy by expanding the domain of the Canadian currency area to the United States. In the new, enlarged entity, the asymmetries between the two Canada's would remain, but the influence and weight of the old economy would be sharply reduced. Monetary union would not solve the rigidity problem in the old economy directly.

On the one hand, Courchene and Harris, as well as Grubel, tend to see strong compatibilities between the United States and most of Canada, so the benefits from reducing the influence of the resource sector would not be offset by costs associated with asymmetric structures and shocks elsewhere. Murray, on the other hand, is less sanguine, especially about asymmetric responses to commodity price shocks. If terms-of-trade movements are one indicator of compatibility, Figure 5 suggests considerable divergence between the two countries. The work of Bayoumi and Eichengreen (1994) and Carr and Floyd (2000) provides further evidence on asymmetries in real shocks.

There is also uncertainty about the likely effect of currency union on the mobility of workers between the two countries. Capital and skilled workers are already highly mobile, but Courchene and Harris worry that migration has been mainly in one direction, with a brain drain of skilled workers and professionals in response to higher U.S. wages and living standards. They hold the depressed Canadian dollar responsible for part of the income disparities and see currency union as a way of improving Canada's relative position.

The likely effect of currency union on the migration of unskilled workers is unclear. Shifts in relative prices against the resource sector are expected to expose the sector to strong adjustment pressures. In the face of nominal wage rigidities, such pressures will be met by the elimination of jobs. If labour mobility is limited, policy makers will face major adjustment problems. There is no evidence that unskilled workers will be more willing or able to move into U.S. jurisdictions than among Canadian regions. The eventual outcome could resemble the recent European experience, where declining sector-specific competitiveness has resulted in higher unemployment, with relatively little geographic or intersectoral migration of labour.

## DETERMINING THE DIRECTION OF CAUSALITY

IN THE DEBATE SURVEYED ABOVE, causality has been assumed to run from an exogenous decline in world commodity prices to a depreciating Canadian dollar to retardation of manufacturing innovation. There is no agreement on the direction of causality, however, with many economists inclined to think that it may run the other way.

FIGURE 5

TERMS OF TRADE: PERCENT CHANGE

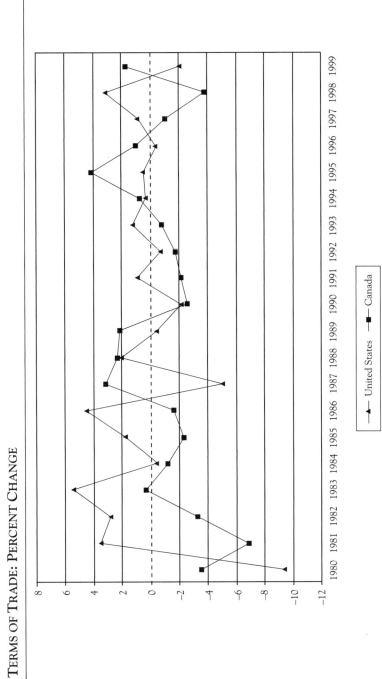

Source: *International Financial Statistics Yearbook 2000.*

Grubel, for one, suggests that causality runs from wage-setting union behaviour via monetary accommodation to currency depreciation. Briefly, labour-union demands for wage increases in excess of productivity gains create unemployment and related market pressures, which are met by the central bank with monetary expansion. While the policy is intended to stimulate aggregate demand, it allows prices to rise along with nominal wages and thereby keeps the growth of real wages in check. The rise in domestic prices relative to those abroad causes the home currency to depreciate (Coricelli, Cukierman and Dalmazzo 2001).

Here, too, there are echoes of the European experience. Indeed, it was a vicious cycle of this kind that induced Austria to adopt the hard-currency peg to the German mark many years ago in an attempt to break the link from wages to prices and exchange rates (Arndt 1982). The policy worked extremely well: it imposed discipline on both wage-setting and price-setting in Austria and forced both into conformity with the inflation targets of the Bundesbank. Courchene and Harris refer to the Austrian case in their discussion of a possible fixed rate scenario for Canada.

Grubel questions the causal link from world commodity prices, arguing that the econometric evidence is not very strong. As an alternative — or additional — explanation, he cites some evidence which relates the depreciation of the Canadian dollar to the growing debt of Canadian governments, and particularly to the foreign-currency denominated component of the debt. Servicing and repaying the foreign portion of debt places downward pressures on the Canadian dollar. The role of external indebtedness does not normally receive much attention in economists' models of exchange rate determination. There is mounting evidence, however, that external debt burdens may have contributed to the difficulties in Southeast Asia in 1997 and in Argentina in 2002.

In Grubel's view, the evidence overall is too scanty to permit a firm conclusion with respect to the causes of Canada's depreciating dollar. He notes, however, that a depreciation gives producers in non-resource sectors room to raise prices, profits and wages. This sows the seeds for future problems when world commodity prices rise. When that happens and the Canadian dollar appreciates, hysteresis effects will make it difficult for these industries to reduce wages and prices. They will then find themselves in a weakened position of global competitiveness as exports fall and imports rise.

Labour market behaviour and rigidities may be endogenous to the exchange rate regime. Before Austria adopted its hard currency peg to the German mark, workers and labour unions fully expected the negative employment effects resulting from their wage-setting behaviour to be met by the central bank with monetary accommodation, while the inevitable increase in prices induced by monetary accommodation would in turn be met by devaluation of the schilling.

After adoption of the hard-currency peg, Austrian monetary policy came to be credibly tied to that of the Bundesbank, ruling out monetary accommodation of excessive wage increases. Hence, wage inflation would result in unemployment and lost output. The pattern of wage-setting changed drastically, with nominal wage settlements disciplined by productivity growth and by the inflation target of the Bundesbank.

From this perspective, it is easy to see why monetary and exchange rate policy autonomy may appear as a curse rather than a blessing. Austrians who lived through both periods — those before and after the hard-currency peg — have little difficulty deciding which regime they prefer.

## CHOOSING THE PROPER FORM OF MONETARY COOPERATION

A S NOTED EARLIER, exchange rate fixity may be achieved in a number of ways, running from the softer varieties of pegged but adjustable rates to the hard peg of the currency board, dollarization and, finally, currency union. Although soft pegs would help achieve some of the objectives discussed in the foregoing pages, they do not resolve many of the risks which the move away from floating rates is intended to eliminate.

Most of the available options can be implemented unilaterally by Canada. With the exception of currency union, they do not require active U.S. participation. The choice between soft and hard pegs would depend to some extent on the importance of the structuralist critique of floating rates. As the history of devaluations in Iceland suggests, soft pegs may not solve the problem, because governments are not always able to resist pressure from the resource sector to devalue the currency whenever world competition becomes too intense.

Among hard pegs, currency board, dollarization and monetary union are the viable options, although the Argentinian debacle and the apparent role of excessive foreign indebtedness raise major questions about the long-run sustainability of currency boards and even dollarization (Alexander and von Furstenberg 2000; Berg and Borensztein 2000a; Wagner 2000; Willett 2001). While exit strategies are indeed more limited and entail higher costs than soft pegs, the recent Argentinian experience suggests that a currency board cannot prevent governments from running policies which undermine the viability of the system and even a currency board will be abandoned when the costs of maintaining it are high enough. The Argentinian crisis has dealt the credibility of the currency board option a serious blow.

Does this mean that the set of viable hard pegs has been reduced to just two — dollarization and currency union? There is no doubt that exit from both is more difficult. Indeed, exit may be more difficult from dollarization than from currency union, because it would create a more serious institutional vacuum at the level of central banking and monetary policy. Exit from a currency union like the EMU would be difficult, but the institutional and policy vacuum would be less serious.

Canadian proponents of closer monetary integration may argue with considerable justification that policy mismanagement of the Argentinian type is not possible in Canada, so that the currency board remains a viable option, along with dollarization and currency union. That is probably correct, except that Canada carries a significant external debt burden, which could cause problems over time in the context of a currency board.

In the end, any move toward greater monetary coordination, whether unilateral or joint, will require reforms of policies and structures in participating countries. A lesson from the European experience is the importance of preparedness. Beginning with the European Monetary System and culminating in the convergence criteria of the Maastricht Treaty, Europe insisted on reforms prior to entry (Hochreiter 2000). The one significant exception was the failure to implement labour market reforms and that failure may yet come to haunt the EMU. Labour market rigidities should be on the agenda of any move toward greater fixity of exchange rates.

In preparing for the EMU, Europe's policy makers understood the need for reforms designed to reduce policy and structural differences. The Maastricht Treaty and its focus on convergence reflect that recognition. Ideally, labour-market reforms should also have been undertaken, but the political will was not there. Hughes Hallett and Viegi (2001) have argued that failure to implement labour-market reforms ex ante exposes a currency union to additional risk.

Furthermore, if McCallum, Murray and others are correct in their claim that the issue is more one of strengthening the Canadian dollar than one of monetary integration, then labour market and other structural reforms may be a way of bringing about a stronger Canadian dollar. This suggests that Canada might do well to pursue structural reforms before making any commitments in the direction of exchange rate fixity.

## THE POLITICS OF MONETARY UNION

ALTHOUGH MANY PROPONENTS of North American currency union see the EMU as a model, it is important to recall that political rather than economic motives have typically been the driving force behind economic integration in Europe. Time and again, when the case for further integration was difficult to make on economic grounds, political arguments saved the day. There is no counterpart to this important force in North America. Economic arguments must carry a much greater share of the case for monetary cooperation.

There is very little political interest in monetary union in the United States. Although an element of public opinion is sympathetic to the notion that closer monetary cooperation is in the enlightened interest of the United States, because it will contribute to stability in the region, the public at large and the U.S. Congress are indifferent.

As unilateral initiatives involving currency boards and dollarization have increased throughout the hemisphere, some observers have argued that the United States has no choice but to get involved. This argument is strengthened further by ongoing integration in the areas of trade and foreign investment, which are creating an integrated economic space in which greater monetary cooperation will become essential.

The emergence of the euro may drive the United States to seek greater monetary coordination in the western hemisphere in order to limit the euro's ability to encroach on the dollar's role as the world transaction and reserve currency. But these are long-run arguments at best (McKinnon 2000).

While it is clear that there is not much political support for greater monetary cooperation in the United States, it is unclear whether there is broad political support in Canada. Without such support it will be difficult for Canada to build a case; furthermore, Canadians wish to preserve some form of cultural independence from the United States.

While there may not be political support for monetary union, there would be widespread support for a stronger Canadian dollar. Canadian policy makers could do worse than to focus on strengthening the currency, an objective which would be well served by structural reforms in labour markets and elsewhere in the economy. In seeking to strengthen the dollar, they will create conditions that may make currency union a stronger option in the future.

## CONCLUSION

IT IS NOT EASY TO MAKE A CASE for currency unification (and, by extension, most other forms of exchange rate fixity) in Canada. Neither the existing Canadian monetary union nor the proposed one satisfies all the requirements for an optimum currency area. Recent Canadian macro-economic experience says that greater monetary coordination is not needed, because Canada is outperforming the United States on the inflation front. Nor does the country need to be rescued from major policy misadventures. And, finally, the political climate on both sides of the border is indifferent, if not hostile, to the idea of closer monetary cooperation.

Interestingly, similar arguments accompanied virtually the entire history of European economic integration. On nearly every occasion when Europe took a major step forward, including Maastricht, there were voices proclaiming that the attempt was doomed. But the process continued and monetary union is a reality today. Traditional economic considerations, both for and against, were not strong enough to provide clear-cut guidelines. That is why a healthy political tail wind was needed to move the ship along.

An important feature that distinguishes the current Canadian debate from its European antecedents is the structuralist hypothesis linking exchange rates to modernization. It remains to be seen whether this argument stands up. A great deal more analytical work and empirical evidence are needed, not only on the allegedly deleterious effects of floating rates on growth and industrial structure, but on the curative effect of monetary union.

Much of the Canadian case for monetary integration is based on structural asymmetries within the country, whose influence monetary union with the United States would mute but not eliminate. To opponents of monetary union, the argument is one of strengthening the value of the Canadian dollar, a goal which can be accomplished without formal monetary integration and within the present Canadian political climate.

While the economic arguments are deficient and the political support weak at this juncture, there are forces at work that seem to make monetary integration in the hemisphere inevitable in the longer run.

## BIBLIOGRAPHY

Alexander, V., and G.M. von Furstenberg. "Monetary Unions — A Superior Alternative to Full Dollarization in the Long Run." *North American Journal of Economics and Finance* 11, 2 (2000): 205-225.

Amano, R., and S. van Norden. "A Forecasting Equation for the Canada-U.S. Dollar Exchange Rate." In *The Exchange Rate and the Economy*. Ottawa: The Bank of Canada, 1993, pp. 266-71.

Arndt, S.W. *The Political Economy of Austria.* Washington, D.C.: AEI Press, 1982.

_____. "Super-specialization and the Gains from Trade." *Contemporary Economic Policy* 16, 4 (1998): 480-85.

_____. "Offshore Sourcing and Production-Sharing in Preference Areas." In *Fragmentation: New Production Patterns in the World Economy*. Edited by S.W. Arndt and H. Kierzkowski. New York: Oxford University Press, 2001, pp. 76-87.

Arndt, S.W., and A. Huemer. "North American Trade After NAFTA: Part I & II." *Claremont Policy Briefs*. Claremont: Lowe Institute of Political Economy, April and July 2000, pp. 1-4.

Bayoumi, T., and B. Eichengreen. "One Money or Many? Analyzing the Prospects for Monetary Unification in Various Parts of the World." Princeton: *Studies in International Finance* 76 (1994).

Berg, A., and E. Borensztein. "The Choice of Exchange Rate Regime and Monetary Target in Highly Dollarized Economies." International Monetary Fund Working Study No. 29, February 2000a.

_____. "Full Dollarization: The Pros and Cons." IMF *Economic Issues* 24 (2000b).

Carr, J.L., and J.F. Floyd. "Real and Monetary Shocks to the Canadian Dollar: Do Canada and the United States form an Optimum Currency Area?" *North American Journal of Economics and Finance* 13, 1 (2000): 1-19.

Coricelli, F., A. Cukierman and A. Dalmazzo. "Economic Performance and Stabilization Policy in a Monetary Union with Imperfect Labour and Goods Markets." Discussion Paper No. 2745, CEPR, March 2001.

Courchene, T.J., and R.G. Harris. "North American Monetary Union: Analytical Principles and Operational Guidelines." *North American Journal of Economics and Finance* 11, 1 (2000): 3-18.

De Grauwe, P. *The Economics of Monetary Integration*, Third edition. Oxford: Oxford University Press, 1997.

Eichengreen, B. *European Monetary Unification: Theory, Practice, and Analysis.* Cambridge: MA: MIT Press, 1997.

Emerson, M. et al. "One Market, One Money: An Evaluation of the Potential Benefits and Costs of Forming an Economic and Monetary Union." *European Economy* 44 (1990).

Frankel, J.A., and A.K. Rose. "The Endogeneity of the Optimum Currency Area Criteria." *Economic Journal* 108, 449 (1998): 1009-25.

Grubel, H.G. "The Merit of a Canada-U.S. Monetary Union." *North American Journal of Economics and Finance* 11, 1 (2000): 19-40.

Gylfason, T. "Fix or Flex? Alternative Exchange Rate Regimes in an Era of Global Capital Mobility." *North American Journal of Economics and Finance* 11, 2 (2000): 173-189.

Harris, R.G. *Determinants of Canadian Productivity Growth: Issues and Prospects.* Discussion Paper No. 8. Ottawa: Industry Canada, December 1999.

_____. *The New Economy and the Exchange Rate Regime.* Discussion Paper No. 0111. Adelaide: Centre for International Economic Studies, Adelaide University, March 2001.

Hochreiter, E. "Exchange Rate Regimes and Capital Mobility: Issues and Some Lessons from Central and Eastern European Applicant Countries." *North American Journal of Economics and Finance* 11, 2 (2000): 155-171.

Hughes Hallett, A. and N. Viegi. "Labour Market Reform and Monetary Policy in EMU: Do Asymmetries Matter?" Discussion Paper No. 2979, CEPR, September 2001.

Kenen, P.B. "The Theory of Optimum Currency Areas: An Eclectic View." In *Monetary Problems of the International Economy.* Edited by R.A. Mundell and A.K. Swoboda. Chicago: University of Chicago Press, 1969, pp. 41-60.

Krugman, P. "Lessons of Massachusetts for EMU." In *Adjustment and Growth in the European Monetary Union.* Edited by F. Torres and F. Giavazzi. New York: Cambridge University Press, 1993, pp. 241-69.

McCallum, John. "Seven Issues in the Choice of Exchange Rate Regime for Canada." *Current Analysis*. Toronto: Royal Bank of Canada, February 1999, pp. 1-10.

_____. "Engaging the Debate: Costs and Benefits of a North American Common Currency." *Current Analysis*. Toronto: Royal Bank of Canada, April 2000, pp. 1-9.

McKinnon, R.I. "Optimum Currency Areas." *American Economic Review* 53, 4 (1963): 717-25.

_____. "On the Periphery of the International Dollar Standard: Canada, Latin America, and East Asia." *North American Journal of Economics and Finance* 11, 2 (2000): 105-21.

Mundell, R.A. "A Theory of Optimum Currency Areas," *American Economic Review* 51, 4 (September 1961): 657-65.

Murray, J. "Why Canada Needs a Flexible Exchange Rate." *North American Journal of Economics and Finance* 11, 1 (2000): 41-60.

Murray, J., S. van Norden and R. Vigfusson. "Excess Volatility and Speculative Bubbles in the Canadian Dollar: Real or Imagined?" Technical Report No. 76. Ottawa: Bank of Canada, July 1996.

OECD. *OECD Economic Outlook*, No. 67. Paris: Organisation for Economic Co-operation and Development, June 2000.

Schreyer, P. "The Contribution of Information and Communications Technology to Output Growth: A Study of the G7 Countries." OECD STI Working Paper 2000/2. Paris: OECD, March 2000.

Soltwedel, R., D. Dohse and C. Krieger-Boden. "EMU Challenges to European Labour Markets." IMF World Economic Outlook 2000: Supporting Studies (January 2001): 184-210.

Tower, E., and T.D. Willett. "The Theory of Optimum Currency Areas and Exchange rate Flexibility." Princeton Special Papers in International Economics, No. 11, May 1976.

Wagner, H. " Which Exchange Rate Regimes in an Era of High Capital Mobility?" *North American Journal of Economics and Finance* 11, 2 (2000): 191-203.

Willett, T.D. "Truth in Advertising and the Great Dollarization Scam." *Journal of Policy Modeling* 23, 3 (2001): 279-89.

*Michael Hart*
*Carleton University*

# 11

# Canada, the United States and Deepening Economic Integration: Next Steps

> The cause of freedom rests on more than our ability to defend ourselves and our allies. Freedom is exported every day we ship goods and products that improve the lives of millions of people. Free trade brings greater political and personal freedom....Economic freedom creates habits of liberty. And habits of liberty create expectations of democracy.
>
> George W. Bush, February 27, 2001

## INTRODUCTION

The security and well-being of its citizens stand at the very pinnacle of any government's responsibilities; trade, economic and security policies are central to fulfilling these responsibilities. For Canada and the United States, the border is a key focal point in achieving mutual economic and security objectives. On September 11, 2001, Canadians and Americans alike were brutally and tragically reminded of the vulnerability of their common border. The immediate — and understandable — response at the border to the outrage of the terrorist attacks in New York and Washington threw into sharp relief growing problems with border management that have arisen with deepening integration and growing cross-border linkages. This integration is likely to become even more intense.

Discussions earlier in 2001 had already indicated that there was swelling support for further facilitating the cross-border movement of goods and people. A growing number of analysts and commentators were suggesting that the level of trade had reached the point at which traditional approaches to border administration had become dysfunctional. Since 1985, the value and volume of cross-border trade and foreign direct investment (FDI) between Canada and the United States have quadrupled. Two hundred million people crossed the border in 2000 and the value of cross-border trade in goods and services reached C$700 billion. The leading sectors of both economies are now those most engaged in international exchange, and in both countries, the basis of prosperity is more and more knowledge-based production that knows no borders.

## Trade and the Canadian Economy

### Total Trade in Goods and Services, 1997-2000

| Year | (in billions of current C$) | | | U.S. Share (percent) | | Share of GDP (percent) | |
|---|---|---|---|---|---|---|---|
| | Exports | Imports | GDP | Exports | Imports | Exports | Imports |
| 1997 | 345 | 331 | 878 | 81.8 | 67.5 | 39.1 | 37.5 |
| 1998 | 371 | 359 | 902 | 84.8 | 68.2 | 41.2 | 39.8 |
| 1999 | 412 | 385 | 958 | 86.8 | 67.3 | 43.1 | 40.2 |
| 2000 | 474 | 426 | 1,039 | 87.2 | 64.3 | 45.6 | 41.0 |

### Trade as a Share of GDP, 1990-2000

| | 1990 | 1991 | 1992 | 1993 | 1994 | 1995 | 1996 | 1997 | 1998 | 1999 | 2000 |
|---|---|---|---|---|---|---|---|---|---|---|---|
| Total Exports | 25.7 | 25.0 | 27.0 | 30.1 | 34.0 | 37.3 | 38.4 | 39.1 | 41.2 | 43.1 | 45.6 |
| Goods | 22.4 | 21.6 | 23.4 | 26.2 | 29.7 | 32.9 | 33.6 | 34.3 | 35.8 | 37.6 | 40.2 |
| Services | 3.3 | 3.4 | 3.6 | 3.9 | 4.3 | 4.4 | 4.8 | 4.8 | 5.4 | 5.4 | 5.4 |
| Total Imports | 25.7 | 25.7 | 27.4 | 30.2 | 32.9 | 34.3 | 34.4 | 37.5 | 39.8 | 40.2 | 41.0 |
| Goods | 20.8 | 20.6 | 22.1 | 24.4 | 27.1 | 28.5 | 28.6 | 31.6 | 33.6 | 34.1 | 35.0 |
| Services | 4.9 | 5.1 | 5.3 | 5.8 | 5.8 | 5.7 | 5.8 | 5.8 | 6.2 | 6.0 | 6.0 |

### Canada and the United States: Two-way Trade, 1990-2000

| | Value (in millions of current C$) | | | Annual Growth (percent) | | |
|---|---|---|---|---|---|---|
| | Goods | Services | Total | Goods | Services | Total |
| 1990–2000 (average) | 366,204 | 49,140 | 415,343 | 11.6 | 9.9 | 11.4 |
| 1997 | 454,140 | 57,923 | 512,063 | 12.8 | 8.0 | 12.3 |
| 1998 | 503,293 | 63,248 | 566,541 | 10.8 | 9.2 | 10.6 |
| 1999 | 558,722 | 67,982 | 626,704 | 11.0 | 7.5 | 10.6 |
| 2000 | 627,208 | 72,762 | 699,970 | 12.3 | 7.0 | 11.7 |

Source: Department of Foreign Affairs and International Trade, *Trade Update 2000* and *2001*.

THE RESPONSE OF THE TWO ECONOMIES to the challenges posed by freer bilateral trade and investment has been both remarkable and positive. Nevertheless, the results have created new bilateral tensions, challenges and opportunities. The growing web of economic linkages joining the two countries, the result of the cumulative impact of billions of discrete daily decisions by consumers and producers alike, points to the need for policy responses on both sides of the border that will have an important bearing on the quality and pace of further integration. Deepening interaction is exposing policies and practices that stand in the way of more beneficial trade and investment. Cumbersome rules of origin, discriminatory government procurement restrictions, complex antidumping procedures, intrusive countervailing duty investigations, burdensome regulatory requirements, vexatious security considerations, onerous immigration procedures and other restrictive measures remain in place, discouraging rational investment decisions and deterring wealth-creating trade flows. The key to resolving many of these issues can be found in better ways and means to manage the border.

In the aftermath of September 11, both governments have begun to strengthen ways and means to counter threats to the security of North America. Reinforcing administration of the border by increasing customs, immigration and related resources, however, is likely to aggravate economic problems and miss addressing security requirements. Instead, the two governments need to work together to effect longer-term and effective solutions that ensure the security of Canadians and Americans alike, while safeguarding the economic life line that joins the two countries.

This study[1] argues that there are compelling security and economic reasons for Canada and the United States to pursue a bold and coordinated approach to ensure that the Canada-U.S. border remains open as a conduit for trade, tourism and investment between the two countries and less vulnerable to disruption by terrorist and other threats. The economic imperative can best be addressed through some fresh thinking and new arrangements that go beyond the current free-trade agreement. Security and related issues need an aggressive effort by police, intelligence, immigration, and allied enforcement bodies to coordinate their activities, share information and cooperate along the full spectrum of their common interests. These two endeavors should be pursued in tandem and should mutually reinforce one another. The objective of both efforts should be to create a North America that is more open, more secure and more prosperous.

## THE IMPACT OF FREER TRADE

ANALYSIS OF THE PROSPECT for any Canada-U.S. initiative to facilitate cross-border trade and investment must proceed from an assessment of the extent to which the Canada-U.S. Free Trade Agreement (FTA) and the North American Free Trade Agreement (NAFTA) — as well as the World Trade Organization (WTO) negotiations — have worked. The economic indicators are impressive, including increasing two-way flows in portfolio and direct investment, deepening integration of capital markets, rising mergers, acquisitions and strategic alliances, growth in the cross-border licensing of product and process technologies, continuing two-way flows in patent and other intellectual property exchanges, and escalating telecommunications traffic. Two-way movements of goods, services, capital, ideas and people are burgeoning, reflecting the extent to which Canadians and Americans alike are taking advantage of reduced barriers and increased opportunities in each other's markets.[2]

Ironically, freer trade's success both supports and undermines the case for further initiatives. Obviously, if the bilateral FTA and trilateral NAFTA have benefited both Canada and the United States, more effort along the same lines should be even better. However, unlike economic, trade and industrial circumstances in the first half of the 1980s, which made the business, economic and political case for a FTA persuasive, circumstances today, in large measure because of the FTA, seem less troublesome. Positive changes in trade and production patterns make the case for tackling the remaining barriers to trade and investment, while real, seem less compelling. This may be short-sighted. The need for a bilateral border initiative must, of course, rest on a judgment that remaining barriers are sufficiently troublesome to warrant a major effort by the two governments to resolve them, but such a judgment must also be informed by broader concerns related to Canada's longer-term economic prospects, U.S. interest in those prospects, and their impact on broader security and related considerations.

In order for Canadians to maintain, let alone improve, their standard of living, Canada needs a confident, dynamic, outward-oriented business sector. It needs entrepreneurs and investors convinced that they can do well in the Canadian economy and persuaded that the policy and regulatory framework supports, rather than undermines, their efforts. In the words of Derek Burney (2000), former Canadian ambassador to the United States, "...benign neglect of the USA by Canada can be very damaging to our well-being. Managing this complex relationship has to be a top priority for our government, whether they like it or not....here is also scope for bold examination and analysis of new policy options for broader cooperation."

The events of September 11 dramatically altered the perspective of most Canadians. Benign neglect went out the window — the need for a bold initiative became both urgent and compelling.

---

### CANADA-U.S. BORDER FACTS

- *About 70 percent of Canada's trade with the United States (by value) moves in or out of the United States by truck. About 11 million trucks crossed the border in 2000, or about 30,000 per day; about 100,000 passenger vehicles also cross every day; the Ambassador Bridge between Windsor and Detroit alone handles some 7,000 trucks a day, or one every minute in each direction, 24 hours a day; on September 13, 2001, the line-up of trucks waiting to cross the bridge into the United States stretched 36 kilometres.*

## CANADA-U.S. BORDER FACTS (CONT'D)

- Cross-border industrial linkages and the application of just-in-time production technologies have made an increasing number of plants on both sides of the border extremely vulnerable to delays; the automotive sector, for example, estimates that unexpected shutdowns due to the late arrival of parts can cost the industry up to $25,000 per minute, costs that will ultimately be reflected in the price consumers pay for vehicles.

- About 75 percent of bilateral trade in goods moves through one British Columbia and four Ontario border crossings: at White Rock-Blaine, two at Windsor-Detroit and one each at Fort Erie-Buffalo and Sarnia-Port Huron; these border crossings have reached their physical limit in processing both goods and people under current border management arrangements.

- Some 200 million individual crossings take place at the Canada-U.S. border each year, an average of more than half a million every day; 30 million cross in the Detroit-Windsor corridor; another 30 million use the Buffalo-Niagara corridor; and a further 20 million cross between British Columbia and the state of Washington.

- In a typical year, 15 million Canadians travel to the United States for visits of one day or more to break up the long winter, visit friends and relatives, conduct business or otherwise pursue legitimate objectives; over the course of the winter, some 1.2 million Canadians spend one night or more in Florida.

- On the Canadian side of the border, there are 135 land-border points, 140 inland offices, 203 airports (13 international), 187 commercial vessel clearance points and 313 small marine points. Many of these are small and do not operate on a 24-hour basis. The United States similarly staffs the 135 Canada-U.S. land-border points as well as pre-clearance facilities at eight Canadian airports, but given its much denser population base, it maintains many more inland offices, airport facilities, commercial vessel clearance points and small marine points.

- The land border is more than 5,000 miles long. Policing that border is a difficult task. Nevertheless, both Canadian and U.S. officials agree that more than 99 percent of the people who cross the border are properly documented, do so for legitimate purposes and do not pose a risk to either country.

## THE IMPACT OF SEPTEMBER 11

BEEFED-UP EFFORTS TO SECURE THE BORDER in response to the threat of terrorist attack had an immediate and devastating impact on the border's role as an economic conduit, particularly on the Canadian side of the border. Canadians, more than Americans, are acutely aware of the role the border plays in their economic well-being.

More than ever, the two-way movement of goods and services across the Canada-U.S. border is Canada's economic life line. The extent of economic integration or linkages between the two countries has reached the stage that Canada's economic well-being has become directly tied to an open and well-functioning bilateral border. Failure to maintain, and even enhance, an open border will have a corrosive impact on Canada's continued economic prosperity.

Problems in the administration of the Canada-U.S. border had been obvious well before September 11.[3] On the economic side, the evidence of a dysfunctional border was mounting, in part because of the success of the FTA and the NAFTA in encouraging the restructuring of the two economies, promoting the more efficient use of resources on a continental basis and allowing trade to flow more freely. Physical infrastructure and human resources were stretched to the limit. Heightened security concerns after September 11 extended those resources beyond their capacity. The Coalition for Secure and Trade-Efficient Borders, a coalition of some 40 Canadian business associations, for example, has expressed the strong concern of its members over the threat a tighter border poses to the economies of both nations. It issued a statement on November 1, 2000, calling on the two governments to move expeditiously to create a secure perimeter around North America and a more open border between Canada and the United States.[4]

Both Canada and the United States want to: 1) maintain a secure border; 2) encourage the rapid movement of legitimate travellers and promote efficient customs administration and clearance of freight; and 3) enforce similar laws by interdicting the movement of illegal drugs and smuggling of all kinds, apprehending illegal migrants, halting money laundering, precluding terrorism of any kind and otherwise preventing or deterring criminal activities. These goals are broadly shared by the two governments. The differences are matters of detail and emphasis.

Border agents on both sides of the border administer a wide range of legal and regulatory requirements related to security, safety, the economy and the like. The clearance of a shipment of goods through either Canadian or U.S. customs, for example, requires that officials at the border be satisfied that: 1) the goods; 2) the truck, train, plane or ship; and 3) the driver or operator are all eligible for entry. Eligibility of the goods may involve considerations related to customs (tariffs, rules of origin and similar issues), health, safety, labeling, government procurement, trade remedies, taxes, environmental concerns and more. The truck, train, plane or ship must be certified to meet safety and similar requirements. The driver or operator must satisfy immigration requirements regarding citizenship, visas, criminal records, professional certification, labour regulations and similar matters. In each case, Canadian and U.S. laws seek to safeguard security, health, safety and other important policy goals.

In most instances, the differences in objectives, approach and rationale of a wide range of Canadian and U.S. laws and regulations relating to both security and economic well-being are minor and unimportant. Those differences that do exist are matters of detail, the result of differing regulatory styles, histories, legislative practices and implementation experiences. In the final analysis, however, they are marginal in their impact. The need is not for harmonization, but for more sharing of information, cooperation and coordination, both within each country and between Canada and the United States.

Officials on both sides of the border are aware of every detail of difference; many perceive their livelihoods to depend on these differences. It is not surprising, therefore, to find ministers being briefed about the importance of some of the differences and being told that resolving these differences is not a 'simple' matter. That is true, insofar as it goes. Eradicating the differences that exist could, in many instances, prove a complex matter; it is also, in most instances, an unimportant one. What counts is that the two governments share objectives and have confidence in outcomes. That is a much more important objective, and one that is much easier to attain. Mutual recognition agreements, for example, offer a technique that falls short of the tyranny of harmonization to big-economy standards while meeting the political requirement of democratic governance of the market. Canada and the United States have already a number of such agreements and need to consider more. A compelling issue for both governments, therefore, is to analyse the tasks currently being performed at the border and then separate those that must continue from those that can be eliminated or managed elsewhere.

In recognition of the extent of their shared objectives, as well as in an effort to reduce costs and facilitate legitimate travel and commerce, Canadian and U.S. officials over the course of the 1990s initiated a series of programs and dialogues aimed at finding ways to make the border more open, effective and efficient. Such programs as CANPASS and INSPASS seek to facilitate travel by frequent, low-risk individuals. Other initiatives — from the Shared Border Accord, announced in 1995, to the Canada-U.S. Partnership Forum, formed in 1999 — seek to make better use of emerging technologies, find ways to streamline the implementation of border policies, share information and coordinate activities, and otherwise make existing laws and policies work more effectively.

425

The basic goal of these various initiatives was described well in 1996 by then Minister of National Revenue, David Anderson: to create: "a hassle-free border for honest travellers and businesses, and a brick wall for those who try to smuggle or break other laws at this border." (*New York Times*, October 4, 2001) Experience to date, however, suggests more may be required. Anderson's successor, Martin Cauchon, called for "a revolution in the way we manage our common border," while International Trade Minister Pierre Pettigrew has suggested that "our two nations can lead by example and act as a model for an increasingly interconnected world, where borders must be seen as welcoming thresholds, not forbidding barriers." Paul Cellucci, U.S. ambassador to Canada, has echoed these comments, noting that "we have to talk about being more consistent [in policies]. We don't want Canadian citizens or U.S. citizens to be spending three or four hours trying to cross the border....If we don't want to go down that road we need to use technology and some more consistent policies to make it more convenient."(*National Post*, April 2, 2001 and June 30, 2001; *Globe and Mail*, August 2, 2001)

Many of these initiatives were very useful, but in the aftermath of September 11, they clearly suffer from two basic weaknesses: 1) they address conditions that no longer exist; and 2) they do not enjoy sufficient political support to give officials, particularly those engaged in enforcement, the necessary incentive to overcome problems and think outside the box. Previous initiatives sought to operate within existing domestic and international legal frameworks. New initiatives should assume a willingness to effect fundamental change and address the full range of barriers and administrative hurdles that remain in place.

## THE EXTENT OF REMAINING TRADE AND INVESTMENT BARRIERS

THE PUBLISHED INVENTORIES of the continuing bilateral irritants maintained by trade officials for both governments suggest that the remaining barriers are significantly less onerous in depth and extent than those in place at the beginning of the 1980s. Nevertheless, barriers remain in place that constrain bilateral trade and investment flows and hamper the creation of a more open border regime. The inventories confirm that freer trade has proved highly successful in underwriting a significant level of deepening cross-border integration, but they also suggest that in order to reap the full benefits of deeper integration, the two governments must address three fundamental issues:

1.  the role of the physical border in conditioning trade and investment decisions, including the costs of compliance and the potential costs created by delays;

2.  the impact of regulatory differences, again involving costs of compliance (both intergovernmental agreements and the pressures of silent integration have accelerated regulatory convergence and narrowed differences, but they have neither eliminated existing differences nor discouraged new differences from emerging in regulatory design, objectives, implementation and compliance); and

3.  the need for the two governments to manage the relationship and strengthen institutional and procedural frameworks to iron out differences and reduce conflict.

These issues, of course, are closely interrelated so that progress toward improving one would spur progress toward improving the others. An improvement in tariff and tariff-related programs and standards issues, for example, would have an important bearing on customs and border administration. In addition, a number of related issues, such as the implementation of immigration and security policies, can have an important bearing on trade and investment flows and would benefit from a concerted, joint effort to find better approaches. As George Haynal, former Assistant Deputy Minister in Canada's Department of Foreign Affairs and International Trade, responsible for relations with the United States, explained in an essay written before September 11:

> A process of policy convergence is already well in train....Its end product is still hard to identify, but clearly it is building a level of integration that extends beyond the economy....The question is less whether we need to negotiate new instruments to further the process, but whether the public realm is capable of keeping up with emerging forces pushing us into deeper integration. (Hart, Dymond and Robertson 2000)

## AN AGENDA FOR OPENING THE CANADA-U.S. BORDER FURTHER:

- For customs and border administration, *more progress needs to be made on various initiatives to facilitate, streamline and even eliminate the need for routine customs clearance of both people and goods;*
- *for* tariffs and related programs, *such as rules of origin, industry on both sides of the border would benefit from the reduction and harmonization of most favoured nation (MFN) tariff levels, obviating the need for many of these programs;*
- *for* product and process standards and regulations, *much more progress can be made to develop either common standards or greater acceptance of equivalence, mutual recognition, common testing protocols and similar provisions;*

427

---

### AN AGENDA FOR OPENING THE CANADA-U.S. BORDER FURTHER (CONT'D)

- *for* services, *there is room to move beyond commitments on market access to greater reliance on common standards and mutual recognition; sectoral discussions related to* financial, transportation, telecommunications and professional services *would also provide further scope for reducing discrimination and enhancing trade and investment opportunities, and increasing healthy competition on a broader basis;*

- *for* government procurement, *the rules should advance from the limited, entities method pursued in the* GATT/WTO *Procurement Agreement and expanded in the* FTA/NAFTA *to a full national-treatment approach, mandating governments throughout the region to purchase goods and services for their own use on a non-discriminatory, fully competitive basis, at least insofar as North American suppliers are concerned;*

- *for* trade remedies — *antidumping and countervailing duties* — *the rules should evolve beyond* WTO-like *procedural safeguards to common rules about competition and subsidies, reducing the scope for anticompetitive harassment and procedures;*

- *for* competition policy, *more effort should be devoted to setting out common goals and providing a basis for cooperative enforcement procedures;*

- *for* investment, *stronger provisions should be made for enforcement by the domestic courts of jointly agreed rules of behaviour; and*

- institutionally, *the two governments need to move beyond the ad hoc intergovernmental arrangements of the* FTA *and the* NAFTA *toward more permanent supranational institutions.*

It is clear that Canada would benefit from reducing by a significant margin what Helliwell and McCallum (1994) have called the "border effect."5 Despite multilateral and bilateral efforts to diminish the impact of the border, they calculate that the propensity for Canadian firms to buy and sell domestically is 12 times higher than their propensity to do business internationally. By way of contrast, the auto pact has virtually eliminated the border effect for trade in automotive products for the states and provinces in which the auto industry is concentrated. The fortuitous circumstances of concentrated ownership that encouraged the negotiation of the auto pact in 1964 also allowed for a high level of cross-border integration over the subsequent 25 years. The development of the auto industry in Ontario since 1965 has been one of the major policy-induced success stories of the twentieth century. More efficient trade and production, and the resulting high-quality jobs, are directly attributable to a reduced border effect.[6]

If Canada and the United States can succeed in further reducing the border effect for more industries, there is no reason why more Canadian-based firms and industries cannot become similarly more specialized and productive, leading to more beneficial trade and investment, better jobs and higher incomes. This kind of progress could have an important bearing on such non-trade issues as the exchange rate and monetary policy, the "brain drain," cross-border merger and acquisition activity and U.S. confidence in Canada's reliability as an economic and security partner. In effect, it could help to reduce what some analysts have called the "Canada discount"[7] — the extent to which both Canadian and foreign investors factor in such extra costs of doing business in Canada as higher taxes and lower productivity levels — and induce more firms to establish or stay in Canada.

Trade policy alone will not eliminate the Canada discount, but unless trade policy is included in the mix of fiscal and other policy initiatives aimed at creating a more resilient and competitive economy, the results will prove disappointing. As Harris (2000) concludes:

> The phenomenal U.S. growth during the 1990s, with low inflation and low unemployment, has had a two-fold effect. First, it has quashed a lot of doubts by anti-market proponents as to the performance and merits of U.S.-style market capitalism. Historically, [Canadian] antipathy towards this model of economic development has precluded getting too close to the United States. Second, the fact that the United States has done so well relative to Canada has raised the export dependency of Canada on the United States and increased the potential benefits to catch up with the United States. Together with a lack of progress on the multilateral front this implies that deeper Canada-U.S. integration is the only realistic option for progress in developing significant market access.

Integration is a natural process flowing from the impact of billions of discrete and seemingly unrelated decisions. Policy, however, can smooth or hinder this process. Geography and history suggest that Canada's economic destiny lies with the U.S. market. More than a third of Canada's economic activity is now generated by exports to the U.S. market and nearly a third of its consumption of goods and services originates in the United States. The extent and depth of this integration are being driven not only by corporate and public policy decisions, but even more by individual Canadians and Americans in their daily decisions about what to eat, wear, drive, read and otherwise spend their resources on. Overwhelmingly, those choices favour North American products. Markets and suppliers in the United States are now the overwhelming preference of Canadian firms and individuals, and Canadian markets and suppliers have assumed a growing importance to U.S. firms and consumers. To manage this growing level of integration, the two governments negotiated a free-trade agreement in the mid-1980s. An accelerating and deepening integration now indicates that more robust instruments may be required to manage relations and ensure that Canada has a voice in the further evolution of a more integrated North American economy. As Burney points out:

> History demonstrates that we can harness our proximity to the United States to our advantage without compromising our identity or our right to disagree. We are best served by rules, agreements, and treaties which reflect genuine compromise and help temper the enormous power imbalance and by a sense of priority and political will which reinforce the importance of this relationship.

From the other side of the border, former U.S. Ambassador to Canada, Gordon Giffin, adds:

> Canada and the United States share much more than geography, and it is our shared values that provide the foundation for this task [a new border accord]. The good news is that a lot of work has already been done by thoughtful people on both sides. Now we need the mutual commitment to get it done. (*Maclean's*, October 22, 2001)

## A COMPREHENSIVE BILATERAL INITIATIVE

FOR SOME OF THE ISSUES that can be addressed jointly, such as customs administration or standards, U.S. interests are roughly similar to those of Canada; for others, such as trade remedies and government procurement, U.S. perspectives are somewhat different. Individually, many of these issues do not appear to have much political curb appeal. Experience has taught Canadian officials that it is hard to make stand-alone progress on standards or government procurement preferences. Taken together, however, the issues listed above add up to a surprising level of continuing differential treatment for suppliers on one side of the border or the other, and these differences form the basis for the continued high level of border administration, despite a decade and a half of freer trade. They are the kind of problems that grow in importance as integration deepens. As the Europeans have learned, they need to be tackled after the successful implementation of the first level of regional integration. Their resolution requires the two governments to take further steps to reduce discrimination and, in those instances where de jure non-discrimination may still mask de facto discrimination, make greater use of such instruments as mutual recognition, joint rule-making, and cooperative enforcement mechanisms.

Many of these issues, of course, are already on the bilateral agenda, and specific aspects may be resolved in due course as part of ongoing efforts to address individual problems. Obviously, if a policy or measure that causes conflict is inconsistent with existing trade agreement obligations, dispute settlement is one way to resolve the matter. Most of the difficult disputes, however, are in areas where the rules are vague or inconsistent, requiring political settlement; in such circumstances, dispute settlement cannot substitute for negotiations. Issue-by-issue consultations and negotiations can also prove useful, but usually more so for the United States than for Canada. There are many examples of Canada negotiating pragmatic solutions to accommodate U.S. interests or concerns, from softwood lumber to durum wheat; there are not many examples in the other direction, the 1965 auto pact being a prominent exception. The exigencies of the highly fragmented U.S. political system make it very difficult for U.S. officials to accommodate foreign interests on an issue-by-issue basis, while the capacity to exercise raw power makes it relatively easy to insist that foreign governments accommodate single-issue U.S. interests.

Before the FTA negotiations were joined in 1986, Canada sought to replicate the success of the auto pact in other sectors with the 1983 sectoral initiative. Officials learned once again how difficult it is to build political support for narrowly conceived or issue-specific initiatives (Hart, Dymond and Robertson 1994). Most governments, but particularly the U.S. government, need comprehensive initiatives in order to build the necessary broad base of support to overcome highly focussed opposition groups. Canada's trade and investment relationship with the United States is too big and important to rely on the inertia created by existing channels of communication. It requires dynamic and creative management of the agenda.

In order to gain appreciable support in the United States, a bilateral initiative must be sufficiently broad and creative to capture the imagination of leading U.S. political figures. While a broad initiative is needed to attract U.S. attention, willingness to address a wide range of specific issues important to individual U.S. political and commercial interests is critical to sustain any initiative. Canada will have to come to grips with some difficult issues. Any initiative that makes significant progress in reducing the dysfunctional impact of the border will involve serious commitments by Canada. Agriculture provides a good example, particularly the current system of supply management and the state-trading practices of the Canadian Wheat Board. The United States will want to explore how both function to advantage Canadian producers. It should be noted, however, that Canada will also be under intense pressure in the new round of WTO negotiations to deal with these issues. Similarly, some Canadian cultural protection programs will be hard to defend in any bilateral initiative. Again, however, these programs are already facing mounting pressures, generated by technological and market factors, as well as critical scrutiny under existing trade agreement dispute settlement provisions. Within a bilateral initiative, there may be greater opportunity to find some accommodation and pursue Canadian export interests as well. Without a bilateral initiative, such policies may erode in ways that Canada can neither manage nor control.[8]

Although Canada will come under intense pressure to accommodate U.S. interests, there is no guarantee that the United States will accommodate enough Canadian interests to justify opening negotiations at the bilateral level. The incentive for the United States is not of the same order as Canada's, although the events of September 11 have altered the balance to some extent. For every dollar of trade that crosses the border, there is an American at one end and a Canadian at the other. The absolute value of U.S. interests at stake is roughly equal to Canadian interests, but their relative value is not — the U.S. economy is now some 15 times larger than the Canadian economy, and U.S. international economic interests are dispersed more widely around the globe.

As the world's premier economy, the United States enjoys advantages that place it ahead of all others in attracting investment. As the world's only remaining superpower, it is also hard for U.S. officials to see the need for accommodating the interests of others. The Washington mindset that the rest of the world should adjust to U.S. policy preferences and choices is hard to undo. Nevertheless, past experience demonstrates that Canadians have been reasonably successful in moving U.S. officials along with good ideas, particularly good ideas embedded within broad initiatives. The FTA negotiations, for example, appeared hopeless at times, but, in the end, Canada managed to satisfy many of its objectives because U.S. political leaders could not abide the failure of the negotiations. Only by pursuing an initiative that is bold, broad and deep will it be possible to test the extent to which U.S. interests can be sufficiently engaged to accommodate Canadian priorities.

The range of issues that needs to be addressed to effect a more open border regime, therefore, is most likely to be resolved within a broadly based initiative. A comprehensive approach, however, risks raising Canadian fears about closer trade and economic ties with the United States. Canadians may react positively to efforts to resolve specific issues. They are prepared to accept that facilitating trade and investment will benefit Canadian firms and consumers, but many would shy away from imposing sanctions on third parties to meet U.S. foreign policy objectives. They are prepared to see more streamlined customs and immigration procedures, but would be wary of common approaches to controls on guns and drugs. Again, however, as we discuss below, the events of September 11 have altered the balance dramatically. Nevertheless, to succeed, a comprehensive approach needs to be carefully explained to ensure that Canadians — and Americans — appreciate the difference between efforts to reduce the wide spectrum of regulatory and other barriers to increased cross-border trade and investment and efforts to establish a more formal type of arrangement, such as a customs union or common market. Neither country is interested in erasing the border as an important political fact and symbol; but both countries have an interest in reducing or even eliminating the dysfunctional economic impact of border administration.

Much of the agenda outlined above can be achieved without taking the additional step of negotiating a full-fledged customs union or common market.[9] The added benefit of a customs union or common market lies in the ease with which some specific issues could be resolved, such as the burdensome nature of rules of origin. The benefits of proceeding to a customs union or common market, however, may not outweigh the resultant complications, particularly those only indirectly related to facilitating border administration. Many of the issues on the agenda provide room, within the context of a comprehensive initiative, for finding mutually beneficial ways to cooperate and reduce regulatory burdens. No initiative is likely to resolve all issues, but with sufficient will and imagination, a comprehensive round of discussions may produce breakthroughs on some of the more intractable ones.

## SECURITY, ENFORCEMENT AND A MORE OPEN BORDER

IN CONSIDERING WAYS AND MEANS to address the increasingly dysfunctional economic impact of border administration and remaining trade barriers, it is useful to distinguish between efforts to ensure compliance with a host of regulatory requirements and efforts to enforce laws and other matters that fall within the ambit of police and security. Most of the requirements administered at the border involve regulatory matters and are secondary to the primary objective of maintaining a secure border. A key aspect of any effort to ensure the more efficient and effective operation of the border, therefore, involves identifying those aspects of the clearance process that can be satisfied away from the border or eliminated altogether.

Much of the customs clearance of goods, for example, involves onerous information and reporting requirements that could be satisfied on a basis similar to normal domestic reporting requirements for firms in both economies. Much of this reporting requirement operates as if the two economies were not joined by a free-trade area. As well, most customs requirements — for example, origin certificates — involve matters that could be eliminated easily by harmonizing MFN tariff levels and other similar steps. A well-designed initiative to identify those remaining aspects of border administration that could be either eliminated or addressed away from the border would contribute greatly to making the border function more effectively.

Similarly, virtually all travel across the border involves properly documented and eligible individuals pursuing legitimate objectives, from business to tourism. Much of the work of immigration officers, therefore, is routine and makes at most a marginal contribution to safety and security. Again, a well-designed initiative aimed at identifying how these routine requirements can be either eliminated, performed away from the border or satisfied by relying on more modern technologies would pay handsome dividends in creating a more efficient, effective and secure border and a better functioning North American economy.

Evidence from a variety of ports-of-entry indicates that attempts to cross the border by those who pose a potential threat to either Canadians or Americans are rare and isolated, particularly relative to the huge number of crossings. Every port-of-entry, of course, is vulnerable to penetration by undesirable elements, but experience indicates that the more 'serious' criminals have ample space — and resources — to bypass port-of-entry controls without much effort. The solution to any real threat lies in devoting more resources to intelligence gathering, information sharing and entry by individuals and goods from non-North American points of origin, rather than to increasing routine inspections at the Canada-U.S. border.

Some Canadians have expressed alarm that moving in this direction would require the two countries to establish a 'common perimeter.' It is hard to take this concern seriously; a de facto North American perimeter is a matter of long standing. The decision to maintain a North American security perimeter and pursue a North American economic space was decided many years ago, based on agreements ranging from the NATO and NORAD to the auto pact and the NAFTA. The issue after September 11 is how, in the face of the terrorist threat, the two countries can strengthen the perimeter that already exists or address security issues within their common economic and security space.

Both Canada and the United States are committed to controlling illegal immigration, drugs, terrorism and other criminal activities. More resources at the border, however, seem unlikely to achieve better results, absent extraordinary further investments in human and physical infrastructure. Increasing resources to such an extent, furthermore, risks causing considerable collateral damage to economic interests.[10] Rather, the two governments need to work with each other at every level to institutionalize contacts, enhance cooperation and share information on matters small and large. They could make much greater efforts to invest in intelligence-gathering and gradually focus ever larger parts of that effort on initial entries into North America. They could also make far greater investments in infrastructure and technology (both at ports-of-entry and the corridors leading to such ports). These investments should not proceed on the basis of current inspection methodologies, but rely much more on risk assessments and random inspections. They should also target more resources toward preclearance programs for goods, vehicles and people. Finally, they need to engage in discussions about increasing the level of convergence in Canadian and U.S. policies governing such matters as cargo and passenger preclearance programs, law enforcement programs of all types and immigration and refugee determination procedures.[11]

To combat terrorism and other illegal activity, Canada and the United States need rapid and timely exchanges of information on criminals and other individuals who may pose a security risk. Although there is information sharing at the moment, it may need to be upgraded significantly, and some of the information data bases need to be combined and made available at the border. Information from law enforcement agencies, immigration agencies, the courts and other institutions may need to be jointly accessible, at the border, in real time. There is a need for much greater collaboration and better information management.[12] The data base management tools and software developed in the last five years, as well as leading-edge networking software, can be deployed at the border and connected to main data bases in Canada and the United States.

## BROADER IMPLICATIONS

IN ASSESSING THE PROS AND CONS of any border initiative, it is important to keep in mind that failure to address the kinds of issues identified above will have a slow but corrosive impact on decisions to invest in Canada. As the smaller partner in North America, Canada must face the hard truth that the United States is by default the preferred location. That preference is predicated on a wide range of considerations, starting with the size and proximity of the U.S. market. For any entrepreneur, it is usually more profitable to service the small market from the large market rather than vice versa. That preference was strongly reinforced by the U.S. reaction to the events of September 11. Businesses are likely to respond to a tighter border by choosing, quite reasonably, to locate in the larger market.

In addition, U.S. advantages, ranging from tax levels to research policies, act as a powerful magnet. Ironically, Canada's long-standing desire to diversify trade by strengthening ties with Europe, Japan and other countries would be improved if the impact of the border between Canada and the United States could be reduced. The challenge for Canada has always been to adopt policies that offset, to some extent, the natural attraction of U.S. investment locations. Canada is failing to meet this challenge. Trade policy alone cannot offset this failure, but trade negotiations can play an important part in reversing the trend. As global integration deepens and the competition for investment intensifies, Canadians need to pay careful attention to what is required to make Canada an attractive location within North America for new or expanded investments. The FTA made a large contribution. A more open and predictable border can make a further contribution.

Finally, in considering any initiative, it is important to distinguish between the impact of proximity and the role of laws, policies and agreements. Much of the political debate in Canada in the past was predicated on a simplistic tendency to equate the two. For good or for ill, proximity to the United States is a fact of life; through laws, policies and agreements Canadians and Americans address the problems and opportunities proximity creates. As Allan Gotlieb, former Canadian Ambassador to the United States, observed:

> [Canadians] believe the United States has an obligation to be nice to us whether or not we are nice to them. But if our political survival does not depend on relations with the United States, our prosperity does. That is why the greatest foreign policy challenge for Canada is the management of our relations with the United States. (*National Post*, August 7, 1999, B11)

For Canada, proximity ensures that the United States will exercise an overwhelming presence in every aspect of Canadian life, from culture to tax levels. As John Kenneth Galbraith observed many years ago, "I was brought up in southwestern Ontario where we were taught that Canadian patriotism should not withstand anything more than a five dollar wage differential. Anything more, and you went to Detroit." (*Saturday Night*, January 1985) Whether governments like it or not, the stick by which matters are measured in Canada is provided by the United States. For most Canadians, the issue is not how well Canada may do on the UN Human Development Index, but how well Canada stacks up against the United States in income levels and in access to goods and services. Trade and other policies can be used to reduce the disparities that now exist between Canadian and U.S. economic performance.

A comprehensive Canada-U.S. bilateral trade and investment initiative provides a unique basis for resolving a wide range of issues between Canada and the United States that will strengthen Canada's attractiveness as an investment location to serve Canadian, North American and world markets. Additionally, in the aftermath of September 11, it will provide a basis upon which the two governments can create a mutually beneficial framework to address security issues. Failure to tackle some of the issues raised earlier will have a subtle, harmful impact on investor confidence in the Canadian economy. As a result, given other advantages naturally enjoyed by the United States, Canadians will slowly but inexorably see the gap between U.S. and Canadian standards of living widen, as more and more of Canada's brightest individuals and most productive firms seek their destiny in the United States rather than in Canada.

## THE CONFIDENCE FACTOR

IN ORDER TO PROCEED TO THE DISCUSSION of a more open border, therefore, Canada will need to address the strongly held perception in the United States — wrong as it may be — that Canada is either unwilling or unable to do what needs to be done to ensure a secure North American perimeter. Whatever the merits of this perception, unless and until Americans are confident that Canadians fully share their determination to make North America secure, they will continue to insist on a much more vigilant approach to their northern border. Already Congress has allocated resources that will allow the principal agencies responsible for security at the Canadian border to triple their resources.[13] In the short term, these extra resources may ease some of the congestion arising from tighter security measures at the border. In the longer term, however, they run counter to the economic interests of both countries. As the Europeans learned when their economic integration deepened, open borders are critical to ensuring that the benefits from integration are widely shared.

As a first step toward establishing a more open border, the federal government, therefore, will need to shore up U.S. confidence in Canada's ability to do its share in securing North America's common perimeter. Meeting this challenge will require some fundamental re-evaluation of recent Canadian policies and practices, a re-evaluation that has strong support among Canadians. Specifically, Canada needs to revamp the implementation of immigration and refugee laws and rethink some of the policies and practices that have developed in recent years.[14] They have become increasingly captive of special interests, are out of step with the values and preferences of most Canadians[15] and are inimical to the changed circumstances. As the government has already indicated, Canada also needs to tighten the way it deals with internal security, from tax deductions for terrorist-sympathizing groups to money laundering and other criminal operations exploited by terrorist groups. Finally, Canada may need to reconsider its military preparedness. Canada's military forces have shrunk steadily over the past decade and its equipment has become more and more dated. Canada's capacity to meet its various domestic and international military obligations is severely stretched.[16]

There is no need to apologize for past policies and practices, nor a need to feel embarrassment about re-examining various laws and regulations. A cataclysmic event that few could have predicted has raised concern and anxiety throughout society. Every government has moved to reconsider its spending and program priorities and re-calibrate the most appropriate balance between freedom and security. Canada needs to tighten security not to deter the 200,000-plus immigrants and refugees it welcomes every year, but because of the 250 or so among them who may pose a risk and wish Canadians or Americans harm.[17]

Nothing is more important in a multicultural society than providing citizens and residents with the confidence that new arrivals have been properly screened and vetted for security. Without such confidence, the inevitable reaction will be fear based on concern about those who are different. Similarly, in a world that feels markedly less safe than before September 11, military preparedness, the capacity to gather and analyse intelligence, and resources available to police and other enforcement bodies assume a new priority.

These are matters that concern not only Americans, but also Canadians. Addressing them, therefore, is not just a matter of a means to an end, but also a matter of things that need to be done on their own merit. In addition, making improvements on these fronts will be an important contribution to restoring U.S. confidence in Canada as an economic and security partner and should provide a more receptive atmosphere within which to pursue the issue of the border. If the government succeeds in rebuilding U.S. confidence, Canada will be better positioned to work with the United States to take the necessary steps to create a more secure common perimeter and a more open joint border.

## BILATERAL OR TRILATERAL APPROACHES?

A S CANADA-U.S. TRADE HAS MUSHROOMED, so has U.S.-Mexico trade. Canada-Mexico trade, however, remains at minuscule levels, representing less than 1 percent of total North American trade flows. An examination of investment flows yields a similar picture. There is as yet very little evidence of the emergence of a North American economy. Instead, there now exist two robust and mutually beneficial bilateral trade and investment relationships joined at the hip by a common free-trade agreement. Mexican trade is concentrated in the southwestern quadrant of the United States, but is gradually spreading north and east, while Canadian trade is concentrated in the northeastern quadrant, but is expanding steadily west and south.

That is one reality. The second is that while Canada and Mexico may share many concerns and issues, the political economy of those issues in the United States is not the same for each country. Both relationships have long histories and are important to the United States, economically and geopolitically, but they have followed divergent paths and responded to different imperatives. The negotiation of the NAFTA stimulated a high level of interest in finding or promoting common elements in the three relationships, but more recent efforts have met with limited success. The three trade ministers meet periodically to discharge their responsibility as the NAFTA Commission. The three foreign ministers have met on occasion, as have business leaders and other elites, with a view to promoting the evolution of a North American community. These efforts may eventually bear fruit, but the results to date are modest.

Finally, the Mexican response to the September 11 events has been even more cautious than Canada's. Without the long history of shared security, military and police cooperation, the Mexican capacity to make an immediate contribution proved severely constrained. Furthermore, the long history of strained relations between the two countries was echoed in a much more muted popular response to the terrorist attacks. Mexican President Vicente Fox has attempted to make amends but is finding it difficult to muster support in his government or to gain a hearing in Washington.

These harsh realities place the United States, in particular, in a difficult position. Canada and Mexico may have many similar objectives to pursue in negotiations with the United States, but the United States has different priorities and sensitivities that arise in each relationship. What it may be prepared to do in negotiations with Canada, it would find very difficult in negotiations with Mexico. Issues that are critical to building support in the United States for negotiations with Mexico are irrelevant in Canada. In short, the idea of deepening and expanding the NAFTA into a North American customs union or common market, as has been suggested by President Fox, raises much more daunting considerations than the mere matter of negotiating bilateral NAFTA-plus accords to address border and security concerns.

In the Canada-U.S. FTA and the NAFTA, the three governments succeeded in tackling and resolving the relatively easy trade and investment issues. Their efforts met with considerable success, first in facilitating cross-border trade, evident in the spectacular increase in bilateral trade flows, and second in changing moods and mindsets, evident in the structural changes that have taken place. What has *not* emerged, however, is a North American economy or community. Governments and businesses now must decide whether they want to take steps to further strengthen and deepen the existing bilateral relationships or actively promote and pave the way for a much more integrated North American economy.

At one level, Canada and Mexico could pursue their own initiative with the United States to explore what may be needed and what is feasible. Such discussions could be pursued in parallel, with officials from both countries prepared to discuss their progress with each other. At a second level, officials could look at what needs to be done to create the rules and institutions required to truly integrate the three economies. The first is a strategy to address immediate needs and concerns; the second is geared to a long-term vision for North America and can be addressed at a slower pace.

Chris Sands (2001), a U.S. analyst, suggests that Canada may be unnecessarily concerned with proving to the United States that it should be treated differently from Mexico in the area of economic and security policy development. The Bush administration has adopted the lens of *realpolitik* in classifying countries according to U.S. interests and priorities. Of primary concern to the United States is its relationship with large powers such as Russia and China, which can decisively influence the character of the international system and can be called upon to assist with rogue regimes and hostile powers. In the second tier are those countries that project power in a regional context, such as Japan and Brazil. Canada occupies a place in the third tier, among countries that lack significant military or regional influence but remain a part of vital U.S. interests. For them, the Bush administration sees strengthened trade and financial ties as key. In the fourth and fifth tier are "failing" and "failed" states that are so preoccupied with their domestic problems that they have little to offer internationally. The administration sees Mexico, Colombia and Saudi Arabia among the "failing" states but considers their stability to be of vital interest to the United States. Paradoxically, prior to September 11, the Bush administration was criticized for underestimating the strategic importance of 'failed states' such as Afghanistan and Sierra Leone, but now they have taken on renewed importance as potential havens for terrorist organizations (Rice 2000; Stohl 2001).

On the basis of these considerations, it is prudent to pursue an initiative aimed primarily at facilitating cross-border trade and enhancing North American security, initially on a bilateral Canada-U.S. basis and without prejudice to the advisability or necessity of including Mexico or eventually incorporating any results into the NAFTA framework. Initially, it is more important to define the issues and the feasibility of their resolution than to focus on their form or the institutional basis for administering the results of any new commitments. Similarly, it is not necessary, at this stage, to determine whether Mexico should participate in any future discussions that may move beyond the initial focus on the border and security. They can be addressed similarly, on the basis of the results of preliminary discussions and in light of Mexican interests and capacity.

## CONCLUDING OBSERVATIONS

IN THE SUMMER OF 2001, *New York Times* reporter Anthony DePalma provided the policy community with an entertaining read. In *Here: The Biography of the New North American Continent*, he posits the interesting thesis that, despite their disparate histories and characters, the three countries of North America have more in common than they think and the NAFTA is drawing them ever closer together. Drawing on his experience as the *Times* bureau chief in Mexico City and Toronto, he concludes that "our border will not disappear, not any time soon. But what may fade away are the misunderstandings and ignorance that have plagued North America for so long." (DePalma 2001, 354)

If nothing else, DePalma captured well an issue that was gaining increasing attention in Canada. Given developments in the global economy, the intensification of private-sector led integration in North America and the stresses created by diverging Canada-U.S. economic performance, a growing number of commentators believed that the time had come for Canada and the United States to consider jointly whether or not to take steps to remove or constrain the remaining barriers to cross-border trade and investment.[18] The combined success of the Canada-U.S. FTA, NAFTA and WTO negotiations had exposed policies and practices that impeded further growth in trade and investment. Various political and think tank commentators had concluded that the remaining problems were most likely to be resolved on the basis of a comprehensive initiative that would capture the imagination of political leaders on both sides of the border and generate the level of support necessary to overcome narrowly focussed opposition.

The tragic events of September 11 fundamentally altered the equation. An issue that could previously have been weighed and debated became an issue for early and decisive action. Disruptions at the border rapidly convinced a growing number of Canadians and Americans that their governments needed to take determined steps to keep the border open as a conduit for trade, tourism and investment and make it less vulnerable to disruption by terrorist and other threats. On the security side, the crisis of September 11 pointed to the need for aggressive and cooperative efforts by police, intelligence, immigration and allied enforcement bodies to coordinate their activities, share information and cooperate along the full spectrum of their common interests. From an economic perspective, it indicated the need for some bold thinking and new arrangements.

Proceeding in this direction, of course, will have implications that go beyond trade and commercial considerations. Some Canadians, for example, are concerned that closer commercial ties might drag Canada into applying U.S. geopolitical trade barriers that are inimical to Canadian values and interests. Others worry that closer trade and commercial integration could undermine the federal and provincial governments' ability to nurture Canadian culture and identity. Still others fear that further negotiations could require Canada to share its resources without the adequate capacity to ensure it benefits from those assets. Some Canadians are suspicious that their governments' approach to health care, education, regional development and other defining policies could be compromised.

These are serious concerns to which there must be serious answers. Some of these fears relate more to the forces of proximity than to the nature of the rules in place to manage the flow of cross-border exchanges of goods, services, capital and technology. Canadians can do little about the fact that they live next door to the world's largest, most energetic economy, but the negotiation of better rules can provide an improved basis for managing the frictions created by proximity and ensure that Canadians are able to reap the full benefits of their geography. Others are matters that would need to be addressed with care in the negotiation of the terms and conditions that would apply. Like Canadians, Americans also have worries that must be addressed. As in the 1985-87 FTA negotiations, the essence of any negotiation involves resolving such issues and finding mutually acceptable compromises. The two governments must engage each other, analyse the issues as they emerge and determine what can be accommodated and what cannot.

## ENDNOTES

1   A longer version of this study was published as *Common Borders, Shared Destinies: Canada, the United States and Deepening Integration* (Hart 2001).

2   Rugman (2000) argues that globalization involves deepening intraregional trade in each of the three regions of the global economy, with FDI playing a larger role than trade in creating links at the interregional level.

3   Earlier in 2001, the Canadian Manufacturers and Exporters Association warned that the border had become dysfunctional, and complained about overburdened and congested highways, lengthy delays at border inspection stations, deteriorating and inadequate infrastructure, poor highway security for travellers, and looming gridlock on major trade corridors. *National Post*, October 12, 2001.

4   Coalition for Secure and Trade-Efficient Borders, *Statement of Principles*, November 1, 2000.

5   By comparing trade between provinces and between states and provinces of comparable size and geographic separation, Helliwell and McCallum (1994) estimated that the border effect was in the order of 17 in 1988 (i.e., the propensity for trade between Canadian provinces was 17 times higher than that for trade between the provinces and equally sized and distant states). While one may quarrel about some of their assumptions, the quality of the evidence on which they relied or the methodology of the study, Helliwell and McCallum make a provocative case that borders continue to have an important effect on trade, investment and distribution patterns. In a later study, Helliwell (1998) estimated that the FTA had reduced this border effect to a factor of 12 by 1996, but that there was little prospect for a further reduction.

6   Some public policy commentators have expressed concern that the gap between Canadian and U.S. productivity levels did not shrink during the first decade of freer trade. Two reasons suggest themselves: 1) during the same period, the U.S. economy, responding to deregulation and the impact of technological breakthroughs, experienced a major spurt in productivity growth, outpacing the improvements in Canada's own performance; and 2) a range of Canadian policies and attitudes continue to hamper further improvements, including reluctance to

accept the benefits of full competition in such sectors as dairy, air transportation, and financial services. The decision not to allow the restructuring of the financial services sector to become more globally competitive, for example, had an obvious impact on the performance of the Canadian economy as a whole and on subsequent investment decisions across a range of sectors. The important issue, of course, is not the gap between productivity levels, but whether Canada is pursuing policies that make sense and benefit Canadians.

7   See D'Aquino and Stewart-Patterson (2000) for a discussion of this concept and ideas on how to eliminate its impact.

8   For those worried about Canada's productivity performance, each of these policies contributes to undermining Canadian productivity improvements and thus undermining the future prosperity of Canadians. More than just U.S. interests are at stake in adjusting these policies to the demands of deepening integration and greater competition.

9   In economic literature, a customs union is the second level of regional integration following a free-trade area, and it involves the establishment of a common external trade policy that allows free circulation of goods and services within the customs union. The third level involves the establishment of a common market, which allows for the free circulation of all factors of production (goods, services, capital and technology), and it is followed by an economic union which usually involves a single currency and monetary policy. The further governments move along the integration spectrum, the more they need institutions of common governance and the greater the implications become for sovereign decision-making. The distinction between free-trade areas and customs unions is built into GATT Article XXIV, the provision that sets out the basic trade rules governing regional preferential trade arrangements. Interestingly, it is not carried over into the much newer General Agreement on Trade in Services (GATS): the scope of GATS Article V relates to regional integration agreements in general. Such distinctions ease the task of economic and legal analysis, but they do not necessarily reflect the fluidity and complexity of modern economic interaction and linkages. In a world in which tariffs have become relatively minor barriers to trade, and non-tariff barriers have assumed much greater importance, establishment of a common external tariff is not a major issue. Additionally, the FTA already anticipates elements of a common market but does not include critically important elements of a customs union. Further bilateral negotiations would provide an opportunity to deal creatively with specific problems without necessarily meeting all of the exigencies of a specific economic or legal category.

10  James Ziglar, then Commissioner of the U.S. Immigration and Naturalization Service (INS) testified before the Senate Appropriations Subcommittee on Treasury and General Government, October 3, 2001, that in the first six months of 2001, 4,000 criminal aliens (half of the total number of criminal aliens detained by the INS), were arrested at the Canadian border. It is worth noting that this number represents 0.004 percent of the people crossing the border, that the relatively high arrest level at the northern border is due in part to high levels of cooperation with Canadian authorities, and that most of these arrests involve relatively minor drug offences. Additionally, media reports the week of November 5 suggested that the U.S. Border Patrol

arrested some 14,000 illegal aliens trying to cross the Canada-U.S. border in 2000, while Canadian authorities apprehended some 7,000 headed in the opposite direction. Again, this represents a miniscule number, particularly in view of the more than one million illegal aliens arrested on the U.S. southern border every year.

11  See testimony by Demetrios Papademetriou and Deborah Meyers, U.S. House Subcommittee on Immigration and Claims, April 14, 1999, for a more detailed exposition of similar views.

12  Then INS Commissioner Ziglar's testimony before both Senate and House Committees on October 3 and 11, 2001, included a catalogue of proposed and potential ways to enhance cooperation and coordination, but also included ominous suggestions for unilateral measures to increase his agency's presence at the border and implement Section 110 of the Illegal Immigration Reform and Immigrant Responsibility Act. Section 110, which would require the documentation of every alien (including Canadians) entering and exiting the United States, is currently suspended due to the practical difficulties of implementing it at land border crossings. Governor Ridge, as Homeland Security Advisor and the first Secretary of the new Department of Homeland Security, has expressed renewed determination to implement Section 110.

13  The U.S. Congress in October 2001 appropriated a further US$609 million to strengthen security along the Canada-U.S. border, money that will be used to buy new equipment, and triple the number of customs and immigration officers from 1,773 to 5,319 and the number of border patrol officers from approximately 300 to 900 (*Globe and Mail*, October 10, 2001, A5). Canada relies on some 2,400 customs officers, as well as 560 immigration officers and other officials, including the RCMP and local police, to back them up to enforce Canadian laws and regulations at the Canada-U.S. border. Current full-time, two-way strength maintained at the border by the two countries thus exceeds 5,000 customs, immigration and related officers.

14  It is important to note here that recent changes in the law are not enough. In order to meet both immigration and security objectives, the government will have to provide the system with sufficient resources, as well as the will to make decisions appropriate to the changed circumstances. Undisciplined immigration and refugee policies will become increasingly unpopular and unsustainable. Canada needs immigrants, but it also needs security and an open border with the United States. All three goals can be pursued on a basis compatible with Canadian values and preferences.

15  Polling after September 11 indicated an impressive 85 percent of Canadians want the government to adopt 'much tougher' immigration and refugee laws and 76 percent believe Canada should harmonize antiterrorism laws with the United States as quickly as possible (*National Post*, September 29, 2001).

16  See Desmond Morton, "What are we asking of our forces?" *National Post*, November 15, 2001, A14, for a thorough overview of the issues facing Canada's military in the new circumstances.

17  It is important to distinguish between fairness and security considerations. Many Canadians have expressed concern that Canada's refugee determination system is far too generous and allows economic migrants to jump the queue and come in as political refugees. The system represents a security threat, however, only insofar as

it encourages refugee claimants to be less than truthful. A closer look at security concerns need not compromise in any way Canada's willingness to keep its doors open to legitimate refugees and qualified immigrants.

18    The *Ottawa Citizen* reflected this fascination in a series of opinion pieces and editorials that ran over the course of the last two weeks of August 2001.

# BIBLIOGRAPHY

Burney, Derek. "Accessing the U.S. Market." Notes for Remarks to the Aerospace Industries Association of Canada, 39th Annual General Meeting, Ottawa, September 18, 2000.

D'Aquino, Thomas, and David Stewart-Patterson. *Northern Edge: How Canadians Can Triumph in the Global Economy.* Toronto: Stoddart, 2000.

DePalma, Anthony. *Here: The Biography of the New North American Continent.* New York: Public Affairs, 2001, p. 354.

Harris, Richard G. "North American Economic Integration: Issues and a Research Agenda." Background paper prepared for an Industry Canada Roundtable on North American Linkages. Ottawa: Industry Canada, September 7, 2000.

Hart, Michael. *Common Borders, Shared Destinies: Canada, the United States and Deepening Integration.* Ottawa: Centre for Trade Policy and Law, 2001.

_____. "Roundtable on Canada-U.S. Free Trade: Is It Time for Round Two?" *Canadian Foreign Policy* 7, 3 (September 2000): 1-14.

Hart, Michael, Bill Dymond and Colin Robertson. *Decision at Midnight: Inside the Canada-U.S. Free Trade Negotiations.* Vancouver: UBC Press, 1994, pp. 57-62.

Helliwell, John. *How Much Do National Borders Matter?* Washington: Brookings Institution, 1998, p. 115.

Helliwell, John, and John McCallum. "National Borders Still Matter for Trade." *Policy Options/Options politiques* 16 (1994): 44-8.

Rice, Condoleezza. "Campaign 2000: Promoting the National Interest." *Foreign Affairs* 79, 1 (January/February 2000): 45-62.

Rugman, Alan. *The End of Globalization: Why Global Strategy is a Myth and How to Profit from the Realities of Regional Markets.* London: Amacom, 2000.

Sands, Chris. "Canada and the United States After September 11." Speech to the Alumni Association at The Norman Paterson School of International Affairs, Carleton University, Ottawa, November 8, 2001.

Stohl, Rachel. "Bush Policy on Failed States is Lacking." CDI Weekly Defence Monitor 5, 16 (April 19, 2001). Available at: http://www.cdi.org/weekly/2001/issue16.

# Part III
## Policy Convergence or Divergence?

Kirk A. Collins     &     James B. Davies
University of Ottawa        University of Western Ontario

*12*

# Tax Treatment of Human Capital in Canada and the United States: An Overview and Examination of the Case of University Graduates

## INTRODUCTION

THIS STUDY REVIEWS THE CURRENT TAX TREATMENT of human capital in Canada and the United States. Its primary focus is on personal income tax (PIT), but it also touches on social security contributions, sales taxes and other forms of taxation. It shows how the net effect of the tax system can be assessed by means of effective tax rates (ETRs) on different kinds of human capital. The result is a picture of the incentive effects for human capital accumulation of both the Canadian and U.S. tax systems. We find that the tax systems in both countries create disincentives for human capital accumulation. Overall, ETRs on human capital appear to be higher in Canada. For high earners in Canada, the ETR can be sizable indeed; on the other hand, one of the lowest ETRs in North America is that on talented Canadians who move to pursue careers in the United States after graduation. The existence of the American opportunity may dampen the disincentive effects of Canadian taxes on investment in education for the most able.

One should be careful in the interpretation of our results. For example, tax disincentives to invest in human capital may not necessarily be a central reason Canada has lagged behind the United States in the development of its high tech sector or in the growth of manufacturing productivity over the last decade. This disappointing performance may have a human capital connection, but the reason for it may lie in the failure of the Canadian education system to provide the right *kinds* of education and training, or it may lie in high post-graduation tax rates, which make Canada a bad location for high-performing "stars." The latter issue is distinct from the question of whether taxes act as a disincentive for human capital formation; investment and location decisions are related, but must be carefully distinguished.

The ETR on human capital is simply the percentage gap between before- and after-tax rates of return. While there have been many attempts to estimate rates of return on human capital in both Canada and the United States over the last 40 years, oddly, there has not been a focus on the ETR. This is in contrast to the situation with regard to physical capital, where it has been recognized since the early 1980s that the ETR is the key tool for summing up the incentive effects of the tax system on investment.

The ETR can be used both conceptually and quantitatively to explore the impacts of various tax provisions, as in the case of physical capital, where differences across industries, type of capital, size of firm, and financial structure have been studied and a considerable lack of uniformity found (Boadway, Bruce and Mintz 1984; McKenzie, Mansour and Brule 1998). In the case of human capital, one can examine differences according to several variables, including earnings level, gender and how education is funded. This of course opens up a wealth of possibilities for comparative study in an international context; so much so, in fact, that the present study should be regarded as preliminary and exploratory. Much more study is needed of both countries, separately and comparatively.

Our methods are illustrated by two sets of calculations. First, we illustrate our analytical framework through calculations using the basic features of the Canadian and U.S. tax systems, and stylized assumptions about earnings and the earnings gains for education. Second, we attempt to provide estimates with a stronger empirical basis through the use of the 1998 Survey of Consumer Finance (SCF) for Canada and the March 1998 Current Population Survey (CPS) for the United States. These are the standard income surveys for the two countries and cover both earnings and income tax payments, using similar methods.

The study is organized as follows. The second section provides the conceptual framework. The third section is a discussion of the tax treatment of human capital in Canada and the United States, the results illustrated by means of our stylized examples. The ETRs based on the SCF and CPS surveys are provided in the fourth section,[1] while the fifth section discusses the implications for North American economic integration and for policy.

## CONCEPTUAL FRAMEWORK

WHILE THE QUALITATIVE ANALYSIS on the way taxation affects human capital investment is well developed in the literature, there is a gap on the quantitative side. In the work on physical capital, much use has been made of the concept of marginal effective tax rates (METRs). These have been estimated for different kinds of capital, industry and methods of finance. In general, it is found that there are large differences in METRs, implying distortions in the allocation of physical capital. Surprisingly, while a parallel concept can be developed readily for human capital, to the best of our knowledge this has not occurred in the literature.[2]

We have investigated and developed the conceptual basis for the calculation of ETRs on human capital investment. Since human capital investment tends to be lumpy, these ETRs are best defined for a particular level of education — for example, high school, community college or university first degree. By observing how these ETRs vary across the population (e.g., by income level and gender) we can tell which types of individuals get the most encouragment from the tax system for human capital investment.

The ETR for human capital formed, for example, in obtaining a bachelor's degree equals the wedge between the before- and after-tax rates of return on a university first degree. In the absence of tuition fees or other direct costs of schooling, a zero ETR would result from proportional labour income taxes or proportional sales taxes on a comprehensive base (exempting human capital inputs). These taxes reduce both after-tax foregone earnings during education, and after-tax earnings after graduation, by the same proportion. In contrast, progressive taxes increase ETRs, since the tax on the extra earnings due to education is at a higher rate than that which would have been paid on foregone earnings. As well, regressive taxes, such as the payroll taxes observed in Canada and the United States, will have the opposite effect for some workers.

The theoretical possibility of having a tax regime that produces a zero ETR illustrates an important point. We can tax the returns to human capital without distorting the incentive to invest in human capital. This is because implicitly subsidizing foregone earnings, and explicitly subsidizing tuition and other direct costs (e.g., by making them tax-deductible), requires less revenue than is collected by taxes levied at the same rate on earnings. Thus, what constitutes a "low" ETR differs from what one might expect. Normally, one thinks of a significant positive tax rate as a necessary evil; in the case of ETRs on capital, however, rates above zero are not necessary.

In order to set out how different tax features affect ETRs on human capital, we provide some notation and simple analytical results. First, the ETR is defined as the gap between gross- and net-of-tax rates of return to a whole program of study, $r_g$ and $r_n$:

(1)   $ETR = (r_g - r_n) / r_g.$

This definition, which is built on the use of internal rates of return, follows the methodology applied in computing ETRs on personal financial assets by Davies and Glenday (1990).[3]

Now, suppose that an individual aged $t$ is planning to engage in a program of education or training that will take $n$ years of study. We will assume that after this program is completed the individual will stay in the labour force until age $T$. Students may continue to earn while going to school. Their wage rates can vary over time, perhaps increasing while they are still in school and likely rising in real terms over much of their lifetime after graduation. Actual before-tax earnings are given by $E_t$, which is the product of the wage rate and hours worked. Before-tax earnings in the absence of the educational program would have been $E_t^*$, where we assume that $E_t^* < E_t$ in the $T - n$ years after graduation. Foregone earning costs of education, $FE_t$, are thus $E_t^* - E_t$ in the first $n$ years. In addition to these costs, there are direct costs, $C_t$, which, in the absence of loans, occur only in the first $n$ years.[4] After-tax variables will be denoted by $E_t^a$, $E_t^{a*}$, $FE_t^a$, and $C_t^a$.

Rates of return on the investment described can be calculated as internal rates of return via the usual approach. The gross private rate of return, $r_g$, is thus the discount rate which makes the present value of the net income streams the same, whether the individual opts to invest or not:

(2) $$\sum_{t=1}^{T} \frac{E_t - C_t}{(1 + r_g)^{t-1}} = \sum_{t=1}^{T} \frac{E_t^*}{(1 + r_g)^{t-1}} .$$

For the sake of illustration, suppose that the length of the schooling program, $n$, is one year. Also, rearrange Equation (2) so all the $t = 1$ terms are on one side and the remaining terms on the other:

(3) $$E_1^* - E_1 + C_1 = \sum_{t=2}^{T} \frac{E_t - E_t^* - C_t}{(1 + r_g)^{t-1}} .$$

| Costs of | Benefits of |
| Education | Education |
| Before-Tax | Before-Tax |

The left-hand side of Equation (3) represents the costs of the education program, made up of foregone earnings, $E_1^* - E_1$, and direct costs, $C_1$. The right-hand side is the present value of future earning increments due to education, $E_t - E_t^*$, net of any deferred direct costs (such as loan repayments).

Again, for the sake of illustration, suppose that the yearly benefits of education, $E_t - E_t^* - C_t$, are constant. Then, because $T$ is typically large, we have

$$E_s^* - E_s + C_s \approx \frac{E_w - E_w^* - C_w}{r_g} \; ,$$

where subscripts $s$ and $w$ denote the schooling and working periods. We now have a simple expression for the before-tax rate of return, $r_g$, and a parallel expression for the after-tax rate of return, $r_n$:

$$(4\text{i}) \quad r_g \approx \frac{E_w - E_w^* - C_w}{E_s^* - E_s + C_s} = \frac{Annual \; Return \; Before \; Tax}{Cost \; of \; Education \; Before \, Tax} \; ; \; \text{and}$$

$$(4\text{ii}) \quad r_n \approx \frac{E_w^a - E_w^{a^*} - C_w^a}{E_s^{a^*} - E_s^a + C_s^a} = \frac{Annual \; Return \; After \; Tax}{Cost \; of \; Education \; After \, Tax} \; .$$

Now, let $m_w$ be the fraction of the annual earning increment in the working period, EI, that is paid in tax:

$$(5\text{i}) \quad E_w^a - E_w^{a^*} = (1 - m_w)(E_w - E_w^*) = (1 - m_w)EI \; .$$

Similarly, we can define the fraction $m_s$ of foregone earnings, FE, during education that would have been paid in tax:

$$(5\text{ii}) \quad E_s^{a^*} - E_s^a = (1 - m_s)(E_s^* - E_s) = (1 - m_s)FE \; .$$

Ignoring direct costs for the time being, with the help of this new notation, Equations (1) and (4i) and (4ii) give

$$(6) \quad ETR\big|_{C=0} = \frac{r_g - r_n}{r_g} = \frac{m_w - m_s}{1 - m_s} \; .$$

This expression is simple and powerful. It indicates that, in the absence of direct costs, the tax system is non-neutral for human capital if, and only if, the increase in earnings resulting from education is taxed at a different rate than would have been applied to foregone earnings. The most obvious possibility is that the graduated rates under PIT will make $m_w > m_s$, resulting in a positive ETR. However, social security and unemployment insurance contributions are sizable, and since contributions are capped at maximum insurable earnings, the schedules are regressive. If contributions are in large part equivalent to taxes (i.e., benefits are paid out in a fashion that departs substantially from actuarial fairness), then these schemes work towards $m_w < m_s$ for workers whose EIs fall entirely or partly above maximum insurable earnings. It should also be borne in mind that sales taxes reduce real earnings; proportional sales taxes on a comprehensive consumption base would give $m_w = m_s$, or neutrality. However, some necessities are widely exempt from sales tax in North America (e.g., food, children's clothing, etc.) or are taxed at a lower rate. This again suggests that $m_w > m_s$, reinforcing the tendency of the PIT to produce a positive ETR.

Equation (6) also makes a number of other insights possible. Among them we note the following:

- If both $m_w$ and $m_s$ increase by the same amount, $m_w - m_s$ stays constant but the ETR increases.

- An equi-proportional rise in $m_w$ and $m_s$ causes an increase in the ETR.

These insights have a direct application to human capital ETRs in North America. Think of $m_w$ and $m_s$ as federal tax rates. If, as is the case in Canada and in some U.S. states, provincial or state income tax rates are either an exactly- or approximately-proportional blowup of federal rates, then they cause an equi-proportional rise in $m_w$ and $m_s$. On the other hand, some U.S. states (e.g., Illinois, Pennsylvania, Michigan) levy proportional income taxes, thereby adding an equal amount to $m_w$ and $m_s$.

One may ask: What would raise the ETR more — equi-proportional additions to $m_w$ and $m_s$ or equal absolute additions? An equal yield comparison is needed in order to answer this question. In general, the size of the percentage increase in $m_w$ and $m_s$ needed to produce the same revenue as an equal absolute increase in all tax rates will depend on the distribution of taxpayers and taxable incomes across income brackets. However, in the simple case where there are just two tax brackets, it is possible to show that the increase in the ETR will always be greater under the equi-proportional adjustment. There should be at least a tendency in this direction even when there are more brackets.[5]

Moving to the more general case, we need to take into account tuition and other direct costs; the student loan amount, $L$; student loan repayments, $iL$, where $i$ is the interest rate; the rate of tax relief on student loan payments, $d$; and credits for tuition and other expenses, $A$. Making the appropriate adjustments to the costs and returns and using the relationship $ETR = 1 - {r_n}/{r_g}$, we have

$$(7) \quad ETR = 1 - \left[ \frac{(1 - m_w)EI - i(1 - d)L}{(1 - m_s)FE + (C'_s - L - A)} \right]\left( \frac{EI - iL}{FE + C'_s - L} \right)^{-1},$$

where $C'_s$ is direct cost before both tuition credits and student loans.

Using Equation (7), we note the following:

- Increases in tuition credits, $A$, or in interest deductibility, $d$, unambiguously reduce the *ETR*.

- The *ETR* is affected by several factors that may be, to some extent, under the government's control (e.g., tuition fees, student loan amounts and interest rates on student loans) but are *outside* the tax system.

- A rise in tuition and other direct costs, $C'_s$, raises the *ETR*. The inference is that both the net and gross rates of return fall, but $r_n$ more so than $r_g$, since $C'_s$ is larger in relation to both returns and costs when the latter are measured after — rather than before — tax.

## A Comparison of Tax Features in Canada and the United States

MOST OF THE MAJOR COMPONENTS of the Canadian and U.S. tax systems have implications for human capital. In this section, we focus on the effects of the PIT, payroll taxes, sales taxes and the corporate income tax. The main features of current student loan plans are also described.

### Personal Income Tax

TRADITIONALLY, THE CANADIAN PIT provided relief for the direct costs of education and training, but did not allow a deduction or credit for interest paid on student loans. While the 1998 federal budget made 17 percent of the interest on qualified student loans creditable, Collins and Davies (2001) found that this had little effect on the ETR on university-level human capital.[6]

In contrast to the Canadian system, the traditional approach in the United States was not to allow a deduction or credit for most direct costs of education and training but to provide interest deductibility on student loans. Thus, it could be said that the Canadian PIT followed a "consumption tax" approach to human capital, while the U.S. system followed more of an "income tax" approach. This contrast has been eroded, however, since not only has student loan interest become partially creditable in Canada, but substantial credits for tuition and other fees were introduced in the United States in 1997.

Note that the tax relief on tuition and other direct expenses provided by the Canadian PIT comes not from a deduction (as in the strict cash-flow approach) but from a credit for 17 percent of tuition (and additional mandatory fees starting in 1997) paid to approved postsecondary institutions, plus 17 percent of an "education amount." The education amount was $80 per month prior to 1996 but was gradually raised to $200 per month between 1996 and 1998. Unused credits can be carried forward to future tax years (since 1997), or they can be transferred to a spouse, parent or grandparent (up to a limit of $5,000, minus the part of the credit used by the student to reduce his or her tax liability to zero). The latter measures ensure that the implicit federal subsidy on direct costs of education is close to a uniform 17 percent rate. Adding provincial tax, the average rate of relief is about 26 percent. While these arrangements work against the negative effect of progressivity on returns, one must recall that most of the human capital costs are in the form of foregone earnings and are thus unaffected. It is also important to point out that while the education amount credits are intended to offset non-tuition direct costs of education and training, they are paid as a lump sum and are therefore akin to a system of student grants.

Currently, in the United States, student loan interest is deductible up to a limit of $2,500, and this deduction is phased out beyond middle-income levels. There are two mutually exclusive tuition credits. The Hope Scholarship Tax Credit provides a 100 percent credit on the first $1,000 of tuition and fees and 50 percent on the next $1,000 for the first two years of postsecondary education.[7] For tax years after 2001, the $1,500 maximum will be indexed for inflation. The Lifetime Learning Credit is provided at a 20 percent rate on the first $5,000 of tuition and fees (this is scheduled to rise to $10,000 after December 31, 2002). Both credits are phased out for single taxpayers with modified adjusted gross income (AGI) in the $40,000 to $50,000 range and for couples filing jointly with modified AGI between $80,000 and $100,000.[8] It should also be noted that neither credit may be claimed if a taxpayer is making tax-free withdrawals from an education Individual Retirement Account (IRA) in the same year. Finally, these credits may be claimed either by a parent or by the student.

A rough comparison highlights the generosity of Canadian (as opposed to U.S.) tuition credits: note that typical fees at the bachelor's level in Canada are now about $4,500, while in the United States they average about $6,100. Assuming that the student and his or her family can make full use of the credits, in Canada, he or she would receive a (federal plus provincial) benefit of $1,709; in the United States there would be a federal benefit of $1,500 and a range of state-level benefits. It would appear, therefore, that tax credits in relation to tuition fees may be somewhat more generous, on average, in Canada. In addition, it should be noted that for U.S. students who attend private institutions, or out-of-state public schools, fees are far above the average, and tax credits are therefore relatively less important.

The PIT systems on both sides of the border also provide tax-sheltered saving for education. First, in both cases, taxpayers now may withdraw funds from their Registered Retirement Savings Plans (RRSPs) or IRAs (as of December 31,

1997) to fund education expenses.[9] This means, for example, that parents can "over-save" in their RRSPs or IRAs and withdraw funds to pay for their children's university education. In Canada, the use of RRSP saving for the taxpayer's own education, or that of a spouse, has been encouraged further since 1998 by the fact that withdrawals (up to $10,000 annually and $20,000 in total) are now tax-free, as long as they are restored to the RRSP within 10 years. These provisions may be especially attractive to high-income taxpayers. In contrast, among those with employer-based pension plans, the use of (deductible) IRAs in the United States is limited to lower income groups, as the $2,000 annual contribution limit is phased out on single incomes (AGI) of between $31,000 and $41,000 and on married couples' joint incomes of between $51,000 and $61,000 (year 2000 limits). Further, annual contribution limits to RRSPs – at $13,500, or 18 percent of earnings in 2000 – are generally higher than those to IRAs.[10]

Both countries have tax-sheltered saving vehicles dedicated to education: Registered Education Saving Plans (RESPs) in Canada and education IRAs in the United States. Contributions are non-deductible, but income within the plans accrues tax-free. Upon withdrawal for education purposes, there is no tax liability in the United States, while in Canada withdrawals are taxed in the hands of the student (i.e., generally at very low rates). Contribution limits are higher in Canada — C$4,000 per year, per beneficiary, as opposed to US$2,000 in the United States — and are encouraged by means of Canada Education Saving Grants (CESGs) of up to $400 per student, per year. CESGs were introduced in 1998. In view of these features, the Canadian scheme likely has a significantly larger negative impact on ETRs than does the U.S. program. As Collins and Davies (2001) found, CESGs can substantially reduce ETRs.

In summary, it is likely that the sheltered savings provisions under the Canadian federal PIT are currently more encouraging to human capital formation than the corresponding provisions in the United States. Greater use can be made of both deductible retirement savings plans and non-deductible education savings plans in Canada to fund higher education. This is because of the higher contribution limits and the use of grants tied to RESP contributions. A further important point is that phase-outs in the United States eliminate these forms of assistance for high-income taxpayers.

In the last section, we indicated that one underlying impact of a PIT system on human capital ETRs arises from "progressivity" (i.e., from the graduated structure of marginal tax rates[MTRs]). It is widely felt that the Canadian PIT is more progressive than that of the United States, and on that basis it might be expected that ETRs in Canada have a tendency to exceed those in the United States (which could perhaps be reversed by differences in deductions and credits). We will now investigate whether this inference is reliable.

Let us first inspect the Canadian and U.S. federal tax schedules that applied in the year 2000[11]:

| FEDERAL MARGINAL TAX RATES BY TAXABLE INCOME, 2000 | | | | | |
|---|---|---|---|---|---|
| Canada | | U.S. Singles | | U.S. Couples Filing Jointly | |
| Income (C$) | Rate (percent) | Income (US$) | Rate (percent) | Income (US$) | Rate (percent) |
| 0 | 17 | 0 | 15.0 | 0 | 15.0 |
| 30,004 | 25 | 26,250 | 28.0 | 43,850 | 28.0 |
| 60,009 | 29 | 63,550 | 31.0 | 105,950 | 31.0 |
| | | 132,600 | 36.0 | 161,450 | 36.0 |
| | | 288,350 | 39.6 | 288,350 | 39.6 |

It is not readily apparent from this panel why the Canadian PIT is generally said to be more progressive than its U.S. counterpart. The tax rate in the lowest bracket is higher in Canada, and the top marginal rate is less than in the United States. The view that the Canadian system is more progressive is probably based on the fact that we move more quickly into the top brackets. This is especially true since Americans receive personal exemptions of $2,800; standard deductions of $4,400 and $7,350, respectively, for single taxpayers and couples filing jointly; and more liberal itemized deductions (e.g., for mortgage interest). Hence, in 2000, a Canadian could have entered the third (and top) tax bracket with a total income of just C$60,009, whereas a single American would have needed at least US$70,750 to enter the third tax bracket and a couple filing jointly at least US$118,900. With the greater generosity of U.S. itemized deductions, the contrast is even more dramatic.

A further important consideration has to do with state and provincial PITs. In 1999, provincial PIT revenue accounted for 64.9 percent of the Canadian total; in the same year, state PIT revenue accounted for 22.4 percent of the U.S. total.[12] Until 2000, all Canadian provinces but Quebec levied their provincial PIT as a proportion of basic federal tax — the so-called "tax-on-tax" approach; and even Quebec's independent PIT schedule did not depart significantly from this standard. The provinces are now free to use whatever tax schedule they like, but, in 2000, four still used the tax-on-tax approach (Newfoundland, Prince Edward Island, Saskatchewan and Alberta); and it is fair to say that the schedules of the other six provinces still correspond approximately to the federal schedule. The result is that one can think of the overall Canadian PIT structure as a roughly proportional blow-up of the federal structure. For the purposes of this study we assume proportionality.

State income taxes present a richer tapestry. Seven states (Alaska, Florida, Nevada, South Dakota, Texas, Washington and Wyoming), which encompassed 16.3 percent of the U.S. population in 1999, levy no income tax. At the opposite extreme, California, with 12.2 percent of the population, levied a highly graduated tax with six brackets and MTRs ranging from 1 to 9.3 percent in 2000. New York State had five brackets with marginal rates varying from 4 to 6.85 percent. Many other states (e.g., Illinois, Michigan, Pennsylvania), in contrast, levy flat income taxes.

The great variety of state income taxes makes it difficult to model simply for the kind of exercise we are carrying out in this section. This is one reason why, in addition to this section's illustrative calculations, we later provide results based on survey evidence, in which individuals report all income taxes paid.

We have reviewed the income taxes levied by the 10 most populous states that levy tax. Together, they comprise 46.6 percent of the U.S. population. In this group, seven states, including the two largest, levy a graduated tax. Therefore, we feel that for the illustrative calculations in this section, an assumption of state-to-federal tax proportionality is a reasonable approximation.

To try to guess which of the Canadian and U.S. income tax schedules is the more progressive simply by eyeballing them is not an adequate way to proceed. We need a more careful comparison. One way to do this might be to convert all U.S. dollar figures to Canadian dollars, and see how some measure of local progressivity varies in each schedule as we ascend the real income scale.

There are two problems with this. First, Canadians and Americans who are deciding whether to invest in human capital do not have the same real earnings and, in terms of our notation, do not face the same $EI$ and $FE$. Thus, to compare progressivity at a given level of real income is not a relevant experiment; Canadians are generally located at lower real income levels, and this fact must be taken into account. Second, the appropriate measure of progressivity for our purposes is $(m_w - m_s)/(1 - m_s)$, or the ETR level that would prevail if the costs of human capital investment were purely foregone earnings. This is not a standard measure of progressivity.[13] So, a custom approach is required.

We proceed by comparing the situations of different well-defined types of human capital investors in both countries. We focus on individuals investing in full-time postsecondary schooling. We assume that their foregone earnings are two-thirds of the amount they would earn if they worked full-time and that the $EI$ produced as a result of one year of schooling equals 10 percent of possible full-time earnings in the year of investment.[14] Assumptions on earnings, tuition fees, loan amounts and tuition credits will be based on the experience in both countries as of the year 2000. Calculations of tax liabilities will take into account the full range of deductions.[15] All individuals are assumed to be single and childless. While the latter assumption is realistic for the schooling period, it is not a realistic assumption for a lifetime of earnings. This is of special concern in the U.S. case, where married couples are typically taxed jointly and are always taxed on a separate schedule from single individuals. We are especially likely to overestimate taxes on women in the United States.[16]

Table 1A sets out our illustrative calculations for Canada. It shows the situation of earners at the 25th, 50th, 75th and 90th percentile of the earnings distributions for three different demographic groups: 23-year-old male and female university graduates and 33-year-old male university graduates. We focus mainly on university graduates at the start of their working careers, in order to get an idea of the ETRs they face on their last year of university education. The alternative would be to look at high school graduates of university age, but that raises the issue that students who decide not to attend a postsecondary institution are not representative of those who do. The 33-year-olds were studied partly to get an idea of tax effects for mature students but also to incorporate cases where the earnings increments from schooling are taxed in the top bracket.[17]

Columns 3 to 5 of Table 1A show our $E_s^*$, $m_s$ and $m_w$ figures, and Case I shows $(m_s - m_w)/(1 - m_s)$, or the bare-bones ETR in the absence of foregone earnings or any distortions other than progressivity. For all but 3 of the 12 individual types, we get $m_w > m_s$ and positive ETRs. The latter range from 4.2 to 15.0 percent.

Interestingly, the ETRs shown in Case I of Table 1A do not show a monotonic trend with income. If the ETRs are charted as a full function of income, they actually show a saw-tooth pattern – alternately jumping whenever the EI crosses into a higher tax bracket, then falling. What is happening is roughly as follows: the tax rate $m_w$ is close to the MTR, whereas $m_s$ is closer to the average tax rate (ATR). The MTR (and therefore $m_w$) takes a small number of large jumps, while the ATR (and therefore $m_s$) rises steadily with income. The highest MTRs are found where the MTR takes the biggest absolute jumps — not at high income levels but at a total income of $7,231 and a taxable income of $30,004, where the federal plus provincial effective MTR jumps from 0 to 24.9 percent and from 24.9 to 33.1 percent, respectively.

Case II of Table 1A shows the effect of the direct costs of education, not counting tuition and education credits and student loans. All the ETRs rise substantially — by an average of 5.8 percentage points across the individual types shown. The ETR range is now from 7.4 to 18.9 percent. This powerful effect on the ETR of a variable outside the tax system is important to note. In recent years, in Canada, there has been a large increase in tuition fees for postsecondary students. In the absence of countervailing action in the form of increased tax credits or loans, the result would have been a substantial increase in human capital ETRs.

Case III of Table 1A introduces tuition and education amount credits. These reduce the ETRs by an average of 7.1 percentage points or by more than the direct costs added in Case II. Also note that the reductions in the ETR are greater at lower income levels. Hence, once education credits are taken into account, there is a greater tendency for the ETRs to rise with income than was evident initially.

It should be noted that our results on the education credits assume that the student gets the full value of the credits, even if they are not needed to reduce his or her tax burden to zero. In other words, amounts deferred to later tax years, or transferred to other family members, are treated as being of equal value to the student as cash-in-hand. This somewhat exaggerates the value of these excess credits.

Finally, in Case IV of Table 1A we add a typical annual student loan amount of $2,500. Like education credits, student loans reduce the ETR. On average, the ETR declines by 2.9 percentage points — a sizable effect, although smaller than that of education credits. Once again, the largest effect is for the lowest earners, strengthening the upward trend of the ETR with income.

These calculations are, of course, subject to qualifications, a number of which have been noted already. The simplified framework of Equation (7) prevents us from taking the hump-shaped age profile of earnings into account. If this profile were modelled, the EIs in several cases would ascend into the top tax bracket, and the ETR would rise. However, we are not able here to account for tax-sheltered education saving and the CESGs that provide substantial assistance for members of higher income groups, who are most likely to exploit these opportunities. Further, as has been emphasized in much recent literature, METRs on middle earners in Canada are substantially increased by the phase-out of sales tax credits and the Canada Child Tax Benefit, over a wide middle-income range. Thus, a more complete analysis could raise relative ETRs for middle earners.

Table 1B provides U.S. results corresponding to those of Table 1A. Here we assume that direct costs of education are US$7,500 per year (as opposed to C$5,500 in Canada). In the columns with education credits, it is assumed that all students receive the maximum value of the Hope credit ($1,500).[18] While this exaggerates the current value of credits for those who have been in postsecondary education for more than two years ($1,000), we note that the Lifetime Learning Credit is slated to double in maximum value to $2,000 in 2003. A student loan amount of $4,000 is assumed.[19]

**TABLE 1A**

**ILLUSTRATIVE CALCULATIONS OF ETRS: CANADIAN UNIVERSITY GRADUATES, 2000 (PERCENT)**

| Sex and Age | Quantile | $E_s^*$ | $m_s$ | $m_w$ | Case I ETR | Case II ETR | Case III ETR | Case IV ETR |
|---|---|---|---|---|---|---|---|---|
| Males, 23 | 25 | $26,000 | 0.249 | 0.249 | 0.0 | 7.4 | −2.4 | −7.1 |
| | 50 | 34,476 | 0.254 | 0.331 | 10.3 | 15.8 | 8.7 | 6.1 |
| | 75 | 43,000 | 0.275 | 0.331 | 7.8 | 13.2 | 6.8 | 4.3 |
| | 90 | 58,000 | 0.302 | 0.331 | 4.2 | 9.1 | 3.8 | 1.7 |
| Females, 23 | 25 | 22,000 | 0.249 | 0.249 | 0.0 | 8.3 | −2.7 | −8.3 |
| | 50 | 28,000 | 0.265 | 0.249 | 0.0 | 7.0 | −2.2 | −6.7 |
| | 75 | 36,608 | 0.261 | 0.331 | 9.5 | 15.0 | 8.1 | 5.5 |
| | 90 | 42,185 | 0.276 | 0.331 | 7.6 | 13.1 | 6.5 | 4.2 |
| Males, 33 | 25 | 34,338 | 0.254 | 0.331 | 10.4 | 15.9 | 8.8 | 6.2 |
| | 50 | 43,004 | 0.276 | 0.331 | 7.6 | 13.1 | 6.5 | 4.2 |
| | 75 | 55,000 | 0.298 | 0.331 | 4.7 | 9.7 | 4.3 | 2.1 |
| | 90 | 70,475 | 0.315 | 0.4174 | 15.0 | 18.9 | 14.9 | 13.6 |

Notes: $E_s^*$ = Full-time, full-year earnings.
$m_s$ = Tax rate on foregone earnings.
$m_w$ = Tax rate on earnings increment.
Case I: No direct costs, no tax credit, no loans.
Case II: Direct costs = $5,500; no tax credit, no loans.
Case III: Direct costs = $5,500; tuition and education amount credits; no loans.
Case IV: Direct costs = $5,500; tuition and education amount credits; student loan = $2,500.
Source: Authors' calculations. See text for details.

As noted earlier, a widespread expectation would likely be that U.S. ETRs should be lower than Canadian ones. In fact, we find that the comparison is about evenly split. Focussing only on progressivity (Case I), the estimated Canadian ETRs exceed the U.S. figures for only 5 of the 12 individual types. Furthermore, in Cases III and IV, with direct costs and credits modelled, ETRs are lower in Canada than in the United States for 13 of the 24 individual types. As pointed out earlier, the results are affected by the fact that it is not possible in these illustrative calculations to take into account a realistic hump-shaped age profile of earnings. Also, we are using the U.S. tax schedule for single people only. The survey-based estimates presented later in the study, which are not subject to these limitations, show that Canadian ETRs generally dominate those in the United States.

**TABLE 1B**

**ILLUSTRATIVE CALCULATIONS OF ETRs: U.S. UNIVERSITY GRADUATES, 2000 (PERCENT)**

| Sex and Age | Quantile | $E_s^*$ | $m_s$ | $m_w$ | Case I ETR | Case II ETR | Case III ETR | Case IV ETR |
|---|---|---|---|---|---|---|---|---|
| Males, 23 | 25 | $20,000 | 0.132 | 0.137 | 0.6 | 5.8 | −2.3 | −7.0 |
| | 50 | 28,985 | 0.137 | 0.137 | 0.0 | 4.3 | −2.1 | −5.5 |
| | 75 | 38,000 | 0.137 | 0.137 | 0.0 | 3.5 | −1.7 | −4.3 |
| | 90 | 48,000 | 0.160 | 0.263 | 12.3 | 15.3 | 11.5 | 10.5 |
| Females, 23 | 25 | 18,000 | 0.124 | 0.137 | 1.6 | 6.6 | −1.8 | −6.8 |
| | 50 | 25,000 | 0.137 | 0.137 | 0.0 | 4.7 | −2.3 | −6.2 |
| | 75 | 32,155 | 0.137 | 0.137 | 0.0 | 4.0 | −1.9 | −5.0 |
| | 90 | 41,289 | 0.137 | 0.232 | 11 | 13.9 | 9.6 | 8.5 |
| Males, 33 | 25 | 31,000 | 0.137 | 0.137 | 0.0 | 4.1 | −2.0 | −5.1 |
| | 50 | 42,000 | 0.137 | 0.254 | 13.5 | 16.3 | 12.2 | 11.3 |
| | 75 | 60,000 | 0.193 | 0.263 | 8.7 | 12 | 8.5 | 7.4 |
| | 90 | 79,130 | 0.225 | 0.263 | 4.9 | 8.2 | 5.3 | 4.0 |

Notes:   $E_s^*$ = Full-time, full-year earnings.
       $m_s$ = Tax rate on foregone earnings.
       $m_w$ = Tax rate on earnings increment.
       Case I: No direct costs, no tax credit, no loans.
       Case II: Direct costs = $7,500; no tax credit, no loans.
       Case III: Direct costs = $7,500; tuition credit; no loans.
       Case IV: Direct costs = $7,500; tuition credit; student loan = $4,000.
Source: Authors' calculations. See text for details.

Finally, Tables 1A and 1B indicate that to achieve a very low ETR, one would pursue one's education in Canada then move to reap the rewards in the United States. One's $m_s$ would be quite high, as shown in Table 1A, while one's $m_w$ would be similar to, or perhaps smaller than, that of the United States, as shown in Table 1B. Since the Canadian $m_s$ is larger than that of the United States, one's "basic" ETR (i.e., before direct costs, education credits and loans enter the picture) would be negative. For example, if a Canadian university graduate in the 90th percentile moved to the United States on graduation, his or her ETR, on this basis, would be −5.6 percent.

It should be noted that recent federal budgets in both countries have reduced taxes, and that further reductions are scheduled for coming years. What impact will these changes have on the ETRs? In the Canadian case, the centrepiece is a reduction in tax rates on middle- and upper-middle-income earners.

The former middle federal tax rate is being reduced to 22 percent, from 25 percent in 2000 and 26 percent in 1999. In addition, a new tax bracket, to run from taxable income of about $61,000 to $100,000, is being carved out of the old top tax bracket. Instead of the former 29 percent federal rate, this new group will face only a 26 percent MTR. A reduction in the bottom tax rate, from 17 to 16 percent, is also occurring. Extending our earlier Case III calculations (i.e., no student loans) to incorporate these changes gives an average ETR reduction of 1.8 percentage points for our 12 individual types. The dominant effect on the results comes from the rate changes in the middle tax brackets. The 25th quantile males, and female 23-year-olds, see a small *increase* in their ETRs, while the median and 75th quantile earners get the largest reduction. ETRs also decline for all of the 33-year-old male university graduates.

In the U.S. case, the Bush tax cuts, recently signed into law, will reduce MTRs at all levels. The current marginal rates of 15, 28, 31, 36 and 39.6 percent are being replaced by rates of 10, 15, 25 and 33 percent. As in the Canadian case, the largest proportional cuts in MTRs are in the middle brackets. However, there is also a substantial cut in the bottom bracket. Again, using Case III (no student loans), we find that the Bush tax cuts will reduce human capital ETRs at all levels.

Our discussion has ignored the fact that low- and middle-income earners are eligible for a variety of tax credits, some of which are refundable. It also ignores the fact that many recent studies have found that METRs of low- and middle-income taxpayers present special features when compared with those of taxpayers at higher income levels. For the lowest earners in the United States, for example, the Earned Income Tax Credit generates a large *negative* MTR; but when taxpayers are in the phase-out range for such credits, their MTRs can be greater than those of taxpayers with higher incomes. Could this mean that our observations about the effect of tax schedules on ETRs in Canada and the United States are misleading?

While tax credits and other tax features undeniably affect MTRs for some postsecondary students, we believe that, overall, the impacts on the cost side of ETR calculations are likely small. This is because most of the tax features in question are aimed at families with children. Only a small fraction of postsecondary students fall in this category. In addition, the income maintenance problems of postsecondary students are not generally addressed by governments through the same tax/transfer means as those of non-students. Rather than receiving refundable tax credits, students are given bursaries and loans. Such programs can, of course, offset the incentive effects coming from ETRs, but they clearly lie on the expenditure rather than tax side and thus fall outside the scope of our study.

Turning to the return side of the ETR calculation, we would expect that the main effect of taking all credits into account would be to increase $m_w$ for lower quartile and median earners. These are the individuals who will likely experience higher MTRs over their working lifetime as a result of credit phase-outs. While the impact could be significant, we do not believe it would be so large as to overturn our conclusion that ETRs on human capital in Canada are small to moderate, and there should be special concern about ETRs on high earners.

## PAYROLL TAXES

BOTH CANADA AND THE UNITED STATES operate largely unfunded "pay-as-you-go" social security plans, as well as unemployment insurance schemes.[20] If these plans were run on an actuarially fair basis, they should have no effect on human capital accumulation in the absence of liquidity constraints. In practice, the plans are so far from being actuarially fair that we are closer to the truth if we treat contributions simply as taxes.

Unlike the PIT, payroll taxes are set up with a regressive structure. The typical pattern is to have a flat rate for contributions on earnings (minus a small exempt amount in some cases) up to some threshold income, or "maximum insurable earnings," beyond which marginal contributions fall to zero. This structure means that payroll taxes add to $m_s$ and may or may not add to $m_w$. In cases where incremental earnings due to education fall entirely above maximum insurable earnings, there is no addition to $m_w$; where this increment straddles the earnings cap, the addition to $m_w$ will be less than the payroll tax contribution rate. In either of these cases, payroll taxes will raise $m_s$ more than $m_w$, and the ETR is likely to decline.

Greater reliance on the social security scheme to generate pensions in the United States has led to much larger maximum insurable earnings there than in Canada: in 2000, for example, they stood at US$76,200 in the United States, as opposed to C$37,600 in Canada. Thus, for most Americans, social security adds as much to $m_w$ as it does to $m_s$ — which will raise the ETR. In contrast, higher earners in Canada may experience no increase in $m_w$ due to their Canada Pension Plan (CPP) contributions. For these individuals, CPP acts like an increase in $m_s$, which will reduce the ETR.

Tables 2A and 2B show the result of adding social security and CPP contributions to Cases I and IV for 23-year-old male and female university graduates and 33-year-old male graduates.[21] In the United States, there is a small increase in the ETR, in most cases, but a sizable decrease for the 90th-quantile 33-year-old male graduates, whose earnings gains from education lie above the social security contribution cap. In Canada, the tendency for ETRs to rise is confined to fewer people than in the United States; both the 75th and 90th quantiles see reductions. Hence, the difference in both countries' social security schemes tends to reduce ETRs on high earners in Canada relative to the United States.

On the employer's side, there may be incentive effects insofar as the employer finances specific human capital accumulation. The costs of this investment include wages paid to workers for time they spend learning rather than producing, costs that an employer will be willing to share if the learned skills are relevant to the firm (Becker 1964). These costs are inflated by the employer's portion of payroll taxes, implying a positive effective tax on the portion of human capital investment which is paid for by employers. The higher rate of social security contributions in the United States implies that this effect should be stronger there than in Canada.

## TABLE 2A

## ILLUSTRATIVE CALCULATIONS OF ETRs, CPP AND SALES TAX EFFECTS: CANADIAN UNIVERSITY GRADUATES, 2000 (PERCENT)

| Sex and Age | Quantile | $E_s^*$ | Case I ETR with CPP | Case IV ETR with CPP | Case I ETR with CPP and Sales Tax | Case IV ETR with CPP and Sales Tax |
|---|---|---|---|---|---|---|
| Males, 23 | 25 | $26,000 | 0.0 | −6.2 | 0.0 | −1.8 |
| | 50 | 34,476 | 10.4 | 6.9 | 12.8 | 12.7 |
| | 75 | 43,000 | 3.4 | 0.0 | 4.2 | 3.7 |
| | 90 | 58,000 | 1.6 | −0.9 | 1.9 | 1.6 |
| Females, 23 | 25 | 22,000 | 0.0 | −7.1 | 0.0 | −2.0 |
| | 50 | 28,000 | 0.0 | −5.8 | 0.0 | 1.8 |
| | 75 | 36,608 | 5.9 | 2.3 | 7.4 | 6.9 |
| | 90 | 42,185 | 3.3 | 0.0 | 4.1 | 3.6 |
| Males, 33 | 25 | 34,338 | 10.7 | 7.2 | 13.2 | 13.1 |
| | 50 | 43,004 | 3.3 | 0.0 | 4.1 | 3.6 |
| | 75 | 55,000 | 1.8 | −0.8 | 2.3 | 1.6 |
| | 90 | 70,475 | 13.5 | 12.2 | 16.9 | 17.3 |

Notes:   $E_s^*$ = Full-time, full-year earnings.
Case I: No direct costs, no tax credit, no loans.
Case IV: Direct costs = $5,500; tuition and education amount credits; student loan = $2,500.
CPP: Rate = 3.9 percent on earnings between $3,500 and $37,600.
Sales Tax: Rate + 13.4 percent
Source: Authors' calculations. See text for details.

## TABLE 2B

## ILLUSTRATIVE CALCULATIONS OF ETRS, CPP AND SALES TAX EFFECTS: U.S. UNIVERSITY GRADUATES, 2000 (PERCENT)

| Sex and Age | Quantile | $E_s^*$ | Case I ETR with Social Security | Case IV ETR with Social Security | Case I ETR with Social Security and Sales Tax | Case IV ETR with Social Security and Sales Tax |
|---|---|---|---|---|---|---|
| Males, 23 | 25 | $20,000 | 0.7 | −4.2 | 0.7 | −1.1 |
| | 50 | 28,985 | 0.0 | −3.6 | 0.0 | −1.6 |
| | 75 | 38,000 | 0.0 | −2.9 | 0.0 | −1.3 |
| | 90 | 48,000 | 13.2 | 12.7 | 14.3 | 15.0 |
| Females, 23 | 25 | 18,000 | 1.7 | −3.6 | 1.8 | −0.2 |
| | 50 | 25,000 | 0.0 | −4.0 | 0.0 | −1.7 |
| | 75 | 32,155 | 0.0 | −3.3 | 0.0 | −1.5 |
| | 90 | 41,289 | 11.9 | 10.6 | 12.8 | 13.0 |
| Males, 33 | 25 | 31,000 | 0.0 | −3.4 | 0.0 | −1.5 |
| | 50 | 42,000 | 14.6 | 13.7 | 15.7 | 16.2 |
| | 75 | 60,000 | 9.4 | 9.1 | 10.2 | 11.0 |
| | 90 | 79,130 | −2.9 | −3.5 | −3.2 | −2.8 |

Notes:  $E_s^*$ = Full-time, full-year earnings.
Case I: No direct costs, no tax credit, no loans.
Case IV: Direct costs = $7,500; tuition credit; student loan = $2,500.
Social Security: Contribution rate = 6.2 percent on earnings up to $76,200.
Sales Tax: Rate + 5.9 percent
Source: Authors' calculations. See text for details.

## SALES TAX

ONE OF THE MAJOR DIFFERENCES in tax structure between Canada and the United States is that Canada relies much more heavily on sales tax revenue. The Canadian federal government levies a lucrative VAT-type Goods and Services Tax, while the U.S. federal government collects no general sales tax. Totalling all sales and excise taxes for 1999 (and referring to the total as "sales tax" for short), we find that U.S. consumers paid sales tax equal to 5.9 percent of aggregate consumer expenditure, as opposed to Canadians' 13.4 percent.

As discussed earlier, if a proportional sales tax were levied on a comprehensive tax base, it would be neutral with respect to human capital formation, in the absence of other taxes. However, in the presence of a PIT with graduated rates or other distortions, this is no longer the case. It is interesting to see how much of

467

an effect the U.S. and Canadian sales tax regimes could have on estimated ETRs under the simplifying assumption of proportionality. While actual sales taxes exempt or zero-rate some necessities, the high excise taxes levied by Canada on alcohol, tobacco and gasoline tend to be regressive. The result is that the assumption of proportionality is a reasonable approximation for present purposes.

Tables 2A and 2B show estimates of ETRs for the two countries, taking into account sales tax under the proportionality assumption. ETRs rise in both countries when we take sales tax into account — by a fairly small amount in the United States but by as much as 5 or 6 percentage points for some of the individual types in Canada. This is an interesting illustration of the principle that to add even seemingly reasonable taxes to an already high level of taxation can have surprisingly distorting effects.

## CORPORATE INCOME TAX

WHILE WE DO NOT PROVIDE ESTIMATES of the effects of corporate income tax (CIT) on human capital ETRs, it is nonetheless interesting to note some of its qualitative effects. Our comments apply to both Canada and the United States.

The CIT affects incentives for both specific and general human capital accumulation occurring through on-the-job training (OJT). In the case of specific training, both the wages paid to trainees and much of the direct costs are deductible from the CIT. This corresponds to immediate expensing of the investment. Structures and equipment used in training, however, are treated in the same way as the firm's other capital expenditures. In other words, its costs are deducted in the form of interest and a capital consumption allowance over the life of the assets. This implies a small departure from neutrality in the treatment of specific human capital but is still a close approximation to neutrality.

The CIT may also have implications for general OJT. Theory predicts that employees should pay for the costs of this training in the form of lower wages. However, the direct costs of providing this training are reduced, due to their deductibility from CIT. Hence, CIT provides a substantial implicit subsidy to general OJT. It is not clear whether the effective rate of subsidy is more or less than that provided to postsecondary institutions. However, this subsidy is worth keeping in mind when one hears claims that subsidies to postsecondary institutions distort the pattern of human capital investment away from OJT and toward formal education and training, with supposed damage in terms of the quality of training. It may be that the effective rate of subsidy to private sector training is not less than that to college and university education.[22]

## STUDENT LOAN PLANS

AS DISCUSSED EARLIER, student loan plans interact with human capital ETRs. They provide benefits that loom larger in relation to after-tax costs and returns and therefore increase after-tax rates of return more than before-tax rates. The result is a decline in the human capital ETR. We captured this effect, to an extent, in Case IV, Tables 1A, 1B, 2A and 2B.[23]

In Canada, the federal and provincial governments cooperate in providing an integrated system of student loans under the umbrella of the Canada Student Loan Plan (CSLP). These are subsidized student loans, the principal form of subsidy being that as long as students meet certain criteria (mainly, maintaining full-time status), no interest accumulates or is paid prior to graduation. Eligibility for loans is needs-tested, and individual students have different limits on the amount they can borrow. In recent years, in part due to rising tuition fees, the student participation rate in the CSLP has been rising, and amounts borrowed have increased. In 1998, the Department of Finance estimated that students taking loans would have an average debt of about $14,000 upon graduation.

There has been some discussion in recent years about the implementation of an income-contingent student loan plan in Canada (Rowley 1993). Such a plan would reduce the ex post net benefits of student loans for high earners and increase them for low earners; the result would be a reduced (downward) impact on the human capital ETR for the former group and a stronger downward effect for the latter. While an in-depth discussion of the incentive effects created thereby would take us too far off course, it should be noted that such a plan would discourage human capital investment by the most able students and encourage it among the less able, at least for those who expect to stay in Canada after graduation. Furthermore, to the extent that those who leave could escape repayment, emigration by the most able holders of student loan debt would be encouraged.

Federal student loan plans in the United States are the Ford Direct Student Loan Program and the Federal Family Education Loan Program. For the former, the education institution acts as an intermediary for the dispensing of funds, which come directly from the federal government; for the latter, students have the option of borrowing from a private lending institution, but the government still guarantees the loan. Like the CSLP, these are both subsidized programs and are dispensed on the basis of need.

Unsubsidized programs in the United States, which were introduced for the 1992-93 academic year and are not based on need, provide students with an alternative means of borrowing. Interest on these loans accumulates while the student is in school and is added to the total cost of borrowing. Studies show that this type of borrowing is on the rise — see *Trends in Student Aid* (2000) — now comprising roughly 48 percent of the federal education loan volume.[24] Since the leveraging benefit of unsubsidized loans is less than that of other student loans, it would be expected that their impact on human capital ETRs would be relatively small.

## ESTIMATING EFFECTIVE TAX RATES ON FIRST DEGREE UNIVERSITY STUDIES USING SURVEY DATA

THE PREVIOUS SECTION PROVIDED illustrative calculations that take into account a wide range of tax features. The simple framework of Equation (7), however, has certain limitations. It is assumed that earnings after graduation are constant for the remainder of the lifetime, which may lead to an underestimation of the tax burden on incremental earnings due to education. Also, results must be based on hypothetical tax scenarios that can only approximate the tax experience of real individuals.

In order to provide more empirically-based estimates of human capital ETRs, we have made further calculations using the cross-section data provided by the 1998 SCF for Canada and the CPS for the United States. In both cases, we have drawn samples of full-time, full-year workers (in order to ensure that we capture the full returns to human capital investment). We create hypothetical lifetime earnings and tax scenarios by assuming that graduates with a particular level of education earn at the same earnings quantile throughout their life. We assume that the observed cross-section earnings and taxes for particular age groups will continue to apply for those same age groups in the future (no adjustment is made for wage growth or future changes in the tax system). The life-cycle path of earnings is projected using quantile age profiles of earnings that have been smoothed using the methods devised by Burbidge, Magee and Robb (1988) and Magee, Burbidge and Robb (1991).[25]

### DATA

THE SCF AND CPS ARE LARGE ANNUAL SURVEYS that provide the standard data for the study of income distribution and related characteristics in their respective countries. Respondents are sampled in the spring of each year, after they have completed their income tax returns. Earnings and tax information are reported for the year preceding the surveys (1997). Sample sizes are 68,633 and 253,044 for the SCF and CPS, respectively.

Our sample includes only individuals aged 19 to 65 who were full-time, full-year workers. The definition of a full-year worker is someone who was employed for 52 weeks during the year of the survey (the self-employed are excluded). We also confine our sample to workers who had either graduated from high school and taken no further schooling or who had received a bachelor's degree but no higher qualification. The definition of earnings includes only wage or salary income.

TABLE 3

EARNINGS AND INCOME TAX RATES: CANADIAN FULL-TIME, FULL-YEAR WORKERS, 1997 (BY QUANTILE, SMOOTHED DATA)

| | High School Graduates | | | University Graduates | | |
| | Quantile | | | Quantile | | |
| Age | 25 | 50 | 75 | 25 | 50 | 75 |
|---|---|---|---|---|---|---|
| Males: Earnings | | | | | | |
| 23 | 16,119 | 23,000 | 34,008 | 26,000 | 34,476 | 43,000 |
| 33 | 25,169 | 35,175 | 46,020 | 34,338 | 43,004 | 55,000 |
| 43 | 30,000 | 39,453 | 52,942 | 43,834 | 53,621 | 69,992 |
| 53 | 30,000 | 41,962 | 56,004 | 45,000 | 56,992 | 70,000 |
| 63 | 26,000 | 34,000 | 44,822 | 40,000 | 47,003 | 67,592 |
| Males: ATR (percent) | | | | | | |
| 23 | 11.9 | 17.3 | 20.8 | 16.2 | 21.9 | 22.0 |
| 33 | 16.0 | 19.6 | 23.7 | 21.4 | 25.4 | 29.8 |
| 43 | 19.5 | 23.4 | 25.8 | 22.1 | 26.5 | 33.6 |
| 53 | 15.0 | 21.3 | 25.9 | 22.5 | 29.7 | 30.7 |
| 63 | 15.8 | 19.6 | 22.3 | 23.3 | 24.1 | 28.4 |
| Females: Earnings | | | | | | |
| 23 | 12,605 | 18,200 | 26,000 | 22,000 | 28,000 | 36,608 |
| 33 | 17,323 | 24,250 | 31,874 | 27,976 | 38,000 | 45,681 |
| 43 | 20,020 | 27,000 | 34,647 | 35,295 | 45,000 | 54,964 |
| 53 | 21,600 | 28,341 | 35,000 | 38,445 | 49,455 | 56,063 |
| 63 | 16,536 | 22,307 | 31,243 | 30,000 | 35,317 | 54,461 |
| Females: ATR (percent) | | | | | | |
| 23 | 9.5 | 14.0 | 16.0 | 17.4 | 18.1 | 19.4 |
| 33 | 11.8 | 17.2 | 18.5 | 17.6 | 21.5 | 24.9 |
| 43 | 12.1 | 16.5 | 20.0 | 19.4 | 26.3 | 28.6 |
| 53 | 16.4 | 18.2 | 19.4 | 21.9 | 21.5 | 28.4 |
| 63 | 13.5 | 15.4 | 18.6 | 21.2 | 20.2 | 24.9 |

Source: Authors' calculations, using the 1998 SCF. See text for details.

## TABLE 4

### EARNINGS AND INCOME TAX RATES: U.S. FULL-TIME, FULL-YEAR WORKERS, 1997 (BY QUANTILE, SMOOTHED DATA)

| | High School Graduates | | | University Graduates | | |
| | Quantile | | | Quantile | | |
| Age | 25 | 50 | 75 | 25 | 50 | 75 |
|---|---|---|---|---|---|---|
| Males: Earnings | | | | | | |
| 23 | 14,000 | 20,000 | 25,986 | 20,000 | 28,985 | 38,000 |
| 33 | 20,185 | 28,000 | 38,000 | 31,000 | 42,000 | 60,000 |
| 43 | 23,000 | 33,000 | 45,000 | 35,000 | 50,000 | 70,000 |
| 53 | 25,000 | 35,000 | 47,000 | 36,000 | 52,000 | 70,000 |
| 63 | 24,000 | 32,097 | 43,000 | 35,000 | 55,000 | 80,000 |
| Males: ATR (percent) | | | | | | |
| 23 | 8.3 | 10.3 | 12.0 | 11.7 | 13.3 | 15.0 |
| 33 | 11.3 | 11.8 | 14.0 | 13.3 | 16.3 | 19.0 |
| 43 | 11.5 | 12.2 | 15.5 | 14.3 | 17.7 | 18.8 |
| 53 | 12.4 | 13.4 | 16.5 | 13.9 | 18.0 | 18.8 |
| 63 | 12.0 | 13.2 | 15.5 | 14.3 | 18.6 | 23.1 |
| Females: Earnings | | | | | | |
| 23 | 12,000 | 16,000 | 20,280 | 18,000 | 25,000 | 32,155 |
| 33 | 15,000 | 20,000 | 27,000 | 25,000 | 33,000 | 45,000 |
| 43 | 16,000 | 22,000 | 30,000 | 25,000 | 34,000 | 48,000 |
| 53 | 16,000 | 22,000 | 30,000 | 25,000 | 35,000 | 48,129 |
| 63 | 15,648 | 22,300 | 30,000 | 19,000 | 30,000 | 43,000 |
| Females: ATR (percent) | | | | | | |
| 23 | 6.8 | 8.1 | 10.1 | 11.6 | 12.4 | 14.5 |
| 33 | 7.4 | 10.6 | 11.5 | 12.4 | 15.0 | 18.6 |
| 43 | 8.1 | 10.7 | 12.0 | 12.4 | 14.7 | 18.7 |
| 53 | 8.1 | 10.7 | 12.0 | 12.4 | 14.6 | 18.4 |
| 63 | 9.1 | 11.8 | 12.0 | 10.3 | 13.5 | 17.4 |

Source: Authors' calculations, using the 1998 CPF. See text for details.

As the Canadian PIT is levied on an individual basis, it is straightforward to obtain a measure of the total income tax paid by an individual in the SCF. Because some of this tax is due on non-labour income, however, the portion of the tax that is deemed to have been paid on labour earnings must be imputed. We have assumed that the taxes paid by individuals fell at the same rate on their various sources of income.[26] We thus compute the ratio of taxes paid to total income, or the ATR. We then multiply wage and salary income by the ATR to compute the tax paid on earnings.

In the case of single taxpayers in the United States, we apply the same procedure as in the Canadian case. However, in the case of married couples, the procedure differs, as couples in the United States are taxed on separate schedules from single individuals. The great majority of married couples elect to be taxed jointly (being taxed separately is rarely advantageous); for individuals in such couples, we compute the couple's joint ATR and then apply this to each partner's labour income to compute their respective taxes paid on earnings.[27]

Tables 3 and 4 show selected data from our age profiles for the 25th, 50th and 75th quantiles in Canada and the United States, respectively. There is quite a pronounced hump in the shape of the age profiles of earnings in Canada. In the United States, however, female high school graduates and male university graduates do not experience a decline of earnings at the end of the working life-cycle, at the 50th and 75th quantiles. Also note that the greater inequality in the U.S. earnings structure shows up in the form of larger percentage differences between the 25th and 75th quantiles than in Canada.

The ATRs shown in Table 3 for Canada range from between 9.5 percent for the youngest 25th percentile female high school graduates to 33.6 percent for the 75th percentile 43-year-old male university graduates. In contrast, the range in the United States is from 6.8 percent, for the same young female group as in Canada, to 23.1 percent for the oldest male university graduates at the 75th percentile.

## ASSUMPTIONS ON THE COSTS AND BENEFITS OF EDUCATION

WE ASSUME THAT INDIVIDUALS who attend university register at age 19, stay at university for four years and enter the labour force at age 23 with a four-year bachelor degree. While in school, students forego the income they would have earned in the labour market. In our base case, this lost income is based on the median earnings of high school graduates.[28] Given that students are only in school for eight months (of full-time study), it is assumed they are able to work for the remaining four. Due to the search costs and uncertainty involved in finding a job, we calculate summer earnings as being one-third of foregone earnings, less 20 percent.[29]

Students also bear the costs of tuition and additional expenses of going to school. For Canadian students, we use Statistics Canada data to compute the average tuition and fee burden, based on arts programs across Canada for the 1997-98 academic year. A figure of $3,253 was obtained for tuition, and we assume that additional direct costs add up to $1,000. For American students, we use data from *Trends in College Pricing*, published by the College Board (1998) in the United States, to calculate corresponding values. The data used in this study are based on the *Annual Survey of Colleges* (College Board 2000), which covers over 3,200 postsecondary institutions across the United States. An average tuition of $5,739 is obtained, and additional costs of $1,000 are assumed.[30]

## RESULTS

TABLE 5 SHOWS OUR MAIN RESULTS. It compares the median experience of men and women in Canada and the United States. Note that the estimated gross and net rates of return exceed 10 percent in all cases, except for Canadian males, whose net rate of return is 8.8 percent. The estimated rates of return are consistent with those from the recent labour economics literature (e.g., Ashenfelter and Krueger 1994; Card 1995). Note also that the gross and net rates of return to university education are higher for women than for men in both countries. This reflects the fact that the male-female wage differential is greater for high school graduates than for university graduates.

Table 5 indicates that the ETRs for median earners are higher in Canada (15.9 percent) than in the United States (8.5 percent), averaging across the sexes. This is a robust result that comes through consistently when we look across quantiles and use alternative assumptions. It is also worth noting that men are indicated as facing higher ETRs than women, in both countries. This is a reflection of the graduated MTRs that characterize the PIT systems in both countries. On average, since men earn more than women, they enter higher tax brackets and experience a greater reduction in their net returns to education.

## TABLE 5

### INTERNAL RATES OF RETURN (IRRS) AND ETRS FOR FIRST-DEGREE UNIVERSITY STUDY, CANADA AND THE UNITED STATES, 1997

|  | Gross IRR | Net IRR | ETR |
|---|---|---|---|
| **Male** |  |  |  |
| Canada | 0.109 | 0.088 | 0.196 |
| United States | 0.128 | 0.116 | 0.094 |
| **Female** |  |  |  |
| Canada | 0.140 | 0.123 | 0.121 |
| United States | 0.132 | 0.122 | 0.076 |

Note: Median earnings of university graduates are compared with the median earnings of high school graduates to measure the returns to education. Foregone earnings during education are based on median earnings of high school graduates.

Source: Authors' calculations, using the 1998 SCF and CPS.

For women, higher gross returns and lower ETRs provide a plausible explanation for their rising postsecondary enrolments in relation to men, a trend that is apparent in both countries.

Tables 6 to 9 break down our results, by quantile, for men and women in both countries. They do so using two different approaches to estimating the counterfactual no-university earnings scenario for university graduates. How much would university graduates have earned had they not gone to university? The best evidence we have on this is provided by the earnings histories of otherwise similar workers with only a high school diploma. We use two different approaches in the attempt to identify these otherwise similar workers. In both cases, we control for age and gender and continue to confine our attention to full-year, full-time workers. In the first approach, we identify "clone" high school graduates; in other words, we impute counterfactual earnings by looking at the amount earned by workers at the same quantile of the distribution of earnings among high school graduates. Thus, for example, we impute the amount that someone at the 70th percentile among university graduates would have earned at age 40 — had he only received a high school diploma — by using the amount earned by a high school graduate of the same age at the 70th percentile for high school graduates. Without engaging in a full-scale econometric study of earnings determinants (which is beyond the scope of our study), we believe that this is the best approach with the available data.

In order to get some idea of the sensitivity of our results, we also compute rates of return and ETRs for a "median" case, where counterfactual earnings are imputed using those of median high school graduates in all cases. This produces less satisfactory results. As Tables 6 to 9 show, for the clone case we get plausible gross and net rates of return for all quantiles, and the variation in these IRRs across quantiles is fairly smooth and not too large. In contrast, for the median case, IRRs for the bottom quantiles tend to be negative or, in some cases, not uniquely defined mathematically. Also, there is a strong upward trend in the rates of return as we move to higher earners, which simply reflects the fact that counterfactual earnings are not increasing.

Highlighting the clone results for Canadian males and females (Tables 6 and 7) shows that ETRs are clearly higher in the top half of the earning distribution, although they do fluctuate up the earnings scale increases. The estimated ETR for the 90th male quantile – 0.311 – is especially striking, although it is a bit of an anomaly. The corresponding results for the United States (Tables 8 and 9) also show an overall rise of ETRs with income, although there is a mild decreasing trend from the lowest quantiles to the median for females. The U.S. results also show a smoother progression of ETRs up the income scale, which, we believe, reflects a smaller sampling variation in the much larger U.S. data set.

# TABLE 6

## IRRs and ETRs, Canadian Males, 1997

| | Case | Quantile | | | | | | | | | | | | | |
|---|---|---|---|---|---|---|---|---|---|---|---|---|---|---|---|
| | | 20 | 25 | 30 | 40 | 50 | 60 | 62.5 | 65 | 70 | 75 | 80 | 85 | 87.5 | 90 |
| Gross IRR | Clone | 0.116 | 0.117 | 0.119 | 0.116 | 0.109 | 0.097 | 0.094 | 0.092 | 0.088 | 0.085 | 0.082 | 0.085 | 0.085 | 0.090 |
| | Median | −0.060 | 0.008 | 0.037 | 0.074 | 0.109 | 0.140 | 0.148 | 0.156 | 0.172 | 0.190 | 0.210 | 0.241 | 0.256 | 0.290 |
| Net IRR | Clone | 0.099 | 0.101 | 0.103 | 0.099 | 0.088 | 0.074 | 0.078 | 0.078 | 0.070 | 0.067 | 0.065 | 0.072 | 0.072 | 0.062 |
| | Median | −0.115 | −0.003 | 0.027 | 0.062 | 0.088 | 0.112 | 0.122 | 0.133 | 0.146 | 0.163 | 0.176 | 0.212 | 0.222 | 0.231 |
| ETR | Clone | 0.147 | 0.137 | 0.134 | 0.147 | 0.193 | 0.237 | 0.170 | 0.152 | 0.205 | 0.212 | 0.207 | 0.153 | 0.153 | 0.311 |
| | Median | −0.917 | 1.375 | 0.270 | 0.162 | 0.193 | 0.200 | 0.176 | 0.147 | 0.151 | 0.142 | 0.162 | 0.120 | 0.133 | 0.203 |

Note: The clone case assumes that a university graduate would have earned the same amount as a high school graduate at the same quantile (among high school graduates), if the university graduate had not gone to university. The median case assumes that the university graduate would have earned the same amount as a median high school graduate.

Source: Authors' calculations, using the 1998 SCF.

# TABLE 7

## IRRs and ETRs, Canadian Females, 1997

| | Case | Quantile | | | | | | | | | | | | | |
|---|---|---|---|---|---|---|---|---|---|---|---|---|---|---|---|
| | | 20 | 25 | 30 | 40 | 50 | 60 | 62.5 | 65 | 70 | 75 | 80 | 85 | 87.5 | 90 |
| Gross IRR | Clone | 0.157 | 0.158 | 0.158 | 0.148 | 0.140 | 0.136 | 0.135 | 0.133 | 0.129 | 0.120 | 0.116 | 0.108 | 0.104 | 0.097 |
| | Median | 0.045 | 0.068 | 0.087 | 0.114 | 0.140 | 0.166 | 0.173 | 0.180 | 0.194 | 0.210 | 0.223 | 0.238 | 0.247 | 0.258 |
| Net IRR | Clone | 0.142 | 0.141 | 0.144 | 0.136 | 0.123 | 0.121 | 0.121 | 0.116 | 0.110 | 0.102 | 0.097 | 0.088 | 0.091 | 0.083 |
| | Median | 0.035 | 0.056 | 0.078 | 0.103 | 0.123 | 0.149 | 0.156 | 0.160 | 0.172 | 0.187 | 0.197 | 0.209 | 0.218 | 0.229 |
| ETR | Clone | 0.096 | 0.108 | 0.089 | 0.081 | 0.121 | 0.110 | 0.104 | 0.128 | 0.147 | 0.150 | 0.164 | 0.185 | 0.125 | 0.144 |
| | Median | 0.222 | 0.176 | 0.103 | 0.096 | 0.121 | 0.102 | 0.098 | 0.111 | 0.113 | 0.110 | 0.117 | 0.122 | 0.117 | 0.112 |

Note: The clone case assumes that a university graduate would have earned the same amount as a high school graduate at the same quantile (among high school graduates), if the university graduate had not gone to university. The median case assumes that the university graduate would have earned the same amount as a median high school graduate.

Source: Authors' calculations, using the 1998 SCF.

## TABLE 8

## IRRs AND ETRs, U.S. MALES, 1997

| | Case | Quantile | | | | | | | | | | | | | |
|---|---|---|---|---|---|---|---|---|---|---|---|---|---|---|---|
| | | 20 | 25 | 30 | 40 | 50 | 60 | 62.5 | 65 | 70 | 75 | 80 | 85 | 87.5 | 90 |
| Gross IRR | Clone | 0.117 | 0.120 | 0.122 | 0.125 | 0.128 | 0.134 | 0.136 | 0.137 | 0.140 | 0.142 | 0.145 | 0.151 | 0.155 | 0.160 |
| | Median | N/A | −0.009 | 0.046 | 0.092 | 0.128 | 0.162 | 0.171 | 0.179 | 0.196 | 0.215 | 0.236 | 0.264 | 0.278 | 0.299 |
| Net IRR | Clone | 0.110 | 0.113 | 0.114 | 0.116 | 0.116 | 0.121 | 0.122 | 0.125 | 0.126 | 0.127 | 0.129 | 0.134 | 0.135 | 0.141 |
| | Median | N/A | −0.032 | 0.035 | 0.082 | 0.116 | 0.149 | 0.156 | 0.164 | 0.180 | 0.198 | 0.217 | 0.242 | 0.255 | 0.273 |
| ETR | Clone | 0.058 | 0.056 | 0.069 | 0.075 | 0.097 | 0.094 | 0.103 | 0.088 | 0.101 | 0.106 | 0.110 | 0.114 | 0.130 | 0.120 |
| | Median | N/A | −2.538 | 0.237 | 0.114 | 0.097 | 0.082 | 0.086 | 0.082 | 0.081 | 0.080 | 0.082 | 0.084 | 0.084 | 0.085 |

Note: The clone case assumes that a university graduate would have earned the same amount as a high school graduate at the same quantile (among high school graduates), if the university graduate had not gone to university. The median case assumes that the university graduate would have earned the same amount as a median high school graduate. N/A = Not available.

Source: Authors' calculations, using the 1998 CPS.

## TABLE 9

## IRRs AND ETRs, U.S. FEMALES, 1997

| | Case | Quantile | | | | | | | | | | | | | |
|---|---|---|---|---|---|---|---|---|---|---|---|---|---|---|---|
| | | 20 | 25 | 30 | 40 | 50 | 60 | 62.5 | 65 | 70 | 75 | 80 | 85 | 87.5 | 90 |
| Gross IRR | Clone | 0.117 | 0.121 | 0.127 | 0.129 | 0.132 | 0.135 | 0.136 | 0.136 | 0.137 | 0.141 | 0.145 | 0.154 | 0.156 | 0.156 |
| | Median | N/A | 0.037 | 0.068 | 0.104 | 0.132 | 0.162 | 0.169 | 0.175 | 0.189 | 0.207 | 0.227 | 0.253 | 0.266 | 0.282 |
| Net IRR | Clone | 0.106 | 0.111 | 0.119 | 0.119 | 0.122 | 0.123 | 0.124 | 0.118 | 0.123 | 0.126 | 0.128 | 0.137 | 0.139 | 0.135 |
| | Median | N/A | 0.025 | 0.060 | 0.094 | 0.122 | 0.150 | 0.156 | 0.157 | 0.174 | 0.191 | 0.207 | 0.231 | 0.243 | 0.252 |
| ETR | Clone | 0.091 | 0.083 | 0.064 | 0.077 | 0.074 | 0.086 | 0.086 | 0.131 | 0.102 | 0.108 | 0.114 | 0.110 | 0.109 | 0.133 |
| | Median | N/A | 0.319 | 0.113 | 0.098 | 0.074 | 0.075 | 0.077 | 0.103 | 0.079 | 0.077 | 0.086 | 0.085 | 0.086 | 0.108 |

Note: The clone case assumes that a university graduate would have earned the same amount as a high school graduate at the same quantile (among high school graduates), if the university graduate had not gone to university. The median case assumes that the university graduate would have earned the same amount as a median high school graduate. N/A = Not available.

Source: Authors' calculations, using the 1998 CPS.

# IMPLICATIONS FOR NORTH AMERICAN ECONOMIC INTEGRATION AND POLICY

THERE ARE TWO ISSUES with regard to North American economic integration where the tax treatment of human capital is important. One has to do with the incentives to accumulate human capital within each country; the other with incentives for the flow of human capital across the border. This latter issue has been much in the news recently in Canada, in the form of the "brain drain" controversy. We will comment on these two issues in turn.

The analysis of human capital ETRs is an important building block in assessing the tax effects on the domestic accumulation of different forms of capital, but it is not the whole story. As we have seen, there is reason to believe that human capital ETRs in Canada may, on average, be higher than those in the United States. Does this mean that Canadians will invest less in human capital than Americans? Furthermore, does it mean that industry will be more intensive in physical capital in Canada than in the United States? The answer to both these questions is: "not necessarily."

Whether or not Canadians will invest relatively less in human capital than Americans depends on the tax treatment of personal savings and investments, as well as on the human capital ETR. It has been calculated that in Canada, about 70 percent of personal investment income is effectively tax-free. Middle- and upper-middle-income Canadians can, for the most part, be viewed as being on a consumption tax regime. A similar statement could be made for the corresponding group in the United States. Given that many in this group will face significant positive ETRs on human capital, there is an incentive effect acting in the direction of physical, as opposed to human, capital accumulation; this effect would seem to be stronger in Canada. Turning to higher income levels, however, as taxpayers encounter positive taxation of personal investment income, they can expect to do so at higher rates in Canada than in the United States, given the higher MTRs under joint federal and provincial income taxes. The relative slant toward physical capital investment, therefore, might be less for the highest earners in Canada.

It is important to note that the relative incentive for personal investment in human versus physical capital in the two countries – assuming that people remain in their country of origin – does not dictate which country's economy will be most human capital intensive. This is because some people will migrate and some physical capital will migrate. As to the latter, it is quite possible that there is a bias toward physical capital investment at the personal level but against physical capital for the overall economy. It is well-known that over the last decade Canada has suffered from a relatively low level of business investment, which has been blamed for much of our lagging productivity growth. It may well be that the economy as a whole is suffering from too low a physical to human capital ratio, while at the same time many personal investments are distorted away from human capital.

Although there has been increasing concern about emigration from Canada to the United States, particularly of highly skilled workers, flows at the moment are still a small fraction of the labour force. Thus, the outflow of human capital from Canada to the United States, overall, has probably had only a small impact on the existing stock of human capital. Nevertheless, in particular fields (e.g., computer programming and medical services), the effects of this have already been sizable; and, if current trends continue, these flows will become increasingly significant.

It is important to note that even if ETRs in Canada were no different from those in the United States, it would not make us impervious to the brain drain. This is because the decision to emigrate is affected by the tax treatment of returns to education but not by the treatment of costs. In other words, only half of what shows up in an ETR is instrumental in such a decision. If costs were more highly subsidized *and* returns more heavily taxed in Canada, Canadian ETRs would not differ greatly from those in the United States. However, there would be a strong tax incentive to emigrate.[31] Thus, policy initiatives aimed at reducing human capital ETRs in Canada will only have a payoff on the emigration front if they are directed at taxing returns less, rather than subsidizing costs more.

Personal incentives to invest in non-human capital also need to be considered, and international movements of both physical and human capital are important.[32] It would therefore be naïve to evaluate tax policy toward human capital strictly in terms of the size of the tax wedge affecting personal investment in human capital. It does appear that Canadians face more of a tax disincentive for education than do Americans. However, if the policy goal is to promote growth and development in Canada, even by way of a strategy to build up a knowledge-based economy, it is not obvious that the chief priority must be to reduce human capital ETRs. Reducing tax disincentives for firms to invest in Canada and for high earners to locate here may be more effective.

Further, in considering the importance of these policy priorities, it is clear that the *way* in which human capital ETRs are reduced is of crucial importance. Providing larger implicit or explicit subsidies for human capital investment will stimulate more education and training, but it will not reduce the incentive for the most highly educated and able workers to relocate to the United States. Reducing MTRs on upper-middle and high earners, however, would both reduce the disincentive to invest in human capital and induce more high-end workers to remain in Canada.

## CONCLUSION

FOR THE PAST TWO DECADES, ETRs have been used to assess the incentive effects of the tax system on investment in physical capital, but this has not been done for human capital investment. This study has developed a framework that allows us to sum up the tax treatment of human capital through the use of ETRs. We find that ETRs on human capital in Canada and the United States vary considerably but can be quite large, particularly for higher earners. Overall, Canadians are subject to higher ETRs than their American counterparts. Because they earn more on average, men face higher ETRs than women, in both countries, which may help to explain the secular trend toward a lower male to female ratio in college and university enrolment.

In the context of North American integration, one is naturally interested in knowing how tax patterns in Canada and the United States may affect not only domestic investment in human capital but also migration decisions and the brain drain. We have pointed out that ETRs are determined by the tax treatment of both the costs and returns to investment. More liberal tax treatment of costs (e.g., through enlarged education credits or sheltered saving for education) will reduce ETRs and encourage human capital formation. However, once education is finished, these tax benefits are largely over. If returns are taxed more heavily in one country than in another, then some of the increased human capital that has been formed will likely flow to the other country. Clearly, there are increasing concerns that such a dynamic is at work in Canada.

If the government wants to use the tax system both to encourage more human capital investment — particularly in high tech areas — and to encourage highly qualified people to locate in Canada, it should reduce the taxation of the *returns* to human capital investment. More generous student assistance may be desirable for a range of reasons, but there must also be a reduction in ATRs on higher earners. If Canadian policy makers find such an approach unpalatable, then it must be accepted that higher earners will tend to migrate to the United States. The magnitude of that flow depends on the elasticity of migration with respect to the tax differential – something outside the scope of this study but deserving of further research.

The last several years have seen many changes in the funding and tax treatment of higher education that have had complex effects in both countries. In both countries there has been a rise in tuition fees, which, as we have shown, increases ETRs. At the same time, education tax credits have been made more generous in both countries. Our illustrative calculations suggest that, except for individuals who pursue expensive out-of-state or private education in the United States or who do not make full use of the available relief, the tax credits now provided reduce ETRs more than tuition fees increase them. The enhancements to sheltered education saving in Canada, and other initiatives such as the introduction of deductibility for interest on student loans, have also tended to reduce ETRs. Thus, there has been significant initiative taken on the costs side of the ledger to reduce human capital ETRs in Canada. Our concern is that the full benefits of this initiative will not be reaped if sufficient action is not taken on the returns side in order to prevent increased losses of highly qualified workers to the United States. The PIT reductions that are currently scheduled are a step in the right direction, but in the face of large parallel reductions in the United States, they may not be sufficient to tip the balance in Canada's favour.

Finally, we should emphasize our finding that taxes other than the PIT have significant effects on human capital ETRs, some of which are intuitive. We have seen, for example, that the much lower earnings threshold at which marginal payroll taxes go to zero in Canada than in the United States offsets the effects of our progressive income taxes, to an extent, and reduces ETRs for higher earners. This highlights the importance of thinking about human capital when considering any changes to payroll tax structure. However, some of the effects of other taxes are less obvious. We have demonstrated, for example, that with a pre-existing progressive income tax, the introduction of additional taxes tends to increase ETRs on human capital even if those additional taxes are proportional. Thus, broad-based sales taxes like the PST and the GST, and even flat provincial or state PITs, increase ETRs. This is unquestionably true in Canada, which relies relatively more heavily on sales tax than the United States.

While we believe we have generated some interesting insights, there is a great deal of additional research that needs to be done on the incentive effects of taxes affecting both human and physical capital investment in Canada and the United States. While work on physical capital is more developed, we need more comparisons of METRs on physical capital in both countries. As well, it is important to recognize that there has been no thorough overall study of ETRs on personal financial investments, in either country. A framework similar to that used here should be used to study ETRs on those earning more advanced university degrees and other qualifications. This would shed further light not only on incentive effects on human capital investment but also on migration incentives. In addition to work on higher university degrees, studies also need to be done on other post-secondary work (e.g., college education, professional programs, etc.) to assess the impact of ETRs on different human capital investment decisions. Finally, it would be desirable to disaggregate by field or program of study to get an indication of how the tax structure treats graduates of different disciplines. We hope that there will be considerable future research on these topics.

# ENDNOTES

1   We would like to thank John Burbidge for his generous assistance in estimating the age-earnings quantile profiles used in the fourth section of this study.

2    As we were preparing the final draft of this study in the summer of 2001, we became aware of Mintz (2001), which was forthcoming in October. Mintz also advocates the calculation of human capital ETRs and embeds components of such ETRs in estimates of net labour costs, by industry, for the year 2000. While Mintz's methods and objectives differ from ours, his conclusion, that ETRs are heavier in Canada than in the United States, is similar.

3    An alternative is to define the ETR as the ratio of the present value of net taxes on labour income over a lifetime to the present value of lifetime earnings (Mintz 2001). While the two approaches will often produce similar results, this is not always the case. We prefer the approach followed here, in part because it does not require any assumption about individuals' discount rates.

4    When education is debt-financed, amounts borrowed during schooling can be modelled as reductions in $C_t$, and repayment (both principal and interest) will be caught in positive $C_t$ after graduation. See Collins and Davies (2001).

5    To illustrate, suppose there are just two brackets, with $m_s = 0.15$ and $m_w = 0.30$. In order to produce the same revenue as an increase of, say, 0.05 in both marginal rates, an equi-proportional increase of 11.1 percent in both tax rates would be needed. The equal absolute increase of 0.05 points would raise the ETR from 0.1765 to 0.1875. The equi-proportional increase would raise the ETR from 0.1765 to 0.2245.

6    The value of the credit is enhanced when provincial income taxes are also taken into account. There is no limit on the amount of interest that may be claimed. Unused credits may be carried forward for up to five years, but are not transferable to other taxpayers.

7    These limits are in U.S. dollars. Throughout this study, dollar magnitudes for the United States are reported in U.S. dollars, and those for Canada are reported in Canadian dollars. According to current markets, the Canadian dollar is worth about US$0.64; according to purchasing power, however, it is worth about US$0.75 - $0.80.

8    AGI equals gross income minus IRA contributions, alimony and a few other smaller items.

9    Canadians have long been allowed to make tax-free RRSP withdrawals two years after the contributions are made. In the United States, there is a general 10 percent penalty on early withdrawals. As of December 31, 1997, exceptions were introduced for qualified higher education expenses and for up to $10,000 of a first-time home purchase.

10    Limits for those with the lowest incomes are greater in the United States, since they are the maximum of $2,000 per person, or 100 percent of earnings. For a Canadian taxpayer, the RRSP contribution limit is less than for a single U.S. taxpayer, up to an income of about C$17,000.

11    The middle marginal tax rate in Canada was reduced from 26 to 24 percent on July 1, 2000. Thus, the 25 percent rate reported in the table is an average figure for the year as a whole. Effective January 1, 2001, the 17 percent rate was reduced to 16 percent, the middle rate fell to 22 percent, and a new bracket extending from about $61,000 to $100,000 was created with a rate of 26 percent.

12    There are also local income taxes in the United States, generally levied at rates of 1 percent or less. New York City, however, levies tax at 4 percent. Note that the burden of state and local income taxes is reduced by the fact that they are deductible against federal tax: the same is not true for provincial taxes in Canada.

13    It is interesting to ask, however, how it is related to a standard measure of local progressivity, the ratio of the marginal to the average tax rate (ATR). The two measures become closely related if students specialize completely in studying (i.e., have zero earnings) and if the incremental earnings due to study are all taxed at a single marginal tax rate (MTR). In that case, $m_s$ equals the ATR, $m_w$ is the MTR, and our measure is a straightforward transformation of the standard measure of local progressivity.

14    There is a large body of literature that estimates human capital earnings equations, which provide estimates of the percentage gain in earnings due to an additional year of schooling. Conventional estimates put the average return at about 7 to 8 percent. Careful work on ability bias and measurement error suggests the true gains may exceed 10 percent (Ashenfelter and Krueger 1994; Card 1995). Our assumed rate of return lies between these two sets of estimates.

15    By referring to the published tax statistics of the two countries, we ascertained the total income levels that, on average, generate the taxable incomes at the threshold of each tax bracket. Since deductions rise with income, this also involves adjusting the marginal tax rates within brackets so as not to exaggerate the calculated tax liabilities.

16    The lower incomes in the first few brackets of the tax schedule for single individuals are about 60 percent of the corresponding bracket limits for couples that file jointly. Since this is roughly the same ratio as that of average husbands' to wives' earnings, using the single taxpayer's schedule for all men provides a reasonable guide to typical tax rates, whether men are single or married. The same clearly is not true for women.

17    It can be argued that a limitation of the assumptions embedded in Equation (7) is that workers in fact have a hump-shaped age profile of earnings. One could argue that the earnings increment from education should be regarded as increasing the hump that would be there in the absence of additional schooling. Hence, the *EI* will be taxed at higher rates as the individual moves toward the peak of the age-earnings profile.

18    Parents or students may claim the credit. As in the Canadian case, we are not discounting the value of the credit to the student if it is claimed by the parent.

19    The direct costs are composed of $6,100 in tuition fees and $1,400 in other expenses. The student loan amount is about the same fraction of these direct costs as the $2,500 amount in the Canadian case.

20    In addition, Canada has some general payroll taxes at the provincial level (see Mintz 2001).

21    We have not done a comparison of unemployment insurance (UI) contributions in both countries. In the United States, UI schemes differ from state to state, making it more difficult to model the system simply than in the case of social security.

22 Heckman and Klenow (1997) argue that in the United States the balance favours private sector training.

23 Tables 1A, 1B, 2A and 2B understate the impact, however, since the fact that interest on loans may be completely subsidized during schooling cannot be captured in the discrete one-schooling-period framework used.

24 Based on the 1999-2000 school year.

25 Our application of these methods uses a parabolic kernel function and cross-validated bandwidths. For an intuitive explanation, see Burbidge and Davies (1994).

26 An alternative would have been to assume that labour earnings are more "basic" than other income sources, and treat the latter as the marginal source of income. We view human and physical capital investments as being made simultaneously, however, so this approach does not suit our purposes.

27 Once again, some might suggest that the "secondary" earner's income be treated as marginal; in our view, however, one no longer can identify reliably whose earnings are marginal in a married couple.

28 Throughout the text, we use median earnings of high school graduates as the counterfactual for *all* university graduates. Sensitivity to this assumption was tested by assuming, alternatively, that a university graduate at percentile X would have earned the amount observed to have been earned by a high school graduate of the same age at percentile X among high school graduates. The alternative counterfactual changes numerical results but leaves our qualitative results mostly unchanged.

29 This approach is similar to that of Stager (1994).

30 It should be noted that tuition fees are much more dispersed in the United States than in Canada. One consequence is that the $5,739 fee reflects the experience of a relatively small group. Students attending public schools in-state had significantly lower fees, and students attending private or out-of-state public universities generally had much higher fees.

31 Likewise, there would be an added disincentive for Canadian graduates of U.S. universities to return to Canada.

32 For a discussion of physical capital movements, see Beaudry and Green (2001), Chapter 6 in this volume.

# BIBLIOGRAPHY

Ashenfelter, O., and A. Krueger. "Estimates of the Economic Return to Schooling From a New Sample of Twins." *American Economics Review* 84 (1994).

Beaudry, Paul, and David A. Green. "Canada-U.S. Integration and Labour Market Outcomes: A Perspective within the General Context of Globalization." In *North American Linkages: Opportunities and Challenges for Canada*. Edited by Richard G. Harris. Calgary: University of Calgary Press, 2003. Chapter 6.

Becker, Gary. *Human Capital*. First Edition. New York: Columbia University Press, 1964.

Boadway, Robin, Neil Bruce and Jack Mintz. "Taxation, Inflation and the Effective Marginal Tax Rate on Capital in Canada." *Canadian Journal of Economics* 17 (1984).

Burbidge, John, and James Davies. "Household Data on Saving Behavior in Canada." In *International Comparisons of Household Saving*. Edited by James Poterba, Chicago: University of Chicago Press 1994.

Burbidge, John, Lonnie Magee and Leslie Robb. "Alternative Transformations to Handle Extreme Values of the Dependent Variable." *Journal of the American Statistical Association* 83 (1988).

Card, D. "Using Geographic Variation in College Proximity to Estimate the Return to Schooling." In *Aspects of Labour Market Behaviour: Essays in Honour of John Vanderkamp*. Edited by L. Christofides, E.K. Grant and R. Swidinsky, Toronto: University of Toronto Press, 1995.

College Board, The. *Trends in College Pricing*. Washington DC: The College Board, 1998. Available at: http://www.collegeboard.com.

_____. *Annual Survey of Colleges*. Washington DC: The College Board, 2000. Available at: http://www.collegeboard.com.

Collins, Kirk A., and James B. Davies. "Taxing Investments in Higher Education." University of Western Ontario, 2001. Mimeograph.

Davies, James B., and Graham Glenday. "Accrual Equivalent Marginal Tax Rates for Personal Financial Assets." *Canadian Journal of Economics* 23 (1990).

Heckman, James J., and Peter J. Klenow. "Human Capital Policy," University of Chicago, 1997. Mimeograph.

Magee, Lonnie, John Burbidge and Leslie Robb. "Computing Kernel-smoothed Quantiles From Many Observations." *Journal of the American Statistical Association* 86 (1991).

McKenzie, Kenneth J., Mario Mansour and Ariane Brule. *The Calculation of Marginal Effective Tax Rates*. Working paper 97-15. Technical Committee on Business Taxation, Department of Finance, Ottawa, 1998.

Mintz, Jack. *Most Favored Nation: Building a Framework for Smart Economic Policy*. Toronto: C.D. Howe Institute, 2001.

Rowley, Robin. "Income Contingency and the Repayment of Student Loans." *Journal of Income Distribution* 3(2) (1993).

Stager, A.A. David. "Returns to Investment in Ontario University Education, 1960-1990, and Implication for Tuition Fee Policy." *Council of Ontario Universities*, December 1994.

*Bev Dahlby*
*University of Alberta*

# 13

# *Economic Integration: Implications for Business Taxation*

## INTRODUCTION

> ...[A]s national economies become more integrated, and as barriers to trade in goods and services fall, the importance of international taxation for the efficient functioning of capital markets will become a central concern. (Slemrod 1995)

THE INTEGRATION OF GLOBAL CAPITAL MARKETS, the decline in transportation and communications costs, and the removal of tariffs and many regulations governing the movement of goods and services are having profound effects on our business tax system. The growth of trade and direct investment with Mexico and the United States is one aspect of this global economic integration. As the volume of trade in goods and services and direct investment among the North American Free Trade Agreement (NAFTA) partners increases, business taxation issues will become increasingly important.

This study deals with the implications of economic integration for Canada's business tax system. It is organized into five sections, beginning with the first, which introduces the subject matter.

In the second section, we review international trends in business taxation to see whether there is evidence of a "race to the bottom." We find that while statutory corporate income tax (CIT) rates have declined over the last 20 years, the reliance of the Organisation for Economic Co-operation and Development (OECD) countries on taxes on corporate profits, measured either as a share of total tax revenues or as a percentage of gross domestic product (GDP), has not changed dramatically.

The third section describes a model of the international tax system which is consistent with some of the stylized facts described in the previous section. The model suggests that the foreign tax credit systems of the major capital exporting countries — the United States, the United Kingdom and Japan — underpin the

CIT systems of the smaller capital-importing countries, and that the corporate tax systems will not whither away as long as the capital-exporting countries retain their foreign tax credit systems. However, the model also suggests that globalization of capital markets may lead to the abandonment of the foreign tax credit system if an increasing share of the capital-exporting countries capital is invested abroad. In that event, the smaller capital-importing countries would probably greatly reduce their rates of capital taxation.

In the fourth section, we review some of the empirical evidence concerning the effects of the international tax system on business decision-making. A number of econometric studies have indicated that foreign direct investment (FDI) by multinational enterprises (MNEs) is quite sensitive to levels of international taxation. The evidence concerning the MNEs' use of transfer pricing to shift profits from high-tax to low-tax countries is more mixed, which is not surprising, given the necessity of trying to infer the MNEs' behaviour from examining their "tracks in the snow." We also review the evidence and policy issues concerning the debt placement policies of corporations with regard to both inbound and outbound investment.

In the final section of the study, we consider a policy issue that may emerge as North American economic integration proceeds: Should Canada, Mexico and the United States adopt a formula apportionment system in levying their CITs? Formula apportionment, which Canada and the United States use to determine the CIT bases of their provincial and state governments, might seem to be the logical conclusion to North American integration. It has been suggested that formula apportionment would reduce administration and compliance costs and pressures to shift profits to low-tax jurisdictions through transfer pricing and debt placement. A closer look at North American formula apportionment reveals that the adoption of fiscal apportionment would pose a number of difficult problems, but many of these issues, such as harmonization of tax bases, will inevitably arise whether we adopt formula apportionment or not.

## INTERNATIONAL TRENDS IN CORPORATE TAXATION: IS THERE A RACE TO THE BOTTOM?

CONCERNS HAVE BEEN EXPRESSED THAT, in an era of high capital mobility and footloose industries, tax competition will lead to an inexorable decline in taxes levied on businesses, shifting the tax burden to the relatively immobile inputs, labour and land. Some view this as a threat to the financial and political underpinnings of the welfare state, which is based on the redistribution of income. In this section, we review international trends in business taxation to see whether there is evidence of a race to the bottom.

## FIGURE 1

### CIT RATES OF G7 COUNTRIES, 1982-2001

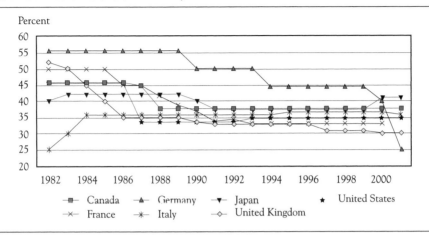

Source: Bartlesman and Beetsma (2000) and Ernst and Young (2001).

## FIGURE 2

### CIT RATES OF SELECTED OECD COUNTRIES, 1982-2001

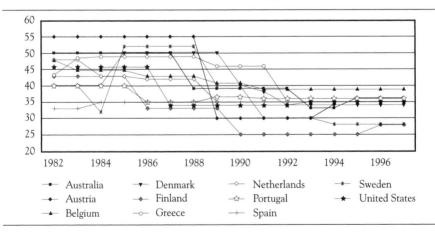

Source: Bartlesman and Beetsma (2000) and Ernst and Young (2001).

FIGURE 3

REDUCTIONS IN CIT RATES BETWEEN 1982 AND 2001

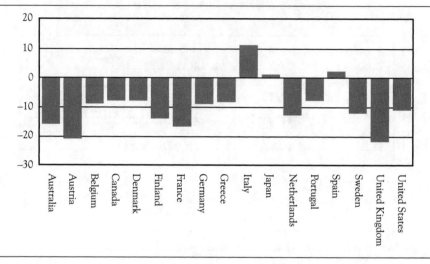

Source: Bartlesman and Beetsma (2000) and Ernst and Young (2001).

Figures 1 and 2 show the trend in CIT rates in the G7 and other selected OECD countries during the 1982-2001 period.[1] These figures indicate that there has been a long-term decline in the CIT rates imposed by these 17 countries. In 1982, the unweighted average CIT rate was 44.4 percent. By 2001, it had declined to 33.6 percent. Furthermore, the variance or dispersion in CIT rates has also declined. In 1982, the tax rates ranged from 25 percent in Italy to 56 percent in Germany, and the standard deviation was 7.84. In 2001, the tax rates ranged from 28 percent in Sweden to 41 percent in Japan, and the standard deviation was 4.05. In addition, a number of countries, including Canada, have announced their intention to reduce their CIT rates in the next few years.[2] While there has been a general trend to lower CIT rates, there are some exceptions. Italy, Japan and Spain had higher CIT rates in 2001 than they had in 1982 (Figure 3). The Nordic countries jacked up their CIT rates in the mid-1980s and then drastically reduced them over the period 1989-91.

There is an interesting time pattern to the tax rate changes surrounding the 1987 cut in the U.S. CIT from 46 to 34 percent.[3] In the period before the 1987 U.S. tax cut, there was no discernable trend in the CIT rate. In 1983 and 1985, the average statutory CIT rate increased, while in 1984 and 1986 it declined, largely because of the United Kingdom's rate reduction, in stages, from 52 percent in 1983 to 35 percent in 1986. By contrast, in the five-year period following the 1987 U.S. tax cut, the average tax rates declined each year. Six countries in sample — Australia, Austria, Denmark, France, Greece and Sweden — cut their tax rates by more than 10 percentage points in the 1988-92 period. Certainly, the 8 percentage point cut in the Canadian CIT rate in 1987-88 was widely acknowledged as a measure required to keep the Canadian corporate tax system competitive with the United States. A study by Grubert, Randolph and Rousslang (1996) indicates that the average foreign tax rate on dividends received by U.S. MNEs fell from 44.7 percent in 1984 to 34.3 percent in 1992, mirroring the change in the U.S. corporate tax rate, and they conclude that this change "was primarily caused by the change in foreign country average tax rates rather than a shift in earnings and profits from high- to low-tax countries." There is, therefore, some evidence that the tax rate cuts in the late 1980s and early 1990s were initiated by the American (and possibly the British) CIT rate cuts.

Did the statutory tax rate cuts in the late 1980s and early 1990s lead to significant declines in revenues collected from the corporate sector? Changes in the relative importance of CIT can be measured either in terms of its share of total tax revenues or by measuring CIT revenues in relation to GDP. Figure 4 shows that between 1965 and 1997, taxes on corporate income as a share of total tax revenues declined by 4.6, 3.8, 7.2 and 7.0 percentage points in Canada, Germany, Japan and the United States, respectively. In Italy and the United Kingdom, the share of total tax revenues rose by 2.4 and 5.0 percentage points, respectively.

However, it is hard to attribute the declining share of CIT revenues in Canada and the United States to these CIT rate cuts, because the most significant declines occurred in the 1965-85 period, before the major statutory rate reductions in those countries. The large declines in Japan and Germany can hardly be attributed to tax rate cuts because there were no significant CIT rate cuts in those countries during that period.[4] Other factors besides rate cuts have been responsible for the long-term decline in the share of tax revenues from CIT.[5]

Figure 5 shows the trend in taxes on corporate income as a percentage of GDP. For the OECD as a whole, taxes on corporate income *increased* as a percentage of GDP from 2.2 percent in 1965 to 3.3 percent in 1997. For Canada, Germany and the United States, there were declines in the ratio of corporate taxes to GDP, but the declines were relatively small, especially in the case of Canada. Most of the decline in Canada and the United States occurred in the 1965-85 period, before the statutory rate reductions in 1987-88. Thus, broadly speaking, there is no evidence of a major shift away from taxes on corporate income among the OECD countries or that cuts in the statutory CIT rates were directly responsible for the decline in CIT revenues.

## FIGURE 4

### TAXES ON CORPORATE INCOME AS A PERCENTAGE OF TOTAL TAXATION

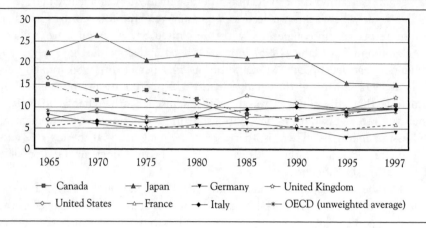

Source: OECD Revenue Statistics (1999, Table13).

## FIGURE 5

### TAXES ON CORPORATE INCOME AS A PERCENTAGE OF GDP

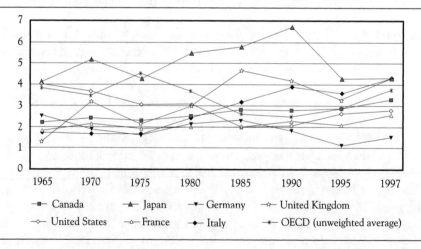

Source: OECD Revenue Statistics (1999, Table12).

One reason why CIT revenues did not abruptly decline in the face of statutory rate reductions in Canada, the United States and the United Kingdom is that the statutory rate reductions were accompanied by tax base broadening measures. Table 1 shows the changes in the statutory tax rates on retained earnings in the manufacturing sector in 10 countries between 1979 and 1994, drawn from a study by Chennells and Griffith (1997). The table also shows the changes in the present value of the capital cost allowances and other deductions on one dollar of investment. The tax rate reductions in Canada, the United States, the United Kingdom and Ireland were accompanied by reductions in the present value of the allowances, and this would have offset, to some degree, any of the revenue reductions from the statutory rate reductions.

It is the combination of the statutory tax rate, capital cost allowances, investment tax credits and other deductions that determine the average and marginal effective tax rates on business income. The average effective tax rate on investment can be defined as the rate at which the tax system reduces the present value of the income stream from a project. Differences in average effective tax rates between countries may affect the location of new investment projects. The marginal effective tax rate (METR) measures the tax that is imposed on an increment in investment spending which just earns the minimum required rate of return for investors. Differences in METRs between countries may affect the location of incremental investments on existing projects.

Table 1 also shows the Chennells and Griffith calculations of the average and effective marginal tax for inbound (source country) and outbound (residence country) investments. Low average and marginal effective tax rates on inbound investment make a country more attractive for FDI. Low average and marginal effective tax rates on outbound investment give a country's domestic firms an advantage in exploiting investment opportunities in other countries. For most countries, average and marginal effective tax rates on inbound and outbound investments declined between 1979 and 1994, but the declines in the average and marginal effective rates were generally smaller than the declines in the statutory rates because of the offsetting changes in investment allowances, as noted above. With regard to inbound investment, the Chennells and Griffith calculations indicate that (not surprisingly) Ireland had the lowest average effective tax rate at 15.9 percent, while Japan had the highest at 32.1 percent, in 1994. Canada had the third highest average effective tax rate at 26.7 percent. With regard to outbound, Germany had the lowest rate at 20.0 percent, while Italy had the highest at 32.6 percent. Canada ranked sixth at 24.7 percent. The empirical evidence on the effect of international taxes on investment will be discussed in more detail in the fourth section under the heading of FDI.

## TABLE 1

### STATUTORY AND EFFECTIVE TAX RATES FOR SELECTED COUNTRIES, 1979 AND 1994

| Country | Year | Statutory CIT Rate | Net Present Value of Allowances | Source Country Tax Rates | | Residence Country Tax Rates | |
|---|---|---|---|---|---|---|---|
| | | | | METR | EATR | METR | EATR |
| Australia | 1979 | 50.0 | 0.71 | 80.6 | 36.5 | 33.6 | 30.6 |
| | 1994 | 33.0 | 0.73 | 50.7 | 27.5 | 35.6 | 25.1 |
| Canada | 1979 | 43.0 | 0.94 | 42.9 | 30.2 | 44.3 | 29.5 |
| | 1994 | 34.3 | 0.73 | 45.1 | 26.7 | 40.7 | 24.7 |
| France | 1979 | 50.0 | 0.81 | 53.6 | 32.6 | 30.3 | 25.5 |
| | 1994 | 33.3 | 0.81 | 49.1 | 24.7 | 24.8 | 21.1 |
| Germany | 1979 | 61.8 | 0.76 | 60.6 | 31.6 | 54.8 | 27.1 |
| | 1994 | 52.2 | 0.80 | 27.5 | 24.9 | 35.5 | 20.0 |
| Ireland | 1979 | 45.0 | 1.00 | 14.0 | 26.2 | N/A | N/A |
| | 1994 | 10.0 | 0.71 | 33.8 | 15.9 | N/A | N/A |
| Italy | 1979 | 36.3 | 0.84 | 35.0 | 22.2 | 35.3 | 28.6 |
| | 1994 | 53.2 | 0.76 | 23.6 | 22.3 | 110.1 | 32.6 |
| Japan | 1979 | 52.6 | 0.70 | 51.9 | 27.8 | 43.5 | 30.3 |
| | 1994 | 50.9 | 0.70 | 61.0 | 32.1 | 52.9 | 28.5 |
| Spain | 1979 | 33.0 | 0.73 | 51.4 | 25.3 | 41.5 | 32.0 |
| | 1994 | 35.0 | 0.70 | 44.6 | 25.5 | 33.5 | 25.2 |
| United Kingdom | 1979 | 52.0 | 1.00 | 17.5 | 29.0 | 43.1 | 29.1 |
| | 1994 | 33.0 | 0.73 | 36.1 | 23.4 | 31.6 | 24.1 |
| United States | 1979 | 49.6 | 0.87 | 41.5 | 28.6 | 40.2 | 30.5 |
| | 1994 | 39.3 | 0.78 | 42.6 | 25.9 | 37.2 | 25.4 |

Source: Chennells and Griffith (1997).

# INTERNATIONAL TAX COMPETITION

## TAXING CAPITAL IN A SMALL OPEN ECONOMY

THIS SECTION OF THE STUDY PROVIDES an analytical framework for discussing the taxation of capital in a small open economy (SOE) in which goods and services and financial capital are perfectly mobile across international boundaries. We investigate the following questions: What rate of taxation should an SOE impose on return to capital? Will tax competition lead to the abandonment of source-based capital taxes such as the CIT? Can we explain why SOEs continue to levy CITs?

There is a well-known (among academic public finance economists) proposition concerning a country's optimal tax structure which states:

Proposition 1: The government of an SOE should not impose a source-based tax on the return to capital if it can set other taxes (such as destination-based consumption taxes, wage taxes and profit taxes) at their optimal values.[6]

This proposition is based on the argument that if capital is perfectly mobile, any source-based capital tax will increase the cost of capital to the economy by the full amount of the tax. This means that the burden of source-based capital taxes will be shifted to relatively immobile inputs such as labour and land (i.e., resources that are in fixed supply) because investors will have to be compensated for any tax that is imposed by the SOE, otherwise they will not invest in the economy. The increase in the gross return to capital means that less capital will be invested, total output will decline and input decisions will be distorted because there will be an increase in the cost of capital in relation to prices of labour and land. Since the same effective distribution of the tax burden can be achieved by taxing labour and land directly, without creating this distortion in production decisions, it is more efficient to tax labour and land directly and eliminate the source-based taxes on capital.

This is a very strong proposition that seems to suggest that the continued existence of source-based capital taxes in many countries is a policy error. Alternatively, one might argue that the proposition is not relevant today because, while capital is highly mobile, it is not perfectly mobile. Still, the proposition can be viewed as a prediction about the long-run trend in the tax mix as economic integration proceeds and a borderless capital market becomes a reality.

We will focus on some of the reasons why governments may continue to levy source-based capital taxes — the existence of pure profits, the desire to shift the tax burden to foreigners, and concerns about the distributional equity of the tax burden.

This study focusses on one aspect of Proposition 1: the availability of optimal taxes on labour and land. In particular, Proposition 1 only holds if a 100 percent tax rate is imposed on the economic profits that are generated by land or other resources that are in fixed supply to the economy. Economic profit, which is sometimes referred to as pure profits or economic rent, is the return to an input in excess of its opportunity cost. Taxes on economic profit are usually considered to be non-distortionary taxes, and therefore the optimal rate for such taxes is 100 percent.

Two points should be emphasized. First, there are economic rents in our economy. Clearly, at current world market prices, at least some of Alberta's oil and gas deposits generate economic rents. Of course, economic rent is a general concept that is not restricted to land and resources, as the quarter of a billion dollars paid to the baseball player, Alex Rodriguez, clearly indicate. However, this study will focus on the economic profits generated by land or resources that are in fixed supply. While the existence of economic rents cannot be doubted, there is a considerable difference of opinion concerning the magnitude of these rents.[7]

Second, it is clear that our tax system is not "optimal" in the sense that governments do not tax away all of the economic rents. There are limitations on the taxation of economic rents because these rents cannot be readily measured, and if the rate of tax on pure profits becomes too high, investors will find ways of characterizing pure profits as other forms of income, which are taxed at lower rates. For example, Gordon and Mackie-Mason (1995) argue that if the tax rate on pure profits exceeds the tax rate on wage income, recorded economic profits will quickly disappear because the owners of firms would pay themselves very high wages and salaries that would be taxed at the lower rate. Thus, information problems prevent governments from imposing 100 percent taxes on pure profits.

What is the implication of a government's inability to completely tax away pure profits? There is a second proposition which states:

> Proposition 2: If the government of an SOE cannot impose a 100 percent tax on pure profits, then it should impose positive tax rates on labour income and a source-based tax on capital.[8]

This proposition explains why an SOE will tax capital — to get at the economic rents that are otherwise incompletely taxed. The question is: Do the limitations on the taxation of pure profits justify the continued existence of high rates of source-based capital taxes in SOEs?

In a technical appendix (available from the author upon request), the optimal tax rates on labour income and capital are derived for an SOE where the tax rate on pure profits is constrained to be less than 100 percent. The optimal tax rates are found by equating the marginal cost of raising an extra dollar of tax revenue from taxing labour income, $MCF_{tL}$, with the marginal cost of raising an additional dollar of tax revenue by raising the tax on the return to capital employed in the economy, $MCF_{tK}$. To the extent that these taxes distort the allocation of resources in the economy by reducing the incentive to work or to invest in the economy, the marginal cost of funds (MCF) will be greater than one. With the optimal set of taxes, the cost of raising revenue is the same for all taxes. In measuring the MCF, we have also incorporated the possibility that distributional preferences may affect the choice of taxes. In particular, a society may place a lower value on a dollar tax burden imposed on the recipients of pure profits than on a dollar of tax burden imposed on labour income if profits accrue disproportionately to the rich or to foreigners, or if it is felt that individuals are not "entitled" to profits.

The optimal tax rate on capital for an SOE is given by the following formula:[9]

$$(1) \quad \tau_K = \frac{(1-\tau_\pi)(\varepsilon_{Kw} - \varepsilon_{Lw})[1 - \beta(1-\tau_L\eta_{Lw})]}{\beta(\varepsilon_{Lc} - \varepsilon_{Kc})(1 - \tau_\pi)\eta_{Lw} + \varepsilon_{Lw}\varepsilon_{Kc} - \varepsilon_{Kw}\varepsilon_{Lc}} \quad ,$$

where

- $\tau_\pi$ is the tax rate on pure profit, $0 \le \tau_\pi \le 1$;
- $\varepsilon_{Kw}$ is the elasticity of demand for capital, $K$, with respect to the wage rate, $w$;
- $\varepsilon_{Lw}$ is the elasticity of demand for labour, $L$, with respect to the wage rate;
- $\varepsilon_{Kc}$ is the elasticity of demand for capital, $K$, with respect to the cost of capital, $c$;
- $\varepsilon_{Lc}$ is the elasticity of demand for labour with respect to the cost of capital;
- $\beta$ is the distributional weight reflecting society's valuation of a dollar of pure profits compared to a dollar of wage income, $0 \le \beta \le 1$;
- $\tau_w$ is the ad valorem tax rate on wage income; and
- $\eta_{Lw}$ is the elasticity of the labour supply with respect to the after-tax wage rate, $0 \le \eta_{Lw}$.

This formula for the optimal tax rate on capital is consistent with Propositions 1 and 2 — the optimal tax rate on the return to capital invested in the economy should be zero if the tax rate on pure profits is one, and a positive tax rate should be imposed if $0 \le \tau_\pi < 1$. Furthermore, the tax rate on capital will tend to be higher when the optimal tax rate on labour is higher and when the distributional weight on profit income is lower. Note that the optimal tax rate on capital is independent of the labour supply elasticity if $\beta = 0$. Otherwise, the effect of the labour supply elasticity on the optimal $\tau_K$ is equal to

$$(2) \quad \frac{\partial \tau_K}{\partial \eta_L} \overset{>}{\underset{<}{\phantom{=}}} 0 \quad as \quad (\varepsilon_{Kw} - \varepsilon_{Lw})\tau_w \overset{>}{\underset{<}{\phantom{=}}} (\varepsilon_{Lc} - \varepsilon_{Kc})\tau_K.$$

This condition implies that if a change in the capital-labour ratio from the wage tax is greater than the change in the capital-labour ratio from the capital tax, an increase in the labour supply elasticity will induce greater reliance on capital taxation.

Few other general results can be gleaned from this formula. However, if it is assumed that aggregate production is based on a Cobb-Douglas production function and $\beta = 0$, then the optimal tax rate on capital is equal to

$$(3) \quad \tau_K = (1 - \tau_\pi)\alpha_\pi,$$

where $\alpha_\pi$ is the share of pure profits in total income. In other words, if the shares of labour, capital and the fixed input in total output are constants (a characteristic of an aggregate Cobb-Douglas production function), and the government only cares about the burden of taxes on labour, then the optimal tax rate on capital in an SOE is equal to the after-tax share of profits in total income. With a Cobb-Douglas production function and $\beta > 0$, the optimal $\tau_K$ will be increasing in $\alpha_\pi$ if $\tau_w \geq \tau_K$.

We calculate the optimal tax rates for an economy in which production is given by a Cobb-Douglas production function, with labour and capital shares of income equal to 75 percent and 20 percent, respectively. This implies that pure profits represent 5 percent of total income or 20 percent of non-labour income. The labour supply elasticity is assumed to be 0.15. Finally, the computation of the optimal tax rates is based on the constraint that pure profits and wages are taxed at the same rate (i.e., $\tau_\pi = \tau_w$) and that the tax system generates revenues equal to 29.4 percent of total output. Given these parameter values and constraints, the optimal tax rates are $\tau_K = 0.00345$, $\tau_w = \tau_\pi = 0.367$ if $\beta = 1$ and society places the same value on wages and profit, and $\tau_K = 0.065$, $\tau_w = \tau_\pi = 0.351$ if $\beta = 0$ and society is only concerned about the effect of the tax system on wage earners. By way of comparison, calculations by McKenzie, Mansour and Brule (1997, p. 27) indicate that the average METR on capital under the current Canadian tax system is in the 22 to 27 percent range. Obviously, other parameter values would generate somewhat different values, but these calculations suggest that the optimal tax rates on capital income are much lower than the rates of taxation on capital that are currently imposed by the Canadian tax system.

Again, one might question the relevance of this conclusion because 1) the Canadian economy does not face perfectly elastic supplies of capital or perfectly elastic demands for Canadian export products, and 2) this model does not reflect an important feature of the taxation of capital in Canada — the presence of the CIT and the existence of foreign tax credits on dividends paid to foreign investors in the United States, the United Kingdom, Japan and other countries. A CIT is a tax on both economic profits and the return on equity financed capital. Changes in the CIT rate simultaneously increase the rate of taxation of economic profit and the METR on capital in the economy. The model described above does not link the rate of taxation on profits to the rate of taxation on capital, and this linkage may be important in explaining the current rate of taxation of capital. Also, it has long been recognized that the foreign tax credit system means that if the Canadian CIT is fully credited by foreign governments, an increase in the CIT rate on foreign owned capital is effectively borne by the treasuries of foreign governments. This means that a significant share of the CIT burden may be exported to foreigners, which greatly enhances the attractiveness of levying a CIT. In the following section, we outline a simple model of the optimal CIT rate in an SOE where foreign tax credits are available to foreign investors.

## The Marginal Cost of Public Funds From Levying a CIT in an SOE

In an SOE, the user cost of capital is determined by the rates of return on debt and equity that foreign investors require in order to make investments in the economy comparable to investments in other countries.[10] The cost of capital to the firm will therefore depend on the CIT rate in the economy, $u$, and the availability of foreign tax credits. Foreign governments limit the foreign tax credit to the rate of taxation that would be applied in their home country, $u_f$. On the one hand, if the government of the SOE sets its CIT rate above $u_f$, then foreign investors will require a higher rate of return in order to make investments in the SOE, and the cost of capital to firms in the economy will increase. This is illustrated in Figure 6. On the other hand, if the government of the SOE sets its tax rate below $u_f$, the taxes in the SOE are fully credited and the user cost of capital will not be affected by changes in the SOE's CIT rate.

This assumes that there are no other distortions in the CIT system. In particular, it assumes that capital cost allowances equal the true economic rate of depreciation. If capital cost allowances are less than the economic rate of depreciation, then the user cost of capital will also increase as the CIT rate increases below $u_f$. Whether or not the cost of capital is constant or increasing in the CIT rate below $u_f$, there will be a "kink" in the cost of capital schedule at $u_f$ when the maximum foreign tax credit is reached. This kink in the cost of capital schedule means that there will be a vertical discontinuity or "jump" in the MCF for the CIT when the CIT rate equals $u_f$.

It also assumes that the MNE cannot defer the additional tax due to the home country by retaining profits in the foreign subsidiary and not remitting dividends to the parent in the home country, or that the MNE is not able to use the low burden to offset high tax burdens in other countries in calculating total foreign tax credit on dividends from the MNE's foreign subsidiaries. (These issues will be addressed in the fourth section.)

## FIGURE 6

### TAXES ON CORPORATE INCOME AS A PERCENTAGE OF GDP

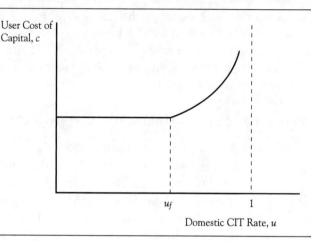

Source: Author's calculations.

In the technical appendix, we derive an expression for the marginal cost of public funds for a CIT, $MCF_u$, for an SOE. The model is highly simplified. There is only one sector. The CIT is levied at the same rate on all firms in the economy. The firms' debt-equity ratios are assumed to be fixed and independent of the tax. It is assumed that there is one foreign government that provides a full tax credit up to its CIT rate, $u_f$.

The model should be regarded as a prototype that illustrates how capital mobility and foreign tax credits affect the MCF for the CIT. The model does not capture the important distortions that are created when different effective CIT rates are imposed on different sectors of the economy. It does not reflect any distortions in the debt-equity ratios of firms as a result of the CIT and does not include other important aspects of international taxation such as transfer pricing or international debt placement.

Within the context of this very simple model, the marginal cost of public funds from the CIT can be shown to equal the following:

$$(4) \quad MCF_u = \frac{-S_c \phi K + \beta[\Pi + (1 + S_c)(1 - u)\phi K]}{\Pi_{corp} + [\tau_K(\varepsilon_{Kc} + \varepsilon_{Lc} S_c) - u S_c]\phi K + \tau_l(\varepsilon_{Kw} + \varepsilon_{Lw} S_c)\phi K},$$

where

- $S_c$ is the change in labour income when the cost of capital increases by one dollar (i.e., $S_c = \dfrac{L}{K} \cdot \dfrac{dw}{dc} = \dfrac{-\varepsilon_{Kw}}{\varepsilon_{Lw} - \eta_{Lw}} < 0$);

- $\phi$ is the rate of increase in user cost of capital as the CIT rate increases (i.e., $\phi = \dfrac{dc}{du}$);

- $\Pi$ is total economic profit;

- $\Pi_{corp}$ is total corporate profits; and

- $\tau_K$ is the METR under the corporate tax system.

As in all marginal cost of public funds formulas, the numerator reflects the burden of a tax rate increase and the denominator reflects the rate of increase in total tax revenues from a tax rate increase. In this model, the burden of an increase in the CIT rate falls on wages and profits, if an increase in the CIT rate increases the user cost of capital for firms. The first term in the numerator is the burden of a small increase in the corporate tax rate that falls on labour, and the second term is the (distributionally weighted) burden that falls on the recipients of the economic rent. In the denominator, the first two terms reflect the increase in CIT revenues and the third term is the rate of change in tax revenues from the wage tax.

The general formula is rather complex, but some insights can be gained from considering the case where $u < u_f$ and the user cost of capital is independent of the CIT rate in the SOE. In this case $\phi = 0$ and if $\beta = 1$, the $MCF_u$ is equal to

$$(5) \quad MCF_u = \frac{\Pi}{\Pi_{corp}},$$

or the ratio of pure profit to corporate profit. Since corporate profits include the return on shareholders' equity, corporate profits exceed pure profit and therefore the $MCF_u$ is less than one. The underlying reason why the $MCF_u$ is less than one is that the CIT burden on the return to shareholders' equity is exported to foreigners when $u < u_f$. The ratio $\Pi/\Pi_c$ is the fraction of the tax burden that is not exported to foreigners. The notion that the $MCF_u$ can be less than one because part of the tax burden is borne by foreign governments' treasuries is not new. The Carter Commission justified the retention of the CIT on the basis of tax exporting through the foreign tax credit. More recently, Thirsk (1986) and Damus, Hobson and Thirsk (1991), by using a computable general equilibrium model for the Canadian economy, demonstrated that the marginal excess burden from the CIT might be relatively low because of tax exporting.[11]

We calculate the MCF for the CIT and the payroll tax by using the same values of the variables and parameters that were used to simulate the optimal capital tax rate in the previous section. Parameter values have been chosen to roughly reflect the tax rates in the non-manufacturing sector of the economy, as described in McKenzie, Mansour and Brule. In particular, the parameters reflect an average METR of 22.8 percent when the average statutory tax rate is 44.3 percent. It is assumed that the average capital cost allowance rate is 6 percent, which is less than the economic depreciation rate of 10 percent, in order to illustrate the effect of this additional distortion. (This assumption might be rationalized by noting that capital cost allowances are not indexed and therefore decline in value with the rate of inflation.) The simulation model implies that the elasticity of capital with respect to the CIT rate ($u = 0.433$) is $-0.67$, which is very close to the estimated elasticity of FDI with respect to the host country tax rates in a number of econometric studies (Hines 1999). Figure 7 shows the MCF for the CIT and the wage tax when the tax rate on labour income in 30 percent. As expected, the $MCF_u$ is (generally) less than one when $u < u_f$. When $u$ hits $u_f$, further increases in the CIT rate push up the user cost of capital at a faster rate because the marginal tax rate increases are no longer credited against foreign taxes, and the $MCF_u$ jumps from 1.026 to 1.318. When the $u$ increases to 50 percent, the $MCF_u$ increases to 1.507. Note that the $MCF_{\tau L}$ for $\tau_w = 0.30$ increases only slightly as $u$ increases and is equal to 1.055 when $u = u_f = 0.40$. Both the $MCF_u$ and the $MCF_{\tau L}$ are smaller than in some other studies because this model does not take into account all of the distortions created by these taxes.

One conclusion that is suggested by these calculations is that there is a wide range of tax rates on labour such that the optimal CIT rate will be equal to $u_f$. The model does not imply that the optimal CIT rate has to be equal to $u_f$. However, there is likely to be a wide range of parameter values such that $u_f$ is the optimal CIT rate because it maximizes tax exporting with a minimal distortion to the allocation of resources in the economy.

Table 2 shows the computed values of the MCF for the CIT and the wage tax. Case 1 shows the values of the MCF in Figure 7. Case 2 shows the MCF when tax policy is only concerned about the well-being of workers. In this case, the optimal CIT rate is 0.445 and the optimal tax rate on labour is 0.297. Cases 3 and 4 show that the $MCF_u$ is higher when the share of pure profits in total income is lower. However, in both of these cases, the optimal CIT rate is the foreign rate, 0.40. Thus the model predicts that an SOE will want to levy its CIT at a rate that is close to the CIT rate of its major source of foreign investment, in our case the United States.

## FIGURE 7

## THE MARGINAL COST OF PUBLIC FUNDS FOR THE CIT AND THE WAGE TAX

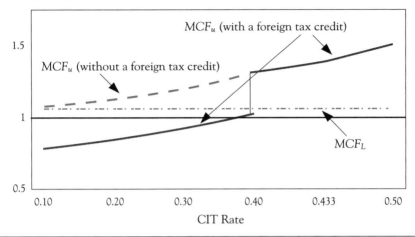

Marginal Cost of Public Funds

$MCF_u$ (with a foreign tax credit)

$MCF_u$ (without a foreign tax credit)

$MCF_L$

CIT Rate

Source: Author's calculations.

## TABLE 2

## COMPUTATIONS OF THE MARGINAL COST OF PUBLIC FUNDS FOR THE CIT AND THE WAGE TAX

| | Case 1 | | Case 2 | | Case 3 | | Case 4 | |
|---|---|---|---|---|---|---|---|---|
| | $\beta = 1$, $\alpha_\pi = 0.05$ | | $\beta = 0$, $\alpha_\pi = 0.05$ | | $\beta = 1$, $\alpha_\pi = 0.02$ | | $\beta = 1$, $\alpha_\pi = 0.125$ | |
| CIT Rate | $MCF_u$ | $MCF_{tL}$ | $MCF_u$ | $MCF_{tL}$ | $MCF_u$ | $MCF_{tL}$ | $MCF_u$ | $MCF_{tL}$ |
| 0.10 | 0.783 | 1.049 | 0.396 | 1.040 | 0.719 | 1.049 | 0.894 | 1.047 |
| 0.20 | 0.844 | 1.051 | 0.466 | 1.043 | 0.798 | 1.052 | 0.918 | 1.048 |
| 0.30 | 0.917 | 1.053 | 0.558 | 1.046 | 0.902 | 1.054 | 0.952 | 1.050 |
| 0.40 | 1.026 to 1.318 | 1.055 | 0.682 to 0.968 | 1.049 | 1.045 to 1.413 | 1.057 | 1.002 to 1.151 | 1.051 |
| 0.433 | 1.388 | 1.056 | 1.028 | 1.051 | 1.478 | 1.058 | 1.186 | 1.052 |
| 0.50 | 1.507 | 1.058 | 1.178 | 1.053 | 1.648 | 1.061 | 1.248 | 1.053 |

Other parameter values: $u_f = 0.40$, $\tau_L = 0.30$, $\alpha_L = 0.75$, $\eta_{Lw} = 0.15$, $\delta = 0.10$ and $a = 0.06$.

## THE TAX TREATMENT OF FOREIGN EARNINGS BY CAPITAL-EXPORTING COUNTRIES: FOREIGN TAX CREDITS VERSUS THE EXEMPTION SYSTEM

CAN THE MODEL EXPLAIN WHY SOME COUNTRIES, such as the United States, provide credits for taxes paid on foreign investment income? In this section, we examine a capital exporter's decision regarding the adoption of a foreign tax credit system whereby foreign income taxes are credited against the income taxes that it imposes, or an exemption system whereby the government exempts active business income earned abroad from further domestic taxation.[12] (The exemption system is also sometimes referred to as a territorial CIT.) In particular, we extend the analysis in Gordon (1992) to explain why, or under what circumstances, capital-exporting countries provide a tax credit to their taxpayers for taxes paid on foreign earnings. Gordon's key insight is that a dominant capital-exporting country like the United States would take into account the effect of its tax system on the tax rates chosen by smaller capital-importing countries like Canada. (In technical terms, the dominant capital-exporting country acts as a Stackelberg leader in forming its international taxation policies.) In particular, a dominant capital-exporting country would recognize that small capital-importing countries will tend to match its CIT rate if it adopts a foreign tax credit regime, but will not impose significant capital taxes if the capital-exporting country chooses an exemption system.

---

### TABLE 3

### TREATMENT OF FOREIGN SOURCE INCOME

|  | Interest | Dividends |
|---|---|---|
| Australia | Credit | Exempt |
| Canada | Credit | Exempt |
| France | Credit | Exempt |
| Germany | Credit | Exempt |
| Ireland | Credit | Credit |
| Italy | Credit | Credit |
| Japan | Credit | Credit |
| Spain | Credit | Credit |
| United Kingdom | Credit | Credit |
| United States | Credit | Credit |

Source: Chennells and Griffith (1997, 104, Table B.3).

---

## FIGURE 8

### THE DEADWEIGHT LOSS FROM A CIT WITH A FOREIGN TAX CREDIT

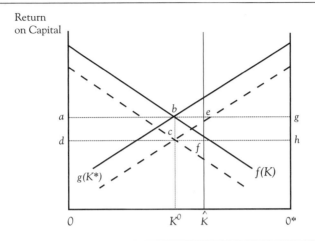

Source: Author's calculations.

It should be noted that there is a third alternative — the deduction system, whereby the capital-exporting country taxes the net-of-foreign-tax return on its residents' investments from abroad. Feldstein and Hartman (1979) show that a dominant capital exporting country, such as the United States, would always prefer the deduction system to the foreign tax credit system. As Table 3 indicates, all major OECD countries use either the exemption or credit systems, and their failure to adopt the deduction system is puzzling. Gordon (1992) suggests that this might be due to the inability to tax foreign source income. In any case, because deduction systems have not been adopted by the OECD countries, we have restricted the analysis to the choice between the credit and exemption systems.

With a foreign tax credit regime, the equilibrium capital allocation is described in Figure 8, where $f(K)$ is the marginal productivity of capital in the large capital-exporting country and $g(K^*)$ is the marginal productivity of capital in the rest of the world (ROW). Capital invested in the capital-exporting country is measured to the right of $0$, and capital invested in the ROW is measured to the left of $0^*$. It is assumed that the ROW is made up of many SOEs, which take the cost of capital and the tax policy of the dominant capital-exporting country as given. For simplicity, it is assumed that the world's capital stock is fixed (i.e., reductions in the return to capital do not affect savings rates). This model assumes that the residents of the dominant capital-exporting country own $\hat{K}$ units of capital, with the remainder of the world's capital stock owned by residents of the capital-importing countries. In the absence of taxation, $K^0$ units of capital are invested in the capital-exporting country, and $\hat{K} - K^0$ units of capital are invested in the other countries. If the capital-exporting country introduces a CIT with a foreign tax credit, the net rate of return on investment in the capital-exporting country will be given by the dashed line below $f(K)$. However, because of the foreign tax credit, the small capital-importing countries will also levy a source-based CIT at (approximately) the same rate, and therefore the net rate of return on investment in the capital-importing countries, given by the dashed line below $g(K^*)$, will also shift down by the same amount. The allocation of capital between the capital-exporting and the capital-importing countries, therefore, does not change as a result of taxation of capital.

Is this a good arrangement from the perspective of the capital-importing countries and the dominant capital-exporting country? First, the equilibrium is obviously advantageous for the capital-importing countries because they collect tax revenues equal to *bghc* while reducing the net incomes of their residents by *eghf*. In other words, the burden *befc* is shifted to the residents of the capital-exporting country, and the marginal cost of public funds from the CIT from the capital-importing countries' perspective is $(eghf)/(bghc) < 1$.

## FIGURE 9

### THE DEADWEIGHT LOSS FROM A CIT UNDER THE EXEMPTION SYSTEM

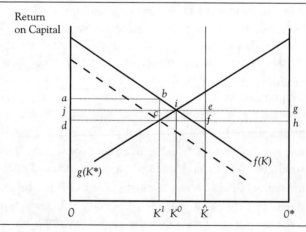

Source: Author's calculations.

Now consider the equilibrium from the capital-exporting country's perspective. The total tax revenue raised by the capital-exporting country is the area *abcd*. This revenue is raised by reducing the return to the owners of domestic capital by the area *aefd*. In other words, the CIT with a foreign tax credit has an excess burden or deadweight loss of *befc* and its MCF is equal to $(aefd)/(abdc) = (1 - \Phi)^{-1} > 1$, where $\Phi$ is the fraction of the capital owned by the capital-exporting country's residents that is invested in other countries. Therefore, the marginal (and average) cost of public funds from taxing capital under the credit system for the capital-exporting country is higher when the proportion of its capital stock that is invested in other countries is larger.

Could the capital-exporting country do better if it dropped its foreign tax credit system and adopted the exemption system? Suppose the capital exporting country switched to the exemption system. In this case, illustrated in Figure 9, the net return on capital in the capital-exporting country declines by the effective tax rate on capital, but now the capital-importing countries would not levy a (significant) tax on the return to capital. Consequently, in the new equilibrium, the after-tax return in the capital-exporting country equals the rate of return on capital in the ROW, and there is a reduction in capital invested in the dominant capital-exporting country from $K^0$ to $K^1$. The capital exporting country collects tax revenues equal to *abcd*, but this imposes a loss equal to *abij*, on its workers (and the owners of fixed inputs) and a loss of *jefd* on the owners of capital in the capital-exporting country.[13] Consequently, the territorial CIT has a deadweight loss equal to *bic* + *iefc*. The first component of the deadweight loss is the loss associated with the reduction in the use of capital in the capital-exporting country. The second component is the loss of surplus on capital invested abroad.

Which tax system is superior from the perspective of the capital-exporting country — the foreign tax credit system or the exemption system? Suppose the capital-exporting country makes its choice solely on efficiency grounds (i.e., it chooses the tax system with the lower deadweight loss for a given amount of tax revenue). In the technical appendix, it is shown that the difference in the deadweight loss per dollar of tax revenue between the exemption system and the foreign tax credit system is equal to

$$
(6) \quad \Delta = \frac{\left(\varepsilon_{Kc} + 0.5\varepsilon^*_{Kc}\right)\left(\tau_K \varepsilon_{Kc} \varepsilon^*_{Kc}\right)}{(\varepsilon_{Kc} + \varepsilon^*_{Kc})^2} - \frac{\varepsilon^*_{Kc}\left(1 - \tau_K \varepsilon_{Kc}\right)}{\varepsilon^*_{Kc} + \left(1 - \tau_K \varepsilon^*_{Kc}\right)\varepsilon_{Kc}}\left(\frac{\Phi}{1 - \Phi}\right),
$$

where $\varepsilon_{Kc}$ is the elasticity of demand for capital in the capital-exporting country, $\varepsilon^*_{Kc}$ is the elasticity of demand for capital by the ROW, (both defined as positive values in this context), and $\tau_K$ is the effective tax rate on capital under the exemption system. When $\Delta$ is positive, the foreign credit system is preferred to the exemption system by the dominant capital-exporting country because the deadweight loss per dollar of tax revenue is lower under the credit system (and vice versa). While the condition in Equation (6) is rather complex, two important tendencies can be discerned. First, the tax credit system will be more attractive the more elastic the demand for capital in either the capital-exporting country or the capital-importing countries. This occurs because the deadweight loss under the credit system is independent of the elasticity of demand for capital in either region, while the deadweight loss under the exemption system is increasing in the elasticities of demand for capital. Second, and most important for our purposes, the credit system is preferred to the exemption system if the proportion of the capital stock invested outside the capital-exporting country is sufficiently small. If $\Phi$ is below some critical value, the capital-exporting country will adopt a CIT with a foreign tax credit and its CIT rate will be determined largely by domestic considerations (i.e., taking into account the MCF for the other taxes that it levies and the marginal benefits from additional public spending).

The critical value of $\Phi$, such that the capital-exporting country is indifferent between the exemption and the foreign tax credit system, is equal to 0.58 if production in both the capital-exporting country and the ROW is based on Cobb-Douglas production functions, with $\alpha_L = 0.70$ and $\alpha_\pi = 0.05$, and equal to 0.27 if $\alpha_L = 0.70$ and $\alpha_\pi = 0.10$.[14] It seems likely that less than one-quarter of U.S. residents' capital is invested abroad, and therefore this model may explain why the U.S. government has chosen to adopt the foreign tax credit system. Furthermore, if the capital-exporting country adopts tax policies that place a higher distributional weight on the burden borne by labour than on capital, then the credit system will be favoured to a greater degree than this analysis indicates because the exemption system places a higher burden on labour than the foreign tax credit system.

This model suggests that economic integration and the globalization of capital markets may have implications for the choice between the credit and exemption systems and therefore the level of capital taxation in the SOEs. Globalization of the capital market may imply that a larger fraction of the capital-exporting countries' capital stock will be invested abroad, either for portfolio diversification reasons or because economic growth and the demand for capital is greater in the capital-importing countries than in the capital-exporting countries. As a result, the advantage in using the credit system will trend to decline and at some point the capital-exporting countries may switch to the exemption system.[15] If that happens, the SOEs would abandon, or at least greatly reduce, their source-based taxes on capital incomes. If savings worldwide are relatively insensitive to the rate of return, then the switch is likely to have detrimental long-run effects from a global perspective. If, however, as endogenous growth models predict, the long-run economic growth rate is directly related to the return on savings, then the switch might raise global welfare.

To recapitulate, we have described a model of the international tax system that appears, at least on the surface, to be consistent with at least some of the stylized facts regarding the trends in capital taxation described in the second section. The model suggests that the foreign tax credit systems of the major capital exporting countries, the United States, the United Kingdom and Japan, underpin the CIT systems of the smaller capital-importing countries. The CIT rate reductions by the OECD countries in the 1988-92 period were a predictable response to the 1987 CIT rate cut in the United States, and possibly the earlier U.K. tax cuts. The model suggests that tax competition in a global capital market will not necessarily lead to the withering away of the corporate tax systems as long as the capital-exporting countries retain their foreign tax credit systems. However, the model also suggests that globalization of capital markets may lead to the abandonment of the foreign tax credit system if an increasing share of the capital from capital-exporting countries is invested abroad. In that event, the smaller capital-importing countries would probably greatly reduce their rates of capital taxation.

## THE IMPACT OF INTERNATIONAL TAXATION ON BUSINESS DECISIONS

WHILE THE PRECEDING MODEL DESCRIBES some of the stylized facts concerning the international tax system, it does not account for other aspects of international tax-setting behaviour. For example, a number of countries — Australia, Canada, Denmark, Ireland, Mexico and Sweden — have cut (or have announced their intention to lower) their CIT rates significantly below the CIT rates in the United States and Japan. The model in the third section predicts that small capital-importing countries should not set their CIT rates significantly below the CIT rates of the major capital-exporting countries that provide foreign tax credits. Even though the U.K. rate is now only 30 percent, a weighted average foreign tax credit rate, based on FDI shares from Japan, the United States and the United Kingdom, would not explain the CIT rate-setting behaviour of most of these countries.[16] Furthermore, the model does not explain the apparent success that Ireland has had in attracting FDI by adopting a 10 percent CIT rate for manufacturing activity.

The inability of the tax credit model to account for the recent CIT rate cuts and the Irish FDI boom may be due to the fact that the model neglects some key aspects of the international taxation system, such as the deferral of dividends to the parent company, the averaging of taxes from high- and low-tax countries in calculating the foreign tax credits, the existence of international tax havens, and the fact that tax policies in many countries have to deal with both inbound and outbound FDI. We will deal with each of these issues in turn.

The foreign tax credit model outlined in the third section implicitly assumes that foreign earnings are taxed on an accrual basis. However, under the U.S. tax system, the active business income of a U.S. foreign subsidiary is only taxed when a dividend payment is made to the U.S. parent.[17] Consequently, a U.S. MNE can defer or postpone the residual U.S. tax liability that arises when the host country tax rate is less than the U.S. rate by retaining the profits in the foreign subsidiary. Deferral reduces the present value of the future U.S. tax liability and in the limit reduces it to zero. With deferral, the subsidiary's cost of capital will be an increasing function of the host country's tax rate, even if it is less than the U.S. rate. A higher host country CIT rate, therefore, will tend to discourage investment.

Furthermore, in calculating its foreign tax credits, a U.S. MNE is able to use the low tax burdens in some countries to offset its excess tax credits on investments in other high-tax countries. By averaging taxes from high- and low-tax sources, the MNE can avoid being put in an excess tax credit position, such that its foreign tax credits exceed its overall U.S. tax liability.[18] Consequently, an increase in the CIT rate in a low-tax country may push up the MNE's overall tax rate, and therefore may not be fully credited at the margin. In that case, an increase in the host country's CIT rate increases its user cost of capital even though its rate is below the U.S. rate, with a potentially deleterious effect on the incentive to invest in the host country. In terms of the model of the CIT described in the third section, deferral and averaging could mean that the $MCF_u$ for the host country is equivalent to the no tax credit case in Figure 7 for $u < u_f$, and that the optimal CIT rate from the host country's perspective might be considerably lower than $u_f$. Indeed, Gordon (2000, p. 30) has concluded "it does not appear that the use of tax credits can explain the survival of taxes on capital income, given that profits from foreign subsidiaries are taxed only at repatriation and with worldwide averaging."

The extent to which deferral and worldwide averaging have effectively converted the U.S. credit system into an exemption system is basically an empirical question. Slemrod (1990) analyses FDI in the United States from countries using the exemption and foreign tax credit systems over the 1962-87 period, and concludes that FDI from exemption countries was not more sensitive to U.S. tax rate changes than FDI from countries providing foreign tax credits. Auerbach and Hassett (1993) also find no difference in the tax responsiveness of

FDI in the United States from countries using the exemption or the foreign tax credit systems. However, Hines (1996) finds that FDI from countries with exemption systems is much more sensitive to the state CIT rates than FDI from countries with foreign tax credit systems. He finds that a 1 percent increase in a state's tax rate reduces the share of manufacturing capital by exemption countries from 9 to 11 percent when compared to foreign tax credit countries, and that foreign investors from exemption countries are much more likely to invest in states with zero CIT rates than investors from foreign tax credit countries. Finally, Shah and Slemrod (1991) examine the FDI flows into Mexico over the 1965-87 period and test whether a measure of U.S. MNE foreign tax credit status affects FDI from the United States to Mexico. They find that in the deficit tax credit case, the U.S. tax rate, not the Mexican tax rate, affects FDI to Mexico. In general, however, both the U.S. and Mexican tax rates affect FDI to Mexico. Thus the empirical results indicate that neither view of the foreign tax system — as a de facto exemption system because of deferral and worldwide average or as a pure foreign tax credit system — provides an adequate description of the impact of a host country's CIT tax rates on FDI, and therefore the $MCF_u$ should be thought of as a weighted average of the MCF under the two systems.

The tax credit model in the third section also ignores the opportunities MNEs have to structure transactions among affiliated companies to take advantage of tax havens and other low-tax countries through transfer pricing and debt placement policies.

Finally, the model set out in the third section assumes that countries are either capital importers or capital exporters. Many countries, such as Canada, have significant levels of both inbound and outbound foreign investment. Tax policies are no longer simply dictated by a country's role as capital-importing or capital-exporting and have to reflect the fact that a country is both a capital importer and a capital exporter.

With these caveats to the foreign tax credit model in mind, we will review some of the literature on the impact of international taxation on FDI, transfer pricing policies and debt placement.

## FDI

OVER THE LAST 15 YEARS, a number of studies have found that international taxation has a significant effect on both inbound and outbound U.S. FDI. Hines (1999) has written a recent survey of this literature and concludes that a substantial number of studies have indicated that the elasticity of FDI with the tax rate is around –0.6. He further concludes that "the large response elasticity of FDI with respect to tax rates, therefore, may contribute to tendencies of governments to 'race to the bottom' with competitive tax reductions for footloose FDI" (p. 312).

Here we will briefly discuss a few of the empirical studies that either were not included in Hines' survey or have a special significance because they deal with Canada, Mexico and other countries besides the United States.

As noted above, Shah and Slemrod estimate an econometric model of FDI in Mexico financed by a transfer of funds from U.S. parents and from affiliates' retained earnings over the 1965-87 period. They find that flows of FDI financed by transfers and retained earnings are sensitive to the METR in Mexico (with elasticities of –0.79 and –1.5, respectively) and that the elasticity of FDI financed by retained earnings "with respect to the Mexican statutory tax rate is –0.56 and with respect to the differences in Mexican and U.S. taxes is –2.8 (all calculated at 1987 values). A change in the credit status of MNEs toward excess credit positively influenced their decisions to reinvest rather than to repatriate their earnings, with an estimated elasticity of 1.9 at 1987 values" (p. 485).

Devereux and Griffith (1998) analyse the location decisions of U.S. MNEs in Europe between 1980 and 1994 and find that a one percentage point increase in the host country's average effective tax rate reduced the probability of investment in the United Kingdom, France and Germany by 1.3, 0.5 and 1.0 percentage points, respectively. They also conclude that "the average effective tax rate does not play a significant role in the choices between producing in Europe abroad as opposed to either exporting to Europe or not serving the European market at all" (p. 363).

Cummins (1996) investigates how taxes affect the allocation of an MNE's production between domestic and foreign affiliates, and the degree of substitutability among the parent and its affiliates' labour and capital, by analysing the production decisions of a sample of U.S. MNEs with Canadian affiliates between 1980 and 1994. He concludes that:

> U.S. MNEs are able to substitute factor inputs between their domestic and Canadian affiliates rather easily, except domestic and foreign labour which are complements. The elasticity estimates imply that an increase in capital taxation that leads to a 10-percent increase in the relative price of domestic capital would lead to at least a 10-percent decrease in the steady-state ratio of domestic to foreign capital. This level of substitution suggests that countries may face increasing pressure on corporate tax revenues, as companies shift production to the lowest tax countries. (p. 26)

A study of Canadian MNEs with U.S. foreign affiliates by Altshuler and Cummins (1998) also concludes that capital invested in the parent and affiliate is highly substitutable.

McKenzie and Thompson (1997) analyse the differences between the user cost of capital in Canada and the United States for the 1971-96 period. They find that the user cost of capital (outside the manufacturing sector) is generally higher in Canada than in the United States, primarily because Canadian real interest rates are higher, but also because the Canadian tax system is less favourable for investment than the U.S. system. They also find that differences in the cost of capital have a small but significant effect on the relative investment rates in machinery and equipment (but not in structures) in Canada and the United States.

One of the most recent studies on the effect of taxation on international investment is by Grubert and Mutti (2000), who analyse how host countries' average effective tax rates affect U.S. MNEs in the foreign manufacturing affiliates' capital stocks in 60 countries. They find that the host country tax rate has a significant effect on foreign affiliates' capital stocks, with an elasticity of –3.23 when compared to the average effective tax rate for countries with an open trade policy, like Canada. They also find that the capital's responsiveness to the host country tax rate is lower in countries with more restrictive trade policies. In addition, Altshuler, Grubert and Newlon (1998) find that the responsiveness of FDI in manufacturing by U.S. MNEs to host country tax rates seems to have increased (roughly doubled) between 1984 and 1992. Their results provide further support for the notion that globalization has made foreign investment decisions more sensitive to international tax rate differentials.

Our selective review of the literature, combined with the more comprehensive review by Hines, indicates that a country's international tax regime and its average and marginal effective tax rates on investment have a significant impact on levels of FDI. Furthermore, these econometric studies suggest that as economic integration proceeds, tax competition for internationally mobile capital will be stronger.

## TRANSFER PRICING

THE TAX REVENUE THAT A COUNTRY GENERATES through its business tax system obviously depends on how the tax system affects capital investment and employment decisions. However, the tax system can also be affected by firms' financial and accounting decisions, affecting recorded revenues and costs. Through transfer pricing and debt placement, MNEs may be able to shift reported profits across national boundaries, and this may have a major impact on the tax revenues that a country receives through its corporate tax system. Here, we examine some of the issues and empirical evidence regarding the impact of transfer pricing. The next subsection deals with debt placement policies.

The prices that are used to establish the value of goods and services traded between related corporations are known as transfer prices. Through the use of transfer prices, corporations can "shift" reported profits across national boundaries by increasing or lowering the value of the goods and services transferred within the corporation. To maximize its global after-tax profit, an MNE, headquartered in a country that uses the exemption system or is in an excess foreign tax credit position, will want to increase profits (by increasing the reported revenues or reducing reported costs on intrafirm transactions) for its operations in low-tax countries, and reduce reported profits (by reducing reported revenues and increasing reported costs on intrafirm transactions) of operations in high-tax countries.[19] Such changes in reported profitability can occur without any changes in the MNE's geographic distribution of investment or output.

The OECD countries have implemented measures to protect their tax bases from profit shifting through transfer pricing, and firms now have to justify the transfer prices that are used for transactions with related parties. In biannual surveys conducted by Ernst and Young, MNEs consistently rank transfer pricing as the most important international tax issue facing them.[20] In setting transfer prices, Canada and other OECD countries have adopted the "arm's length principle" (i.e., the appropriate transfer price is the one that would be established if the transaction occurred between unrelated parties). Establishing the appropriate transfer price is often difficult because many of the goods or services transferred within an MNE may be unique, with no close counterparts in the marketplace. This is especially true of intellectual property such as patents, trademarks or special services like management.

In general, five different methods are used to calculate transfer prices — comparable uncontrolled price, resale price, cost plus, profit split and comparable profits.[21] Different transfer pricing methodologies will result in different allocations of profits between the buyer and the seller, and therefore different allocations of taxable profits between the home and host country on transactions between a parent and its subsidiary. Thus countries may have conflicting interests concerning which transfer pricing methodology to use.

Other factors, in addition to the efforts of governments to control or restrict the use of transfer pricing for profit shifting, may limit an MNE's use of transfer pricing to minimize its worldwide tax payments. First, transfer prices that are out of line with market prices may change employees' incentives concerning what to produce and how to produce it, leading to a less efficient organization. Second, a firm may have to change the location of some of its activities in order to take advantage of transfer pricing opportunities, and this change may lead to less efficient geographical organization production and sales activities. Third, if the foreign subsidiary is not 100 percent owned by the parent, then transfer prices that shift reported profits from the subsidiary to the parent are detrimental to the interests of the minority shareholders, as well as the host country's treasury. Minority shareholders may have greater access to information on the extent of profit shifting than the host government, and they may have legal recourse to unfair transfer pricing policies. Profit shifting may also lower share prices for affiliates and make profit shifting through transfer pricing a less attractive option for the parent company.

Despite these obstacles to transfer pricing, there is considerable anecdotal evidence that MNEs shift profits in order to reduce their total tax bill. Bartelsman and Beetsma (2000) cite the example of the German car producer, BMW, "...whose tax payments in Germany as a share of its worldwide tax payments dropped from 88% in 1988 to 5% in 1992 and −16% in 1993. BMW's financial director publicly stated that his corporation tried to shift cost to where taxes were highest, which was Germany" (p. 1). In view of the director's comments, it is not surprising that Germany has recently reduced its CIT rate.

While theoretical models and anecdotal evidence suggest that profit shifting through transfer pricing should be a pervasive activity, econometric studies have yielded mixed results concerning the existence and economic significance of transfer pricing. The empirical literature on transfer pricing has recently been surveyed by Newlon (2000), who concludes:

> A number of studies provide evidence consistent with income shifting by MNEs. There are, however, several reasons to be cautious about the interpretation of this evidence. First, some studies find evidence consistent with little or no income shifting. Second, firms and MNEs are heterogeneous in numerous ways that cannot be observed from the data and may confound the results of these studies. We cannot rule out the possibility that tax rates may be correlated with unobservable factors that affect the profitability of MNE affiliates. (p. 230)

We will focus on three recent studies that were not included in Newlon's survey. Bartelsman and Beetsma search for evidence of profit shifting by analysing the effect of tax rate differentials on the ratios of the value of output to labour costs in the OECD countries over the 1979-97 period. (Their hypothesis is that if MNEs engage in transfer pricing, the value-of-output to labour ratios should be lower in high-tax countries.) Their econometric results are consistent with this hypothesis and suggest that a 1 percent increase in the corporate tax rate for an OECD country reduces reported profits by 1 percent, so that with production constant, there is no increase in tax revenues. When the effects on production and investment are taken into account, the corporate profit tax base declines by 4 percent and leads to a 3 percent decline in corporate tax revenues. In other words, Bartelsman and Beetsma's results suggest that the OECD countries are on the negatively sloped part of the Laffer curve for corporate tax revenues.

Swenson (2001) searches for evidence of transfer pricing by analysing the prices of U.S. imports of manufactured goods from Canada, France, Germany, Japan and the United Kingdom from 1981 to 1988. She developed a transfer pricing model in which a firm's cost of using transfer prices increases with the square of the deviation from the (unobserved) arm's length price. (These costs reflect the resources that the firm has to use to implement and justify its transfer prices as well as any expected penalties imposed by governments in the host and home countries.) The model predicts that transfer prices from firms headquartered in exemption system countries should be proportional to the differences in the CIT rates of the United States and the home country, and decreasing in the U.S. tariff rate. She finds a statistically significant transfer pricing effect on U.S. import prices, but the overall effect is rather small — a 5 percent reduction in the home country tax rate would lead to only a 0.008 percent increase in U.S. import prices.[22] However, as Swenson points out, this import price effect was observed for total imports, which include both interaffiliate and non-affiliate trade, and therefore the implied effects on affiliate trade are considerably larger. Furthermore, there were significant differences in the magnitude of the import price effects across different industries, and in certain sectors such as automobiles (an important component of Canada-U.S. trade), the import price effect was considerably larger. Nevertheless, the overall effect on U.S. tax revenues from the transfer pricing effect on imported manufactured goods from the countries included in the study is likely to be very small. Obviously, the Swenson and Bartelsman-Beetsma studies reach drastically different conclusions regarding the economic significance of transfer pricing.

Hoffman (2001) investigates transfer pricing by analysing the tax to asset ratios of 94 Canadian corporations with an international presence (either as a Canadian parent with a foreign subsidiary or as a Canadian subsidiary with a foreign parent) over the 1987-94 period. He utilized (confidential) data based on the Corporation Sample File developed by Finance Canada. Hoffman hypothesizes that a firm's ratio of income tax to assets would be higher if the corporation had affiliate corporations in countries with CIT rates that were higher than in Canada, and vice versa. The regression equations that he estimates are similar in form to those estimated by Harris, Morck, Slemrod and Yeung (1993) and include various categories of expense, tax credit and debt leverage variables as control variables. The tax variables are entered either as the differential between the Canadian and the other countries' tax rates, or as a dummy variable indicating that the firm had affiliates in high-tax or low-tax regions (compared to Canada).[23] Both ways of entering the tax variable in the regressions produce similar qualitative results.

## TABLE 4

### ESTIMATED COEFFICIENTS OF THE TAX DIFFERENTIAL VARIABLE IN THE TAX-TO-ASSET RATIO REGRESSIONS BY HOFFMAN (2001)

| Country | Entire Sample | Private Corporations | Public Corporations | Canadian Parent | U.S. Parent | ROW Parent | Manufacturing | Non-Manufacturing |
|---|---|---|---|---|---|---|---|---|
| Australia | | √ | X | | √ | | √ | √ |
| Belgium | √ | | X | √ | X | | √ | |
| Brazil | X | X | | X | X | | | X |
| France | √ | √ | | √ | √ | √ | | |
| Germany | X | X | √ | X | √ | | √ | |
| Hong Kong | √ | √ | √ | √ | X | | X | √ |
| Ireland | √ | | X | √ | X | X | X | |
| Italy | | √ | | | √ | | | |
| Japan | √ | √ | √ | √ | | | | √ |
| Mexico | | X | √ | | √ | X | | |
| Netherlands | √ | √ | | √ | √ | X | | |
| New Zealand | X | X | | X | X | √ | | |
| Singapore | √ | √ | | √ | X | | √ | √ |
| Spain | X | X | | | √ | X | √ | X |
| Switzerland | | √ | | | √ | √ | | √ |
| United Kingdom | √ | √ | √ | | √ | √ | √ | X |
| United States | X | X | X | X | √ | | | X |
| Tax Havens | X | | √ | X | X | √ | X | |

Note:   A "√" indicates a statistically significant tax coefficient estimate consistent with tax-motivated transfer pricing and an "X" denotes a statistically significant tax coefficient estimate inconsistent with tax-motivated transfer pricing.

Source:  Hoffman (2001, 161, Table 5-26).

Table 4 summarizes Hoffman's results for the tax differential specifications. In the estimates for the entire sample of corporations, there were eight consistent coefficient estimates and six inconsistent estimates (including the coefficient estimate on the tax differential with the United States). The subsample that yielded results that were most consistent with tax-motivated transfer pricing was the 25.5 percent of corporations that were subsidiaries of a U.S. parent. For this subsample, there were 10 consistent coefficient estimates (including the U.S. tax differential coefficient) and 7 inconsistent coefficients. For the U.S. parent subsample, with the high-tax/low-tax regional dummy specification, 7 out of the 22 estimated tax coefficients were consistent with tax-motivated transfer pricing, and the only inconsistent coefficient estimates were for Africa, where, as

Hoffman argues, political instability and exchange rate risks could override tax considerations in setting transfer prices. Hoffman finds that a 1 percent change in Canada's tax rate could lead to a change in Canadian tax liability for a representative corporation of between $0.113 million and $2.280 million, depending on the location of the subsidiary. Although the statistical results are mixed, there is enough evidence of tax-motivated transfer pricing for Hoffman to conclude that "lower Canadian corporate tax rates would reduce the degree of income shifting, thus increasing the Canadian tax base…" (p. 127).

## DEBT PLACEMENT

FDI CAN BE FINANCED IN A NUMBER OF WAYS:

- equity supplied by the parent or an affiliated foreign subsidiary;
- third-party debt borrowed in the home country or the host countries;
- internal debt from the parent to the foreign subsidiary; or
- retained earnings of the foreign subsidiary.

These different ways of financing the FDI may lead to significantly different tax payments in the home and host countries and affect the worldwide total tax burden of the MNE.[24] In particular, the geographic location of an MNE's debt determines in which country interest deductions are made and in which country the income is taxed. These issues are of importance to Canada, both as an importer and as an exporter of FDI. We begin by examining the debt placement issues that arise from inbound FDI. Later, we examine debt placement issues arising from FDI investment by Canadian-based MNEs.

### Debt Financing of Inbound FDI

In our discussion of the debt placement issues on inbound FDI, we assume that the parent company is incorporated in the United States because it is our largest source of FDI and the U.S. government has adopted policies that have potentially important impacts on the debt placement policies of its MNEs. The U.S. government has adopted interest allocation rules which affect the foreign tax credits that U.S.-based MNEs can claim on foreign-source income. Detailed descriptions of the interest allocation rules can be found in Altshuler and Mintz (1995), Shaviro (2001) and Graham (2001). The current U.S. rules, which were enacted in 1986, allocate a fraction of the domestic interest expense incurred by a parent corporation to its foreign-source income. The fraction of the domestic interest allocated to foreign source income, $\alpha$, is the ratio of the MNE's foreign assets minus foreign debt to its worldwide assets net of foreign debt. The impact of the interest allocation rules depends on the tax credit position of the U.S. MNE.

If an MNE's average foreign tax rate is less than the U.S. rate, $u^* < u_{us}$, and it is in a deficit credit position, then the interest allocation rules have no impact on the firm's U.S. tax liability. The increase in U.S. tax on domestic operations (due to the allocation of interest to foreign source income) is completely offset by the reduction in U.S. tax levied on the foreign source income. An extra dollar of third-party interest expense reduces the MNE's worldwide taxes by the U.S. tax rate, $u_{us}$, whether it is incurred by the parent or by its foreign subsidiary (Graham, Table 3). Therefore, the interest allocation rules do not change the firm's incentives regarding borrowing by the parent versus borrowing by the foreign subsidiary.

If $u^* > u_{us}$ and the MNE is in an excess credit position, then the interest allocation rules increase the amount of tax that the MNE has to pay to the U.S. treasury, with no offsetting reduction in tax paid to the host country. An extra dollar of third-party interest expense reduces its worldwide tax bill by $(1 - \alpha)u_{us}$ if it is incurred by the parent corporation and by $u^*$ if it is incurred by the foreign subsidiary (Graham, Table 3). This strengthens the incentive (that exists in the absence of the interest allocation rules) for the MNE's foreign subsidiary to incur debt, thereby reducing the tax payments in the host country.[25] Altshuler and Mintz show that U.S. interest allocation rules raised the user cost of capital of U.S. MNEs on their investments abroad (by about 8 percentage points for Canadian FDI) and in the United States, when compared to purely domestic firms.

The empirical literature dealing with the effect of the U.S. tax system on the debt financing strategies of U.S. MNEs has been surveyed recently by Graham. Here we will only discuss briefly three studies that have a Canadian dimension. Hogg and Mintz (1993) analyse the debt and distribution behaviour of 28 Canadian subsidiaries of U.S. MNEs between 1983 and 1989. They hypothesize that because of the change in the interest allocation rules and the decline in the U.S. CIT rate in relation to the Canadian rate after 1986,

- U.S. subsidiaries would increase their debt after 1986;
- interest, management fees, royalties and certain other expenditures (cross-border charges) paid by the foreign subsidiary to the U.S. parent would increase; and
- retained earnings of Canadian foreign subsidiaries would decline and dividend payments would increase.

Their data indicate that the majority of Canadian foreign subsidiaries increased their debt and dividend payments, as hypothesized, but cross-border charges did not change significantly. Hoffman re-examines the Hogg-Mintz data on cross-border charges and finds that there was a timing response, with cross-border charges temporarily reduced in 1986 and shifted to 1987 in anticipation of the lowering of the U.S. tax rate in that year.

Altshuler and Mintz examine the debt allocations of 17 large U.S. MNEs between 1986 and 1991. They find that the debt-to-asset ratios of the Canadian subsidiaries increased from 0.14 to 0.48 for firms that were in an excess foreign tax credit position, while the Canadian foreign subsidiaries of U.S. firms that were in a deficit tax credit position for at least one year during the 1986-91 period increased their debt asset ratios by a smaller amount, from 0.21 to 0.42. Their regression analysis indicates that a 1 percentage point increase in the interest allocation ratio raises the ratio of foreign subsidiary debt to worldwide debt by 0.53 points for a parent with excess tax credits.

Jog and Tang (2001) examine the effect of the Canadian CIT rate on the debt-to-asset ratios of 388 large non-financial corporations operating in Canada between 1986 and 1994. They distinguish the firms by their ownership — Canadian-controlled (CC) or foreign-controlled (FC) — and on the basis of whether the corporation had foreign affiliates (FAs) or not (NFAs). Their econometric analysis indicates that the debt-asset ratios of Canadian corporations, especially CCNFAs, rise with increases in the Canadian CIT rate.[26] The relative sensitivity of the CCNFAs debt-asset ratios is somewhat surprising, given the usual emphasis in the literature on the flexibility that firms with foreign affiliates have in financing their investments. However, Jog and Tang also find that an increase in the Canada-U.S. tax rate differential increases the debt-asset ratios of CCFAs and FCFAs in relation to CCNFAs. This finding shows that the tax rate differential has the predicted effects on firms with an international nexus.

The econometric analysis by Jog and Tang indicates that the Canadian CIT rate and the Canada-U.S. tax rate differential affect the debt behaviour of Canadian-controlled corporations with foreign operations. We now turn to a discussion of some of the issues connected with the Canadian tax treatment of debt used to finance foreign investment by Canadian-controlled corporations.

## Debt Financing of Outbound FDI

Table 5 describes the basic features of the Canadian tax treatment of foreign-source income.[27] Here we will deal only with the tax treatment of the active business income of foreign subsidiaries of Canadian corporations. This income, if it is earned in a country with which Canada has a tax treaty, is classified as exempt surplus and is exempt from further taxation at the corporate level in Canada. The Canadian parent corporation can borrow to finance an investment in a foreign subsidiary and deduct its interest expenses from its Canadian taxable income, even though the income earned by the subsidiary will be exempt from CIT in Canada. Everything else being equal, the corporation will minimize its worldwide tax bill by borrowing in the country that has the highest tax rate, because this will give it the largest deduction of its interest expense. Consequently, the corporation has the incentive to borrow in Canada and finance the foreign subsidiary through equity if the Canadian tax rate is greater than the tax rate in the host country.

Canada has an extensive network of tax treaties, and in many of these countries — such as Barbados, Cyprus, Ireland and Israel — the effective CIT rates are substantially below Canadian rates, especially for non-manufacturing activities. Arnold, Li and Sandler (1996) note that Canada has no specific rules regarding the allocation of interest expenses, but this is a common situation. Other countries, such as Australia, Germany and France, have only limited rules regarding the allocation of interest expenses. The United States is the only country with a comprehensive set of interest allocation rules and, as we have seen, these rules are not entirely satisfactory from the perspective of U.S. MNEs or the foreign countries where they operate.

## TABLE 5

### CANADIAN TAX TREATMENT OF FOREIGN SOURCE INCOME

| Passive Business Income | Active Business Income | |
|---|---|---|
| | **Designated Treaty Country** | **Non-treaty Country** |
| Property income (interest, dividends, rents, royalties); if earned in a controlled foreign corporation; designated as Foreign Accrual Property Income . | Classified as exempt surplus; exemption system used; no further Canadian CIT imposed on dividends from a foreign subsidiary; PIT imposed when distributed to Canadian shareholders; qualifies for dividend tax credit. | Classified as taxable surplus. Tax credit system; the foreign tax credits are calculated on a country by country basis and are equal to the lesser of foreign income tax paid or the Canadian income tax payable on the foreign source income. Excess foreign tax credits may be carried back for three years and forward for seven years to reduce Canadian income tax. |
| Taxed on an accrual basis, with a tax credit for foreign taxes paid. | Canada has over 75 tax treaties with other countries; over 90 percent of Canadian foreign investment is in treaty countries. | |
| A controlled foreign corporation is one controlled by not more than five Canadian residents. | Based on the assumption that the foreign tax rate is equivalent to the Canadian tax rate; this may not be true in all cases. | Deferral is possible. |

Borrowing in Canada to finance investments abroad that come back to Canada as exempt surplus reduces the revenues generated by the CIT in Canada and effectively subsidizes Canadian direct investments in other countries. For example, consider an investment project in Canada financed by debt that requires a 20 percent rate of return to be profitable because it is taxed at 40 percent. A similar investment in a foreign subsidiary would only require a 16.7 percent return if the host country has a 10 percent CIT rate and if the interest is deducted by the Canadian parent.

Is the potential cross-subsidization of FDI a good thing? Although the research by Cummins cited earlier suggests that capital is highly substitutable between a parent and a foreign subsidiary, and therefore the implicit subsidy to FDI may reduce domestic investment in Canada, the relationship between foreign and domestic investment is often complex and likely varies from company to company and project to project. Devereux (1996) describe some alternative investment scenarios and the possible linkages between domestic investment and FDI:

1. A purely domestic firm spots a new opportunity in a foreign market. It is cheaper to produce abroad to service this market: no effect on domestic investment.
2. A shift in costs occurs, which makes it cheaper to produce a good abroad rather than at home: a negative effect on domestic investment — possibly one-for-one — with the rise in foreign investment.
3. A change in internalization factors makes it cheaper to produce abroad rather than to license a third party: no effect on domestic investment.
4. A firm aims to produce a new product which requires an intermediate good — for example, a design produced by R&D; the R&D takes place domestically, but production of the final good is cheaper abroad: a positive relationship between domestic investment and outward FDI.

Given the complexity of the relationship between domestic investment and FDI in other countries, it is difficult to say, in the absence of more research on this topic, whether the implicit tax incentives for outbound FDI lead to the expansion or the contraction of domestic employment and investment.

Brean (1997) defends Canada's relatively favourable tax treatment of FDI by Canadian MNEs on the grounds that FDI generates externalities (through the promotion of R&D and head-office activities), and therefore the social rate of return to FDI likely exceeds its private rate of return. While this is probably true in some situations (scenario 4 above), it is also true that some domestic investments generate beneficial externalities, and therefore it would be better to subsidize all externality-generating investments (if we can identify them) rather than provide relatively favourable treatment for FDI.

Given the uncertainties about the relationship between domestic investments and FDIs and the relative magnitude of their positive externalities, the Technical Committee on Business Taxation (the Mintz Committee) recommended that Canada adopt a "level playing field" approach, such that domestic and foreign investment receive similar tax treatment. The committee considered the adoption of interest-allocation formulas, but rejected this approach as either not feasible or potentially highly distortionary for domestic and foreign investment decisions. In the end, the Mintz Committee recommended the adoption of a "tracing" procedure (with a minimum threshold of $10 million of indebtedness related to foreign investments) whereby deductions of interest expense on debt used, directly or indirectly, to finance FDI would be disallowed. The committee recognized that strict enforcement of a tracing procedure is difficult, if not impossible, but felt that a limited attempt to produce a more neutral tax treatment of domestic investment and FDI was desirable. Furthermore, the debt placement issue provided additional support for reducing the CIT rates on non-manufacturing activities that the Mintz Committee recommended and the federal government announced in 2000.

## NORTH AMERICAN INTEGRATION AND FORMULA APPORTIONMENT

WHILE GLOBAL FORCES ARE AFFECTING the business tax system, the growth of trade and direct investment with Mexico and the United States will also shape our business tax system. As North American economic integration proceeds, with increasing volumes of trade in goods and services and direct investment among the NAFTA partners, business taxation issues will become increasingly important. In this section, we discuss briefly one of the business tax harmonization issues that will emerge as the NAFTA deepens Canada's economic linkages with the United States and Mexico.

At some point, we may want to consider whether the taxation of international business income should continue to be based on "separate accounting", whereby corporate profits are measured and taxes assessed on the basis of the geographic distribution of each unit's business, or whether "formula apportionment" should be used to allocate the North American profits — or even the global profits — of companies operating in Canada, the United States and Mexico. As we have seen in the previous section, transfer pricing and debt placement issues make determining the geographic allocation of income increasingly difficult, arbitrary and costly. As McDaniel (1994, p. 705) expresses it, "At some point, identifying what is 'U.S. income,' or 'Canadian income' or 'Mexican income' may be as irrelevant as identifying 'California income' and 'Nebraska income' became for corporations doing business in the United States...."

Since both Canada and the United States use formulas to allocate CIT bases among the provinces and states, it is natural to consider the possibility of using an allocation formula for the CIT base among the NAFTA partners.[28] In addition, the possibility of using formula apportionment has been considered to allocate the CIT base within the European Union (McLure and Weiner 2000) and to allocate worldwide corporate profits (Mintz 1998; Weiner 1999).

There are many questions that have to be addressed in evaluating the merits of switching to a formula apportionment system. What formula would be used? Who would it apply to? What would it apply to? Would formula apportionment apply to companies' worldwide or only their North American incomes? Would formula apportionment reduce the pressure of tax competition? Would it lower administration and compliance costs?

*What formula would be used?* In Canada, the allocation of a company's corporate tax base among the provinces (in which it has a permanent establishment) is based on a formula that gives equal weight to a province's shares of its sales and payroll. For example, suppose a corporation has two permanent establishments, one in Ontario and one in Alberta, with half of its payroll in Ontario and half in Alberta. If four-fifths of its sales are made in Alberta, then 65 percent — $(1/2)(1/2) + (1/2)(4/5)$ — of its total taxable profits would be allocated to Alberta. The corporation's provincial CIT rate would be $0.65u_{AB} + 0.35u_{ONT}$.

In Canada, all of the provinces use the same allocation formula. In the United States, the state governments set their own apportionment formulas, and four different systems are used by the 46 states that levy a state CIT. Thirteen states use a formula that gives equal weight to sales, payrolls and property, and 23 states "double-weight" sales (i.e., the share of sales in a state has a 50 percent weight, while payrolls and property each have a 25 percent weight). The other 10 states either weight sales by more than 50 percent or have an elective system (see Anand and Sansing 2000, 190, Table 1). The lack of a common formula means that corporate profits may be over- or under-taxed in relation to a common allocation formula, and it adds to compliance costs of U.S. businesses.

If the NAFTA partners were to adopt a formula apportionment system, it is clear that they would have to agree on a common formula to avoid the problems that are encountered at the state level in the United States. But what formula should they adopt? Unfortunately, economics does not provide much guidance on how to divide the "corporate pie", other than to suggest that the formula's incentive structure should maximize (or at least preserve) the size of the pie. Each country would presumably want the formula that would give it the largest share of the corporate tax base. Anand and Sansing have shown that if labour and capital are not completely mobile between jurisdictions, net exporters (like Canada and Mexico) prefer a higher weight on input shares, and net importers (like the United States) prefer a higher weight on sales.

Certainly, the adoption of formula allocation among countries has a large potential for redistributing the corporate tax revenues. Shackelford and Slemrod (1998) used data on 230 U.S. MNEs to estimate the impact on U.S. tax revenues of adopting an equally weighted sales, payroll and property allocation formula for their worldwide income. For this sample of companies, they found that U.S. tax revenues would be 38 percent higher ($386 million as opposed to $279 million) with formula apportionment. Shackelford and Slemrod did not indicate which countries would have lost revenue under formula apportionment, but given the importance of Canada and Mexico as locations for U.S. FDI, we can only presume that Canada would have lost revenues under this formula.

One might predict that if formula apportionment is adopted, the chosen formula will preserve the status quo allocation of CIT revenues among the NAFTA partners. However, subsequent changes in exchange rates could substantially change the allocation of revenues, even if the formula replicates the status quo allocation of revenues at the existing exchange rate. A decline in the Canadian dollar would reduce the share of tax revenues allocated to Canada, and exchange rate uncertainty would make corporate tax revenue even more volatile than it is currently. The adoption of an allocation formula would be much more attractive under a fixed exchange rate regime or with a common currency.

*Who would the formula apply to?* Under the Canadian system, the allocation formula is applied separately to each corporation on the basis of the geographic distribution of its permanent establishments. The incomes of companies with a significant common ownership are not jointly allocated under the Canadian allocation system. The absence of a unitary or consolidated reporting requirement means that there is still an incentive for profit shifting among affiliated companies if there are significant differences in the tax rates in the jurisdictions in which they operate. If formula apportionment were adopted among the NAFTA partners, it would be best to apply it to corporate groups with a significant degree of common ownership.

*What would it apply to?* Formula apportionment works best when governments use the same definition of the tax base. In Canada, there is a high degree of tax base harmonization because 7 of the 10 provinces use the federally defined CIT base, while the other 3 provinces that collect their own CIT have adopted tax bases that are very similar to the federal base. As a consequence of this high degree of tax base harmonization and the use of a common formula, the provincial allocation system is considered a model for other countries (McLure and Weiner 2000, 287). In the United States, there is less tax base harmonization among the states, but the system works reasonably well.

With the growth of trade and integration of capital markets, there is increasing pressure on governments and regulatory bodies to adopt common accounting standards. If the NAFTA partners were to adopt formula apportionment, it would produce even greater pressures for harmonization of accounting standards and definition of tax bases. Given the relative sizes of the U.S., Canadian and Mexican economies, harmonization will in effect mean that Canada and Mexico will adopt U.S. accounting conventions and tax base definitions.

*Would formula apportionment apply to companies' worldwide or only their North American incomes?* In light of the opposition of European countries to California's attempt to tax the worldwide profits of corporations, it is likely that only the latter could be implemented.

*Would formula apportionment reduce the pressure of tax competition?* While formula apportionment might reduce the incentive for companies to use debt placement to shift profits among their North American operations, formula apportionment and unitary assessment would not entirely eliminate the incentive to use transfer pricing. For example, transfer prices could be used to increase the reported sales revenues from the country with the lowest tax rates, especially for exports from North America.

With formula apportionment, there are still strong competitive pressures to have the same or lower tax rates as in other jurisdictions, because the allocation formula converts the CIT into a tax on employment, sales and investment in jurisdictions with above-average tax rates and a subsidy for employment, sales and investment in jurisdictions with below-average tax rates (McLure 1980; Dahlby 2000). For example, if Canada had a higher tax rate than the United States or Mexico, the cost of hiring an additional worker in Canada would be equal to the Canadian wage rate plus the increase in taxes that the firm has to pay as a result of having more of its taxes attributed to Canada because its Canadian payroll has gone up. The cost of hiring an additional worker in Mexico or the United States would be the wage rate less the reduction in tax resulting from increasing the share of its profits attributed to a low-tax jurisdiction. With formula apportionment, jurisdictions feel the pressure of tax competition through its impact on a firm's average tax rates as well as through the mobility of capital and labour. Consequently, the pressures for tax rate competition might be greater under formula apportionment than under separate accounting.

In addition, there would be more scope to export taxes, for example, by increasing the use of taxes that are deductible from the CIT base. This might distort the tax policies of the federal governments in Canada, Mexico and the United States. However, formula apportionment would remove the need for withholding taxes on interest, dividends and royalties within North America.

This would eliminate some of the capital market distortions created by with-holding taxes.

*Would formula apportionment lower administration and compliance costs?* As we have seen, formula apportionment would reduce, but not eliminate, an MNE's incentive to use transfer pricing and debt placement to shift profits among its North American affiliates. The magnitude of these cost savings, while difficult to estimate, would be one of the main advantages of adopting formula allocation for the North American CIT base.

# ENDNOTES

1    These CIT rates are the "headline" rates, which are the national CIT rates on re-tained earnings. They do not include subnational rates or surcharges which are important in some countries, like Canada. They are used to illustrate the changes in the CIT rates of individual countries and not to compare the level of corporate taxation in different countries.

2    Australia and Denmark reduced their CIT rates to 30 percent in 2002.

3    See Lyons (1996) for a description of the 1986 U.S. tax reforms and their impli-cations for international taxation. As Lyons notes, the 1986 reforms in the United States were largely implemented for domestic tax policy reasons.

4    This does not imply that the revenues collected from a CIT are not affected by the CIT rate. A constant tax rate may lead to a decline in the CIT share of reve-nue if other countries cut their rates, which leads to the erosion of the country's CIT base through declines in investment, transfer pricing or international debt placement.

5    See Department of Finance (1998) for a discussion of the factors that have led to the long-term decline in CIT revenues as a percentage of GDP.

6    See, for example, Gordon (1986) and Bruce (1992).

7    Many left-wing commentators seem to think that the entire return to capital is an economic rent, while right-wing commentators seem to deny, or at least overlook, the existence of economic rents in discussing tax policy.

8    See, for example, Huizinga and Nielsen (1997) and Keen and Marchand (1997).

9    All of the own and cross-price elasticities of demand are negative and $\varepsilon_{Lw} < \varepsilon_{Kw} < 0$ and $\varepsilon_{Kc} < \varepsilon_{Lc} < 0$ (see Keen and Marchand). This implies that the denominator is positive and the numerator is greater than or equal to zero. See Sorensen (2001) for a derivation of the optimal tax rate on capital in a model with imperfect capital flows between countries.

10    Only a thumbnail sketch of the model is presented here. A more detailed descrip-tion of the model is contained in a technical appendix which is available from the author upon request.

11 It should also be noted that the Damus-Hobson-Thirsk model also assumed that the demands for Canadian exports were not perfectly elastic, which provides another avenue for exporting the CIT burden.

12 The tax treatment of foreign source income has been addressed by Feldstein and Hartman (1979), Bond and Samuelson (1989) and Oakland and Xu (1996), among others.

13 This analysis ignores any loss of tax revenue from taxes on labour income or pure profits. See Gravelle and Smetters (2001) for an analysis of the incidence of a territorial CIT imposed by the United States.

14 These calculations are based on the assumption that the tax rate on capital under the exemption system would be 0.15. The higher the tax rate, the more likely it is that the credit system will be preferred to the exemption system.

15 The adoption of the exemption system has been raised in the United States in the context of "fundamental" tax reform that would shift the U.S. tax system to a consumption tax base.

16 Australia, Canada and Ireland receive over 65 percent of their FDI from Japan and the United States (Chennells and Griffith 1997, p. 85, Table A.1).

17 For a description of the U.S. treatment of foreign source income and an analysis of the repatriation decision by U.S. foreign MNEs, see Ault and Bradford (1990) and Hines and Rice (1994).

18 Excess foreign tax credits can be carried forward to offset taxes in future years, but future tax credits are obviously worth less than an immediate tax credit.

19 In setting its transfer prices, a firm headquartered in a country with a foreign tax credit system would only be concerned about the difference in tariff rates between the home and host country if it is in a deficit tax credit position, because all income is subject to the home country tax rate. However, deferral and the worldwide average of foreign tax credits may also create incentives for an MNE from a tax credit country to take advantage of differences in statutory tax rates in setting transfer prices (Swenson 2001).

20 See Ernst and Young. International Taxation. Available at: http://www.ey.com/global/content.nsf/canada/tax_-_international_tax_-_transfer_pricing.

21 See Hoffman (2001, pp. 18-22) for a description of these alternative methods.

22 The relatively small import price effect measured by Swenson may be due to the fact that many manufactured goods may not present the opportunities for profit shifting through transfer pricing that are provided by intangible property such as patents and trademarks.

23 Harris, Morck, Slemrod and Yeung use a similar high-tax, low-tax region dummy variable technique in their study of transfer pricing by U.S. MNEs.

24 In addition, the tax treatment of the MNE's FDI will depend on whether it is made through a foreign branch of the MNE or through a subsidiary incorporated in the foreign country.

25 Shaviro (2001, p. 33) notes that the interest allocation rules may export the U.S. parent's interest expense "even if the taxpayer is more highly leveraged (in relation to assets) abroad than at home...." For example, suppose that both the U.S.

parent and its foreign subsidiary have 100 in assets, 50 in (third-party) debt and 5 in interest expense. The interest allocation formula would allocate one-third of the U.S. parent's interest expense to the dividend income received from the foreign subsidiary.

26    Computations by Jog and Tang indicate that while a reduction in the CIT rate would lead to an offsetting increase in the CIT base as a result of a decline in firms' debt levels and interest deductions, tax revenues would still decline.

27    For more details see Arnold, Li and Sandler (1996).

28    CITs are not levied at the state level in Mexico.


## ACKNOWLEDGMENTS

I WOULD LIKE TO THANK KEN MCKENZIE for his comments on the first draft of this paper.


## BIBLIOGRAPHY

Altshuler, Rosanne, and Jason Cummins. *Tax Policy and the Dynamic Demand for Domestic and Foreign Capital by Multinational Corporations.* Working Paper 97-4, Technical Committee on Business Taxation. Ottawa: Department of Finance, 1998.

Altshuler, Rosanne, Harry Grubert and Scott Newlon. *Has U.S. Investment Abroad Become More Sensitive to Tax Rates?* NBER Working Paper 6383. Cambridge MA: National Bureau of Economic Research, 1998.

Altshuler, Rosanne, and Jack Mintz. "United States Interest-Allocation Rules: Effects and Policy." *International Tax and Public Finance 2*, 1(1995): 7-36.

Anand, Bharat, and Richard Sansing. "The Weighting Game: Formula Apportionment as an Instrument of Public Policy." *National Tax Journal* 53, 2 (2000): 183-99.

Arnold, Brian, Jinyan Li, and Daniel Sandler. *Comparison and Assessment of the Tax Treatment of Foreign-Source Income in Canada, Australia, France, Germany and the United States.* Working Paper 96-1, Technical Committee on Business Taxation. Ottawa: Department of Finance, 1996.

Auerbach, Alan, and Kevin Hassett. "Taxation and Foreign Direct Investment in the United States: A Reconsideration of the Evidence." In *Studies in International Taxation.* Edited by Alberto Giovannini, R. Glenn Hubbard and Joel Slemrod. Chicago: University of Chicago Press, 1993, pp. 119-44.

Ault, Hugh J., and David F. Bradford. "Taxing International Income: An Analysis of the U.S. System and Its Economic Premises." In *Taxation in the Global Economy.* Edited by Assaf Razin and Joel Slemrod. Chicago: NBER and University of Chicago Press, 1990, pp. 11-52.

Bartelsman, Eric, and Roel Beetsma. *Why Pay More? Corporate Tax Avoidance through Transfer Pricing in OECD Countries.* CESifo Working Paper No. 324. Center for Economic Studies, University of Munich, 2000.

Bond, Eric, and Larry Samuelson. "Strategic Behaviour and the Rules of International Taxation of Capital." *Economic Journal* 99 (December 1989): 1099-1111.

Brean, Donald. "Policy Perspectives on Canadian Tax Treatment of the Foreign Source Income of Canadian-based Multinational Enterprise." Working paper, Faculty of Management, University of Toronto, 1997.

Bruce, Neil. "A Note on the Taxation of International Capital Income Flows." *The Economic Record* 68 (1992): 217-21.

Chennells, Lucy, and Rachel Griffith. *Taxing Profits in a Changing World.* London: The Institute for Fiscal Studies, 1997.

Cummins, Jason. "The Effects of Taxation on U.S. Multinationals and their Canadian Affiliates." Working Paper 96-4, Technical Committee on Business Taxation. Ottawa: Department of Finance, 1996.

Dahlby, Bev. "Tax Coordination and Tax Externalities." *Canadian Tax Journal* 48, 2 (2000): 399-409.

Damus, Sylvester, Paul A.R. Hobson and Wayne R. Thirsk. "Foreign Tax Credits, the Supply of Foreign capital, and Tax Exporting." *Journal of Public Economics* 45 (1991): 29-46.

Department of Finance. *Technical Committee on Business Taxation Report.* Ottawa, 1998.

Devereux, Michael. "Investment, Saving, and Taxation in an Open Economy." *Oxford Review of Economic Policy* 12, 2 (1996): 90-108.

Devereux, Michael, and Rachel Griffith. "Taxes and the Location of Production: Evidence from a Panel of U.S. Multinationals." *Journal of Public Economics* 68 (1998): 335-67.

Ernst and Young. *Worldwide Corporate Tax Guide.* New York, 2001.

Feldstein, Martin, and David Hartman. "The Optimal Taxation of Foreign Source Investment Income." *Quarterly Journal of Economics* 93 (1979): 613-29.

Gordon, Roger. "Taxation of Investment and Savings in a World Economy." *American Economic Review* 76 (1986): 1086-102.

_____. "Can Capital Income Taxes Survive in Open Economies?" *The Journal of Finance* 47, 3 (July 1992): 1159-80.

_____. "Taxation of Capital Income vs. Labour Income: An Overview." In *Taxing Capital Income in the European Union.* Edited by Sijbren Cnossen. Oxford: Oxford University Press, 2000, pp. 15-45.

Gordon, Roger H., and Jeffrey K. Mackie-Mason. "Why is There Corporate Taxation in a Small Open Economy? The Role of Transfer Pricing and Income Shifting." In *The Effects of Taxation on Multinational Corporations.* Edited by Martin Feldstein, James R. Hines, Jr. and R. Glenn Hubbard. Chicago: NBER and University of Chicago Press, 1995, pp. 67-91.

Graham, John. *Taxes and Corporate Finance: A Review.* Working paper, Duke University, 2001.

Gravelle, Jane, and Kent Smetters. *Who Bears the Burden of the Corporate Tax in the Open Economy?* NBER Working Paper No. 8280, 2001.

Grubert, Harry, and John Mutti. "Do Taxes Influence Where U.S. Corporations Invest?" *National Tax Journal* 52, 4 (2000): 825-39.

Grubert, Harry, William Randolph and Donald Rousslang. "Country and Multinational Company Responses to the Tax Reform Act of 1986." *National Tax Journal* 49, 3 (1996): 341-58.

Harris, David, Randall Morck, Joel Slemrod and Bernard Yeung. "Income Shifting in U.S. Multinational Corporations." In *Studies in International Taxation*. Edited by Alberto Giovannini, Glenn Hubbard, and Joel Slemrod. Chicago: University of Chicago Press, 1993, pp. 277-308.

Hines, James R. "Altered States: Taxes and the Location of Foreign Direct Investment in America." *American Economic Review* 86, 5 (1996): 1076-94.

_____. "Lessons from Behavioral Responses to International Taxation." *National Tax Journal* 52, 2 (1999): 305-22.

Hines, J.R. Jr., and E.M. Rice. "Fiscal Paradise: Foreign Tax Havens and American Business." *Quarterly Journal of Economics* 109 (1994): 149-182.

Hogg, Roy, and Jack Mintz. "Impact of Canadian and U.S. Tax Reform on the Financing of Canadian Subsidiaries of U.S. Parents." In *Studies in International Taxation*. Edited by Alberto Giovannini, Glenn Hubbard and Joel Slemrod. Chicago: University of Chicago Press, 1993, pp. 47-76.

Hoffman, Michael. "International Taxation and the Income Shifting Behaviour of Multinational Enterprises." Ph.D. Dissertation, Department of Economics, University of Alberta, 2001.

Huizinga, Harry, and Soren Bo Nielsen. "Capital Income and Profit Taxation with Foreign Ownership of Firms." *Journal of International Economics* 42, 1-2 (February 1997): 149-65.

Jog, Vijay, and Jianmin Tang. "Tax Reforms, Debt Shifting and Tax Revenues: Multinational Corporations in Canada." *International Tax and Public Finance* 8, 1 (2001): 5-26.

Keen, Michael, and Maurice Marchand. "Fiscal Competition and the Pattern of Public Spending." *Journal of Public Economics* 66 (1997): 33-53.

Lyons, Andrew. *International Implications of U.S. Business Tax Reform*. Working Paper 96-6, Technical Committee on Business Taxation. Ottawa: Department of Finance, 1996.

McDaniel, Paul R. "Formulary Taxation in the North American Free Trade Zone." *Tax Law Review* 49, 4 (1994): 691-744.

McKenzie, Kenneth, Mario Mansour and Ariane Brûlé. *The Calculation of Marginal Effective Tax Rates*. Working Paper 97-15, Technical Committee on Business Taxation. Ottawa: Department of Finance, 1997.

McKenzie, Kenneth, and Aileen Thompson. *Taxes, the Cost of Capital, and Investment: A Comparison of Canada and the United States*. Working Paper 97-3, Technical Committee on Business Taxation. Ottawa: Department of Finance, 1997.

McLure, Charles. "The State Corporate Income Tax: Lambs in Wolves' Clothing." In *The Economics of Taxation*. Edited by Henry Aaron and Michael Boskin. Washington DC: The Brookings Institute, 1980.

McLure, Charles, and Joann Weiner. "Deciding Whether the European Union Should Adopt Formula Apportionment of Company Income." In *Taxing Capital Income in the European Union*. Edited by Sijbren Cnossen. Oxford: Oxford University Press, 2000, pp. 243-92.

Mintz, Jack. The Role of Allocation in a Globalized Corporate Income Tax. IMF Working Paper 98/134. Washington DC: International Monetary Fund, 1998.

Newlon, T. Scott. "Transfer Pricing and Income Shifting in Integrating Economies." In *Taxing Capital Income in the European Union*. Edited by Sijbren Cnossen. Oxford: Oxford University Press, 2000, pp. 214-42.

Oakland, William, and Yongsheng Xu. "Double Taxation and Tax Deduction: A Comparison." *International Tax and Public Finance* 3, 1 (1996): 45-56.

OECD Revenue Statistics. Paris: Organisation for Economic Co-operation and Development, 1999.

Shackelford, Douglas, and Joel Slemrod. "The Revenue Consequences of Using Formula Apportionment to Calculate U.S. and Foreign-Source Income: A Firm-Level Analysis." *International Tax and Public Finance* 5, 1 (1998): 41-59.

Shah, Anwar, and Joel Slemrod. "Do Taxes Matter for Foreign Direct Investment?" *The World Bank Economic Review* 5, 3 (1991): 473-91.

Shaviro, Daniel. "Does More Sophisticated Mean Better? A Critique of Alternative Approaches to Sourcing the Interest Expense of American Multinationals." Working paper, New York University Law School, 2001.

Slemrod, Joel. "Tax Effects on Foreign Direct Investment in the United States: Evidence from Cross-Country Comparison." In *Taxation in the Global Economy*. Edited by Assaf Razin and Joel Slemrod. Chicago: University of Chicago Press, 1990, pp. 79-117.

_____. "Free Trade Taxation and Protectionist Taxation." *International Tax and Public Finance* 2, 3 (1995): 471-89.

Sorensen, Peter. *International Tax Coordination: Regionalism versus Globalism*. Economic Policy Research Unit (EPRU) Working Paper 01-08. University of Copenhagen, 2001.

Swenson, Deborah. "Tax Reforms and Evidence of Transfer Pricing." *National Tax Journal* 54, 1 (2001): 7-26.

Thirsk, Wayne R. "The Marginal Welfare Cost of Corporate Taxation in Canada." *Public Finance* 41 (1986): 78-95.

Weiner, Joann. *Using the Experience in the U.S. States to Evaluate Issues in Implementing Formula Apportionment at the International Level*. OTA Paper 83. Washington DC: Office of Tax Policy Analysis, 1999.

Gerard W. Boychuk     &     Keith G. Banting
University of Waterloo        Queen's University

*14*

# The Paradox of Convergence: National versus Subnational Patterns of Convergence in Canadian and U.S. Income Maintenance Policy

## INTRODUCTION

DURING THE POSTWAR ERA, the welfare states developed by the Organisation for Economic Co-operation and Development (OECD) countries were highly diverse. In 1974, for example, social spending as a proportion of gross domestic product (GDP) varied widely, ranging from 8 percent in Japan to 27 percent in the Netherlands. Program structures also varied enormously, to the point that analysts could identify distinct models of social policy, each reflecting a different conception of the state's social role. Esping-Andersen (1990), for example, pointed to three models of welfare capitalism: a social-democratic Scandinavian model; a liberal Anglo-Saxon model; and a corporatist Christian Democratic model. Other analysts have suggested extensions to the typology, adding a "southern model" here or an "Australian model" there.[1] This very welter of categories proved a simple point: there was no defining model of the welfare state among OECD nations during the postwar era.

In the contemporary period, the pressures generated by globalization have raised questions about the scope for diverse social policy regimes. Do countries still have the capacity to chart distinctive social futures in an era defined by deeper integration of the global economy? Or are pressures for harmonization slowly leading advanced industrial democracies to converge on a common approach to social policy? These questions take on a special urgency in Canada. Public opinion surveys suggest that many Canadians associate their sense of national identity and collective accomplishment with their social programs. However, these same polls — and wider debates — reflect an underlying anxiety that increasing economic integration with the United States is narrowing Canada's scope for a distinctive social policy path.

This study examines this issue in the North American context. In so doing, it seeks to extend the existing literature in the field by examining several possible objections to previous research — objections that point to the possibility of time lags in the link between economic integration and policy convergence, or that emphasize the importance of supplementing studies at the national level with an examination of subnational patterns. The study therefore looks for evidence of lagged effects, and greater cross-border convergence when attention is focussed at the regional level. The findings provide little evidence of lagged effects, which raises doubts about arguments positing a slow but inexorable convergence of Canadian programs on U.S. norms. The findings on the regional level, however, are surprising — paradoxical, in fact: it is federal programs, not provincial ones, that show the strongest pattern of cross-border convergence at the regional level. This outcome challenges a number of pervasive assumptions about the role of national and regional programs in responding to economic integration in North America.

## THE SCHOLARLY LITERATURE

THERE IS NOW A SUBSTANTIAL BODY OF LITERATURE that is sceptical of the proposition that globalization is generating social policy convergence across OECD countries. Few countries can escape the need to adjust their social policy regimes to the new economic order, but differences in national politics still condition the way in which countries react, mediating the impact of economic pressures on the social contract. As a result, there is no reason to presume that social policy will converge on a single approach to the social needs of citizens.

The evidence for this conclusion takes different forms. Banting (2000) points out that social spending as a proportion of GDP in OECD countries continues to inch upward, and there is no overall pattern of convergence in the proportion of their national resources that different countries devote to social programs. Similarly, neither the detailed analysis of taxation trends in Olewiler (1999) nor the analysis of both taxation and public expenditures in Garrett (1998) find evidence of significant convergence across OECD countries. These themes recur in a variety of other studies, including Esping-Andersen (1996), Iversen (2001), Krugman (1996), Martin (1996) and Swank (1998, 2001).

This emerging consensus does not extend automatically, however, to a second form of economic integration — the emergence of regional trading blocs such as the European Union (EU) and the North American Free Trade Agreement (NAFTA). Europe presents a fascinating case. In the postwar era, the welfare states of Europe were especially diverse, reflecting the primacy of national political traditions on the continent that first gave the world both the nation state and the welfare state. Each of Esping-Andersen's three worlds of welfare capitalism has deep roots here; however, these historic differences are now challenged by a powerful integrative project. The political determination to build an ever closer union, the creation of supranational political structures, and the introduction of a single monetary regime and common currency have generated pressures that go well beyond those implicit in the global economy alone (Leibfried and Pierson 1995). It is, therefore, not surprising that there is stronger evidence of convergence in social policy within the EU than across the OECD nations generally. Social spending as a share of GDP shows a clear pattern of convergence, although it is worth noting that this pattern is as much due to considerable spending increases in southern countries like Portugal, Spain and Greece, as it is to the slowing of growth in northern Europe (Banting 2000).

Even in the EU, however, the depth of convergence should not be overstated. Convergence in spending co-exists with national diversity in program structures. The diverse social policy models across EU nations tend to respond differently to similar economic pressures. Despite the member states' adoption of a formal resolution in favour of a voluntary convergence in social protection regimes, a study by the European Commission could find no consistent pattern of convergence implicit in the program adjustments of the 1980s: "There has certainly been a convergence in the problems to be solved ... [but] there is no clear evidence of convergence of social protection systems in the Community of the 1980s" (Commission of the European Communities 1994; Montanari 1995). The 1990s witnessed more intense pressures, especially with the approach of monetary union, and there has been a trend toward more market-sensitive forms of social intervention across the continent (Rhodes 1998). Nevertheless, there is still no single European model of the welfare state on the horizon.

But what of the North American case? The NAFTA does not create the same depth of economic integration as the EU, and there is no prospect for supranational political institutions on the horizon. Nevertheless, there are reasons to anticipate that pressures for social policy convergence would be strong. Despite the mythologies woven around social policies by many Canadians, comparative analysts of the welfare state tend to regard the Canadian and U.S. approaches to social policy — especially outside of health care — as variations on the same "liberal" model of the welfare state. Moreover, the overwhelming dominance of the U.S. market and the deeply asymmetrical relationship between the two countries would seem to create especially potent pressures for convergence.

Despite these differences, the conclusions that emerge from previous research echo findings elsewhere. Studies suggest that the differences between the two systems, while perhaps small, do in fact matter (Card and Freeman 1993). Core programs like pensions and health care continue to evolve along separate pathways, reacting differently to common pressures. Convergence has emerged in specific programs, to be sure, the clearest cases being unemployment insurance and child benefits. Nevertheless, the overall picture is one of persisting differences (Banting 1997a, 1997b; Banting, Hoberg and Simeon 2000; Boychuk 1997, 1999; Skogstad 2000). Over the last two decades, social programs have been restructured in both countries; some benefits have been cut and some expanded. To quote from one recent survey:

> As the century drew to a close, the Canadian and American welfare states were as different as they were in the mid-1970s, the high-water mark of the postwar welfare state. The two systems have changed, and they are different in different ways than they were in the 1970s. But convergence is not the big story. In social policy at least, the conclusion seems clear. The border still matters. Distinctive cultures and politics still matter. The costs of distinctiveness may be rising, but significant degrees of freedom remain. (Banting 2000)

## POSSIBLE OBJECTIONS TO THE RECENT RESEARCH

THESE CONCLUSIONS ABOUT THE CANADIAN SCOPE FOR CHOICE might be called into question from two perspectives. The first objection, which might be labelled the "lagged-effect" argument, contends that the full logic of economic integration is still unfolding and that a pervasive pattern of convergence between the Canadian and U.S. policy systems is sure to emerge over time. There are two forms of this argument: the economic version holds that there is a natural sequencing in adjustments to integration (with the first wave emerging in industrial structures) and that pressures to narrow tax and expenditure differentials will build over time; the cultural version holds that economic integration will inevitably produce greater cultural integration between the two countries, as media and other linkages steadily pull Canadian attitudes more firmly toward U.S. norms. In this scenario, Canadians will start to bring more U.S. values into their own politics, and Canadian social programs will slowly come to resemble those south of the border. This objection is impossible to counter fully, as evidence of continuing policy divergence can always be dismissed simply on the grounds that the anticipated lag is longer. However, the potential objection does point to the need to update the analyses of both countries' trajectories.

A second possible objection is that convergence is not evident in federal programs or aggregate national social policy indicators because these are not the best places to look. A weakness of previous studies is that they have tended to focus on federal programs in the two countries, or to rely on some average program or a single statistical aggregation of provincial and state programs. This focus on federal programs or aggregate nation-wide indicators might miss important dynamics. There are several reasons to suspect that cross-border convergence would emerge earlier, and more forcefully, at the provincial rather than federal level. First, provinces and states have control over some of the policy levers that are most important in adjusting to increasing economic integration and competitive pressures, including programs with significant implications for labour markets. Second, both countries have recently decentralized authority over important social programs: decentralization widens the scope for interprovincial variations in the patterns of social policy development. Third, provinces have distinct economic structures and trading patterns, which generate unique pressures for policy adjustments. Provincial governments may be more sensitive than the federal government to the competitive pressures generated by cross-border economic integration and competition.

Thus, according to Courchene and Telmer (1998), provinces are tailoring their social programs increasingly according to the patterns that prevail in competing U.S. states, usually their immediate neighbours to the south. They write:

> It is time to view Canada as a series of north-south, cross-border economies with quite distinct industrial structures. British Columbia is oriented toward the Pacific Rim and the U.S. Northwest; the energy-based Alberta economy competes with the oil and gas producing regions of the Texas gulf; the breadbaskets of Saskatchewan and Manitoba keep a competitive watch on the U.S. midwest; the Great Lakes economies of Ontario and Quebec are integrated with each other and with their counterparts south of the border; and the fortunes of Atlantic Canada likely will increasingly be linked to the Atlantic Rim and the Boston-New York axis ....

> One of [the consequences] is that the manner in which a Great Lakes economy might want to integrate apprenticeship, training, welfare, UI/EI, education and the transition to work will likely differ from the way a Pacific Rim economy like British Columbia might like to forge the same integration ... the economy diversity across Canada's regions also implies policy diversity, the common term for which is asymmetry. (pp. 289, 291)

This second possible objection, therefore, points to the importance of examining two dimensions of recent social policy experience: the extent of variation in social programs across regions within Canada and the United States; and patterns of cross-border convergence at the regional level. A more careful examination at these levels may well blur the image of two essentially different welfare states co-habiting uneasily on the North American continent.

This study seeks to respond to these possible objections to previous studies. First, it looks for a lag effect by updating previous analyses of the extent of convergence in federal and nation-wide social programs in recent years. Second, it examines the provincial and state levels of social policy more thoroughly, in particular the extent of variation within each of the two countries. Third, it looks for growing similarity between the policy regimes of adjacent cross-border regions.

## METHODOLOGY

IN EXAMINING THESE ISSUES, the study focusses on income maintenance policy. This sector was chosen for two reasons: first, income maintenance programs ought to be particularly sensitive indicators of Canada-U.S. social policy convergence, as they are tightly intertwined with labour market flexibility and encompass several of the areas identified by Courchene and Telmer as being key to divergent responses to economic integration. Second, income maintenance is marked by interesting jurisdictional gradations. Some programs are exclusively federal in nature, including Old Age Security (OAS), the Guaranteed Income Supplement (GIS), unemployment insurance and child benefits. Others fall predominantly under provincial jurisdiction, and include social assistance and workers' compensation. The selection of income maintenance programs thus allows the study to explore whether there is a growing incidence of regional diversity and cross-border convergence as we move from federal to provincial programs.

The following sections undertake a broad quantitative overview of program indicators. A complete study would also require more nuanced, qualitative assessments of issues like changes in the detailed regulations governing access to programs, etc. However, this type of analysis is beyond the scope of this study. We examine four program areas — retirement income policy, unemployment insurance, social assistance and family benefits, and workers' compensation — and compare program evolution along three dimensions: Canadian and U.S. trends at the national level; the extent of interregional variation within each country; and the extent of cross-border convergence at the regional level. To keep the analysis manageable, the examination of cross-border convergence at the regional level focusses on two cases: Ontario and the Great Lakes states; and British Columbia and Washington. A partial exception to this strategy is in the area of retirement income policy. Because pension programs do not embody explicit regional variations (with the exception of modest differences in the benefit structures of the Canada and Quebec Pension Plans[C/QPP]), regional differences in benefits reflect regional differences in incomes rather than policy choices, and there is little to be gained by extending the analysis to interprovincial variations and cross-border convergence at the regional level. The analysis of retirement income policies is therefore limited to trends at the national level.

## RETIREMENT INCOME POLICY

PENSIONS, THE MOST POLITICALLY SENSITIVE of all income-transfer programs, have become the subject of intense policy debates and political struggles across OECD countries (OECD 1998). The demography of aging populations, the long-term slowing of real wage growth, changing family structures and shifting political doctrines have generated intense pressures in many countries. Governments almost everywhere have adjusted, refined or reformed inherited pension programs. Despite pervasive tinkering, however, governments have tended to respond to common pressures in different ways, so that pension programs continue to reflect considerable diversity, in defiance of occasional suggestions for a movement toward "one best practice" (World Bank 1994; James 1997). This continued diversity is driven by two powerful forces. First, pension programs represent a classic case of path dependency, in which past choices constrain future available options.[2] Second, the continuing vibrancy of domestic political traditions across western nations limits the scope for convergence, especially since political leaders often prefer the political cover of a relatively broad coalition supporting pension reforms when they include benefit restrictions (Myles and Pierson 2001; Myles and Quadagno 1997).

This pattern is reflected in the case of Canada and the United States. Both countries have reformed their pension systems during the last 20 years in response to similar demographic, social and economic pressures; yet, the pattern of change reflects divergence rather than convergence, as changes have tended to enhance traditional differences between the two systems.

The first divergence is in the role of public pension programs in seniors' incomes. In the early 1980s, the shares of seniors' incomes that came from public programs, investment income, occupational pensions and earnings were almost identical in the two countries. As Table 1 shows, the two countries have since followed different paths, with public programs playing a larger role in Canada, largely as a result of the maturing of the C/QPP.

Not only have public programs come to play a larger role north of the border, but the structure of these programs in each country also differs in important respects. Both systems can be characterized as having three tiers: a contributory tier with earnings-related benefits; a non-contributory tier of benefits financed from general revenues; and a tax-related tier that supports occupational pensions and private savings. However, the balance across the tiers — especially the first and second — differs significantly, with powerful consequences for retired citizens. In the United States, the dominant tier is the contributory plan, officially entitled Old Age, Survivors and Disability Insurance (OASDI), but commonly known as Social Security. The second tier consists of a means-tested benefit known as Supplementary Security Income (SSI), which is subject to very stringent income and asset tests and plays a comparatively limited role. In Canada, the contributory tier (the C/QPP) is smaller, and more of the load is assumed by the second-tier programs: the OAS, which until 1989 was a universal, flat-rate benefit; and the GIS, an income-tested benefit that supports low- and medium-income elderly Canadians. The relative importance of these tiers in the two countries is illustrated in Table 2.

The difference in structure ensures that public pensions have a larger redistributive impact in Canada. The power of targeted programs is critical to this pattern: close to 40 percent of elderly Canadians, including many who had average earnings before retirement and who have significant assets during retirement, receive a GIS payment. In the United States, the SSI has always had stringent income limits and requires individuals to exhaust most of their assets before they can qualify. As a result, it reaches only about 4 percent of the elderly population.

## TABLE 1

### INCOME SOURCES OF SENIORS, CANADA AND THE UNITED STATES, 1982-96 (PERCENT SHARES FROM VARIOUS SOURCES)

| Year | Public Programs | Investment Income | Other Pensions | Earnings | Other |
|------|-----------------|-------------------|----------------|----------|-------|
| Canada | | | | | |
| 1982 | 43 | 28 | 13 | 11 | 5 |
| 1984 | 46 | 22 | 15 | 12 | 5 |
| 1986 | 48 | 21 | 16 | 10 | 5 |
| 1988 | 49 | 19 | 18 | 9 | 5 |
| 1990 | 46 | 23 | 18 | 7 | 6 |
| 1992 | 49 | 18 | 21 | 6 | 6 |
| 1994 | 50 | 14 | 23 | 7 | 6 |
| 1996 | 49 | 14 | 25 | 7 | 5 |
| United States | | | | | |
| 1982 | 39 | 25 | 15 | 18 | 3 |
| 1984 | 38 | 28 | 15 | 16 | 3 |
| 1986 | 38 | 26 | 16 | 17 | 3 |
| 1988 | 38 | 25 | 17 | 17 | 3 |
| 1990 | 36 | 24 | 18 | 18 | 3 |
| 1992 | 40 | 21 | 20 | 17 | 3 |
| 1994 | 42 | 18 | 19 | 18 | 3 |
| 1996 | 40 | 18 | 19 | 20 | 3 |

Note: Public Programs include Social Security in the United States, and C/QPP and OAS/GIS in Canada. Other Pensions are private pensions, superannuation and annuities, including Railroad Retirement, IRA, Keogh and 401(k) payments in the United States.

Source: Statistics Canada, Survey of Consumer Finances; Social Security Administration, Office of Research, Evaluation and Statistics, Income of the Aged Chartbook 1998. Available at: http://www.ssa.gov/statistics/income_aged/1998/iac98.pdf

TABLE 2

PUBLIC SPENDING ON TIERS OF THE PENSION SYSTEM, CANADA AND THE UNITED STATES, 1999 (PERCENT OF TOTAL SPENDING/REVENUES FOREGONE)

|  | Canada | United States |
|---|---|---|
| Contributory Earnings-related Programs | 33.7 | 68.6 |
| Non-contributory Benefits | | |
| a) Means- or Income-tested | 8.8 | 1.3 |
| b) Universal or Quasi-universal | 29.9 | – |
| Tax Treatment of: | | |
| a) Occupational Pensions | 11.5 | 20.1 |
| b) Voluntary Retirement Savings | 12.9 | 5.2 |
| c) Miscellaneous Credits and Deductions | 3.2 | 4.8 |

Source: Data kindly supplied by Kent Weaver, Brookings Institution.

TABLE 3

RATIO (UNITED STATES TO CANADA) OF THE INCOME REPLACEMENT RATE OF PUBLIC PENSIONS, BY PRE-RETIREMENT INCOME LEVEL, 1999

| Pre-retirement Income ($) | Ratio |
|---|---|
| 10,000 | 0.55777 |
| 15,000 | 0.65659 |
| 20,000 | 0.78832 |
| 25,000 | 1.02996 |
| 30,000 | 1.05511 |
| 35,000 | 1.07566 |
| 40,000 | 1.12708 |
| 50,000 | 1.23460 |
| 60,000 | 1.34213 |
| 70,000 | 1.44966 |
| 80,000 | 1.53158 |
| 90,000 | 1.68636 |
| 100,000 | 1.87595 |

Source: Brown and Ip (2000, Table 3).

The redistributive impact of pension systems can be measured by calculating the proportion of pre-retirement income that is replaced by pension benefits for people at different pre-retirement income levels. Such calculations regularly show that the Canadian package provides greater minimum protection for the elderly, especially for those who had low incomes during their working lives. Contrastingly, in the United States, the emphasis is on actuarial equity, with a closer relationship between contributions and benefits at all income levels.[3] This is confirmed in Table 3, which presents the ratio of the income replacement rate in the United States to that in Canada. Although the two systems are broadly similar in the middle-income levels, the U.S. system replaces a smaller proportion of earnings in the lower-income range and is much stronger in the higher-income range. Moreover, these data understate the difference because they include SSI as part of the U.S. package; as noted above, many of the low-income elderly in the United States do not qualify for this benefit.

Over the last 20 years, both countries have reformed elements of their retirement income policies on a repeated basis, largely in response to similar demographic and economic pressures. In the future, however, these changes will be a source of greater divergence, not convergence. Although the deferred nature of some of the changes means that their cumulative impact will not show up in the data for some time, the direction of change in the two countries is clear. The most striking contrast has been in the balance between benefit reductions and increased revenues. In the United States, virtually all of the adjustment has taken the form of restrictions in benefits, the biggest change being the gradual increase — from 2000 to 2021 — in the age of eligibility for OASDI, from 65 to 67 years of age. There have been no significant general increases in the contribution rate since this pattern of incremental change began in 1977.

On the Canadian side, the balance has been different. There have been some modest restrictions in benefits, but the biggest change has been the phasing-in of significant increases in the contribution rate for the C/QPP. Admittedly, the contribution rate in Canada started from a much lower position — reflecting the larger role of non-contributory plans — and there is a convergence underway between the two systems on this dimension (Figure 1). The differential retirement ages and other features, however, are opening up a growing gap in the role of public pension benefits for average citizens. Moreover, a little-noticed default procedure written into the Canadian legislation in 1997 suggests that increases in contribution rates likely will continue to play a more important role north of the border.[4]

Nor should we anticipate a significant change in the redistributive impact of the two systems. Admittedly, the freezing of the level of earnings exempt from C/QPP contributions (at the 1997 level) will erode one source of redistribution in the Canadian package as a whole; however, the primary source of the redistributive difference lies in the contrasting roles of the OAS/GIS and SSI, and nothing indicates that this historic difference will narrow.

FIGURE 1

CPP AND OASDI, EMPLOYEE PAYROLL TAX RATES, 1965-2009

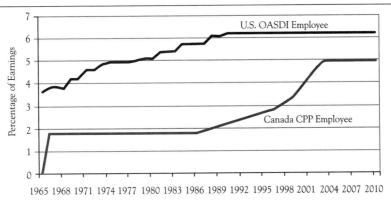

Another difference has grown in recent years. In 1997, Canada decided to invest some CPP revenues into equities through an arm's-length investment board, extending a practice first introduced by the QPP. Since the introduction of the QPP in 1965, the Caisse de dépôt et de placement du Québec has invested a portion of its funds in both direct and portfolio investment in Quebec corporations, establishing a model that the rest of the country has now adopted. In the United States, such a strategy is intensely controversial, especially on the Republican right (Myles and Pierson 2001; Weaver 2003).

With the exception of contribution rates to contributory programs in the two countries, the overall pattern in the retirement income field over the last 20 years is one of divergence. The differences are growing in the overall role of the public sector, the provision of retirement income, the age of entitlement to benefits, investment practices in the case of contributory programs, and redistribution towards the low-income elderly; and the changes already in place are not likely to alter these patterns significantly over time.

## UNEMPLOYMENT INSURANCE

IN CONTRAST TO THE CASE OF PENSIONS, there has been substantial convergence in the field of unemployment insurance over the course of the 1990s. Moreover, this field presents the first evidence of a paradox in the patterns of the income maintenance system. Although unemployment insurance is a federal program, it represents the strongest case of interprovincial variation and cross-border convergence at the regional level.

543

FIGURE 2

## UNEMPLOYMENT INSURANCE GENEROSITY INDEX, CANADA AND THE UNITED STATES, 1986-98

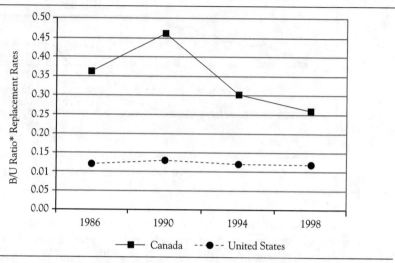

Note: For sources and methodology, see Appendix A.

## THE NATIONAL PERSPECTIVE: STRONG CONVERGENCE

WHILE THERE ARE BROAD ENDURING DIFFERENCES in unemployment insurance between Canada and the United States (such as the existence of maternity benefits in Canada, which are not available in the United States), there has also been strong convergence over the 1990s. To explore the extent of cross-border convergence at the subnational level, the analysis relies on an unemployment insurance "generosity" index, which is calculated by multiplying two elements: the B/U ratio (ratio of beneficiaries to the total number of unemployed persons) by the replacement rate (the average weekly benefits as a proportion of the provincial/state average weekly wage).

The major change has been in the B/U ratio in Canada.[5] Traditionally, the Canadian program provided benefits to a much higher proportion of the unemployed than did the U.S. program. However, a moderate increase in U.S. B/U ratios, combined with a striking drop in Canadian B/U ratios, has resulted in sharp convergence in the two countries' generosity index (Figure 2). Although changes in the B/U ratio are driven in part by economic conditions and changes in labour market structure, a significant element resulted from federal policy changes[6] (Boychuk 2001a; HRDC 1998; McIntosh and Boychuk 2000).

FIGURE 3

DISPERSION IN UNEMPLOYMENT INSURANCE PROGRAMS, PROVINCES
AND STATES, 1985-99 (BENEFICIARIES/TOTAL UNEMPLOYED)

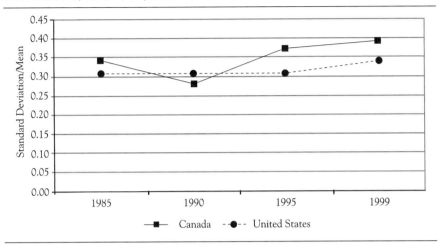

## THE INTERREGIONAL PERSPECTIVE: INCREASING VARIATION

NOT SURPRISINGLY — considering the operation of the federal Employment
Insurance program in Canada — there is little dispersion among provinces in
unemployment insurance benefits as a proportion of provincial average weekly
wages. However, dispersion among provinces in terms of B/U ratios is more significant and has been increasing over the 1990s. Interestingly, the variation in
the B/U ratio among Canadian provinces is now higher than that among U.S.
states, which has increased over the 1990s, though at a more moderate rate
than in Canada (Figure 3).

## THE REGIONAL CROSS-BORDER PERSPECTIVE: GROWING CONVERGENCE

A COMPARISON OF CANADIAN PROVINCES TO U.S. STATES reveals tremendous
differences in the extent to which individual regions have moved toward the
U.S. pattern. In 1990, no province had a generosity index lower than that in
any U.S. state, and this is still the case in Atlantic Canada. However, the number of states with higher generosity indices has increased in relation to all other
provinces, especially Ontario, Alberta and British Columbia. For example,
while no states had higher generosity indices than Ontario in 1990, 22 states
did by 1999 (Figure 4).

FIGURE 4

UNEMPLOYMENT INSURANCE GENEROSITY INDEX, CANADIAN
PROVINCES COMPARED TO U.S. STATES, 1995, 1999

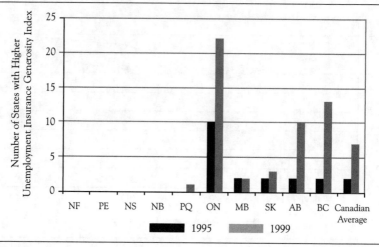

Note: For sources and methodology, see Appendix A.

FIGURE 5

UNEMPLOYMENT INSURANCE GENEROSITY INDEX, ONTARIO AND
GREAT LAKES STATES, 1986-98

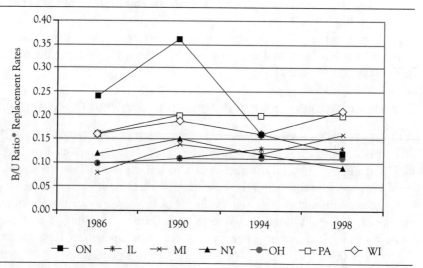

Note: For sources and methodology, see Appendix A.

## FIGURE 6

## UNEMPLOYMENT INSURANCE GENEROSITY INDEX, BRITISH COLUMBIA AND WASHINGTON, 1986-98

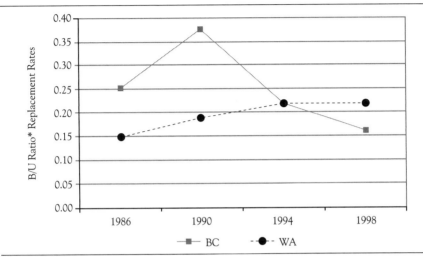

Note: For sources and methodology, see Appendix A.

Cross-border regional convergence is also clear. Ontario's generosity index was significantly higher than those of the Great Lakes states in the mid-1980s, and drew even further away in the late 1980s. By 1998, however, Ontario's index had plummeted to slightly below the Great Lakes states' average (Figure 5). A similar pattern is evident in the indices for British Columbia and Washington, with the B.C. index significantly lower during the late 1990s (Figure 6).

The pattern is clear but paradoxical. Unemployment insurance combines all three of the patterns identified in the introduction: growing convergence with the U.S. pattern, increased interprovincial variation, and growing cross-border convergence at the regional level. The pattern of policy development in unemployment insurance — a purely federal program — looks like what one might expect *if* it were a provincial program, and *if* provinces like Ontario and British Columbia were responding to competitive pressures generated in their respective cross-border regions.

## SOCIAL ASSISTANCE AND FAMILY BENEFITS

SOCIAL ASSISTANCE AND FAMILY BENEFITS constitute a field marked by complex patterns of distinctiveness and convergence. Once again, however, the patterns are paradoxical. Cross-national convergence is strongest in family benefits, which is dominated by the federal government in Canada. There is no strong evidence of cross-national convergence in program areas where provinces dominate, such as social assistance. To explore the patterns in this sector requires a separate examination of social assistance and family benefits, and then a look at the combined impact.

### THE NATIONAL PERSPECTIVE: CONVERGENCE AND DIVERGENCE

#### Social Assistance

Comparing social assistance programs is difficult in the absence of a qualitative examination of social assistance provision in the individual provinces. Data on expenditure and recipiency do not adequately control for variations in economic conditions, especially unemployment rates. However, focussing on benefit levels only risks overlooking important differences in access. This section relies on all three indicators, but these limitations should be borne in mind.

There is little quantitative evidence of convergence in social assistance programs in Canada and the United States. In terms of total expenditures, the broader trend since the early 1980s has been one of divergence. Expenditure differences did narrow at the end of the 1990s, but national-level differences were no less marked at the end of the decade than they were at the beginning (Figure 7). A comparison of the number of beneficiaries in Canada to those in the United States is complicated by the variety of means-tested programs in the United States. In terms of recipiency rates, Canadian rates historically fell between those of Food Stamps (a program with broad coverage but low benefits) and those of Aid to Families with Dependent Children (AFDC)/SSI (programs with narrower coverage but higher benefits). However, as caseloads have fallen more significantly in the United States than in Canada over the 1995-98 period, Canadian rates have come to approximate those for Food Stamps.[7] (Figure 8). Moreover, differences in recipiency rates may well grow further as federally-stipulated time limits begin to take effect in the United States, depending on how states use the discretion granted them under the new system.

FIGURE 7

TOTAL PER CAPITA EXPENDITURES, SOCIAL ASSISTANCE BENEFITS
(ENTITLEMENT PROGRAMS ONLY), CANADA AND THE UNITED STATES,
1980-98

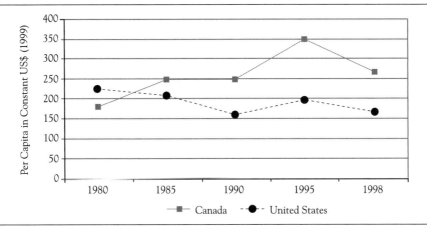

Note: For sources and methodology, see Appendix B.

FIGURE 8

TOTAL BENEFICIARIES, SOCIAL ASSISTANCE PROGRAMS, CANADA AND
THE UNITED STATES, 1980-98

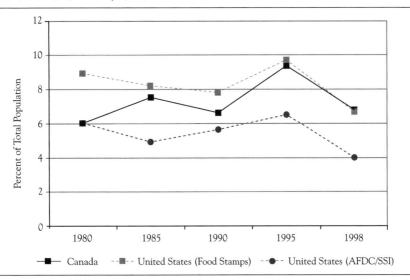

Note: For sources and methodology, see Appendix B.

FIGURE 9

EIC/CCTB, EARNINGS AND BENEFITS, 2000 (FAMILY WITH TWO
CHILDREN)

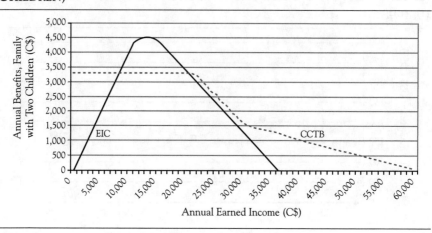

Sources: See Appendix B.

TABLE 4

COMPARISON OF THE U.S. EIC AND THE CANADIAN CCTB,
1993, 1998

|  |  | Beneficiary Families (per 1,000 population) | Total Benefits (constant 1998 US$ per capita) | Average Credit (constant 1998 US$ per family) |
|---|---|---|---|---|
| United States | 1993 | 58.6 | 67.90 | 1,066 |
|  | 1998 | 67.6 | 100.50 | 1,480 |
| Canada | 1993 | 107.3 | 158.80 | 1,865 |
|  | 1998 | 105.5 | 161.40 | 1,789 |

Sources:  Human Resources Development Canada, *Social Security Statistics* (on-line), Tables 106,
107; United States, *Green Book 2000*, Table 14-14.

**Family Benefits**

In contrast, there has been significant convergence in family benefits, which are
dominated by the federal government in both countries. Over the last 30 years,
Canada moved away from a universal family allowance program and established
income-tested refundable tax credits under the Child Tax Credit and, later, the
Canada Child Tax Benefit (CCTB) and National Child Benefit Supplement
(NCBS). (For an overview of these changes, see McIntosh and Boychuk, and
Boychuk 2001a, 2001b, 2002.) Traditionally, the United States has had no child

benefit program, but it has moved in that direction with the adoption of the Earned Income Credit (EIC). There are important differences between the EIC and CCTB: the EIC only provides benefits to families with earned income, unlike the CCTB; and the Canadian program provides support much further up the income scale (Figure 9).

The late 1980s and early 1990s did see a convergence in benefit levels as a result of the massive expansion of the EIC program. From 1985 to 1995, recipiency rates more than doubled and average credit amounts tripled, so that by 2000, the total value of benefits under the program was over eight times that of 1985, in real terms (United States, Greenbook 2000, Table 14-14). The result was a notable convergence in per capita expenditures and the average credit per family, as shown in Table 4. However, this convergence almost certainly began to fade again after the 1998 inception of the CCTB and the NCBS when the Canadian government began to devote more resources to the child benefit program (Boychuk 2001a).

Nevertheless, in comparison to the postwar period, when Canada had a universal family allowance and the United States had no such benefit, the two countries have clearly moved closer together.

### The Integrated Impact

The paradox of the conflicting patterns of convergence in federal family benefits and divergence in provincial social assistance shapes the combined impact of these programs in Canada and the United States. The levels of combined federal and provincial/state social assistance benefits for families with no earned income have not converged significantly from the mid-1980s until now (Figure 10). This is because the Canadian package for such families combines social assistance and family benefits, whereas such families receive no benefit from the EIC in the United States.

In contrast, there has been a marked convergence in income maintenance benefits in Canada and the United States for low-income families with some earned income (Figure 11). The domestic roots of convergence are found in two trends: most important has been the massive growth in the EIC program; however, a secondary factor has been declining real social assistance rates in Canada, since partial benefits can be received by some families with income roughly equivalent to minimum wage in some provinces.

FIGURE 10

SOCIAL ASSISTANCE AND FAMILY BENEFITS (ENTITLEMENT PROGRAMS
ONLY), CANADA AND THE UNITED STATES, 1986-99
(SINGLE PARENT, 1 CHILD, NO EARNED INCOME)

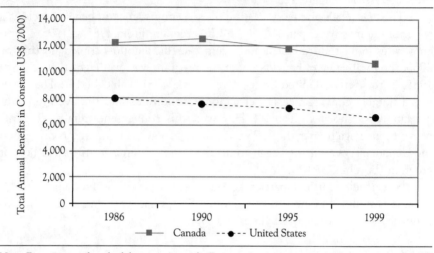

Note: For sources and methodology, see Appendix B.

FIGURE 11

SOCIAL ASSISTANCE AND FAMILY BENEFITS (ENTITLEMENT PROGRAMS
ONLY) CANADA AND THE UNITED STATES, 1989-99
(SINGLE PARENT, 1 CHILD, FULL-TIME MINIMUM WAGE)

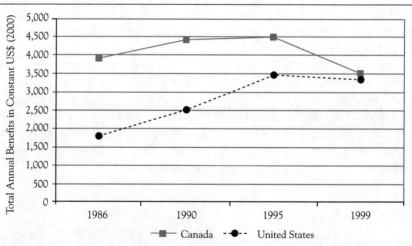

Note: For sources and methodology, see Appendix B.

FIGURE 12

DISPERSION, SOCIAL ASSISTANCE, CANADIAN PROVINCES, 1980-99
(EXPENDITURES PER CAPITA)

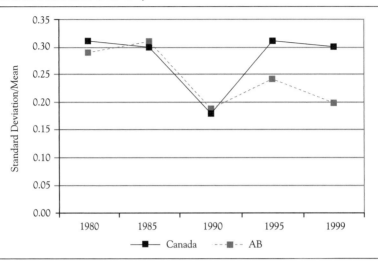

Sources: See Appendix B.

FIGURE 13

TOTAL BENEFIT EXPENDITURES PER CAPITA, SOCIAL ASSISTANCE
PROGRAMS (ENTITLEMENT PROGRAMS ONLY), ONTARIO AND GREAT
LAKES STATES, 1980-99

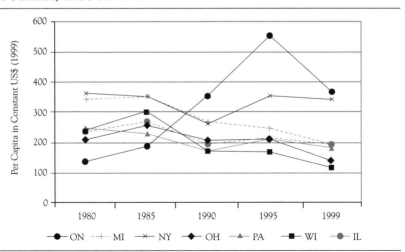

Sources: See Appendix B.

## THE INTERREGIONAL PERSPECTIVE: MIXED PATTERNS OF INCREASING OR DECREASING VARIATION

SOCIAL ASSISTANCE EXPENDITURES, benefit levels and beneficiary rates in the Canadian provinces show little evidence of a consistent pattern of convergence or divergence. For example, dispersion in provincial social assistance expenditures has varied sharply over the 1980s and 1990s, but is no greater at the end of the 1990s than it was in the early 1980s. Variation among provinces decreased sharply in the late 1980s as the two highest-spending provinces (British Columbia and Quebec) came to approximate the provincial average much more closely (Figure 12). A pattern of equally sharp divergence emerged in the early 1990s, driven in part by above-average expenditures in Ontario, British Columbia and Quebec. The most important factor in increasing provincial variation after 1990, however, has been Alberta's strong deviation from national norms in social assistance.[8]

## FIGURE 14

## TOTAL BENEFIT EXPENDITURES PER CAPITA, SOCIAL ASSISTANCE PROGRAMS (ENTITLEMENT PROGRAMS ONLY), BRITISH COLUMBIA AND WASHINGTON, 1980-99

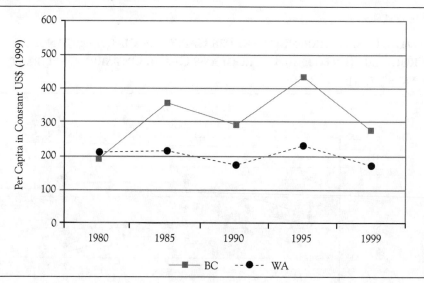

Sources: See Appendix B.

Variation in both provincial-only and combined benefit packages for families with no earned income has remained low and stable from 1986 to the present. Variation in provincial benefits for single-parent families with income equivalent to the Canadian average minimum wage is more significant, and has fluctuated considerably, partly as a result of changes in basic benefit levels and earning exemption policies in individual provinces; however, variation was no higher at the end of the 1990s than it was at the beginning. Variation in provincial benefits for single-parent families at full-time average wage is dampened considerably by the increasingly significant role of federal income-tested benefits, which comprise a significant proportion of total benefits at this income level.

## THE REGIONAL CROSS-BORDER PERSPECTIVE: MIXED CONVERGENCE AND DIVERGENCE

IN THE 1990S, the broad trend in both Ontario and British Columbia resembled something of a roller coaster, with divergence from their respective cross-border counterparts in the first half of the decade, followed by sharp re-orientations in the second half which offset much of the earlier change. In the early 1980s, total social assistance expenditures per capita in Ontario were below those in the Great Lakes states — but approached their standards throughout the decade. The province began to pull away sharply during the first half of the 1990s, only to fall again during the second half of the decade. Overall, however, expenditure levels in Ontario look less like those of its neighbouring Great Lakes states at the end of the 1990s than they did at the beginning (Figure 13). A roughly similar pattern emerges in the case of British Columbia and Washington: sharp divergence in the first half of the 1990s and convergence in the second half. Once again, these indicators of social assistance are no more similar at the end of the decade than they are at the beginning (Figure 14).

# WORKERS' COMPENSATION

OUR FINAL CASE, WORKERS' COMPENSATION, is a purely provincial or state program in both countries. Interestingly, there is no evidence of convergence in these programs; rather, the overall picture is one of moderate but continuing distinctiveness. There is some limited evidence of moderately increasing variation among provinces, but the patterns are not what one might expect to see, given expectations of provincial-level adjustment to U.S. social policies. The picture in Ontario is one of divergence, with maximum benefits becoming higher than those in most Great Lakes states — states that Ontario closely mirrored in the mid-1980s and early 1990s. Conversely, in British Columbia and Washington, there is striking convergence; however, it occurs from the U.S.

side, with Washington coming to approximate the relatively unchanged program in British Columbia much more closely.

## THE NATIONAL PERSPECTIVE: CONTINUING NATIONAL DISTINCTIVENESS

THERE ARE BROAD DIFFERENCES in the parameters of workers' compensation programs across Canadian provinces and U.S. states (Sullivan 1998).[9] The percentage of a claimant's wage used to calculate benefit entitlements is (again, with a few exceptions) uniformly higher in Canada than in the United States, and this difference has not diminished over time.[10] Similarly, differences in waiting periods — which are uniformly longer in the United States — have not diminished over time. Finally, some states have maximum benefit periods and/or maximum limits on total benefits, neither of which exist in the Canadian provinces. Differences in these program parameters have remained largely unchanged over the course of the past 20 years, and the overall pattern is one of continuing distinctiveness. Despite these differences, average weekly maximum benefits across provinces and states have remained very close in both countries in real terms, with differences hovering between 3 and 6 percent over the 1987-99 period.[11] Excluding medical costs — which differ markedly between the two countries — the total cost of compensation for work-related disabilities and fatalities has also been very similar in the two countries, in real dollar terms.[12]

## FIGURE 15

## DISPERSION IN WORKERS' COMPENSATION, CANADIAN PROVINCES, 1987-99 (MAXIMUM BENEFITS AND TOTAL BENEFIT PAYMENTS)

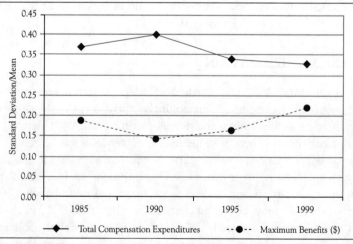

Sources: See Appendix C.

## THE INTERREGIONAL PERSPECTIVE: LIMITED INCREASED VARIATION

THERE IS SOME VARIATION AMONG PROVINCES, both in terms of the percentage of wages used to calculate benefits, as well as in the waiting periods for compensation; however, these differences are muted and, while there have been some minor shifts over time in individual provinces, this variation has not been increasing (Appendix C, Table C1). The evidence on program operation is mixed. Levels of variation among provinces in total compensation costs per capita (which are obviously strongly driven by labour force composition) have decreased somewhat over the 1990s (Figure 15). However, variation in maximum benefits (the more clearly policy-driven of the two indicators) has been increasing moderately over the 1990s. Thus, there is limited evidence of moderately increasing variation at best.

## THE REGIONAL CROSS-BORDER PERSPECTIVE: GREATER DIVERGENCE

THE PATTERNS THAT EMERGE when we examine Ontario and British Columbia in relation to their cross-border neighbors are not what we might expect. The percentage used to calculate benefits as a proportion of net earnings was decreased from 90 to 85 percent in Ontario in 1997, bringing replacement rates closer to those in U.S. states. At the same time, however, a notable increase in maximum benefits occurred in Ontario. While maximum benefits appeared roughly average among Great Lakes states at the beginning of the 1990s, Ontario's maximum benefits were the highest of all jurisdictions by the end of the decade, despite the fact that maximum benefits as a percent of median household income remained stable in all of the Great Lakes states (Figure 16).

A comparison with Michigan highlights the growing difference between Ontario and its closest neighbouring state, within the context of a relatively unchanging program structure. Neither Michigan nor Ontario have time limits or global benefit limits, although Michigan's seven-day waiting period is considerably longer than Ontario's one-day period. Both have relatively similar benefit determination schedules (80 percent of "spendable" income in Michigan; 85 percent of net average earnings in Ontario). As of 1987, maximum benefits as a percentage of median household income were lower in Ontario than in Michigan; however, this position reversed by the early 1990s so that by 1999, maximum benefits were over 25 percent higher in Ontario. It is not surprising that in 1998, total compensation costs per capita were over 36 percent higher in Ontario than in Michigan.

The workers' compensation systems in British Columbia and Washington, in terms of percentage replacement of wages and maximum weekly benefits in dollar terms, are virtually identical (60 to 75 percent gross in Washington; 75 percent gross in British Columbia). In neither jurisdiction are benefits time- or amount-limited. Per capita costs are higher in Washington ($196 in 1998, as opposed to $151). Together, these two jurisdictions have the highest overall compensation costs per capita in both countries. The similarities that exist between the two jurisdictions, however, are obviously not the result of harmonizing British Columbia's workers' compensation system to U.S. norms; rather, while workers' compensation program parameters and maximum benefit levels remained relatively unchanged in British Columbia since the mid-1980s, significant changes took place in Washington state. Between 1987 and 1999, maximum weekly benefits in Washington increased by just under 80 percent, in real terms (Figure 17). Thus, workers' compensation in British Columbia and Washington provides an interesting example of upward harmonization of U.S. social benefits to Canadian levels of social provision.

## FIGURE 16

### WORKERS' COMPENSATION, MAXIMUM BENEFITS, ONTARIO AND GREAT LAKES STATES, 1987-99 (PERCENT OF MEDIAN HOUSEHOLD INCOME BY STATE OR PROVINCE)

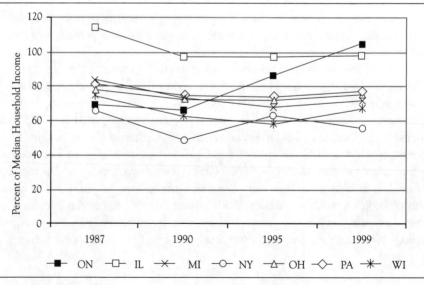

Sources: See Appendix C.

FIGURE 17

WORKERS' COMPENSATION, MAXIMUM WEEKLY BENEFITS, BRITISH
COLUMBIA AND WASHINGTON, 1987-99 (CONSTANT US$)

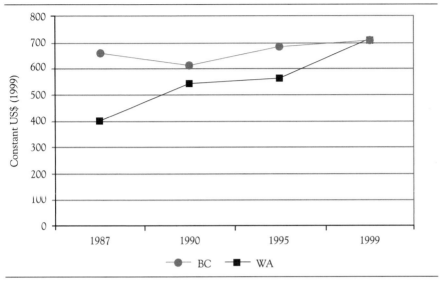

Sources: See Appendix C.

## SUMMARY AND CONCLUSIONS

THIS STUDY HAS SOUGHT TO EXTEND EXISTING RESEARCH on the extent of
convergence in the social programs of Canada and the United States. Previous studies have concluded that the large number of adjustments in social
programs in the two countries over the last two decades has not produced a
pervasive pattern of convergence. Although specific programs have become
more similar — especially unemployment insurance and family benefits — the
overall pattern is one of two societies adjusting to common pressures in different ways, and thereby preserving, or even enhancing, small differences that
matter. This study considers three possible objections to those studies:

1. There may be a lag in the impact of economic integration, and a pervasive pattern of convergence may still predominate over time.

2. By focussing on federal programs and national aggregates of provincial
   and state programs, the research may miss growing regional diversity in
   both countries that would qualify the image of distinctive approaches
   to social policy on either side of the border.

3. By focussing on federal programs and national aggregates, the research may also miss cross-border convergence at the regional level.

The study finds little evidence of a lagged effect. Recent policy changes have not reflected an increasingly pervasive pattern of convergence. The major cases of convergence identified in earlier research — unemployment insurance and family benefits — remain the classic cases. Recent changes in some major areas, such as retirement income programs, generate greater divergence; and differences between other Canadian and U.S. programs, like social assistance and workers' compensation, were as great at the end of the 1990s as at the beginning. As anticipated in the introduction, this does not disprove the lagged-effect hypothesis, as a more pervasive pattern of convergence may be just around the corner. At a minimum, however, the corner seems to be getting further away.

The most interesting findings relate to interprovincial variation and cross-border convergence at the regional level. Focussing on variation within Canada and the United States as well as between them does blur the image of two different welfare states co-existing uneasily on the North American continent. Nevertheless, the findings here are also paradoxical. Most commentary has emphasized the scope for growing interprovincial diversity and cross-border convergence in programs managed by provincial governments, especially in the wake of greater decentralization in both Canada and the United States. However, the strongest patterns of convergence are to be found in programs controlled by the federal government in Canada, unemployment insurance and family benefits. Changes in unemployment insurance — a purely federal program — approximate what one would expect if it were a provincial program, and if provinces like Ontario and British Columbia were responding to competitive pressures in their respective cross-border regions. In contrast, provincial programs like social assistance and workers' compensation show less consistent evidence of greater interprovincial variation and cross-border convergence. The most powerful convergence in these areas, support for low-wage families, is driven primarily by federal components of the system in both countries — child benefits in Canada and the EIC in the United States.

These paradoxes, if they persist, may prove important for our understandings of the processes of adaptation to economic change in federal systems. The propositions advanced by scholars like Courchene, about growing diversity in provincial programming and a greater provincial focus on cross-border economies, do not show up in our data. The findings reported here also have implications for our understanding of the Canadian federation system, and the distinctive responsiveness of federal and provincial programs to the regional diversity that characterizes Canada. To pursue those implications fully, however, is a subject for other studies and other times.

# ENDNOTES

1    See, for example, Castles (1989) and Ferrera (1996).

2    Mature "pay-as-you-go" pensions present the clearest example of path-dependent constraints on future change. Proposals for a shift to a funded program confront a formidable "double payment" problem; current workers would have to pay for existing pension commitments at the same time as they save for their own retirement.

3    For an assessment of replacement rates at different income levels in the two systems as they existed in the late 1980s, see Banting (1997a, Table 7.6).

4    Under the revised legislation, if the chief actuary of the CPP concludes that the plan is not sustainable, the federal and provincial governments are obliged to agree on needed changes. If they do not agree, contribution rates will increase automatically to meet half of the anticipated deficiency (phased in over three years), and indexation of CPP benefits will be frozen for three years. According to the Brookings Institution's Kent Weaver, this makes reliance on contribution rate increases more likely in Canada than in the United States, where in fact they are likely to remain off the agenda (Weaver 2003).

5    There are only moderate differences in the replacement rate between the two countries, which have remained largely stable over the 1985-2000 period.

6    For an analysis which attempts to untangle the effects of policy changes from changes in labour market structure, see HRDC (1998).

7    More recent comparisons of beneficiary rates are hampered by the lack of more recent state-level data on SSI. However, there is little evidence — considering the most recent national data on Temporary Assistance for Needy Families (TANF) recipiency in the United States and social assistance recipiency in Canada — that Canadian rates are converging on the U.S. average.

8    It is unclear to what extent this divergence is the result of deliberate policy shifts (especially in 1993) or unemployment rates that have tended to be significantly below the national average.

9    In both Canada and the United States, workers' compensation is largely a provincial or state issue (Sullivan, p. 214). In Canada, workers' compensation is provided by no-fault government monopolies. In the United States, there are a variety of forms of public, private and self provision, with only six states offering workers' compensation through an exclusive state fund (Burton and Thomason 2000). As Burton and Thomason note: "...in all North American jurisdictions, benefit levels and eligibility conditions are established by statute. These statutes also create agencies charged with the responsibility of administering the program." (p. 293)

10    In Canada, the average is between 80 and 90 percent of net, and 66 $^2/_3$ percent of gross in U.S. states. (We have not calculated equivalencies between net and gross percentages; however, judging from the use of gross and net incomes in state and provincial calculations, the Canadian net income parameters are likely equivalent to roughly 75 percent of gross.)

11    Measuring these benefits as a percentage of median family income gives figures that are higher in Canada than the United States. These differences have remained remarkably stable over time.

12    Burton and Thomason have developed an impressively rigorous approach to estimating the overall cost of workers' compensation in different jurisdictions. See also Thomason, Schmidle and Burton (2001).

## BIBLIOGRAPHY

Banting, Keith. "The Social Policy Divide: The Welfare State in Canada and the United States." In *Degrees of Freedom: Canada and the United States in a Changing World*. Edited by Keith Banting, George Hoberg and Richard Simeon. Montreal: McGill-Queen's University Press, 1997a.

_____. "The Internationalization of the Social Contract." In *The Nation State in a Global/Information Era*. Edited by Thomas Courchene. Kingston: John Deutsch Institute for the Study of Economic Policy, Queen's University, 1997b.

_____. "What's a Country For? The Social Contract in the Global Era." Working Paper No. 11, School of Policy Studies, Queen's University, November 2000.

Banting, Keith, George Hoberg and Richard Simeon. "North American Integration and the Scope for Domestic Choice: Canada and Policy Autonomy in a Globalized World." In *Capacity for Choice: Canada in a New North America*. Edited by George Hoberg. Toronto: University of Toronto Press, 2000, pp. 252-98.

Boychuk, Gerard W. "Are Canadian and U.S. Social Assistance Policies Converging?" *Canadian-American Public Policy* 30 (July 1997): 1-55.

_____. "Resemblance and Relief: Social Assistance Provision in the American States and Canadian Provinces." *American Review of Canadian Studies* 29, 2 (Summer 1999): 259-85.

_____. "Aiming for the Middle: Challenges to Federal Income Maintenance Policy." In *How Ottawa Spends, 2001-2002: Power in Transition*. Edited by Leslie A. Pal. Don Mills: Oxford University Press, 2001a, pp. 123-44.

_____. "À la remorque de l'OCDE ? Sécurité du revenu et valorisation du travail au Canada et aux États-Unis." *Lien social et Politiques* 45 (2001b): 41-53.

_____. "Social Union, Social Assistance: An Assessment." In *Perspectives and Directions: The Social Union Framework*. Edited by Tom McIntosh. Regina: Canada Plains Research Centre, 2002, pp. 51-67.

Brown, Robert, and Jeffrey Ip. "Social Security — Adequacy, Equity, and Progressiveness: A Review of Criteria Based on Experience in Canada and the United States." *North American Actuarial Journal* 4, 1 (2000): 1-19.

Burton, Jr., John F., and Terry Thomason. "The Cost of Workers' Compensation in Ontario and British Columbia." In *Workers' Compensation: Foundations for Reform*. Edited by Morley Gunderson and Douglas Hyatt. Toronto: University of Toronto Press, 2000.

Card, David, and Richard B. Freeman. "Introduction." In *Small Differences that Matter: Labor Markets and Income Maintenance in Canada and the United States*. Edited by David Card and Richard B. Freeman. Chicago: University of Chicago Press, 1993.

Castles, F.G. "Social Protection by Other Means: Australia's Strategy of Coping with External Vulnerability." In *The Comparative History of Public Policy*. Edited by F.G. Castles. Cambridge: Polity Press, 1989, pp. 16-55.

Commission of the European Communities. *Social Protection in Europe: 1993*. Luxembourg: Office of the Official Publications of the European Communities, 1994.

Courchene, Thomas, and Colin Telmer. *From Heartland to North American Region State*. Toronto: Centre for Public Management, Faculty of Management, University of Toronto, 1998.

Esping-Andersen, Gøsta. *The Three Worlds of Welfare Capitalism*. Princeton NJ: Princeton University Press, 1990.

_____. Editor. *Welfare States in Transition: National Adaptations in Global Economies*. London: Sage, 1996.

Ferrera, Maurizio. "The Southern Model of Welfare in Social Europe." *Journal of European Social Policy* 6, 1 (1996): 17-37.

Garrett, Geoffrey. "Global Markets and National Politics: Collision Course or Virtuous Circle?" *International Organization* 52 (1998): 787-824.

Human Resources Development Canada. *1998 Employment Insurance Monitoring and Assessment Report*. 1998. Available at: http://www.hrdc-drhc.gc.ca/ei/employ/sp121898/sum.shtml.

Iversen, Thorben. "The Dynamics of Welfare State Expansion: Trade Openness, De-industrialization, and Partisan Politics." In *The Politics of the Welfare State*. Edited by Paul Pierson. Oxford: Oxford University Press, 2001, pp. 45-79.

James, Estelle. "Canada's Old Age Crisis in International Perspective." In *Reform of Retirement Income Policy: International and Canadian Perspectives*. Edited by Keith Banting and Robin Boadway. Kingston: School of Policy Studies, Queen's University, 1997, pp. 29-48.

Krugman, Paul. *Pop Internationalism*. Cambridge, MA: MIT Press, 1996.

Leibfried, Stephan, and Paul Pierson. "Semisovereign Welfare States: Social Policy in a Multitiered Europe." In *European Social Policy: Between Fragmentation and Integration*. Edited by Stephan Leibfried and Paul Pierson. Washington, DC: Brookings Institution, 1995, pp. 43-77.

Martin, Andrew. *What Does Globalization Have to Do with the Erosion of the Welfare State: Sorting Out the Ideas*. Program for the Study of Germany and Europe, Working Paper Series No. 7.5, Harvard University Center for European Studies, 1996.

McIntosh, Tom, and Gerard W. Boychuk. "Dis-Covered: EI, Social Assistance and the Growing Gap in Income Support for Unemployed Canadians." In *Federalism, Democracy and Labour Market Policy in Canada*. Edited by Tom McIntosh. Montreal and Kingston: McGill-Queen's University Press, 2000, pp. 65-159.

Montanari, B. "Harmonization of Social Policies and Social Regulation in the European Community." *European Journal of Political Research 27*, 1 (1995): 21-45.

Myles, John, and Paul Pierson. "The Comparative Political Economy of Pension Reform." In *The New Politics of the Welfare State*. Edited by Paul Pierson. Oxford: Oxford University Press, 2001, pp. 305-33.

Myles, John, and Jill Quadagno. "Recent Trends in Pension Policy Reform: A Comparative View." In *Reform of Retirement Income Policy: International and Canadian Perspectives*. Edited by Keith Banting and Robin Boadway. Kingston: School of Policy Studies, Queen's University, 1997, pp. 247-71.

OECD. *Maintaining Prosperity in an Aging Society*. Paris: OECD, 1998.

_____. PPP Web site. Available at: http:/www.oecd.org/std/ppp/pps.htm.

Olewiler, Nancy. "National Tax Policy for an International Economy: Divergence in a Converging World." In *Room for Manoeuvre? Globalization and Policy Convergence*. Edited by Thomas Courchene. Kingston: John Deutsch Institute for the Study of Economic Policy, Queen's University, 1999.

Rhodes, Martin. "Subversive Liberalism: Market Integration, Globalization and West European Welfare States." In *Regionalism and Global Economic Integration: Europe, Asia and the Americas*. Edited by William Coleman and Geoffrey Underhill. London and New York: Routledge, 1998.

Skogstad, Grace. "Globalization and Public Policy: Situating Canadian Analyses." *Canadian Journal of Political Science 33*, 4 (2000): 805-28.

Sullivan, Terry. "Outcome Research: Payer and Provider Applications in Canada and the United States." In *Integrated Health Management*. Edited by Jeffrey S. Harris and Ronal R. Loeppke. Washington: American College of Occupational and Environmental Medicine, 1998.

Swank, Duane. "Funding the Welfare State: Globalization and the Taxation of Business in Advanced Market Economies." *Political Studies 46*, 4 (1998): 671-92.

_____. "Political Institutions and Welfare State Restructuring: The Impact of Institutions on Social Policy Change in Developed Democracies." In *The New Politics of the Welfare State*. Edited by Paul Pierson. Oxford: Oxford University Press, 2001.

Thomason, Terry, Timothy P. Schmidle and John F. Burton, Jr. *Workers' Compensation: Benefits, Costs and Safety Under Alternative Insurance Arrangements*. Kalamazoo MI: W.E. Upjohn Institute for Employment Research, 2001.

United States House of Representatives, Committee on Ways and Means. *Greenbook: Overview of Entitlement Programs*. Washington: Government Printing Office, 1992, 1996, 2000.

Weaver, R. Kent. "Cutting Old-Age Pensions." In *The Government Taketh Away: The Politics of Pain in the United States and Canada*. Edited by Leslie Pal and R. Kent Weaver. Washington DC: Georgetown University Press, 2003 pp. 41-70.

World Bank. *Averting the Old Age Crisis: Policies to Protect the Old and Promote Growth.* Washington: World Bank and Oxford University Press, 1994.

# APPENDIX A

# UNEMPLOYMENT INSURANCE AND MISCELLANEOUS DATA

## MISCELLANEOUS DATA USED IN AUTHORS' CALCULATIONS

### Purchasing Power Parities

All purchasing power parities (PPPs) are taken from the OECD's *PPPs for GDP- Historical series,* in downloadable MS-Excel format from the OECD PPP site. Available at: http:/www.oecd.org/std/ppp/pps.htm.

### Real Dollar Deflators

All values in U.S. real dollars are calculated using U.S. CPI-U, as reported in Table No. 768, Consumer Price Indexes (CPI-U) by Major Groups, 1980-1999, United States, Census Bureau, *Statistical Abstract of the United States,* 2000. All values in Canadian real dollars are calculated using CANSIM CPI (label D28608), accessed electronically. Available at:
http://datacentre.chass.utoronto.ca/cansim/search.html#retrieve.

### Population

All U.S. population figures are taken from United States, Census Bureau, *Statistical Abstract of the United States,* 2000, Table 20. Resident Population by State: 1980-1999. All Canadian population figures are taken from Statistics Canada, *Canada Year Book 2000,* Table 3.9 — Population by Age, Canada, the Provinces and Territories.

### Median Household Income

United States: Census Bureau, *Statistical Abstract of the United States,* 2000, Table 742—Median Income by State in Constant (1998) Dollars: 1988-1998. Canada: Statistics Canada, *Income Distribution by Size,* various years. Cat. 13-207-XPB. Table 34 — Percentage Distribution of Families and Unattached

Individuals by Income Groups and Provinces. (Table includes median income for all households by province.)

## UNEMPLOYMENT INSURANCE CALCULATIONS

### B/U Ratios

Calculated by authors, following methodology in Canada, Human Resources Development Canada, *1998 Employment Insurance Monitoring and Assessment Report*. Available at:
http://www.hrdc-drhc.gc.ca/ei/employ/sp121898/sum.shtml.

### Unemployment Insurance Generosity Index

Calculated by authors. B/U ratio (as above) multiplied by unemployment insurance replacement rates (average weekly benefits/average weekly wage). See sources below.

## UNEMPLOYMENT INSURANCE SOURCES

### United States, Total Number of Unemployed

United States, Census Bureau, *Statistical Abstract of the United States*, 2000, Table 680—Total Unemployed and Insured Unemployed by State: 1980-1999.

### United States, Average Weekly Unemployment Insurance Benefits and Total Unemployment Insurance Beneficiaries

United States, Census Bureau, *Statistical Abstract of the United States*, Table —State Unemployment Insurance, by State and Other Areas, various years.

### United States, Average Weekly Wage

United States, Department of Labour, *ET Handbook No. 394*. Available at:
http://www.workeforcesecurity.doleta.gov/external/lpext.dll/HB/HB%2039/lnk 75.html.

### Canada, Total Number of Unemployed

CANSIM. Electronic Access. Unemployment/15+/Annual Averages, Series: D984892, D985286, D985568, D985850, D986132, D986414, D986696, D986978, D987260, D987542, D987824.

### Canada, Total Number of Beneficiaries

Canada, Human Resources Development Canada, *Social Security Statistics: Canada and the Provinces, 1974/75 to 1998/99*, Table 223 — Employment/Unemployment Insurance, Annual Average Number of Regular Beneficiaries, by Province and for Canada, Fiscal Years ending March 31, 1974-75 to 1998-99.

### Canada, Average Weekly Unemployment Insurance Benefits

CANSIM, Labels D730479-730489, electronic access.

### Canada, Average Weekly Earnings

Statistics Canada, *Employment, Earnings and Hours, 2000*. Cat. 72-002-XPB. Table 9 — Average Weekly Earnings, All Employees, Industrial Aggregate.


# APPENDIX B

# SOCIAL ASSISTANCE AND FAMILY BENEFITS — METHODOLOGY

## TOTAL EXPENDITURE AND BENEFICIARY COMPARISONS

### Canada

Comparisons of social assistance expenditures are based on data for provincial and municipal social assistance benefit expenditures. For years prior to the end of the Canada Assistance Plan in 1996, these include federal transfers.

### Total Social Assistance Expenditures

Canada, Human Resources Development Canada, *Social Security Statistics*, Table 438 — Provincial and Municipal Social Assistance Program Expenditures, by Province and for Canada, 1980-81 to 1998-99.

## Total Social Assistance Beneficiaries

Canada, National Council of Welfare, Historical Provincial and Territorial Sta-tistics. Available at:
http://www.ncwcnbes.net/htmdocument/reportprowelfare/appendix.htm.

Canada, National Council of Welfare, Fact Sheet: Welfare Recipients. Available at:
http://www.ncwcnbes.net/htmdocument/principales/numberwelfare.htm.

## United States

Social assistance expenditure and beneficiary data include AFDC and SSI, excluding benefits to the aged, which in Canada fall under the rubric of pensions rather than needs-tested social assistance. Notably, these figures exclude expenditures for housing benefits, which are not available on a state basis in comparable form across the time period examined here.

Two recipiency rates for the United States are presented. The first includes only AFDC/TANF and SSI for the non-aged. However, there is a wide range of programs (including housing benefits and Food Stamps) which may be considered social assistance, but for which individuals need not be AFDC/SSI recipients. Calculating the total number of beneficiaries of all these social assistance programs is complicated by the fact that a large number of people are recipients of more than one program. The second recipiency rate is based on Food Stamps, on the assumption that beneficiaries of all other programs receive Food Stamps. As not all beneficiaries of other social assistance programs receive Food Stamps, this recipiency rate still understates the total number of persons who receive some form of needs-tested benefits in the United States; although it is a closer approximation of this total than AFDC/SSI.

## Total Beneficiaries and Expenditures

United States, Department of Health and Human Services, Administration for Children and Families. Change in TANF Caseloads 7/00-9/00. Available at:
http://www.acf.dhhs.gov/news/stats/welfare.htm.
United States, Department of Health and Human Services, Administration for Children and Families. Change in TANF Caseloads. Available at:
http://www.acf.dhhs.gov/news/stats/caseload.htm.

United States, Social Security Administration, *Social Security Bulletin: Annual Statistical Supplement*, various years.

Table 9.G.2 — AFDC/TANF, Average Monthly Numbers of Families and Recipients of Cash Payments and Total Amount of Payments by State.

Table 7.B.1 — Supplemental Security Income, Number of Persons Receiving Federally Administered Payments and Total Annual Amount, By Category. (Authors' calculations of total recipients and payments to the non-aged only.)

United States, Census Bureau, *Statistical Abstract of the United States,* various years. Table 630 — Federal Food Stamp Program by State.

United States, House of Representatives, Committee on Ways and Means, *Greenbook 2000.* Table 15-9 — Food Stamp Recipients by Jurisdiction, Selected Fiscal Years, 1975-1999.

## SOCIAL ASSISTANCE AND FAMILY BENEFIT COMPARISONS

SOCIAL ASSISTANCE BENEFIT CALCULATIONS FOR THE UNITED STATES include entitlement programs only — programs for which individuals, if eligible, automatically receive benefits. Many low-income individuals in the United States may be eligible for numerous programs (the most important is federal housing benefits) under which benefits may be considerable (housing benefits in some states can be the equivalent of AFDC/TANF benefits), but which recipients may or may not receive. Under such entitlement programs as AFDC, SSI and Food Stamps, recipients who meet program requirements receive benefits.

### Full-time Employment at Minimum Wage

The comparisons do not compare benefit packages at minimum wage rates in each province and state, but rather earnings equivalent to the U.S. federal minimum wage, in order to eliminate the distortionary effects of differences in minimum wage rates across provinces and states. Social assistance and family benefits for single parents with children are drawn from the U.S. *Greenbook.* The *Greenbook* benefit figures are adjusted to represent benefits for a single-parent family with one child, rather than with two in order to make the family unit comparable to the family unit used in National Council of Welfare (Canada) data. In addition, benefits are adjusted to reflect benefit packages at earned income equivalent to fulltime employment at the federal (rather than state) minimum wage, in order to minimize the impact of variation in minimum wage rates. In making these adjustments, the authors relied on earnings exemption data provided in Urban Institute, *State TANF Policies as of July 1999,* Table II.A.1 Earned Income Disregards for Benefit Computation, July 1999. (Prior to TANF, earnings exemptions were uniform across states, with the exception of

federally-granted state waivers. Under TANF, however, earnings exemptions vary.) These data are also available electronically from the Urban Institute's Welfare Rules Database. Available at:
http://newfederalism.urban.org/nfdb/index.htm.

A minimum-wage equivalent to the U.S. federal minimum wage is calculated for Canada using OECD PPPs. Benefit packages for families at this earning equivalent are then calculated on a province-by-province basis, using benefits and earnings exemption information (National Council of Welfare) and tax credit adjustments (various sources.)

While the amounts of benefit packages are not based on actual minimum wage rates in the provinces and states, they do roughly approximate benefit levels that would be received at minimum-wage employment in the Canadian provinces (see Table B1).

## Sources

Canada, National Council of Welfare, *Welfare Incomes*, various years.

Benefit calculations for the United States are drawn from information on AFDC/TANF, the Food Stamps program, and EIC presented in United States, House of Representatives, Committee on Ways and Means, *Greenbook*, various years.

## CCTB/EIC EARNINGS AND BENEFITS

Calculated by authors.

## Sources

Canada Customs and Revenue Agency. *Your Canada Child Tax Benefit*. Available at: http://www.ccra-adrc.gc.ca/E/pub/tg/t4114eq/t4114eq-06.html.

United States, House of Representatives, Committee on Ways and Means, *Greenbook 2000*. Table 13-12—Earned Income Credit Parameters, 1975-99.

## TABLE B1

## U.S. FEDERAL AND CANADIAN PROVINCIAL MINIMUM WAGE RATES, 1999

|  | Minimum Wage ($ domestic) | Minimum Wage ($US, PPP=1.17) |
|---|---|---|
| U.S. Federal | 5.15 | 5.15 |
| Newfoundland | 5.25 | 4.49 |
| Prince Edward Island | 5.40 | 4.62 |
| Nova Scotia | 5.50 | 4.70 |
| New Brunswick | 5.50 | 4.70 |
| Quebec | 6.90 | 5.90 |
| Ontario | 6.85 | 5.85 |
| Manitoba | 6.00 | 5.13 |
| Saskatchewan | 6.00 | 5.13 |
| Alberta | 5.65 | 4.82 |
| British Columbia | 7.15 | 6.11 |
| Canadian Mean | 6.02 | 5.15 |

Sources: U.S. federal minimum wage rate from United States, Census Bureau *Statistical Abstract of the United States, 2000*, Table 699 – Federal Minimum Wage Rates: 1950-1999. Canadian minimum wage rates from Canadian Council on Social Development, Minimum Wage Rates, Canada and the Provinces. Available at: http://www.ccsd.ca/fs_minw.htm.

# APPENDIX C

# WORKERS' COMPENSATION

## DATA AND METHODOLOGY

ONE OF THE MAIN DIFFICULTIES when we compare total expenditures and beneficiaries in Canada to those in the United States is the starkly differing relationship between workers' compensation programs and the health care system in each country. In Canada, injured workers have access to universal health care, regardless of whether they file a successful workers' compensation claim. In the United States, the provision of health care under workers' compensation (which workers might otherwise have to pay through private insurance, or out-of-pocket) provides a considerably stronger incentive to file workers' compensation claims. Likely as a result of this dynamic, waiting periods in the United States are, with very few exceptions, uniformly longer than in Canada. In addition, medical costs comprised a much higher proportion of total workers' compensation costs in the United States than in Canada. Finally, due to the incentive effects for injured workers to apply for compensation in order to receive medical benefits, compensation costs are likely higher in the United States than they would be in the context of a universal health care system.

## Sources

### Maximum Benefits, Percent of Wage for Benefit Calculation, Waiting Periods

All data on program parameters and benefit levels in Canadian provinces and U.S. states are taken from United States Chamber of Commerce, *Analysis of Workers Compensation Laws*, various years.

### Total Compensation Expenditures

United States, Social Security Administration, *Social Security Bulletin: Annual Statistical Supplement, 2000*. Table 9.B.3—Workers' Compensation Benefits, By Type of Insurer and Medical Benefits, by state, 1998. (Total non-medical compensation benefits calculated by authors as total compensation minus "medical amount".)

Canada, Human Resources Development Canada, *Social Security Statistics*, Table 250—Workers' Compensation, Total Payments, by Province and for Canada, 1974-97 and Table 246—Workers' Compensation, Expenditures for Medical Care and Funeral Services, By Province and for Canada, 1974-97. (Total non-medical payments calculated by authors as total payments minus payments for medical care and funeral services.)

## TABLE C1

### WORKERS' COMPENSATION PROGRAM PARAMETERS, CANADIAN PROVINCES, 1990-99

|  | Percent of Wages 1990 | Percent of Wages 1999 | Waiting Period (days) 1990 | Waiting Period (days) 1999 |
|---|---|---|---|---|
| Newfoundland | 90 (net) | 80 (net) | 1 | 1 |
| Prince Edward Island | Fixed ($450 per month) | 80 (net for 39 weeks, then 85 percent) | 1 | 1 |
| Nova Scotia | 90 (net) | 75 (net for 26 weeks, then 85 percent) | 3 | 2 |
| New Brunswick | 80 (net) | 85 (net) | 1 | 3 |
| Quebec | N/A | 90 ("weighted net") | Same day | Same day |
| Ontario | 90 (net) | 85 (net) | 1 | 1 |
| Manitoba | 75 (gross) | 90 (net for 24 months, then 80 percent) | 1 | 1 |
| Saskatchewan | 90 (net) | 90 (net) | Next day | Next day |
| Alberta | 90 ("weighted net") | 90 ("weighted net") | 1 | 1 |
| British Columbia | N/A | 75 (gross) | 1 | 1 |

Note:   N/A = Not Available.
Source:   United States Chamber of Commerce, Analysis of Workers Compensation Laws, various years.

# Comment on:

## THE PARADOX OF CONVERGENCE: NATIONAL VERSUS SUBNATIONAL PATTERNS OF CONVERGENCE IN CANADIAN AND U.S. INCOME MAINTENANCE POLICY

Comment by James Gaisford
University of Calgary

DO REGIONAL TRADE AGREEMENTS like the NAFTA lead to convergence in social programs? In this paper, Boychuk and Banting attempt to examine the degree of convergence between Canadian and U.S. income maintenance programs. More specifically, consideration is given to retirement income policy, unemployment insurance, social assistance and family benefits, and workers' compensation. A novel feature of the paper is that the programs are assessed for the degree of convergence not only at the national level, but also between Ontario and the Great Lakes states and between British Columbia and Washington state.

The authors contend that, in spite of similar demographic pressures, the pension policies of the two countries have tended to diverge, rather than converge, over most relevant dimensions of comparison. For example, the Canadian system continues to be more redistributive than that of the United States. While Canada has not followed the U.S. lead in imposing increased age restrictions in response to the aging of the population, it has avoided such reductions in benefits by increasing the contribution rate for the Canada Pension Plan. As the authors acknowledge, this has led to convergence between the Canadian contribution rate and the historically higher U.S. rate, which is shown in Figure 1.

With respect to unemployment insurance, Boychuk and Banting point to a convergence at the national and subnational levels, with simultaneous increases in diversity across Canadian provinces. Despite the authors' claim, there seems to be little that is paradoxical in this. As they note, Canadian pension reform has made Canada's national system less generous, bringing it closer to the average of U.S. states. Further, Canada introduced variations in the generosity of benefits that depend on regional unemployment rates. Consequently, Canada's federal program now shows more cross-border similarity at the regional level with the programs of U.S. states, as well as more diversity across provinces. The authors' emphasis on a "B/U ratio" (beneficiaries/unemployed persons) and a "generosity index" to test for policy convergence also seems problematic. As they acknowledge, these measures are driven partly by economic conditions. As a result, convergence or divergence in these measures is inherently related to convergence or divergence in economic conditions, as well as by changes in economic policy.

On the one hand, there has been significant convergence in family benefits as the United States filled a former void and introduced its Earned Income Benefit, while Canada moved away from universal Family Allowances to the Canada Child Tax Benefit. On the other hand, there has been little qualitative or quantitative convergence between Canadian and U.S. social assistance programs, either at the national or regional level. Further, there is little evidence of any systematic convergence between provincial social assistance programs within Canada; and Alberta, in particular, has diverged significantly.

With respect to the workers' compensation programs, there is also little evidence of convergence, either at the national level between Canada and the United States or across Canadian provinces. While there is no evidence of convergence in maximum benefits between Ontario and the Great Lakes states, the maximum benefits paid by Washington state have converged on those paid by British Columbia.

There appear to be many worthwhile directions for further study with respect to the question of Canada-U.S. convergence in social policy. It would be interesting to examine other regional comparisons, like Alberta versus Texas, and Manitoba and Saskatchewan versus the U.S. Midwest. Adding Quebec to the analysis would be of particular interest because of its cultural and linguistic distinctiveness. Similarly, bringing Mexico into the comparisons would be interesting. Other programs, for example in the areas of health and education, could be analysed. Perhaps most important, it would be worthwhile for further research on the convergence hypothesis to move beyond the discussion of descriptive data in the direction of more formal statistical testing.

*Nancy Olewiler*
*Simon Fraser University*

# 15

# *North American Integration and the Environment*

## INTRODUCTION

E CONOMIES OF THE WORLD ARE BECOMING MORE INTEGRATED because of a host of factors. These include reduced barriers to trade and foreign investment, technological changes in communication and information flows, and relative price changes, like lower transportation costs. Greater integration has, in turn, led to large increases in economic activity, with substantial growth in gross domestic product (GDP) and trade and investment flows in most countries over the past 30 to 50 years.

This study addresses the impact economic integration has had on the natural environment. The focus is on North America. The natural environment of any country or region consists of its natural resources — minerals and energy, aquatic and terrestrial species, forests, soils, water and the atmosphere. While economists typically look at natural resources individually, ecosystems, with their complex relationships among species and physical resources, are the fundamental resource base of a country. The difficulty for environmental and resource economics is that there is no summary statistic like GDP that measures the state of the ecosystems for a region or country. Indicators of environmental quality represent snapshots and time trends of component parts of ecosystems.

Put simply, the key questions asked in this study are as follows:

1. Is economic integration bad or good for the environment?

2. Is environmental regulation good or bad for the economy?

3. Do trade agreements and increasing trade and investment flows undermine a country's regulatory efforts to improve environmental quality?

A very large literature has emerged over the past 15 years to examine these questions. The questions may be simple, but the answers are complex and can be ambiguous. Moreover, there appears to be a large divergence between what the public and many policy makers believe about the impacts of trade and economic growth on the environment and the impact of environmental regulation on the economy and what economists have been observing empirically. This gap is due in part to the complexity of the topic and the absence of consistent sets of high-quality data. But it also reflects the political economy of environmental regulation in an integrating world.

The outline of the study is as follows. A very brief review of why market economies fail to provide the optimal level of environmental quality makes the key point that environmental regulation and clear assignment of property rights are essential for any economy regardless of its degree of integration with other economies. Environmental quality indicators for North America are presented to set the stage for the analysis. While it is very difficult to get consistent and comparable data for all three countries, some interesting trends are illustrated. A series of hypotheses regarding the relationship between trade, growth, the environment and environmental regulation are then examined in some detail. Relevant literature is reviewed and recent data presented. These hypotheses are:

- Stringent environmental regulation undermines a country's competitiveness, leading to job losses and driving investment to countries or regions where environmental regulation is less stringent. This is called the "pollution haven" hypothesis — pollution-intensive industries will seek to locate in regions with low levels of environmental regulation.

- Because of the threat of pollution havens (real or perceived), there will be a race to the bottom (RTTB), in which countries or regions compete for industries by reducing the stringency of their environmental regulation until the lowest common denominator prevails. A weaker version of the RTTB hypothesis is the "no race at all" or regulatory chill hypothesis, which sees governments reluctant to enforce environmental regulations. They mollify environmental interest groups by introducing regulation, but it is not binding on producers.

- Economic growth leads to lower levels of environmental quality. Greater economic integration exacerbates the situation by contributing to higher growth rates in output and incomes.

- Trade agreements interfere with a country's domestic environmental targets and policies.

The debate surrounding these hypotheses affects environmental policy makers. The political economy of environmental policy is driven in part by two perceptions: first, that there is an unambiguous negative effect of integration on the environment; and second, that environmental regulation adversely affects economic growth and productivity. If the facts do not support these perceptions, it means that environmental policies should be a complement to trade and investment policies. It is not a case of a country needing one or the other.

The last section of the study draws on the investigation of the four hypotheses and develops some policy implications for Canada.

## OPTIMAL LEVELS OF ENVIRONMENTAL QUALITY

WHY DO ENVIRONMENTAL PROBLEMS EXIST? Environmental degradation is a by-product of human activity and natural processes. Wastes are generated from production and consumption activities. When property rights to the natural environment are not well defined, there is no incentive for anyone to take into account the impact their waste generation is having on the natural environment and other economic agents. If one can dispose of wastes freely, why incur costs of treating waste products and reducing their deleterious effects? The key problem is that much of the natural environment is an open access resource. No one effectively owns the atmosphere, most water bodies, or even many land resources. Consumers and producers do not bear the full costs of their waste disposal; it is shared by society. Thus, too much waste is produced relative to the social optimum, with an implicit price of waste discharge that is too low. This is an environmental externality that causes ecosystem degradation.

When private property rights exist and are well enforced, those who deposit waste products on another's property are required to clean them up and/or compensate the property owner. An efficient level of waste generation then ensues, because the environmental externality is internalized. However, when environmental externalities are pervasive, affecting many people and producers, and it is difficult to associate an emission with a particular source (like air pollution from automobiles or pesticide runoff from agriculture), assigning private property rights to the environment becomes virtually impossible. Some form of regulatory policy is required.

Degradation can also occur from land uses on private property that do not incorporate impacts on the natural environment. For example, a farmer may drain a wetland to increase acreage on which to plant crops. The decision is based on the expected return from the land in crops, not the potential social value of the land in the form of downstream water purification, erosion control, wildlife habitat, biodiversity enhancement and so on. This too is an externality that occurs because the social value of the wetland is not reflected in market prices. Without some form of government incentive to conserve wetlands, or private initiatives to offer compensation for not draining them, there will be an insufficient supply from society's viewpoint. There is no well-defined market for the products of a wetland.[1] Environmental degradation, therefore, comes from the failure of markets to price all the benefits that arise from the use of the natural environment.

Regulation can take many forms. The two main generic categories are command and control policies and market-based initiatives. Command and control policies directly restrict waste flows or specify the processes that generate wastes. They are like quantity controls in the form of standards. Standards can act directly on waste products by limiting emissions into the natural environment (emission or effluent standards),[2] or they can require producers (or consumers) to install specific types of pollution control and abatement equipment or use specific operating techniques. The latter are called design standards. The chief characteristic of standards is that they require the waste discharger to meet specific conditions set out in the regulations or face a penalty. They do not set an explicit price for the wastes. There may be an implicit price that emerges from the quantity constraints. By contrast, the principle of a market-based initiative is to establish a price for polluting activities. The goal is to set that price at the point where the marginal damage caused by the polluting activity is equal to the marginal cost of controlling emissions. The discharging party (the polluter) then faces this price for each unit of emissions it contemplates releasing into the natural environment. The waste-discharge services of the environment effectively become another input into production or consumption activities and are then used efficiently if no other market distortions exist. Examples of market-based policies include pollution taxes or charges, tradeable pollution permits, and subsidies. Whether governments use command and control or market-based policies depends on a host of factors, including the type of pollutant (its toxicity, whether it is local, regional or global), likely elasticity of response to implicit or explicit pollution prices, administrative feasibility and so on. No single policy instrument is appropriate for all types of environmental problems.

Efficient environmental policy will impose the tax, standards or other policy instruments as directly as possible on the source of the emissions, rather than use indirect policies. For example, an emissions tax on motor vehicle wastes is a more efficient instrument than an excise tax on gasoline, if the environmental target is to reduce air pollution from motor vehicles. The emissions tax provides an incentive for vehicle owners to adjust all aspects of their driving (kilometres driven, the vehicle's characteristics, gasoline used, etc.) to reduce their tax liability. A gasoline tax, or tax on kilometres travelled, may be a good proxy for an emissions tax when it is technically difficult to levy the latter, because air pollutants are highly correlated with gasoline consumption and kilometres travelled. Therefore, a reduction in gasoline use and travel will also decrease emissions. But it will not provide an incentive for drivers to switch to a different type of gasoline that produces fewer emissions unless the tax rate varies by fuel type. As a practical matter, however, it may be physically impossible or administratively prohibitive to use emissions-based policies.

If a country has socially efficient environmental policies in place that internalize environmental externalities, in theory its degree of integration with other countries should not affect the state of the natural environment. Ideally, as investment and trade flows increase and GDP grows, a country's environmental policy will ensure that domestic pollution remains at the optimal level because the price for polluting activity correctly reflects environmental quality targets. In practice, countries do not have optimal environmental policies. Many environmental externalities remain unpriced or unregulated. If this is the case, a greater degree of openness may exacerbate environmental degradation. The theoretical literature examines this issue, typically from the viewpoint of developing versus developed economies. The models assume that developing countries have less stringent environmental regulation than developed countries. Increased trade flows may make them worse off as economic activity expands, bringing with it more waste flows and land use changes that increase environmental degradation (e.g., deforestation, loss of fish habitat). Chichilnisky (1994) assumes that developing countries will have less well-defined property rights and thus more open access environmental resources. This gives them a comparative advantage in these resources. An increase in trade and investment flows will then lead to greater production and use of natural resources and, hence, more environmental degradation. The culprit here is the insufficient definition and enforcement of property rights and policies to use environmental resources efficiently for the benefit of society, not increased integration per se. Copeland and Taylor (1994) model trade between developed (the North) and developing (the South) countries in a general equilibrium analysis. They consider a local pollutant that is confined to each country (i.e., it does not spill over national boundaries). They describe their results in terms of three distinct but related effects of trade and growth on the environment that were first used by Grossman and Krueger (1991). These are:

1. The *scale effect*. Trade liberalization contributes to higher levels of GDP. GDP growth means more production and consumption, and hence more waste production and environmental degradation. Environmental quality will decline if regulatory policies do not keep up with GDP growth (i.e., if optimal environmental policies are not in place). The scale effect may not be monotonic with rising income levels. If environmental quality is income-elastic, a country's inhabitants will want higher levels of environmental quality as incomes rise and thus pressure their governments to introduce more stringent policies that ensure growth does not lead to worsening environmental quality. Higher incomes may also lead consumers and producers to voluntarily reduce their emissions and engage in more environmentally friendly

activities. For example, more recycling and process changes that produce less pollution per unit output may occur.

2. The *composition effect* captures any industrial restructuring that occurs because of trade and economic growth. Trade and growth can affect the pollution intensity of production. With increased trade, if the expanding export sectors are less pollution-intensive than the contracting import-competing sectors, the pollution intensity of a country's output will decline, and vice versa. What happens depends on a country's comparative advantage in pollution-intensive goods. Of course, not all countries can specialize in environmentally friendly goods; some will become relatively more pollution-intensive (if there are no offsetting effects elsewhere). This is one reason for protests against trade liberalization. The composition effect is also connected to scale. Rising incomes may lead consumers (as noted above) to prefer goods that are less environmentally damaging or alter their demand for goods, which in turn affects the mix of pollution-intensive versus environmentally friendly production. Thus, both traded and non-traded goods production and consumption may shift toward having a smaller adverse impact on the environment.

3. The *technique effect* looks at how production technologies change with more trade and higher growth. The effect can go either way — toward less or more environmentally damaging production. Again, it is linked to the other effects. If efficient environmental regulations are in place, or regulations become more stringent as the economic scale rises, they will provide strong incentives for producers to seek new technologies that reduce the cost of meeting environmental targets. The new technologies may result in lower emissions. Alternatively, as the economic scale rises, technologies may become more pollution-intensive as the natural environment degrades and more and more resources and manufactured capital are used to achieve a given level of output.

Copeland and Taylor assume that the North has more stringent environmental regulation than the South because of its higher income level. As trade increases, pollution-intensive industries in the North contract while those in the South expand. The composition effect thus leads to lower levels of pollution intensity in the North and higher levels in the South. The scale effect leads pollution levels to rise in both regions, but it also increases the willingness to pay for environmental quality, thus leading to more stringent regulation. This stimulates the technique effect to kick in and lower pollution per unit output. In their model, if the income elasticity of the demand for environmental quality exceeds one, the technique effect offsets the scale effect and leads to rising environmental quality.[3] This still leaves the composition effect that improves environmental quality in the North, but reduces it in the South. Aggregate environmental quality declines when the average pollution intensity of output rises because of the composition effect in the South. Aggregate output of pollution-intensive goods rises as a result of production specialization in the South and the lack of compensating rises in environmental regulation.[4] Thus, if trade could somehow be balanced so that environmental regulation kept up with rising pollution intensity in the South, then environmental quality would not need to decline. Another implication is that if trade liberalization leads to income convergence (at a higher, not lower, level than before), threats to environmental quality would diminish.

Both Chichilnisky and Copeland-Taylor assume that comparative advantage is dependent on a country's environmental policy and property rights, other things being equal. Developing countries then have a comparative advantage in pollution-intensive goods because they have lower income levels and hence less stringent regulation, in addition to property rights that are not as well defined and enforced as in developed countries. As discussed below, the empirical evidence is mixed. However, there are other problems with the assumptions. A study done for the World Trade Organization (WTO) by Nordström and Vaughan (1999) argues that it is the absolute difference in regulatory stringency that matters for comparative advantage, not measures like pollution abatement and control expenditure (PACE) in each country. Differences in PACE across countries or regions are a common indicator of regulatory stringency used in the literature. This is largely because there is no readily measurable indicator of regulatory stringency (more on this below). The use of PACE, however, is problematic for several reasons. First, PACE data are extremely hard to obtain, if available at all. The United States discontinued its survey of PACE by firms in 1994. Canada has approximately three years of PACE data, collected by special surveys that ended during the budgetary cutbacks of the 1990s. There are, therefore, no plant-level data that can be used to look at effects post-NAFTA. Second, even if PACE data were available, what do they really tell us? A high level of PACE in any given year could indicate that a region previously had very lax environmental targets and was now trying to catch up with other regions. It does not mean, necessarily, that a region had stringent policies. PACE could also be high because a region is rich in other factor inputs that pollution-intensive industries use intensively. These could be either primary or capital resources. Many pollution-intensive industries are also capital-intensive (e.g., chemicals, and oil and mineral refining). Developed countries have a comparative advantage in capital-intensive goods, so the Copeland-Taylor model implies that pollution-intensive production will increase in the North rather than the South. Their results would then be reversed. Aggregate pollution levels should fall, not rise. Ultimately, the effects must be determined empirically. The next section examines a variety of indicators of environmental quality, investment, trade flow and the pollution-intensity of production in North America from the early 1990s (pre-NAFTA or at the time it was adopted) to the most recent year available.[5]

## ENVIRONMENTAL QUALITY TRENDS IN NORTH AMERICA

A S NOTED IN THE INTRODUCTION, there is no universal indicator of environmental quality. Many countries are now collecting a wide variety of data on a number of different indicators, but there is no way to aggregate these largely physical measures to arrive at an overall number. The result is that for North America, there is good news and bad news, and one is left with subjective methods to determine whether overall environmental quality is declining or not. Another difficulty is that indicators are not necessarily measured (or reported) in comparable ways across countries. This is a problem in North America for many indicators. A third problem is that data at the country or even regional level may well hide "hot spots" — regions where environmental quality is much lower than suggested by the aggregate figures because of a concentration of pollutants in that region. This can be due to physical factors (e.g., geography, meteorology, hydrology) or an agglomeration of polluting sources (e.g., industry, agriculture, urban areas). Caution in interpreting the data is thus warranted. Finally, there are insufficient data to get a clear indication of trends for many types of environmental indicators (e.g., biodiversity).

The data presented are thus snapshots and fairly brief time trends. The basic message is that there is good and bad news. The examples below illustrate potential scale, composition and technique effects at work.

### AIR QUALITY

SOME OF THE BEST ENVIRONMENTAL DATA are on air quality. Figures 1 and 2 present air quality data for Canada and the United States for the so-called "criteria pollutants" — sulphur dioxide ($SO_2$), nitrogen oxides ($NO_x$), carbon monoxide (CO), volatile organic compounds (VOC), particulate matter (PM) and ground-level ozone ($O_3$). Mexican data are sparse, as collection began in 1988 and there are still few data on a national level. Data are collected for the criteria pollutants in major cities. The news is generally good for Canada and the United States and improving for Mexico.[6] Ambient concentrations (and/or emissions) of $SO_2$, CO and VOC have declined over time in Canada and the United States, and in major Mexican cities like Mexico City. This is good news, as all these pollutants contribute to health problems, productivity losses and ecosystem damage. However, other criteria pollutants have increased. Ambient levels of $O_3$ have risen in Canada and remain high in Mexico. $O_3$ is a main component of urban smog, formed from emissions of VOC plus $NO_x$ in the presence of sunlight. In the United States, while national emissions of VOC have declined since 1995, many urban areas still have ambient levels that exceed target levels during portions of the year. Emissions of $NO_x$ have remained relatively constant; smog thus remains a problem in U.S. urban areas as well. $NO_x$ emissions in Mexico City have risen 25 percent from 1988 to 1996 and $O_3$ remains a very serious problem for all major Mexican cities. Levels exceed the "good" standard for nine out of 10 days in Mexico City. But generally, smog in Mexican cities is not getting worse. It is just not getting better for the largest cities (although it is improving somewhat in some smaller ones). The health effects of smog include exacerbating lung diseases that induce respiratory inflammation, and other cardiovascular illnesses. It damages materials and reduces agricultural productivity. The major source of VOC and $NO_x$ is motor vehicles.

## FIGURE 1

## CANADIAN ANNUAL AVERAGE AMBIENT LEVELS OF CRITERIA POLLUTANTS, 1979-96

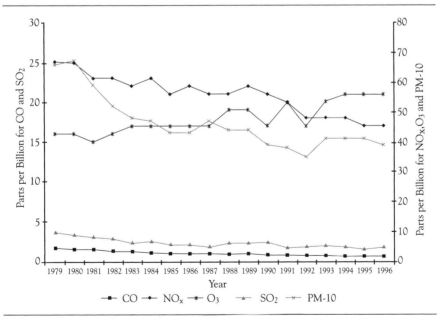

Source:  Environment Canada. *State of the Environment*, "Urban Air Quality," SOE Technical Supplement No. 99-1, National Environmental Indicator Series, Spring 1999. Available at: http://www.ec.gc.ca.

## FIGURE 2

## U.S. TOTAL NATIONAL EMISSIONS OF CRITERIA AIR POLLUTANTS, 1978-97

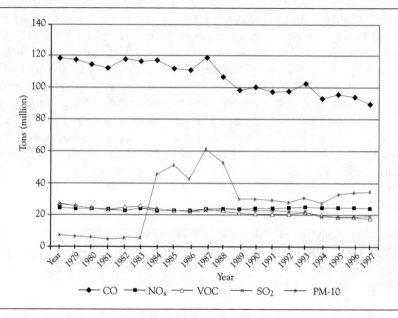

Source:   Environmental Protection Agency. *National Air Pollution Emission Trends, 1900-1998,* "Total National Emissions by Pollutant and Year," Tables 3-13.

Figure 3A shows U.S. fuel consumption by motor vehicles and the average miles per gallon since 1970. There is a U-shaped relationship in fuel consumption, but fuel efficiency has been rising gradually, reflecting fuel efficiency regulation. Miles driven per vehicle per year increased as well (from just under 10,000 miles in 1970 to approximately 12,200 miles in 1998). Canadian data are shown in Figure 3B. Fuel efficiency rose (more kilometres per litre of fuel consumed) from 1976 to 1996; however, kilometres travelled and fuel consumption rose as well. Thus, while fuel efficiency has gone up, energy consumption has not fallen over time. The increase in fuel consumed may reflect a potentially negative composition effect within an industry — the shift to less fuel-efficient vehicles (e.g., sport utility vehicles) because of low real fuel prices and fads. These data may also illustrate the scale effect at work and point to the necessity of targeting policy to the correct environmental indicator. Improvements in fuel efficiency do not lead necessarily to less pollution if the increase in miles driven per year offsets the fuel efficiency gains.

FIGURE 3A

## U.S. MOTOR VEHICLE FUEL CONSUMPTION AND FUEL EFFICIENCY, 1970-98

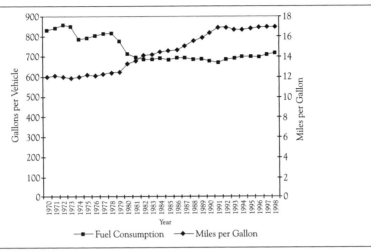

Source: Energy Information Administration. *Annual Energy Review*, 1999, "Motor Vehicle Mileage, Fuel Consumption and Fuel Rates, 1949-1998," Table 2.9.

FIGURE 3B

## CANADIAN AUTOMOBILE FUEL CONSUMPTION, FUEL EFFICIENCY AND KILOMETRES TRAVELLED

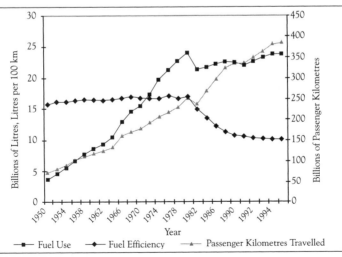

Source: Environment Canada. State of the Environment Indicators, Passenger Transportation. Available at: http://www.ec.gc.ca.

585

## FIGURE 4A

### CANADIAN CO$_2$ EMISSIONS FROM FOSSIL FUELS, 1958-97

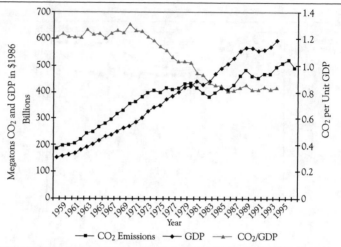

Sources: Data from Environment Canada, 1999 and 2000; *Canada's Greenhouse Gas Inventory, 1997* and *1998*; Statistics Canada (GDP data.).

## FIGURE 4B

### U.S. CO$_2$ EMISSIONS, GDP AND CO$_2$/GDP, 1949-99

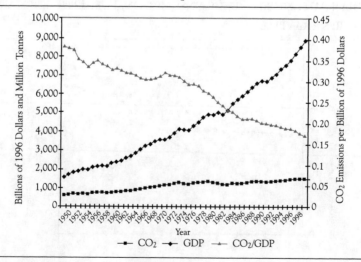

Sources: Environmental Protection Agency. *National Air Pollutant Emission Trends, 1900-1998;* Energy Information Administration. *Annual Energy Review, 1999,* "Energy Consumption per Person and per Dollar of Gross Domestic Product, 1949-1999," Table 1.5.

FIGURE 5

U.S. LEAD EMISSIONS, 1970-98

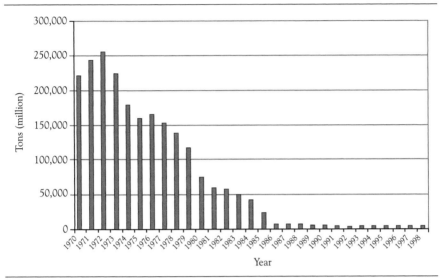

Source: Environmental Protection Agency. *National Air Pollutant Emission Trends, 1900-1998.*

An examination of changes in the emissions and ambient levels of criteria pollutants over time shows that the components of urban air pollution — $NO_x$, VOC and the resulting $O_3$ — are not declining. The major source of these emissions is motor vehicles. It indicates that regulatory policies (discussed below) have not kept up with the increasing number of motor vehicles in urban areas. The number of vehicles has risen because of population and income growth.

Emissions of PM have decreased in Canada fairly consistently since 1979, but follow a very complex path in the United States, with levels rising dramatically in the mid-1980s, then falling until 1995, but now rising again. PM comes from fossil-fuel fired power plants, motor vehicles, construction and natural sources like fires and volcanoes. It is viewed as one of the most serious air pollutants affecting human health, causing cardiovascular problems, cancers and premature death.[7]

Figures 4A and 4B present emissions of $CO_2$ and the ratio of $CO_2$ to GDP for Canada and the United States. While aggregate emissions have risen, the carbon intensity of production is falling. This illustrates a potentially beneficial composition effect. However, the rise in aggregate emissions shows the role of the scale effect and why there is ongoing concern about the relationship between carbon emissions and climate change.

## FIGURE 6A

## U.S. ENERGY CONSUMPTION: AGGREGATE, PER CAPITA, PER DOLLAR GDP, 1949-98

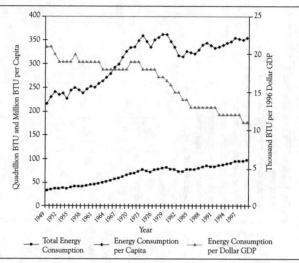

Source: Energy Information Administration. *Annual Energy Review, 1999,* "Energy Consumption per Person and per Dollar of Gross Domestic Product, 1949-1999," Table 1.5.

## FIGURE 6B

## CANADIAN ENERGY CONSUMPTION: PER CAPITA AND PER GDP, 1961-97

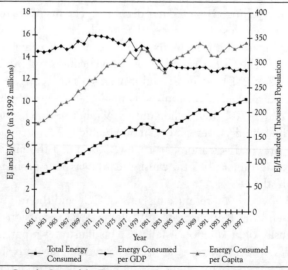

Sources: Environment Canada, State of the Environment Indicators. Available at: http://www.ec.gc.ca/ind; Statistics Canada, *Historical Statistics;* CANSIM C892268 (Population by Age, Sex, Canada).

The final air pollution examples illustrate two success stories for environmental regulation: first, the removal of lead in gasoline; and second, the Montreal Protocol to eliminate the production and use of stratospheric ozone-depleting compounds. Since the ban on leaded gasoline in Canada and the United States, emissions fell dramatically, then stabilized, as Figure 5 indicates for the United States.[8] Mexico introduced unleaded gasoline in 1990 and banned leaded fuel in Mexico City in 2000. The Montreal Protocol of 1987 established a timetable for the elimination of CFCs and other ozone-depleting compounds. CFCs were banned in Canada in 1995.

## ENERGY CONSUMPTION AND THE ENERGY INTENSITY OF OUTPUT

ENERGY USE IS A GOOD INDICATOR of environmental quality impacts because most energy consumed is derived from fossil fuels, and the by-products of consumption release the local and global air pollutants discussed above. Energy production also has widespread environmental impacts, whether it is fossil-fuel based or not (e.g., hydro-electricity and nuclear power). Figures 6A and 6B show energy consumption in the United States and Canada in aggregate, per capita and per unit GDP. While aggregate and per capita consumption have been rising continually, energy consumption per dollar of GDP has fallen since the 1970s, but much more modestly in Canada than in the United States. These data illustrate the competing forces of the scale effect versus what ultimately might be environmentally beneficial composition and technique effects. The technique effect is probably the factor most responsible for the reduction in energy use per unit GDP, as producers and consumers started to use more energy-efficient equipment after the oil-price shocks of the 1970s and the greater environmental awareness (and higher incomes) of the 1980s and 1990s. However, the figures indicate that scale effects still dominate.

## WATER QUALITY

WATER QUALITY IS MEASURED for individual bodies of water. There are no national measures that can be summarized easily. Again, there is good and bad news. Regulatory efforts have reduced significantly the amount of phosphorus released into the Great Lakes since the late 1970s. For example, Figure 7 illustrates the declining phosphorus concentration in Lake Ontario.[9] Phosphorus (and other nutrients, like nitrates) is a major source of the eutrophication of surface waters caused by an overabundance of plant material (largely algae). This reduces the oxygen content of the water, killing fish and other aquatic fauna. Figure 8 illustrates another example of water quality improvement due to regulation — specifically, the ban on PCBs.

## FIGURE 7

## TOTAL PHOSPHORUS CONCENTRATION IN LAKE ONTARIO, 1971-93

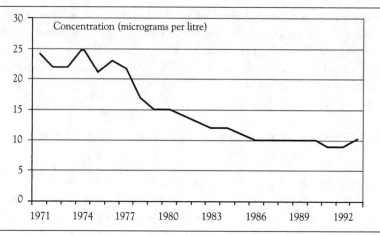

Source: Environment Canada. *Human Activity and the Environment*, 2000, Table 6.3.3.

## FIGURE 8

## CONCENTRATION OF PCBS IN CANADIAN SURFACE WATERS, 1972-79

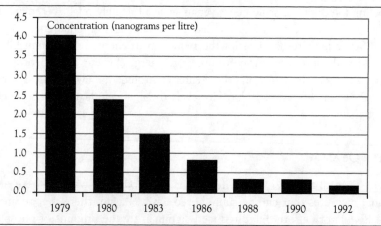

Source: Environment Canada. *Human Activity and the Environment*, 2000, Table 6.3.2.

Recent events in Canada, however, point to the bad news that our water treatment infrastructure has been declining in recent years. There has been an increase in the number of water supplies contaminated by bacteria and parasites. These have resulted in "boil water" advisories for many parts of the country (e.g., more than half of Newfoundland's water supplies, many water districts in the interior of British Columbia and, of course, the highly publicized case of Walkerton, Ontario, as well as more recent problems in North Battleford, Saskatchewan). There are also cases of ground water contamination from pesticides and other persistent toxins. An in-depth examination of water quality in the United States and Mexico is beyond the scope of this study. The evidence in Canada, however, suggests that there are problems.

## WATER SUPPLY

WATER SUPPLY — THE TOTAL AMOUNT available for consumption and use — is another indicator of environmental quality. The simple story is that each country does not have a water supply problem in aggregate, but particular regions are facing potential water shortages due to the depletion of ground water supplies and the total commitment of existing surface waters to current use. Water as a commodity is also a very contentious issue in the NAFTA and other trade agreements. It is beyond the scope of this study to address that issue (indeed it is a study in itself). The key point is that there is concern about the available quantity of water in some regions.

## TOXIC EMISSIONS

TOXIC COMPOUNDS ARE THOSE DEEMED by regulators to pose a threat to human health or ecological processes, or to be highly resistant to chemical and biological breakdown by natural processes and therefore found to persist in the ecosystem after release, or ones that accumulate in the food chain.[10] Table 1 compares toxic emissions in Canada to those in the United States in 1994, for industries at the two-digit SIC level.[11] Note that the emission intensity of releases can differ substantially between the two countries.[12] Canada is over 50 percent more emission-intensive than the United States for virtually all of the most emission-intensive industries: paper and allied products, rubber, plastics, non-metallic minerals, chemicals and chemical products, and refined petroleum and coal. The United States is over 50 percent more emission-intensive in the less pollution-intensive industries, like electrical and electronics, fabricated metal, food, beverages, furniture and fixtures, machinery, leather, and wood and lumber. Overall, emissions per dollar of output from Canadian manufacturing industries are 50 percent higher than releases from U.S. manufacturing. Table 1 illustrates a key point: pollution intensity can differ significantly among similar industries operating in different countries. There are many potential reasons for these differences, including technology, product mix, comparative advantage in pollution absorption (although this is not too convincing, given that these compounds are not assimilated by the natural environment) and of course, regulatory stringency.

591

## TABLE 1

## CANADIAN AND U.S. EMISSIONS OF TOXIC COMPOUNDS TO OUTPUT VALUE RATIOS (E/$Q), 1994

| Canada | | | United States | | |
|---|---|---|---|---|---|
| SIC | Sector | E/$Q | SIC | Sector | E/$Q |
| 10 | Food | 43 | 20 | Food | 260 |
| 11 | Beverages | 27 | | | |
| 15 | Rubber | 3,568 | 30 | Rubber and Plastics | 1,427 |
| 16 | Plastics | 3,430 | | | |
| 17 | Leather | 429 | 31 | Leather | 1,261 |
| 18 | Primary Textiles | 281 | 22 | Textiles | 544 |
| 19 | Textile Products | 452 | | | |
| 25 | Wood | 172 | 24 | Lumber | 710 |
| 26 | Furniture and Fixtures | 567 | 25 | Furniture and Fixtures | 1,534 |
| 27 | Paper and Allied Products | 7,286 | 26 | Paper and Allied Products | 3,456 |
| 28 | Printing and Publishing | 412 | 27 | Printing and Publishing | 212 |
| 29 | Primary Metals | 7,290 | 33 | Primary Metals | 6,077 |
| 30 | Fabricated Metals | 1,099 | 34 | Fabricated Metals | 965 |
| 31 | Machinery | 60 | 35 | Machinery | 147 |
| 32 | Transportation Equipment | 1,090 | 37 | Transportation Equipment | 609 |
| 33 | Electrical and Electronics | 281 | 36 | Electrical and Electronics | 288 |
| 35 | Non-metallic Minerals | 1,797 | 32 | Stone/Glass/Clay | 530 |
| 36 | Refined Petroleum and Coal | 9,293 | 29 | Petroleum and Coal | 1,643 |
| 37 | Chemicals | 11,557 | 28 | Chemicals and Allied Products | 4,844 |
| 39 | Other Manufacturing | 444 | 39 | Miscellaneous Manufacturing | 497 |
| | | | 38[*] | Instruments and Related | 189 |
| | **Canadian Average** | **2,791** | | **U.S. Average** | **1,484** |

Notes:  E/$Q are emissions in pounds per million Canadian dollars.
Emissions = releases plus transfers.
* Instruments and related products are included in SIC 39 in Canada.

Sources:  Canadian emissions: NPRI, 1994; Canadian value-added: Statistics Canada. *Manufacturing Industries of Canada*, Cat. No. 31-2-3-XPB; U.S. emissions: TRI; U.S. value-added: Bureau of the Census, *Annual Survey of Manufacturers M95(AS)-1*; as cited in Olewiler and Dawson (1998).

Table 2 shows that there have been some significant changes in Canadian data since the mid-1990s, with emissions from some of Canada's most pollution-intensive industries, like paper and allied products, chemicals, and primary metals, declining substantially. The decline is due to regulatory changes and voluntary actions by industry to reduce emissions. However, these results are not so optimistic when one looks at aggregate toxic emissions to Canadian environmental resources (air, surface water, land, underground) over the 1993-98 period (Harrison and Antweiler 2003). The top half of Figure 9 illustrates the time trend in toxic releases unweighted by toxicity. The largest decline is in discharges to surface water. There has been an increase in discharges to air, land and underground injection since 1993. One implication of this trend is that polluters may simply be reallocating their wastes to another medium (e.g., away from water and onto soils) in response to differences in the stringency of regulations. The bottom half of Figure 9 presents the toxicity weighted releases. The aggregate levels have risen somewhat over time (up for air and land, down for water and underground injection, except in 1993 for that medium). They suggest that polluters could be shifting from high volume-low toxicity emissions to low emission-high toxicity releases.

TABLE 2

EMISSION AND TOXIC INTENSITY OF CANADIAN MANUFACTURING INDUSTRIES, 1997

| SIC | Industry | Emissions/$Output |
|-----|----------|-------------------|
| 37 | Chemicals | 2,345 |
| 29 | Primary Metals | 1,507 |
| 15 | Rubber | 268 |
| 16 | Plastics | 1,090 |
| 36 | Refined Petroleum and Coal | 1,027 |
| 35 | Non-metallic Minerals | 294 |
| 26 | Furniture and Fixtures | 355 |
| 32 | Transportation Equipment | 153 |
| 30 | Fabricated Metals | 208 |
| 28 | Printing and Publishing | 190 |
| 19 | Textile Products | 365 |
| 27 | Paper and Allied Products | 1,798 |
| 39 | Other Manufacturing | 189 |
| 18 | Primary Textiles | 47 |
| 17 | Leather | 163 |
| 25 | Wood | 155 |
| 33 | Electrical and Electronics | 12 |
| 31 | Machinery | 17 |
| 10 | Food | 31 |
| Average | | 556 |

Note:   Emissions/$Output are the releases of toxic compounds by each industry in pounds divided by the value of industry shipments in millions of Canadian dollars.

Sources: Emissions data from Environment Canada, National Pollutant Release Inventory and Statistics Canada, Manufacturing Industries of Canada, National and Provincial Areas, Cat. No. 31-203-XPB.

## FIGURE 9

### CANADIAN TOXIC EMISSIONS TO ENVIRONMENTAL MEDIA, 1993-98 (UNWEIGHTED BY TOXICITY)

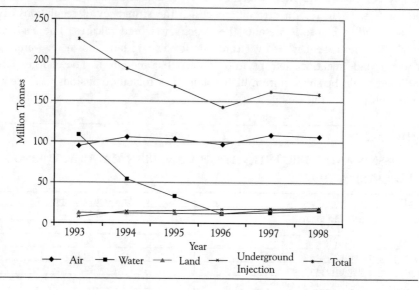

### CANADIAN TOXIC EMISSIONS, 1993-98 (WEIGHTED BY TOXICITY)

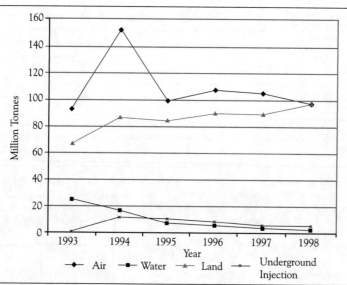

Source: Harrison and Antweiler (2003).

## FOREST COVER

DATA ON FOREST COVER ARE AVAILABLE FROM all three countries for 1990 and 1995.[13] Forest cover is defined as the total number of hectares with either natural forests or plantations. Both Canada and the United States had a very small increase in total hectares — a rise of 0.3 percent in Canada and 1.4 percent in the United States. Total forest cover fell in Mexico by 4.4 percent. However, the sum of total forests in the NAFTA countries rose marginally from 511.2 million to 512.5 million hectares. Thus, aggregate forest cover did not decline after the passage of the NAFTA. These aggregates do not, of course, reflect some significant forest-use issues like the harvest of old growth forests in British Columbia and the Pacific Northwest of the United States. The aggregate data do not take forest quality into account.

Prestemon (2000) examines the impact of the NAFTA on Mexican forest cover by using a general equilibrium model that incorporates land use and ownership characteristics of the country. His theoretical model assumes that a proportion of forestland is in private hands, where landowners maximize their land value by allocating it to timber or other uses, depending on which yields the largest present value of net returns over time. All timber markets are assumed to be competitive. Public forestland is divided into two components — publicly managed and open access. Open access harvests are assumed to represent the illegal poaching of trees: the poachers weigh the value of the tree against the penalties for being caught. There is no interest in long-term sustained management of the forest because there is no security of tenure. Passage of the NAFTA changed a number of factors that affect timber harvests on all land. Effects are complex because of the need to examine both short- and long-term incentives to harvest timber. An important result is that if all forestland is public (with some proportion open access), and if prices rise in a post-trade liberalization environment, forest cover will fall because this raises the return for poaching.[14] The impact of the NAFTA on forest cover is therefore dependent on how forest product prices change and the share of forestland in open access versus private ownership. Mexican forest ownership is complex, with private and public lands held not as open access, but by communities and as *ejidos*, where rights are assigned communally. Public land comprises about 80 percent of total forestland. The federal government regulates harvests on the *ejidos* and requires sustained forest use of the land, so it cannot be interpreted as completely open access forest, although some illegal harvesting does occur. This also means that if timber prices fall, the public forestland cannot be converted to another land use (like agriculture). The community shares in the profits from the timber harvest. There are also protected forests where timber harvests are forbidden.

On the basis of data from Mexico and results from other general equilibrium models, a variety of scenarios is presented for different land-use elasticities, timber and agricultural prices, and the percentage of land under different property rights. If the NAFTA simply removes domestic distortions, forest cover rises modestly with increases in public lands, offsetting reductions in private forest-land. This is because timber prices fall slightly. If the NAFTA causes domestic timber prices to reach international prices, timber prices fall by a much larger amount. There is a large increase in forest cover, reflecting the prediction that virtually all threatened public land is held in timber in perpetuity and all private forests are converted to other uses. Because the majority of Mexico's forests are public, this increases forest cover. These results assume no policy changes on the part of the federal government: for example, if timber prices fall, the government does not decide to reduce the stock of protected forest. The prediction that timber prices in Mexico would fall after the NAFTA seems reasonable, because Mexico is a net importer of timber products. Note that these are long-run changes. Thus, the decrease in forest cover observed from 1990 to 1995 may be consistent with the model, as private landowners harvest their timber then convert their land to other uses. The study thus illustrates what Chichilnisky's study argued — property rights to natural resources are a key determinant of the impact of trade liberalization on the natural environment.

## FISH STOCKS

WORLD RESOURCES (2000) DATA do not isolate fish harvests from the NAFTA countries, as they are presented for geographical regions of the major oceans. However, it is clear that a large number of North American marine fish stocks have declined, some to the point of collapse, like cod. All fisheries in the Atlantic ocean, with the exception of those in the Southwest Atlantic, are characterized as "overfished." The NAFTA, however, is not the cause of overfishing; all these regions were "fully fished" prior to its passage. Chomo and Ferrantino (2000) argue that while harvests in many North American fisheries exceed their sustainable level and declining stocks are a major concern, NAFTA-related policies are unlikely to have had any effect on the stocks. This is because tariffs were already near zero prior to the NAFTA. Where tariffs did exist (for Mexican products), the trade flows are low relative to harvests. Fish stock harvesting techniques and fisheries management have, however, been subjects of trade disputes.[15] Pacific fisheries are somewhat less threatened, but again predictions are that they will be fully fished within the next few years. It is clear that wild fish stocks are an environmental resource whose sustainability is in question.

SOILS AND AGRICULTURE

IDEALLY, ONE WOULD LIKE DATA on land and soil productivity or soil loss over time, but we could not find these types of data for the three countries. Total hectares in agricultural use has declined for Canada and the United States from 1987 to 1997, down less than 0.01 percent in Canada and 4.7 percent in the United States. In Mexico, total cropland has risen by 7.1 percent (perhaps as a result of conversion from forestry?). Overall, cropland has declined about 2.8 percent. Data are also available on average annual fertilizer use per hectare of farmland. Fertilizer use has environmental impacts. Run-off of excess fertilizer (beyond what plants take up) can contaminate ground water and, as noted above, contribute to eutrophication of surface waters. Fertilizer use rose in Canada and the United States, 31.4 percent and 32.5 percent, respectively, but fell almost 24 percent in Mexico. This is an intriguing result, given the cropland data. More intensive farming appears to be occurring in Canada and the United States, but not in Mexico. This may reflect comparative advantages and relative price changes for agricultural goods, product mixes or the type of farming techniques used (composition and technique effects). This is the subject for another study.

CONCLUDING COMMENTS

THIS SOMEWHAT LENGTHY SECTION presents crude environmental indicator data and illustrates that any possible impact on the natural environment of greater economic integration through trade liberalization, investment and economic growth is complex and ambiguous. The list of indicators is by no means complete, so a definite conclusion on the actual impact of integration on the environment cannot be drawn. Different sides in the debate can draw their own conclusions with the use of selected data. What can be said is that the evidence does not support a massive change in either direction for most of the indicators. It may also be that too little time has passed to infer anything concrete. These data provide a modest empirical check on some of the hypotheses examined below.

# HYPOTHESES ON THE LINKS BETWEEN INTEGRATION AND THE ENVIRONMENT

WE EXAMINE FOUR HYPOTHESES to try to determine how greater economic integration affects the natural environment and how environmental regulation affects the economy. In each case, a snapshot of the relevant literature is presented along with some recent data.

## HYPOTHESIS 1: COMPETITIVENESS AND POLLUTION HAVENS

*Stringent environmental regulation undermines a country's competitiveness and provides a strong incentive for capital and jobs to flee to regions with less stringent regulation.*

A NUMBER OF FACTORS MUST BE PRESENT to make a country's competitiveness, jobs and productivity highly dependent on the stringency of its environmental regulation. First and foremost, environmental regulation would have to lead to a decline in a company's profit significant enough to force it to scale back its production or contemplate relocating to a region with less stringent regulation. It is important to focus on profit, not just cost, as both total revenue and total cost can be affected by environmental regulation. To comply with regulations, a firm may have to cut output, incur higher capital costs for new pollution-abatement equipment or face higher operating costs. However, it may change its production techniques and even possibly lower total cost. Any or all of these changes can occur. The type of regulatory policy used also plays a role. Theoretical and empirical literature show that market-based policies are generally more cost effective than command and control policies — they reach the same environmental target at a lower total cost to society, including the cost to the polluter. This should be borne in mind throughout the discussion because, with a few notable exceptions (e.g., the U.S. sulphur dioxide trading program), most environmental regulation in North America has been command and control. Substituting market-based policies for command and control policies could have a significant impact on the cost of compliance.[16]

There has been environmental regulation in Canada and the United States since the 1970s. What has been happening in practice? The early literature (pre-1990s)[17] examining competitiveness and productivity issues finds that PACE was, on average, less than 2 percent of total cost and rarely exceeded 5 percent of total production cost. These results are widely cited and pertain to industry aggregates. There are at least two reasons why these numbers may be an underestimate: pollution-intensive industries (or firms within industries) face higher costs and costs may rise over time as regulations are phased in and gradually become more stringent. An example of the former is found in a study of the U.S. copper industry (Chapman 1991) that examines environmental regulation and worker health and safety. Regulation was estimated to lead to a 20 to 25 percent increase in production cost.[18] In a 1990 study, the U.S. Environmental Protection Agency (EPA 1990) estimated that PACE would rise as a percentage of GDP from an average of 1.7 percent for the 1972-90 period to 2.6 percent by 2000. A key reason why PACE is expected to rise over time is that as (or if) regulation becomes more stringent, firms will move up their marginal abatement cost curves and face higher unit costs of controlling additional increments in pollution. Unfortunately, we cannot test these predictions against more recent data because, as noted above, Canada and the United States currently do not survey and report PACE data. There is thus no current estimate of PACE except in studies of individual sectors and anecdotal information.

It is by no means certain, however, that pollution abatement costs must rise over time. If the regulations induce technological and/or process changes, costs may fall. This might explain why PACE did fall in the United States between 1973 and 1988 (the last year these data were available). PACE as a percentage of total capital expenditure for mineral processing fell from 12.1 percent over the 1973-80 period to 7.4 percent for 1981-88. The decreases for chemicals, pulp and paper and petroleum were from 9.1 to 5.3 percent, 11.7 to 6.5 percent and 10 to 7.1 percent, respectively. By way of comparison, the drop for all manufacturing was from 6.2 to 3.8 percent (United States Department of Commerce, various years). In Canada, a study of the cost of compliance with Ontario's Municipal Industrial Strategy for Abatement regulations found that it was significantly lower than estimated at the time the regulations were first introduced.[19] Other recent evidence supports what has become known as the "Porter hypothesis" — that regulation induces commercially valuable processes or products. Morgenstern, Pizer and Shih (1997) estimate from survey data on PACE that a one-dollar incremental expenditure leads to a 13 cent increase in production cost, on average, across their sample.[20] Berman and Bui (1998) examine oil refineries over the 1977-93 period and find that those facing the most stringent regulation in the United States had the fastest productivity growth, which they attribute to new technology. However, the Porter hypothesis remains controversial (Palmer, Oates and Portney 1995; Porter and van der Linde 1995). For example, Jaffe and Palmer (1997) find that PACE stimulates R&D but provides limited direct commercial value to the firm incurring the abatement cost (but this does not rule out public benefits from the spillover of technological knowledge). Attempts to quantify the cost saving due to regulation-induced technological innovation (Nordström and Vaughan) fail to find very significant impacts. The key message is that environmental regulation adds to a firm's cost of production, but the increments appear to be small, except perhaps for the most pollution-intensive firms. One should also not forget that society is interested in net benefits — the total cost versus total benefits of improving environmental quality. The distribution of these net benefits is often what is of concern to policy makers.

At least two factors are at work on the total revenue side. If firms have any degree of market power and environmental regulation increases their costs, they may be able to pass along these cost increases to consumers of their products. If firms take world prices as given, and other producing countries do not have comparable environmental regulation, then their profits will fall from what they would be without regulation. However, they may be able to brand and market themselves as environmentally friendly and thereby differentiate their products from those of other firms.[21] This would shift their demand curve out if buyers respond positively to the branding. There is some evidence to support the view that investors and consumers do care about a company's environmental record. Cohen and Fenn (1997) examined financial and environmental data from the Standard and Poor's 500 companies, dividing them into "green" firms, which had environmental records better than the median firm, and "brown" firms, which were environmental deadbeats. The green portfolio outperformed the brown in 80 percent of the cases and was statistically significant in 20 percent of all cases. The conclusion is that being green does not appear to penalize the company. Repetto (1995) gets similar results.

Finally, one must compare any potential impact of environmental regulation on a firm's profit to changes in other input prices and availability that may be occurring simultaneously. Econometric techniques can of course do this by specifying all the factors that may influence a firm's decision on how much to produce and where to locate. Evidence from econometric studies finds little support for the pollution haven hypothesis. A brief review of the most recent literature illustrates these findings. See Levinson (1997) and OECD (1997) for a more extensive review of the earlier literature on foreign direct investment (FDI) flows and pollution havens.

There are two strains in the literature — the first examines FDI flows, or trade flows (generally from the United States to other countries), the other looks at interstate investment flows within the United States in response to differences in environmental regulation among states. The FDI studies are reviewed first.

A study by Leonard (1988) for the period 1973-85, and updated by Olewiler (1994) to 1991, finds that while the pollution-intensive industries' (chemicals and mineral processing in these studies) share of total FDI rose over time, the change was minimal — rising from 25.7 percent in 1973 to 28.9 percent in 1991. The share of FDI from chemicals and mineral processing that went to developing countries (alleged to be the pollution havens, an assumption challenged elsewhere in this study) peaked in 1982, and fell thereafter. Similar findings are repeated for later years. Repetto notes that, on the one hand, developing economies receive a much smaller share of U.S. FDI in pollution-intensive industries (5 percent) compared to total U.S. FDI (45 percent). Developed countries, on the other hand, received 24 percent of the pollution-intensive FDI from the United States. Albrecht (1998) examines American FDI inflows and outflows and finds that outward FDI is growing faster in clean industries, while inflows of FDI are growing faster in dirty industries.

## TABLE 3

### INBOUND FDI INTO THE UNITED STATES, 1994 AND 1999

| | 1994 | | | | | | 1999 | | | | | |
|---|---|---|---|---|---|---|---|---|---|---|---|---|
| | All Countries | % of total | Canada | % of total | Mexico | % of total | All Countries | % of total | Canada | % of total | Mexico | % of total |
| All Industries | 45,095 | | 4,585 | | 1,058 | | 271,169 | | 12,228 | | 1,214 | |
| Petroleum | 1,665 | 2.6 | 177 | 2.8 | 2 | 0.1 | 5,558 | 1.7 | 386 | 2.1 | 6 | 0.5 |
| Total Manufacturing | 19,673 | 30.4 | 1,705 | 27.1 | 823 | 48.7 | 72,610 | 22.4 | 5,780 | 32.1 | 968 | 77.3 |
| Food and Beverages | −1,375 | | 480 | 7.6 | D | | −2,285 | | −539 | | −36 | |
| Chemicals | 10,820 | 16.7 | −11 | | D | | 9,416 | 2.9 | 399 | 2.2 | D | |
| Primary and Fabricated Metals | 1,982 | 3.1 | 265 | 4.2 | −1 | | 1,619 | 0.5 | 626 | 3.5 | D | |
| Machinery | 3,826 | 5.9 | 61 | 0.9 | −18 | | 24,132 | 7.4 | 2,217 | 12.3 | −7 | |
| Other Manufacturing | 4,419 | 6.8 | 909 | 14.5 | 590 | 34.9 | 39,729 | 12.3 | 3,078 | 17.1 | −162 | |
| Wholesale Trade | 5,785 | 8.9 | 698 | 11.1 | 45 | | 11,853 | 3.7 | 346 | 1.9 | −105 | |
| Retail Trade | 1,532 | 2.4 | −50 | | −1 | | 2,478 | 0.8 | 95 | 0.5 | D | |
| Depository Insurance | 3,800 | 5.9 | 327 | 5.2 | −29 | | 18,331 | 5.7 | 354 | 2.1 | 97 | 7.7 |
| Finance (except Depository Insurance) | 1,751 | 2.7 | 408 | 6.5 | −14 | | 8,793 | 2.7 | 1,855 | 10.3 | D | |
| Insurance | 2,759 | 4.3 | 488 | 7.8 | * | | 27,014 | 8.3 | 2,203 | 12.2 | * | |
| Real Estate | 259 | 0.4 | −10 | | 3 | 0.2 | 1,341 | 0.4 | 824 | 4.6 | 3 | 0.2 |
| Services | 2,303 | 3.6 | 177 | 2.8 | 53 | 3.1 | 16,876 | 5.2 | −17 | | 56 | 4.5 |
| Other | 5,570 | 8.6 | 664 | 10.6 | 175 | 10.3 | 106,315 | 32.8 | 401 | 2.2 | 122 | 9.7 |

Notes: * Indicates less than $500,000. D indicates information suppressed to avoid disclosure of company data. Minus sign indicates a net outflow.

Source: http://www.bea.doc/gov/bea/di/fdi.21.

## TABLE 4

### GROWTH IN VALUE-ADDED AND EXPORTS, CANADA AND MEXICO, 1990-96 (PERCENT)

| | Value-added Growth | Export Growth |
|---|---|---|
| Canada | 1990-96 | 1990-96 |
| Top Five Industries | 4.60 | 18.50 |
| Bottom Five Industries | −1.70 | 4.30 |
| Average (All Industries) | 1.60 | 11.20 |
| Pollution-intensive Industries | 0.02 | 6.70 |
| Number of Pollution-intensive Industries in Bottom Five | 3.00 | 3.00 |
| Mexico | | |
| Top Five Industries | 10.60 | 27.00 |
| Bottom Five Industries | −3.40 | 5.90 |
| Average (All Industries) | 3.20 | 16.00 |
| Pollution-intensive Industries | 1.90 | 9.40 |
| Number of Pollution-intensive Industries in Bottom Five | 1.00 | 3.00 |

Source: Sawchuk and Sydor (2003, Tables 2 and 3).

Table 3 presents FDI inflows to the United States in 1994 and 1999 from all countries, then isolates those from Canada and Mexico. While aggregate inflows of FDI have increased dramatically in the post-NAFTA period for all pollution-intensive industries except chemicals, the share of inbound FDI in the pollution-intensive sectors has fallen relative to that of services and a number of other less polluting sectors. While this does not contradict Albrecht's findings, it does suggest that the data should be interpreted with care and that a longer time series should be investigated.[22] The World Bank (1998) calculates the net exports of pollution-intensive goods for the 1986-95 period and finds that developing countries do not specialize in these industries. They import more pollution-intensive goods than they export. These results suggest that other components of a country's comparative advantage dominate differential environmental regulation. Examination of data on the growth in industry value-added and exports from 1990 to 1996 in Canada and Mexico shows that pollution-intensive industries are growing more slowly than average and that their export growth is not high.[23] Table 4 shows that pollution-intensive industries, with the exception of rubber and plastics (not shown), are generally among the slowest-growing sectors, with export growth lagging behind that of less pollution-intensive industries. Some even have negative growth in value-added and exports.

The numbers above look at aggregates and do not try to explain FDI, growth in value-added, or trade flows as a function of factors reflecting a country's comparative advantage.[24] A number of studies try to do this. Some examples are given. Xing and Kolstad (1998) perform a cross-sectional regression of U.S. FDI for two industries that are pollution-intensive and four industries that are not. The explanatory variables are corporate tax rates, market size (GDP per capita), industry profitability and the stringency of environmental regulation. Because stringency cannot be measured directly, they use a country's $SO_2$ emission levels in that year as a proxy. The coefficient on $SO_2$ is significant and positive for the pollution-intensive industries, but not for the others, thus supporting the pollution haven hypothesis. The estimated impact was relatively small. For example, a 1 percent increase in $SO_2$ emissions in a country is predicted to attract $0.27 million of additional FDI from the U.S. chemical industry. Total annual FDI by the U.S. chemical industry in recent years was $4 billion, of which most went to developed countries with presumably similar stringent environmental regulation (Nordström and Vaughan, p. 41).

Using an environmental indicator as a measure of environmental stringency is problematic. The level of emissions in any year can be a function of a host of factors including regulatory stringency (e.g., current and past regulation, physical features, characteristics of the pollutant, etc.). Results may also be sensitive to the indicator chosen. For example, in a framework analogous to the one by Xing and Kolstad, Kwan (1999) uses three different environmental quality indicators as proxies for stringency and finds that the results are sensitive to the variable chosen. The pollution haven hypothesis is supported for only one of her variables. What to use as the indicator of regulatory stringency is an unresolved problem in all of the environmental literature.

Low (1992) examines U.S.-Mexico trade patterns for 48 industries that had high PACEs. These industries accounted for 12 percent of all exports to Mexico, but had a growth rate of 9 percent annually prior to the NAFTA, compared to 3 percent for all exports. This could be interpreted as support for the pollution haven hypothesis. But Low also estimates that if pollution abatement cost in Mexico rose to the level of that in the United States (presumably by increasing regulatory stringency), Mexican export earnings would drop by 2 percent. This suggests that changes in trade flows due to environmental regulation are relatively small, and as the data in Table 4 indicate, growth in pollution-intensive sectors has typically been well below that of other sectors. Xu (1999) examines exports of pollution-intensive goods for 34 countries and finds they were unchanged between the 1960s and the 1990s, even though most developed countries brought in environmental regulations in the 1970s. Grossman and Krueger regress U.S. imports from Mexico relative to total imports on factor shares (labour and capital), effective tariffs and PACE. While the coefficient on PACE is positive, it is insignificant. This result is typical of the many studies trying to find support for pollution havens by examining trade and FDI flows. There is either no support for the hypothesis or, if positive, it is small.

Early studies of investment flows within the United States typically found no significant impact of environmental regulation on plant location. One criticism was that insufficient time had passed since the implementation of the regulations. More recent studies still use data that end just as the NAFTA was signed, so there are post-FTA data but no studies examining the post-NAFTA period (Fredriksson and Millimet 2000; List and Co 2000; Gray 1997; Levinson 1996). Levinson's results, for example, suggest that the average state's probability of attracting new domestic firms decreases by 0.89 percent when aggregate PACE increases by one standard deviation. This translates into a loss of 65 production jobs over a five-year period — hardly a substantial effect. List and Co, using the same sort of conditional logit model as Levinson, estimate the probability that foreign investment (FDI inbound to the United States) locates in a state. Their data are on the occurrence of investment, not the level of investment. Their regulatory stringency variables (four proxies were used in different estimations) were highly correlated with the probability of investment, suggesting that foreign investment is more sensitive to regulatory stringency than domestic investment (if we compare their results to Levinson). However, the magnitudes are still not large. The median state's probability of attracting a new foreign firm decreases by 2.07 percent when real PACE per $1000 of value-added rises 10 percent. The state would lose 174 jobs over the 1986-93 period. While they call this impact "large," it would be surprising if it were anywhere close to the investment and job losses that would occur if wage rates rose 10 percent.

These studies also yield what seems at first to be a surprising result. While the effects are still small, the stringency of environmental regulation appears to have an effect on the location of both pollution-intensive and non-intensive plants. In some cases, the impact of environmental regulation is stronger on non-intensive firms than pollution-intensive ones. The authors find this per-plexing and contrary to expectations. It suggests that the pollution haven hy-pothesis is fundamentally flawed because it focusses on the wrong variable. Perhaps studies should be looking at the state of the environment in a region, not the stringency of environmental regulation. The reason industries do not differ is that no one wants to enter a dirty state. Why?

First, U.S. regions with more stringent regulation are ones that, typically, are non-attainment areas. This means that their pollution levels exceed man-dated environmental targets. Under various U.S. policies, no new plant that re-leases emissions can locate in a non-attainment area unless it can find another plant that will reduce its emissions and so offset those from the new entrant. As a result, investment is curtailed. Even industries that do not release much pollu-tion may be affected by these regulations. It should not be surprising that the regulations work — they are meant to keep pollution levels from rising and they do (modestly). This is the objective of the policy. It is not really a test of the pollution haven hypothesis when some regions are constrained and others are not in the degree to which new investment can enter. Second, all firms and their workers may care about the quality of the environment (whether the firms themselves are pollution-intensive or not). People do not want to live in a pol-luted area. Firms do not want to face higher absenteeism due to pollution-related illnesses or future liability for environmental damage suffered by their employees or the community. They may also be liable if they locate on land that was previously contaminated by other firms. Even with assurances that the site was cleaned up, they cannot be sure some unforeseen toxin is not still active at the site and that they will have to clean it up or compensate affected parties. Third, non-attainment areas may also be ones where economic activity in gen-eral is declining because of the quality of life there (or other factors, like weather). The general migration of people and firms from the rust belt to the sun belt of the United States may dominate any environmental regulatory im-pact. Finally, firms may expect that a region that has more stringent regulation today, because it is dirtier than the standard, may increase its stringency even more in the future if pollution levels do not fall to the target level. These results suggest that rather than dwelling on environmental regulation as a deterrent to competitiveness, we might want to focus on environmental quality as a positive attribute for investment and environmental regulation as necessary to ensure improved or sustained environmental quality.

In summary, over 20 years of empirical studies have not supported the hypothesis that a country or region with stringent environmental regulation becomes less competitive and sees its companies and jobs relocate to pollution havens. The popular and political rhetoric still seems to think otherwise.

## HYPOTHESIS 2: THE RACE TO THE BOTTOM OR REGULATORY CHILL[25]

*Economic integration exacerbates destructive competition by countries or regions for industry. Governments will reduce the stringency of their environmental regulation until the lowest common denominator prevails. Or, they will pass regulations they have no intention of enforcing.*

THE RTTB OR REGULATORY CHILL (weak enforcement of regulations) hypothesis is a logical extension of the pollution haven hypothesis. If the pollution haven hypothesis was supported by the data, we might expect to see destructive competition among governments to weaken environmental regulation to the lowest common denominator (that of the havens) or, at best, to pass regulations they have no intention of enforcing. In principle, an examination of the state of environmental regulation within North America can be used to test the RTTB hypothesis. An RTTB hypothesis could be supported if

- regulations are converging among all three countries to some level lower than what prevailed before the NAFTA came into effect;

- regulations have not been weakened on paper, but enforcement is decreasing over time; or

- environmental quality is declining over time.

Taking the last statement first, from the previous section we know it is not possible to state unambiguously whether environmental quality has declined or not. As noted, environmental quality indicators are moving up and down, but clearly not uniformly down. Therefore, the data do not support evidence of an overall decline in environmental quality. As with empirical evidence on environmental quality, it is not an easy task to tackle the other two indicators of an RTTB, because it is impossible to aggregate all the different types of environmental regulation in North America.

### Convergence of Environmental Regulations?

A number of general observations can be drawn from an examination of environmental regulation in North America and how it has changed over time. These will be supported with examples that parallel the environmental indicators examined in the second section.

- There is no evidence of an RTTB in federal environmental regulation in North America. Regulations, if they move at all, are generally converging to more, not less stringent levels.

- While the period 1994-97 was characterized by few new environmental regulations in Canada and the United States, Mexico was making major changes to its environmental regulations, bringing them closer to Canada-U.S. standards.

- There has been a general upsurge in environmental initiatives since the late 1990s in all three countries, but regulatory interest at the federal level is highly variable over time.

Local governments are being given more responsibility for environmental regulation in Canada and Mexico. This may lead to lower levels of environmental quality because local governments, restricted in their capacity to fund environmental capital, have a narrow set of policy instruments and lack expertise. However, there are examples in all three countries of a race to the top to remove waste sites from communities. The NIMBY (not in my back yard) sentiment is alive and well all over North America. Evidence for the convergence of environmental policies is set out below.

1. *Toxic Compounds.* Canada introduced its National Pollutant Release Inventory (NPRI) in 1993, which is largely modelled on the U.S. Toxic Release Inventory (TRI) that began in 1987. Mexico also recently introduced its Pollution Release and Transfer Registry, which is also modelled on the TRI. These are federal government policies that require all companies employing at least 10 people to annually report releases and transfers of designated toxic compounds in quantities in excess of a minimum level. The data reported to the government must also be made available to the public. While the exact wording of the regulations differs and the lists of toxic compounds are not exactly the same in Canada and the United States, the regulations are virtually identical. Canada and the United States have also been converging toward banning the production and consumption of a number of highly toxic compounds (DDT, PCBs, dioxins, furans, mercury in certain uses, etc.) Mexico is beginning to move in the same direction. Canada has

frequently lagged behind the United States in introducing federal regulations governing toxic compounds.[26] The toxic inventory data are readily accessible by the public and could be one reason for strong local initiatives to improve environmental quality.

2. *Federal Air Quality Regulations.* Canada and the United States have ambient air quality targets. They are mandatory federal standards in the United States, enforced at the state level, and non-binding federal guidelines in Canada. Provinces can legislate these objectives as standards or introduce their own targets. Table 5 lists the Canadian targets, with U.S. standards in parentheses. All of the targets meet or exceed guidelines established by the World Health Organization. The figures in the column headed "maximum acceptable concentration" are the current Canadian targets and each serves as the reference point in data comparing actual ambient concentrations to each guideline. The maximum desirable concentration is a long-run goal, and the maximum tolerable concentration is for areas that have been far below the acceptable level. The United States has a set of complex standards for areas that do not meet the standard — the non-attainment regions. Canada has no comparable guidelines. Mexico also has ambient air quality standards similar to those in the United States, but has merged them into an index of air quality. As noted in the previous section, air pollution in the large urban areas typically exceeds their standards. The actual targets shown in Table 5 are not identical in Canada and the United States, but there is no discernable pattern of differences. Sometimes Canadian guidelines are more stringent than those in the United States and vice versa. A key point is that the targets have not changed for many years. Both countries introduced their targets in the 1970s, and they have stayed the same until the late 1990s, when the EPA proposed legislation to tighten standards for PM and ozone. The legislation was stopped by the Supreme Court after a legal challenge by a company, and the EPA is now appealing this decision. There are proposals in Canada to tighten some of its guidelines as well.

3. *Motor Vehicle Fuel Economy Targets.* Canada and the United States have fuel efficiency targets for motor vehicles.[27] Again, the targets are mandatory standards in the United States and non-binding guidelines in Canada. They apply to all new motor vehicles produced each year. The producer has to meet an average fuel efficiency rating for its entire fleet (pooled together). There are separate standards for automobiles and light-duty trucks (including sport utility vehicles). Targets for automobiles were brought in many years ago and very gradually raised.

They have been constant, however, since the mid-1980s. Targets were introduced for light-duty trucks in 1990, with the gradual implementation of higher targets over time. The Canadian targets are identical to those of the United States. This is a good example of where economic integration has contributed to a uniform environmental target independent of whether that target is mandatory or not. Because the North American auto industry is integrated, all Canadian manufacturers meet the U.S. standards. There have been periods when planned tightening of the standards was delayed, but these occurred prior to the NAFTA. Thus, while there is no evidence of an RTTB, the targets appear to be "stuck" at the status quo — their existing level. Canada has recently proposed some tightening of its guideline standards and converting them to standards, but no action has been taken.

**TABLE 5**

**CANADA'S NATIONAL AMBIENT AIR QUALITY OBJECTIVES (NAAQOS)**
**(U.S. STANDARDS SHOWN IN PARENTHESES)**

| Pollutant | Averaging Time | Maximum Desirable Concentration | Maximum Acceptable Concentration | Maximum Tolerable Concentration |
|---|---|---|---|---|
| Sulphur Dioxide | Annual | 11 ppb | 23 ppb (30) | – |
| | 24-hour | 57 ppb | 115 ppb (140) | 306 ppb |
| | 1-hour | 172 ppb | 344 ppb (500)[a] | – |
| Suspended Particulates | Annual | 60 µg/m$^3$ | 70[c] µg/m$^3$ (50) | – |
| | 24-hour | – | 120[c] µg/m$^3$ (65)[b] | 400 µg/m$^3$ |
| Ozone | 1-hour | 50 ppb | 82 ppb (80)[b] | 153 ppb |
| Carbon Monoxide | 8-hour | 5 ppm | 13 ppm (9) | 17 ppm |
| | 1-hour | 13 ppm | 31 ppb (35) | – |
| Nitrogen Dioxide | Annual | 32 ppB ppb (53) | | |
| | 24-hour | – | 106 ppb | 160 ppb |
| | 1-hour | – | 213 ppb | 532 ppb |

Note: a = 3-hour average; b = proposed limit; c = interim provincial. 24-hour guidelines for PM-10 = 50 µg/m$^3$; for PM-2.5 = 25 µg/m$^3$.

Source: Environment Canada. *State of the Environment*, "Urban Air Quality," SOE Technical Supplement No. 99-1, National Environmental Indicator Series, Spring 1999. Available at: http://www.ec.gc.ca. U.S. EPA National Environment Air Quality Standard (NAAQS) levels. Available at: http://www.epa.gov.

4. *Acid Precipitation.* Canada took the lead in the 1980s, pushing the United States toward stronger regulations. Eastern Canada was hard hit by acid precipitation coming from several large Canadian sources (Sudbury mineral smelters, Ontario Hydro, oil refineries) and coal-fired power plants in the eastern and midwestern United States. After years of dragging its feet, the United States introduced legislation for the very innovative tradeable permit market for $SO_2$ — the key pollutant in acid precipitation, in the amendments to the *Clean Air Act* of 1990. The market has been operating since the mid-1990s and has contributed to reductions in $SO_2$ in excess of the targets. Neither Canada nor Mexico participates in this market, nor do they have any tradeable emissions markets. Canada has run some pilot programs for $NO_x$ and has studied a market mechanism for greenhouse gases. In the past few months, there has been a call for more stringent regulation of $SO_2$ in Canada and the United States because of continued concerns over declining environmental quality in those regions of both countries most affected by acid precipitation.

5. *Water Quality.* Mexico has probably the worst water quality among the countries of the Organisation for Economic Co-operation and Development (OECD). Only about 14 percent of its households have treated water. Its delivery and treatment infrastructures are primitive. However, since the NAFTA and joining the OECD, regulatory reform has accelerated. A program launched in 1995 introduces a number of market-based policies like progressive pricing, discharge fees and infrastructure construction. There is a long way to go, but the direction is positive. Canada and the United States have extensive water treatment and delivery systems, with major funding programs introduced in the 1970s. Cuts to public budgets largely eliminated these federal programs in the 1990s. The infrastructure has deteriorated, with resulting decreases in water quality in many regions, as noted in the previous section. Only in the past few years has there been a resurgence in federal attention to the infrastructure. On water quality targets, the United States has mandatory federal standards; Canada has federal guidelines that are not binding. Following the Walkerton incident in 2000, several provinces (e.g., Ontario and British Columbia) have begun the process of implementing binding standards.

6. *Lead and CFCs.* Airborne lead emissions are a major health hazard, especially for children. Lead is a neurotoxin reducing cognitive ability at low levels and leading to permanent brain damage at higher levels. As noted in the previous section, Canada and the United States had eliminated

lead from gasoline by 1990 (the United States was first). Mexico began to eliminate lead from its gasolines in 1990 and continues to phase it out. The regulations are thus being harmonized at the most stringent level. All three countries are signatories to the Montreal Protocol to eliminate the production and use of stratospheric ozone-depleting compounds (ODCs). CFCs and some other ODCs have been eliminated in Canada and the United States. Mexico signed the Montreal Protocol as a developing country, which allows it to phase out ODCs over a longer period. In the mid-1990s, Mexico announced that it will attempt to speed up the phase-out process.

7.  *Natural Resource Management.* This is a huge topic. The key point to make is that all three countries still provide subsidies (including preferential tax treatment for some industries) for the protection and bailout of these extraction industries (e.g., fishing, energy, agriculture and some parts of the forest industry). These subsidies generally lead to faster rates of exploitation than would be the case if market prices prevailed, and thus contribute to environmental degradation. Trade agreements can be "friends of the environment" by not allowing domestic subsidies to violate national treatment provisions. This is one example where very little progress has been made to change regulations to make them more compatible with sustainable resource use. Governments seem to be stuck at the bottom.

8.  *Climate Change.* One hesitates to enter this quagmire. All three countries were signatories to the Kyoto Accord, but to date, only Canada has ratified the treaty (in late 2002). It remains uncertain whether significant progress will be made to meet the Kyoto targets. North America lags behind much of the European Union (EU) in implementing any sort of explicit environmental policy to deal with carbon emissions.[28] Reasons are complex and range from unresolved scientific debate and how to account for carbon sinks to the political power of industrial sectors (the fossil fuel and electricity-generating industries) and regional interests (Alberta, Texas and Alaska). The indicators in the previous section show continued increases in greenhouse gas emissions in aggregate and per capita terms, so this issue is not going to go away while governments study the problem further. It is not clear what role North American integration may be playing in this regulatory stalemate.

## Compliance with Environmental Regulations

One of the major concerns about the NAFTA was that greater integration would lead to less compliance with existing regulations; governments would not publicly announce that they were weakening standards and guidelines, they simply would not monitor polluters as vigorously nor enforce the existing regulations. Mexico's record on compliance was very poor prior to the NAFTA. What happened? The short answer is that we do not know for sure. A major problem is finding and interpreting the data. Ideally, one would like to know monitoring and enforcement inputs and outcomes — how many inspections are actually done, what percentage they are of the possible total, what percentage of those inspected are in compliance, and so on. Typically, these types of data are available only by starting at the local level and working up, as in all three countries, much of the enforcement is local or state/provincial. The definitive work has not yet been written. What follows is just a snapshot of some general observations:

- Mexico has increased efforts at monitoring and enforcement. It works with the United States through the Border XXI initiative to improve inspection frequency and probability of detecting violators. The environmental inspection arm of SEMARNAP (the main environmental/natural resource agency), PROFERA, reports a large reduction in serious violations from 1993 to 1996 (72 percent), and a substantial increase in compliance (43 percent) of maquiladora facilities over the same period (United States-Mexico Chamber of Commerce 1998). It is hard to judge how meaningful these numbers are, but evidence does not suggest an RTTB.[29]

- All three countries suffer from inadequate resources being devoted to compliance. Budgetary cutbacks of the 1990s greatly reduced personnel in Canadian environment ministries. Decentralization of environmental responsibilities to lower levels of government has also contributed to the loss of personnel for monitoring and enforcement. Canada seems stuck in the status quo.

- All three countries have increased their dependence on voluntary compliance.[30] This means working with companies to enable them to undertake environmental audits so they can identify pollution problems, take remedial action and report emissions to government authorities. Voluntary compliance is on the agendas of not only environment ministries but also other organizations dealing with environmental issues (e.g., the OECD, the World Bank, the WTO, environmental non-governmental organizations), but the sort of impact it will have on actual compliance rates is unclear. International branding is also at work. The International Standards Organization (ISO) has created a set of standards for environmental management systems in its ISO-14001 program, created in 1996. This is fully voluntary, but many firms, especially multinational ones, seek the ISO-14001 certification for both themselves and for subcontractors they may use in different countries. All three countries have voluntary eco-certification programs, and Mexico in particular provides incentives to assist companies in meeting the standards.[31] Integration may not have made environment ministries more dependent on voluntary compliance, but it has certainly increased the incentives for companies to eco-brand. While all this seems positive and cooperative, one still worries that the fox is being asked to guard the chicken coop. This is an area to watch.

In summary, there is no support for an RTTB in environmental regulation as a result of greater economic integration. There was a tendency for Canada and the United States to be stuck in the status quo with little initiative on some environmental issues up to the end of the 1990s, but this trend began before the Canada-U.S. FTA and the NAFTA. Regulatory interest has again been sparked by all sorts of environmental concerns from the global (climate change) to the very local (water quality and waste sites). Integration may be playing a positive role in this recent policy upswing — linkage of economies and better information flows have increased the public's awareness of environmental problems and demand for action. Whether the environment can stay on the front burner is uncertain; there have been too many cycles of vacillating interest over the past 35 years for one to be sanguine.

## HYPOTHESIS 3: GROWTH IS BAD FOR THE ENVIRONMENT

*Greater integration leads to higher levels of output and income. This puts more stress on the environment because the scale effect dominates any positive impacts of the composition and technique effects. More income and output mean more consumption and production and, hence, more waste flows, resource use and environmental degradation.*

HYPOTHESIS 3 IS RELATED TO THE FIRST TWO HYPOTHESES. The main theoretical and empirical relationship we examine is the environmental Kuznets curve (EKC). The EKC represents a functional relationship between environmental indicators such as those presented in the previous section and measures of growth, typically GDP per capita. It may also include other explanatory variables. One additional variable that some of the literature has investigated is a country's degree of openness. There are dozens of studies that have estimated EKCs with data across countries at a point in time, and time series within a country, and a few have estimated EKCs with panel data.[32] The theory suggests that if environmental quality is an income-elastic good, the EKC between pollution levels and income will be either falling or an inverted U shape.

The main conclusion from the EKC studies is that there is no consistent relationship between rising GDP and indicators of pollution. The evidence does not show that pollution *must* rise with economic growth, so Hypothesis 3 is only supported for some environmental indicators. Caution is in order because there are many difficulties with this work. For example, where the results yield the inverted U shape, the turning point can be at a per capita income level higher than most countries can hope to achieve for many years. Few countries in the world have per capita incomes higher than US$10,000. While per capita incomes in Canada and the United States obviously exceed this amount, Mexico's is US$3,415 (1995 US$). This can bias both the shape of the curve and the location of the turning point at which pollution starts to fall with increases in per capita GDP.

One example of the type of EKCs that are generated when income and the degree of a country's openness are included in cross sectional data for the late 1990s is found in Olewiler (2001). The study examines the environmental indicators of unsafe drinking water, sanitation availability, deforestation, $SO_2$ in urban areas, and $CO_2$ emissions. The estimated EKCs are

- falling (almost L-shaped) for unsafe drinking water and lack of sanitation — once per capita income levels reach between US$4,000 and US$5,000 (1995 US$), levels of safe water and sanitation approach 100 percent;

- falling for $SO_2$ until per capita income passes US$32,000, at which point the curve begins to slope up again very gradually;

- an inverted U shape for deforestation, with a turning point of about US$30,000; and

- different shapes for $CO_2$, depending on the indicator used. $CO_2$ emissions per capita yield an inverted U shape with a turning point of approximately US$28,000; net $CO_2$ (aggregate emissions minus carbon sequestration) and aggregate $CO_2$ emissions are rising functions.

Openness (exports plus imports as a proportion of GDP) enters each of the equations (except for per capita $CO_2$) negatively; more open countries have lower pollution levels. The openness coefficient is generally not significant (except for per capita $CO_2$), but its inclusion always adds to the equation's explanatory power. Openness thus cannot be said to increase a country's pollution level. This result is consistent with other studies examining openness and environmental impact. Hypothesis 3 remains ambiguous.

## Hypothesis 4: Trade Agreements Undermine Environmental Policy Setting

*Provisions within trade agreements inhibit a country's autonomy in setting environmental policy and therefore prevent a country from reaching its domestic environmental targets.*

IN THE EARLY 1990S, part of the debate over the merits of the NAFTA focussed on its potentially adverse impact on the environment. The maquiladoras on the Mexico-U.S. border free trade zone were cited as being a leading indicator of the forthcoming rise in environmental degradation. The area was already heavily polluted, and many companies operating there were branches of multinational companies from OECD countries. It was a classic pollution haven and NAFTA critics felt this was just the beginning of more degradation if the agreement came into force.

Concern over the environmental impact of the NAFTA by non-government organizations and the public led to the inclusion of an environmental side agreement (the North American Agreement on Environmental Cooperation), language about sustainable development in the preamble of the main agreement, and a strengthening of sanitary and phytosanitary trade requirements. New institutions and programs were set up under the side agreement to address environmental concerns within the NAFTA countries. These institutions included the Commission for Environmental Cooperation (CEC), a trinational body with the authority to investigate allegations of non-enforcement of environmental regulations within each country and to monitor the environmental impact of the NAFTA. The Border Environment Cooperation Commission and the North American Development Bank were established to help provide resources for U.S.-Mexican border communities to improve environmental infrastructure. These joined the Border XXI Program, a set of initiatives to help improve environmental quality and enforcement and provide data on any environmental impact due to the NAFTA.

Concern over the environment thus led to the creation of environmental institutions within the NAFTA. How much impact the environmental institutions have had on environmental quality and environmental regulatory processes is open to debate (and beyond the scope of this study). A casual examination of the activities of the CEC, for example, does not reveal a very impressive list of achievements.[33] One problem is that it need not make all its actions public, so it is difficult for independent assessment to occur. Criticism and praise of the other institutions is also present in the popular and academic literature. Whatever the verdict, it is probably fair to say that environmental concerns do have a higher profile because these institutions exist.

The more pressing issue is the presence in the NAFTA (and other trade agreements) of provisions that inhibit a country's autonomy in setting environmental regulations to meet target levels of environmental quality. This is what Hypothesis 4 asserts. According to Mann (2000) and the IISD (2001)[34], trade laws like the NAFTA can affect environmental policy in a number of ways. These include:

- National treatment (non-discrimination) clauses ensure that parties to the agreement will not be treated less favourably then domestic producers. They forbid the adoption of protectionist measures and give foreign producers equal opportunity to access a country's market. In the context of environmental policy, this means that a tariff on a pollution-intensive good cannot be introduced unless the same good produced within the country faces an identical tax. A related implication is as follows: If the producer of a hazardous or polluting product is only located in a foreign country (there are no domestic producers), how can equal treatment be given? Will tariffs designed to internalize environmental externalities arising in the consumption (or disposal) of the good in the importing country be forbidden? If so, this would give producers of toxic compounds the incentive to locate all production abroad.

- Environmental policies which are disguised barriers to trade cannot be implemented. But what, exactly, is a disguised barrier to trade? The NAFTA side agreement does recognize a country's need to protect its environment. The General Agreement on Tariffs and Trade (GATT) — and now the WTO — also recognized that environmental regulations could be exceptions (limited and conditional) from the other obligations of the agreement.

- Environmental policies might have to be based on sound scientific analysis. This is required for sanitary and phytosanitary regulations, but not for most types of environmental regulations, although there is some uncertainty about the burden of proof required for environmental regulations. But even if "sound science" isn't a direct requirement, it may be a necessary component in the process of setting an environmental regulation — establishing that risk assessment has been done, the environmental objective identified, and an appropriate risk management tool selected. This sort of process, while probably implicitly underlying the determination of environmental policies anyhow, will have to be more explicit and transparent to avoid trade disputes from interfering with domestic environmental policy making. Risk assessment does not need to be done for environmental regulation; but if it is done, and does not use sound science, the regulation could be open to the charge that it is a disguised barrier to trade.

- A country that wishes to establish a regulation different from international standards must prove why the difference is necessary.

- There is a principle that says the least trade restrictive measure consistent with the environmental objective should be used (e.g., the GATT, 1994, Article XX and the NAFTA, Article 2101).

- Product taxes and charges can be levied on imports, but process taxes/charges cannot. For example, a government can levy an excise tax on fuel produced domestically and imported. It cannot put a tax on the energy consumed in producing a tonne of imported steel because that is a tax on the production process.

- These provisions and conditions apply retroactively to policies adopted before the NAFTA came into force. This implies that regulatory decisions taken before the "rules of the trading game" were known can give rise to trade disputes.

- Under the NAFTA, actions can be taken against a country when there is the potential for a trade barrier to exist. It is not necessary to prove that an actual impact has occurred.

These features of trade agreements suggest that there may well be major concern over the ability of policy makers to pursue environmental objectives without running into trade disputes. Many past, present and potential environmental regulations would not survive trade law challenges. However, Mann argues that under most trade agreements (e.g., the GATT and the WTO) it is unlikely that that there would be many cases brought against environmental policies. There are three reasons: First, a trade challenge must be brought by one government against another. Most governments do not spend scarce time and funds looking for environmental regulations to challenge in other countries. This could initiate retaliation and a costly trade war. Second, even if a country loses a case brought against it, there are no penalties (under the WTO), nor does it have to give up the regulation. It must make the regulation consistent with international standards. Under the NAFTA (Article 2018) the regulation would have to be removed or not implemented, but a replacement measure could be introduced. Third, under GATT rules, a ruling does not have to be adopted.

Thus, while there is definitely reason for concern about impingement on domestic regulatory authority, the trade provisions listed above do not seem to be a major threat. Since the NAFTA was adopted, there have been no trade and environment cases initiated between the three governments. A few cases involving the environment have come before the WTO. However, unlike the GATT or the WTO, the NAFTA contains a provision that may be a threat to environmental policy setting. This is the Chapter 11 provision that allows a corporation to bring suit against a government and seek compensation for expropriation of its actual or potential earnings. The provision gives foreign investors rights and remedies that are more extensive than in other trade agreements, going beyond anything in the GATT or the WTO. Chapter 11 was brought in to protect investment in Mexico from appropriation; it was not intended as a way to challenge environmental policy. However, of the 17 actions brought under Chapter 11 (to March 2001), 10 are related to adopted or proposed environmental regulations. The tribunals hearing the cases have generally ruled in favour of the foreign investor (corporations). The tribunals consist of three members, one from each of the member countries. Their deliberations are secret and need not even be published unless one of the parties in the case chooses to do so.

The cases heard thus far suggest that unless they are overturned on appeal, or Chapter 11 is amended, the NAFTA could present a barrier to environmental policy making.[35] Mann (p. 39) concludes that Chapter 11 cases have successfully argued that new environmental laws, especially those with a larger impact on one company than others, expropriate the investor's business and that compensation is required. At least one tribunal has determined decisions (the Metalclad case against Mexico) that the motive for the regulation is not relevant. The tribunal did not mention environmental protection in that case. The expropriation was defined as "covert or incidental interference with the use of property" (p. 32). The case suggests that NAFTA tribunals are using a broad interpretation of expropriation that may challenge a jurisdiction's police power (or peace, order and good government in Canada). Regulators may fear that environmental regulations that interfere with the use of investments to generate profits could fall under Chapter 11, generate suits and require compensation.

This gloomy view is tempered by several factors. First, some of the decisions involving environmental regulations under Chapter 11 are under appeal and may be reversed. Second, the signatories of the NAFTA have expressed some concern with this provision that may lead to its re-examination. However, the uncertainty about the future impact of Chapter 11 and fallout from past decisions could dampen a regulator's enthusiasm for introducing new environmental policies. In the Ethyl Corporation v. Government of Canada Chapter 11 case, Canada tried to ban the import of the fuel additive MMT, which has potential negative health impacts (and damages air pollution equipment in cars), and lost.[36] The government backed down and removed the import ban after the corporation won the case, and had to sign a letter that said there was no proof that MMT is harmful.

Much more could be written on the Chapter 11 cases than can be covered in this study. Until there is a full assessment of the impact of Chapter 11 on environmental regulation, it would be premature to reject Hypothesis 4.

## POLICY IMPLICATIONS FOR CANADA

THE EVIDENCE REVIEWED in this study does not support the view that greater integration of the North American economies must result in lower levels of environmental quality. Some environmental quality indicators have improved, while others have declined, but there is no compelling evidence that the source of the changes in environmental quality is greater economic integration. While the long-term impact on the environment of increased trade and investment flows and higher rates of growth is still not clear, there is no evidence that North American integration has promoted the development of pollution havens or a race to the bottom for environmental regulation. Regulations, if they have moved at all, appear to be converging to at least the status quo level (before the NAFTA) of the country with the most stringent regulations. There appears to be a trend toward tightening regulations and a very slow creep toward the use of more cost-effective market-based policies.

While current features of trade agreements do restrict the set of instruments that policy makers can use to address domestic environmental problems, with the exception of the provisions within Chapter 11 of the NAFTA, these constraints do not appear to be a significant impediment to the adoption of socially efficient policies. Trade agreements may even promote better policy that improves environmental quality. For example, if countries are nudged toward reducing their subsidies to pollution-intensive industries and the primary sectors because they violate principles of national treatment and can be viewed as non-tariff barriers, it could help reduce non-sustainable natural resource production.

The principles incorporated in Chapter 11 and the processes established to adjudicate cases brought under this provision appear to be flawed and may pose a threat to socially efficient environmental policy making. This provision of the NAFTA should be re-examined with the objective of ensuring that maximizing net social benefits is paramount as a justification for environmental regulations.[37] If environmental cases under Chapter 11 continue to favour corporate investors, it could handicap policy makers at all levels of government, but especially local government, who do not have the resources to ensure that their environmental actions do not violate these investment provisions.

Canadian environmental policy is decentralized, with the primary responsibility for many environmental regulations residing at the provincial level. This presents some trade-offs in an integrating North America. Local regulations can be tailored to the specific conditions within the community. Good environmental policy should reflect the marginal damage and abatement costs, resource endowments and other factors within the region. Harmonization of policies is not consistent with efficiency if conditions differ among regions — local pollutants may be regulated most efficiently by local governments. But then, at least two problems emerge in the context of economic integration. First, as noted above, local governments may lack the resources and expertise necessary to ensure that efficient environmental policy is consistent with the principles of trade agreements. Second, while there is no evidence in North America of an RTTB for environmental policies, decentralization may contribute to being stuck with the status quo because policy makers fear introducing policies that deviate from the perceived norm. This is true of Canadian environmental policy at all levels. The Canadian constitution and the political economy of federalism hamper a strong federal role in environmental policy, except in areas of international environmental treaties and where the federal government has carved out a role through regulations like the CEPA.[38] As noted in the previous section, Canadian federal environmental regulations are guidelines, not binding targets. This is in sharp contrast to the United States, were federal regulations are binding and the government can use threats (e.g., withhold state funding) if states are lax in enforcing the regulations. Canada uses moral suasion. This may be the kinder, gentler route to improving the environment, but it also means that Canada may not be moving as fast as it could toward reaching environmental targets. This may actually harm Canadian competitiveness and economic growth over time if, as the empirical studies discussed in this study suggest, investors and people want to move to regions where environmental quality is high, not to pollution havens.

Integration, more particularly the protests against trade and investment agreements, has played a role in making the public more aware of environmental issues. There is pressure on governments, regulatory agencies and corporations to provide more and better information about the environmental impact of integration, as well as their policies and actions. This is a good thing for many reasons. First, an important problem in analysing the relationship between integration and the environment is the lack of data and public access to it. During the years of public sector restraint, a number of environmental data series were terminated. These should be reinstated and expanded so both the public and policy makers know what is happening. Ignorance and misinformation feed the rhetoric from the two extreme sides of the integration and environment debate — those who oppose all trade and investment agreements and those who favour complete integration without environmental safeguards. Second, without information on environmental damages, costs of abatement, trends in emissions and so on, good policy making is impossible. Third, regulators have a higher probability of getting environmental measures implemented without trade and investment challenges if they have all their facts and analyses straight. Fourth, data help corporations and individuals make their own environmentally responsible decisions (i.e., they facilitate voluntary actions to improve environmental quality). Reliable information flows are essential to eco-labeling or branding and pollution prevention programs, for example. Governments can help play a role in these voluntary actions by testing and certifying the information released by companies.[39]

Finally, consider two starkly different scenarios of the relationship between integration and the environment:

> *Scenario I*: Governments will not impose efficient and effective environmental regulations because they are convinced by special interest groups that this will destroy their economy's competitiveness. Subsidies to pollution-intensive and resource-using sectors are maintained to protect jobs and investments in those industries, despite the fact that this contributes to inefficient use of natural resources and environmental degradation, and tilts the playing field against less environmentally damaging industries. Trade and investment agreements are signed without environmental safeguards. Economic growth does indeed occur and output and incomes rise. But pollution also increases because environmental regulations have not kept pace with the increase in economic scale. Only weak regulatory incentives exist to stimulate research and development of new technologies to control emissions and reduce the environmental impact from production and consumption per unit output, because there is no payoff to this sort of investment. The economy appears healthy in the short term, but rising pollution levels continue to degrade the environment to the point where the sustainability of natural and economic systems is threatened. Thresholds are crossed where it will take billions of dollars to repair environmental damage, if indeed repair can be done at all.

> *Scenario II*: Governments use socially efficient environmental policies that balance the costs of improving the environment against the benefits of higher levels of environmental quality. They welcome economic integration and sign trade and investment agreements that have environmental safeguards that work. Growth increases and environmental regulations keep pace to ensure that pollution does not rise above the level consistent with social efficiency. The gains from trade may

even be high enough to "pay for" raising the environmental targets over time. In other words, there are increases in the standard of living from both the perspective of real incomes and environmental quality. Investors want to locate in this country and people want to live there. Some pollution-intensive industries may leave, but many stay and develop better and cheaper ways of controlling their emissions over time so that they become less pollution-intensive.

These scenarios are, of course, overly pessimistic and optimistic. Canada is now at a point between them. The key message is that even if one rejects the hypothesis that economic growth is bad for the environment, it does not mean that economic growth alone will sustain or improve environmental quality. Economic growth and cost-effective and socially efficient environmental policies are essential companions to a healthy environment. As a number of the world's well-known economists and ecologists (Arrow et al. 1995) have stated:

> Economic growth is not a panacea for environmental quality; indeed, it is not even the main issue. What matters is the content of growth — the composition of inputs (including environmental resources) and outputs (including waste products). This content is determined by, among other things, the economic institutions within which human activities are conducted. These institutions need to be designed so that they provide the right incentives for protecting the resilience of ecological systems. Such measures will not only promote greater efficiency in the allocation of environmental resources at all income levels, but they would also assure a sustainable scale of economic activity within the ecological life-support system.

## ENDNOTES

1    Individuals may, of course, bargain with a farmer to preserve his wetland. This has happened in practice, through non-governmental organizations. For example, Ducks Unlimited uses funds from its members (waterfowl hunters) to compensate farmers who preserve wetlands in Canada and the United States. The Nature Conservancy buys ecologically sensitive lands.

2    Emissions refer to waste products released to the atmosphere, while effluents are the wastes discharged into bodies of water. To simplify discussion, discharges of waste to any environmental medium will be called emissions.

3    Antweiler, Copeland and Taylor (1998) use sulphur dioxide as an environmental indicator to estimate scale, composition and technique effects for 44 countries on the basis of 1971-96 data. The composition effect is unclear. Capital appears to flow from middle-income countries to the highest- and lowest-income countries.

Capital migration to high-income countries supports the prediction that pollution intensity will rise in capital-intensive countries if pollution and capital intensity are highly correlated. The move to the lowest-income countries is not consistent with this, but may reflect regulatory stringency. However, they also find that the technique effect dominates the scale effect. For example, a 1 percent increase in economic activity increases $SO_2$ emissions by 0.3 percent (scale effect), but the technique effect reduces these emissions by 1.4 percent, leading to a combined effect of a reduction of 1.1 percent.

4   A variant on the Copeland-Taylor argument for investment is presented by Beladi, Chau and Khan (2000). In their theoretical model, the North is capital-rich and resource-poor, while the South is the opposite. Trade liberalization leads to greater investment by the North in the South's natural resource industries (their example is agriculture), but this simply serves to accelerate the depletion of natural resource stocks through pollution (and presumably extraction rates above replacement rates for renewable resources). The South therefore needs more and more capital over time to produce the same output. This is reflected in an upward sloping demand curve for capital by the South. Pollution levels and environmental degradation are then ever increasing.

5   One problem with many studies examining trade and growth effects on the environment and environmental regulation is that they use data that predate major changes in trade liberalization. This is being remedied now with the publication of work that uses much more recent data. This paper, therefore, does not review much of the literature that is based on data from the 1970s and 1980s. There are many good surveys of this literature. See, for example, Levinson (1997), Nordström and Vaughan (1999), Olewiler (1994) and Jaffe, Peterson, Portney and Stavins (1995).

6   The sources for the Mexican data are Hayward and Jones (1999) and Guzmán (1999).

7   PM is one of the most serious air pollutants worldwide. The numbers given in Figures 1 and 2 are for PM-10, which refers to PM less than 10 microns in size. The current scientific analysis suggests that PM-2.5 may be even more important to monitor, for health reasons. The United States started measuring these emissions in 1990.

8   Canadian data on lead emissions are available from specific sources, but an aggregate indicator could not be located.

9   The success in reducing phosphorus is largely due to Canada-U.S. cooperation through the institution of the International Joint Commission on boundary waters.

10   This is paraphrased from the Canadian *Environmental Protection Act* of 1988. Similar wording occurs in U.S. legislation covering toxic releases.

11   These data come from the National Pollutant Release Inventory (NPRI) for Canada and the Toxic Release Inventory (TRI) for the United States. Dasgupta, Lucas and Wheeler (2002) have collected data on the emission of air pollutants from a sample of 6,000 Mexican manufacturing plants and calculated emission intensity per employee for large, medium and small plants. These data cannot be directly compared to the NPRI and TRI data because the emissions covered are not the same.

However, the ratios for Mexico suggest that the pollution intensity of industries differs among the countries. This should not be surprising, given differences in factor endowments and regulation. For example, the most emission-intensive ratio for Mexico is for petroleum products, a pollution-intensive industry in Canada and the United States as well. Mexico's ratio is 638 pounds per employee for large firms. The ratio in Canada for all toxic releases is 3,486 tons per employee and 770 tons per employee in the United States. The most emission-intensive firms in Mexico, in this sample, are small firms in the wood industry, with a ratio of 1,050 tons of emissions per employee. By way of comparison, the Canadian and U.S. ratios are 16 and 57 tons of emissions per employee, respectively.

12   The data should be adjusted to reflect toxic intensity, not just emission intensity, where toxic intensity reflects the projected toxicity of each of the compounds released by each industry. In Table 1, compounds of what might be very different toxicity are aggregated by weight. See Olewiler and Dawson (1998) for a measure of the toxic intensity of Canadian industries. Lucas, Wheeler and Hettige (1992) derive toxicity measures for U.S. manufacturing industries. In these toxicity-weighted measures, most industries which are emission-intensive are also toxic-intensive. For example, the industries in Canada with the highest overall toxicity are (in descending order of toxicity): refined petroleum and coal, chemicals and chemical products, mining, crude petroleum and natural gas, primary metal, paper and allied products, rubber, plastics and non-metallic minerals. These industries are also the top seven in Table 1.

13   Data on forest cover and the next four categories come from various tables in World Resources Institute (2000).

14   This result is consistent with other studies on deforestation.

15   These are the tuna-dolphin and shrimp-turtle cases that came under provisions of the GATT. The trade disputes were over the ability of a country to extend natural resource conservation regulation extra-territorially. These actions were held in violation of trade and not covered by exemptions for conservation. However, the United States finally prevailed on appeal of the shrimp-turtle case; the WTO has determined that the conservation devices and law are consistent with WTO rules (McKenna 2001).

16   The aggregate cost of compliance with $SO_2$ standards is estimated to have fallen by between 30 and 50 percent under the sulphur trading program, compared to the command and control regulations that it replaced.

17   See Olewiler (1994) for a more detailed summary of the early literature.

18   Unfortunately, the breakdown between environmental regulations versus health and safety is not provided.

19   Donnan (2000) suggests a number of contributing factors in addition to technological change, including the closure of older, less efficient plants.

20   Their standard deviation was high at 69 cents.

21   Environmental branding or eco-labelling is discussed again in Hypothesis 4 and in the fourth section.

22   See, for example, Globerman and Shapiro (2003) for a more comprehensive examination of FDI.

23    The data are taken from Sawchuk and Sydor (2003), Tables 2 and 3.

24    They also cannot isolate individual cases where pollution-intensive firms within an industry are growing.

25    Information in this section is taken from a number of sources, including the Web sites of each country's federal environmental agencies: http://www.ec.gc.ca (Canada), http://www.epa.gov (United States), http://www.ine.gob.mx (Mexico). Other sources include the OECD *Environmental Performance Review* for Mexico (1998), Canada (1995a) and the United States (1995b), and the United States-Mexico Chamber of Commerce (1998).

26    The *Canadian Environmental Protection Act* (CEPA) was introduced in 1988 (replacing other legislation) and amended in 1998 to give the federal government more power to regulate toxic compounds. The U.S. legislation (e.g., CERCLA) was passed prior to the 1988 CEPA.

27    These are the Corporate Average Fuel Efficiency (CAFE) standards for the United States and Company Average Fuel Consumption (CAFC) for Canada.

28    Recent Canadian announcements about climate change policies focus on voluntary actions, technological fixes such as the substitution of fuel cells for internal combustion engines, subsidies to reduce energy consumption, and some form of a tradeable carbon permit market. These policies may contribute to significant changes in carbon dioxide discharge over time, but in the short term may do little. They clearly signify a different strategy than the Europeans, who have introduced taxes. The United States is in a state of flux, with the federal administration signalling that it views climate change as less of a problem than its energy supplies and announcing that it will not ratify Kyoto. Individual U.S. states, however, may be introducing policies to help reduce greenhouse gas emissions.

29    Dasgupta, Hettige and Wheeler (2000) have examined Mexican survey data to determine what factors improve compliance. The key factors include regulatory pressure, environmental training for plant personnel, being a publicly-held firm or a large plant, and education.

30    An example in Canada is the 3P Program — Pollution Prevention Pays — under which companies work with environmental ministries to reduce emissions and use natural resources more efficiently. The participants in the program are, so far, very positive (and excited) about the program.

31    These programs may result in trade actions if they are deemed to be subsidies available only to domestic firms.

32    See Shafik (1994), Seldon and Song (1994, 1995), Barbier (1997) and the other papers in the special issue of *Environment and Development Economics* 2,4 (1997) for examples of EKCs.

33    In fairness to the CEC, some reviews of its work have mentioned that its budget is too small to meet its mandate.

34    The author of the IISD guide is also Mann.

35    The cases are complex, some with policy errors made by the environmental agencies involved. It is beyond the scope of this paper to go into the details of each case.

36    The case is complex and there were problems with the Canadian policy and risk assessment of the compound. There were inadequate data on health risks from

MMT, so Health Canada could not consider MMT a health risk under the 1988 CEPA. MMT is a manganese-based fuel additive that the automobile industry argues damages air pollution equipment in vehicles. MMT is not used in gasoline in the United States, only in Canada. Under CEPA, Canada cannot ban a compound that damages cars, only one that damages people, and they did not have enough scientific evidence to prove at the time that MMT damages people. The 1998 CEPA may have changed the powers of the federal government regarding the definition of toxicity. The Ethyl Corporation was asking for $251 million in damages; it received US$13 million from Canada.

37 Environment ministers from the three NAFTA countries expressed concern about Chapter 11 in 1999. The governing body of the NAFTA may now be interested in revisiting the provisions of Chapter 11 as they apply to environmental regulation. See IISD (2001).

38 Even in the case of international treaties, the federal government may have difficulty implementing conditions in a treaty if provinces refuse to cooperate with the policies under consideration.

39 Recent federal government announcements have indicated that measures taken to help meet global climate change targets and urban smog problems include a large component of information collection and dissemination. The government intends to inform Canadians how certain changes in their driving habits or the type of vehicles they use, etc., will improve things. This is useful policy. However, it should not be the only type of policy in place.

# BIBLIOGRAPHY

Albrecht, J. "Environmental Policy and Inward Investment Position of U.S. Dirty Industries." *Intereconomics* (July-August 1998): 186-94.

Antweiler, W., B. Copeland and S. Taylor. *Is Free Trade Good for the Environment?* Discussion Paper No. 98-11. Vancouver: Department of Economics, University of British Columbia, 1998.

Arrow, K., B. Bohlin, R. Costanza, P. Dasgupta, C. Folke, C.S. Holling, B.O. Jansson, S. Levin, K.G. Maler, C. Perrings and D. Pimentel. "Economic Growth, Carrying Capacity, and the Environment." *Science* (April 18, 1995): 520-21.

Barbier, E. "Introduction to the Environmental Kuznets Curve Special Issue." *Environment and Development Economics* 2, 4 (1997): 369-81.

Beladi, H., N.H. Chau and M.A. Khan. "North-South Investment Flows and Optimal Environmental Policies." *Journal of Environmental Economics and Management* 40 (2000): 275-96.

Berman, E., and L. Bui. *Environmental Regulations and Productivity: Evidence from Oil Refineries*. NBER Working Paper No. 6776, November 1998.

Chapman, D. "Environmental Standards and International Trade in Automobiles and Copper: The Case for a Social Tariff." *Natural Resources Journal* 31 (1991): 449-61.

Chichilnisky, G. "North-South Trade and the Global Environment." *American Economic Review* 84, 4 (1994): 851-74.

Chomo, G.V., and M.J. Ferrantino. *NAFTA Environmental Impacts on North American Fisheries*. Discussion Paper for the First North American Symposium on Understanding the Linkages between Trade and the Environment, 2000.

Cohen, M., and S. Fenn. *Environmental and Financial Performance: Are they Related?* Nashville: Department of Economics, Vanderbilt University, 1997. Mimeograph.

Copeland, B., and S. Taylor. "North-South Trade and the Environment." *Quarterly Journal of Economics* 109 (1994): 755-87.

Dasgupta, S., H. Hettige and D. Wheeler. "What Improves Environmental Compliance? Evidence from Mexican Industry." *Journal of Environmental Economics and Management* 39 (2000): 39-66.

Dasgupta, S., R.E.B. Lucas and D. Wheeler. "Plant Size, Industrial Air Pollution, and Local Incomes: Evidence from Mexico and Brazil." *Environment and Development Economics* 7, 2 (May 2002): 365-81.

Donnan, J. "Environmental Protection and Economic Performance of the 'Countdown Acid Rain' Program in Ontario." Municipal Industrial Strategy for Abatement: 2000. Mimeograph.

Environmental Protection Agency. *Environmental Investments: The Cost of a Clean Environment*, EPA0230-90-084. Washington DC: EPA, 1990.

Fredriksson, P.G., and D. L. Millimet. *Is there a Race to the Bottom in Environmental Policies? The Effects of NAFTA*. September 5, 2000. Mimeograph.

Globerman, S., and D. Shapiro. "Assessing Recent Patterns of Foreign Direct Investment in Canada and the United States." In *North American Linkages: Opportunities and Challenges for Canada*. Edited by Richard G. Harris. The Industry Canada Research Series. Calgary: University of Calgary Press, 2003. Chapter 7.

Gray, W. *Plant Location: Do Different Industries Respond Differently to Environmental Regulation?* Clark University: 1997. Mimeograph.

Grossman, G.M., and A.B. Krueger. *Environmental Impacts of a North American Free Trade Agreement*. NBER Working Paper No. 3914, November 1991.

Guzmán, Francisco. "Air Pollution in Mexico City." Instituto Mexicano de Petróleo, Integrated Program on Air Pollution, *Report of the First Workshop on Mexico City Air Quality*, Massachusetts Institute of Technology, Integrated Program on Urban, Regional, and Global Air Pollution, February 1999. Available at: http://eaps.mit.edu/megacities/workshops/workshop199902/mexico.html.

Harrison, K., and W. Antweiler. "Incentives for Pollution Abatement: Regulation, Regulatory Threats, and Non-governmental Pressures." *Journal of Policy Analysis and Management*. Forthcoming.

Hayward, S., and L. Jones. *Environmental Indicators for North America and the United Kingdom*. Vancouver: The Fraser Institute, April 1999.

IISD. *Private Rights, Public Problems, A Guide to NAFTA's Controversial Chapter on Investor Rights*. Winnipeg: International Institute for Sustainable Development, 2001.

Jaffe, A., and K. Palmer. "Environmental Regulation and Innovation: A Panel Data Study." *Review of Economics and Statistics* 79, 4 (November 1997): 610-19.

Jaffe, A., S. Peterson, P. Portney and R. Stavins. "Environmental Regulation and the Competitiveness of U.S. Manufacturing: What does the Evidence Tell Us?" *Journal of Economic Literature* 33 (1995): 132-63.

Kwan, C. *American Foreign Direct Investment: Finding Evidence of the Industrial Flight Hypothesis.* Department of Economics, Simon Fraser University: 1999. Mimeograph.

Leonard, H.J. *Pollution and the Struggle for the World Product.* Cambridge: Cambridge University Press, 1988.

Levinson, A. "Environmental Regulations and Manufacturer's Choices: Evidence from the Census of Manufacturers." *Journal of Public Economics* 62 (1996): 5-29.

_____. "Environmental Regulations and Industry Locations: International and Domestic Evidence." In *Fair Trade and Harmonization:Prerequisites for Free Trade*, Vol. 1. Edited by J. Bhagwati and R. Hudec. Cambridge and London: The MIT Press, 1997.

List, J.A., and C.Y. Co. "The Effects of Environmental Regulation on Foreign Direct Investment." *Journal of Environmental Economics and Management* 40, 1 (2000): 1-20.

Low, P. "Trade Measures and Environmental Quality: The Implication for Mexico's Exports." In *International Trade and the Environment.* Edited by P. Low. World Bank Discussion Paper 159. Washington: The World Bank, 1992.

Lucas, R., D. Wheeler and H. Hettige. "Economic Development, Environmental Regulations and the International Migration of Toxic Industrial Pollution: 1960-1988." In *International Trade and the Environment.* Edited by P. Low. World Bank Discussion Paper 159. Washington: The World Bank, 1992.

Mann, H. *Assessing the Impact of NAFTA on Environmental Law and Management Processes.* Discussion Paper. First North American Symposium on Understanding the Linkages between Trade and the Environment, 2000.

McKenna, B. "WTO Turns out to be on the Side of the Sea Turtles." *The Globe and Mail*, October 26, 2001, p. B8.

Morgenstern, R., W. Pizer and J. Shih. *Are We Overstating the Economic Costs of Environmental Protection?* Discussion Paper 97-36. Resource of the Future, Washington DC, 1997.

Nordström, H., and S. Vaughan. *Trade and Environment.* Geneva: World Trade Organization, 1999.

OECD. *Environmental Performance Review, Canada.* Paris: OECD, 1995a.

_____. *Environmental Performance Review, United States.* Paris: OECD, 1995b.

_____. *Environmental Performance Review, Mexico.* Paris: OECD, 1998.

_____. *Foreign Direct Investment and the Environment: An Overview of the Literature.* December 1997. Available at: http://www.oecd.org.

Olewiler, N. "The Impact of Environmental Regulation on Investment Decisions." In Benidickson, J., G.B. Doern and N. Olewiler. *Getting the Green Light: Environmental Regulation and Investment in Canada.* Policy Study 22. C.D. Howe Institute, 1994.

_____. "Globalization and the Environment." In *Globalization and the Knowledge Economy: Perspectives for Malaysia*. Edited by M. Ariff and F. Flatters. Malaysian Institute for Economic Research, 2001.

Olewiler, N., and K. Dawson. *Analysis of National Pollutant Release Inventory Data on Toxic Emissions by Industry*. Working Paper 97-16, prepared for the Technical Committee on Business Taxation, Ottawa: Department of Finance, 1998.

Palmer, K., W. Oates and P. Portney. "Tightening Environmental Standards: The Benefit-Cost or the No-Cost Paradigm?" *Journal of Economic Perspectives* 9, 4 (1995): 119-32.

Porter, M., and C. van der Linde. "Toward a New Conception of the Environment-Competitiveness Relationship." *Journal of Economic Perspectives* 9, 4 (1995): 97-118.

Prestemon, J. P. "Public Open Access and Private Timber Harvests: Theory and Application to the Effects of Trade Liberalization in Mexico." *Environmental and Resource Economics* 17 (2000): 311-34.

Repetto, R. *Jobs, Competitiveness and Environmental Regulation: What Are the Real Issues?* Washington DC: World Resources Institute, May 1995.

Sawchuk, G., and A. Sydor. "Mexico and Canada: Changing Specializations in Trade with the United States." In *North American Linkages: Opportunities and Challenges for Canada*. Edited by Richard G. Harris. Calgary: University of Calgary Press, 2003. Chapter 3.

Selden, T. M., and D. Song. "Environmental Quality and Development: Is There a Kuznets Curve for Air Pollution Emissions?" *Journal of Environmental Economics and Management* 27 (1994): 147-62.

_____. "Neoclassical Growth, the J Curve for Abatement, and the Inverted U Curve for Pollution." *Journal of Environmental Economics and Management* 29 (1995): 162-68.

Shafik, N. "Economic Development and Environmental Quality: An Econometric Analysis." *Oxford Economic Papers* 46 (1994): 757-73.

United States Department of Commerce. "Plant and Equipment Expenditures by Business for Pollution Abatement." In *Survey of Current Business*. Washington DC: USDC, various years.

United States-Mexico Chamber of Commerce. *Environmental Issues in Mexico under NAFTA*. May 1998. Available at: http://www.usmcoc.org/n10.html.

World Bank. *World Development Indicators, 1998*. Washington, DC: The World Bank, 1998.

World Resources Institute. *World Development Indicators*. Washington DC: World Resources Institute, 2000.

Xing, Y., and C. Kolstad. *Do Lax Environmental Regulations Attract Foreign Investment?* Santa Barbara: University of California, May 1998. Mimeograph.

Xu, S. "Do Stringent Environmental Regulations Reduce the International Competitiveness of Environmentally Sensitive Goods? A Global Perspective." *World Development* 27, 7 (1999): 1215-26.

# Comment on:

## NORTH AMERICAN INTEGRATION AND THE ENVIRONMENT

*Comment by James Gaisford*
*University of Calgary*

THIS STUDY PROVIDES A VERY GOOD PRIMER on trade and the environment within a North American context. It begins with an overview of why markets typically fail to provide the optimal level of environmental quality, and thus, why government action is called for to clarify property rights and/or provide market-based or direct forms of environmental regulation. It reviews the decomposition of the impact of trade on the environment into scale, composition and technique effects, which was introduced by Grossman and Krueger (1991) and elaborated by Copeland and Taylor (1994). The scale effect, associated with an equal proportional increase in all outputs, typically pushes toward reductions in environmental quality. The composition effect is inherently ambiguous. For example, in response to increased trade, pollution would tend to rise if a country exports pollution-intensive goods, but fall if it imports them. The technique effect generally pushes toward improved environmental quality, given that rising incomes are associated with tighter regulation. Since the overall effects are ambiguous, how trade and integration affect the environment in each specific instance is an empirical question.

The study continues with a useful survey of environmental trends in Canada, Mexico and the United States. The interim conclusion seems to be that the advent of the NAFTA and closer North American integration have not had a dramatic effect on the environment, either for good or bad. One area of possible concern that may have trade linkages is the reduction in forest cover and increased agricultural use of land in Mexico. The overview of environmental trends also points to the need for improved data collection by all three countries.

Olewiler then examines a series of hypotheses on linkages between integration and the environment. The first of these is the pollution haven hypothesis. She cites numerous studies that suggest that countries or regions with more stringent environmental regulations do not become less competitive over time and thereby experience a significant loss of jobs and capital to pollution havens. Interestingly enough, the evidence seems to suggest that investors, as well as individuals, favour regions where environmental quality is high.

Similarly, there is little evidence for the second hypothesis that greater economic integration generates a "race to the bottom" in terms of either regulation or enforcement. Here the available data do not always support systematic econometric testing, so that many of Olewiler's provisional conclusions have to be drawn in the absence of formal studies. Nonetheless, where there is evidence of regulatory convergence, it is generally at a high level. Olewiler does, however, sound two notes of caution. First, Canada and the United States seem to be "stuck in the status quo," at least on some environmental fronts. Second, in Canada and Mexico, local governments are being given more environmental responsibility, and they may ultimately lack the expertise and capital to ensure environmental quality. Partially offsetting this second concern, Olewiler notes that the "not in my back yard" phenomenon is, in fact, propelling the removal of waste sites from many local communities.

The third hypothesis Olewiler investigates is that integration is bad for the environment because integration stimulates growth, which thereby leads to environmental degradation. Since the relationship between many environmental problems and per capita gross domestic product typically follows an inverse U shape, or so-called "environmental Kuznets curve," the real issue is often the income level at which environmental quality begins to rebound. Empirically, this depends on the pollutant in question. Given the per capita income levels in Mexico, the evidence seems to suggest that there may be cause for concern with respect to deforestation and emissions of sulphur dioxide and carbon dioxide.

The final hypothesis Olewiler discusses is that provisions within trade agreements may inhibit a country's ability to set environmental policy. Here, a serious concern is raised over Chapter 11 of the NAFTA, which allows foreign corporations to sue governments in the event of expropriation of actual or potential benefits. While the intent of Chapter 11 is to protect foreign investments from capricious actions by governments, the preponderance of actions to date have involved complaints about environmental regulations. Consequently, Olewiler concludes that: "This provision [of the NAFTA] appears to be flawed and may pose a threat to socially efficient environmental policy making." Here one might go beyond the Olewiler critique. A deeper problem with Chapter 11 is that it effectively oversteps national treatment and gives foreign firms preferential treatment.

## BIBLIOGRAPHY

Copeland, B., and S. Taylor. "North-South Trade and the Environment." *Quarterly Journal of Economics* 39 (1994): 755-87.

Grossman, G.M., and A.B. Krueger. "Environmental Impacts of a North American Free Trade Agreement." NBER Working Paper No. 3914, 1991.

Roger Ware & Tristan Musgrave*
Queen's University

# 16

# Competition Policy and Intellectual Property: Issues of Canadian and American Integration

## BACKGROUND: THE IMPORTANCE OF COMPETITION POLICY IN PROMOTING INNOVATION AND ECONOMIC GROWTH

A REALITY FACING ADVANCED NATIONAL ECONOMIES is that firms must now operate in an environment of increasing global competition. Moreover, antitrust enforcement is on the rise in industrial economies, particularly in the European Union (EU) and the United States. More than 90 countries now have a modern framework of competition law. Indeed, prompted by several recent trends such as globalization, unprecedented merger activity, deregulation and technological advances, antitrust enforcers are now more active than they have been for over a quarter of a century and show signs of getting even busier (The Economist 2000a). Yet, not a great deal is known about the value and role of competition policy in promoting economic efficiency, innovation and economic growth.

The work most often cited as advocating an important role for a strong competition policy is Porter (1990), which advocates strict competition regulation in domestic industries. In a work that focusses on 10 important trading nations over a four-year period, Porter finds that competition policy maintains and promotes domestic competition, which increases innovation, efficiency and, ultimately, economic growth. These are the roots of a nation's competitive advantage in relation to its rivals. This position has been subject to significant criticism, however; its opponents argue that there is insufficient evidence to establish that vigorous enforcement of competition policy leads to higher levels of competition, competitive advantage, or still further, higher rates of growth. Most importantly, there are enormous costs associated with widespread enforcement and also many new efficiency-enhancing technologies that are driving numerous industries to consolidate at an increasing rate. As a result, until evidence proves otherwise, it may be best for a nation to apply its competition policy sparingly.

The underlying theme of Porter's argument is that domestic competition is the key to sustaining and developing a nation's competitive advantage. Domestic

*Currently a law student at McGill University.

rivalry pressures firms to innovate and make more efficient use of their resources — specifically, their labour and capital. Local rivals push each other to lower costs, improve quality and service, and to invest in research and development (R&D) in order to create new future products and processes (Porter, pp. 118-119). A primary result of competition, therefore, is that the general productivity of an industry increases; and when combined with international trade, high industry productivity will generally make the nation as a whole more competitive. Porter credits high levels of competition in many German and Japanese industries as one of the predominant factors that gave these nations the large competitive advantage they enjoyed during the late 1980s. Consequently, as strong domestic competition is an essential determinant of national advantage and economic growth, any factor that can be shown to affect competition will also affect the nation's ability to compete abroad. However, too little competition in any industry may be a serious problem.

The opposite strategy to a vigorous competition policy is for a government to allow horizontal mergers that create "national champions" — firms that are permitted to dominate their particular domestic industries. Porter's evidence suggests that these merged firms generally perform poorly. Efficiency gains from economies of scale or cost savings often prove elusive; they would be best achieved through global production instead of a merger with a domestic rival, and firms that are the most successful internationally are usually those that face active domestic rivalry (Porter, p. 662). Furthermore, by creating a firm that dominates a national industry, the government may be creating an inefficient monopolist that is too politically important to fail. Instead of directing resources into R&D or into improving the efficiency of production, the firm may channel them into rent-seeking activities, such as lobbying different levels of government to preserve its dominance. In the long run, these inefficient activities may culminate in a failing or lagging industry that requires government aid or subsidization to survive. Ultimately, if the government permits a large number of national champions in an economy, national advantage and economic growth may suffer. Currently, this is one of the major fears regarding the proposed bank mergers in the Canadian commercial banking industry. Tough antitrust laws can be part of a solution to these problems.

Porter believes that domestic competition must be buttressed by a nation's commitment to a strict competition policy:

> A strong antitrust policy, especially in the area of horizontal mergers, alliances, and collusive behaviour, is essential to the rate of upgrading in an economy. Mergers, acquisitions, and alliances involving industry leaders should be disallowed... Direct interfirm collusion should be illegal. Cooperative ventures involving direct collaboration between competitors must pass strict guidelines. (p. 663)

Although he states that firms in a failing industry should not be prohibited from merging, and that collusion between firms for the purpose of R&D should be allowed, Porter's stringent prescription for antitrust regulations is based on the assumption that antitrust policy *causes* competition. Indeed, he contends that a nation's antitrust policy will contribute directly to its competitive advantage and to economic growth.

McFetridge (1992) attacks the premise of Porter's argument that antitrust laws cause competition:

> The evidence is that, while it may or may not have had an effect on Japanese competitiveness, Japanese antitrust enforcement cannot be characterized as other than permissive. Similarly, while the German cartel offices are very active, the German statute is highly permissive. It is very difficult to believe that Japanese and German competitive advantage is the result, even in part, of vigorous antitrust enforcement. (p. 137)

McFetridge's observations draw an important distinction between the existence of antitrust laws and their enforcement. Japanese and German markets were highly competitive without a great deal of antitrust law enforcement. It is possible, however, that the existence of relatively weak antitrust statutes and the possibility of punishment were enough to deter many major antitrust violations during the given time period.

In addition, McFetridge proposes that national advantage may actually cause competition, instead of the reverse, as suggested by Porter. If a nation is more productive in a particular industry, it may attract a large number of firms. Conversely, if other industries are less productive, they might suffer from a lack of competition. If this suggestion of reverse causality has any merit, then the importance of competition policy in the broader economic environment is diminished. Antitrust enforcement may indirectly increase national advantage and economic growth by (at most) maintaining competition and innovation, but its role in creating competition will be minimal. In such circumstances, overzealous enforcement may even be harmful to the very industries competition laws are meant to protect.

One problem with antitrust investigations is that they are extremely costly. As demonstrated by the U.S. Justice Department action against Microsoft, lawyers, economists, judges, consultants and expert witnesses, among others, can cost millions of dollars to both taxpayers and the firm in question. Many of these proceedings can last for years. This is particularly true for firms seeking large international mergers, an increasing number of which need to be evaluated separately by competition commissions in the various affected jurisdictions. Most importantly, these cases run the imminent risk of distracting the firm's executives from their corporate goals and reallocating resources from R&D to the defence of the firm. As leading economists Milton Friedman and Alan Greenspan emphasize, the possibility of falling victim to a mistaken antitrust action can have a chilling effect on a dominant firm's efficiency and incentive to innovate (The Economist 2000b). By affecting the actions of an industry's key firm or firms in this way, antitrust investigations have the potential to erode the competitiveness of the whole industry. This is especially true for the "new economy."

Contrary to Porter's observations, recent advances in technology might actually encourage monopolies to innovate, a development that may pose a difficult challenge for antitrust enforcers. As former U.S. Treasury Secretary Larry Summers points out, "innovation is increasingly driven by firms that win temporary monopoly power but enjoy it for only a moment before being replaced by a company with a better product that itself gains a short-lived monopoly" (The Economist 2000b). This suggests that the new economy may be characterized by more monopolies than the old, but that few of them will be able to affect consumers adversely and put up long-run barriers to entry. Indeed, particularly in the production of information goods like computer software, firms may enjoy both supply- and demand-side economies of scale and extremely low marginal costs. As a result, these firms will want to raise production and lower the price of their outputs. But if antitrust regulators limit a firm's ability to compete in rapidly changing markets by, for example, restricting market share or blocking all large horizontal mergers, prices may actually rise, and consumers could be hurt. It may be best, therefore, for governments to tolerate some monopolies in the realization that rapidly changing markets will force these firms to innovate and become more productive; otherwise, their rivals will displace them quickly.

Another consequence of the many new technologies is that they have created excess capacity in many industries and prompted a desire for industry consolidation. In the financial services industry, for example, new retail and communications technologies, computer systems, standardized software and customer data bases have reduced significantly the need for heavily staffed and physically complex commercial bank branches. An overwhelming proportion of the transactions traditionally processed at branches now are provided through alternative delivery channels like automatic tellers, direct debit terminals, the telephone and the Internet (Mathewson and Quigley 1998, p. 4). Consequently, bank mergers can create one-time synergetic gains due to rationalization and may be able to take advantage of economies of scale and scope. Similar gains can be made in many information- or technology-based service or production industries (e.g., insurance and telecommunications). Instead of making large horizontal mergers illegal per se, therefore, as Porter advises, it might be more efficient to view each merger independently and balance any anticompetitive effects against gains due to increases in technical efficiency. If this is done, the industry may become more productive; national advantage may rise as a result.

Although most of Porter's analysis remains to be challenged, it is clear that he may have overestimated the importance of competition policy in promoting innovation, efficiency and economic growth. There can be little argument that over time, intense domestic competition most likely will lead to innovation and an increasingly efficient use of national resources, both of which contribute directly to a nation's competitive advantage. However, Porter does not give sufficient evidence to support his premise that strict competition legislation and its enforcement is a predominant factor that stimulates competition. Even the presence of permissive laws and the possibility of punishment for their violation may be enough to keep the majority of firms in line. If, however, national advantage governs the level of competition that an industry can sustain, antitrust policy may have a reduced role in promoting or sustaining competition. If this is true, governments should be wary of getting carried away in their attempts to protect competition. There are enormous financial and opportunity costs associated with antitrust investigations. In addition, as a result of technological advances, many so-called "anticompetitive activities," including many large mergers and acquisitions, may enhance efficiency. These should not be illegal per se, but they should be subject to the rule of reason. Porter's proscription of such activities would make such flexibility almost impossible. In the long run, the consequences of a government's increasing (and perhaps unnecessary) enforcement of competition policy may be severe in their negative impact on national advantage and economic growth. These criticisms by no means suggest that Porter's hypothesis is incorrect; however, we still have strikingly little evidence to support his proactive conclusions.

# MULTIJURISDICTIONAL ISSUES IN COMPETITION POLICY

## SOME THEORETICAL ISSUES

ABSTRACTING FROM THE REALITIES OF TRADE IN CANADA, we consider first some theoretical issues relating to multiple jurisdictions for competition policy — issues that arise even if the competing jurisdictions have identical laws and objectives for their national competition policy. These issues were first analysed in a pioneering study by Head and Ries (1997) and were followed by a longer, non-technical discussion by Guzman (1998).[1]

Head and Ries work under the assumption that nations with jurisdiction over merging firms pursue an objective of maximizing domestic total surplus in their competition policies. They do not investigate the implications of extraterritorial jurisdiction. Head and Ries derive some basic and important results that are also discussed in Guzman's study. First, the support of independent national jurisdictions for mergers that reduce global surplus depends on the worldwide distribution of production and consumption of the relevant product. A product consumed entirely outside of the relevant antitrust jurisdictions affects them only through profits and not through consumer surplus. Any profitable merger or other activity, therefore, is approved. At the other extreme, if all nations have a symmetric share of world consumption and production, only the mergers that increase world welfare are approved by the national jurisdictions.

When several jurisdictions have independent frameworks, problems arise from the opposing nature of individual countries' objectives. Assume initially that both nations' objectives are the same: both desire to maximize total surplus (or the sum of consumer and producer surplus). We start by identifying several benchmark cases.

### Producers Only in Country A, Consumers Only in Country B

Suppose country A produces a good that, for the sake of argument, is sold only in country B. The effect of this is that all producer surplus is realized in country A, while all consumer surplus is realized in country B. If a merger is proposed between two firms in country A, with no efficiency benefits, the competition authorities there would have no objection, as their total surplus would increase. Country B, however, would suffer losses in consumer surplus as a result of any postmerger price increases. Whether or not the competition authorities in country B can block the merger depends on the degree of extraterritoriality they can exercise with their competition laws. If we assume country B laws have no extraterritoriality, the merger would proceed on the basis of its approval in country A, even though, by assumption, this merger would lower total surplus.

If the efficiency gains accruing from the merger were large enough to lower postmerger prices, total surplus would necessarily increase. Both jurisdictions then would approve the merger, because postmerger surplus would increase in both countries.

Now suppose country B can exercise its competition laws outside its territory in pursuit of its own surplus, but not that of other countries. In the first case, the merger would be prevented by country B: this is the outcome consistent with maximizing total world surplus. In the second, the merger would be permitted, as it is also the outcome that maximizes world welfare. But consider a third case: a merger that involves intermediate efficiency gains, such that prices still increase by a small amount in country B, but total surplus still increases because of the efficiency gains. Country B will now block the merger, even though country A approves it, and the merger has the effect of increasing world surplus.

## Firms in Both Countries A and B, Consumers Only in Country B

The only difference in this assumption is that country B may approve a merger or other action that raises prices if enough of the increase in profits accrues to its own firms. Again, let us assume initially that neither country A or B has extraterritorial jurisdiction. A merger between firms in country A is always approved, whether it increases or decreases total surplus; but a merger between firms in country B that increases total surplus is approved only if enough of the profit gains accrue to those firms. This is likely to occur if country B firms are larger and more efficient than those in country A.

Suppose now that country B can apply its laws extraterritorially, as before. A merger that increases total world surplus because of a substantial efficiency saving is still vetoed by country B if most of the profit increase accrues to the firms in country A. One scenario for this would be a merger between the firms in country A that creates efficiency gains and leads to higher prices and higher profits for firms in both countries. As the efficiency gains and a large part of the profit increase accrue directly to firms in country A, country B will use its extraterritorial power to veto the merger, despite the fact that it increases total surplus.

## Firms Only in Country A, Consumers in Both Countries A and B

Without extraterritoriality, country A (where firms are concentrated but consumers are not) approves activities that increase its own surplus; consequently, it approves all mergers that increase global surplus. Country A also approves some activities or mergers that reduce total surplus, as some of the loss of consumer surplus occurs in country B, which does not have a veto over the merger.

With extraterritoriality, country B blocks all mergers that do not reduce its own prices, including mergers that increase global surplus. Thus it allows only mergers with substantial efficiency gains.

## Firms and Consumers in Both Countries A and B

In the general case (producers and consumers in both countries), each country's attitude toward a potentially anticompetitive activity depends on the weighting of consumer and producer interests within its own country. Guzman analyses this general case, both with and without extraterritoriality. Without extraterritoriality, if production and consumption are distributed asymmetrically, too many mergers and other anticompetitive activities are allowed. This becomes less true the closer the two countries come to a symmetrical distribution of consumption and production.

## TABLE 1

### THE EFFECT OF TRADE ON ANTITRUST POLICY (WITH EXTRATERRITORIALITY)

| Country Characteristics | | Percentage of Global Surplus Taken into Account | | Policy Result in Relation to Optimal Global Policy |
|---|---|---|---|---|
| Percentage of Global Production of Imperfectly Competitive Goods | Percentage of Global Consumption of Imperfectly Competitive Goods | Producer Surplus | Consumer Surplus | |
| 100 | 100 | 100 | 100 | Optimal Regulation |
| 100 | 0 | 100 | 0 | Underregulation |
| 0 | 100 | 0 | 100 | Overregulation |
| 50 | 100 | 50 | 100 | Overregulation |
| 100 | 50 | 100 | 50 | Underregulation |
| x | y | x | y | If x>y: Underregulation If x<y: Overregulation If x=y: Optimal Regulation |

Source: Guzman (1998).

With extraterritoriality, Guzman summarizes the result nicely: "A country that can apply its laws extraterritorially will underregulate anticompetitive behaviour if it is a net exporter and overregulate such behaviour if it is a net importer" (p. 1,520). We reproduce Guzman's Table I above.

A country's antitrust policy is weaker if it cannot apply its laws extraterritorially; indeed, without extraterritoriality, international antitrust policy is weaker than the optimal global policy. When countries cannot apply their laws extraterritorially, the deviation of national policies from the optimal global policy increases as trade between countries grows. This divergence occurs because, as trade increases, the beneficial effects of regulating anticompetitive activities are felt more acutely by foreign consumers, while the costs of preventing local firms from engaging in similar activities continue to be borne entirely at home.

If every nation can exercise extraterritoriality, the toughest law is binding, because an inefficient activity imposes a net loss on at least one country, and that country can prevent the activity through the extraterritorial application of its antitrust laws. Thus every globally inefficient activity is prevented, because it will reduce the surplus of at least one country. On the downside, however, some globally efficient activities are also prevented.

## COMPETITION LAWS: DIFFERENT COUNTRIES, DIFFERENT OBJECTIVES

THE PRECEDING ANALYSIS assumes that competition law in all countries is devoted to the same objective: to maximize total surplus. The reality is not so harmonious, and Canada and the United States provide an important example of antitrust laws that pursue different objectives, particularly with respect to merger policy.

Until the recent Federal Court of Appeal decision in *Superior Propane* (Competition Tribunal 1998), it was widely believed that Canada's *Competition Act* was drafted to allow efficiency gains arising from a merger to play a major role in determining its overall effect on competitiveness. Unfortunately, at present, the treatment of efficiency gains arising from a merger in Canada is subject to a great deal of uncertainty arising from the Competition Tribunal's decision in this case, which oversaw the merger between Superior Propane and ICG, the two dominant retailers in the Canadian propane industry. This case was subsequently remanded by the Federal Court of Appeal, a decision which is currently awaiting a decision on leave to appeal to the Supreme Court of Canada. In the original verdict, the Competition Tribunal followed a total surplus standard in allowing the merger to proceed. This standard is the most favourable to the consideration of efficiency gains likely to arise from a merger: that is, the Tribunal determined that the efficiency gains from the merger would far exceed any anticompetitive costs associated with it, and they allowed it to proceed. Now that this decision has been remanded, however, one has to be cautious in assigning significant weight to efficiency gains in Canadian merger policy.

In the United States, efficiency gains are accorded only a secondary role in determining the competitive effects of a merger. Recent court decisions — together with guidelines on efficiency issued by the Federal Trade Commission (FTC) and the U.S. Department of Justice (1997) — indicate that mergers will be judged on a "price standard," meaning that they will only be permitted if they are not expected to raise consumer prices. On the basis of standard theories of oligopoly behaviour, the only way a merger is likely to lead to lower prices is if it creates substantial gains in efficiency. A range of mergers that increase total surplus, but are also likely to increase consumer prices, would not be allowed under the U.S. guidelines. Interestingly enough, the Competition Tribunal found the Superior Propane-ICG merger to have precisely these attributes.

While the Canadian position on efficiencies is particularly difficult to see at present, it is still interesting to analyse the implications of the Canadian position as set out in the *Merger Enforcement Guidelines* (Consumer and Corporate Affairs Canada 1991) for mergers that have Canada-U.S. cross-border ramifications. The effect of extraterritoriality is, in a sense, to favour the country with the "strictest" antitrust policy. For example, consider the net effect of the preceding framework on Canada-U.S. antitrust policy. The United States follows a consumer surplus standard and pursues vigorous extraterritorial application of its antitrust laws. Canada pursues a total surplus standard but does not attempt extraterritorial jurisdiction. The net result would be to nullify completely Canada's total surplus objective in any mergers or other activities that have cross-border implications.

This important proposition is best illustrated with some hypothetical examples. Suppose a major telecommunications equipment maker in Canada were to propose a merger with a major U.S. supplier. The merger is expected to increase prices but also lead to substantial efficiency savings — the net result of which would be a gain in total surplus. Canada's competition policy before the Federal Court of Appeal decision in *Superior Propane* would permit the merger on the grounds that total surplus would increase. The United States, however, would block the merger, applying its consumer surplus standard extraterritorially. Note that because of the consumer surplus standard, under these assumptions, the United States would block the merger even if it increased total surplus at home.

## INTERNATIONAL POLITICAL ECONOMY "GAMES" WITH MERGER POLICY

THE ABOVE OBSERVATIONS can be illuminated further through a game theory analysis. Let us suppose that the governments of Canada and the United States are making a strategic choice between a merger policy that uses "consumer surplus" as the decision-making criterion, and one that uses "total surplus." The framework also can handle easily any hybrid approaches to merger evaluation, like the "balancing weights" approach recently proposed in Canada by Professor Peter Townley.[2]

To illustrate the idea, if courts in the United States pursue a consumer surplus objective in their merger reviews, it would make sense for Canada to pursue total surplus as its dominant strategy because it would maximize surplus accruing to Canada. A merger between a Canadian and a U.S. company that was expected to increase prices in both jurisdictions but increase total surplus in Canada through offsetting cost savings would, however, be vetoed by U.S. authorities.

Suppose now that the United States was able to exercise extraterritoriality in its antitrust policy, so as to veto any merger that did not meet its own objectives. In this kind of game, as we have suggested, "the toughest policy wins," so that Canada's best response to a U.S. consumer surplus strategy is irrelevant for all mergers with cross-border implications. For purely domestic mergers, however, Canada might still wish to pursue a total surplus strategy.

It is somewhat ironic that the United States, the nation that has been most active in the extraterritorial application of its antitrust laws, has one of the strictest antitrust frameworks, and wishes to export it. In fact, if U.S. trading partners had strict, consumer-oriented competition policies themselves, the United States would be better off with a weaker antitrust framework that uses a total surplus objective, because it would benefit U.S. firms (and raise total surplus). The United States would not choose to exercise its extraterritoriality, because the strong consumerist policies of its trading partners would protect its own consumers from price increases due to any anticompetitive activities on the part of the trading partners. In fact, such a configuration would benefit the United States more than a global policy that maximizes total surplus.

As both international trade and merger activity pick up in intensity, and more mergers feature a marriage of U.S. and non-U.S. companies, the importance of the extraterritorial application of U.S. antitrust laws will continue to increase. In the limiting case, the United States will set competition policy for all of its trading partners. The loss of income and efficiency from the application of the U.S. consumer surplus standard across all developed countries could be substantial.

## EXTRATERRITORIALITY IN PRACTICE

THE REAL FORCE of one jurisdiction's extraterritorial antitrust enforcement hit home in 1996, in the case of Boeing's planned acquisition of McDonnell Douglas (Federal Trade Commission 1997a). The FTC approved the takeover unconditionally, but three days later the EU Antitrust Advisory Committee recommended that the merger be blocked on the grounds that it would harm fair trade. Several U.S. lawmakers were surprised that the EU would attempt to exercise jurisdiction over what appeared to be a merger of two U.S. companies.[3] Although the EU could not actually have blocked the merger, given an adverse finding, it did have authority to impose multibillion dollar fines based on 10 percent of Boeing's world income.

In the *Boeing-McDonnell Douglas* case, both jurisdictions believed that the decisions of the other side's enforcement agencies were taken in a way that reflected their own interest rather than that of global competition. As Kovacic (2001) puts it in a recent article:

> Americans often seem convinced to the point of moral certainty that naked economic nationalism animated the EC's decision, and Europeans usually appear equally persuaded that the FTC's forbearance was certifying proof of a political fix. (p. 808)

Conversely, the United States has also exerted extraterritoriality. In 1996, the FTC required two Swiss pharmaceutical companies that had merged — Ciba-Geigy and Sandoz — to divest key units of their business and license a patent to a competitor as a condition for the approval of their merger (Federal Trade Commission 1997b). The FTC reached its decision on the grounds that the merger in Switzerland could "quash" domestic competition and thus cause harm to U.S. consumers.

The legal basis of U.S. extraterritorial jurisdiction was solidified in the *Hartford Fire* case (Hartford Fire Insurance Co. 1993). The defendants were largely London-based re-insurance companies, who were alleged to have violated the *Sherman Act*. Both sides agreed, however, that the conduct was legal under U.K. law, which applied to the defendant companies. However, the U.S. Supreme Court held that the *Sherman Act* did apply to foreign conduct that was unlawful under the Act and was meant to have, and did have, a substantial effect in the United States.

Prior to *Hartford Fire*, the attempt to apply competition laws extraterritorially was largely through the medium of "positive comity," which is a weaker notion than that of full extraterritoriality. When conflicts arise between two or more nations claiming jurisdiction over a matter, the doctrine of comity exists for resolving them. In fact, this notion is enshrined in the U.S.-EC (now EU) Agreement on Antitrust Cooperation and Coordination. In essence, this agreement says (in Article V) that U.S. and EU regulators may request the other side to initiate appropriate enforcement activities if the requesting party believes that its interests are being adversely affected by anticompetitive practices in the other party's territory.

Unfortunately, the problem with even the notion of positive comity is that it presupposes that one country will take steps to act in the best interests of another — an assumption most economists would consider highly unrealistic. Because of its inherent implausibility, and with the strength of the *Hartford Fire* decision, comity is being superseded by both true extraterritoriality and bilateral treaties that describe the nature of cooperation between two countries on antitrust issues.

A model example of such a treaty is the 1995 Canada-U.S. Agreement on Cooperative Enforcement of Antitrust Investigations, which incorporates comity considerations (U.S. Department of Justice 1995b). If one party believes that its vital interests are affected adversely by anticompetitive activities in the territory of the other, the first party may request the other's antitrust authorities to initiate "appropriate enforcement activities." As with the U.S.-EC agreement, the requested party has full discretion to decide whether to initiate or proceed with any enforcement activities at the other party's request.

## Evidence on the True Objectives of Competition Policy in Different Jurisdictions

As we have noted above, the analytical literature on multijurisdictional issues in merger reviews has made some fairly strong assumptions about the objectives of national competition jurisdictions. In particular, the working assumption has been that national agencies will pursue a policy of total surplus maximization, where the total surplus in question is that accruing only within the agency's jurisdiction. An important question: What support does the evidence from cases provide for or against these assumptions? They could be wrong on two counts: first, decisions could reflect a concern for consumer surplus, not total surplus (U.S. enforcement agencies adopt this position explicitly; Canada has not revealed its "new" position yet, but it is likely to be similar); second, country policies may not be as unilateralist as theorists have hypothesized so far.

Although it is beyond the scope of this study to conduct thorough case evaluations, we will discuss two recent cases that bring to bear on this issue. First are the *Seaspan* and *Norsk* merger cases in Canada, which led to a single Consent Order (Competition Tribunal 1996). Seaspan was a new entrant to the market for ship berthing services in Burrard Inlet, British Columbia, a market that had been controlled hitherto by C.H. Cates and Sons Ltd. After first acquiring Cates, Dennis Washington, the respondent in this case, signed an agreement in 1994 to acquire Seaspan, which gave the merged company virtually complete control of this market. What is interesting about this case, from the perspective of this study, is that the majority of the customers of these ship berthing services are foreign (equivalently, the business is largely an export business). Hence, any harm arising from a substantial reduction in competition (in the form of a loss in consumer surplus) would be experienced mainly by foreigners, not Canadian citizens. Moreover, although this is not mentioned in the Consent Order, the proposed merger would almost certainly have realized non-trivial efficiency savings. Ostensibly, then, this case appears to be one in which the dead weight loss would be experienced largely by foreigners, but the efficiency savings would accrue to Canadians — the strongest case for allowing a merger if a *domestic* total surplus criterion is being applied. The fact that the Competition Bureau opposed the merger suggests that either it had applied a consumer surplus criterion to the consumer harm expected by the small number of Canadian consumers, or it had applied whatever objective function it was using *globally* and not just to Canadian residents.

The second case is the Boeing-McDonnell Douglas merger noted above. Kovacic discusses whether the behaviour of the EC and the U.S. agencies was more than usually dictated by the interests of their "own" firms, Airbus and Boeing, respectively. As Kovacic puts it, "Discussions of the case often feature assertions that economic nationalism guided the analysis of the EC or the FTC" (p. 839). Surely, however, it is unsurprising for nations to use competition policy to pursue their national interest. It is perhaps more surprising when they do not as, apparently, in the Canadian *Seaspan* case.

On the surface, the fact that the FTC raised no objections to the merger is puzzling. The U.S. agency had opposed — vigorously and successfully — the merger of *Staples* and *Office Depot* (Federal Trade Commission 1997c), which had also involved an increase in concentration from three firms to two. When one takes into account, however, the widely accepted conclusion that McDonnell Douglas was no longer competitive in the commercial aircraft business, the FTC finding of "no competitive harm" appears much less controversial. On the EU side, the key issue is not one of objectives, but of methodology: the EU applies the concept of "entrenchment" of dominant position to its analysis of horizontal mergers, a concept that does not appear in North American competition law. Part of the concern in this case stemmed from the belief that the military aircraft capability of McDonnell-Douglas would allow a transfer of useful technology into Boeing commercial aircraft production. This concern was largely based on testimony from rival military aircraft manufacturer Lockheed Martin, and, according to Kovacic, was probably misplaced, as the technology transfer would almost certainly have flowed in the opposite direction, from commercial to military aircraft production.

The evidence of these two cases, while not broad enough to draw strong conclusions, at least suggests that countries often act in their own interests when enforcing competition law, although the *Seaspan* merger case in Canada indicates a broader objective. It would be a worthwhile research project to examine a large set of cases to discern the objectives of the enforcement agency.

## INTERNATIONAL EFFORTS TO CREATE A GLOBAL COMPETITION AGENCY

THE RISING NUMBER OF INTERNATIONAL MERGERS and other practices with international antitrust ramifications, as well as an increasing awareness of the costs imposed by independent investigations by each affected jurisdiction, have prompted several parallel groups to initiate talks aimed at setting up global competition agencies. The best known of these is the International Competition Policy Advisory Committee (ICPAC), appointed by the U.S. Department of Justice, which has issued a report (ICPAC 2000).

## The Global Competition Initiative

THE ICPAC REPORT PROPOSED that the United States and a number of international organizations collaborate to create a forum where government officials, non-governmental organizations (NGOs) and private firms could consult and work toward common solutions regarding competition law and policy (ICPAC, p. 282). Called the Global Competition Initiative (GCI), the purpose of this forum would be to foster dialogue among government officials and other interested parties, directed toward greater convergence of competition law and analysis, common understanding and common culture (ICPAC, p. 29). Most importantly, the GCI could be used as a vehicle to offer technical expertise to developing economies and even mediation and other dispute resolution mechanisms.

The structure of the forum would be relatively simple. Membership would be as inclusive and comprehensive as possible, in order to allow for the broadest scope of views and opinions. It would be open to both developed and developing nations but also would allow NGOs, private firms and other interested parties to play a valuable role, by allowing them both attendance at the forums and a say on the issues to be discussed.

The scope of the agenda would be considerable and would be driven by the interests of its members and other interested institutions. Topics of concern might be: to multilateralize and deepen positive comity; to agree on common consensus disciplines regarding hard-core cartels, merger control laws, appropriate actions of government, and global frontier subjects, like e-commerce; dispute mediation; and even technical services. Put simply, the GCI is an inclusive attempt to set the stage, at a multinational level, for more effective and harmonious national antitrust enforcement and greater international cooperation.

Meetings could take place on an annual or semiannual basis in the form of a set of intergovernmental consultations — similar to the G8 summits, only less formal. The structure of this model is practical because it demonstrates that nations and interested parties can create a vehicle to exchange views, experiences and advice without investing in a permanent staff or an extensive bureaucracy (ICPAC, p. 282). Although many analytical and deliberative dimensions of the GCI are built on approaches initiated by the Organisation for Economic Co-operation and Development (OECD), there is no existing institution that can carry out such a wide range of talks on competition policy matters.

The GCI was proposed as a stage for the discussion of competition matters that have not received sufficient attention from other international organizations. Although the World Trade Organization (WTO) and the OECD are generally concerned with competition policy issues, the scope of their policy coverage is limited.

The WTO is focussed mainly on trade-related government restraints and does not cover all competition policy issues. Not only would any additional coverage of these matters overburden an already complex agenda, but the style of its deliberations would also be completely different from that envisaged for the GCI. The WTO mandate to negotiate rules that are then subject to dispute settlement would be inappropriate and actually run contrary to the purpose of the GCI, where issues would be discussed in a consultative manner. Indeed, the GCI is intended as a place where nations can develop binding agreements, consultations or non-binding agreements of their own accord, without being bound by international law.

Similarly, the OECD is a very important but limited setting where governments have committed themselves to discussing competition policy. Under the Competition Law and Policy Committee (CLP) — as well as within a larger group composed of members of the CLP and the OECD's Trade Committee — competition authorities from the 29 OECD member nations have conducted successful studies regarding competition issues. Indeed, the OECD has been very effective at promoting soft-convergence of competition policies among its members and providing technical assistance to OECD observers and non-members (ICPAC, p. 283). However, the OECD has a number of fundamental flaws that make it a poor organization to act as wider forum for policy debate. For example, many nations that have competition policy laws in place — or are considering incorporating them — are not OECD members and are thus not represented. This is particularly true of developing nations, whose needs may not yet be fully integrated into the OECD deliberations. Furthermore, these committees have had only limited success in resolving policy disputes. As a result, under current formats, neither the WTO nor the OECD is an ideal venue for more extensive meetings on competition issues, so that a forum like the proposed GCI is an attractive alternative.

To a limited extent, meetings like those envisioned by the GCI exist already. For example, the German competition authority has hosted several meetings for enforcement officials around the world. Similar to the Asia-Pacific Economic Cooperation (APEC) forum, the logic behind the GCI is that it will make such meetings more inclusive and formalize them. Nonetheless, it is important to note that the GCI was not proposed to replace any existing structure that examines competition policy issues. If it is created, the GCI will undoubtedly depend on their support and expertise to become a success. The last forum at which supranational cooperation on competition issues was discussed was the Free Trade Area of the Americas (FTAA), which contains a chapter on competition policy.

## INTELLECTUAL PROPERTY ISSUES

As Canadian and American economic integration proceeds, the framework for protection of intellectual property (IP) in the two countries has become increasingly important. In September 2000, the Commissioner of Competition released the final version of the *Intellectual Property Enforcement Guidelines* — the IPEGs (Competition Bureau 2000), which describe the Competition Bureau's position on the enforcement of the *Competition Act* in IP matters. The IPEGs followed by five years the joint release in April 1995 by the U.S. Department of Justice and the FTC of the *Antitrust Guidelines for the Licensing of Intellectual Property* — the U.S. guidelines (U.S. Department of Justice 1995a).

The two sets of guidelines were created primarily from concerns about the *domestic* interaction of competition policy and IP, but it is interesting and important to note their differences in approach. Moreover, we will explore whether these differences may have implications for integration issues between the two countries.

Intellectual property law and competition law have generally been perceived as being in conflict because – loosely speaking – the former creates monopolies and the latter tries to prevent or destroy them. The views of U.S. courts have at least become more sophisticated over the course of the twentieth century. The Federal Court was able to observe in *Atari Games Corp* v. *Nintendo of America* "the aims and objectives of patent and antitrust laws may seem, at first glance, wholly at odds. However, the two bodies of law are actually complementary, as both are aimed at encouraging innovation, industry and competition" (Atari Games Corp. 1992, p. 30). To perceive this complementarity, it is necessary to take a more dynamic and long-run view of competition policy than traditionally has been adopted by the respective enforcement agencies — in other words, to view the goal of competition policy as the realization of long-run efficiency (where some market power might be tolerated) rather than short-run efficiency (Gallini and Trebilcock 1998).

The differences in the two countries' approaches to IP enforcement are in fact far less significant than the similarities. Both sets of guidelines emphasize that IP and competition laws are complementary rather than conflicting and that IP is much like other kinds of property and should be treated as such for the purpose of investigating infractions of competition law. As Willard Tom (1998) put it in a recent speech:

> That an inventor may lay claim to the domain marked out by his intellectual property is no more antithetical to antitrust than that a firm lays

> claim to its factory.... Recognizing the degree to which intellectual property is like other forms of property for antitrust purposes helps us to recognize that the two bodies of law, far from being inevitably conflicting, are instead complementary ways of achieving a common goal. Competition is a spur to innovation and a way to spread the benefits of innovation to the consumer; intellectual property helps the inventor reap the rewards of innovation and thereby preserves the incentive to innovate.

Both sets of guidelines are concerned with creating a framework to encourage innovation. A major difference is that in the United States, the antitrust laws are seen as bearing the burden of promoting innovation, as well as the goal of static efficiency. In Canada, the IPEGs indicate that IP laws bear the primary responsibility for promoting innovation.

The U.S. guidelines introduced the concept of an innovation market, which "consists of the research and development directed to particular new or improved goods or processes and the close substitutes for that research and development" (U.S. Department of Justice 1995a, p. 11). This "innovation" in market definition has been both welcomed and criticized; while certainly it has served to focus attention on the potential of large-scale mergers and other agreements for dampening incentives to innovate, it has also revealed how non-robust our knowledge is about the relationship between market structure and competition. Implicitly, the U.S. guidelines adopt the position that a competitive market structure is likely to foster a higher rate of innovation than a monopolistic one, although the evidence on this old (Schumpeterian) question is still mixed.

In Canada, the Competition Bureau took a more conservative route by not embracing the concept of innovation markets in the IPEGs: "...the Bureau is likely to define the relevant market based on one of the following: the intangible knowledge or know-how that constitutes the IP, processes that are based on IP rights, or the final or intermediate good resulting from, or incorporating, the IP" (Competition Tribunal 2000, p. 11).

The IPEGs draw a fundamental distinction between conduct that constitutes the mere exercising of IP rights (which generally will not be challenged) and conduct that extends beyond such rights, which are subject to the general provisions of the *Competition Act* (Department of Justice 1986). Thus, an infringement of the Act would generally require something more than the mere exercise of the IP rights. The IPEGs are not entirely clear on what this "something more" is required to be, but the general idea seems to be that potential problems can arise where the exercise of the IP rights involves the agreement of a party other than the IP owner. For example, if the owner of a proprietary technology had licensed it to a competitor, then refused to continue to license when the competitor invested in some complementary assets — this might constitute an abuse under the *Competition Act*.

While the U.S. guidelines have their unique attribute in the concept of innovation markets, the IPEGs have theirs in their discussion of Section 32 of the *Competition Act*, which has no parallel in U.S. law. Section 32 deals specifically with anticompetitive conduct involving IP rights. Possible remedies that are allowed include modifying or invoking the rights held by the IP owner. However, the IPEGs make it clear that Section 32 would be invoked very rarely and then with a justification akin to the "essential facility" argument. In other words, if an IP owner, by refusing to license his or her IP, is creating or sustaining a dominant position in a market, then Section 32 might be used to force licensing. Moreover, despite the fact that this "special IP remedy" predates even the 1986 *Competition Act*, it has never been the subject of a judicial decision on merits, and only a couple of cases have progressed to a settlement.

What can we conclude about the differences between IP protection in the two countries and their implications for North American integration? First, we must recognize that so far, the role of IP in competition policy is much less important in Canada than in the United States. Most of the disputed cases in this area arise in the pharmaceutical, biotechnology and software industries, which are smaller — both absolutely and in relation to gross domestic product — in Canada. Nevertheless, some recent competition cases have featured disputes about IP: in the Tele-Direct case, the producer of unbranded phone directories claimed the right to use the Yellow Pages' "walking fingers" trademark (Competition Tribunal 1994); and in the Warner case, the issue was whether Warner could refuse to license its copyrighted recordings to a rival subscription music club (Competition Tribunal 1997). In both these cases, the IP rights were upheld, and the thrust of the IPEGs suggests that the Competition Bureau would not prosecute similar cases if they arose in the future.

## INTELLECTUAL PROPERTY RULES THAT DISCRIMINATE AGAINST CANADIAN COMPANIES

THE UNITED STATES CONTINUES TO DISTINGUISH its patent law from most of the developed world with a "first to invent" requirement for a patent, in contrast with the "first to file" rule employed in Canada and most OECD nations.[4] Prior to the North American Free Trade Agreement (NAFTA), a date of invention for a U.S. patent could only be established in the United States, which clearly discriminated against Canadian companies wishing to register U.S. patents. However, the amended Section 104 of the U.S. *Patent Act* now states that (if an invention is made in a NAFTA country) "that person shall be entitled to the same rights of priority in the United States with respect to such invention as if such invention had been made in the United States" (U.S. Code 2001).

Section 204 of the U.S. *Patent Act* is headed "Preference for United States industry" and essentially states that the holder of a U.S. patent can only assign exclusive rights to a company that will manufacture the product in the United States. We have not been able to find out to what extent this is an impediment to Canadian companies; however, the section begins by restricting itself to "small business firms" and "nonprofit organizations," which would seem to preclude any major established Canadian company.

Another piece of legislation designed to enhance the competitiveness of U.S. firms in relation to their non-U.S. counterparts is the *National Cooperative Research and Production Act* (NCRPA) of 1993 (Dougherty 1999). This legislation was a response to a widespread belief that antitrust fears had inhibited businesses from forming joint ventures, and that as a result U.S. firms were not keeping up with foreign competition. The Act mandates rule-of-reason treatment for any activities that fall within the statutory definition and sets out a new standard for the application of the rule of reason to statutory joint ventures. There is little available evidence on whether the Act has been successful in its aims (Dougherty). There is no restriction on Canadian or other foreign firms registering a joint venture under the Act, however, provided at least one of the participants is a U.S. firm. Whatever the net effect of the Act has been, it seems unlikely that it has served to discriminate against Canadian companies wanting to form joint ventures with U.S. counterparts.

## CONCLUSION

WE HAVE DISCUSSED SEVERAL ISSUES relevant to Canada that concern the multijurisdictional application of competition policies and IP. A notable conclusion in the area of competition policy is that the assertion of extraterritoriality in the application of U.S. antitrust law does diminish Canada's ability to pursue an independent competition policy of its own.

Although there have been suggestions that U.S. IP law discriminates against Canadian companies in several ways, we have found little evidence that it does, either in the statutes or their application.

## ENDNOTES

1   Guzman does not cite the earlier work of Head and Ries, so he may not have been aware of it.

2   Author of an expert affidavit dated August 16, 1999 (exhibit A-2081), filed in Competition Tribunal (1998).

3    Senator Slate Gorton (Republican-Washington) put it this way: "I am outraged the Europeans are asserting antitrust authority in an extraterritorial manner where there is no relevance, other than the fact that we sell airplanes in their market."

4    A pioneering discussion of the economic implications of this difference in patent law is found in Green and Scotchmer (1990).

# BIBLIOGRAPHY

Atari Games Corp. *Atari Games Corp and Tengen, Inc.* v. *Nintendo of America Inc. and Nintendo Co.,Ltd.*, 1992-2 CCH Trade Cases 69,969, 1992.

Competition Tribunal. *Director of Investigation and Research* v. *Tele-Direct (Publications) Inc.* (CT-1994/003). Ottawa: Competition Tribunal, 1994. Available at: http://www.ct-tc.gc.ca.

_____. *Director* v. *Dennis Washington* (CT-1996/001). Ottawa: Competition Tribunal, 1996. Available at: http://www.ct-tc.gc.ca.

_____. *Director* v. *Warner Music Canada* (CT-1997/003). Ottawa: Competition Tribunal, 1997. Available at: http://www.ct-tc.gc.ca.

_____. *Commissioner* v. *Superior Propane Inc.* (CT-1998/002). Ottawa: Competition Tribunal, 1998. Available at: http://www.ct-tc.gc.ca.

_____. *Intellectual Property Enforcement Guidelines.* Ottawa : Industry Canada, September 2000. Available at: http://strategis.ic.gc.ca/pics/ct/ipege.pdf.

Consumer and Corporate Affairs Canada. *Merger Enforcement Guidelines.* Ottawa: Consumer and Corporate Affairs Canada, 1991. Available at: http://strategis.ic.gc.ca/pics/ct/meg_full.pdf.

Department of Justice. *Competition Act.* Ottawa: Department of Justice, 1986. Available at: http://laws.justice.gc.ca.

Dougherty, V. "Antitrust Advantages to Joint Ventures under the National Cooperative Research and Production Act." *Antitrust Bulletin* 44 (1999): 1007-78.

Federal Trade Commission. Acquisitions-Boeing Co., 5 Trade Reg. Rep. (CCH) 24,295. FTC, July 1, 1997; and European Commission (EU), case no. IV/M.877-Boeing/McDonnell Douglas, 1997 O. J. (L 336) 16, 1997a.

_____. FTC Consent Agreement in the Sandoz Ltd., Sandoz Corporation matter of CIBA-Geigy Limited, CIBA-Geigy Corporation, Chiron Corporation, and Novartis AG. File No. 961 0055, Docket No. C-3725, 1997b.

_____. *Federal Trade Commission* v. *Staples, Inc.*, No. 97-701. Washington DC: Federal Trade Commission, 1997c.

Gallini, N.T., and M. Trebilcock. "Intellectual Property Rights and Competition Policy: A Framework for Analysis of Economic and Legal Issues." In *Competition Policy and Intellectual Property Rights in the Knowledge-Based Economy.* Edited by Robert D. Anderson and Nancy T. Gallini. Calgary: University of Calgary Press, 1998.

Green, J., and S. Scotchmer. "Novelty and Disclosure in Patent Law." *Rand Journal of Economics* 21 (1990): 131-46.

Guzman, A. "Is International Antitrust Possible?" *New York University Law Review* 73 (1998): 1501-48.

Hartford Fire Insurance Co. *Hartford Fire Insurance Co. v. California*, 509 U.S. 764, 1993.

Head, K., and J. Ries. "International Mergers and Welfare Under Decentralized Competition Policy." *Canadian Journal of Economics* 30 (1997): 1104-23.

ICPAC. *International Competition Policy Advisory Committee to the Attorney General and Assistant Attorney General for Antitrust.* Final Report. Washington DC: U.S. Department of Justice, 2000. Available at: http://www.usdoj.gov/atr/icpac/finalreport.htm.

Kovacic, William E. "Transatlantic Turbulence: The Boeing-McDonnell Douglas Merger and International Trade Policy." *Antitrust Law Journal* 68 (2001): 805-74.

Mathewson, Frank G., and N. Quigley. *Canadian Bank Mergers: Efficiency and Consumer Gain versus Market Power*, C.D. Howe Institute, 1998.

McFetridge, D. "Globalization and Competition Policy." In *Productivity Growth and Canada's International Competitiveness.* Edited by T.J. Courchene and D.D. Purvis. Kingston: John Deutsch Institute, 1992, pp. 133-80.

Porter, M.E. *The Competitive Advantage of Nations.* New York: MacMillan, 1990.

The Economist. "Antitrust Spaghetti Monti". October 7, 2000a, p. 81.

_____. "The New Economy: Knowledge is Power." September 23, 2000b, pp. S27-S31.

Tom, Willard K. "Licensing and Antitrust: Common Goals and Uncommon Problems." Address to the American Conference Institute, 9th National Conference on Licensing Intellectual Property, October 12, 1998. Available at: http://www.ftc.gov/speeches/other/aciippub.html.

U.S. Code. *Patent Act.* Title 35, Part II, Chapter 10, Section 104, 2001. Available at: http://www.accessgpo.gov/uscode/uscmain.html.

U.S. Department of Justice. *Antitrust Guidelines for the Licensing of Intellectual Property.* Washington DC: U.S. Department of Justice and the Federal Trade Commission, April 1995a. Available at: http://www.usdoj.gov/atr/public/guidelines/ipguide.pdf.

_____. *Canada-U.S. Agreement on Cooperative Enforcement of Antitrust Investigations.* Washingtn DC: Department of Justice, 1995b. Available at: http://www.usdoj.gov/atr/public/international/docs/uscan721.pdf.

_____. *1992 Horizontal Merger Guidelines.* Washington DC: U.S. Department of Justice and the Federal Trade Commission, April 1997 Revision to Section 4 on Efficiencies.

Catherine L. Mann & Diana Orejas*
Institute for International Economics

# 17

# Can the NAFTA Partners Forge a Global Approach to Internet Governance?

## INTRODUCTION

ECONOMIC ACTIVITY IN GOODS, services and information via the Internet is complex and global. By contrast, the highest jurisdictions in charge of government policy and legislation are national. Yet policy choices made by one nation will impinge increasingly on the policy choices made by another. How do the North American Free Trade Agreement (NAFTA) partners differ in their approaches to Internet policy issues? Are they working toward an approach that will reduce conflict and increase benefits from expanded use of the Internet? If the NAFTA partners — with their differing relationships between governments, citizens and business, and varied levels of Internet access and development — can find an approach that meets domestic needs but is also "interoperable" across borders, it could be an important model for global Internet governance.

This study focusses on three policy areas that are particularly affected by the tension between the global marketplace and national jurisdictions and considers the approaches being taken by Canada, the United States and Mexico:

1. Business conduct: Global electronic (e-)businesses pose challenges to both antitrust and consumer protection.

2. Tax regimes: The Internet affects the classification and treatment of both domestic and cross-border transactions, as well as the mode of raising revenues.

3. Information protection: The Internet uses information intensively, so the coverage and method of personal data protection are important.

Right now, each of the NAFTA partners is focussing on establishing approaches and legislation attuned to the domestic arena; there is relatively little attention being paid to the cross-border implications of these efforts or to creating explicit multilateral approaches. So far, this approach to Internet governance

* Now at the International Trade Centre UNCTAD/WTO (ITC).

of "live-and-let-live" works because of existing cooperation arrangements and bilateral agreements, as well as shared experiences in various international Internet and e-commerce working groups under forums like Asia-Pacific Economic Cooperation (APEC), the Free Trade Area of the Americas (FTAA), the Organisation for Economic Co-operation and Development (OECD) and the World Trade Organization (WTO).

## TABLE 1

## OVERVIEW OF THE NAFTA PARTNERS' LEGISLATION AND COOPERATION

| | Mexico | United States | Canada |
|---|---|---|---|
| Legislation | Mostly Federal | Sectoral<br>Self-regulation | Federal<br>Provincial<br>Self-regulation |
| Taxation | VAT at the Federal Level | State Sales Tax | Federal and Provincial GST |
| Oversight Agencies and Enforcement | Procuraduria Federal del Consumidor<br>Instituo Nacional del Consumidor<br>(consumer protection) | Free Trade Commission<br>Department of Justice<br>Internet Fraud Complaint Center (FBI)<br>(antitrust, Internet fraud) | Privacy Commissioners<br>Consumer Affairs<br>Canadian Competition Bureau |
| Private Sector Oversight | | TRUSTe<br>BBBOnline | BBBOnline |
| Cooperation Initiatives | | | |
| Tax Treaties | 1992 Income Tax Treaty (amended 2000) ◄► | | ◄► 1980 Income Tax Treaty (Amended 1983, 1984, 1996, 1997) |
| Technical Assistance | ◄——————————— | | |
| Competition and Deceptive Marketing | 2000 Agreement on Competition Laws ◄► | | ◄► 1995 Agreement on Competition and Deceptive Marketing Laws |
| Consumer Protection | | ◄► www.econsumer.gov/ ◄► | ◄► Consumer Sentinel Database |
| Informal Cooperation | | Consultations, Meetings. Conferences, Routine Contacts between Government Officials ◄► | ◄► |
| Participation in International Forums | APEC<br>FTAA<br>OECD<br>WTO | APEC<br>FTAA<br>OECD<br>WTO | APEC<br>FTAA<br>OECD<br>WTO |

However, the increasing economic integration of these three economies as a result of the Canada-U.S. Free Trade Agreement (FTA) and the NAFTA, accelerated and accentuated by the Internet, demands development of more explicitly interoperable approaches. Policy makers should take up the challenge now to forge a NAFTA approach rather than focus only on the domestic arena. It may be easier than they think.

The next section of the study briefly addresses why it matters that any international understandings emerge. The third section discusses two areas where the NAFTA has already helped to create a common treatment: classification of transactions and protection for trade and intellectual property (IP). The fourth section addresses three areas where the challenge ahead lies: business conduct, tax issues and protection of personal data. The fifth and final section summarizes the NAFTA approach and considers its potential to emerge as a global approach to Internet governance. Table 1 gives an overview of the NAFTA partners' legislation and cooperation on issues key to e-commerce.

## THE POTENTIAL BENEFITS OF THE INTERNET

WHY SHOULD WE CARE whether a NAFTA-based approach to Internet governance might be successful on a global scale? The Internet facilitates trade by enhancing traditional commerce mechanisms and by providing new instruments for transactions. It creates new markets in time, space and information that allow exchanges previously hindered by prohibitive transaction and coordination costs. However, these new markets in time, space and information are increasingly cross-border and hard to trace (challenging tax collection and perhaps increasing fraud), involve personal information (raising concerns about improper use) and may be characterized by "winner-take-all" network externalities. The benefits of the Internet can come only if the policy issues are properly managed.

Conflicting national approaches to Internet governance can jeopardize the potential benefits of more global and efficient markets. Convergence to a single global policy is unrealistic, however, given differences in national cultures, levels of development and so on. New and existing regulations must provide an environment of certainty (protecting consumers, privacy, intellectual property and competition). At the same time, they must allow enough flexibility for national differences to be preserved and provide sufficiently strong incentives for innovation and expansion of the Internet.

A successful governance approach at the NAFTA level would provide an appropriate environment for the expansion of e-transactions and thus contribute to the expansion of trade. Therefore, an Internet governance model that maximizes the benefits of the Internet while managing the policy issues is a key policy tool to increase economic welfare. Building on the NAFTA relationship might be a good way to start.

It is difficult to measure what the potential macro-economic benefits might be, because Internet activities are new and evolving so rapidly (and with great volatility). Even measuring Internet activity and usage is difficult. There are several approaches to getting ballpark estimates of the macro-economic gains. One approach is to aggregate the cost savings and increased economic efficiency associated with the diffusion of network technologies into businesses. A second is to investigate how trade flows might change with broader use of the Internet. A third is to consider the long-run gains from broad structural policy reforms that allow information technologies to take hold.

1. Efficiency gains: Two studies aggregate sector-level estimates of the cost reductions and efficiency gains of using the Internet. Brookes and Wahhaj (2000) suggest that gross domestic product (GDP) growth in the industrial countries might rise by an average of 0.25 percent over the next 10 years. Litan and Rivlin (2001), compiling work on the United States, suggest that productivity gains might be on the order of 0.25 to 0.5 percent.

2. Trade flows: Freund and Weinhold (2000), using a panel of industrial and developing countries, find that a 10 percent increase in the relative number of Web hosts in one country would lead to about 1 percent greater trade in 1998 and 1999, beyond what would have been expected on the basis of a simple gravity model. Considering broad trade liberalization, Brown, Deardorff and Stern (2003) find that global free trade (goods and services) would raise global welfare by about US$2 trillion—augmenting the GDP of the NAFTA partners by more than 5.5 percent each.

3. Structural reforms: The United Nations Conference on Trade and Development (UNCTAD), using a computable general equilibrium (CGE) model,[1] suggests that, in the long run, the GDP in the industrial and developing countries might rise by about 5 and 1.2 percent, respectively. The 5 percent increase for the industrial countries comes to about US$1 trillion, a figure similar to the results suggested by Brookes and Wahhaj, and Litan and Rivlin. The percentage for developing countries is smaller, on the assumption that they need to undertake more policy reforms to achieve the gains.

# A NAFTA APPROACH ALREADY IN PLACE FOR INTERNATIONAL TRADE AND INTELLECTUAL PROPERTY

IN TWO AREAS, there is already a NAFTA approach that differs from the global approach and is more conducive to achieving the benefits of the Internet: classification and coverage of international trade transactions, and treatment and protection of IP.

## INTERNET TRANSACTIONS AND INTERNATIONAL TRADE

A KEY DISTINCTION in the world of international transactions and trade negotiations is whether a product is a good or a service. This distinction is fundamental to the current structure of the WTO because the two functional agreements on trade — the General Agreement on Tariffs and Trade (GATT) and the General Agreement on Trade in Services (GATS) — are characterized by very different commitments toward liberalization by the signatories. The NAFTA, by contrast, has much more similar commitments for goods and services. As Internet transactions increasingly blur the distinction between a good and a service, similar treatments and commitments toward liberalization are important.

Signatories to the GATT (precursor to the WTO and originating in the late 1940s) committed to free trade in goods. While derogations have been common, unless a country explicitly negotiates a tariff, quota or other constraint, the transaction in the good is presumed to receive free trade and non-discriminatory treatment. However, under the GATS (which only came into force as an agreement in 1993), countries make no basic commitment to free trade in services; instead they use schedules of "commitments" to liberalize within certain modes of supply.[2]

Electronic transactions or means of delivery were not explicitly considered in the GATS scheduling process, and how they should be treated is not clear (Mann and Knight 2001). So far, all economies have adhered to the moratorium (agreed to at the 1998 Geneva Ministerial) on any new customs duties on e-transactions. But disquiet over the potential to lose tariff revenue has increased.

In the NAFTA, treatment of goods and services is more similar, with the underlying principle of liberalization preserved. First, with respect to goods trade, tariffs were eliminated between Canada and the United States under the FTA and the NAFTA. By 2003, customs duties will be phased out with Mexico. (Of course, derogations remain in all the bilateral relationships.) Additionally, the three countries agreed to implement uniform customs procedures, documentation and regulations to facilitate trade.

Second, the NAFTA provisions on services are more liberal than those of the GATS. NAFTA uses a "top-down approach" (i.e., all services are covered unless they are specifically excluded in the agreement). The GATS is a "bottom-up" arrangement and applies only to services included in the agreement. This difference is significant when it comes to information technology (IT) and the Internet, as new services arising from technological innovation would be covered automatically by the provisions under the NAFTA and would not require new negotiations.

The NAFTA provisions for cross-border service trade are broad and include production, distribution, marketing, and the sale and delivery of services. While virtually all services are covered by Chapter 12 of the NAFTA,[3] each country excluded "sensitive" sectors from coverage: health, education and cultural industries in Canada; services specifically reserved to nationals by the Mexican Constitution in Mexico (energy and petrochemicals, telegraph services, postal services and railroads, public law enforcement, social welfare, public education); and marine transportation in the United States. Looking forward, liberalization of services key to the effective use and diffusion of the Internet (telecommunications, finance and delivery) will be necessary.

## BALANCING PROTECTION OF INTELLECTUAL PROPERTY AND INNOVATION

INTELLECTUAL PROPERTY LAWS establish the rules for ownership and the rules of digital content, both key to the development of e-commerce. Ongoing international initiatives like the World Intellectual Property Organization (WIPO), FTAA, APEC and OECD are trying to find a way to address IP issues such as rules of ownership, access to content, liability of Internet intermediaries, trademarks and domain names, and data base protection. One of the major Internet challenges for IT legislation is that the Internet is international and the scope of some IP laws is national.

In general, the architects of IP law are faced with balancing the need to protect IP that is expensive to produce but easy to replicate against the desire to promote competition and further innovation that builds on existing knowledge.[4] How have the Internet and e-commerce changed the nature of the balance between users and creators of information? First, the characteristics of information: it is an increasingly important component of the product bundle; by itself, it is "non-rival" (my use does not impede your use); and, in aggregate (as data bases), it has externalities (value beyond just the individual data points). Second, the characteristics of replication: digital delivery of perfect copies is double-edged — sometimes desirable (a data base of medical knowledge underpinning an expert system), sometimes not (a perfect theft). If we look at IP law and e-commerce through this lens, we can see that the enormous potential of e-commerce cannot be realized without guarantees: to sellers that their IP will not be stolen and to buyers that their purchase is an authentic legal product.

Third, the dynamic relationship between protection and innovation: open standards and protocols, and ease of entry have been key to the exceedingly rapid development of the Internet and e-commerce thus far. Network effects mean that the value of information and IP increase with the number of people that can access, use, and augment them (e.g., at an auction site). Protection of IP that limits the ability of firms to create interoperable software will constrain the value of the whole network, as well as keep out new firms and participants. Thus, the extension of 20-year protection under TRIPS (trade-related aspects of intellectual property rights) to so-called "business method" patents (like the Amazon One Click shopping basket) is a concern.

The NAFTA contains a comprehensive multilateral IP agreement whose provisions set high legal standards for the protection and enforcement of rights across a wide range of IP including copyright, trademarks, trade secrets and patents. In addition, the NAFTA protects semiconductors, geographical indications, satellite broadcast signals, industrial designs and sound recordings. The NAFTA benefits are not limited to industries whose primary goods rely on the protection of IP rights but extend to any company that seeks to protect its trademarks, logos or trade secrets.

## A NAFTA Approach in the Making: Business Conduct, Taxation and Privacy

IN THE BUSINESS AREAS OF CONDUCT (competition policy and consumer protection), taxation of domestic and cross-border transactions, and protection of personal information, the NAFTA partners are at different stages of domestic understanding and legislation and have achieved different degrees of multilateral cooperation and consultation. There are, however, good foundations on which to build. In the area of business conduct, there is a deepening relationship based on a positive comity principle. In the area of taxation, there is a need to consider the implications of the Internet for domestic tax administration and the development of a common set of principles for cross-border transactions. In the area of protection of personal information, domestic developments rooted in practicality and flexibility are creating the basis for a multilateral understanding.

### Business Conduct: Competition Policy and Consumer Protection in a Global World

NEW TECHNOLOGIES GIVE CONSUMERS AND PRODUCERS unprecedented access to global markets, which in turn accelerates world economic integration. In general, the resulting interdependence between nations is beneficial for competition and consumers. As more suppliers become available to producers, consumers have a wider choice of products and merchants. Anticompetitive practices are no exception to this trend. Some areas of new technology allow for a large accumulation of market power, which poses new challenges for competition regulators. The scope for large-scale exploitation of consumers, anticompetitive conduct and restraints on innovation is enormous.

E-businesses are global in nature because Web sites can be located anywhere physically and accessed by anyone. This ubiquity raises a number of enforcement challenges in the aggregation and use of market power, forcing cooperation between competition agencies of different countries and thus enhancing the international dimension of competition policy and protection against fraud.

Cooperation among countries becomes increasingly necessary as new technologies allow for a dramatic increase in cross-border transactions. Products that are the expression of ideas ignore borders. Sectors like computers, software, biotechnology, pharmaceuticals, international banking and finance, or international media operate at a global level. In addition, the volume of international trade transactions conducted over the Internet is growing rapidly. There is a need for rules that both businesses and consumers can live with — otherwise e-commerce will not flourish.

## The NAFTA, Competition Policy and Deceptive Marketing Practices

The NAFTA accelerated the pace of North American market integration and is allowing businesses to operate in the three NAFTA countries as they would in the absence of national boundaries. This trend reinforces the need for collaboration in competition policy matters.

Chapter 15 of the NAFTA requires the parties to maintain competition laws and cooperate in their enforcement through mutual legal assistance, notification, consultation and exchange of information. It also provides for a working group of competition and trade officials from the three countries to report and make recommendations on the relationship between competition policy and trade under the NAFTA.

Cooperation between the NAFTA countries in the area of competition policy is not new. At the bilateral level, Canada and the United States have been cooperating since 1959, when Canadian and U.S. officials agreed to notify one another in antitrust matters.[5] Subsequent arrangements established more comprehensive cooperation procedures.[6] In particular, the Canada-U.S. Agreement Regarding the Application of Competition and Deceptive Marketing Practices Laws (Government of Canada, 1990) requires each party to notify the other about enforcement activities that affect the interests of the other party; to cooperate in the detection of anticompetitive activities and deceptive marketing practices; to share information and locate evidence; and to coordinate enforcement investigations of anticompetitive activities and deceptive trans-border marketing practices. In addition, a positive comity provision allows competition officials to request the other country's authorities to investigate suspected anticompetitive activities, thereby eliminating duplication of enforcement and decreasing extraterritorial enforcement concerns (Valentine 2000a, 2000b).

This agreement institutionalized consultation procedures by requiring semiannual meetings. Increased interaction between officials on both sides of the border make communications more efficient. Requests for assistance have become part of the competition enforcement process in Canada and the United States; joint or parallel investigations, as well as informal cooperation between the competition authorities, have become a standard practice. As a result, competition agencies in both countries can better address anticompetitive activities that affect the economies of both parties.

Cooperation with Mexico is more recent, as Mexico's competition law was passed only in 1992. In fact, one of the main purposes of the NAFTA's Chapter 15 was to accelerate and ensure the passage of a competition law in Mexico (Lloyd and Vautier 1999). In 2000, the United States and Mexico signed a competition policy cooperation agreement (U.S. Department of Justice 2000). This agreement is similar to the Canada-U.S. accord discussed above but does not include deceptive marketing practices. Given the short history of Mexican competition policy, technical assistance from Canada and the United States is a key part of the cooperation activities, as Canadian and U.S. enforcement officials are actively involved in the training of Mexican investigators.

Examples of the NAFTA type of cooperation can be found both in the fight against fraud and in antitrust investigations. The Consumer Sentinel Database, for instance, is used by both Canadian and U.S. officials to fight Internet fraud (U.S. Federal Trade Commission 1997). Law enforcement agencies in Canada and the United States have access to this consumer complaints data base that facilitates the identification of fraud schemes. The data base is growing rapidly; Internet related complaints increased from 1 percent of all complaints in 1996 to 22 percent in 1999 (in 1999, there were 18,622 Internet-related complaints, more than half of them about Internet auctions).

Another example of cooperation is the Federal Trade Commission (FTC) "international Internet surf days" initiative that promotes voluntary compliance. On these dates, enforcement agencies look for a particular scam and warn those who are breaking the law. On average, 20-70 percent of Web operators who receive warnings come into compliance with the law (either by taking down their sites or modifying their claims).

At the international level, a recent cooperative initiative regarding consumer protection resulted in the creation of a Web site that provides information on consumer protection legislation in four languages in the 13 participating countries (Canada, Mexico and the United States among them) and allows for the filing of complaints. Although a useful tool for exchange of information, this mechanism does not provide for further cooperation between enforcement agencies.

## Toward a NAFTA Understanding on Business Conduct

The existence of positive comity agreements eases extraterritorial problems. However, positive comity agreements are unlikely to provide a solution for e-commerce as the geographic location of Internet transactions is difficult to establish. This approach might be an option in the future, once international standards on permanent establishment, transactions and jurisdiction are established.

NAFTA-type cooperation does not necessarily lead to harmonized competition and antifraud enforcement procedures in Canada, Mexico and the United States. The text of the agreement does not include any formal commitment on policy harmonization, and national enforcement agencies are ultimately responsible for implementing their different statutes to serve their particular goals. To a certain extent, however, there has been an informal convergence because of the increased exchange between enforcement officials. There is no dispute settlement procedure for competition law matters; as a result, any disagreement between members has to be resolved through cooperation (Pitofsky 1998). With borders becoming increasingly irrelevant to North American e-commerce, there will be a need for more intense cooperation between the NAFTA partners. Eventually, a tripartite enforcement agency might be the most effective means of implementing competition and consumer protection laws.

In very concrete terms, national laws continue to limit information sharing, a stricture that gives the impression there is less cooperation between Canada and the United States than between the European Union and the United States. In Canada, Article 29 hampers information sharing with U.S. law enforcers. Similarly, U.S. legislation prohibits the FTC from disclosing information obtained by compulsory process. Changes in these laws or harmonizing their interpretation could improve enforcement without harming confidentiality. Canada and the United States have comparable consumer and confidentiality laws that would facilitate this process. Integrating Mexico might be more of a challenge. American legislation on information sharing in competition cases states that the United States can enter into an agreement with another competition agency only if it provides a level of confidentiality protection equivalent to that in the United States and if the agency's jurisdiction has a comparable competition law.

## TABLE 2
## TAXATION IN THE NAFTA COUNTRIES

|  | Canada | Mexico | United States |
|---|---|---|---|
| Total Tax Receipts (percent of GDP) | 37.4 | 16.0 | 28.9 |
| Tax Structure (percent of total tax) |  |  |  |
| Personal Income Tax | 37.8 | N/A | 40.5 |
| Corporate Income Tax | 10.5 | N/A | 9.0 |
| Taxes in Goods and Services | 24.7 | 51.3 | 16.2 |
| Other Taxes | 13.6 | N/A | 11.9 |
| Tax Rates |  |  |  |
| Personal Income Tax | 46.0 | 40.0 | 45.6 |
| Corporate Income Tax | 46.1 | 35.0 | 39.5 |
| Taxes in Goods and Services |  |  |  |
| Federal | 7 | 10 to 15 | 0 |
| State/Provincial | 0 to 10 | 0 | 0 to 7 |

Note: The 10 percent VAT in Mexico applies only to the border states.
Sources: Revenue Statistics, 1965-98, OECD; U.S. Federation of Tax Administrators, available at http://www.taxadmin.org/fta/rate/sales.html; Revenue Canada; the Hacienda Publica Mexico.

## INTERNET TRANSACTIONS AND TAX REGIMES

TAX ADMINISTRATION, to a greater or lesser degree, requires knowing the "who, what and where" of the transaction. Policy makers are concerned about the potential erosion of their tax revenues,[7] and businesses want to know their tax liability, so the focus has been on administrating *existing* taxes in the changing environment. [8] However, e-commerce and the Internet blur the who, what and where of transactions. Therefore, tax policy makers should also be asking, "*How* should tax regimes evolve in the face of the Internet?"

### Taxes and Tax Systems in the NAFTA Countries

The three NAFTA partners differ in their dependence on direct and indirect taxes for government revenues (Table 2), the administrative complexity of their systems and the degree of compliance. Only the United States has considered directly the impact of Internet transactions on its tax system, and none of them has considered the international implications of Internet transactions on taxes. Each partner country needs to progress internally in this area. Although bilateral tax arrangements that govern cross-border transactions exist, the NAFTA partners need to work toward a NAFTA-based agreement for apportioning taxes earned on cross-border sales and on income earned.

In the United States, the federal government raises 60 percent of its revenues from individual income taxes and about 10 percent from corporate income taxes; there is no federal sales or value-added tax (VAT). On average, a state raises 25 percent of its revenues from sales taxes, 20 percent from property taxes, 15 percent from individual income taxes and the rest through miscellaneous tax and user charges. For the state sales taxes, the final user (usually at the retail level) pays the taxes, which are applied principally on tangible property (with exceptions) and usually not on services. Business inputs generally are exempt from tax. For the most part, the administrative burden of the sales tax system is due to the 30,000 different applicable tax rates, depending on location. Tax ignorance, as opposed to tax avoidance or evasion, is also a real issue.

As in the United States, most of Canada's federal tax revenues come from income taxes. In addition, there is a federal consumption tax that accounts for somewhat less than 20 percent of revenues. This goods and services tax (GST) of 7 percent is collected on the sale of most goods and services in Canada and is levied on all taxable imports, but not on exports. Similarly, basic groceries, agricultural products, prescription drugs and medical devices have a zero-rate GST. Also exempt are health and medical services, tolls, education, and financial services. Foreign-based organizations providing services in Canada must register for the GST in order to claim input tax credits. This federal set of taxes is augmented at the provincial level, with the provincial sales tax (PST) that varies by province and is only payable on imports that are not for resale. Several provinces have an agreement with the federal government to combine the GST and the PST: the resulting Harmonized Sales Tax (HST) is a 15 percent flat rate.[9]

Mexico appears rather similar to Canada and the United States in the structure of its tax revenue, but the success of its tax administration effort is quite different. At the federal level, 40 percent of total tax is raised through income taxes. Like Canada, Mexico has a federal indirect tax, which accounts for 30 percent of total tax revenues. This VAT of 15 percent is applied to all sales of goods and services but with a broad range of special exemptions: food and drugs have a zero rate, the border regions have a tax rate of only 10 percent, and there are exemptions for entire sectors, including land transportation, agriculture and fishing.[10] The key difference in Mexico, however, is apparently low administrative compliance: Mexico's federal VAT revenues amounted to just 3.3 percent of GDP, while the income tax only 4.6 percent of GDP. With a tax to GDP ratio of just 11.5 percent in 1999, therefore, Mexico is well below the average ratio of 28 percent for OECD countries (OECD 2000).

Recognizing both the complexity and compliance issues, President Fox sent his fiscal reform initiatives to Congress on April 3, 2001. In order to broaden the tax base, he proposed changes to the VAT, eliminating exemptions and the zero percent rate (although as is common with VAT systems, the zero percent rate would still apply for exports). Additionally, he proposed that tax payments be carried out at the time of disbursement, not at the time of sale.[11]

As noted above, only the United States has considered explicitly the impact of Internet transactions on its tax system. When the U.S. Congress passed the *Internet Tax Freedom Act* in 1998, which kept domestic Internet transactions free from any "new" taxes for three years but did not revoke existing sales or use taxes (U.S. Code 1998), it mandated a review of the implications of e-commerce for domestic sales taxes. A majority of members of the Advisory Commission on Electronic Commerce (the Gilmore Commission) supported the view that digital products downloaded over the Internet (including software, books or music) should not be taxed and that in the interest of tax neutrality, their tangible equivalents should also be tax-exempt. The Gilmore Commission completed its review by March 2000 but could not recommend a plan of action to Congress formally because no supermajority view was reached. As services to the final consumer are not often taxed in the United States, this strategy apparently would have classified digital products as services and "harmonized down" the tax treatment of their tangible equivalent.

One objective of the commission's proposal was to encourage states and local governments to harmonize their rates and reduce the myriad state and local taxes (some 30,000), which are administratively cumbersome and encourage tax-strategizing behavior. The National Governors' Association (NGA) is examining how to simplify sales and use taxes by applying computer technologies to tax administration, although not all states are participating in this study effort (NGA 2000). Any tax implications at the international level were not addressed, as the commission did not have the mandate to address cross-border issues.

### How Do Internet Transactions Stress These Tax Regimes?

There are two main forms of tax collection: direct and indirect tax regimes. The Internet challenges them both, but in different ways. For indirect tax regimes, the issue is how to apply sales taxes and VATs when the tax treatment of goods and services differs, where transmission is via e-channels, and when transactions cross borders. For direct tax regimes, the issues are how e-commerce activities should be treated and income apportioned under the rules of permanent establishment, as well as the equity of taxing capital as opposed to labour earnings (Mann, Eckert and Knight, ch. 6).

The indirect tax system used to be simple to administer and audit — thus its popularity. As is clear from the discussion of NAFTA taxes, indirect taxes have tended to become situation-specific (rather than broad-based) as policy makers try to target specific transactions or users. Moreover, the Internet blurs the who, what and where of the transaction, which makes such targeting more difficult. In particular, as cross-border transactions are growing quickly, tax authorities do not have the luxury of considering the domestic environment in isolation.

All told, inconsistencies in the indirect tax system will lead increasingly to tax-strategizing business and consumer behavior both within and across borders. Thus, despite the trend toward more GSTs or VATs in recent years, the pressures exerted by the Internet environment will force countries to re-evaluate their dependence on this regime.

For direct taxes, the key issue is the international apportionment of income earned on Internet transactions. A mixing-and-matching of the two ways to account for business income earned in a cross-border transaction — source-based and residence-based — will subject some income to double taxation.[12] Consequently, bilateral and multilateral tax treaties attempt to allocate income earned to the source and to the residence, by "permanent establishment," and give tax credits to minimize double taxation.[13]

Permanent establishment, in the context of the Internet, is an evolving concept. The Internet facilitates new corporate relationships (partnerships, strategic alliances), new types of intermediaries (application service providers), virtual communities (business-to-business or "B2B" exchanges) and a host of new business models (auctions, reverse auctions). Where profits will be taxed is an important issue, as firms (particularly dot-coms) can relocate easily to jurisdictions where tax laws are more beneficial. Consequently, the allocation of income to different government jurisdictions will become increasingly difficult. As the threat of double taxation increases, so do the incentives for non-compliance. The pressure will be to reduce capital income tax rates.

These observations lead us to examine the third significant source of tax revenues: individual income, which probably remains the least affected by the Internet and e-commerce. Labour, by and large, remains within the same political jurisdiction as the tax authority — which supports the notion of taxation *with* representation.[14] Firms keep close track of how much they pay workers, even in the Internet markets; as a result, labour income can be taxed by the government authority so long as the firms report, audit or declare it. Then, the tax revenue can be apportioned to countries depending on where the value was added. From an administrative standpoint, individual income tax involves the smallest number of transactions to trace and probably the most carefully documented set of transactions, and it is the factor of production least prone (or allowed) to move in response to tax differences: exactly the recipe for an efficient tax regime.[15]

## Toward a NAFTA Tax Agreement

Right now, there is no NAFTA agreement on tax issues; rather these issues are addressed in a bilateral way. Canada and the United States have had an income tax treaty since the 1980s. Changes to the treaty were proposed in September 2000 to clarify the issue of a corporation's residence status and avoid double taxation. Mexico and the United States signed an income tax treaty in September 1992, to avoid double taxation on income and set limits on taxation at the source of royalties, dividends and interest (U.S. Department of the Treasury 1992). With respect to taxation of Internet transactions, there are no explicit North American bilateral or multilateral agreements, but there is ample cooperation and discussion among customs and tax officials in the three countries.[16]

The NAFTA partners should move beyond cooperation and discussion to create an explicit trilateral tax agreement. Each country should be able to maintain a system based on a combination of direct and indirect taxes that meets their redistributive preferences, although pressure will increase to focus taxation on the bigger target (income, not transactions) and at the ultimate source of value (people, not firms). The foundation for tax apportionment among the member countries already exists in the rules of origin agreements, customs and tariff preferences and drawback procedures. Achieving a trilateral tax agreement will deepen the integration of the NAFTA countries by raising tax efficiency, even as each of the partners retains the individual flavor of its relationship between government and citizenry.

## THE INTERNET AND PERSONAL INFORMATION

DATA COLLECTION ON THE INTERNET is pervasive and valuable. E-commerce "cookies" and "bugs" track, collect and compile personal information, which allows the creation and combination of data banks of specific information and preferences. Yet clearly, there is a tension between collectors of information (firms as information aggregators) and providers of information (individual businesses or consumers). Moreover, there is a wide spectrum of businesses, consumers and information, which makes the tension between users and providers of information multidimensional and dynamic.

Is there a role for policy intervention to modulate this tension between the individuals who want to protect their personal information and those who would use it to create new products and services? Are policy makers in the NAFTA countries weighting the various parties in the same way and choosing the same approach to intervention? Not only is the balancing act difficult, but each government sees its role (and citizens see their government's role) in the balancing act differently.

## Treatment of Personal Information by the NAFTA Partners

The U.S. privacy landscape appears wild and unruly — unlike that of the rest of the world. Most countries that protect privacy through national regulation, including Canada and Mexico, have opted for comprehensive data protection laws. These laws establish government data protection agencies, require registration of data bases and call for institutions to seek consent before processing personal data. However, the NAFTA partners may be more similar than it first appears. The way the different protection agencies implement and enforce the privacy environment has yielded similar outcomes, which bodes well for achieving a clearly stated set of principles and an integrated approach for the NAFTA as a whole.

In the United States, the protection of personal information relies on a mix of legislation, self-regulation and regulatory enforcement. About 600 federal and state laws protect the confidentiality of personal information. They take the form of sectoral protections (e.g., for financial information) that, when combined with self-regulatory provisions and case law, loosely cover American citizens' bank records, cable television subscriptions, children's online activities, credit reports, video rental records, library loans, medical records, tax records and telephone services.[17] The number of privacy laws is rising: in 2000, U.S. state legislatures debated about 4,000 legislative privacy proposals, which became more than 300 new laws. Furthermore, two federal laws were passed that include privacy protection for financial and medical information, and omnibus privacy legislation was considered by the 2001 U.S. Congress (Fowler 2001).

A hallmark of the U.S. approach is that innovation and self-regulatory commitments are backed up by oversight and enforcement. It includes innovative approaches to protecting information in a way that the user controls, and they emanate from both individual firms and standards groups. Widely available and inexpensive software programs, like Junkbusters and Anonymizer, permit users to block sites from sending cookies. The Platform for Privacy Preferences (P3P)[18] is a browser-embedded software that allows users to specify the type of information they are willing to divulge and whether or not it can be shared with third parties.

In terms of self-regulation, organizations such as BBB*Online* and TRUSTe provide guidelines, as well as an enforcement mechanism, through the use of Web site privacy seals. Such seals are awarded to companies meeting specific standards, such as a satisfactory complaint record and the posting of privacy policies that meet the standards of notice, disclosure, choice, consent and security. Codes of conduct, like the Better Business Bureau's BBB*Online* Code of Online Business Practices and Privacy Programs provide merchants with privacy guidelines to implement.

These self-regulatory efforts are backed up with oversight and enforcement by private-sector interest groups like the Electronic Privacy Information Center and government agencies. The FTC has considered several cases (e.g., Double-Click/Abacus, eToys, Amazon and others) where questionable data protection practices have emerged. In some cases, the onslaught of publicity by privacy groups, or just the threat of FTC consideration, has changed the behavior of firms; but not always.

In Canada, personal information is protected by federal as well as provincial and territorial legislation. For some time now, privacy legislation at the provincial level has covered the collection, use and disclosure of personal information held by *government* agencies.[19] Since 1994, comprehensive privacy legislation in Quebec has also covered personal information in the provincially regulated *private* sector. This legislation gives Canadians a general right to access and correct their personal information and provides oversight through an independent commissioner authorized to receive and investigate complaints.

Comprehensive privacy legislation was passed in April 2000. Bill C-6 (*Personal Information and Electronic Documents Act*) lists 10 principles for fair information practices (accountability, identification of purpose, consent, limited collection, limited use, disclosure and retention, accuracy, safeguards, openness, individual access and verification of compliance). It states that any organization covered under the Act must obtain an individual's consent to collect, use or disclose any personal information. Individuals have a right to access the information held on them by organizations, challenge its accuracy and request that it be kept private. Personal information includes name, age, opinions, evaluations, comments, "intentions," dispute records (such as complaints to a business) and loan or credit records. The Act will come into force in three stages.

The first two phases cover federal transactions. As of January 2001, the Act has applied to personal information about customers or employees (except "personal health information," which came under coverage as of January 2002)[20] that is collected, used or disclosed by "federal works, undertakings or businesses" in the course of commercial activities. Federal works, undertakings and businesses include organizations like the banks, telephone companies, cable television and broadcasting companies, firms engaged in interprovincial transportation, and air carriers. The Act also applies to personal information shared or disclosed for profit, or any kind of benefit, outside the borders of Canada, as well as across provincial or territorial borders, where the information itself is the subject of the transaction.[21]

By January 2004, the Act will cover the collection, use or disclosure of personal information in the course of any *commercial* activity within a province, including provincially regulated enterprises like retail stores. It will apply to all personal information in all interprovincial and international transactions by all organizations in the course of their commercial activities. The federal government may exempt organizations and/or activities in provinces that have their own privacy laws that are substantially similar to the federal law.[22]

The Act does not require companies to obtain explicit consent: "consent can be either express or implied" (Privacy Commissioner 2001). It does not apply when organizations use personal information for journalistic, artistic or literary purposes, or personal and domestic purposes. It does not define what constitutes "sensitive data" nor does it prohibit the collection of such data. The Act also lists several specific situations where personal information (including data that can be considered sensitive in Europe) may be collected, used or disclosed without the knowledge or consent of the individual. However, it requires organizations to take into account the sensitivity of the information in determining the form of consent sought for its collection and recommends that an organization "should" generally seek express consent when the information is likely to be considered sensitive. It does require that more sensitive information be safeguarded by a higher level of protection.

Industry Canada is the guardian of the interpretation of the legislation. Use and disclosure of personal information without the knowledge or consent of the individual is regulated by Industry Canada, which limits secondary uses of the data and provides sufficient and adequate safeguards for this type of data (Industry Canada 2001).

Mexico has not yet passed any comprehensive new legislation regarding privacy issues but has amended existing regulations to address the challenges of information sharing on the Internet. A new chapter in the Mexican Consumer Protection Law (*Ley Federal de Proteccion al Consumidor*) includes provisions for transactions made through e-media, optic media or other new technologies, which address the issue of confidentiality of information provided by consumers.

Under these provisions, suppliers of services must: use information provided by consumers in strict confidence; transmit such information to third parties only with the explicit authorization of the consumer or by legal order; use appropriate technology to ensure the safety of consumer information; provide the consumer with information about where and how to make a claim or find additional information on a product; avoid commercial practices that could mislead or confuse consumers about the goods or services offered; and provide necessary warnings of unsuitable content for vulnerable population groups like children, the elderly and the sick.

As for government activities, the Mexican Penal Code protects against the disclosure of personal information held by government agencies. The law prohibits e-surveillance in cases of electoral, civil, commercial, labour or administrative matters and expands protection against unauthorized surveillance to cover all private means of communications, not merely telephone calls. In addition, messages sent over the Internet have the same protection in Mexico as communications sent by mail. Furthermore, the Mexican Constitution and Federal Criminal Law punish the unauthorized opening of correspondence and any other kind of written messages.

**Economic Theory as a Guide to Policy to Protect Personal Information**

The flow of information is important for economic development and key to the efficient functioning of some sectors of the economy. Information flows have increased greatly in recent years and will grow further with the spread of the Internet. While they pose new regulatory challenges and open new opportunities for abuse, electronic exchanges of information also present a unique opportunity for economic growth and integration. As new national, regional and local regulations are developed to address the challenges posed by the Internet, conflicting regulations could impose restrictions on data exchanges. In this way, they could reduce the potential benefits of the new technologies and disrupt important sectors of the economy (Mann, Eckert and Knight, pp. 37-41; Mann 2001).

There are two approaches that policy makers can take to try to achieve the proper balance of rights and make sure that the spillover inherent in the collection of information is internalized by the information aggregators. Under the first, they can mandate a comprehensive approach to the way information aggregators treat data. Under the second, they can focus on creating market incentives for innovation so that aggregators improve the range of choices on whether or not, and how, data are collected, compiled and cross-referenced. Which approach better balances the benefits of aggregation of personal information with individual preferences for restrictions?

The economic theory of the second shows best that neither the market nor the mandate approach can achieve the highest levels of economic well-being for a *country* as a whole. And in neither case are all *individual* demands met. On the one hand, because there are many users and few aggregators, the market approach is likely to yield an incomplete set of information-use policies and so may not meet the privacy preferences of each unique user. On the other hand, the rules-oriented mandate approach is a sort of "one-size-fits-all" policy that assumes every person or business will have the same preferences on the way information is revealed: those spelled out in the rules. People and businesses are not all alike in their attitudes to privacy, however, so again, some specific preferences will not be met.

In either case, the network benefits of the Internet will be lost — in the first case, because of a fear that personal information will be lost, and in the second, because there is too little "personalization." It is difficult to institute a measure to find which approach would create the greatest number of happy users. This is why we cannot rank these alternative policies in terms of their impact on efficiency or society's well-being.

What, then, is the difference between the two approaches? Under the market approach, firms would have incentives to try to satisfy the privacy demands of individuals, particularly if those demands were effectively communicated to the aggregators and backed by government enforcement. The incentives would come in part from the very network benefits that would be lost if the privacy policy were too weak and users defected. In contrast, under the mandate approach, the private sector would have fewer incentives to innovate to resolve market imperfections (there is one set of rules for everyone), and the problem of enforcement remains. In today's technologically dynamic environment, it is crucial to retain the incentive for private sector response. This need can make one wonder about the effectiveness of a strict rules-based environment.

### Toward a NAFTA Framework for Data Protection

The challenge of international privacy legislation is to protect information from misuse while allowing international flows of data. The NAFTA partners appear to be taking very different approaches to regulating privacy: Canada has opted for new, comprehensive legislation while the United States relies heavily on self-regulation. Mexico is struggling with basic protections, but the wording of its new law is quite strict.

How different are these approaches, in fact? A key observation is that Canadian legislation, while comprehensive, is actually quite open to the self-regulatory and agency enforcement model currently being followed by the United States. The language on "explicit consent" and the role of Industry Canada put Canadian practice into a self-regulation model, albeit one backed up by private sector and federal agency enforcement. Despite Mexico's strict language, the three countries are, in fact, not too far apart in practice.

Moreover, while there is no common NAFTA approach yet, there is regular contact between the regulating authorities of the three countries, furthering the consultative and practical ties that will form the foundation for a NAFTA framework for the protection of personal data. In the end, the increasing economic integration of North America will be the market incentive that leads to a set of privacy solutions to meet the needs of the differing populations.

What will the NAFTA privacy framework look like? It will keep the national legislation, but the private sector will have the incentives to continue to innovate privacy solutions to meet the needs of the different populations in the NAFTA marketplace. This market-driven set of innovations will need to be backed up with federal enforcement by Industry Canada, the FTC and their Mexican counterpart. These three agencies will need to work more closely together to create a common environment of oversight and enforcement.

One model for this arrangement is the positive comity agreements. When more than one country has the authority to investigate, a positive comity referral makes sure that officials closest to the problem take charge to avoid duplication of effort. For example, in the area of competition law, Canada and the United States have an advanced set of cooperation mechanisms in place: each country has its own laws, but they are compatible enough to allow for coordination of procedures.

## Conclusion: A NAFTA Approach or a Global Model?

BUSINESS CONDUCT, TAX REGIMES AND PERSONAL INFORMATION are areas where there are potential conflicts between national jurisdictions of policy and the economics of the Internet marketplace. Policy makers must recognize the demands of their constituents (the voters). In this fast-paced technologically dynamic environment, however, they must avoid predetermining solutions or codifying exclusionary rules. The key is to create incentives for the private sector to help manage the differences between individuals and businesses and the problems of cross-border jurisdictional overlap. Because the private sector reaps the rewards from network benefits, as well as niche markets, it will seek interoperable approaches to solve the problems of spillover and jurisdictional overlap. Interoperable policies should allow national policies to reflect national differences yet also allow the network benefits of the global marketplace to flourish. The imposition of tight rules and mandates runs the risk of locking in suboptimal and non-interoperable solutions. However, *to make sure that the market works toward these goals, policy makers, along with private sector representatives, must back up private sector efforts with oversight and enforcement.*

In all three countries, new regulations are being developed to deal with the new economic reality of the Internet. Because of economic integration and the NAFTA institutional structure, there is substantial ongoing interchange between businesses and between government personnel. As a result, while domestic legislation is not homogeneous, it is not confrontational. Right now, problems arising from differences are addressed through bilateral agreements, cooperation arrangements and other forms of informal cooperation, such as information sharing, discussions, technical assistance and training. The three countries should build on these working relationships to create a NAFTA tax agreement, a NAFTA framework for information protection and a North American understanding on business conduct.

NAFTA procedural cooperation would not necessarily lead to common rules or harmonized procedures. Countries have different histories and cultures, enforce different statutes, seek different welfare goals and respond to concerns that reflect different levels of economic development. The North American approach comes less from negotiated agreements and more from sustained informal interaction, from a daily exchange of information. North American researchers, government officials and private citizens meet frequently and exchange ideas. Growing economic integration has increased the interaction between public servants and private businesspeople of the three countries in all sectors and at all levels. Government officials in all three countries have come to know their North American counterparts personally; their e-mail and phone contacts have become a routine means for consultation that, in time, will translate into more uniform interpretation of the situation and generate the most appropriate response.

At a minimum, the "North American model" allows the NAFTA countries to benefit from each other's experience with different policy approaches and permits the adoption of policies that have proved to be more successful, while adapting them to fit existing legislation and particular domestic situations. The greatest advantage of the North American approach is its flexibility. If a particular line of action is unsuccessful or impractical it can be changed easily. Even among the NAFTA partners, a detailed set of international agreements would be more difficult to reach, given the different cultures, histories and legislative processes.

Can this NAFTA model be exported to the rest of the world? Canada and the United States closely resemble each other in their economic systems and living standards, although they differ substantially in the way their citizens perceive the role of the government. Mexico differs both politically and economically. *However, these countries are more similar than might appear at first in their attitude toward the role of the private sector as leader, with the government and advocacy sectors in a backup role. In addition, they are similar in their emphasis on practicality and flexibility, rather than the advocacy of strict rules.*

Are a NAFTA tax agreement, a framework for information protection, and an understanding on business conduct exportable as models for other countries? The key ingredient in their exportability is not economic integration, level of development or "trust" in government, but rather a mutual respect between the private and public sectors, working together to achieve common goals.

# ENDNOTES

1   Adjusted to be consistent with the other work. See discussion in Mann, Eckert and Knight (2000, p. 24).

2   This is an extremely cursory overview of the WTO and its two main components, the GATT and the GATS. For more detail and analysis, see Jackson (1997); for a good "side-by-side" comparison of the rights and obligations under the GATT versus the GATS, see Snape and Bosworth (1996).

3   Financial services and telecommunications are covered in separate chapters of the NAFTA.

4   This section draws on Mann, Eckert and Knight (2000, pp. 117-20). See also Maskus (2000) for a comprehensive analysis of the economics of intellectual property, as well as empirical analysis and policy discussion.

5   This informal notification and consultation arrangement is known as the Fulton-Rogers Agreement.

6   The 1985 Canada-U.S. Treaty on Mutual Legal Assistance in Criminal Matters (Government of Canada 1990) provided specific mechanisms, like search warrants or orders for oral examination, to assist investigations.

7   Efforts to measure the potential loss of tax revenues are difficult because of dynamic response. For the United States, Goolsbee and Zittrain (1999) calculate a loss over the next few years of less than 2 percent of sales tax revenues. For the full range of countries around the world, Teltscher (2000) also finds tax revenue losses of less than 1 percent overall, although the figure is higher for some countries.

8   See *International Tax Review* (1999, 2001) for a review of how the following countries and regions interpret existing tax law for e-commerce: Australia and New Zealand, Canada, Germany, India, Ireland, Israel, Japan, Latin America, the Netherlands, Singapore, South Africa and the United Kingdom. Updates are available at *International Tax Review* No 4 (2002).

9   The HST applies to Nova Scotia, New Brunswick and Newfoundland.

10  Exemptions for goods transactions include sales of land; residential buildings (but not hotels); construction materials; books; magazines; certain authors' copyrights; currency; shares; credit instruments; and sales by non-profits, farmer groups, labour unions or government agencies. Exemptions for rendered services include those from state and local governments; social security institutions; official education; insurance; banking; public entertainment; medical services; and public transportation by land (except for rail transport). Zero-rated goods include food, water, patent medicines, farm equipment and chemicals. International freight and international air passenger service are among the zero-rated services. Imports are subject to the same VAT (the taxable value of tangible goods is the value declared for import duties plus the duties). Exports have a zero percent VAT rate. This provides an incentive for exporters, as they have the right to the refund the VAT charged by others on supplies and services used in the production of exports.

11  Secretaria de Hacienda y Credito Publico at http://www.shcp.gob.mx.

12  In general, income earned by U.S. firms and individuals is taxed at U.S. rates regardless of where the income was earned — the so-called residence-based taxation. Other countries, particularly developing countries, tax income earned by non-resident firms operating in the country — the so-called source-based taxation (Maguire 1999).

13  See the OECD Model Tax Convention, which is a blueprint many countries have used as a framework for bilateral tax treaties. It apportions tax responsibility and revenue so as to avoid double taxation of income earned through foreign investment. See http://www.oecd.org/pdf/M00005000/M00005346.pdf for a PDF version of the most recent information on the articles of the model convention.

14  This is not to say that labour cannot move; but it is relatively less mobile than firms, particularly at the margin of e-commerce.

15  The questions of fairness inevitably arise when labour income is taxed at a relatively higher rate than capital income. Evasion of labour and capital income taxation is one reason for choosing the VAT or GST systems. In addition, tax systems are often used to redistribute income across geography, as well as class. These issues remain. But the reduced ability to tax value-added, transactions or corporations raises the stakes for finding appropriate answers and charting a course toward changing tax regimes to reflect the realities of the global and networked production space and marketplace.

16  At a conference in Washington DC on April 30, 2001, the Mexican Finance Minister confirmed that there is ample cooperation between Mexican and U.S. officials, but such cooperation has been more difficult lately given the change in the U.S. administration and the delays in Treasury Department appointments.

17  Also, specific U.S. legislation restricts certain practices, like the unauthorized use of identification and passwords: this is more of a fraud than a privacy issue.

18  The World Wide Web Consortium (W3C), an international academic and industry body devoted to applications, engineering standards setting and research, developed P3P.

19  Except in Prince Edward Island and Newfoundland.

20  Health Canada is coordinating a federal/provincial/territorial working group, the Protection of Personal Health Information Working Group, to develop a Harmonization Resolution for the treatment of personal health information in Canada. While not legally binding, this resolution would set voluntary principles for the protection of personal health information across Canada in the public and private sector. Some Canadian jurisdictions already have legislation to deal specifically with the collection, use and disclosure of personal health information by provincial health care organizations and other approved individuals and agencies. (Alberta, Ontario, Saskatchewan and Manitoba have such legislation. To date, however, only Manitoba's *Personal Health Information Act* is in force.)

21  In addition, it will cover all businesses and organizations engaged in commercial activity in the Yukon, the Northwest Territories and Nunavut.

22    There are other laws that contain provisions to protect the privacy of Canadians. The federal *Bank Act* regulates the use and disclosure of personal financial information by federally regulated financial institutions. Similarly, provincial statutes regulate the activities of financial institutions like credit unions and insurance companies. In addition, consumer protection laws at the federal and provincial levels offer limited protections and remedies against illegal and unethical business practices that may constitute an infringement of privacy.

## BIBLIOGRAPHY

Brookes, Martin, and Zaki Wahhaj. *The Shocking Economic Effect of B2B*. Global Economics Paper No. 37, Goldman Sachs, February 3, 2000.

Brown, Drusilla K., Alan V. Deardorff and Robert M. Stern. "Impacts on NAFTA Members of Multilateral and Regional Trading Arrangements and Tariff Harmonization." In *North American Linkages: Opportunities and Challenges for Canada*. Edited by Richard G. Harris. Calgary: University of Calgary Press, 2003. Chapter 9.

Fowler, Alexander. "Privacy by Compliance?" *Professional Ethics Report* 14, 1 (Winter 2001). Available at http://www.aaas.org/spp/dspp/sfrl/per/per24.htm.

Freund, Caroline, and Diana Weinhold. *On the Effect of the Internet on International Trade*. International Finance Discussion Papers 2000-693. Washington DC: Federal Reserve Board, December 2000.

Goolsbee, Austan, and John Zittrain. "Evaluating the Costs and Benefits of Taxing Internet Commerce." *National Tax Journal* 52, 3 (1999): 413-28.

Government of Canada. *Treaty between the Government of Canada and the Government of the United States of America on Mutual Legal Assistance in Criminal Matters (with Annex)*. Signed March 18, 1985, in force January 24, 1990. Canada Treaty Series (CTS) 1990/19. Available at:
http://www.lexum.umontreal.ca/ca_us/en/cts.1990.19.en.cfm.

_____. *Agreement between the Government of Canada and the Government of the United States of America Regarding the Application of their Competition and Deceptive Marketing Practices Laws*. Signed and in force August 1, 1995. Canada Treaty Series (CTS) 1995/15. Available at:
http://www.lexum.umontreal.ca/ca_us/en/cts.1995.15.en.cfm.

Industry Canada. *The Personal Information and Electronic Documents Act: A Primer on Its Privacy Provisions*. 2001. Available at:
http://www.e-com.ic.gc.ca/english/privacy/632d30.html.

*International Tax Review*. Deloitte Touche Tohmatsu. London : Euromoney PLC Institutional Investor, September 1999.

_____. "E-commerce." Deloitte Touche Tohmatsu. London : Euromoney PLC Institutional Investor, 2001.

Jackson, John H. *The World Trading System: Law and Policy of International Economic Relations*. Cambridge: MIT Press, 1997.

Litan, Robert E., and Alice M. Rivlin, eds. *The Economic Payoff from the Internet Revolution*. Washington, DC: Internet Policy Institute and Brookings Institution Press, 2001.

Lloyd, P.J, and K.M.Vautier. *Promoting Competition in Global Markets*. Northampton MA: Edward Elgar Publishing, 1999.

Maguire, Ned. "Taxation of E-commerce: An Overview." *International Tax Review* (September 1999): 3-12.

Mann, Catherine L. "International Internet Governance: Oh What A Tangled Web We Could Weave." *Georgetown Journal of International Affairs* 11, 2 (Summer/Fall 2001): 79-86.

Mann, Catherine L., and Sarah Cleeland Knight. "Electronic Commerce in the World Trade Organization." In *The WTO After Seattle*. Edited by J. Schott. Washington: Institute for International Economics, 2000: 253-68.

Mann, Catherine L., Sue E. Eckert and Sarah Cleeland Knight. *Global Electronic Commerce: A Policy Primer*. Washington: Institute for International Economics, 2000, pp. 24, 37-41, and Chapter 6.

Maskus, Keith. *Intellectual Property Rights in the Global Economy*. Washington: Institute for International Economics, 2000.

NGA. Streamlined Sales Tax project, December 22, 2000. Available at: http://www.nga.org/nga/newsRoom/1,1169,C_PRESS_RELEASE^D_1067,00.html.

OECD. *OECD Economic Surveys, Mexico 2000*. No. 13. OECD, July 2000.

Pitofsky, Robert. "Competition Policy in a Global Economy — Today And Tomorrow." Speech delivered at The European Institute's Eighth Annual Transatlantic Seminar on Trade and Investment, Washington DC, November 4, 1998. Available at: http://www.ftc.gov/speeches/pitofsky/global.htm.

Privacy Commissioner. *Guide for Businesses and Organizations to Canada's Personal Information Protection and Electronic Documents Act*. Part I of Act in force in three phases beginning January 1, 2001. Available at: http://www.privcom.gc.ca/information/guide_e.asp?V=Print.

Snape, Richard N., and Malcolm Bosworth. "Advancing Services Negotiations." In *The World Trading System: Challenges Ahead*. Edited by Jeffrey J. Schott. Washington: Institute for International Economics, December 1996.

Teltscher, Susan. *Revenue Implications of Electronic Commerce: Issues of Interest to Developing Countries*. United Nations Conference on Trade and Development (UNCTAD), April 2000. Mimeograph.

U.S. Code. *Internet Tax Freedom Act*. 1998. Available at: http://www.accessgpo.gov/uscode/uscmain.html.

U.S. Department of Justice. *Agreement between the Government of the United States of America and the Government of the United Mexican States Regarding the Application of Their Competition Laws.* Signed and in force July 11, 2000. Available at: http://www.usdoj.gov/atr/icpac/5145.pdf.

U.S. Department of the Treasury. *The United States-Mexico Tax Treaty.* Signed on September 18, 1992. Available at: http://www.mac.doc.gov/nafta/8504.htm November 4, 2001.

U.S. Federal Trade Commission. Consumer Sentinel Database. 1997. Available at: http://www.consumer.gov/sentinel.

Valentine, Debra. "Cross-Border Canada-U.S. Cooperation in Investigations and Enforcement Actions." *The Canada-United States Law Journal* 26 (2000a): 271-97.

_____. "The Management and Resolution of Cross-Border Disputes as Canada and the United States Enter the 21st Century." Speech presented at the Canada-U.S. Law Institute, Case Western Reserve University, Cleveland, April 14-16, 2000b.

*Comment on:*

## CAN THE NAFTA PARTNERS FORGE A GLOBAL APPROACH TO INTERNET GOVERNANCE?

*Comment by Steven Globerman*
*Western Washington University*

T HE MOTIVATION FOR THE STUDY by Mann and Orejas is their view that the emergence and growth of the Internet is a phenomenon that is fundamentally altering the nature of international commerce, thereby elevating the importance of intergovernmental cooperation across a range of public policy issues. In particular, the Internet has effectively reduced transaction and coordination costs that are primarily related to distance. As a consequence, the overall volume of international transactions can be expected to grow at a faster rate, all other things constant. This development is desirable, as increased international economic integration can be expected to improve national productivity and real income levels. At the same time, the growth of electronic (e-)commerce is making the approach to public policy issues more complex in a number of areas. Mann and Orejas highlight three areas in particular for the focus of their concerns: 1) competition policy and consumer protection; 2) taxes and national tax systems; and 3) the security of privacy and personal information.

The broad concern expressed by Mann and Orejas that is common to all three areas is whether national enforcement of laws and regulations will be rendered increasingly suboptimal by the enhanced geographical mobility of final outputs and factor inputs associated with the spread of e-commerce. In this regard, the authors' thesis is that the continued growth of the Internet will pose serious challenges to the effectiveness of public policies unless countries closely coordinate, if not harmonize, their laws and regulations addressing competition, tax and privacy protection regimes. For example, e-commerce will render residence-based tax regimes more problematic to administer, as it is more difficult to identify the location of buyers and sellers engaged in e-transactions than it is to identify the location of participants in "conventional" transactions. Moreover, it is easier for commercial parties to "arbitrage" tax differences by shifting the geographical location of electronic Web sites than it is to arbitrage by shifting the location of physical assets. As another example, the ability of national and local governments to identify and punish individuals and companies committing business fraud and other violations of commercial and competition law might be emasculated, to the extent that those individuals and companies will use Web sites located in jurisdictions with much weaker legislation and regulations governing the relevant violations.

Against this background, Mann and Orejas see potentially large benefits in international cooperation to address the governance of e-commerce. However, they also see great problems in accomplishing such cooperation, given profound cross-country differences in underlying commercial laws and regulations, as well as differences in social attitudes toward individual privacy, the fairness of specific types of taxes and so forth. While such differences are relevant to the NAFTA trading region, the NAFTA partners are sufficiently similar in these broad dimensions that Mann and Orejas believe meaningful cooperation and coordination is possible among them in matters of Internet governance. Indeed, their study is essentially a call for increased cooperation and coordination within the NAFTA.

In general terms, the issues raised by Mann and Orejas reflect the broad tradeoffs at a national level that are associated with the harmonization of regulations and standards in international commerce. Potential benefits derived from increased international trade and investment must be set against potential costs associated with adopting regulations and standards that depart from those that would be "ideally" chosen under autarky. It is certainly not inevitable that the benefits will always outweigh the costs. The authors make a circumstantial case for the benefits of closer intergovernmental coordination of Internet governance, exceeding the relevant costs within the NAFTA regime. While I do not find their case unreasonable, neither do I find it persuasive. The magnitude of the benefits is related to the impact that e-commerce will have on international trade. My own reading of the evidence on this impact is much more equivocal than their reading. Indeed, some recent evidence calls into question whether international trading propensities have been affected at all by e-commerce, while other evidence suggests that e-commerce is encouraging closer international economic integration only in selected economic activities (Leamer and Storper 2001; Globerman, Roehl and Standifird 2001). Certainly, the preponderance of available evidence indicates that retail consumers who shop on the Web strongly prefer to shop on domestic Web sites in order to avoid costs of transportation and currency exchange, as well as to speed delivery. Trust in domestic brand name merchandisers is also an important factor underlying a home country purchasing bias (Lynch and Beck 2001). Against this background, Mann and Orejas might be overly enthusiastic about the impact that the Internet will have on international business activity, as well as the Internet's influence on the geographical mobility of markets and factors of production.

The benefits of closer intergovernmental coordination are also related to the "deadweight losses" associated with socially inefficient arbitrage of tax rate and regulatory differences that are facilitated by e-commerce on the one hand, but discouraged by closer coordination on the other. As noted above, international transactions using the Internet have not grown at the rate that early enthusiasts prophesied. This is not to say, however, that tax and regulatory reform at the national level would not be beneficial for the NAFTA governments. In particular, a move away from taxing income to taxing consumption will arguably enhance incentives to invest in physical and human capital, and thereby promote faster real income growth. The taxation of consumption should also permit a simplification of tax laws so that there are fewer exemptions and deductions in the taxation of labour and capital income. Interestingly, the authors suggest that the spread of e-commerce argues for an increased emphasis on taxation of labour income, as labour is a relatively immobile factor of production.

Mann and Orejas suggest that the costs of closer coordination would be low, given existing cooperation among the current NAFTA governments on issues of antitrust enforcement and privacy protection, as well as international taxation. Whether even closer cooperation will continue to have relatively low costs, at the margin, is unclear, particularly as the authors do not put forward a specific agenda for cooperation. Indeed, it might be argued that there could be too much cooperation if it results in the imposition of an Internet governance regime that hampers or stifles "market innovation." Mann and Orejas acknowledge this concern in expressing their support for private sector solutions to Internet governance problems. However, this acknowledgment further obscures the precise role that governments should play in Internet governance.

The existing contacts among national governments on matters of taxation, antitrust and the like reflect the already high degree of policy interdependence created by the activities of multinational companies. For example, transfer pricing practices of multinationals create powerful pressures, threatening the sustainability of international differences in business taxation, while the growing mobility of skilled labour is causing governments to pay closer attention to international differences in marginal income tax rates on high-income earners. Further, large international mergers and acquisitions, such as General Electric's recently aborted takeover attempt of Honeywell, are highlighting differences in antitrust practices among developed countries, which in turn are mobilizing international companies to push for greater international harmonization of antitrust practices. Against this background, the starting point that I would propose for a study of Internet governance would be whether and precisely how the growth of e-commerce is changing the existing benefits and costs of closer harmonization of national policies in the areas identified by Mann and Orejas. I suspect that the adoption of this focus would lead to more precise suggestions for ways in which the NAFTA governments could cooperate more closely, or perhaps even, in some cases, ways in which they might cooperate less closely.

## BIBLIOGRAPHY

Globerman, Steven, Thomas W. Roehl and Stephen Standifird. "Globalization and Electronic Commerce: Inferences From Retail Brokering." *Journal of International Business Studies* 32, 4 (2001): 749-68.

Leamer, Edward, and Michael Storper. "The Economic Geography of the Internet Age." *Journal of International Business Studies* 32, 4 (2001): 641-66.

Lynch, Patrick, and John C. Beck. "Profiles of Internet Buyers in 20 Countries: Evidence for Region-Specific Strategies." *Journal of International Business Studies* 32, 4 (2001): 725-48.

## About the Contributors

**Ram Acharya** is an economist with the Micro-Economic Policy Analysis Branch at Industry Canada, where he has conducted research on the pre- and post-merger performance of Canadian firms and on Canada-U.S. economic integration regarding trade and investment. He was a policy analyst at the Department of Foreign Affairs and International Trade, where he conducted research on Canada-U.S. regional market integration and analysis of international trade and investment performance in Canada. He received his Ph.D. in economics from the University of Ottawa in 1999.

**Sven D. Arndt** is the C.M. Stone Professor of Money, Credit and Trade and the Director of the Lowe Institute of Political Economy at Claremont College in California. His research interests include trade theory and policy, globalization and production fragmentation, and regional economic integration. He is the managing editor of *The North American Journal of Economics and Finance* and was the co-editor of *World Economy*, an annual document on trade policy. He has served as Director of the Office of International Monetary Research at the U.S. Treasury and as President of the North American Economics and Finance Association. He received his Ph.D. in economics from the University of California at Berkeley.

**Keith G. Banting** is Director of the School of Policy Studies at Queen's University in Kingston. His research interests lie in the area of comparative public policy, and the welfare state of western nations in particular. He obtained his Ph.D. from Oxford University. He has been a visiting scholar at a number of institutions, including the London School of Economics and the Brookings Institution. He also served as a Research Coordinator for the Royal Commission on the Economic Union and Development Prospects for Canada. He is the author of *Poverty, Politics and Policy*, a study on the politics of social policy in Britain, and *The Welfare State and Canadian Federalism*, which explores the implications of federal institutions for income security programs.

**Paul Beaudry** is a Professor of economics and the Canada Research Chair at the University of British Columbia, an associate at the Canadian Institute for Advanced Research and a Faculty Research Fellow at the National Bureau of Economic Research. He obtained his Ph.D. in economics from Princeton University. His main research fields include macro-economics, contract theory and labour economics. He is also the author of numerous publications and has written for periodicals such as the *Canadian Journal of Economics*, the *Journal of Monetary Economics* and the *American Economic Review*.

**Eugene Beaulieu** is an Assistant Professor in the Department of Economics at the University of Calgary. He received his Ph.D. in economics from Columbia University. Prior to his doctorate, he worked as an economist for the Government of Kenya and the Bank of Canada. He focusses his research on international trade, commercial policy and economic development. He also conducts empirical research on the political economy of trade policy and the labour market effects of trade policy. His work has been published in journals such as the *Review of International Economics*, the *Journal of Economic History* and the *Canadian Journal of Economics*.

**Gerard W. Boychuk** is an Assistant Professor in the Department of Political Science at the University of Waterloo. He received his Ph.D. in political science from Queen's University. His research interests include public administration, public policy, and Canadian and U.S. politics. He is the author of *Patchworks for Purpose: The Development of Provincial Social Assistance Regimes in Canada* (1998). He is a co-investigator, with Debora Van Nijnatten, in a multiyear project comparing the public policies of U.S. states and Canadian provinces in the fields of environmental protection and social policy. He also has acted as a consultant to Human Resources Development Canada on public policy comparisons between Canada and the United States.

**Drusilla K. Brown** is an Associate Professor of economics at Tufts University. She received her Ph.D. from the University of Michigan in 1984. She was appointed Assistant Professor at Tufts University in 1985 and promoted to Associate Professor in 1992. She is also a member of the advisory board of the North American Economics and Finance Association. Her primary area of research is in the application of large-scale applied general equilibrium models to the study of international economic integration in the western hemisphere. Recent publications have appeared in the *Economic Journal*, the *Journal of International Economics* and the *Journal of Development Economics*.

**Kirk A. Collins** is a part-time Professor of economics at the University of Ottawa. Presently, he is completing his Ph.D. at the University of Ottawa and is doing research on human capital, taxation and policy issues. He is also professionally affiliated with the Canadian Economics Association and the American Economic Association. He recently co-authored a study on the tax treatment of human capital in Canada, with Jim Davies, for the Institute for Research on Public Policy. Other papers include *Winning at Hide and Seek: The Tax Mix and the Informal Economy*, co-written with Dan Brou, and *Endogenous Leisure, Human Capital and Taxes*.

**Bev Dahlby** is a Professor of economics at the University of Alberta and a Fellow of the Institute for Public Economics. He received his Ph.D. from the London School of Economics. He is currently researching the theory and measurement of the marginal cost of public funds, and he has work in progress on topics ranging from the Alberta pension plan to public pensions, provincial business taxes and the taxation of the mining sector in Canada. He has served as an associate editor of *Canadian Public Policy* and on the editorial board of the *Canadian Tax Journal*. His research has appeared in periodicals such as the *Journal of Political Economy*, the *Journal of Public Economics*, *International Tax and Public Finance* and the *Canadian Journal of Economics*.

**Jim Davies** is a Professor of economics and the RBC Financial Group Fellow (EPRI) at the University of Western Ontario. He received his Ph.D. from the London School of Economics. His research interests include inter-generational models of income distribution, marginal tax rates and lifetime tax incidences. He is the author of two books, including *Reforming Capital Income Taxation in Canada: Efficiency and Distributional Effects of Alternative Options* (1987), with France St-Hilaire. He has served as a special advisor to the federal Department of Finance and has consulted widely. He is a Research Fellow of the C.D. Howe Institute and of the CESifo Network at the University of Munich. In 1999, he joined the editorial boards of the *Canadian Tax Journal* and the *Review of Income and Wealth*.

**Alan V. Deardorff** is the John W. Sweetland Professor of International Economics and a Professor of economics and public policy at the University of Michigan. His current research interests include the role of labour standards in international trade policy, the interactions among domestic economic policies in an international environment and the determinants of bilateral trade patterns. With Robert Stern, he has developed the Michigan Model of World Production and Trade, which is used to estimate the effects of trade agreements. He has served as a consultant to the U.S. Departments of Commerce, Labor, State, and Treasury and to international organizations, including the OECD and the World Bank. He has published numerous articles on various aspects of international trade theory and policy. He received his Ph.D. from Cornell University.

**James D. Gaisford** is a Professor of economics at the University of Calgary. Currently, he is the Undergraduate Coordinator for the Department of Economics and is also the Associate Director of the Centre for International Financial and Economic Research at Loughborough University, United Kingdom. He earned his Ph.D. from Queen's University. His research focusses primarily on the areas of international trade, agricultural economics and liberalization in former command economies. His academic work has been published in periodicals such as the *International Economic Journal*, the *Journal of Economic Development*, the *Canadian Journal of Agricultural Economics*, *World Economy* and the *Journal of International Trade and Development*.

**Steven Globerman** is currently Ross Distinguished Professor of Canada-U.S. Business and Economic Relations and Director of the Centre for International Business at Western Washington University. He was previously a faculty member at Simon Fraser University and York University and has been a visiting faculty member at a number of other universities in North America and Europe. His research interests encompass a range of topics in international economics and industrial organization, and he is widely published in professional journals. He has consulted extensively for both private and public sector organizations and served on the research staffs of two Canadian government Royal Commissions.

**David Green** is an Associate Professor of economics at the University of British Columbia. His areas of interest include wage inequality, wage and income distribution and the labour market impacts of social policy. His work includes *Cohort Patterns in Canadian Earnings and the Skill-Based Technical Change Hypothesis*, co-written with Paul Beaudry, and *The Effects of Minimum Wage on the Distribution of Teenage Work*, with Harry Paarsch.

**Richard G. Harris** is the Telus Professor of Economics at Simon Fraser University and a former Fellow of the Economic Growth Program of the Canadian Institute for Advanced Research. His major area of specialization is international economics, and the economics of integration in particular. During the 1980s, he worked extensively on the economic modelling of the impact of the Canada-U.S. Free Trade Agreement and subsequently on the NAFTA. He has served as a consultant to a number of Canadian government departments, international organizations and corporations in the area of international economics. In addition to a number of technical articles, he has published policy-oriented books and articles on Canada-U.S. free trade, international macro-economics, economic growth, the Asia-Pacific region and Canadian public policy.

**Michael Hart** is a Professor of international affairs at the Norman Patterson School of International Affairs at Carleton University. He is a former official in Canada's Department of Foreign Affairs and International Trade, where he specialized in trade policy and trade negotiations. He was involved in the Canada-U.S. free trade negotiations, the North American free trade negotiations and various GATT, textile and commodity negotiations. He was founding director of the Centre for Trade Policy and Law and stepped down in September 1996 after a second term as director. He holds M.A. and A.B.D. degrees from the University of Toronto and is the author, editor and co-editor of more than a dozen books, and numerous articles and chapters in books on international trade issues.

**Keith Head** is an Associate Professor in Asian commerce strategy at the Faculty of Commerce, University of British Columbia, where he teaches courses on international business management and public policy analysis. He has a Ph.D. from the Massachusetts Institute of Technology and a B.A. (Economics) from Swarthmore College. His research interests include foreign direct investment, international trade policy, multinational enterprises, industrial organization and economic geography. His current research focusses on the immigrants' impact on trade and the effects of trade liberalization on North American manufacturing. He won the Killam Teaching Prize in 2000, and is the author of *Elements of Multinational Strategy* and numerous chapters and articles in economic books and journals.

**Catherine L. Mann** has been a Senior Fellow at the Institute for International Economics since 1997. She has served at policy making institutions in Washington: previous positions include Assistant Director in the International Finance Division and Officer at the Federal Reserve Board of Governors, and senior staff member for the Chief Economist of the World Bank. In addition to her work at the Institute, she is Adjunct Professor of management at the Owen School of Management at Vanderbilt University and is currently teaching at the Johns Hopkins School for Advanced International Studies. Her recent work has focussed on the economic and policy issues of global information, communications and technology, with a particular emphasis on the economics of privacy, tax and intellectual property. She received her Ph.D. in economics from the Massachusetts Institute of Technology.

**Tristan Musgrave** is currently a student in the Faculty of Law at McGill University. Previously, he was a research and teaching assistant at Queen's University, where he received his M.A. in economics. His research interests include competition policy, intellectual property laws and globalization.

**Nancy Olewiler** is a Professor of economics at Simon Fraser University who previously taught at Queen's University. She obtained her Ph.D. in economics from the University of British Columbia. Her research is focussed on environmental policy and the impact of environmental regulations on foreign investment, environmental tax shifting and policy instruments for greenhouse gases. From 1990 to 1995, she was the managing editor of *Canadian Public Policy*, and from 1996 to 1998 she served as a member of the Technical Committee on Business Taxation, created by the federal government to propose changes to business taxes in Canada. She has published a variety of academic papers, texts and policy studies in the areas of taxation, natural resources and environmental economics.

**Diana Orejas** is currently working in Geneva for the Enterprise Management Development Section of the International Trade Centre UNCTAD/WTO (ITC). She designs and implements training and counselling programs aimed at increasing the international competitiveness of small and medium enterprises in developing countries. Prior to ITC, she worked on NAFTA- and FTAA-related research at the Institute for International Economics in Washington, DC. She holds an M.A. in international relations and international economics from Johns Hopkins University.

**Pierre-Paul Proulx** is Professeur honoraire at the Université de Montréal and an economics consultant. He is a graduate of the University of Ottawa, University of Toronto and Princeton University, where he received his Ph.D. in economic sciences. His recent projects have dealt with topics such as the competitiveness of large cities in North America, trade and foreign direct investment flows between European and North American countries, growth by country and region in Europe and by state in the United States, as well as globalization and productivity.

**Someshwar Rao** is the Director of the Strategic Investment Analysis Directorate, Micro-Economic Policy Analysis Branch, Policy Sector, at Industry Canada. He is responsible for managing research and analysis associated with issues related to trade, investment, productivity, the new economy and policy modelling. He is also responsible for the Industry Canada Research Publications Program. Prior to joining Industry Canada in 1992, he worked as a senior economist at the Economic Council of Canada for over 15 years. He was actively involved with the preparation of the Council's Annual Review and two major reports on the

Canada-U.S. Free Trade Agreement and Canada's competitive position. He also served as acting director of the group that was responsible for the development of CANDIDE, a disaggregated model of Canadian industry. He has published extensively on both micro- and macro-economic issues. He obtained his Ph.D. in economics from Queen's University.

**John Ries** is an Associate Professor and an advisor to the M.B.A. Strategic Management specialization at the University of British Columbia. He obtained his Ph.D. in economics from the University of Michigan. He teaches courses on international business, international trade policy, government and business, and the Asian business environment. He has been a consultant to the Canadian government and has published articles in numerous academic journals, including the *American Economic Review*, the *Journal of International Economics*, the *Journal of Industrial Economics* and the *Canadian Journal of Economics*.

**Gary Sawchuk** is a Senior Economist, Strategic Initiatives, with the Business Frameworks and Taxation Directorate of the Micro-Economic Policy Analysis Branch at Industry Canada. He holds a Ph.D. from the University of Manitoba and an M.P.A. from Harvard University. He is presently working at benchmarking Canada's innovation performance and maintains research interests in the areas of international trade and Canada-U.S. economic relations.

**Lawrence Schembri** is the Research Director of the International Department of the Bank of Canada. He obtained his Ph.D. in economics from the Massachusetts Institute of Technology. His research is focussed mainly on international economics. He has published papers on the impact of trade liberalization on employment, productivity growth and competitiveness, and international trade in services. His work has appeared in journals such as the *Journal of International Economics, Business History* and the *Canadian Journal of Economics*.

**Nicolas Schmitt** is a Professor of economics at the Université de Genève, on leave from Simon Fraser University. His main teaching areas are industrial organization, international trade and micro-economics. He obtained his Ph.D. in economics from the University of Toronto. He currently focusses his research on the role of vertical restraints in international markets, trade liberalization and the "brain drain" in Canada. His published work includes papers on non-tariff barriers, market integration and market structure, which have appeared in journals like the *International Economic Review, American Economic Review* and the *Journal of International Economics*.

**Daniel M. Shapiro** is a Professor in the Faculty of Business Administration at Simon Fraser University. He received his Ph.D. from Cornell University. He was a Director of the Executive M.B.A. program at Simon Fraser University and a Wing Lung Bank Fellow at the School of Business in Hong Kong Baptist University, and he has more than 20 years of experience as a business educator and researcher. He has served as a consultant to the Anti-Inflation Board, Investment Canada, the Bureau of Competition Policy, the OECD, the World Bank and the City of Vancouver. As a consultant, he worked in various sectors, including foreign investment, mergers, competition policy, strategy and industrial policy. He has published books and monographs, and over 30 articles in scholarly journals. His research interests include industrial organization, managerial economics, and business and public policy.

**Prakash Sharma** is a Senior Research Coordinator with the Micro-Economic Policy Analysis Branch at Industry Canada. Previously, he was with the Department of Foreign Affairs and International Trade (DFAIT), where he was a Senior Research Coordinator and Deputy Director of the Trade and Economic Analysis Division. He has also taught at the University of Ottawa. Before obtaining his Ph.D. in economics from Carleton University in Ottawa, he studied economics at the University of Heidelberg in Germany. His policy analysis and research work relates to international trade and investment. A number of his papers are available on the DFAIT Web site under policy analysis documents.

**Robert M. Stern** is Professor of economics and public policy (Emeritus) at the University of Michigan. He received his Ph.D. in economics from Columbia University. He has served as consultant to the U.S. Departments of Labor, State, and Treasury, the U.S. Agency for International Development, the United Nations Conference on Trade and Development, the Economic Council of Canada, and economic committees of various countries worldwide. He has collaborated with Alan Deardorff since the early 1970s in developing the Michigan Model of World Production and Trade. His research focusses on multilateral trade agreements and the economic effects of regional trading arrangements .

**Aaron Sydor** is a Senior Policy Research Advisor with the Trade and Economic Analysis Division at the Department of Foreign Affairs and International Trade. Formerly, he was an economist with the Micro-Economic Policy Analysis Branch at Industry Canada. His research interests include international trade and investment and issues related to foreign ownership. He received his M.A. in economics from Carleton University and his B.A. in economics from Brock University.

**Mykyta Vesselovsky** is currently a Ph.D. candidate in economics (A.B.D.) at Carleton University. His research interests include international economics and industrial organization. He was previously a research assistant in the Department of Economics at Carleton University. He has done quantitative research for several working papers on international trade and tariffs, productivity growth, technology shocks and international competitiveness.

**Roger Ware** is a Professor of economics at Queen's University and the Director of LECG, a leading international economic consulting services firm located in Toronto. In 1993-94, he held the T.D. McDonald Chair in Industrial Organization at the Competition Bureau in Ottawa, advising the Commissioner on a wide range of competition policy topics and cases. His research interests are focussed on antitrust economics, intellectual property and the economics of the banking sector. He has published articles in all of these areas, as well as numerous other publications in scholarly journals on industrial organization issues. He obtained his Ph.D. from Queen's University.